A CLASSIFIED COLLECTION OF TAMIL PROVERBS

A
CLASSIFIED COLLECTION
OF
TAMIL PROVERBS

REV. HERMAN JENSEN

"AN OUNCE OF MOTHER WIT IS WORTH A POUND OF LEARNING"

GYAN

Published by

GYAN

Gyan Publishing House
5, Ansari Road
Daryaganj, New Delhi-110002
Phone: 011-47034999, 9811692060
E-mail: books@gyanbooks.com

Distribution Network
gyanbooks.com
India, USA, Canada, UK, Australia, France

ISBN : 978-81-212-4507-4 (HB)
First Published, 1897

2nd Impression 2020

Printed at: Gyan Press, Delhi.

A Classified Collection of Tamil Proverbs
Author: Herman Jensen

A CLASSIFIED COLLECTION

OF

TAMIL PROVERBS

BY THE

REV. HERMAN JENSEN,

Danish Missionary, Madras.

"AN OUNCE OF MOTHER WIT IS WORTH A POUND OF LEARNING."

MADRAS:

THE METHODIST EPISCOPAL PUBLISHING HOUSE.

LONDON:

TRÜBNER AND CO.

1897.

THE LUZ, 19*th April*, 1897.

FROM

THE HON'BLE S. SUBRAMANIA AIYAR, B.L., C.I.E.,
Dewan Bahadur.

DEAR SIR,

I have no doubt that your forthcoming collection of Tamil proverbs will prove highly useful and interesting. The collection of sayings in the West by the side of these proverbs would enable many people to see how much similarity in ideas exists between the East and the West.

As regards the translation into English the ideas underlying those proverbs have been well brought out. I wish every success to your laudable undertaking.

Yours sincerely,
(Signed) S. SUBRAMANIEM.

From

C. W. Tamotharam Pillay, Esq., B.A., B.L.

The edition of proverbs brought out by the Rev. Mr. Jensen is decidedly an improvement upon its predecessors. Its classification under appropriate heads gives it a superior aspect, facilitating one to lay his hand on what he wants which he cannot do in a collection simply alphabetically arranged, the advantage of which is also combined in the edition by the index of the initial words.

Notwithstanding that there are slight errors of grammar and spelling, which a European compiler cannot but fall into, the book, I believe, will be of great use to both the Tamilians and foreigners.

(Signed) C. W. Tamotharam Pillay.

Madras, 23*rd April*, 1897.

PREFACE.

About twenty years ago, when I got Percival's collection of Tamil proverbs into my hands, I had only been a short time in India, and had as yet got no insight into Indian thought and literature. I had read only a couple of small Tamil story books, but when reading these I had already perceived that the Indians could hardly tell a story without introducing some proverbs into it. My attention was thus at an early period of my life in India drawn to proverbs, and I began to study Percival's collection. I got, however, very little out of my study, as Percival had only given a translation of the Tamil proverbs, and had given no hints as to their meaning. So in those days I got no insight whatever into the real household proverbs, but had almost to rest satisfied with the many aphorisms, or what we in Tamil call நீதிமொழி, of which we find large numbers in all our Tamil proverb collections. Yet, from what I had seen in the story books and in Percival's collection I had got an interest in these terse, blunt and poetic sayings; and year after year on getting deeper into the thought and life of India, and at the same time becoming acquainted with more and more of the proverbs, my interest in them steadily increased. And whenever I met with a new proverb either when talking with the people or reading Tamil books, I always looked for it in Percival's collection, and if he had not got it, I took a note of it; and at times I tried to have some of them explained by the common people.

While I was thus leisurely prosecuting the study of Tamil proverbs, the Rev. J. Lazarus, B.A., began to prepare a "Dictionary of Tamil Proverbs." I looked forward to the publication of this book with very great interest, but when it appeared, I was somewhat disappointed with it, partly because Mr. Lazarus had not given a translation of the proverbs and partly because his explanation of the proverbs seemed to me, from the insight I had got into the proverbs through years of study, not always to be the right one. But the book roused my interest afresh, and I took a Tamil munshi for about three years to go through all the proverbs I had found in other collections, and those I now found in Mr. Lazarus's book, and also those I had collected myself. This study with my munshi together with the kind help I got from other Tamil people led me to a fuller understanding of Oriental proverbial literature, and after a couple of years investigation, I got the idea of publishing a collection of these beautiful national sayings. But no sooner had I began to realize the idea, than I felt how much easier it was to get an idea than to carry it out. And hundreds of times, when going on with this work, have I felt the force of the Tamil proverb: "I stepped into the water without knowing its depth."

When the idea of publishing a collection of Tamil proverbs occurred to me, I saw at once that I had great difficulties to face. I had the difficulty of two languages, both of which were foreign to me. I had the fear—and still have it—that it might be too much for a foreigner to venture on the publication of Tamil proverbs, as proverbs undoubtedly form the most difficult branch of a nation's literature to comprehend. Besides this, it was clear to me that if I were to publish Tamil proverbs, I could not adopt the usual alphabetical order, but would have to arrange them into groups. Another difficulty—and without comparison the most important one—was to get the proper meaning of the proverbs, not as some pandits may please to explain them, but as common men and women understand them, when they use them in their every day life. Another difficulty, again, was to have these thousands of proverbs before me sifted. What was to be taken, and what to be left out? It always seemed to me that our collections of proverbs suffered from a great evil, *viz.*, that they contained too many useless sayings, too many aphorisms and too many repetitions of the same proverbs.

With these difficulties before me I started, hoping that the proverb would prove true: "Little strokes at last fell great oaks," or as we say in Tamil: "Stroke upon stroke will make even a grindstone creep."

When going into the study of Tamil proverbs one finds that little has been done in the way of making a scientific investigation of them. All proverbs, sayings and aphorisms we meet with in our

Tamil proverb collections we generally call Tamil proverbs, but these two terms—*Tamil* and *Proverbs*—raise two great questions: Are they all Tamil originally, and are they all proverbs? When comparing the Tamil proverbs with the Telugu ones, we find a good number almost word for word the same. And I remember when once walking with a friend in the streets of Poona, that he quoted two Marathi proverbs, both of which we have literally in Tamil. At Bombay I once happened to look into a Marathi proverb collection, and when I asked for a translation of the first proverb in the book I found it to be ours: "The dancing girl, who could not dance, said that the hall was not big enough." But which is which in our Tamil proverb collections. They are all called Tamil.

Again, is it right to insert in our collections of proverbs hundreds and hundreds of aphorisms, classical sayings (நீதிமொழி) and common sayings, when these only communicate a truth in a general way, without making use of any sort of illustration? It seems to me that we should not allow "the confusion of proverbs with mere precepts or maxims destitute of proverbial significance and character" to go on. Each in its proper place. I have not left them out altogether, but tried to insert only such as are common, and at the same time contain rare words or idiomatic phrases.

To show what I mean by aphorisms and precepts, I shall quote a few here:—கண்டவன் எடானோ?—உயிருள்ளமட்டும் தைரியம் விடலாமா?—முதலிலே கெட்டிக்காரன் முடிவிலே சோம்பேறி.—வேலை அதிகம் சம்பளம் கொஞ்சம்.—இச்சித்த காரியம் இரகசியமல்லவே.—கள்ளனுக்கு ஊர் எல்லாம் பகை.—குடித்தனம் ஒன்றுபண்ணினால், நன்மை வரும் தீமை வரும்.—கேட்டவை எல்லாம் நம்பாதே, நம்பினதெல்லாம் சொல்லாதே.—தீமைபேசுகிறவன் தீமையாளிதான்.—புதிய காரியங்களில் புதிய யோசனை வேண்டும்.—தருமத்தைப் பாவம் வெல்லாது.—இருவராலே ஆகாத காரியம் ஒருவராலே ஆகுமா?—செலவு அதிகம் வரவு போதாது.

Here are a few more of the same kind, but a little more classical in their grammar:—குணமில்லாத வித்தை எல்லாம் அவித்தை.—தீரக்கற்றவன் தேசிகன் ஆவான்.—பழிக்கு ஆனோர் சிலர், பழிபடுவோர் சிலர்.—உருவத்தினாலேயல்ல இன்பப்பேச்சினால் கிளி நன்குமதிக்கப்படும்.—உதிரத்துக்கு அல்லவோ உருக்கம் இருக்கும்.—அறம் பொருள் இன்பம் எல்லாருக்குமில்லை.—தீயாரைச்சேர்ந்து ஒழுகல் தீது, தீயார் பண்செய்வனவும் தீது.—சொல்லும் சொல் ஆக்கமும் கேடும் தரும்.—நல்ல நினைவை அனுசரித்தலே கெட்ட நினைவை நீக்கல்.—குலஸ்திரீ தன் பர்த்தாவையும், பரஸ்திரீ தன் மேனியையும் பேணுவார். இல்லறமல்லது, நல்லறமன்று. மனையாள்

விடியுமுன் எழுந்து வீட்டுப்பணி செய்வாள்.—But where would be the end of it, if these were to be passed off as proverbs? A fine collection, quite a Mahabharata, might be made out of them. The literature of India abounds in them. From the Mahabharata, Hitopadesa, ஔவையார் and other books, we could easily get a beautiful collection of aphorisms and sayings counted by thousands.

Many of the proverbs met with in books have so often been handled by pandits, that we meet with the same proverb in a number of forms. The same is the case with a number of proverbs, which, just because they are in common use all over the country, have become slightly altered when wandering about the country from place to place and from caste to caste. As they are in spite of slight changes the same proverb, they ought either to be put down together or references ought to be made from one to the other, as Captain Carr has tried to do in his collection of Telugu proverbs. If this is not done, they cannot but give the inexperienced student of proverbs a great deal of trouble; and to me they have been a real worry, as I had to find them all out, in order that I might not in this collection repeat two proverbs that are the same. Here are a few examples of this kind:—

கண்ணில் குத்தின விரலைக் கண்டிப்பார் உண்டோ=கண்ணில் பட்ட கையைத் தறிப்பாரில்லை=கைதப்பிக் கண்ணில் பட்டால் கையைக் கண்டிப்பதுண்டா=கைவிரல் கண்ணில்பட்டால் கையை என்ன பண்ணலாம்=விரல் கண்ணில் குத்தினது என்று வெட்டிப்போடுவார்களா=விழியிலே குத்தின விரலை அறுப்பாருண்டா.—அம்பட்டன் குப்பையைக் கிளறினால் மயிர்மயிராய்ப் புறப்படும்=கிண்டக் கிண்ட அம்பட்டன் குப்பை மயிரே புறப்படும்.—அமாவாசைப் பருக்கை என்றைக்கும் அகப்படுமோ=நித்தியம் கிடைக்குமா அமாவாசைச்சோறு.—அப்பிடாவுமில்லை வெட்டுக்கத்தியுமில்லை=அவனுக்குக் கப்படாவுமில்லை வெட்டுக்கத்தியுமில்லை=கப்படாவுமில்லை வெட்டக் கத்தியுமில்லை.—உடம்பு முழுதும் நனைந்தவருக்குக் கூதல் என்ன=அற நனைந்தவருக்குக் கூதல் என்ன=முட்ட நனைந்தார்க்குக் குளிரில்லை=முழுதும் நனைந்தவருக்கு ஈரமில்லை=முற்றும் நனைந்தவருக்கு ஈரம் ஏது.—இருந்தும் கெடுத்தான் செத்தும் கெடுத்தான்=திருவாய்த்தான் இருந்தும் கெடுத்தான் செத்தும் கெடுத்தான்=சீவரத்துக் கிராமணி இருந்தும் கெடுத்தான் செத்தும் கெடுத்தான்=சியபுரத்துப் பள்ளி செத்தும் கெடுத்தான் இருந்தும் கெடுத்தான்.—கடலிலே ஏற்றம் போட்ட கதை=சமுத்திரத்தில் ஏற்றம் போட்டதுபோல்=சமுத்திரத்தில் ஏற்றம்போட்டுத் தண்ணீர் இறைத்தாற்போல்.—வேலையற்ற அம்பட்டன் மகளைப் பிடித்துச் சிறைத்தானும்=வேலையில்லாத அம்பட்டன் ஆட்டைச் சிரைத்தானும்=மினைக்கெட்ட அம்பட்டன் பூனையைச் சிரைத்தானும்

=வேலை மினக்கெட்ட அம்பட்டன் பெண்சாதி தலையைச் சிரைத்தானாம்.—கூழ் புளித்தது என்றும் மாங்காய் புளித்தது என்றும் உணராமல் சொல்லலாமா=வாய் புளித்ததோ மாங்காய் புளித்ததோ.—உடைந்த சங்கு ஊது பறியுமா=ஒட்டை சங்கு ஊது பறியாது.—அரைக்குடம் ததும்பும் நிறைகுடம் ததும்பாது=குறைகுடம் தளம்பும் நிறைகுடம் தளம்பாது=குறைகுடம் கூத்தாடும்=நிறைகுடம் தளும்பாது.—கட்டாந்தரையில் கொட்டக் குட்டிச்சுவரில் நெறிகட்டினதாம்=குட்டிச்சுவரில் தேள்கொட்டிக் கட்டுத்தறியிலே நெறிகட்டுமா=திண்ணைக்குத் தேள் கொட்டிற்று தண்ணீர்மிடாவுக்கு நெறிகட்டிற்று=தென்னமரத்தில் தேள்கொட்டப் பனைமரத்தில் நெறிக்கட்டினதுபோல்=தென்னைக்குத் தேள்கொட்டப் பனைக்கு நெறிகட்டினதுபோல்.—ஊர் மெச்ச நடவாமல் உடல் மெச்ச நடக்கிறவனைப்போல்=உடலுக்கோ பால்வார்த்து உண்பது, ஊருக்கோ பால்வார்த்து உண்பது=ஊருக்குப் பால்வார்த்து உண்கிறாயா உடம்புக்குப் பால்வார்த்து உண்கிறாயா=உடல் மெச்சப் பால் குடிக்கிறாயா, ஊர் மெச்சப் பால் குடிக்கிறாயா.—நிழல் நல்லது முசிறு பொல்லாதது=மரம் நல்லதுதான் முசுடு கெட்டது.

The above are only a few examples of the many repetitions of the very same proverb.

There is another way of changing a proverb, *viz.*, by putting the second half of a proverb at the beginning, so that we get two proverbs out of one. As an instance:—பட்ட காலிலே படும், கெட்ட குடியே கெடும், changed into:—கெட்ட குடியே கெடும் பட்டகாலிலே படும்; இருந்தகால் மூதேவி, நடந்தகால் சீதேவி, changed into:—நடந்த காலிலே சீதேவி, இருந்த காலிலே மூதேவி.

As my aim in making this collection has been practical rather than scientific, I have not tried to solve all these difficulties in any other way than by trying my best to avoid all repetitions. But with reference to this there is much for any one to do who would try to give us a scientific collection of Tamil proverbs. In such a work we should also expect to see what we call *Tamil proverbs* sifted, so that we might learn where they have originated, as in a good English collection of proverbs we can see where each had its origin—in Greece, in Italy, in Spain, in Germany or elsewhere.

This collection of proverbs is a selection from the thousands that are given in our Tamil proverb collections, and also from the many I have come across when reading Tamil books and conversing with Tamil people. Though I feel sure that there are a good number of real household proverbs I have not given that ought to be in such a collection as this, I am at the same time convinced that there cannot be very many. Once a man gave me 200 proverbs which he had collected at Madura, but among them all I found only two new ones which were not more or less a repetition of what I had.

The Tamil proverb collections from which I have got help are:—A bazaar book containing about 2,000 proverbs without any English. உவமைச்சொல் அகராதி, a collection of about 5,000 Tamil proverbs published in 1872, which is with reference to real household proverbs, far superior to Percival's. The book is out of print but can be seen in our public libraries. Then there is Percival's collection of about 6,000 proverbs with an English translation. A very useful little "Handbook of Tamil Proverbs and Phrases" was published in 1888 by Mr. P. Satya Nesan, B.A., containing 500 proverbs only, but with translation, application and many similar English proverbs. The last collection that appeared was Mr. Lazarus's "Dictionary of Tamil Proverbs." This book is now the largest collection we have, and so far it makes its predecessors superfluous. Mr. Lazarus has not translated the proverbs, but to every one he has given a hint as to its meaning.

The other books from which I have chiefly drawn are the Tamil story books and Sastras. Of such I shall mention a few: கதாமஞ்சரி, கதாசிந்தாமணி, பஞ்சதந்திரம், கிளிக்கதை, முப்பத்திரண்டு பதுமைகதை. Pandit S. M. Natesa Sastri's "Folklore in Southern India," which has a number of proverbs and Tamil stories to illustrate them. A magazine published some years ago called: "The Saguna Bodhini Series." A book called இராமநாடகம் is, though written in poetry, full of proverbs. This is still more the case with "Vinoda Rasamanjari" by A. Viraswami Chettiar, late Pandit in the Madras Presidency College. This book is simply interwoven with Tamil Proverbs. "Mathar Neethy" is another story book containing many fine proverbs; and the same may be said of a book called: குடும்பசம்ரக்ஷணி. "The Viveka Chintamani," a monthly magazine, published by Mr. C. V. Swaminatha Iyer in Triplicane, has for the last year had a number of Tamil proverbs with Tamil explanation in every issue. The Sastras translated from Sanskrit into Tamil contain hardly any proverbs except the Mahabharata. This royal storehouse of something of everything that India has produced contains a good number of proverbs interspersed throughout the huge volume. So even with reference to proverbs the Bengali proverb almost holds good: "What is there after the Mahabharata?"

Dear as these beautiful little proverbs are to Tamil people, I have for years wondered that so little has been done to make them known to Europeans, specially to European ladies, who have, or, at least, could have, so much influence with Indian women. Percival gave a translation to his collection and left it there. But a mere translation of a real proverb will not in most cases bring us into contact with its homely meaning. Take as an instance Percival's:—இளையாள் இலை தின்னி, மூத்தாள் காய் அறிவாள், translated: "the younger sister feeds on leaves, the elder is accustomed to fruit;" in this case the translation is wrong, but even if it were translated properly, it would have no meaning to a European. As Percival says, "In many instances the application has equally puzzled both myself and others to whom I have applied for information." To be sure, there's the rub in trying to explain proverbs. And consequently Percival left out the application, although he says that foreigners destined to spend the best part of their life among the Tamil people will find their proverbs of inestimable value. But in many cases a Tamil proverb without its application is to a foreigner almost like an unbroken cocoanut to a dog, as the Tamil saying is. Mr. P. Satya Nesan in his collection began in the right way, but did not go far enough; Mr. J. Lazarus, on the other hand, had his thoughts chiefly directed on collecting all the Tamil proverbs into one book. Hence Tamil proverbs as such have hitherto been handed over to us like a chaos.

My desire, as I have already indicated, has been first to make the application of each proverb clear, and next to divide them into families. As far as I have succeeded in grasping the meaning, so far almost have I succeeded, I suppose, in getting them into their proper families. But it is hard to get such a register of sin, as proverbs almost are, into a systematic order. The phenomena of sinful life are so manifold, and the reflections on it so numerous that the difficulties sometimes seemed to me insurmountable. Be it remembered, that as long as I was working at the arranging of them I had not at hand the English index nor the two glossaries and the many references from one proverb to another, and from one family to another, that are now before the reader. But in spite of all the difficulties and drawbacks, it seems to me that it is only when we have arranged the proverbs in groups or families that we are able to see what the proverbs teach us. I do not look upon the arrangement introduced by me as at all final. Far from it. What I have done I wish to be considered a beginning only, or a little attempt at cultivating the ground. Many of the proverbs are imperfectly explained, partly because their meaning has not been fully grasped, and partly because many of them to be well understood ought to have a little story attached to them. They might be divided into more families, and all the minor families might again be grouped into main families, as I have tried to do at the beginning of the book, and also at the end of it.

As the result of bringing the proverbs into groups, though I have in many cases not achieved what I have aimed at, one can easily get an insight into the social, ethical or domestic thoughts contained in them. Take as an instance the family on fate and fortune. There may within this family be a few that would have fitted in better somewhere else, and in some other family may be a few that might have been inserted under fate and fortune; but one can at once by the help of the arrangement of the book get an insight into what the Tamil proverbs teach on such a subject. I have also observed that the dividing of the proverbs into families is a great advantage in the study of the Tamil language itself. Though each proverb in a family may be said to harp on one and the same string, the thought is expressed in a variety of terms, some of which are synonymous. Look for instance at the family on ostentation or டம்பம்—one of the chief Indian sins, according to the proverbs at least—in what a variety of language is vanity rebuked! Another advantage of the family arrangement is that as a number of similar proverbs are brought together, they need less explanation; for apart from a few that are misplaced, the heading of each chapter —though in many cases it has been difficult to find an adequate heading—gives the key to the meaning of all that are included under it. It is a matter of consequence that though the proverbs in each family allude to the same thing, they are in most cases not synonymous. In the chapter on a mother, it is at once evident that most of the proverbs have little or nothing connecting them but this, that they refer to a mother. In the same chapter we get also a good insight into the way in which India regards a mother in all her capacities. In an hour's time one can by studying the chapter on a mother get some real knowledge of her position in India,—a knowledge which one could hardly get from any other sources. The references from one number to another all through the book are not to be taken as references to synonymous proverbs. This holds good in a few cases, but more often the references mean only that the reader would do well to compare the particular proverb with another, because they are closely related in thought or in language. As related individual proverbs are referred to each other, so are whole families referred to each other by the numbers given below the different chapters.

In selecting English equivalents for the Tamil proverbs I have used the following books:—W. Carew Hazlitt's "English Proverbs and Proverbial Phrases." "A Handbook of Proverbs," which is a republication of Ray's collection of English Proverbs. Captain Carr's "Telugu Proverbs" A collection of Marathi Proverbs. And "Eastern Proverbs and Emblems" by the Rev. J. Long.

A few words on the characteristics of Indian proverbs compared with the English, as they have struck me while working on them, may not be out of place, though I have not made a study of this subject.

When going through an English collection of proverbs, one is struck by the number of proverbs referring to the weather and the seasons. India has very few proverbs of this kind. In India we have the South-West monsoon from May to October, and the North-East monsoon from November to April, and there is the end of it. The characteristic of the weather in England is change, while in India it is regularity. It would be thoroughly out of place in India to say:—"A woman's mind and winter wind change oft." For the big chapter in this book on "Sorrow and lamentation of women" I could hardly find any equivalent from the English. The English woman has been respected, while her Indian sister has met with very little respect, hence her lamentation, and her revolting in bitter terms against her oppressors. Again, in India we have no girls or young ladies. We meet in India with female children and wives, as the Indian woman passes at once from being a child to being a wife. But in Europe young women have a fine time for their development, both physical and intellectual, before they get married. In this transition period, then, there is a rich sphere for English proverbs, but as there is no such period in India, there are no such Indian proverbs. Even a widow is not overlooked by the English proverbs, as she sometimes aspires, if possible, to marry again, but the Indian widow has no such aspiration, for she is a mere widow, a முண்டைச்சி, a contemptible thing! Woman's dress plays a part in English proverbs, but it is jewelry which is here the all-important thing; hence the tailor's shop plays the same part in Europe as the goldsmith's in India. In India a woman has had no trouble in dressing up in order to make an attractive appearance in Society, as her parents arranged her marriage for her while she was still a child. Even if she is a monkey—exceedingly ugly—she will be married.

The Tamil proverbs referring to vanity and ostentation outnumber the English and are at the same time very pointed. There is almost no end to the Tamil proverbs on the wicked tendency in the human race to see their enemies destroyed. Though India is saturated with superstition, it seems to me, strange to say, that we meet with more English than Tamil proverbs on superstition. The Tamil proverbs almost altogether leave out criticism of superstition, ceremonies, gods and temples, in short, all that refers to religious life. Even on caste there are comparatively few. Folly and laziness are regarded so differently by the Indians and the English that it is impossible to find English equivalents for the Tamil.

The meaning of an English and a Tamil proverb may be the same, but the habits, customs and climate have formed them so differently. As an instance, we say in Tamil: "Ears (ornamented) with palmyra-leaves are better than ears with no ornaments;" for this we might put the English:—"Better a bare foot, than no foot at all;" to go bare-footed in the Northern countries of Europe, especially in winter-time, would be very hard, but in India it is difficult to understand this English proverb, as all Indians still enjoy the great privilege of going bare-footed.

One great peculiarity about the Tamil or Dravidian proverbs is that the animals we meet with are but dumb figures brought in merely for the purpose of illustration. In the Panchatandra, on the other hand, all animals are imbued with sense and characteristics: they think, talk, move and behave in every way like man. Nay, some animals in those ancient days seem even to have been reading the Vedas. The Aryans have given life to all their animals. The Dravidians, on the contrary, seem not to have seen much in animals; in their proverbs, at least, they have not attributed anything like intellect to them, except perhaps a little to the cat. The shrewd and sensible elephant represents in Tamil proverbs outward greatness only. The gentle cow gives milk. The buffalo is for ploughing. Sheep are as stupid as their shepherd. The dog's faithfulness is unknown. Dogs, pigs and crows are dirty and greedy animals. The ass is ever obstinate, but has willingly or unwillingly to submit to hard work and hard treatment; its fate is a hard and pitiful one, indeed; in the hands of the washerman it fares as badly as the monkey in the hands of the mendicant. The doctor and medicine for the poor ass is to go and roll itself in the dust of the street. Whatever is done to an ass, it cannot become a horse; in this sense the horse is used for something great and grand. But as the animals are brought in only in order to illustrate, and not for their own sake at all, they are of little interest in this connection.

I have always been much struck with the complaining, the sighing, the groaning under the tyranny of men and of fate that underlies so many of the Indian proverbs. This is also the case with the Indian songs, hence also almost all tunes in India are full of melancholy. The triumphant tone does not pervade anything Indian. In all departments of Indian literature it is as if the goddess of the earth, Bhûmidêvi, stood personified, groaning under the burden heaped upon her. This feeling has found very strong expression in the Bhagavatgita:—

Arjuna.

Slayer of Madhu! Yet again, this Yôg,
This Peace, derived from equanimity,
Made known by thee—I see no fixity
Therein, no rest, because the heart of men
Is unfixed, Krishna! rash, tumultuous,
Wilful and strong. It were all one, I think,
To hold the wayward wind, as tame man's heart.

Krishna.

Hero long armed! beyond denial, hard
Man's heart is to restrain and wavering;
Yet may it grow restrained by habit, Prince!
By want of self-command. This Yôg, I say,
Cometh not lightly to th' ungoverned: (who need it!)
But he who will be master of himself
Shall win it, if he stoutly strive thereto.

The Song Celestial.—E. ARNOLD.

But why so much ado about nothing? Why take so much trouble about these proverbs? What is the good of it? Who cares for these obsolete childish things? Perhaps some old grandmother, when telling stories to women and children inside the houses who are half asleep on their mats, may make some use of them. But we men of the nineteenth century, what on earth have we to do with obsolete proverbial literature, some may ask. My answer is that it is well known that the more a nation develops the more its proverbs die out; but though Europe has now for many hundreds of years been developing, there are many proverbs still in circulation among the different nations of Europe, and some of these proverbs will not die out as long as there is a tongue on earth to speak them. Whether we look to the West or to the East we find that figurative speech always has great influence over the masses. I suppose this was the reason why Jesus, who "knew what was in man," "spake unto the multitude in parables; and without a parable spake he not unto them." It is interesting to observe that the latest Tamil drama: "Lilavati-Sulochana" written by an educated man, P. Sambandam, B.A., contains about a score of Tamil proverbs. If proverbs are still largely in use by the masses, if they still form a part of their daily language, used in practical life for practical purposes, it is clearly our duty to know them, if we want to exert any influence on the people.

When we read biographies of great men, we often see these great men attribute much of their greatness to their mother's influence on them in their early life. A mother, or a home, does lay the first foundation in every child's heart for its future, and in most cases the foundation laid by the mother or by the women of the home, has a most important effect on the moral life afterwards. In this case India is no exception to the rule. But from where does the Indian mother get thoughts by which to educate her children at home? When a child is naughty, or when a daughter has quarrelled with her mother-in-law and comes home, does an Indian mother in such cases in order to rebuke or comfort quote from the Bhagavatgita, or from the Upanishads? Does she from these books try to inculcate in the child's heart what the different *indriyas* mean? that some of them are to be subdued, others again to be developed?

The Indian mother has her own practical way at home.

Legends, stories and proverbs are her storehouse; from these she obtains material for rebuking, for sneering, for warning, for encouraging, for comforting and for praising. The proverbs and maxims are India's practical ethics. The Indian proverbs are not antiquarian curiosities, but living and stern realities, and hence perhaps more celestial than the so-called "Celestial Songs" of the Bhagavatgita.

By a good knowledge of Indian proverbs one is enabled, as it were, to feel the moral pulse of the Indian people, and a sound insight into the proverbial literature of India is like getting a microscope by which one can look deeply into the recesses of the native heart. Nothing else can throw so much light on the daily practice of the Indians as do the proverbs. And if one could publish the obscene ones also, which often contain most striking truths, we should see still deeper into the misery of the country. But the obscene ones with which I have met in our collections, and in intercourse with the people, I have left out. I have, however, reason to believe that there are many obscene ones besides the few that I have seen and heard; and that they are freely used by the great majority of the common people even in their children's presence. The children are often, I am told, made to laugh over them.

Proverbs are merciless in their criticism of sinful life, and they always aim at putting things right. As already said, the Indian mothers nurse their sons and daughters with them. By proverbs satire is pronounced over folly and over wickedness. By a proverb a crowd or a household is made to smile pleasantly, that otherwise might have got into a hot fight. In proverbs lies buried an endless store of criticism, encouragement, humour, sorrow and complaint, referring to all classes of mankind from the unborn child to the grey-haired veteran. And as the Hindu—and we might for that matter say the whole world—likes to hurt without hurting (சுடாமல் சுடுகிறது), that he may not burn his own fingers, he has in the proverbial literature material by the help of which he can indirectly express his sorrow and joy, his approval or disapproval. By proverbs the shrewd and avaricious Brahmin is criticised; the calculating and careful Chetty is held up to ridicule or indirectly praised; the shepherd's stupidity and the kuravan's rudeness is brought out; the ungrateful and deceitful friend is mercilessly rebuked; the life of immoral women is censured in strong terms; vanity is ridiculed; the dulness and indifference of the Pariah is sarcastically blamed. No wonder that many of the proverbs are universal in their application, for human life is much the same all the world over. Anger, pride, arrogance, selfishness, avarice, passion, dissimulation, falsehood and many more sins that keep society at a low level, are all of them universal, and it is with such that the proverbs deal.

The Rev. J. Long in his "Eastern Proverbs and Emblems" says with reference to the Chinese proverbs—he has it from "Scarborough's Chinese Proverbs":—"Used as quotations, the value of proverbs in China is immense. So used in conversation, they add a piquancy and a flavour which greatly delight the Chinese and make mutual intercourse more easy and agreeable. But it is to the missionary that the value of an extensive acquaintance with Chinese proverbs is of the highest importance. Personal experience, as well as the repeated testimony of others, make us bold to assert, that even a limited knowledge of Chinese proverbs is to him daily of inestimable value. A proverb will often serve to rouse the flagging attention of a congregation, or to arrest it at the commencement of a discourse. A proverb will often serve to produce a smile of good nature in an apparently ill-tempered audience and so to call forth a kindly feeling which did not seem before to exist. And very often a proverb aptly quoted will serve to convey a truth in the most terse and striking manner, so obviating the necessity for detached and lengthy arguments whilst they fix at a stroke the idea you are wishing to convey." The same author remarks: "Like the proverbs of Solomon (நீதிமொழி), the Psalms, Bunyan's 'Pilgrim's Progress,' and the 'Arabian Nights,' they speak in a language 'understanded of the people'."

And from Archbishop Trench he quotes: "Anyone who by after-investigation has sought to discover how much our rustic hearers carry away, even from sermons to which they have attentively listened, will find that it is hardly ever the course or tenor of the argument, supposing the discourse to have contained such; but if anything has been uttered as it used so often to be by the best Puritan preachers, tersely, pointedly, epigrammatically, this will have stayed by them, while all the rest has passed away.

Great preachers to the people, such as have found their way to the universal heart of their fellows, have ever been great employers of proverbs."

Pandits when inserting proverbs in the books they have made, or in books translated by them, have often tried to refine the language in which they are expressed. They are always trying to employ big words and highflown terms, not knowing as yet that simplicity is the highest beauty. I think it is our duty, when we meet with pandit-refined proverbs to bring them back to their original form. I could give many examples of this kind, but I shall confine myself to one: *பன்றியோடு இணங்கின* or *கூடிய கன்றும் மலம் தின்னும்.* The common form of this proverb is: *பன்றி பின் போகிற கன்றும் பீ தின்னும்.* *பீ* is not an indecent word in a Hindu home as yet. Would that no worse words were used in Hindu houses! Real life has dictated the proverbs, and as they are used in real life, so they should be quoted. Their meaning, their words and their grammar are alike practical and simple, why then dress them up in a pandit's dress? When they die, let them die; but as long as they are realities, and play an important part in the life of the nation, we should let them go in their natural simplicity, and honour them in their natural dress.

The Two Tamil Indexes.

I might perhaps be blamed for arranging the proverbs into families, because this arrangement makes it almost impossible for us to find any individual proverb, when we wish to see it. It is, however, almost equally difficult to do this with the alphabetic arrangement, if one does not happen to remember the first word, which is often no easy thing, as it may be a most insignificant word, an *இந்த* or *அந்த* or *எந்த* or *ஒரு* or any other little word which has no relation to the meaning of the proverb. I have, however, furnished the book with an index, or alphabetical glossary, containing the first word of each proverb, so that if the first word is remembered it is easy to find any proverb.

I have noticed by experience that there are words within the proverbs that by and by stick to the mind; while we forget the first word of a proverb, we remember words within it. I have therefore also provided this book with an index of words from within each proverb arranged alphabetically.

This latter glossary is given not only to help the reader to find the proverbs, but also in order to supply a vocabulary of the most important words found in them. The student who takes an interest in Tamil can easily, whenever he meets with a word in other books, or in conversation, and wishes to see how the word is used in proverbs, turn to the two indexes, find the word, and see the use of it and also its translation. As to translation, however, he may not always find direct help, as the translation of a proverb cannot but be somewhat free, if we are to get the meaning out of it by a translation.

To those who might prefer the proverbs arranged according to the letter, and not according to the spirit, the two glossaries will be of great help, as they can at once find out for themselves where the words horse, elephant, monkey, snake, poison, medicine, doctor, Brahmin, Pariah, Chetty, rain, wind, sickle, thali, husband, wife, woman, destiny and such like words appear.

I have in conclusion to express my thanks to all who have helped me in this work. My munshi, Mr. Vasudeva Pillai, has been my chief help in making the proverbs clear to me and in giving me their homely applications. He has also supplied me with a few hundreds of new proverbs, not found before in any collection I have come across. But after I had gone through the thousands of proverbs and phrases with my munshi, and as far as possible ascertained their meaning and their application, had selected those out of them that I wanted, had translated them into English, added their application, furnished some of them—about 1,500—with corresponding English proverbs, brought them into families, and made a copy of it all, there was one thing still to be done, and that was to make a thorough revision of the English part of the book. For this last, but very important part of the undertaking the Rev. A. C. Clayton of the Wesleyan Mission came to my assistance, and for the generous help he has given me I shall ever feel most grateful. For about a year and a half Mr. Clayton has almost daily worked at the revision of my English manuscripts, going over most of them twice at least. The proverbs being in a simple language, their translation ought also to be simple and plain. But it is very difficult to translate an Eastern proverb into English so that its meaning may be clearly understood and it is still more difficult to do it so that the language of the translation may be in harmony with the original in directness and simplicity. So whatever the reader finds of idiomatic beauty in the English translation and application is almost all owing to the deep interest Mr. Clayton has taken in this work and the perseverance with which he has sought to improve it.

To my great sorrow Mr. Clayton was transferred up-country at the beginning of this year. When he left there were still about 1,000 proverbs to be carried through the press, and up-country Mr. Clayton found it impossible to correct the proofs as quickly as I desired. Mr. A. Moffat, M.A., B.SC. of the Christian College has been kind enough to help me in correcting what was still left to be carried through the press. The Rev. N. Devasahayam, B.A., of the Leipzig Mission has also kindly gone over all the proof-sheets.

HERMAN JENSEN.

VEPERY, MADRAS.
24th April, 1897.

INDEX TO THE ENGLISH HEADINGS.

A

CLASSIFIED COLLECTION

OF

TAMIL PROVERBS.

GOD.

கடவுள்.

These Sentences about God are not Proverbs, but Aphorisms.

கடவுள் துணை.

God (is our) help, *or* The Lord is our help.

This little sentence is put above the Title of almost every Hindu book.

கடவுள் துணை or தெய்வமே துணை are the most common. But we meet also with:

கணபதி துணை ; ஸ்ரீராம ஜெயம் and other expressions.

1. அன்புக்கு ஒருவனே.
God is love. (Upanishad.)

2. அறியாத வஸ்து or மனோவாக்குக்கு எட்டாதவன்.
The unknown God, *or* The One that cannot be reached by mind or by words.

3. அரிது அரிது அஞ்சு எழுத்து உணர்தல்.
Exceedingly difficult it is to know the five letters.

The '*five letters*' refer to famous incantation, or the highest spiritual wisdom, or God's Name.

"*The best way to see divine light, is to put out thine own candle.*"

> "Some say that eight plain hold all truth,
> And some that it doth dwell in five!
> No wonder that such living fools
> Exalt Vishnu, and Siva praise."

CH. E. GOVER: *The Folk-Songs of Southern India.*

4. அவன் அசையாது, அணுவும் அசையாது.
Unless God move, not an atom will move.
God is the hidden power behind everything.

5. ஈசனுக்கு ஒப்பு இங்கு ஒன்றுமில்லை.
Nothing here is equal to God.

6. உள்ளக் கருத்து வள்ளலுக்குத் தெரியும்.
The secrets of the heart are known to God. (Psalm 44, 21.)

7. எள்ளுக்குள் எண்ணெய்போல எங்கும் நிறைந்திருக்கிறான்.
God pervades all, as the oil in the oil seed.

8. ஒருவராயிருந்ததில் அவருக்குச் சந்தோஷமில்லை.
God did not feel joy in being alone (and hence he created). (Upanishad.)

9. சப்த பிரம்மத்தினால் அசப்த பிரம்மம் பிரகாசிப்பிக்கிறது.
The invisible God is made to shine by the revealed God. (Upanishad.)

10. சப்த பிரம்மம் பரபிரம்மம் இரண்டையும் அறியவேண்டியது.
We should know both the revealed and the unrevealed God. (Upanishad.)

11. தன்னிலேயே தான் இருப்பான்.
God is the self-existing. (Vishnu Puràna.)

12. தீதுறும் பாவச் செய்கை அற்றவன் தேவன்.
He who is without sin is God.

13. தெய்வ வணக்கமே நரக வாசலை அடைக்கும் தாழ்.
The worship of God is the bolt that shuts the gates of hell.

14. நாராயணன் ஒருவன்தான், இரண்டாவதன் ஒருவனுமில்லை.
God is one, there is no second to him.

15. பரபிரம்மத்தைத் தியானம் செய்வதினால், பிரகாசிக்காமலிருந்த விஞ்ஞானமானது பிரகாசமாகிறது.
By meditation on God the spiritual wisdom in man, which is unilluminated will become radiant. (Upanishad.)

16. புகை நுழையாத இடத்திலேயும் அவன் நுழைவான்.
Even where smoke cannot enter He can enter.
Said also about a crafty person.

GOD AND MAN.

17. ஆகாசத்திலிருந்து அறுந்துவிட்டேன், பூமிதேவி ஏற்றுக்கொண்டாள்.
I was torn off from heaven, but God's (Bhumidevi's) mercy received me on earth.
So says one who stands alone and helpless in this world.

18. அகதிக்கு ஆகாசமே துணை.
Heaven helps the helpless.

19. அடிக்கும் ஒரு கை, அணைக்கும் ஒரு கை.
(God's justice and love) smite with one hand, and embrace with the other.

20. அரசன் அன்று கொல்லும், தெய்வம் நின்று கொல்லும்.
A king kills on the day of the offence, God stands (delays) and kills.
"*God stays long, but strikes at last.*"
"*Though the mills of God grind slowly, yet they grind exceeding small;*
Though he stands and waits with patience, with exactness grinds he all." (Tennyson.)

21. ஹரியும் சிவனும் ஒன்றல்ல என்கிறவன் வாயிலே மண்!
May earth fall into the mouth of him who says, that Vishnu and Siva are not one!

22. ஆட்டுக்கு வால் அளவு அறுத்து வைத்திருக்கிறது.
God has cut the tail of the sheep as it is. 28.
God has limited each person's power.

23. ஈசனுடைய அடியார் மனம் எரிந்து புகைந்தால், வீண்போகுமோ?
Shall it be counted as nothing that the hearts of God's worshippers burn and smoke? 24.

24. எளியாரை வலியார் அடித்தால், வலியாரைத் தெய்வம் அடிக்கும்.
If the mighty oppress the weak, God will punish the mighty. 23, 30.

25. ஏழை பிள்ளைக்குத் தெய்வமே துணை.
God is the protector of the helpless children. (Psalm 72, 4.)
"*Where God helps, nought harms.*"

26. கண்ணைக் கெடுத்த தெய்வம் கோலைக் கொடுத்தது.
God who deprived him of sight gave him a staff (*i.e.*, mental acuteness).
"*God never shuts one door, but he opens another.*"
"*A blind man's wife is in God's keeping.*" (Kashmiri Proverb.)

27. கிழவியும் காதம், குதிரையும் காதம்.
The old woman finished her ten miles, and so did the horse.
The story is that a man having performed the proper religious ceremonies hastily mounted his horse and set off for heaven. At the same time an old woman performed some ceremonies, with all her heart slowly and carefully, and her real piety brought her to heaven before the man on horseback.
"*God knows well which are the best pilgrims.*"

28. குதிரை குணம் அறிந்து அல்லவோ தம்பிரான் கொம்பு கொடுக்கவில்லை.
Is it not because God knew the disposition of the horse that He has not given it horns. 22.
"*God sends the shrewd cow short horns.*" "*Curs'd cows have short horns.*"

29. குழந்தையும் தெய்வமும் கொண்டாடின இடத்தில்.
Children and God prefer to be where they are made much of.

30. கெடுப்பாரைத் தெய்வம் கெடுக்கும்.
Those that destroy others will be destroyed by God. 24.

31. சுவாமி இல்லை என்றால் சாணியைப் பார்; மருந்தில்லை என்றால் பாணத்தைப் பார்; பேதி இல்லை என்றால் (நேர்) வாளத்தைப் பார்.
If you say there is no God, look at the cowdung; if you say, there is no medicine, look at the fireworks; if you say, there is no purgative, look at the croton seed. 130.

The cowdung of which the image of Ganesa is formed does not get worm eaten like other cowdung, because a grass root is put through it. The fireworks being made of 'medicines' or chemicals burn splendidly. And the *croton tiglium* never fails as a purgative.

32. தலைவன் சொல் கேள், நன்னெறி தவறேல்.
Listen to the word of God and don't turn from the good path.

33. தான் ஒன்று நினைக்க, தெய்வம் ஒன்று நினைக்கிறது.
While man thinks one thing, God thinks another.

34. திருவாக்குக்கு எதிர்வாக்கு உண்டோ?
No word can go against God's word.

35. தூங்காதவனே நீங்காதவன். .
He who is ever active is never moved.

36. பூனையானது தன்னைத் தழுவத்தெரியாத சக்தியற்ற குட்டியைத் தன் வாயில் கவ்விச் செல்வதுபோல்.
As the cat takes its young one which is unable to crawl and carries it, (so God takes the helpless and carries him, till he learns to cling to God as the young monkey clings to its mother).

These illustrations from the cat and the monkey are called: மார்ச்சால நியாயம் and மர்க்கட நியாயம்.

37. தெய்வமில்லாதையா பொழுது போகிறதும், பொழுது விடிகிறதும்.
Is it because there is no God, that the sun sets and rises?
Said ironically to a disbeliever in God as the Designer.

38. தெய்வம் காட்டும், ஊட்டுமோ?
God will show us a way but will he put food into our mouth?
"*God helps those who help themselves.*"
"*God gives every bird its food, but does not throw it into the nest.*"
"*God reaches us good things with our own hand.*"

39. தெய்வசித்தமிருந்தால், செத்தவனும் எழும்புவான்.
If it be the will of God, even the dead will rise.

40. முன்னவனே முன் நின்றால், முடியாத காரியம் உண்டோ?
If the first one (God) stand before us, there is nothing which we cannot do.
"*What God will, no frost can kill.*"

41. வையம்தோறும், தெய்வம் தொழு.
Whatever world you inhabit (through the different transmigrations) worship God.

FATE.

விதி.

NO ONE WILL ESCAPE WHAT GOD HAS PREDICTED.

42. அயன் இட்ட கணக்கு ஆருக்கும் தப்பாது.
No one shall escape God's account.

43. அயன் இட்ட எழுத்தில் அணுவளவும் தப்பாது.
In what God has written there will not be an atom of failure.

44 அயன் அளந்தபடி.
According to God's measure.

45. அன்றைக்கு எழுதினதை அழித்து எழுதுவானோ?
What God has written before that He will not destroy and re-write.
" *That which must be, will be.*"

46. அயன் அமைப்பை ஆராலும் தள்ளக்கூடாது.
No one can cast off God's decree.

47. இட்ட எழுத்துக்கு ஏற ஆசைப்பட்டால் கிடைக்குமா?
If we want more than God has appointed, shall we get it?

48. இல்லது வராது, உள்ளது போகாது.
That which does not exist will not come into existence, and that which exists will not be annihilated.

49. ஊசி முனையில் தவம் செய்தாலும் உள்ளதுதான் கிடைக்கும்.
Even if a man make penance standing on the point of a needle, he will not get more than was destined for him. 56.

50. ஊத்தை போனாலும், உள்வினை தீராது.
Though dirt may be got rid of, inherited fate will not expire.

51. எண்ணெய் போக முழுகினாலும், எழுத்துப் போகத் தேய்ப்பாருண்டா?
One may bathe so as to wash off oil, but who can rub himself so as to free himself from fate.

52. எழுதின விதி அழுதால் தீருமா?
Though one weeps, will the fate written (by Brahmà) be removed?

53. கோட்டையில் (or நாட்டையாள) பெண் பிறந்தாலும், போட்ட புள்ளி (எழுத்து) தப்பாது.
Though a woman is born in a fort (in a royal family), she will not escape her fate.

54. ஜாதிக்குத் தக்கப் புத்தி, குலத்துக்குத் தக்க ஆசாரம்.
No one will be able to rise above the range of understanding and the religious customs that belongs to his caste.

55. தலை எழுத்து இருக்க, தலையைச் சிரைத்தால் போகுமா?
Since the letters of fate are on your head, will your fate leave you because you shave your head.

56. தலைகீழாய்த் தவம் செய்தாலும், கூடுகிற (or கிடைக்கிற) காலம் வந்து தான் கூடும்.
Though you stand on your head to do penance you will only succeed in your aim at the time of success. 49.
Success is attained not by effort, but by Fate.

59. தாரமும் குருவும் தலைவிதிப்படி.
You get your wife and your priest according to destiny. 3429.
"*Marriages are made in heaven.*" "*In time comes she whom God sends.*"

60. துள்ளித் துள்ளிக் குதித்தாலும், வெள்ளிப்பணமும் கிடையாக்காலத்தில் கிடையாது.
However much a man exerts himself, he will not get even a silver coin as long as fate is against him.

61. பிரமதேவன் போட்ட புள்ளிக்கு இரண்டாமா?
When God has made a mark, there is no erasing of it.

62. மண்டையில் எழுதி, மயிரால் மறைந்ததுப்போல்.
The fate written in our heads is hidden by our hair.
We cannot read our fate.

63. வந்த கூத்து ஆடித்தானே தீரவேண்டும்.
If he begins a dance at all, he must finish it.
"*You must dree your ain weird.*"

64. வியாதிக்கு மருந்து உண்டு, விதிக்கு மருந்து உண்டா?
There is medicine for diseases, but is there any medicine for fate?

FATE DECIDES SUCCESS.

65. அடுத்து முயன்றாலும், ஆகும் நாள் தான் ஆகும்.
Though a man exerts himself over and over again, he shall only get what he seeks at the appointed day.
"*Man doth what he can, and God what he will.*"

66. ஆற்று மணலிலே தினம் புரண்டாலும், ஒட்டுகிறதுதான் ஒட்டும்.
Even if a man roll himself daily in the river sand only what sticks to him will stick.
"*No butter will stick to his bread.*"

67. முத்து அளக்கிறவளும் பெண்பிள்ளைதான், மூசப்பயறு அளக்கிறவளும் பெண்பிள்ளைதான்.
The woman who measures pearls is but a woman, and she who measures spoiled beans is but a woman. 567.
Fate makes these outward differences.
"*Every man hath his own planet.*"

68. *விதித்த விதியைவிட, வேறு நடக்குமா?*
Will anything but what is destined happen to men?
" *That which must be, will be.*"

69. *வருந்தி அழைத்தாலும், வாராது வாராது.*
Though we beg and call, that which will not come, will not come.
" *Every man has his lot.*"

TRANSMIGRATION OR INHERITED DEEDS.

வினை.

70. *அவன் அவன் செய்த வினை, அவன் அவனுக்கே.*
The deeds of each individual will follow each individual (into the next world).
" *As you make your bed, so must you lie on it.*"

71. *கர்மத்தினாலே வந்தது, தர்மத்தினாலே போகவேண்டியது.*
What has come over one by inheritance, must be got rid of by virtuous acts.

72. *காளை போன வழியே கயிறு போகும்.*
Wherever the bull runs, its rope will follow. 75.
Whatever one has done, good or evil, will follow him.
" *As you sow, so you shall reap.*"

73. *செய்த வினை செய்தவர்க்கு எய்திடும் (வரும்).*
What a person has done in a former birth, will come upon him again.

74. *கூலி குறைத்தாயோ, குறைமரக்கால் இட்டாயோ?*
Did you reduce your servants' wages, or did you measure with a scanty measure?
Said to one, who has a hard lot in this life; implying that the cause of it must be some bad actions done in a former birth. (This may be said in a quarrel in order to stop the mouth of an opponent.)

75. *தன் நிழல் தன்னோடே வரும்.*
Our shadow will follow us. 72.

76. *தன் வினை தன்னைச் சுடும், ஒட்டப்பம் வீட்டைச் சுடும்.*
His own deeds will burn him, and a cake will burn the house.
Patanattu Pillayar, the poet, used to eat with men of all castes, which is contrary to Hindu rule. His sister seeing this and thinking him better dead than so defiled baked a cake with poison in it and gave it to him. The sage knowing her purpose, took the cake and placed it among the tiles on the roof of her house. By a miracle it set the house on fire. Thus the evil woman's deed was requited.

77. *தினை விதைத்தவன் தினை அறுப்பான், வினை விதைத்தவன் வினை அறுப்பான்.*
He who sows millet, reaps millet, he who sows deeds (good or bad) will reap accordingly.

78. முற்பிறப்பில் செய்த வினை, இப்பிறப்பில் மூண்டது (from மூள்).
Deeds done in a former birth, burn in this birth.

79. வந்த வினை போகாது, வரா வினை வராது.
The fruits of deeds done in a former birth will not go, and the fruits that do not come will not come.

80. வரும் வினை வழியில் நிற்காது.
The approaching result of deeds done in a former birth does not stop on the road.

81. விட்டகுறை தொட்டகுறை விடுமோ?
The defects that were unremedied in a former birth, and the defects we now yield to, will not forsake us.

The faults and failings of a former birth affect a subsequent birth.—This proverb is sometimes used about little things put off yesterday, that have to be done to-day.

FORTUNE.

அதிஷ்டம்.

THE FICKLENESS OF FORTUNE.

82. ஆகும் காலம் ஆகும், போகும் காலம் போகும்.
At the time for possessing it is possessed, at the time for losing, it is lost.

" *Joy and sorrow are next-door neighbours.*"

83. அம்பா பாக்கியம் சம்பா விளைந்தது, பாவி பாக்கியம் பதராய் விளைந்தது.
By Amba's fate good rice grew up, by my miserable fate grew up only chaff.

" *Fortune and misfortune are two buckets in a well.*"

84. அதிஷ்டமும் ஐசுவரியமும் ஒருவர் பங்கல்ல.
Good fortune and riches are never one man's share (Anyone may be lucky enough to get them).

85. அதிஷ்டம் ஆறாய் பெருகுகிறது.
Fortune (if it comes) comes like a river in flood.

In the rainy season Indian rivers will often suddenly rise many feet in a few hours.

86. குப்பை உயர்ந்தது, கோபுரம் தாழ்ந்தது.
The dunghill is raised, the tower is sunk.

Said from envy to hurt a person who is getting on well in this world.

" *To-day a king, to-morrow nothing.*"

87. சுகதுக்கம் சுழல் சக்கரம்.
Joy and grief are a whirling wheel. 2910.

" *Change of fortune is the lot of life.*"

88. சுகம் தக்கிறதுமில்லை, விரதம் தக்கிறதுமில்லை.

Well-being does not last, and penance does not last.

These two do not abide in anyone.

89. தங்கம் எல்லாம் தவிட்டுக்கு மாறுகிறது.

All the pure gold changes into bran.

In time of adversity or famine the well-to-do are reduced to beggary. *Cf.* The story of the prodigal son and that of the five Pandavas in exile.

" *To-day in finery, to-morrow in filth.*"

" *The highest spoke in Fortune's wheel may soon turn lowest.*"

90. முப்பதுவருஷம் வாழ்ந்தவனுமில்லை, முப்பதுவருஷம் தாழ்ந்தவனுமில்லை.

There is no one who has prospered for thirty years, and no one who has met with adversity for thirty years.

" *Fortune and glass soon break, alas !* "

UNLUCKINESS.

91. அதிஷ்டமில்லாதவனுக்குக் கலப் பால் வந்தாலும், அதையும் பூனை குடிக்கும்.

Even if an unlucky man gets a (large) measure of milk the cat will drink it. 96.

" *He who is born to misfortune stumbles as he goes, and though he fall on his back will fracture his nose.*"

92. அளகாபுரி (or குபேரன் பட்டணம்) கொள்ளையானாலும், கொடுத்து வைக்காத பாவிக்கு ஒன்றுமில்லை.

Even when Alagapuri (the city of the God of riches) is plundered, the unlucky wretch will get nothing. 1706, 1750.

93. சனியன் பிடித்தவளுக்குச் சந்தையிலும் கந்தை அகப்படாது.

A woman possessed by Sani will not get even a rag in a big market.

Sani is the most malignant of the planets; hence 'a woman possessed by Sani' means a very unlucky, unfortunate woman.

94. சனியன் பிடித்தவள் சந்தைக்குப் போனாலும், புருஷன் அகப்படமாட்டான்.

Though a woman possessed by Sani go to the (crowded) market she won't get a husband.

95. நாள் செய்கிறது, நல்லவர்கள் செய்யமாட்டார்கள்.

Good people cannot do what a lucky day can do. 2211.

All Hindus have a very great belief in the efficacy of auspicious days.

96. பால் குடிக்கப் பாக்கியமில்லாதவன் விலைப்பால் வாங்கினாலும், அதையும் பூனை குடித்ததாம்.

Though the man who is not fated to drink the milk, buy it for a price, the cat will drink it. 91.

The story is that a woman having lost all her children, bought a child from some poor people, but even it died.

"*He that was born under a three-half penny planet shall never be worth twopence.*"

97. போலை பொறுக்கப் போச்சாம், பூனை குறுக்கே போச்சாம்.

A vain woman went to pick up a little fuel, but a cat came across her path.

For a cat to cross one's path is a bad omen. The meaning of the proverb is that an unlucky person cannot attempt the smallest deed without being checked by bad omens.

"*Whither goest thou, misfortune? To where there is more!*"

98. விடியாமூஞ்சி வேலைக்குப் போனாலும் வேலை அகப்படாது, வேலை அகப்பட்டாலும் கூலி அகப்படாது.

Though the unlucky seek work, he will not find it, and even if he get work he will get no pay for it.

LUCK.

99. அதிஷ்டமிருந்தால், அரசு பண்ணலாம்.

If a man be lucky he may get a country to rule.

"*Luck is all.*"

100. அதிஷ்டவான் மண்ணைத் தொட்டாலும் பொன்னாகும்.

The fortunate need only touch earth, and it becomes gold.

101. அவசாரி ஆடினாலும் அதிஷ்டம் வேண்டும், திருடப்போனாலும் திசை வேண்டும்.

If one play the harlot, luck is needed; and if one go to steal, fortune is needed.

102. அவனுக்குச் சுக்கிரதிசை அடிக்கிறது.

The favourable influences of the planet Venus is upon him.

"*Fortune's favourite.*" 109.

103. அழகு இருந்து அழும், அதிஷ்டமிருந்து உண்ணும்.

Where there is Beauty there will be weeping; where there is luck there will be eating.

104. அழகு சோறு போடுமோ, அதிஷ்டம் சோறு போடுமோ?

Will beauty feed you, or will fortune feed you?

105. ஆகும் காலம் மெய் வருந்தவேண்டாம், தேங்காய்க்கு இளநீர்போல சேருமே.

At an auspicious time, there is no need to fatigue one's body; success will then come of itself as the juice gathers in the green cocoanut.

"*When God wills, all winds bring rain.*"

106. ஆனை உண்ட விளாங்கனிபோல்.

Like the wood-apple eaten by the elephant.

Though it swallowed this hardshelled fruit whole, only the shell could be found in its stomach, the pulp had all been digested. In this way wealth disappears leaving only trouble. 2034.

107. குதிரை ஏற அதிஷ்டம் இருந்தால், சூத்தின்கீழ் வந்து நுழையாதா?

If you are destined to ride a horse, will it not come and place itself under you?

"*He danceth well to whom Fortune pipeth.*"

108. கொடுக்கிற தெய்வம் முகம்மேல் (or மூஞ்சியிலே or சூத்திலே) அடித்துக் கொடுக்கும்.

When God gives, he will throw his gifts at us.

If we are lucky fortune will be forced on us. 2138.

109. சுக்கிரதிசை அவன் சூத்திலே அடிக்கிறது.

Fortune strikes him behind. (It comes unexpectedly.) 102.

110. யோகவான் பல்லக்கு ஏறுவான்.

He who has luck in his favour will ride in a palanquin.

111. வந்தால் சும்மா வரும், வாராமல் போனால் ஒன்றும் வராது.

If (fortune) comes, it will come of itself; if it does not come, nothing will come.

THE UNLUCKY BRINGS MISFORTUNE WITH HIM.

112. ஆகாத நாளையில் பிள்ளை பிறந்தால், அண்டை வீட்டுக்காரனை என்ன செய்யும்?

A child is born on an unlucky day, what harm can it do to the next door neighbours?

That it will bring ruin on its own relations is implied. 441.

113. உள்ளதையும் கெடுத்தாள் உதறுகாலி வந்து.

When a woman with twitching feet came into the house, she destroyed what was in the house. 117.

114. என் வீட்டுக்குப் பூவாய்வர, பொன்னும் துரும்பாச்சுது.

When she came to my house as a young flourishing girl, my gold became an unlucky straw.

The mother-in-law may say so about daughter-in-law.

115. *சீதை பிறக்க, இலங்கை அழிய.*

By Sita's birth Ceylon was destroyed.

Said of one who is the ruin of a family.

116. *தம்பி பிறக்க, தரைமட்டம் ஆச்சுது.*

When the younger brother was born all was levelled to the ground.

By his ill luck or by his bad behaviour.

117. *துடைகாலி வந்ததும், எல்லாம் துலைந்துபோச்சுது.*

No sooner had the woman with the affected walk (looked upon as unlucky) entered the house, than all was lost.

Both this and No. 113 refer to an unlucky girl being married into the family.

"*An ill marriage is a spring of ill fortune.*"

118. *ராகுத் திசையில் வாழ்ந்தவனுமில்லை, இராஜா திசையில் கெட்டவனுமில்லை.*

No one prospers under the influence of the star Rahu, and no one is ruined under the influence of the star Raja.

Rahu is the ascending node, believed to be a monstrous dragon.

119. *பரணி அடுப்புப் பாழ்போகாது.*

A hearth kindled on the second lunar day will burn always.

120. *பரணியில் பிறந்தால், தரணி ஆளலாம்.*

A person born under the planet Bharani will rule the world.

"*Better be lucky born than a rich man's son.*"

121. *வந்ததும் அப்படியே, சிவன் தந்ததும் அப்படியே, எனக்கு முன் என் அதிஷ்டம் போய் நிற்கிறது.*

What came was thus, and what God gave was the same; my fate goes before me, stands there (and takes away my luck).

i.e., I am unfortunate wherever I go; I had a husband, but I am as poor as ever; God gave me a child, but even that died.

PRIEST: GURU.

குரு.

122. *அடுத்து வந்தவர்களுக்கு ஆதரவு சொல்லுகிறவன் குரு.*

Only he is a priest who speaks encouraging words to those who come to him for shelter.

123. *காரண குரு, காரிய குரு.*

The priest for the sake of truth, and the priest for material gain.

The former has his mind set on essential truth and seeks the spiritual benefit of his disciples. While the latter seeks only his own interest.—A very interesting story about a Karya priest is told by Pandit S. M. Natesa Sastri in his Folklore in Southern India. pp. 179.

124. குப்பையும் கோழியும்போல குருவும் சிஷனும்.
The priest and his disciple are as close as the dunghill and a fowl.
As the fowl by constant scratching finds tho seeds, &c., in the dunghill, so the disciple by constant enquiry finds out the truth that the Guru knows.

125. குப்புற விழுந்து தவம் செய்தாலும், குருக்களுக்கு மோக்ஷமில்லை.
Though a priest make penance lying flat on his face he will not be saved.

126. புண்ணியமில்லாத வழிகாட்டி வீண்.
An ungodly spiritual guide is worthless.
"*He preaches well that lives well.*"

127. பொறி வென்றவனே அறிவின் குருவாம்.
He who has conquered the five senses (*or* the flesh) will be a priest of wisdom.

VEDA OR SPIRITUAL WISDOM.

வேதம்.

128. அந்தணர்க்குத் துணை வேதம்.
The Veda is the strength of the Brahmins.

129. ஆலயம் அறியாது ஓதின வேதம்.
The temple does not know the Veda you recite.
The temple in this case represents "the Holy of Holies" or heaven itself. Said to one who preaches according to his own idea, and not according to the recognised scriptures.

130. சாஸ்திரம் பொய் என்றால், கிரகணத்தைப் பார்.
If you say the Shastras are false, look at the eclipse. 31.
The eclipse that occurs as foretold in the Shastras is a proof of the truthfulness of the Shastras.

131. சுருதி குரு சுகானுபவம் மூன்றும் ஒத்தது மெய்பொருளாம்.
When the sacred writings, the priest, and one's own happiness are all in harmony, we have the truth. 134.

HEAVEN.

மோக்ஷம்.

132. அற்றது பற்று எனில், உற்றது வீடு.
If you get out of bondage, heaven is yours. 137.
In com. language: பற்றில்லாமல் போனால், இருக்கிறது மோக்ஷவீடு.

133. இடுவது பிச்சை, பெறுவது மோக்ஷம்.
What you give to another is alms, what you gain for yourself by that alms is 'bliss.'

134. சுருதி சுகானுபவம் இரண்டும் ஒத்தால் முக்தி.
Where the sacred writings and one's own happiness are in harmony there is salvation. 131.

"*He that will enter Paradise must have a good key.*"

135. சுவர்க்கத்திலே தோட்டியும் சரி, தொண்டமானும் சரி.
In heaven a scavenger and king Tondamán are alike.

"*We shall lie all alike in our graves.*"

136. சுவர்க்கத்துக்குப் போனாலும், கக்கத்தில் அக்ஷயப்பாத்திரமா?
Even when we go to heaven, shall we have an old pot under our arm? 2943, 3361.

"*When he dieth he shall carry nothing away.*" Psalm 49, 17.

137. பந்தம் கெட்டு, மோக்ஷம் காணியாச்சியாகும்.
If the fetters of sin be destroyed salvation is one's own. 132.

138. சூக்ஷமத்தில் இருக்கிறது மோக்ஷம்.
Salvation is a minute essential, *or*, Salvation is not a matter of multa but of multum.

SIN, FAULT, DEFICIENCY.

பாவம், குற்றம், குறை.

EVERY MAN HAS HIS FAULTS.

139. அத்திப் பழத்தைப் பிட்டுப்பார்த்தால், அத்தனையும் சொத்தை (or புழு).
If we break and examine a fig-fruit, it is all decayed (or wormeaten).

Outwardly fine, but inwardly rotten.

140. ஊர் என்று இருந்தால் சேரியும் இருக்கும்.
Where there is a Hindu village, there is also a Paria village.

Where there is something good, there is also something evil.
Also used like "of course." Have you thieves in your village? Have you water near your house? To such questions this proverb is an affirmative reply.

"*It is in courts as it is in ponds; some figs, some frogs.*"

141. இலுப்பைப் பூவைத் திருப்பினால், இரண்டு புறமும் பொத்தல்.
If we turn the Bassia flower, holes will be found on both sides.

142. எல்லாத்துக்கும் ஒரு சொட்டு உண்டு. 2998, 3000, 3011, 3014, 3017.
Everything has its defect.

"*Lifeless, faultless.*"

143. எல்லாத்துக்கும் உண்டு இலையும் பழுப்பும்.
Every tree has fresh leaves and decayed ones.

Defects are found in everyone.

"*No garden without its weeds.*"

144. எல்லார் வீட்டுத் தோசையிலும் ஓட்டை.
Whosoever makes a pancake, there will be holes in it.
Refers to a particular thin kind of pancake made by the Brahmins for Ekadasy festival.

145. ஔவையார் மேலும் குற்றம், அண்ணாவியார் மேலும் பழுது உண்டு.
There is fault in Avvai and there are defects in teachers.
Avvai was a famous Tamil poetess.
"*Shew me a man without a spot, and I'll shew you a maid without a blot.*"

146. கறந்த பாலும் எச்சில், பிறந்த பிள்ளையும் எச்சில்.
Fresh drawn milk is impure, and a new born baby is impure. 3004.
"*There is none without a fault.*"

147. காகமில்லாத ஊர், பாவமில்லாத ஊர்.
A village without crows is also without sin.

148. பாவம் பெரியோரையும் தொட்டுக் கொண்டாடும்.
Sin lays hold even of great people triumphantly.

149. முத்திலும் சொத்தை உண்டு, பவழத்திலும் பழுது உண்டு.
There are defects in pearls and flaws in coral.
"*A good garden may have some weeds.*

150. வீட்டு வீட்டுக்கு மண் அடுப்பேதான், பொன் அடுப்பு இல்லை.
All houses have an earthen fire-place, a fire-place of gold exists nowhere.
Refers to the degenerate state of mankind with its wants and sorrows.
"*Every man has his fault.*"

"NO ONE SEES HIS OWN FAULTS."

151. இமைக் குற்றம் கண்ணுக்குத் தெரியாது.
The eye cannot see the defect of the eye-lid. 2089, 3214.

152. கெடுமதி கண்ணுக்குத் தோன்றாது.
Wickedness is not manifest to the eye.

153. தன் குற்றம் கண்ணுக்குத் தோன்றாது.
One's own faults are not seen by one's own eye.
"*Men's years and their faults are always more than they are willing to own.*"

154. தன் முதுகு தனக்குத் தெரியாது.
No man can see his own back.
"*That man sins charitably who damns none but himself.*"
"*If the camel could see his hump, he would fall down and break his neck.*"

155. பித்தனுக்குத் தன் குணம் நூலினும் செவ்வை.
A crazy man thinks his behaviour straighter than a straight line.
" *Folly is wise in her own eyes.*"
" *Ignorance is the mother of impudence.*"

TO CONDEMN IN OTHERS WHAT WE OURSELVES DO.

Faults of other men ye question,
Not the fault that ye have done!
Like chaff your neighbour's vices winnow,
Like a false die hide your own.

DUTT'S: *Lays of Ancient India.*

156. அக்காளைப் பழித்துத் தங்கை அவசாரியானாள்.
The sister who blamed her elder sister became a harlot herself.
" *Every one should sweep before his own door.*"

157. அசலார் குற்றம்போல் தன்குற்றம் பார்த்தால், பின் தீது உண்டோ மன்னுயிருக்கு?
Would there be any more evil in man, if each one would observe his own faults as he observes the faults of his neighbour?
" *We carry our neighbour's failings in sight; we throw our own crimes over our shoulders.*"

158. ஓரக்கண்ணனைப் பழிக்கிறான், ஒற்றைக் கண்ணன்.
The one eyed man mocks the man who squints.
" *The pot calls the kettle black.*"
" *The raven said to the rook, stand away, black-coat!*"

159. தன்னைச் சிரிப்பது அறியாதாம் பல்லாவரத்துக் குரங்கு, தன் ஊரைச் சிரிக்குமாம்.
It is said, that the monkey of Pallavaram, without knowing that the village laughed at him, laughed at the village.
" *Those who live in glass-houses should not throw stones.*"

160. தாயைப் பழித்துத், தங்கை அவசாரி ஆடுகிறாள்.
After blaming her mother, the younger sister played the harlot herself.
" *Virtues all agree, but vices fight one another.*"

161. மகளுக்குப் புத்திச் சொல்லித், தாய் அவசாரி போனாளாம்.
The mother after warning her daughter, played the harlot herself.
" *Let him that has a glass skull not take to stone throwing.*"

162. மூக்கு அறுந்த மூளி, காது அறுந்த மூளியைப் பழித்தாளாம்.
The person who had a defective nose blamed the one who had a defective ear.
" *Point not at others' spots with a foul finger.*"

THE SIN OR FAULT IN ONE PERSON, THE BLAME OR PUNISHMENT ON ANOTHER.

163. அண்டை மேலே கோபம், கடாவின் மேலே காட்டினது போல (or ஆறினதுபோல்).

Like wreaking on the goat the anger he felt towards his neighbour.

" *Since he cannot revenge on the ass, he falls on the pack-saddle.*"

164. அண்ணன் பேரில் இருந்த கோபத்தை நாய் பேரில் ஆற்றினான்.

The anger he felt towards his elder brother, he cooled on the dog.

" *He that cannot beat his horse beats the saddle.*"

165. அவலை நினைத்துக்கொண்டு, உரலை இடிக்கிறான்.

Thinking of the steeped rice he beat the mortar.

Being angry with a superior whom he cannot harm he ill-treats some one in his power. *Cf.* சுடாமல் சுடுகிறது, to burn without burning, to punish indirectly, *or:* ஒன்றைச் சாக்கிட்டு மற்றொன்றைத் திட்ட, making one thing an excuse for reproaching another.

166. அம்மி மிடுக்கோ, அரைப்பவள் மிடுக்கோ?

Is the power in the grinding stone or in the woman that grinds? 169.

Said when blame is laid not on the person who is the real sinner, but on a person who has been led into sin.

167. இழவு சொன்னவன் பேரிலேயா பழி?

Should you blame him who *announces* a death?

" *Messengers should neither be beheaded nor hanged.*"

168. உண்டவன் உண்டுபோக, என் தலை புண்டு போகிறதா?

Some one ate it and ran away; am I to lose my head for it?

" *Many without punishment, none without sin.*"

169. எய்தவன் இருக்க, அம்பை நோவானேன்?

Why blame the arrow, when he who discharged it is there? 166.

170. கத்திரிக்காய் சொத்தை என்றால், அரிவாள்மணை குற்றம் என்கிறாள்.

If you say that the brinjals are decayed, she says it is the fault of the knife by which they were cut.

171. கரும்பு கசக்கிறது வாய்க் குற்றம்.

If the sugar-cane tastes bitter, the fault is in the mouth of the eater.

If one dislikes a good thing or a good person, the fault lies in himself.

172. காக்காய் ஏறினதும், பனம் பழம் விழுந்ததும்.

The crow ascended the palm tree, and the fruit fell down.

The fruit was quite ripe, and it needed a slight touch to make it fall and this the crow accidentally gave, and was wrongly blamed for the fall of the fruit. This thought is commonly expressed by: காகதாளி நியாயம், or more commonly: தொட்டவன்பேரில் பழி, and is applied to a person, who happens to show the flaw in a thing, that was broken before he touched it.

173. கோஊூரான் அவசாரி போக, குண்ணத்தூரான் தண்டம் கொடுக்க.
The woman from Ko-village played the harlot, but the woman from Gunnatur-village got the punishment.

174. சித்திரத்து கொக்கே, ரத்தினத்தைக் கக்கு!
O, beautiful stork, vomit the jewel!
Said by an innocent person who is blamed for a theft.

175. செல்லம் செருக்குகிறதா? வாசல்படி வழுக்குகிறதா?
Was it indulgence that made you slip? Was the entrance to the house slippery? 3336.
Said to a spoiled child who blames something or somebody else for its faults.

176. தலை வெட்டி பழிபோடலாமா?
You have cut the head off. Is it right to blame somebody else?

177. பழி ஓரண்டை, பாவம் ஓரண்டை.
The blame on one side, the sin on another.
"*One doth the scath, and another has the scorn.*"

178. முகம் ஆகாதிருந்தால், கண்ணாடி என்ன செய்யும்?
If your face is ugly, what can the mirror do?
Don't blame anything else for faults caused by yourself.

MISCONSTRUCTION.

179. அன்பற்ற மாமியாருக்குக் கால் பட்டாலும் குற்றம், கைபட்டாலும் குற்றம்.
Whether your foot or your hand touch an unkind mother-in-law, it is wrong.
"*Faults are thick where love is thin.*" 185, 2765, 2838, 3643.

180. அன்பற்ற மாமியாருக்குக் கும்பிடுகிறதும் குற்றம் தான்.
Even a bow to an unkind mother-in-law will be taken as an offence.
"*Where there is no love, all are faults.*" 2770.

181. ஆமை பிடிப்பார், மல்லாத்துவார், நாம் அது சொன்னால் பாவம்.
They will lay hold of a tortoise and turn it on its back; but to mention it is a crime.
"*Speak what you will, bad men will turn it ill.*"

182. பாவி கொடுமை பாலும் புளிக்கிறது.
The heinousness of my sin will turn milk sour.
By my hard fate even the good I do to others is misconstrued.
"*All are not thieves that dogs bark at.*"

183. பேசினால் வாயாடி, பேசாதிருந்தால் ஊமைப் பயல்.
If I speak, I am called a babbler; if I am silent, I am called a dumb fellow.
"*It is hard to please all parties.*"

184. *மாமியார் துணி அவிழ்ந்தால், வாயாலும் சொல்லக்கூடாது, கையாலும் காட்டக்கூடாது.*

If the mother-in-law's dress becomes unfastened, you must not tell her of it, nor show her it (for fear of offending her).

"*If you want a pretence to whip a dog, it is enough to say he ate up the frying pan.*"

185. வேண்டாம் பெண்சாதி கைப்பட்டால் குற்றம், கால் பட்டால் குற்றம்.

If a wife disliked by her husband touch him with her hand or her foot, it is wrong.

"*When love fails we espy all faults.*"

"*To crazy ship all winds are contrary.*" 179, 2770.

WILFUL SIN.

186. *அறிந்து அறிந்து செய்கிற பாவத்தை அழுது அழுது தொலைக்கவேண்டும்.*

One will have to weep endlessly to expiate sin done wilfully. 728.

187. *கழுவிக் கழுவிப் பின்னும் சேற்றை மிதிக்கிறதா* (com. *மெரிக்கிறதா*)?

After washing your feet, will you walk in the mud?

188. எட்டி எட்டிப் பார்த்து, குட்டிச்சுவரில் முட்டிக்கொள்ளுகிறதா?

After seeing a ruined wall, why should you go and knock your head against it?

How is it that you allowed yourself to sin wilfully?

189. குட்டிச்சுவரில் முட்டிக்கொள்ள வெள்ளெழுத்தா?

Are you so blind as to run your head against a ruined wall?

Doing what one knows to be foolish or wrong.

190. *பார்த்திருந்தும் பாழுங்கிணற்றிலே விழுகிறதா?*

Though you see an empty well, will you go and fall into it?

191. *விளக்கைப் பிடித்துக்கொண்டு கிணற்றிலே விழுகிறதா?*

Will you go and fall into a well with a lamp in your hand?

"*Run not into ruin with your eyes open.*"

FAULT-FINDING.

192. *ஒருவன் தலையிலே மாணிக்கம் இருக்கிறது என்று வெட்டலாமா?*

Would it be right to cut off another person's head, because you think there is a gem in it?

Why suspect without reason? 3327.

"*Defaming others is the greatest of all sins.*"

"*Throw much dirt and some will stick.*"

"*He that would hang his dog, gives out first, that he is mad.*"

193. குற்றம் பார்க்கில் சுற்றமில்லை.
If you look at men's faults you will have no friends.
"*Deem the best of every doubt, till the truth be tried out.*"

194. தன் தப்பு பிறருக்குச் சந்து.
One's own faults are an opportunity for others. 742.
"*The vulgar keep no accounts of your hits, but of your misses.*"
"*In an enemy spots are soon seen.*"

195. தூர்ந்த கிணற்றைத் தூர்வாராதே.
Do not clear a well that has been filled up. 443, 459, 460.
Cf. மறந்துபோன சங்கதியைக் கிளறாதே. Don't stir up what is forgotten.
"*Do not rake the gutters.*"
"*Let sleeping dogs lie.*"

196. பகையாளிக்குப் பருப்பிலே நெய்விட்டதுபோல.
Like adding *ghee* to an enemy's favourite food.
A man's misfortunes are as pleasant to his enemies as clarified butter is to the Hindu palate. 247, 1842.

"AS YOU MAKE YOUR BED, SO YOU MUST LIE ON IT."

197. அகப்பட்டுக்கொள்வேன் என்றோ கள்ளன் களவு எடுக்கிறது?
Does a thief steal expecting that he will be caught?
No one sins thinking that he will have to suffer for it.

198. அடாது செய்தவன் படாது படுவான்.
If one does what is unseemly, he will suffer what he should not suffer.
"*Fly that pleasure which paineth afterwards.*"

199. அஷ்டமத்துச் சனியை வட்டிக்கு வாங்கினதுபோல.
Like buying Saturn (a malignant star) in his worst shape with borrowed money.
i.e., Wilfully courting utter destruction by one's folly.
"*He that courts injury will obtain it.*"

200. அழிவழக்குச் சொன்னவன், பழிபொறுக்கும் மன்னவன்.
A man who defends a false case is a king who tolerates crime.
i.e., Must take the consequences of his crime sooner or later.
"*Trickery comes back to its master.*"

201. உதைத்தகால் புழுக்கிறபோது அல்லவோ புழுக்கும்.
When the time comes for worms to consume the kicking foot, will they not consume it?
In due course destruction will come even to the haughtiest.
"*Every ill man hath his ill day.*"
"*Vengeance belongeth to me, saith the Lord.*"

202. உப்பு தின்கிறவன் தண்ணீர் குடிப்பான்.
He who eats salt, will drink water. 2704.

As surely as a thirsty man drinks water, so surely will a sinful man incur punishment.

203. உருட்டப்புரட்ட உள்ளதும் உள்ளுக்கு வாங்கும்.
By reason of fraud and trickery, the truth within you will shrivel up. 3334.

"*Ill sowers make ill harvest.*"

204. உருட்டும் புரட்டும் ஒடுக்கும் சிறப்பை.
Frauds and tricks will reduce a man's greatness.

"*Most of our evils come from our vices.*"

205. உனக்கும் பேபே, உன் அப்பனுக்கும் பேபே!
To you *Bêbê*, and to your father *Bêbê*!

A man pressed by his creditors was advised by a friend, to whom also he owed money, to escape from their importunities by feigning madness. The debtor accordingly did so, replying to them all like an idiot, *Bêbê!* The plan was successful and the creditors were deceived. Then the friend asked that the debt due to himself should be paid. But he himself received the treatment he had advised the deceitful debtor to use to the others. The proverb is also used about children who have no respect for older persons.

"*Trickery comes back to its own master.*"
"*He falls into the pit, who leads another into it.*"

206. குட்டிக்கலகம் பண்ணுகிறவன், குட்டுப்பட்டுச் சாவான்.
He who causes quarrels in a family will be cuffed to death.

"*As a man lives so shall he die; as a tree falls, so shall it lie.*"

207. சூதன் கொல்லையிலே மாடு மேயும்.
A bullock will feed in the cheat's garden. 456, 1806.

"*Deceiving and being deceived.*" (2 Tim. 3, 13.)
Cf. "*He went out shearing, he came home shorn.*"

208. சூதும் வாதும் வேதனை செய்யும்.
Deceit and quarrelling will end in suffering.

"*The biter bit.*"

209. தின்னத் தெரியாமல் தின்று, பேலத் தெரியாமல் பேலுகிறது.

A vulgar proverb meaning that he who eats without moderation, will suffer pain.

"*He who swims in sin will sink in sorrow.*"

210. பசிக்குப் பனம்பழம் தின்றால், பித்தம் பட்ட பாடுபடட்டும்.
If he *will* eat the palmyra fruit because he is hungry, let him suffer the biliousness it causes.

Said in condemnation of those who find their chief good in sensuous enjoyment.

"*Gather thistles, expect prickles.*" "*Dead-sea fruit.*"

211. பண்ணின பாவத்தைப் பட்டுத் தொலைக்கவேண்டும்.

We must suffer for the sin we have done and so atone for it.

212. பூ மலர்ந்து கெட்டது, வாய் விரிந்து கெட்டது.

Blossoms open and die, your mouth opens and destroys you. 2503.

Blossoms fade away after opening fully; the mouth opens to say what it should not, and ruins the speaker.

"*The evil that cometh out of thy mouth flieth into thy bosom.*"

213. பொருள் போனவழியே துக்கம் போகும்.

In the way the wealth went, sorrow will follow.

He who gains wealth unfairly, gets sorrow too.

"*Evil-gotten good never proveth well.*"

214. மரத்தின் பழம் மரத்தண்டை விழும்.

The fruit falls near the tree.

The results of your deeds will come upon yourself.

"*A drunken night makes a cloudy morning.*"

215. மல்லாந்து உமிழ்ந்தால் (com. முழிந்தால்) மார்மேலே விழும்.

If you spit up while lying on your back, what you spit out will fall on your breast.

"*Who spits against heaven, it falls on his head.*"

216. மறந்த உடைமை மக்களுக்கு ஆகாது.

Forgotten property is no good to any one.

If one forgets something somewhere and the people of the place keep the forgotten property as their own, it will be injurious both to them and to their off-spring.

217. மோசநாசம் கம்பளி வேஷம்.

A person who cheats and ruins will himself come to wear a common blanket only.

Said as a warning to him who deceives or uses false measures; or when family property is divided and one of the family secretes jewelry or other valuable things.

218. வாய்கொழுப்பு சீலையால் வடிக்கிறது.

The insolence of his mouth trickles through his cloth. 1287.

An impatient man while waiting for his rice abused the woman who was boiling it, and she threw it all into his lap, and the hot water in which it was boiled drained away from the rice, soaked through his clothes and scalded him.

"*Pride goes before and shame follows after.*"

Cf. 2605 *ff.*

DECEIT, HYPOCRISY AND DISGUISE.

மோசம், பாசாங்கு, வேஷம்.

" And no marvel; for even Satan fashioneth himself into an angel of light."

FALSE FRIENDSHIP.

219. அவன் ஒரு குளிர்ந்த (com. குளுந்த) கொள்ளி.
He is a smouldering firebrand. 1929.
Said of dissembling enemies.

220. அரிவாளும் அசையவேண்டும், ஆண்டை குடியும் கெடவேண்டும்.
The sickle will move, but his Master's family will be ruined.
He feigns working for his master's gain, but his thoughts are on ruining him.

221. ஆர் குடிகெடுக்க, ஆண்டிவேஷம் போட்டாய்?
When you disguised yourself as a mendicant, whose family did you intend to ruin?
Said of one who feigns piety in order to gain an evil influence.
" *What is good a friar never loved.*"

222. எட்டினுல் குடுமியைப் பிடிக்கிறது, எட்டாவிட்டால் காலைப் பிடிக்கிறது.
If he can reach it, he will pull your hair; if not, he will seize your legs. 356.
Said of one who tries to ruin a superior, either by open attacks or by secret intrigue.
" *I ask your pardon, coach, I thought you were a wheelbarrow, when I stumbled over you.*"
" *A knavish confession should have a care for absolution.*"

223. ஈரச்சீலை போட்டுக் கழுத்து அறுப்பான்.
He will tie a wet cloth round your neck and then cut your throat.
Sudden treachery.
" *They scratch you with one hand, and strike you with the other.*"

224. கட்டிக்கொடுத்த சோறும், கற்றுக்கொடுத்த சொல்லும் எதுவரைக்கும்?
Boiled rice tied up in a cloth (provision for a journey), and a word you have learned, how long will these last?
The food will be eaten up at the first stopping place and a thing learnt as a parrot learns is soon forgotten. Said of one who by following the interested advice of a third party, finds that all the profit he makes goes into the other's hands, whilst the advantage to himself is but momentary.

225. கண்டதைக்கொண்டு காலைவாரி அடிக்கிறது.

Through what he sees, he knocks your legs from under you.

A person says to a friend—but a false friend—"I think, I am going to get good employment"; the false friend replies, "Don't take it, I will get you a place with double that salary," and so causes him to lose what he might have had.

"*In the fair tale is foul falsity.*"

226. குளிர்ந்த (com. குளுந்த) கொள்ளியாயிருந்து, குடியைக் கெடுக்கலாமா?

Is it right to destroy the family by pretending to be a cheering firebrand? 2188.

"*It is time to fear when tyrants seem to kiss.*"

227. கொல்லைக்குப் பல்லி, குடிக்குச் சகுனி.

He is a *Palli* plant (*Buchnera*) to the garden, and Saguni to the family.

The *Palli* plant (*Buchnera*) saps the soil of the garden, while Saguni, the councellor of Duryodhana in Mahabhárata, ruined the Kaurava family completely.

"*He knows one point more than the devil.*"

228. சிரித்துக் கழுத்து அறுக்கிறது.

To smile on a man, and then cut his throat. 231, 229, 3101.

"*A snake in the grass.*"

229. சோற்றைக் கொடுத்துக் கழுத்தை அறுக்கிறது.

Giving a man a meal and then cutting his throat. 228, 231.

"*Full of courtesy, full of craft.*"

230. தலையைத் தடவி மூளையை உரிவான்.

He will pat your head gently and take out your brains.

"*He covers me with his wings, and bites me with his bill.*"

231. தேற்றிக் கழுத்தை அறுக்கிறது.

Comforting you and cutting your throat. 228, 229.

"*It is an ill sign to see a fox lick a lamb.*"

232. தேனும் பாலும் போலிருந்து, கழுத்தை அறுத்தான்.

He was like honey and milk, but cut my throat.

"*The fowler's pipe sounds sweet, till the bird is caught.*"

233. பகையாளி குடியை உறவாடி கெடுக்கவேண்டும்.

The family of an enemy must be destroyed by friendliness.

"*Fair words and wicked deeds deceive wise men and fools.*"

234. மடிமாங்காய் போட்டு, தலைவெட்டுகிறது.

Putting mangoes into a man's lap, and then beheading him for stealing them. 782.

Ruining an enemy by treachery.

235. மோந்தாற்போல முகத்தைக் கடிக்கிறது.

He bites one in the face, while he makes it appear as if he would only smell one's head.

To "smell the head" is as tender an act as kissing among Europeans.

236. கையைப்பிடித்துக் கள்ளை வார்த்து, மயிரைப்பிடித்துப் பணம் வாங்குகிறதா?

After receiving you with a friendly grasp of the hand, and giving you toddy to drink, will they not lay hold of your hair and take your money?

237. பள்ளத்திலே இருந்தால் பெண்சாதி, மேட்டிலே இருந்தால் அக்காள்.

In the valley he treats her as his wife, on the hill he treats her as his elder sister.

Said of a man who will take every base advantage if he has no fear of being detected.

"*Do in the hole as thou wouldst do in the hall.*"

238. கைகொடுத்துக்கொண்டே கடையாணி பிடுங்குகிறான்.

While he seems to give a helping hand (in pushing the conveyance), he takes out the linch-pin. 772.

Cf. 913 *ff.*

HYPOCRISY.

"How many like to mask their lives,
Wash clean and seem upright,
And yet be black as hell."

CH. E. GOVER: *The Folk-songs of Southern India.*

239. அகோர தபசி விபரீத சோரன்.

He performs severe penance outwardly, but he is a great rogue.

"*All saint without, all devil within.*"

"*Hypocrisy is a sort of homage that vice pays to virtue.*"

240. அடிநாக்கிலே நஞ்சும், நுனிநாக்கிலே அமிர்தமுமா?

At the bottom of the tongue is poison; will there be sweetness at the tip? 255.

"*A honey tongue, a heart of gall.*"

241. அண்டைவீட்டுப் பார்ப்பான் சண்டை மூட்டித் தீர்ப்பான்.

The Brahmin in the next house breeds a quarrel and settles it.

He gains honour or profit by settling quarrels that he has himself aroused. 256, 264, 271.

"*Reynard is still Reynard, though he put on a cowl.*"

242. அமுக்கினால்போலிருந்து அரணை அழிப்பான்.

He pretends to be submissive, but he will destroy a fort.

"*Cats hide their claws.*"

243. அரிச்சந்திரன் வீட்டுக்கு அடுத்த வீடு.

The next house to that of Harishchandra.

Harishchandra was a king in the ancient time famous for never having uttered a lie. The proverb is said ironically about a person who pretends to be honest, but is a well known liar.

244. அழுகள்ளன், தொழுகள்ளன், ஆசாரக்கள்ளன்.
A weeping hypocrite, a worshipping hypocrite and a ritualistic hypocrite. 123.
"*An ill man is worst when he appeareth good.*"

245. அவன் ரொம்ப வைதிகமாய் (or சீலமாய்) பேசுகிறான்.
He talks very piously.
"*Honey in his mouth, words of milk; gall in his heart, fraud in his deeds.*"

246. ஆடவிட்டு வேடிக்கை பார்க்கிறது.
Setting them going and watching the fun. 266, 292.
Instigating strife and making profit out of it.

247. ஆடு நனைகிறது என்று கோனாய் அழுகிறதாம்.
It seems that the wolf wept, because the sheep got wet.
"*Crocodile's tears.*" 196.
"*Crows bewail the dead sheep and then eat them.*"
"*Beware of the geese when the fox preaches.*"

248. ஆண்டியைக் கண்டால் லிங்கன் என்கிறான், தாதனைக் கண்டால் ரங்கன் என்கிறான்.
If he meet a Saivite mendicant, he speaks of Siva; if he meet a Vaishnavite mendicant, he speaks of Vishnu. 2838.
"*He hath a cloak for his knavery.*"

249. ஆம்புடையானைக் (com. அகமுடையான்) கொன்ற அற (or பழி) நீலி.
After killing her husband she feigns sorrow. 256, 288.

250. இங்கே தலை காட்டுகிறான், அங்கே வால் காட்டுகிறான்.
Here he shows his head, and there his tail.
He will not show himself boldly in his true character.
"*If you be false to both beasts and birds, you must like the bat, fly only by night.*"

251. இடாள் தொடாள், மனுஷாள்மேலே செத்த பிராணன்.
She will neither give to them nor touch them, but she is dying for love of them!
Said of one who makes great professions of kindness, but does not dream of carrying them out.
"*She loves the poor well, but cannot abide beggars.*"

252. இது என் குலாசாரம், இது என் வயிற்றுசாரம்.
This is the law of my caste, and this is the law of my belly. 851.
Potters are never Vaishnavas; but the potters at Srirangam were compelled by the Vaishnava Brahmins to put the Vaishnava mark on their foreheads; otherwise the Brahmins would not buy their pots for the temple. One clever potter, having considered this difficulty, after making the Saivite symbol (*Vibhoothi*) on his forehead put a big Vaishnava mark on his stomach. When rebuked for so doing by a Brahmin, he replied as above.

252*a*. இந்தப் பூனையும் பால் குடிக்குமா?
Will *this* cat drink milk? 2874.

A cat generally sits as if it thought of no mischief, but no sooner does it see an opportunity of doing wrong than it avails itself of it.—A demure humbug.

" *He looks as if butter would not melt in his mouth.*"
" *Though the cat winks a while, yet sure she is not blind.*"

253. இராவண சந்நியாசிபோலிருக்கிறான்.
He is an ascetic like Ravana.

That is, 'He is a hypocrite,' for a true ascetic (*sannyasi*) should have nothing to do with women, but Rávana carried off Seeta the wife of Ráma.

" *An artful fellow is a devil in a doublet.*"

254. உதடு பழஞ்சொரிய, உள்ளே நெஞ்சு (or வயிறு) எரிய.
His lips rain fruit, his heart within is on fire. 2369.

" *A flattering speech is honied poison.*"

255. உதட்டிலே உறவும், நெஞ்சிலே பகையும்.
Friendship on his lips, hatred at heart. 240.

" *Bees that have honey in their mouths have stings in their toils.*"

256. எடுத்து மூடிவிட்டு எதிரே வந்து நிற்பாள்.
She will take it and hide it, and come and stand before you (as if innocent). 249.

" *Hiders are good finders.*"

257. ஏகாதசி திருடியை ஏற்றடா ரதத்தின்மேல்.
Oh sir, this thief steals on a holy day (Ekádasi) so put him on the idol's car.

Said in mockery of the pretended piety of a notorious swindler.

258. என்காணும் தாதரே, ஆண்டி புகுந்தீர்? இதுவும் ஒரு மண்டலம், பார்த்துவிடுவோம்.
Oh Vaishnavite mendicant, have you become a Saivite? (*He replies*) I will try for forty days what gain this brings. 1193.

259. ஒன்றும் அறியாளாம் கன்னி, ஒடிப்பிடித்ததாம் ஆறுமாத ஜன்னி.
This young woman acts the innocent but she has been a wreck for six months.

The evident consequences of her immorality make her pretended innocence absurd. Used about sham virtue.

260. கண்டால் ஒரு பேச்சு, காணாமல்போனால் ஒரு பேச்சு.
When he sees you, one word; when he does not see you, another. 261, 262.

261. கண்டால் காமாச்சி நாயகர், காணாவிட்டால் காமாட்டி நாயகர்.
When speaking *with* him, you speak as to a respectable person; when you speak *about* him, you speak as if he was a fool.

" *He that speaks me fair and loves me not, I'll speak him fair and trust him not.*"
" *He that praiseth publicly will slander privately.*"

262. கண்டால் முறைசொல்லுகிறது, காணாவிட்டால் பேர் சொல்லுகிறது.
When speaking to him, you give him his title, when speaking of him, you merely mention his name.

"*He who praises in praesentia, and abuses in absentia, has with him pestilentia.*"

263. கத்திரிக்கொல்லையில் கூத்து (or வேடிக்கை) பார்க்கிறதுபோல.
Like looking at a theatrical performance in a garden of *brinjals*.

Said to a person who pretends to go out to see a performance and avails himself or herself of the opportunity to do mischief. A *brinjal* is an edible vegetable.

264. கள்ளனுமாகி விளக்கும் பிடிக்கிறான்.
He is himself a thief, and yet he brings the lantern. 141, 256, 271.

"*If thou dealest with a fox think of his tricks.*"

265. கறந்த மேனியாய்ப் பேசுகிறது.
Your speech is as pure as new drawn milk! 3118.

Said sarcastically to one who makes great professions of truthfulness.

"*Nobody so like an honest man as an arrant knave.*"

266. குத்திவிட்டு வேடிக்கை பார்க்கிறது.
To incite (*or* provoke) one to do a thing, and then enjoy the fun. 246.

267. கும்பிடும் கள்ளர் குழைத்திடும் கள்ளர்.
Rogues who pretend to be religious, and rogues who smear themselves with sacred ashes.

"*Full of courtesy, full of craft.*"

268. கூட்டோடே (or பொந்தியோடே) கைலாசம் சேர்வாய்.
Would that you could go to heaven with your body!

Said sarcastically to one who pretends to be pious.

"*No rogue like the godly rogue.*"

269. கை கண்ட வேசிக்குக் கண்ணீர் குறைச்சலா?
Does a clever prostitute lack tears? 275.

270. கையில் ஜெபமாலை, கக்கத்தில் கன்னக்கோல்.
He has a rosary in his hand, and under his arm he has an implement for breaking through the walls of houses.

"*Hypocrisy can find out a cloak for every rain.*"

271. கோழி திருடியும் கூடிக்குலாவுகிறான்.
Though he has stolen the fowl he joins the others in going about searching for it. 241, 256, 264.

"*May the man be damned and never grow fat, who wears two faces under one hat.*"

272. சேற்றிலே மேய்கிற பிள்ளைப் பூச்சிபோல.

Like the mole-cricket grazing in the mud. 2835.

Though the mole-cricket (gryllus) lives in mud, the mud does not stick to its body; it is not defiled by the mud. Thus according to one Hindu philosophy, man's soul is not defiled by living in this material world.

A Hindu once asked a Christian preacher, if he could not become a Christian at heart, and outwardly remain a Hindu. To this question the Christian quoted the above phrase.

273. தீவாள் திடுக்கிடுவாள், திண்ணைக்கு மண் இடுவாள், வருகிற கிழமைக்கு வாசலுக்கு மண் இடுவாள்.

She is wicked, but professes fear; she will repair the verandah facing the street, and next week she will repair the entrance to the house.

She is known for what she is, but she is as clever in hiding her misdeeds as she is in doing them.

"*If a man is practised in disguise, he cheats most discerning eyes.*"

274. நாட்டுக்கு நல்ல துடைப்பம், வீட்டுக்குப் பீத்தத் துடைப்பம்.

He is a fine broomstick in the country, but he is a worn-out broomstick at home.

Said of one who has a good name abroad, but is known at home as a bad character.

275. நீலிக்குக் கண்ணீர் நிமையிலே.

A silly woman has her tears in her eye-lids. 269.

She is ever ready to shed tears either from silliness or deceitfulness.

"*Women laugh when they can, and weep when they will.*"

276. பகிடியைப் பாம்பு கடித்ததுபோல.

Like the jester that was bitten by a snake.

Applied to one who so often tells lies that if he happen to speak the truth no one will believe him. Or, to a child that constantly feigns sickness to avoid going to school, and is not believed to be ill when it is really sick.

"*He that sweareth till no man trust him, he that lieth till no man believe him, he that borroweth till no man will lend him, let him go where no man knoweth him.*"

277. பக்தியோடே பாகற் (com. பாவல்) காய்ச் சட்டியோடே தீயுது.

She is so pious that she forgets cooking and allows the food to burn in the pot.

"*Much praying but no piety.*"

278. பசுத்தோல் போர்த்துப் புலிப்பாய்ச்சல் பாய்கிறது.

To put on a cow's skin, and leap like a tiger. 282.

"*A wolf in sheep's clothing.*"

279. பரம்பரை ஆண்டியோ, பஞ்சத்துக்கு ஆண்டியோ?

Are you an hereditary mendicant, or are you only a mendicant because of the famine? 123, 2065, 2852.

Is your piety genuine, or merely for gain?

280. பறைச்சேரி மேளம் கலியாணத்துக்கும் கொட்டும், கல் எடுப்புக்கும் கொட்டும்.

A Paria drum is beaten at weddings, and also beaten at funerals.

Said of a double-dealing unreliable person, who is as ready for good as for evil. 181.

" *A conscience as large as a shipman's hose.*"

281. பாம்புக்குத் தலைகாட்டி, மீனுக்கு வாலைக் காட்டுகிறது.

Showing his head to snakes, and his tail to fish.

If among wicked people, he will speak and act as they do; if among good people, he will try to appear good. 180.

282. பார்த்தால் பூனை, பாய்ந்தால் புலி.

If you look at him he is a cat, if he springs he is a tiger.

Demure wickedness. 278.

283. மனதிலே ஒன்று, வாக்கிலே ஒன்று.

One thing in his heart, another thing in his words.

" *All are not friends that speak one fair.*"

284. மைலங்கி மைலங்கி பூ எங்கே வைத்தாய்? வாடாதே, வதங்காதே அடுப்பிலே வைத்தேன்.

O, you dissembling woman, where did you put the flowers? (*She replies*) In order that they should not shrivel and fade I put them in the fire-place.

Deceitful excuses. Said for instance to a girl who feigns inability to fetch water from the well, but after escaping her duty, goes and plays, and while playing exerts herself far more than she would have needed to do to bring the pot of water.

285. ருத்திராக்ஷப் பூனை உபதேசம் பண்ணினதுபோல.

Like a cat putting on a rosary and teaching religion.

Said of a religious teacher who makes his religion a cloak for sin.

" *Beads about the neck and the devil in the heart.*"

" *They are not all saints that use holy water.*"

286. விசுவாசக் கொக்கு நடமாடிச் செத்ததாம்.

It is said, that a pious crane died from wandering about.

Said in derision of the excellent professions of a false friend.

287. வித்தைக் கள்ளி மாமியார் விறகு ஒடிக்கப்போனாளாம், கல்தாழை முள்ளு கொத்தோடே தைத்ததாம்.

The cunning mother-in-law went to gather firewood, and it seems she was pricked by the thorns of an aloe!

The aloe mentioned has no thorns, so her excuses for not bringing the wood were not believed. Said of a person who makes excuses that are not plausible.

288. வெட்டிப்போட்டுக் கட்டிக்கொண்டு அழுகிறது.

To strike a person down and then embrace him and weep over him. 249.

289. வேஷமோ தவவேஷம், மனதிலோ அவவேஷம்.
If we look at his appearance, it is the appearance of a religious ascetic, but if we look at his heart, it seems false.

"*He has one face to God, and another to the devil.*"

290. வைக்கோற் கட்டுக்காரனை ஒப்புக்குக்கட்டி அழுதாப்போல.
Like one who deceitfully embraced and wept over a man who was carrying a burden of straw.

He pities the bearer for having to carry such a heavy burden, and gets him to give him a little straw for his cow. Interested sympathy.

291. வைக்கோல்கார்கொண்டு மாய்ந்து மாய்ந்து அடித்தானும்.
He beats you fatally with a straw.

Said of a father or mother or master who constantly threatens to beat naughty children, or lazy servants, but never does it.

Cf. Kashmiri '*Kokun haput*' 'Father's bear,' *i.e.*, nothing to be afraid of.

"*If you cannot bite, never show your teeth.*"

292. பிள்ளையும் கிள்ளி, தொட்டிலும் ஆட்டுகிறது.
Pinching the child, while swinging it in the cradle. 246.

Said also about God, who has placed man as an unhappy being in this world, but at the same time granted him the holy books to comfort him.

Cf. 913 *ff*. 2338 *ff*. 2373 *ff*.

ROGUERY, CRAFTINESS.

பொல்லாப்பு, தீமை.

"TO A ROGUE A ROGUE AND A HALF."

292*a*. அஞ்சனக்காரன் முதுகில் வஞ்சனைக்காரன் ஏறினான்.
The cheat has got up on the back of the conjurer.

"*The fox knows much, but more he that catcheth him.*"

293. அவன் கெட்டான் குடியன், எனக்கு இரண்டு டிராம் வாரு!
That drunkard is done for, but give me a drink!

"*A pickthank, a picklock, both are alike evil: the difference is, that trots, this ambles to the devil.*"

294. ஆயக்காரனுக்குப் பிரமஹத்திக்காரன் சாக்ஷி.
The murderer of a Brahmin is fit witness for a tax collector.

"*To a rogue a rogue and a half.*"

295. எல்லாரும் ஆளின்கீழே நுழைந்தால், இவன் ஆளின் நிழல்கீழே நுழைவான்.
When every one else creeps under him, this man will creep under a man's shadow. 298.

296. கெட்டதுபட்டது கிருஷ்ணாங் குளம், அதிலும் கெட்டது அத்திப்பட்டாங்குளம்.
Those who live near the Krishna-Pond in Madras are wicked, but those who live near the Attipattan-Pond are worse.

297. சுவாமியாருக்குச் சுவாமி வேண்டும்.
One big rogue needs another to check him.
" *To a hard knot a hard wedge.*"

298. தடுக்கின்கீழே நுழைந்தால், கோலத்தின்கீழே நுழைகிறது.
If one creeps in under the mat, the other one will creep under the *Kolam*.
The *Kolam* is a design drawn at the threshold of a Hindu house. 295.
" *One trick is met by another.*"

299. போக்கிரிக்குப் போக்கிரி வேண்டும்.
A blackguard needs a blackguard. 300, 415, 1389, 2285.
" *Set a thief to catch a thief.*" " *To a rude ass a rude keeper.*"
" *Devils must be driven out with devils.*"

300. மாமியாருக்கு மாமியார் வேண்டும்.
One mother-in-law needs another mother-in-law. 415.
She can only be outwitted another mother-in-law.
" *One heat expels another.*"

FROM BAD TO WORSE: MAKING BAD WORSE, AND "MISFORTUNES SELDOM COME SINGLY."

301. அகதி பெறுவது பெண்பிள்ளை அதுவும் வெள்ளி பூராடம்.
The destitute woman bears a female child and this happens under an evil star.
The climax of ill-luck: the woman is destitute, the infant is a female, and the time of its birth is inauspicious.

302. அங்கே என் அடிமகளே! கஞ்சிக்கு அழுகிறாய், இங்கேவா அடி, காற்றாய்ப் பறக்கலாம்.
Why my girl, you are crying there for gruel, come over here and you may fly like the wind.
A neighbour who sees a daughter-in-law weeping says this implying that the girl does get something to eat now, but if she leaves that house she will get nothing, and so go from bad to worse.

303. அஷ்டதரித்திரம் தாய் வீடு, அதிலும் தரித்திரம் மாமியார் வீடு.
My mother's house, was as poor as poor can be, but my mother-in-law's house is still worse!
While unmarried and staying at home with her mother, the girl was badly off; but after she was married and sent to her mother-in-law's house, she found still greater poverty.
" *Out of the frying pan into the fire.*"

304. அழுகிற வேளை பார்த்து, அக்குள் பாய்ச்சுகிறான்.
Seeing a woman in sorrow he thrusts his hand into her arm-pit.

305. ஆம்புடையான் செத்து அவதிப் படச்சே (or ஆவிப்பறக்கச்சே), அண்டை வீட்டுக்காரன் அக்குளிலே பாய்ச்சுகிறான்.
While her husband was dying, her neighbour thrust his hand into the arm-pit (of the sorrowing wife). 326.

He took advantage of her unprotected state. Said about persons who take a mean advantage of another's misfortunes.

306. ஆயத்துக்குப் பயந்து, ஆற்றிலே நீந்தினதுபோல.
Being afraid of paying the tax he swam the river.

Incurring great risks in order to escape slight troubles.

" *He leaps into a deep river to avoid a shallow brook.*"

307. இடறின காலிலேயே இடறுகிறது.
The leg that has stumbled stumbles.

One fall into sin leads to more falls.

308. உடம்பு எங்கும் சுடுகிறது, அழலை (நெருப்பை) மடியிலே கட்டுகிறாய்.
Though your body is burning all over, yet you put fire into your lap.

Making bad worse.

309. எரிகிற கொள்ளியை எறித்தள்ளினதுபோல.
As a burning firebrand was made to flare higher.

To excite a person already excited.

310. எலிக்குப் பயப்பட்டு வீட்டைச் சுடுகிறதா?
Should one burn down one's house for fear of rats? 322, 330, 339.

311. ஒட்டைக் கூத்தன் பாட்டுக்கு இரட்டை தாழ்பாள் போட்டதுபோல.
She bolted the door doubly against *Ottaikuttan*'s song.

The story that illustrates this proverb is found in "*Vinodarasamanjari,*" pp. 271. A king had a favourite poet *Ottaikuttan*, his queen had another. The king's poet was envious of the queen's poet, and had him imprisoned. The queen hearing this went into her room and bolted the door. At night when the king came to see his queen, she said she would not let him in till her favourite had been released from prison. On hearing this the king sent his own poet to sing outside the queen's door. So that the queen might think that her request had been complied with. But the queen knew at once that the song did not come from her favourite, and became more angry with the king and bolted the door with another bolt. Thus the king's stratagem only made matters worse. The proverb is used when a person is displeased with, or sorry for something that has happened, and somebody tries to soothe him, but only succeeds in irritating him still more.

" *As water in a smith's forge, that serves rather to kindle than quench.*"

312. ஒழுக்கு வீட்டிலே வெள்ளம் வந்ததுபோல.
As a flood came into a leaky house.

" *One ill calls another.*"

313. கண் புண்ணிலே கோல் இட்டதுபோல.
Like putting a probe into a wound in the eye.
"*To add fuel to the fire.*"

314. கலக் கந்தை கட்டிக்கொண்டு காணப்போனேனாம், இருகலக் கந்தை கட்டிக்கொண்டு எதிரே வந்தாளாம்.
When I went clad in a number of rags to see her, she met me clad in double the quantity of rags. 324, 325, 722.
She counterfeited poverty more cleverly than I did, and I could therefore not get the help out of her that I expected.
"*When Greek meets Greek, then comes the tug of war.*"

315. கள் உண்ட குரங்கு.
A monkey that has drunk toddy. 320, 321.
It is naturally mischievous but becomes worse after drinking toddy.

316. காலம் போன காலத்தில் மூலம் வந்து குறுக்கிட்டதுபோல.
Like getting piles in one's old age.
The sufferer is already weak, but the piles will make him still worse.

317. காற்றும் மழையும் கலந்து அடித்தாற்போல.
Like being beaten by wind and rain at the same time.

318. கிணறு தப்பித் துரவில் விழலாமா?
After escaping the common well, should one go and fall into a *Turavu?* 319.
A *Turavu* is a big well.

319. கிணற்றுக்குத் தப்பித் தீயிலே பாய்ந்தான்.
Having escaped the well, he jumped into fire. 318, 338.
"*Out of the frying pan into the fire.*"

320. குரங்கின் கையில் கொள்ளி அகப்பட்டதுபோல.
Like a monkey getting hold of a firebrand.
It will do endless mischief.
"*One mischief falls upon the neck of another.*"

321. குரங்கு கள்ளும் குடித்து, பேயும் பிடித்து, தேளும் கொட்டினால், என்ன கதி ஆகும்?
If a monkey drinks toddy, is possessed by a devil and stung by a scorpion, what will be its fate?
If a person gives room for one moral evil after another, how will he end? The three evils referred to are the three evil principles (*Mala*) self-will, delusion, lust, often mentioned, in the Hindu philosophy. 315, 462.
"*But evil men shall wax worse and worse.*" (II. Tim. 3, 13.)

322. கொசுகுக்கு அஞ்சி குடிபோகிறதா?
Will a family remove to another house for fear of mosquitoes? 310, 330, 339.

323. கோல் இழந்த குருடனைப் போல.
Like the blind man that lost his stick. 2135.
He was already badly off, but fell into a worse plight.

324. சிற்றப்பன் வீட்டுக்குப் போய் சிற்றாடை வாங்கி வரலாம் என்று போனாளாம், சிற்றப்பன் பெண்சாதி ஈச்சம் பாயை இடுப்பில் கட்டிக் கொண்டு எதிரே வந்தாளாம்.

It is said, that she went to her uncle's house in the hope of getting a small cloth, but she met her uncle's wife wearing only a palm-leaf mat round her waist. From bad to worse. 314, 325.

325. சீலை இல்லை என்று சின்னாய் (சிறிய தாய்) வீட்டுக்குப் போனாளாம், அவள் ஈச்சம் பாயைக் கட்டிக்கொண்டு எதிரே வந்தாளாம்.

She went to her maternal aunt because she had no cloth, but her aunt came to meet her clad in a palm-leaf mat. 314, 324.

326. தாடி பற்றிக்கொண்டு எரியச்சே, சுருட்டுக்கு நெருப்பு கேட்டானும்.

While one man's beard was burning, another man asked him for a light for his cigar. 305.

"*If my beard is burnt, others try to light their pipes at it.*"

Kashmiri: "*My beard is on fire, and he comes to warm his hands at the blaze.*"

327. நாய் வாயிலே கோலை இட்டதுபோல்.

Like putting a stick into the mouth of a dog.

To irritate some one causelessly.

"*A man may make his own dog bite him.*"

328. நெருப்பிலே நெய்யை விட்டதுபோல.

Like pouring ghee (butter) into fire.

Making matters worse.

"*To cast oil in the fire is not the way to quench it.*"

329. பட்ட காலிலே படும், கெட்ட குடியே கெடும்.

The leg that has been hurt will be hurt, and the ruined family will be ruined.

This is *the* proverb signifying that: "*Misfortunes never come singly.*"

330. பிச்சைக்காரனுக்குப் பயந்து அடுப்பு மூட்டாததுபோல.

Fearing beggars, she did not kindle a fire on the hearth.

To avoid giving to the poor, she starved herself. Stinginess. 310, 322, 339

331. பிச்சைக்காரன் சோற்றிலே சனீஸ்வரன் புகுந்ததுபோல.

As *Sani* entered into the beggar's food.

Life was hard to the beggar, and misfortune embittered it. *Sani* is a most malignant planetary deity.

332. பிச்சைக்குப் பிச்சையும் கெட்டது, பின்னையும் ஒரு காசு நாமமும் கெட்டது.

He did not get the alms he went for, and the money he had spent to adorn his forehead with his caste-mark was also lost.

333. முதலே தூர்ப்பலம், அதிலும் கர்ப்பிணி.
First of all, she is weak, and secondly she is pregnant.
A great trouble is coming, but there is not strength to meet it.

334. முண்டைக் கண்ணிப் பிள்ளை இரண்டு கண்ணும் நொள்ளை.
The child of the woman with bulging eyes, was blind in both eyes.
Kashmiri: "*Misfortune after misfortune.*"

335. மரத்திலிருந்து விழுந்தவனை பாம்பு கட்டித்ததுபோல (or மாடு மெரித்தது or தேர் ஓடினதுபோல).
As the snake bit (*or* the ox trampled on *or* the car ran over) the man who had fallen from a tree.
"*Pour not water on a drowned mouse.*"

336. முன்னே பிறந்த காதை விட, பின்னே பிறந்த கொம்பு பலம்.
The horn that was born last was stronger than the ear that was born first. 2495.
In a certain firm the employes longed to be rid of the strict manager, but when they had ousted him another came who was still worse.
"*King Log and King Stork.*"

337. விரல் சுற்றின் பேரில் அம்மி (or உரல்) விழுந்ததுபோல.
Like a grinding stone (*or* a mortar) falling on a whitlow.

338. விலங்கு வேண்டாம், தொழுவில் இருக்கிறேன் (or மாட்டிக்கொண்டேன், or போடு என்கிறான்).
I did not want the fetters, but here I am in the stocks. 319.
I was displeased with the work I had, and got the work I applied for, but I find that I am worse off.

339. வீட்டை என் இடித்தாய்? மூட்டைப் பூச்சிக்குப் பயந்து.
Why did you break down your house? I did it for fear of bugs. 310, 322, 330.
"*Burn not your house to fright away the mice.*"

340. வீணாய் உடைந்த சட்டி வேண்டியது உண்டு, பூணாரம் என் தலையில் பூண்ட புதுமையை நான் கண்டதில்லை.
Plenty of pots are uselessly broken, but I never saw a pot put as an ornament round my head. That would be something fresh.
The story is as follows:—A woman used to break a pot on her husband's head for every tenth sin he committed. The husband got tired of this and went away to a friend's house, but here he found the wife breaking a pot on her husband's head for every fault he did; and she did it so, that the mouth of the pot jumped over and fell down round the visitors neck and stuck there like a necklace.
"*Home is homely, and too homely sometime, where wives' footstools to their husbands' head climb.*"

340*a*. கேடு வரும் பின்னே மதிகெட்டு வருமுன்னே, யானை வரும் பின்னே மணி ஓசை வருமுன்னே.

Loss of sense precedes (spiritual) degradation as surely as the sound of the bells precedes the elephant.

" *Coming events cast their shadows before them.*"

" *Quem deus vult perdere primum dementit.*"

340*b*. விநாசக்காலே விபரீதப்புத்தி.

In times of degeneration people get a perverted mind.

Cf. 792 *ff.* 2958 *ff.*

SELFISHNESS.

தன் காரியத்தில் புலி.

341. அண்ணனுக்குப் பெண் பிறந்தால், அத்தை அசல் நாட்டாள்.

If the elder brother gets a daughter, his sister becomes a stranger to him.

All his kindness was formerly directed to his sister, but now all goes to his own child. நாட்டாள் is sometimes written நாடாள். The proverb then implies that the sister who has a son will not seek a wife for him among strangers, but will demand her elder brother's daughter for him.

342. அரைக்கிறவன் ஒன்று நினைத்து அரைக்கிறான், குடிக்கிறவன் ஒன்று நினைத்துக் குடிக்கிறான்.

He who grinds the ingredients thinks of one thing and grinds, he who drinks the medicine thinks of something else, and drinks.

A doctor only thinks of the profit he will get by the medicine he is preparing, the sick person only wonders whether it will cure him or not. Each thinks of his own interests.

343. அவரவர் அக்கரைக்கு அவரவர் பாடுபடுவார்.

Each one will exert himself for his own interest.

344. அள்ளுவது எல்லாம் நாய் தனக்கு என்று எண்ணுமாம்.

The dog seems to think that whatever is taken is intended for it.

Mean people greedily desire everything they see. 354.

345. ஊரார் வீட்டு (com. ஊராமூட்டு) நெய்யே, என் பெண்சாதி கையே.

The ghee (butter) belonged to the village, but my wife's hand distributed it.

The husband and his wife were at a village feast. She was asked to help in distributing the food; as the ghee was not her own, she gave her husband much more than she would give him at home. Used about liberality with others' goods. 3185.

" *'Tis good feasting in other men's houses.*"

346. ஊரார் வீட்டுச் சோற்றைப்பார், ஒசுபாடி வயிற்றைப்பார்.
Look at the villagers' rice; look at this shameless man's stomach.

He eats as often as he can and as much as he can at others expense. A proverb about selfish greed.

347. எங்கள் வீட்டுக்கு வந்தால் என்ன கொண்டுவருகிறாய், உங்கள் வீட்டுக்கு வந்தால் என்ன தருகிறாய்?
If you come to our house what will you bring me? if I go to your house what will you give me?

The same proverb is found in Telugu.

" *What's your's is mine, what's mine, is my own.*"

348. எது எப்படிபோனாலும், தன் காரியம் தனக்கு.
However matters go he thinks only of his own affairs.

" *He is a slave of the greatest slave who serveth nothing but himself.*"

349. எரிகிற வீட்டிலே பிடுங்கிறது லாபம்.
Whatever you are able to secure from a burning house is a gain.

When supplies are bought for a wedding or for any grand occasion, or for some government contract, the person who manages the affair will secure something for himself; this is specially true of police and lawyers in their management of cases. 359.

" *It is good fishing in troubled water.*"

" *Every little helps.*"

350. எறும்புக்குத் தன்கையால் எண்ஜாண் உடம்பு.
Even an ant is eight span long, if measured by its own hand.

Every little man thinks himself great, because he measures himself according to his own standard.

351. ஆல் பழுத்தால் அங்கே, அரசு பழுத்தால் இங்கே.
When the banyan is ripe he is there, and when the peepal (Ficus religiosa) is ripe he is here. 2737.

Wherever there is something to be had, there the greedy man is to be found.

352. ஒரு கோமுட்டியைக் கழுவில் போட்டதற்கு ஒன்பது கல எள்ளு ஆச்சுதே, ஊர் கோமுட்டிகளை எல்லாம் கழுவிலே போடு என்றானாம்.
A man once said: If I get nine big measures of sesamum seed for impaling one merchant, then impale all the merchants in the village.

Other people's sufferings are nothing to such a man, if he only gains by it.

" *He sets any house on fire only to roast his eggs.*"

353. ஓணான் வேலிக்கு இழுக்கிறது, தவளை தண்ணீருக்கு இழுக்கிறது.
The lizard drags its prey to the hedge, the frog drags its prey to the water.

Every man tries to secure what he has gained to himself.

" *All draw water to their own mill.*"

354. கஞ்சி வரதப்பா என்றால், எங்கே வரதப்பா என்கிறான்.

If the one says, O *Kanji Varathappa*, the other replies:—where is the gruel?

A certain Vaisnavite at Conjevaram was praying to the God, *Kanji Varathappa;* a beggar who stood near by asking for alms, heard the name of the God imperfectly, and thought that the Vaisnavite said *Kanji varukirathappa, i.e.* "Some gruel is coming." Not seeing it he said *Engé Varathappa, i.e.* "Where is the gruel?" The proverb is really a pun on the two words *Kanji* and *Varathappa* and is used when one appropriates remarks to himself that were uttered with no reference to him. 344.

355. கடைக்குக் கடை ஆளாய்தான் இருப்பான்.

There is a person in each *bazaar* (shop) to sell things.

Each merchant does his best to sell his own goods.

356. கிட்டினால் ராமா கோவிந்தா, கிட்டாவிட்டால் ஒன்றுமில்லை.

If we get what we want, we worship the idol as Rama or Govindan, if we do not get it, the idol is nought. 222, 2186, 2732.

357. குடிக்கிற பாலைக் கமர் வெடிப்பிலே வார்க்கிறதா?

Do you pour the milk for drinking into a crevice in the ground.

Used about foolish expenditure of money on selfish litigation or pleasure. 367, 622, 2621.

"*A penny weight of love is worth a pound of law.*"

358. கோணி கொண்டது, எருது சுமந்தது.

The bull carried all that the sack held.

Said about selfish avarice.

"*In the world there be men, that will have the egg and the hen.*"

359. சந்தடி சாக்கிலே கந்தப்பொடி காற்பணம்.

Taking advantage of your being so busy, he gets a pice-worth of scented powder for himself into your bill. 349.

Said of one who selfishly seeks to get profit for himself out of others. If a carriage is lent to such a person to convey him one mile, he is sure to keep the vehicle all day to pay a number of visits. If he goes shopping with you he makes you pay his bill.

360. செத்தவன் வீட்டிலே கெட்டவன் ஆர்?

Who is the loser in the dead man's house?

At a funeral, some outsiders take a pride in distributing the food and sweets which the near relatives have provided and are clever at making plans for disposing of the dead man's property. Said of those who are liberal with the property of others.

"*To cut large slices of another man's loaf.*"

361. சுயகாரிய துரந்தரன், சுவாமி காரியம் வழ வழ.

He is smart about his own business, he lets God's things slip.

"*Greedy are the Godless.*"

361*a*. தலைமகள் அறுத்தாலும், தானே வாழவேண்டும்.
Though the eldest daughter has her *thali* cut off, her mother will not care if she is well off herself.

A selfish mother will not mind when her daughter is made a widow.

" *Close sits my shirt, but closer my skin.*"

362. தனக்கு என்றால் பிள்ளையும் களை வெட்டும்.
If it be for himself even a child will weed.

" *He feathers his own nest.*"

363. தன் காரியத்தில் புலி.
He is a tiger in his own affairs.

" *A man is a lion in his own cause.*"

364. தன் காரியம் என்றால், தன் சீலை பதைக்கும்.
If it concerns his own affair, even his cloth will be restless.

" *Every man wishes water to his own mill.*"

365. தாய்முலைப்பாலிலும் உப்பு பார்ப்பான்.
He will find salt in the milk from his mother's breast. 2899.

Said of one who is over suspicious in every thing concerning himself.

366. தானும் வாழுகிற காலத்தில், வயிறு சிறுக்கும் மதியும் பெருக்கும்.
When she is married, her stomach will become small and her sense great.

While a girl is in her mother's house she has nothing to do but eat, but when she goes to her husband's house she will find little time to eat and will have to be constantly on the alert to economise.

367. தான் குடிக்காத பாலைக் கவிழ்த்துவிடுகிறதா?
Should you spill the milk you can't drink ?

Even children will use this proverb when another child is unwilling to share some sweets or fruits with them. 357.

" *The Dog in the manger.*"

368. தேவடியாள் இருந்து, ஆத்தாள் செத்தால் கொட்டு முழக்கம், தேவடியாள் செத்தால் ஒன்றுமில்லை.
If the dancing girl be alive, and her mother dies, there will be beating of drums; but if the dancing girl dies there will be no such display.

To get the favour of the dancing girl, many men will attend her mother's funeral; but if the dancing girl herself die, there is nothing to be gained by attending her funeral. In like manner:—If somebody die in a rich man's house, all people will attend that they may gain his favour; but if the rich man die, no one will care as nothing more is to be had from him in future.

369. நல்ல நாச்சியார் கடைந்த மோர், நாழி முத்துக்கு நாழிமோர்.
A measure of buttermilk churned by a good woman was sold for a measure of pearls.

Said of a person who overvalues his own worth. 3248.

" *No one calls his own buttermilk sour.*"

370. நான் என்றால் இளக்காரம், என் பீ (சொத்து) என்றால் பலகாரம்.
He cares nothing about me personally, but he considers even my filth a cake. 2733.

Servants and subordinates care little for their masters or superiors, but they care for his wealth if they can make anything out of it.

371. நீயும் நானும் அடா, சாறும் சோறும் அடா!
You and I, sir; sauce and food, sir.

i.e., We shall get on together by ourselves as well as food and sauce. Said by a wife to a husband as a reason why he should leave the joint-family, in his father's house.

372. பார்த்திருக்கத் தின்று, முழித்திருக்கக் கை கழுவுவான்.
Though I saw him, he went on eating; and though I watched him, he washed his hands.

He finished his meal without giving me a share. Said of one who enjoys himself selfishly.

373. பிள்ளைப் பேறு பார்த்ததும் போதும், என் அம்புடையானைக் கட்டி அணைத்ததும் போதும்.
There has been enough of your help in my confinement, and of your embracing my husband.

One woman told another that she would like to help her at the time of her confinement. Her intention was however to get access to the husband of the latter with whom she was in love. Hence the rebuke. Used of the interested help of deceitful friends.

374. வாழைபழம் தின்னாத குரங்கு இல்லை.
There is not a monkey that does not eat plantains.

Every one looks for his own profit.

Or வேண்டாம் என்கிற குரங்கு உண்டா?
Is there a monkey that says, I don't want?

375. வெட்கம் கெட்டாலும் கெடட்டும், தொப்பை இட்டால் போதும்.
Let me lose my respect (if necessary); I am satisfied, if I get fat.

Said of one who seeks profit at any cost.

Cf. Kashmiri: "A fat man has no religion."

Cf. 1054 *ff.*

DISGRACE.

வெட்கமில்லாமை, முறையில்லாமை, வெட்கப்படுத்தல்.

376. அங்கத்தை ஆற்றிலே அலசொணாதா?
Couldn't you wash your body in the river?

Said to a very wicked fellow, whose badness it is impossible to amend.

377. அடி அதிரசம், குத்து கொழுக்கட்டை.
A thrashing is a sweetmeat, and a cuff is a cake. 403.

No sense of shame in him.

378. *அடித்தது ஆட்டம் பிடித்தது பெண்டு.*
To beat people is a joke to him and he treats any woman he gets hold of as he likes. 391.

Used of unprincipled tyranny.

379. *அம்மாள் கெட்ட கேட்டுக்கு முக்காடு ஒன்றா?* (or *ஒரு கேடா?*)
Is one veil sufficient to cover a woman's wickedness? 417.

Is modesty a sufficient cloak for immorality?

380. *அவன் மிதித்த* (com. *மெரித்த*) *இடம் பற்றி எரிகிறது.*
The place on which he treads will take fire.

Said of the very wicked and the very unlucky.

381. *அவன் சாயம் வெளுத்துப்போய்விட்டது.*
His colour has been well bleached out.

Just as a cloth loses its colour and value through much washing, so he, having been found out in his deceit, is dishonoured.

382. *அவிழ்த்துவிட்ட கோழி.*
A fowl that is let loose. 390, 411.

One who goes about doing whatever he likes, not feeling shame before anyone.

383. *ஆட்டுக்கும் மாட்டுக்கும் முறையா, காட்டுக்கும் பாட்டுக்கும் வரையா?*
Have sheep and cows moral laws, and have woods and songs any limit?

Said ironically of those who have no shame in their misdeeds.

384. *ஆற்றித்தூற்றி அம்பலத்தில் வைக்கப்பார்க்கிறான்.*
(Or *என்னை பவிஷு ஆற்றுகிறான்.*)
He tries to winnow me in public.

He tries to bring disgrace on me in public.

385. *இந்த அமாவாசைக்கும் வெட்கமில்லை, வருகிற அமாவாசைக்கும் வெட்கமில்லை.*
This new moon he has no shame, nor will he have any next new moon.

No shame now and none hereafter.

386. *இறைச்சி தின்றாலும் எலும்பைக் கோத்துக் கழுத்தில் அணிகிறதா?*
Though a person eats flesh, why string the bones and hang them round his neck?

It is bad enough to do evil, but still worse to make it public.

387. *உத்தமனுக்கும் தப்பிலிக்கும் ஓலை என்னதற்கு?* (for *தப்பிலி*, *போக்கிரி* or *ஒசுப்பாடி* or *ஒக்கட்டான்* are used.)
Written bonds are not needed for honest men or rogues.

The good man will do his duty without them, the rogue will not do his duty though he has signed a hundred.

388. *என் முகத்திலே கரி பூசினாயே.*
Thou hast smeared my face with charcoal. 1026.

You have disgraced me.

Or *என் முகத்திலே கரி தடவாதே* (or *சாணி போடாதே*).
Don't smear my face with charcoal (*or* cowdung).

389. என்பேரில் தப்பிருந்தால், என்னை மொட்டை அடித்துக் கழுதைமேல் எற்றிக்கொள்.
If I am wrong, shave my head and make me ride on an ass.
Put me to shame, if I am wrong in what I have done or said.

390. ஏடாகூடக்காரனுக்கு (or வம்புக்காரனுக்கு) வழி எங்கே? போகிறவன் தலைமேலே.
Where is the path of a rash man? Over a quiet man's head. 382, 411, 415.
"*Bold and shameless men are masters of the world.*"

391. கண்டதே காக்ஷி, கொண்டதே கோலம்.
What you see is a sight, and what you get is an ornament. 378.
Applied to those who give way to all sorts of evil, not knowing that everything is the result of *Maya*, illusion.

392. கெட்ட குடி கெட்டது, பூராவாய்க் குடி அப்பா!
You are drunk, drink plenty old fellow.
A sneer about drunkards and debtors. Why stop drinking or borrowing?

393. கொழுக்கட்டைக்குத் தலையுமில்லை, கூத்தாடிச்சிக்கு (or கோயில் ஆண்டிச்சிக்கு or குடியனுக்கு) முறையுமில்லை.
The cake has no point, and the dancing girl (*or* the female mendicant *or* the drunkard) does not regard the ties of relationship.
A dancing girl is invariably a harlot.

394. சிறைச்சாலைக்கு அழகில்லை, தேவடியாளுக்கு முறையில்லை.
A prison has no beauty, and a dancing girl does not regard the ties of relationship. 3593.

395. நானும் வந்தேன், நாற்றமும் போச்சுது.
When I entered the home, the smell disappeared.
A Mahomedan young man whose father sold salt fish, married the daughter of a dealer in sweet perfumes, and after the wedding the girl came to her father-in-law's home to live with her husband. At first she could not bear the smell of the fish, but after a while she became used to the odour and ceased to perceive it and was conceited enough to suppose that her presence had driven it away. The meaning of the proverb is, that those who live in an atmosphere of sin become blind to the disgrace of sin.

396. சூத்தை வழித்து முக்காடு போட்டாற்போல்.
A vulgar proverb satirising sham prudery.

397. சொரணைகெட்டவன் சொந்தக்காரன்.
A shameless fellow will win. 415, 416.
As he has no shame, he does anything he likes.
"*He that has no modesty has all the town for his own.*"

398. தடிக்கு அஞ்சாத பாம்பு.
A snake that does not fear the stick.

399. தலைக்குமேல் வெள்ளம் ஜாண்போனால் என்ன, முழம்போனால் என்ன?
When a flood rises over one's head, what does it matter whether it rises only a span or a cubit?
When one is completely discredited, further disgrace makes no difference.

400. திருடிக்குத் தெய்வமில்லை, அவசாரிக்கு ஆணையில்லை.
A thief does not fear God, and a harlot is not bound by an oath.
"*The tears of a whore and the oaths of a bully may be put into the same bottle.*"

401. திருப்பதியில் மொட்டை அடித்ததுப் போதாமல், ஸ்ரீரங்கத்தில் சிரிப் பாய்ச் சிரிக்கவந்தான்.
Not thinking it enough to have been shaved bald at Tirupati, he came to Shrirangam to become a laughing-stock.
Not satisfied with the first shame, he seeks another.

402. துவைத்துத் தோள்மேல் போட்டுக்கொண்டான்.
He has dipped it in water and put it on his shoulder. 1318.
Dipping a cloth in water makes it heavier. Said of one who adds sin to sin and makes a public display of his wickedness.
Danish: "*He has bitten of the head of all shame.*"

403. தோளின்பேரில் தொண்ணூறு அடி அடித்தாலும், துடைத்துப்போடு வான்.
Even though he be beaten ninety-nine times on his shoulder, he will rub the smart off. 377, 413.

404. பத்துப்பேர் மெச்சப் படிக்கிறதிலேயும், ஆயிரம்பேரை அடிக்கிறதிலே யும், நாலுபேர் மெச்ச நடிக்கிறதிலேயும், மிடாமிடாவாகக் குடிக் கிறதே கெட்டிக்காரத்தனம்.
It is more praiseworthy to drink pot after pot of toddy than to study so as to be praised by ten persons, or to conquer a thousand people, or to dance so as to be praised by four.
Used ironically of the degenerate who despise goodness and praise wickedness.
"*Hell will never have its due, till it have its hold of you.*"

405. பனைமரத்திற்கு நிழல் இல்லை, பறையனுக்கு முறையில்லை.
The palmyra palm yields no shade, and a Paria does not regard the ties of relationship.
A reference to the incestuous habits of certain Parias.

406. பீ தின்கிறதுபோல் கனவு கண்டால், பொழுதுவிடிந்தால் யாருக்குச் சொல்லுகிறது.
If one dreams that he eats dirt, to whom can he tell it at day-break.
If one secretly leads a bad life he will be ashamed to tell of it to others.

407. பூராடக்காரனோடு போராடி முடியாது.
No one can fight with a man born under the star *Purádu*.
Those born under this star are wicked and insolent.

408. பெற்ற தாயுடன் போகிறவனுக்குப் பத்தம் ஏது?
Will the man who lies with his own mother regard any ties? 424, 3593.

409. பெற்ற தாயைப் பெண்டுக்கு அழைப்பான்.
He will call his own mother to be his wife. 408.

Boundless wickedness.

410. பெற்றாரை நினையாத தறுதலை.
A wicked child that has no respect for his parents.

411. போக்கற்ற நாய்க்குப் போனதெல்லாம் வழி.
A dog without an aim, a road that goes in every direction! 382, 390.

Said of a wicked person who goes where he likes and does what he likes.

412. முட்ட (or முழுதும்) நனைந்தவனுக்கு ஈரமில்லை பேனுமில்லை. (or முக்காடு என்ன?)
One who is soaked through, is not wet, and has no lice about him. (*or* does not want a veil?)

Applied to men utterly shameless or utterly poor. (This is the vulgar form of the proverb.)

413. முப்பது செருப்பு தின்றவனுக்கு மூன்று செருப்பு பணிகாரம்.
To him who has eaten thirty shoes, three will be like a cake. 403.

A man who has been beaten with a shoe thirty times will not mind being beaten thrice.

414. மருந்து தின்றால் பிழைப்பாய் என்றால், மயிர்தான் தின்னமாட்டேன் என்கிறான்.
If you say to him, Take medicine and you will live, he replies, I won't take a drop of it.

Said of those who are so bad that they will not hear about improvement.

415. ராஜன் பெரிதோ, போக்கிரி பெரிதோ?
Is the king or the blackguard the greater? 299, 300, 390, 397.

In a fight or quarrel the shameless man is the greater, as he will not refrain from using any abuse or device.

"*Beware of him who regards not his reputation.*"

416. வெட்கம் கெட்டவன் ஊருக்குப் பெரியவன்.
One who is lost to all shame is the big man of the village. 397, 415.

417. வெட்கம் சிக்கி விட்டு வெளிப்பட்ட மூளிக்கு முக்காடு ஒரு கேடா?
When an utterly shameless woman appears in the public, is a veil all she needs? 379.

418. வெட்கத்தை விற்று அக்குளிலே அடக்கிக்கொண்டுபோகிறான்.
He has sold his honour, and put it under his arm.

Said of one who has done a shameless thing which he tries to hide.

"*Who hath horns in his bosom, let him not put them on his head.*"

419. வைய வைய வைரக்கல், திட்டத் திட்டத் திண்டுகல்.
Abuse him and he will become a lasting stone, scold him and he will become a flint.

A shameless fellow. Also used about one who in spite of all his injustice prospers in this world.

WICKEDNESS.

பொல்லாப்பு, தீமை.

THE WICKED INTENT ON WICKEDNESS.

420. கள்ளன் புத்தி திருட்டுமேலே.
A thief's mind is on stealing. 529.
"*Ill doers are ill thinkers.*"

421. கெடுவான் கேடு நினைப்பான்.
The wicked think only of wickedness. 422.

422. தான் திருடி அசல்வீடு நம்பமாட்டான், கூத்திக்கள்ளன் பெண்சாதியை நம்பான்.
He who is a thief himself can't trust his neighbour, and he who keeps a concubine can't trust his wife.
A wicked person cannot believe good of others.
"*A thief thinks every man steals.*"
"*He that does not speak truth to me does not believe me when I speak truth.*"
"*Do well and doubt no man; do ill and doubt all men.*"

423. மூக்கறையன் கதைபோல் பேசுகிறான்.
He speaks like the noseless man in the story.
A certain man who had no nose was always ridiculed in his village. To make the other people as badly off as himself, he began at certain times to praise God and to thank him that he had enabled him to see him. When he thus burst out in loud praise, people gathered round him, and asked what they should do to see God. His advice was, that they should cut off their noses. This they did one after another. And though they could not see God, they pretended that they could out of very shame. Thus wicked people will try to draw good people over to their own wicked ways.
"*A hog that is bemired, endeavours to bemire others.*"

THE DOER OF GREAT EVILS, WILL NOT FEAR TO COMMIT SMALLER ONES.

424. ஆத்தாளோடு போகிறவனுக்கு அக்காள் ஏது, தங்கச்சி ஏது?
What is an elder or a younger sister to him who lies with his own mother? 408, 3593.

425. கொலைக்கு அஞ்சாதவன் பழிக்கு அஞ்சுவானா?
Will he be afraid of blame, who is not afraid of committing murder?

426. மலை முழுங்கின மாதாவுக்குக் கதவு சுண்டாங்கி.
To a mother who has swallowed a mountain, a door is but a bit of seasoning.

427. மாரியத்தாளை பெண்டு பிடிக்கிறவனுக்குப் பூசாரி பெண்சாதி எம்மாத்திரம்?
What is the priest's wife to him, who seduces the Goddess of Small-pox herself?

HE WHO COMMITS SMALL EVILS, WILL SOON COMMIT GREAT ONES.

428. *கடுகு களவும் களவுதான், கர்ப்பூரக் களவும் களவுதான்.*
Theft of mustard is theft, and theft of camphor is theft.
Camphor is sacred, and used in the worship of all the gods.
"*Sin is sin whether big or small.*"

429. *காதை அறுத்தவன் கண்ணைக் குத்தினாலும் குத்துவான்.*
He who cuts off the ears of a person, may also stab his eyes.
"*Small faults indulged are little thieves, that let in greater.*"

430. *கையை உடைத்துவிட்டவன் தலையை உடைத்தாலும் உடைப்பான்.*
He who breaks one's hand, may also break one's head.
"*He that will steal an egg, will steal an ox.*"

431. *இன்றைக்கு இலை அறுத்தவன் நாளைக்குக் குலை அறுக்கமாட்டானோ?*
Will not he who steals leaves to-day, steal a cluster of fruit to-morrow?
To do a little evil will lead to doing greater.—Or, said of one who is overanxious to see the result of his labour. In this case: *மாட்டான்* for *மாட்டானோ.*
"*He who hath done ill once will do it again.*"

432. *இன்றைக்கு சின்னதுக்கு வந்தது, நாளைக்குப் பெரிதுக்கு வரும்.*
He who came for a little to-day, will come for a big thing to-morrow.
Said often by mothers to their children.
"*He that will steal a pin will steal a better thing.*"

Cf. 424 *ff.* 2013 *ff.*

KILL EVIL AT ITS VERY BIRTH.

433. *குட்டிப்பாம்பை அடித்தாலும், குற்றுயிராய் விடப்போகாது.*
Though it be only a young snake you beat, it won't do to leave it half dead.

434. *தீ மிஞ்சவைத்தாலும், பகை மிஞ்ச வைக்கப்படாது.*
Though you may cherish fire to excess, don't cherish hatred to excess (but kill it at once). 454.

435. *ஜாண் பாம்பானாலும் முழத்தடி வேண்டும்.*
Though the snake be only a span long, a stick a cubit long is needed to kill it.

436. *பாம்பை முட்டையிலே, புலியைக் குட்டியிலே, கொல்லவேண்டும்.*
A snake must be killed while in the egg, and a tiger while it is young.
"*Destroy the lion while he is but a whelp.*"

437. முளையில் கிள்ளாததை முற்றினால், கோடாலிகொண்டு வெட்ட வேண்டும்.

What is not nipped at the bud but left to mature, will have to be felled with an axe. 3299.

Neglected evil is hard to destroy.

Cf. 3299 *ff.*

MISCELLANEOUS PROVERBS ABOUT WICKEDNESS.

438. அதமனுக்கு (vulg. அதலைக்கு) ஆயிரம் ஆயுசு.

A vile man lives a thousand years. 446.

"*A bad thing never dies.*" "*An ill stake standeth longest.*"
"*A creaking door hangs on its hinges.*"

439. அந்த ஊர் மண் மெரிக்கவே, தன்னை மறந்துவிட்டான்.

As soon as he put his foot on the soil of that village, he went to the bad.

440. அவசாரி என்று ஆனைமேலே ஏறலாம், திருடி என்று தெருவில் வரலாமா?

A prostitute may ride an elephant in the streets, but can a thief come into the streets?

Some sins are condoned.

"*No law for lying.*"

441. ஆகாத வேளையில் பிள்ளை பிறந்தால், அப்பனையும் ஆத்தாளையும் கொல்லுமே ஒழிய, பஞ்சாங்கஞ் சொன்ன பார்ப்பானை என்ன செய்யும்?

If a child is born at an inauspicious time though he ruins both his father and mother, what harm can he do to the Brahmin who tells his horoscope? 112.

Said in mockery of a wicked person who invokes all kinds of evil on those whom he hates.

442. எட்டுப்படி அரிசி ஒரு கவளம், ஏழு ஊர் சண்டை ஒரு சிம்மாளம்.

Eight measures of rice is only a mouthful to her, and the quarrels of seven villages makes her jump with joy. 450.

A description of a shrew.

443. எண்டி பாட்டி மஞ்சள் குளித்தாய் (என்றால்), பழைய நினைப்பு அடா பேராண்டி!

If the grandson asks, O, old woman, why are you adorning your body with saffron? she replies. O my grandson my old passions have returned. 459.

After losing her husband or getting somewhat old, a woman should not adorn herself with saffron. If she does, it shows that she wants to attract men. Used of hidden vice that springs up again.

444. ஐயோ என்றால் ஆறுமாசத்துப் பாவம் சுற்றும்.

If I pity you, six month's sin will surround me. 461.

To pity a wicked person and forbear with him is considered a great sin.

"*If you pity rogues, you are no great friend of honest men.*"

445. கடைகெட்ட மூளிக்குக் கோபம் கொண்டாட்டம்.
Anger is fun to a wicked woman.

446. கள்ளிக்கு நாடு எல்லாம் காடு.
The *Kalli* weed (*Euphorbia*) grows all over the country. 438.
"*Weeds grow apace.*" "*Ill weeds grow fast.*"

447. காலம் கண்ட பெருச்சாளி.
He is a bandycoot who has seen many days.
A bandycoot is a large animal of the rat tribe very strong and cunning. Used of a knowing rascal.

448. காலங்கெட்டுக் கறுப்புகோழி வெள்ளைமுட்டை இடுகிறது.
The black hen that wasted its time lays a white egg.
This is not exactly a proverb. Used about the present evil age (Kaliyuga).

449. குரங்கு புண் ஆறாது.
A monkey's wound never heals.
A monkey is too restless to let its wounds heal, and so the human race through its constant activity in wickedness cannot amend its ways. A philosophical saying.

450. தண்டுக்கு ரொட்டி சுட்டுபோடுகிறவள்.
She makes bread for the army. 442.
i.e., She is a camp follower, a term of abuse.

451. திருட்டுப்பயல் கலியாணத்தில் முடிச்சு அவிழ்க்கிறவன் பெரியதனம்.
At the marriage of a thief the pick-pocket is the *best-man*.
If the master is a wicked man, he will have servants still worse.

452. திருட்டுக்கு நவமணி.
In thieving he shines like the Nine Gems.
A capital rogue. A first class scamp. The *Nine Gems* were nine learned men in the court of Vikramaditya the Great.

453. தேளுக்குக் கொடுக்கிலே விஷம், தேவடியாளுக்கு உடம்பிலே விஷம், உனக்கோ சர்வாங்கம் விஷம்.
Scorpions have poison in their tail, harlots in their body, but as to you, your whole body is poison!
An expression of contempt for a wicked person.

454. நெருஞ்சிமுள் தைத்தாலும், குனிந்து பிடுங்கவேண்டும்.
If a thorn runs into the foot, one must stoop to take it out. 434.
Be careful even with little evils.—If a mean fellow abuses you, bear it humbly.

455. நெருப்பைக் கண்டு மிதித்தாலும் (com. மெரித்தாலும்) சுடும், காணாமல் மிதித்தாலும் சுடும்.
Whether you tread on fire knowingly or unawares, it will burn.
Evil is evil whether seen or not.

456. பாம்பு ஆட்டி பாம்பிலே (சாவு), கள்ளன் களவிலே (சாவு).
(Death) comes to the snake who has lived as a snake, and to the thief who has lived as a thief. 207.

As one lives, so will he die.

" *The wolf must die in its own skin.*"

Or பாம்பாட்டிக்குப் பாம்பிலே சாவு, கள்ளனுக்கு களவிலே (or கழுவிலே) சாவு.
Death come to the snake-charmer from his snake, and to the thief from his theft (*or* on the impaling tree).

i.e., Retribution follows a person from his own wickedness.

457. புளியமரத்தில் ஏறினவன் பல் கூசினால் இறங்குவான்.
He who has climbed a tamarind tree will come down when his teeth are set on edge.

People will do evil as long as they can. The fruit of the tamarind tree is proverbially sour.

458. போக்கிரி (or முரட்டு) தனத்துக்கு முதல் தாம்பூலம் கொடுக்கவேண்டும்.
We must honour the great rogue by giving him *betel* first.

He is to be marked out as the worst rogue.

459. போன சனியனைத் தாம்பூலம் வைத்து அழைத்ததுபோல.
Like recalling *Sani* (the planet Saturn) by giving him betel.

The folly of re-instating a bad servant helper, or friend. Only harm will come of it. *Sani* is the most malignant of all the heavenly bodies.

460. போன சுரத்தைப் புளி இட்டு அழைத்ததுபோல்.
Like bringing a fever back again by giving tamarind. 459, 742.

Refers to difficulties one has got over, but in which one wilfully entangles himself again. Specially used of evil habits, given up for a time and then resumed.

" *Misfortunes when asleep are not to be awakened.*"

461. முகத்திலே முழித்தாலும், மூன்று நாளைக்குச் சோறு அகப்படாது.
If you look into the face (of a wicked person) you will not get food for three days. 444.

462. முப்பதும்போய், மூன்றும் தள்ளினவள்போல பேசுகிறாள்.
She speaks like an experienced person who has passed her thirtieth year, and given up the three restraints. 321, 443.

The *three restraints* are modesty, shame, arrogance (வெட்கஞ்சிக்கி வீறுப்பு). 321.

463. வர வர மாமியார் கழுதைபோல் ஆனாள்.
The mother-in-law became gradually like an ass.

Said of a person who becomes worse and worse in evil-doing chiefly through envy.

PRIDE AND ARROGANCE.

கொர்வம், அடங்காமை.

464. அடங்காப் பாம்புக்கு ராஜா மூங்கில்தடி.
A bamboo stick is the king of an insolent snake.
"*Restive horses must be roughly dealt with.*"

465. அடுத்த வீட்டுக்காரனுக்கு அதிகாரம் வந்தால், அண்டை வீட்டுக்காரனுக்கு இரைச்சல்.
If their neighbour is promoted to authority the people next door will be in for all the noise.
"*A great lord is a bad neighbour.*"

466. அடுத்த வீட்டுக்காரனுக்கு அதியோகம் (or அதிஷ்டம்) வந்தால், அண்டைவீடு குதிரைலாயம்.
If a neighbour is fortunate he will buy up the next house for a stable.
He will oppress his neighbours as king Ahab oppressed Naboth. (1 Kings 21.)

467. அவரா சுறுக்கே, அரிவாள்மணை கருக்கே?
Is he sharp? Is the kitchen knife sharp?
Used ironically by a wife to describe the ability of her husband, if he is arrogant.—Or said of a wicked man who says that in future he will do right.

468. அவனுக்கு ஆகாசம் மூன்றுவிரல்கடை (or அளவு).
To him the sky is only three fingers above him (*or* long).
Said of an exceedingly proud person.
"*He is on the high ropes.*"

469. அறுத்துக்கொண்டதாம் கழுதை, எடுத்துக்கொண்டதாம் ஓட்டம்.
It seems that the ass broke loose and took to its heels.
Said of a stupid and obstinate fellow who suddenly leaves his home or his work and runs away.
"*Who drives an ass, and leads a whore, hath pain and sorrow evermore.*"

470. ஆர் அடா, விட்டது மானியம்? நானே விட்டுக்கொண்டேன் மானியம்!
What, you fellow, who gave you that property? I have given it to myself!
Said of one who does things as seems proper to him.—Or of an inferior, who takes undue authority on himself.

471. இருந்த நாள் எல்லாம் இருந்துவிட்டு, ஊர்ப் பறையனுக்குத் தாரை (com. தார) வார்த்ததுபோல.
Like keeping it all this time and at last giving it as a present to a village-Pariah. 503.
Said of one who, in his foolish pride, keeps some valuable too long, because he can't get the price for it he wants, and of one who will not give his daughter in marriage because he cannot get a sufficiently wealthy bridegroom for her, and at last finds that the girl has been seduced.
"*Better to bow than break.*"

472. உன்னைக் கொடுப்பேனே ஒருகாசு, உன்னோடு போச்சுது புரட்டாசி.
Do you think I will give you a coin? with you the month of September is gone.

During the month of Purattasi (September—October) Vaishnava mendicants receive large presents, but when the month is over they may not expect much. Said to remind an inferior who arrogantly magnifies his claims on the respect and help of others that he can't have all he wants.

473. ஒழுங்கு ஒரு பணம், சளுக்கு (or டம்பம்) முக்கால்பணம்.
For outward show a whole coin, and for vanity three quarters of a coin. 1643.

474. கட்டுக்கு அடங்காப் பிடாரி.
A scamp who does not submit to rules!

Used about an unmanageable child or person.

475. குருவுக்கு மிஞ்சின சிஷ்யன்.
A disciple greater than his Spiritual Guide (*Guru*). 479, 1391.

Said of a proud and insolent fellow.

"*A halter and a rope for him that will be pope without all right and reason.*"

476. சுண்டக்காய் சுண்டக்காயே, எனக்கு முந்தி வந்திருக்கிறாயே?
A *Shunda* fruit (*Solanum*) is but a *Shunda* fruit (*i.e*, small and insignificant); how have you come before me?

Said by a big man in contempt of a humble person.

477. சொருகிக்கிடந்த அகப்பையும் சோறு அள்ளப் புறப்பட்டது.
The ladle that was stuck in the thatch as useless has begun to scoop up rice.

Said of a person who has been overlooked or not thought of, but who suddenly makes his appearance with an air of injured dignity.

478. டம்மாரக்காளைபோல் அலையாதே.
Do not go about like a noisy young bullock.

Said of an unruly person.

479. தடிக்கு மிஞ்சின மிடா.
He is a pot that is greater than a stick! 475.

i.e., It is not afraid of being broken by the stick; though any stick can break a pot. Said of a subordinate who is insolent to his master.

480. தலைக்குத்தலை பெரியதனம் (or நாட்டாமை).
One head is arrogant to the other. 481.

Said of wicked and unruly people, who will submit to no one.

481. தாலி அறுத்தவள் வீட்டிலே தலைக்குத் தலை பெரியதனம்.
In a widow's house (lit. one who has taken off her *thali*) all are masters. 480, 2869.

482. தான் தோன்றி பெருமாள் (com. தான் தோணி, or தான் தோன்றி தம்பிரானாயிருக்கிறான்).
He goes about imagining himself a God.

"*He is so full of himself that he is quite empty.*"

483. தானே கவர்னர், தன் புத்தி பட்ளர்.
He thinks himself a governor, and his intellect a butler.
There is an obscene form of this proverb.

484. தானுய்த் தின்று தலையாய்ப் போகவேண்டும்.
He wants to eat everything himself, and to become the head of everybody.
Said of a person who adds insolent arrogance to selfish greediness.

Or: தானே தின்று தன் தலையே பெருகவேண்டும்.
He wants to keep everything for his own enjoyment, and aims at raising his own head gloriously.

485. தீட்டின மரத்திலே கூர் பார்க்கிறது.
To try the sharpness of the knife on the knife-board. 492.
To be haughty and impertinent towards those who have given us help.

486. துரைவீட்டு நாய் நாற்காலிமேல் ஏறினதுபோல.
Like the dog that jumped up on the gentleman's chair.
"*Every man a little beyond himself is a fool.*"

487. நானும் பூசாரி, எனக்கும் சுவாமி ஆட்டமுமுண்டு.
I too am a *Pujari*, even I can dance like a God.
Sarcastically used to a person, who pretends that he can speak with authority on important subjects. A *Pujari* is a Sudra priest in the temple of a local tutelary deity.
"*Every ass thinks himself worthy to stand with the king's horse.*"

488. நான் ஆம் ஆம் என்றால், ஹரி ஹரி என்கிறான்.
If I say yes, yes, he says Hari, Hari. 2837.
He will not agree with what I say.

489. நீ செத்தால், உலகம் எல்லாம் எலும்பாய்ப் போகுமோ?
If you die, will the whole world become skeleton?

490. பட்டிமாட்டுக்குக் கட்டை கட்டினதுபோல.
Like tying a log to a skittish cow's neck.
Haughty and wicked persons are not rectified by the punishment they get.

491. பிடிவாதம் குடிநாசம்.
Obstinacy is a family's destruction. 1899.

492. பெற்றதாய் இடத்திலேயா கற்ற வித்தை காட்டுகிறது (or ஓதுகிறது).
Do you show off the tricks you have learned to your own mother? 485.
Said of a disobedient and haughty child or man, who has learnt bad ways, but tries to deceive the experienced.

493. மா கனப் பட்டதெல்லாம் ஒரு திரணம், மாட்டுக்காரப்பையனுக்குச் சரணமா?
Greatness is but a straw; shall I then bow down to a cowherd's boy?

494. வற்றிற்றும் கள்ளு வறண்டாளாம் சாணாத்தி, ஊறிற்றும் கள்ளு உதித்தாளாம் சாணாத்தி.

When the toddy dries up, (in the hot season) the toddy-drawer's wife will shrivel up, when the toddy flows (in the cooler weather) she will become plump.

Said of an inferior, who, as long as he has his master's favour, is haughty and unjust towards others, but if he loses that, will behave fairly again. *Toddy* is the fermented juice of certain palms, and is an intoxicant.

495. விரைக்குவிட்ட காய்ப்போல.

Like fruits let go to seed.

Such fruits are useless for food. The term is used of an arrogant person whose indolence his master puts up with till the work entrusted to his skill is finished, and then he is at once dismissed (அதிக பிரசங்கி or அடங்காதவன் or மிஞ்சிபோனவன்).

OBEDIENCE, DISOBEDIENCE, HUMILITY AND HUMILIATION.

அடக்கம், சிறுமைப்படுத்தல்.

496. அகப்பை குறைத்தால், மட்டத்துக்கு வருவான் (or கொழுப்பு எல்லாம் அடங்கும்).

If his spoon is made smaller, he will be manageable; (*or* his fatness will be reduced). 501,512.

Used of a forward child that needs a little management.

497. அடக்கம் ஆயிரம் பொன் தரும்.

Submission will yield a thousand gold coins.

"*Humility often gains more than pride.*"

> "By hearing Scripture man acquires;
> By doing it his soul aspires;
> The utmost love is conquering sense,
> Which cometh of obedience."
>
> E. Arnold: *Indian Idylls.*

498. அவன் வால் அறுந்துபோச்சுது.

His tail has been cut off. 508.

His pride has been subdued.

"*His comb has been cut.*"

499. ஆடி ஓய்ந்த பம்பரம்போல.

Like a top that has done spinning. 500.

Said of one who has been humbled.

"*His heart went into his boots.*"

500. *ஊசல் ஆடி தன் நிலையில் நிற்கும்.*
The swing swings, but comes to a standstill. 499, 507.
Wickedness will come to an end some day.
" *Blow the wind ever so fast, it will lower at last.*"

501. *எடாகூடம் பேசினால், அகப்பை சூனியம் வைப்பேன்.*
If you speak haughtily I will only give you an empty ladle. 496.
i. e., I will give you no food.—Commonly said to children, servants or daughters-in-law.
" *I will take you down a peg.*"

502. *காலால் இட்ட வேலையை, கையால்* (or *தலையால்*) *செய்வான்.*
The work pointed out to him by (his master's) foot, he will do with his hands (*or* head). 2639.
A highly obedient person.

503. *சொன்னபடி கேட்டால், மாப் (மாவு) படைப்பேன்* (or *கொடுப் பேன்*), *கேளாவிட்டால் மண்ணை வெட்டிப்படைப்பேன்.*
If you obey, I will bake bread for you ; but if you don't, your bread shall be dust. 471,2843.
" *Better to bow than to break.*"

504. *தலைமேலே இடி இடித்தாலும், தான் குனியான்.*
Even if he be struck on the head by lightning, he will not bend.

505. *தாழ்ந்தது தங்கம், உயர்ந்தது பித்தளை.*
The humble are pure gold, the proud are brass.

506. *தாழ்ந்து நின்றால், வாழ்ந்து நிற்பாய்.*
If you be humble, you will remain prosperous.
" *Better bend the neck than bruise the forehead.*"

507. *தேர் ஓடி தன் நிலையில் நிற்கும்.*
The car may run, but it will come to a standstill. 500.
Said about a proud and over-bearing person, or about a wicked husband who leaves his wife for years, but is sure to return at last.

508. *பல்லுப் பிடுங்கின பாம்புபோல்.*
He is like a snake that has had its teeth drawn (*i.e.*, is harmless). 498, 510.

509. *பழைய பொன்னனே பொன்னன், பழைய கப்பரையே கப்பரை.*
Ponnan has become old Ponnan, the vessel has become an old vessel. 535.

There was once a servant, who found a vessel full of gold buried in the earth. He did not remove it, but went daily to look at it. At the same time he became proud and unruly. His master watched him closely, and found out about the treasure, which he took secretly. When the servant found that his treasure was gone, he resumed his usual docility and when asked for the reason of the change in his bearing, he replied as above. This is said of one who suddenly becomes rich, but as suddenly loses his wealth.

510. பெட்டிப்பாம்புபோல் அடங்கினான்.
He is now as gentle as a snake in a box. 508.
After being caught and punished, he fears to do evil.

510*a*. பேச்சுப் பேச்சு என்னும் (பேசும்); பெரும் பூனை வந்தால் கீச்சுக் கீச் சென்னும் கிளி.
The parrot will imitate your speech but when the big cat comes near, it will screatch in fear. 1483.
Said of a boaster who knows his own littleness and is put to shame in the presence of his superiors.

511. மடங்காக் குதிரைக்குச் சவுக்கு அடி.
Beat an unruly horse with a whip. 198.

512. வயிற்றில் அடித்தால் எல்லாம் போகும்.
If your stomach be beaten, it is all up with you. 496.
i.e., If a proud and mischievous fellow gets no food, his arrogance will come to an end.

513. வீட்டுக்கு அடங்காத பிள்ளையை ஊரார் அடக்குவார்கள்.
The villagers will master a child who will not obey his own relations.
i.e., Public opinion must be respected, even by the most rebellious.

THE PERMANENCE OF EVIL.

திருப்புதல், மாற்றல்.

514. அரைக்காசுக்கு அழிந்த கற்பு ஆயிரம் பொன் கொடுத்தாலும் கிடைக்குமா?
Even if you give a thousand gold-pieces, can you regain the chastity lost for half a copper coin?
Guilt is easily acquired, but not easily got rid off.
"*What is done can't be undone.*"

515. ஆயிரஞ்சொன்னாலும், அவசாரி சமுசாரி ஆகமாட்டாள்.
Though she be advised a thousand times, a prostitute will not become a wife.
"*What is bred in the bone will never be out of the flesh.*"

516. இராமேசுரத்துக்குப் போனாலும், சனீசுரன் தொலையவில்லை.
Though he went on a pilgrimage to Rameswaram, his evil destiny is not expiated. 519, 520.

517. உண்டு உறியில் இரு என்றால், உருண்டு தெருவிலே விழுகிறான்.
Though I tell him to eat and make himself at home, he goes rolling about and falls in the streets.
Said of one who is well advised but will not reform.

518. எட்டிக்குப் பால்வார்த்து வளர்த்தாலும், தித்திப்பு உண்டாகுமா?
Will the strychnine-plant ever grow sweet, even if milk is poured round its roots?
It will remain bitter and poisonous. Evil will always be evil.
"*'Tis is hard to break a hog of an ill custom.*"

519. ஐங்காதம் போனாலும், தன் பாவம் தன்னோடே.
Though he go fifty miles, his sin will be with him. 516, 520.

520. காசிக்குப்போனாலும், கருமம் தொலையவில்லை.
Though he went to Benares, his sins are not expiated. 516, 519, 523, 2241, 2520.
"*He who goes a beast to Rome, a beast returns.*"

521. குடிக்கிறவன் வாயைச் சுற்றிச் சூடு போட்டாலும், குடியை விடான்.
Even though you burn a drunkard round his mouth, he won't give up drinking.
The permanence of bad habits. (Prov. 27, 22.)

522. கெட்டபால் நல்லபால் ஆகுமா?
Can spoiled milk become good milk?

523. கெட்டவன் கங்கை ஆடினால், பாவம் தீருமா?
Will a bad man get rid of his sin by bathing in the Ganges? 520.
"*If we be enemies to ourselves whither shall we fly?*"

524. கையை அறுத்துவிட்டாலும், அகப்பை கட்டிக்கொண்டு திருடுவான்.
Though his hand is cut off, he will fasten a ladle to the stump of his arm and steal with that. 757.

525. செருப்பால் அடித்தாலும், திருட்டுக்கை நிற்காது.
Though you strike him with your slippers, his thievish habits (*lit.* hand) will not cease.

526. செவிடன் காதிலே சங்கு ஊதினாற்போல்.
Like blowing a conch in the ear of a deaf man.
Said of giving good advice to those who will not heed it.
"*He that will not be saved needs no sermon.*"

527. சொல்லச்சொல்ல மட்டி மண்ணைத் தின்கிறான்.
However much a self-willed man is warned, he eats earth. 532.

528. தங்கத்தைக் குவிக்கிறேன் என்றாலும், தன் புத்தி விடுகிறதில்லை என்கிறான்.
Though I say to him, I will heap up pure gold for you; he says, My (bad) nature won't leave me.

529. திருடனுக்குத் திருட்டுப்புத்தி போகாது.
The thievish nature of a thief will not leave him. 420.

530. *பாய்கிற மாட்டுக்குமுன்னே வேதம் சொன்னாற்போல.*
Like repeating the Vedas before a bull about to gore you.
It is impossible to check wickedness in full career.

531. *பித்தனுக்குப் புத்தி சொன்னால், கேட்பானா?*
If we warn a rogue, will he listen? 155, 2563, 2707.
"*He has the greatest blind-side, who thinks he has none.*"
"*Who is so deaf, or so blind as is he, that wilfully will neither hear nor see.*"

532. *வேண்ட வேண்ட, தாண்டவம் (கூத்து) ஆடுகிறான்.*
Though I entreat him over and over again to cease, yet he dances wildly. 527.
Said of one who will not give up his wicked ways.
"*They that be in hell think there's no other heaven.*"

Cf. 675 *ff.* 839 *ff.* 873 *ff.*

REDUCED CIRCUMSTANCES.

நொந்துபோகுதல், இளைத்துப்போகுதல்.

533. *அவசாரியிலே வந்து, பெருவாரியிலே போகிறது.*
What has been gained by playing the harlot, is lost in the plague.
"*Ill got, ill spent.*"

534. *அவள் பலத்தை மண்கொண்டு ஒளித்தது.*
Her power is hidden by earth.
"*Her day is over.*"

535. *அவன் ஓடிப்பாடி நாடியில் அடங்கினான்.*
He has been running and singing (*i.e.*, has been arrogant), but his pulse has sunk. 509, 553.
அவன் நாடி அடங்கிபோச்சுது, his pulse is brought down; he has come to his senses at last. Said of one who has lost his property and his pride too.
"*Reckless youth makes rueful age.*"

536. *அவன் சிறகு ஒடிந்த பறவை.*
He is a bird with broken wings.
"*He is on his last legs.*"

537. *அவன் வாழ்வு நண்டு குடுவை உடைந்ததுபோல.*
His career came to an end like the breaking of the vessel (*Kuduvei*) in which crabs were carried.
A *Kuduvei* is a small earthen vessel. When this broke all the crabs crawled away. Used for instance when the death of a mother leaves a large family of children with no one to look after them.

538. அழிந்து பழஞ்சோறாய்ப்போச்சுது.
It is boiled rice gone bad. 560.
Used of lost goods, of broken health, and of a ruined character.

539. ஆடாதும் ஆடி ஐயனாருக்குக் காப்பும் அறுத்து ஆச்சுது.
Having behaved as he ought not to have behaved, he had to take off even his bracelets and give them to the God Ayanar.
"*He made his money fly.*"

540. ஆனை இருந்து அரசாண்ட இடத்தில் பூனை இருந்து புலம்பி அழுகிறது.
In the place where he once lorded it as an elephant, he now lords it like a weeping cat!
"*Pride breakfasted with plenty, dined with Poverty, and supped with Infamy.*"
"*Pride goes before a fall.*"

541. ஆனைமட்டும் ஆதாளி அடித்துப்போட்டு ஆந்தைபோல முழிக்கிறான்.
He has done his best to play a grand part in the world; now he blinks like an owl.
"*Many there be that buy nothing with their money but repentance.*"

542. ஈ என்று போயிருக்கிறான்.
(He has become so feeble that) he can only say "*Ee.*"

543. உப்புச்சட்டி வறை ஓடும் தோற்றுவிட்டான் (or ஏலம் போட்டுவிட்டார்கள்).
Even his salt-pan and pot-sherd were sold by auction.
The bitterest poverty.

544. உலக்கை தேய்ந்து உளிப்பிடி ஆச்சுது.
The rice-pounder is so worn, that it is like the handle of a chisel.
Said of things worn out, or of an impaired intellect, or decayed dignity.

545. என் அப்பன் கூத்தாடி, எனக்கு ஒன்றும் தெரியாது, பிச்சைபோடு.
My father was an acrobat; I know nothing; give me alms!
Charity claimed on account of the worthiness of one's ancestors.
"*What matters it to a blind man that his father could see?*"

545*a*. எங்கப்பன் பிறந்தது வெள்ளிமலை (or கைலாசம்), எங்காய் (*i. e.*, எங்கள் தாய்) பிறந்தது பொன்மலை (or மகாமேரு).
My father was born on a Silver Mountain (*or* Kailasa), my mother was born on a Gold Mountain (*or* Mount Meru). 851.
Kailasa is Siva's heaven. *Meru* is a fabulous mountain often identified with the Himalayas. The proverb is used sarcastically about people who have come down in the world but still vaunt their high origin.

546. கந்தைத் துணியும் கரிவேஷமும் (or கோலமும்) ஆனான்.
His clothes are a rag and his garb is all charcoal.
Said of a person reduced to utter poverty.

547. கம்மாளன் பணம் கரியும் பொரியுமாய்ப் போய்விட்டது.
The goldsmith's money has become charcoal and sparks.
Goldsmiths are said to gain much by trickery, but their wealth goes as quickly as it comes.

548. கழுதை தேய்ந்து கட்டெறும்பு ஆச்சுது.
The ass is worn down to an ant.

Said of one who rushes into licentiousness and is ruined in goods, or health.

549. கள்ளுக்கு இரண்டு, கருவாட்டுக்கு இரண்டு.
I have spent a couple of coins on toddy and a couple on salted fish.

i.e., I spent a little here and a little there, and thus have spent all I had. When the husband thus recounts to his wife a number of trifling expenses to excuse himself for having spent all his wages, his wife replies, in order to ridicule him:—

வண்ணானுக்குக் குறுணி (நெல்) கொடுத்தேன், கேள், கழுதை கேள்! அம்மட்டனுக்குக் குறுணி கொடுத்தேன், கேள், கழுதை கேள்! என்கிறீர்களே!

What you say is this: I gave a measure of rice to the washerman. Listen, you donkey listen! and I gave a measure to the barber. Listen, you donkey listen!

By this she implies that her husband has given away money that ought to have gone to household expenses.

"*Haste makes waste, and waste makes want, and want makes strife between the good man and his wife.*"

550. காசுக்கூண்டு கரிக்கூண்டாய்ப் போச்சுது.
The vessel in which money was kept, is now used for charcoal.

551. குடல் அறுந்த நரி எந்தமட்டும் ஓடும்?
How far will a fox run that has lost its entrails (*i.e.*, its strength)?

A degenerate man's day will soon be over.

552. குடியில் பிறந்து, குரங்கு ஆட்டம் ஆடுகிறான்.
He was born in a good family, but now he behaves like a monkey.

Said of one who has brought himself down by a bad life.

553. குந்தினையா குரங்கே, உன் சந்தடி அடங்கே.
O monkey, are you sitting down? Is your chatter subdued? 535.

Used of one whose prosperity and impudence have both met with disaster.

"*Better it is to suffer and fortune to abide, than hastily to climb and suddenly to slide.*"

554. கெட்ட ஊருக்கு எட்டு வார்த்தை.
A decayed village needs eight words.

It is hard to describe a decayed country, its literature and its religion, in such a way as to make them seem respectable.

555. கோவில் சோற்றுக்குக் குமட்டின தேவடியாள், காடிச் சோற்றுக்குக் கரணம்போடுகிறாள்.
The dancing girl who was formerly more than filled with good food in the temple, now turns a somersault to get a poor man's rice.

556. சந்தனம் தெளித்த கையாலே சாணி தெளிக்க ஆச்சுது.
It has come to this, that the hand that formerly sprinkled sandal is now sprinkling cow-dung water. 567.

557. தேரைவால்போல சுத்த சூனியம் ஆச்சுது.
It is as completely gone as a frog's tail.

Complete loss of wealth or honour.

558. நண்டும் குடுவையும் நடுத்தெருவில் உடைந்ததுபோல.
As the pot holding crabs broke in the midst of the street. 537, 787.

Applied for instance to the death of the chief person in a family; who protected the others and kept the property and the family together.

559. நாளுக்குநாள் நரியாய்ப்போகிறது.
Day after day it grows into a jackal.

Said of circumstances that become worse daily; or character, property, health or beauty that deteriorates.

560. நொந்த நூல் அழிந்துபோகிறது.
Spoiled thread is destroyed. 538.

561. பட்டப்பகல் விளக்குப் பாழ் அடைந்ததுபோல.
Like a lamp that has become worthless in broad daylight.

Said of one who has been reduced in circumstances till his appearance in public is as ineffective as the shining of a lamp in clear daylight.

562. பத்து கப்பல் வந்தாலும் பறந்த கப்பல், எட்டுக்கப்பல் வந்தாலும் இறந்த கப்பல்.
If ten ships come they fly away, if eight ships come they are dead. 1216.

The idea is, that no amount of wealth is of any use to a spendthrift.

"*A great fortune in the hands of a fool is a great misfortune.*"

"*Many would have been worse, if their estates had been better.*"

563. பூ விற்ற கடையிலே புல் விற்கவும், புலி இருந்த காட்டிலே பூனை இருக்கவும், சிங்கம் இருந்த குகையிலே நரி இருக்கவும், ஆனை ஏறினவன் ஆடு மேய்க்கவுமாச்சுதே.
It has come to this that grass is sold in the flower market, that a cat lives in the forest where the tiger lived, that a jackal occupies the den where the lion lived, and that he who used to ride on an elephant now herds sheep!

A saying of the good king *Nala*, while wandering about with his queen, *Damayanti*, after he had lost his kingdom; now quoted about losses of property and fortune.

564. மக்கி மண்ணாயிருக்கிறான்.
He is turned into dust.

565. மச்சை அழித்தால், குச்சுக்கும் ஆகாது.
If you break down a big building, you can't build a hut (out of the materials). 569.

566. மண்ணைக்கீறி மண்ணிலே படுத்திருக்கிறார்கள்.
They are scratching the soil and lying in the dust.

Said of people reduced to beggary.

567. முத்து அளந்த கையால், மூசப்பயறு அளக்க வந்தது.
The hand that measured pearls has come to measure spoiled pulse. 67, 556.

568. வற்றலாய்க் காய்ந்த வடகம் (com. வடவம்) போல் வற்றி.
It has dried up and shrivelled like a '*Vadavam.*'

Vadavam is a mixture of herbs and spices used for curry, made into balls and dried in the sun.

569. வாழ்ந்தவன் கெட்டால், வறை ஓட்டுக்கும் ஆகான்.
If a prosperous man is reduced in circumstances, he is not worth a pot-sherd. 565, 2599.

"*The highest tree hath the greatest fall.*"

Cf. 2314 *ff.*

ON PEOPLE WHO HAVE COME DOWN IN THE WORLD.

570. மொண்டு தின்கிற வீட்டிலே, கொண்டுதின்று முடியுமா?
In a house where they fared sumptuously, how will they fare, if they have to buy food for each meal?

Formerly they had a large store to draw on at will, but now they have to buy in very small quantities for each meal.

571. கொள்ளை அடித்துத் தின்கிறவனுக்குக், கொண்டுதின்னத் தாங்குமா?
Will he who used to get his livelihood by robbery, submit to buy his meals and eat?

572. போரோடு தின்கிற மாட்டுக்குப், பிடுங்கிப்போட்டுக் கட்டுமோ?
Will the cow that is used to eat from the stack be satisfied with handfuls?

Those who have been accustomed to luxury will not appreciate poverty.

573. மழைபெய்து நிறையாதது, மொண்டுவார்த்து நிறையுமா?
If it could not be filled by the rain, will it be filled by water that is drawn and poured into it?

Used of misfortunes for which there is no remedy.

ENVY AND JEALOUSY.

பொறாமை.

574. அசல்வீடு வாழ்ந்தால், ஐந்துநாள் பட்டினி கிடப்பாள் (or பரதேசம் போகிறது).
If the neighbouring house prospers, she will starve herself for five days (*or* she will go on a pilgrimage).

"*An envious man waxes lean at the fortune of his neighbour.*"

575. அண்டைவீட்டுக்காரி பிள்ளை பெற்றாள் என்று அசல்வீட்டுக்காரி இடித்துக்கொண்டதுபோல.
Like the woman who struck her own stomach when she heard that her next door neighbour had borne a child. 580, 586.

576. ஆடு கொழுக்கிறதெல்லாம், இடையனுக்கு லாபம்.
All the fatness of the sheep is profit to the shepherd.

When one in a family prospers, but is unwilling to help his relations, they will say this; meaning that his present stinginess does not matter as his wealth will come to his relatives at his death.

577. ஊருக்கு ஓமல் (com. ஓம்மல்), வீட்டுக்கு வயிற்றெரிச்சல்.
Fame abroad, envy at home.

"*Malice seldom wants a mark to shoot at.*"

578. ஊர் எல்லாம் வாழ்கிறது என்று வீடு எல்லாம் அழுது புரண்டாலும் வருமா?
Though a household weeps and rolls on the ground (in envy) saying, The whole village prospers, will (prosperity) come (to that household)?

"*Malice drinketh its own poison.*"

579. எதிரிக்குச் சகுனத்தடை என்று மூக்கை அறுத்துக்கொள்ளுகிறது போல.
Like cutting off your nose as a bad omen to your enemy!

Said of one who hurts himself in trying to injure some one whom he hates.

"*Envy shoots at others and wounds herself.*"

"*Cutting off one's nose to spite one's face.*"

580. ஒப்படியாள் (com. ஓரகத்தி or ஒப்புடையாள்) பிள்ளை பெற்றாள் என்று ஒக்கப் பிள்ளை பெறலாமா?
When her husband's brother's wife gets a child, can this woman also get one (because she is envious)? 575, 586.

581. கணக்கப்பிள்ளை பெண்சாதி கடுக்கன்போட்டுக்கொண்டாள் என்று காரியக்காரன் பெண்சாதி காதை அறுத்துக்கொண்டாளாம்.
When the accountant's clerk's wife saw that the accountant's wife had put on an ear-ring, she cut off her own ears!

582. கல் எறிக்குத் தப்பினாலும், கண் எறிக்குத் தப்ப முடியாது.
Though one may escape the throwing of a stone, one can't escape the glance of an (envious) eye.

"*A jealous man's horns hang in his eyes.*"

583. சத்துரு பொறாமை தனக்கே தண்டனை.
An enemy's envy is a punishment to him.

584. குழந்தை காய்ச்சலும், குண்டன் (or குள்ளன்) காய்ச்சலும் பொல்லாது.
The envy of children and servants (*or* dwarfs) is dangerous.

It is generally thought in India that a dwarf is very cunning and very bad.

585. நன்றாயிருந்தாலும் பார்க்கமாட்டார்கள், கெட்டாலும் தாங்கமாட்டார்கள்.
If you are well off they envy you; if you are reduced in circumstances they shun you.

586. பிள்ளை பெற்றவளைப் பார்த்து, மலடி பெருமூச்சுவிட்டு அழுததுபோல.
As the barren woman sighed and wept when she saw her who had a child. 575, 580.

587. பொறாமை நெஞ்சிலே கொள்ளிக்கட்டையால் சுடவேண்டும்.
Envy in the heart must be branded with a firebrand.

588. மாமியாருக்கு கண் மண்டை பிதுங்கிப்போகிறது.
The eyes of a mother-in-law will burst out of her head.
She is proverbially jealous of the love that exists between her son and his wife.

589. மூக்கறையனுக்கு வாழ்க்கைப்பட்டால், முன்னும் போகவிடான், பின்னும் போகவிடான்.
If a woman is married to a man with a defective nose, he will not let her walk before him or after him.
He is jealous lest she should like other men. Also said of a master who is jealous of his authority.
"*As jealous as the man that searched a hollow walnut for his wife's leman.*"

590. நான் கெட்டாலும், எதிரி வாழவேண்டும்.
Even if I am ruined, let my enemy prosper.
This proverb is unique.

JUSTICE AND INJUSTICE, PARTIALITY AND IMPARTIALITY.

ஓரம், அநியாயம், நியாயம்.

591. அடி என்கிற மந்திரியுமில்லை, பிடி என்கிற ராஜனுமில்லை.
There is no minister to say 'Strike' and no king to say 'Arrest.'
Said when persons act according to their own base desires.

592. ஆயக்காரன் அஞ்சு பணம் கேட்பான், அதாவெட்டுக்காரன் ஐம்பது பணம் கேட்பான்.
Bogus officials will ask for fifty coins; the real tax-collector demands only five.

593. எள்ளுக்காய்ப் பிளந்த விவகாரம்.
A dispute that is decided as clearly as a sesamum bean splits. 598.
The sesamum bean splits longitudinally into two even parts. Used of the decisive settlement of a dispute.

594. ஒரு கண்ணிலே வெண்ணெ தடவிக்கொண்டு, ஒரு கண்ணிலே சுண்ணாம்பு தடவிக்கொண்டு பார்க்கிறதுபோல.
He looks at people after having smeared one eye with butter, and the other with lime. 762.
i.e., He looks favourably on some and severely on others.—Said when there are two boys or two daughters-in-law in a family, of whom one is favoured, and the other misused by one of his or her parents.

595. ஒருகண் மூடி, ஒருகண் முழிக்கிறது.
Shutting one eye, and keeping the other open.
"*To get on his blind side.*"

596. ஒருதலை வழக்கு நூலிலும் செவ்வை.

A partial statement is straighter than a straight line.

A partial statement will seem clear, and a partial judge will make his judgment seem more righteous than the law itself.

597. ஓரம் சொன்னவன் ஆருக்கும் ஆகான்.

A partial man is unpleasant to everybody! 3468.

598. கண்ணாலே கண்டதை எள்ளுக்காய்ப் பிளந்தாப்போல சொல்லவேண்டும்.

What you have seen with your eyes you should state as plainly as a sesamum bean splits. 593.

599. கேட்பாருமில்லை, மேய்ப்பாருமில்லை.

There is no one (in this community) to inquire, and no to herd you.

i.e., Every does what he likes. Often used by women.

600. மண்ணிலிருந்து வழக்கு ஓரம் சொல்லாதே.

Standing on the earth (*i.e.*, the Goddess Prithivi) do not speak partially.

The Goddess Earth (Prithivi, Bhumadevi) is a special guardian of truth.

601. மரத்தாலி கட்டி அடிக்கிறது.

To tie a wooden *thali* and beat her.

In former days if people were unable to pay their taxes, unjust rulers would take the women's jewels, even their gold *thalis*, and beat them and give them wooden *thalis* instead. The *thali* is a marriage-token (corresponding to the European wedding-ring) tied round the neck of the bride.

602. மரியாதை ராமன் வழக்குத் தீர்த்தாப்போல.

As *Mariyathei Raman* settled disputes.

Mariyathei Raman was a judge in the ancient kingdom of the Chola kings, the hero of many tales, famous for the acuteness of his judgments. See the *Kathamanjurii*, &c.

603. வாழ்ந்த மகள் வந்தால் வர்ணத் தடுக்கு இடு, கெட்ட மகள் வந்தால் கிழிந்த தடுக்கு இடு.

When the prosperous daughter pays a visit, they say, Put the fine mat for her to sit on; when the poor daughter pays a visit, they say, Put the old torn mat for her.

Respect of persons.

604. வெள்ளரிக்காய் விற்ற பட்டணம்.

This is a town where cucumbers are sold!

i.e., A place where everything can be had except justice.

Cf. கேள்விமுறையில்லாத ஊர். A village without management.

Cf. 702 *ff.* 1357 *ff.*

STRIFE AND SLANDER.

சண்டை, கலகம்.

605. அஞ்சு ஊர் சண்டை சிம்மாளம், அங்கலம் அரிசி ஒரு கவாளம்.
She jumps with joy over the quarrels in five villages, and she eats a big measure of rice at a mouthful. 196.

Used of a woman who is mighty in strife, and delights to hear about quarrels.

606. அங்கிடு தொடுப்பிக்கு அங்கு இரண்டு குட்டு, இங்கு இரண்டு சொட்டு.
A slanderer and talebearer will get two claps there and two cuffs here. 1545.

"*A tale-bearer will tell tales of you as well as to you.*"
"*The most dangerous of wild beasts is a slanderer; of tame ones, a flatterer.*"
"*A gossip speaks ill of all, and all of her.*"

607. அண்டை வீட்டுச் சண்டை கண்ணுக்குக் குளிர்ச்சி.
A quarrel in a neighbouring house is a pleasure to the eye.

608. அவன் தொட்டுக்கொடுத்தான், நான் இட்டுக்கொடுத்தேன்.
He gave a touch, but I gave a blow.

The one did a little injury, but the other, returned it with interest.

609. ஆத்தி (or அகத்தி) நாரு கிழித்தாற்போல உன்னைக் கிழிக்கிறேன்.
I will tear you to pieces as the fibres of *Atti* trees are torn to pieces!

A kind of rope is made from the fibre of this tree.

610. ஆனை கண்ட பிறவிக்குருடர்கள் அடித்துக்கொண்டதுபோல.
As the men born blind quarrelled about the elephant.

The folly of disputing about things concerning which one has no information. The proverb is from a story about four blind men who quarrelled over their different ideas about an elephant, which is intended to show, that it is useless for men to dispute about the unknown God.

611. உள்நாக்கும் தொண்டையும் அதிர அடைத்ததுபோல.
Like shutting up one's palate and throat.

Said of one who sulks after a quarrel.

612. உனக்கு ஆச்சு எனக்கு ஆச்சு ஒரு கை பார்க்கவேண்டும்.
The hand must see whether it is yours or mine.

i.e., We must fight the matter out.

613. எச்சிலைக்கு நாய் அடித்துக்கொண்டு நிற்கிறதுபோல.
Like a dog keeping on fighting for an old plate made of leaves.

Said of children who quarrel about sweetmeats, &c. Hindus usually eat from plates made of leaves which are thrown away after being used once.

614. எடுத்துக் கவிழ்த்துப் பேசுகிறான்.
He speaks so as to upset you!

i.e., He speaks rudely.

615. என் கை வெல்லம் தின்கிறதா? or என் கையிலே எலும்பு இல்லையா?
Does my hand eat sugar? *or* Are there no bones in my hand?
A threat, meaning that the speaker can strike as well as speak.

616. ஒரு வீடு அடங்கலும் பிடாரி (or பக்ஷாரி).
A house full of termagants!
A noisy quarrelsome household.

617. கடா பின்வாங்குகிறது பாய்ச்சலுக்கு இடம்.
When a goat draws back, it is to get room to butt!
Applied to one who feels himself superior in a quarrel, and therefore quietly waits for the moment, when he can give a decisive blow.—Also to a big dog and a cur.—"Dignity and impudence."

618. கலகம் பிறந்தால், நியாயம் பிறக்கும்.
If there be a quarrel the rights of the matter will come out.
If quarrels, misunderstandings and debts, are examined by outsiders, the truth will be found out. Used by the innocent or injured party.

619. கலகத்திலே போனபிற்பாடு, கால்மாடு தலைமாடா?
Are feet and heads distinguished after strife has begun? 1303.

620. காற்றுக் காற்றோடே போச்சுது.
The wind is gone with the wind.
i.e., Let our quarrel be forgotten.

621. கீழ்க்காது மேற்காது மூளி, சண்டைக்கு ரணபத்திரகாளி.
That wretched woman has no jewels for any part of her ears, but she is good at a quarrel.

622. குட்டையைக் கலக்கிப் பருந்துக்கு இரை இடுகிறது.
Disturbing the water in a pool, and giving food to kites. 375.
A quarrel ruins the peace of a family and disperses its wealth among lawyers.

623. குருவிக்கூண்டை கோலால் கலைத்ததுபோல.
Like destroying the nest of a bird with a stick. 3086.
Used of slander or strife that breaks up a family.

624. குறவழக்கும் இடைவழக்கும் கொஞ்சத்தில் தீராது.
Disputes of hunters and shepherds are not easily settled.
The quarrels of stupid people are hard to settle.

625. சண்டைமுகத்தில் உறவா?
Will relationship count in a quarrel? 628, 1303.

626. சாக்ஷிக்காரன் காலில் விழுவதைவிட, சண்டைக்காரன் காலில் விழுவது நல்லது.
It is better to fall at the feet of him with whom you have quarrelled than to fall at the feet of a witness.
In this proverb straightforwardness is recommended. Perhaps also there is the idea, that the witness of a crime is more difficult to silence than the person wronged.

627. சொன்னதைச் சொல்லு அடி! சுணைகெட்ட மூளி!
O shameless woman, say what you said!

628. படுகளத்தில் ஒப்பாரியா?
Does relationship count on the battle field? 625.

629. பேச்சுக்குப் பேச்சுச் சிங்காரமா?
Is there any beauty in speaking words against words?
Said sarcastically about endless disputes.

630. மது பிந்து கலகம்போல இருக்கிறது.
It is like the quarrel caused by a honey drop.
Applied to quarrels arising from trifles.
"*Contend not about a goat's beard.*" "*A storm in a tea-pot.*"

631. மாரைத் தட்டி மனதிலே வை.
Beat your breast and remember.
When one of the disputants uses a bad word, the other beats his own breast to make himself remember it, that he may return it with interest. Tamil abuse is most fluent and most indecent, and neither men nor women hesitate to use the most obscene words.

632. மௌனம் கலகநாசம்.
Silence is the end of a quarrel.

633. வந்தது (or எட்டினது) சண்டை, இறக்கடி கூடையை!
I have a quarrel with you! Set your basket down! 634.
i.e., We must have our quarrel out. Quoted about a woman of quarrelsome disposition, to whom strife is a delight.
"*A man that will fight may find a cudgel in every hedge.*"

634. வல்லிடி வழக்குச் சொல்லடி மாமி.
O mother-in-law, tell me how you wantonly caused that quarrel. 633.
Said to a person who stirs up strife without cause.

635. வெறும்வாய் மெல்லுகிற அம்மையாருக்கு நாழி அவல் அகப்பட்டது போல.
It is like a measure of bruised rice to a woman who has been working her jaws on nothing.
A sarcastic description of the joy that a quarrelsome woman finds in strife.
"*Arthur could not tame a woman's tongue.*"

THE WORTHLESS.

உதவாதவன்.

"GIVE NOT THAT WHICH IS HOLY UNTO DOGS."

636. எலும்பு கடிக்கிற நாய்க்குப் பருப்புசோறு ஏன்?
Why give pulse and rice (*i.e.*, good food) to a dog, that is biting bones? 1198.
A dog is regarded as an unclean animal in all the East, because, along with the village pigs, it plays the part of scavenger.
"*What should a cow do with a nutmeg?*"

637. ஒரு சந்தி பானை நாய் அறியாது.
A dog does not know a vessel used on fast-days from a common pot. 647.

Nothing is sacred to the wicked.

638. கலசத்துக்குத் தெரியுமோ கர்ப்பூர வாசனை?
Will a (common) pot know the smell of Camphor?

" *He sprinkles incense on a dunghill.*"

639. கழுதைக்குத் தெரியுமா கஸ்தூரி (or கந்தப்பொடி) வாசனை?
Will an ass know the odour of musk? 849.

640. காட்டுப்பூனைக்குச் சிவராத்திரி விரதமா?
Will a wild cat observe the fast of *Sivaratri*? 651.

The *Sivaratri* is a monthly vigil in honour of Siva, but a cat will kill and eat animals and birds even on that night. No time is sacred to the wicked.

641. குங்குமம் சுமந்த கழுதை பரிமளம் அறியுமா?
Will the ass that bears a load of *Kunkuma* (a fragrant plant) enjoy the odour of it?

642. குரங்கின் தலையில் கரகம் வைத்துக் காளிகும்பிட்டதுபோல.
Like putting a pot of sacred water on the head of a monkey and worshipping *Kali*!

Kali is a malignant deity, who is supposed to be highly infuriated at any breach of the ceremonies in her temples. The most clever and capable person is always employed to carry the pot of sacred water in her presence. To give such a sacred trust to a careless man, would be incurring the Goddess' vindictive spite. The proverb is used of a person who employs a well-known fool to perform a duty that is to be done with the greatest care.

643. குரங்கு கையில் பூமாலை அகப்பட்டதுபோல.
Like a monkey getting a garland of flowers into its hands!

644. சிறுபிள்ளை கட்டின சிற்றாடைபோல.
Like a little girl wearing a small cloth. 3317.

A child too young to understand why she should wear clothes will untie her cloth and perhaps forget it altogether and run about naked. Said of one who does not appreciate his privileges, and also of one put into a position for which he is unworthy.

645. தனக்கு என்றால் புழுக்கை கலம் கழுவி உண்ணாள்.
Knowing that the pot is for herself the slave-woman will not clean it before she eats from it.

Said about people who only do what work they are compelled to do, and are utterly careless about personal neatness and comfort.

646. நக்கிற நாய்க்குச் செக்கு என்றும் சிவலிங்கம் என்றும் தெரியுமா?
A dog is not able to distinguish an oil mill from a *linga*.

The *linga* is a conical stone emblem of the god Siva. The oil mill is made out of the bole of a large tree. The two are very slightly alike. The proverb means that degraded people cannot distinguish between sacred and secular things.

647. நாய்க்குத் தெரியுமா தேங்காய் ருசி?
Does a dog appreciate the sweetness of a cocoanut? 637.
"*A pebble and a diamond are alike to a blind man.*"

648. பறைச்சி வெற்றிலைபோட்டால், பத்துவிரலும் சுண்ணாம்பு.
When a Paria woman chews betel, her ten fingers will be smeared with lime (through slovenliness).

649. பன்றிக்குட்டிக்கு ஒரு சந்தி ஏது?
What has a young pig to do with a fast day?

650. புழுக்கை ஒழுக்கம் அறியாது, பித்தளை நாற்றம் அறியாது.
A slave does not understand good conduct, and brass does not know a bad smell. 676.

651. பூனைக்கு இல்லை தானமும் தவமும்.
A cat does no charity and no penance! 640.

652. பேடி கையில் ரம்பை அகப்பட்டதுபோல.
Like *Rambha's* falling into the hands of a eunuch.

Rambha is one of the celestial courtezans in *Swerga*, the heaven of Indra. No eunuch would be better off if he caught her. Hence the proverb is used about good fortune happening to those who are unable to make use of it.

THE APPARENTLY WORTHLESS ARE USELESS.

653. ஓதி பெருத்தால், உரலாமா?
Can the *odina* tree be made into a mortar when it has grown big? 662.

Wood from the *odina* is no use at any time. The worthless will always be useless.

654. ஓதியமரம் தூணாமோ, ஒட்டாங்கிளிஞ்சல் துட்டு ஆமோ?
Will an *odina* tree make a pillar? Will a shell serve as a coin?

655. கங்கையிலே முளைத்தாலும், பேய்ச்சுரைக்காய் நல்ல சுரைக்காய் ஆகாது.
Even if it grows in the *Ganges*, a bad gourd will not become a good one.

The River *Ganges* is usually said to purify everything that comes in contact with its sacred waters.

656. கல் எல்லாம் மாணிக்கக் கல்லாமா?
Is every stone a precious stone? 2498.

657. கங்கையிலே பிறந்த நத்தை சாலக்கிராமம் ஆகாது.
A snail born in the *Ganges* will not become a *Salagramu* stone.

The *Salagrama* is an ammonite worshipped by the Vaishnavas because its spirals are supposed to contain or typify Vishnu.

658. காட்டுப் பேய்ச்சுரைக்காய் கறிக்கு ஆகுமா?
Will a wild gourd ever become fit to season food?

659. குப்பையிலே முளைத்த கீரை கப்பலுக்குப் பாய்மரமாகுமா?
Will a vegetable grown on a dunghill make a mast for a ship?

THE WORTHLESS MAY BE OF USE.

660. அழுக்குச் சீலைக்குள்ளே மாணிக்கம்.
A ruby may be found within a filthy cloth. 2407.
An apparently worthless man may have a good soul.
" *A little body often harbours a great soul.*"

661. ஒடிந்த கோலானாலும், ஊன்றுகோலாகும்.
Although a broken stick, it may be of use to lean on.

662. ஒதியமரமும் சமயத்துக்கு உதவும்.
Even an *odina* tree may be useful on occasion. 654.

663. ஓட்டைபானையில் சர்க்கரை இருக்கும்.
A broken pot will hold sugar.

664. குப்பையிலே முளைத்த கொடி கூரையில் ஏறினதுபோல.
As the creeper that grew on a dunghill spread over the roof of the house.
This may also be used as a sneer against one who is thought to be an upstart.

665. சிறு துரும்பு பல்லுக்குத்த உதவும்.
Even a little straw may serve as a tooth-pick.

666. சேற்றிலே முளைத்த செந்தாமரை.
The red lotus that grew in the mud.
Women will use this about a beautiful child born of ugly parents. Men will say this about a child with a noble disposition born in a mean family.

667. நத்தை வயிற்றிலே முத்து பிறக்கிறது.
In the womb of an oyster, pearls are born.

Cf. 2005 *ff.*

THE WORTHLESS CANNOT ATTAIN TO WHAT IS NOBLE.

668. அக்கிராரத்தில் பிறந்தாலும், நாய் வேதம் அறியுமா?
Though a dog is born in a Brahmin street, will it know the Veda?
There are several other forms of this proverb.

669. குட்டிநாய் கொண்டு வேட்டை ஆடுகிறதா?
Is a pup any good in hunting?

670. கூலிக்குக் குத்துகிறவளைக் கேளிக்கை ஆடச் சொன்னாற்போல.
Like telling a woman who pounds rice for hire, to dance. 674.
The graceful art is beyond her.
" *An emmet may work its heart out, but can never make honey.*"

671. கொட்டிக்கிழங்கு வெட்டுகிறவள் கோவிலில் வந்து ஆடுவாளா?
Will a woman, who is digging up eatable roots, come to a temple and dance?

672. ஸ்ரீரங்கத்துக் காக்காயானுலும், கோவிந்தம் பாடுமா?
Though a crow be born at *Srirangam*, will it be able to say "*Govinda*"?

Srirangam is a sacred place of the Vaishnavas near Trichinopoly, *Govinda* is a name of Vishnu. The meaning is, that circumstances cannot alter character. To be in a holy place will not make a bad man good.

673. திருடனை ராஜன் முழிமுழிக்கச் சொன்னுல், முழிப்பானு?
If a thief is told to look with the (bold) eye of a king, will he be able to do so?

A thief is afraid of being found out, and the fear in his heart prevents him from simulating the fearless look of a king.

674. நெல்லு குத்துகிறவளுக்குக் கல்லு பரிக்ஷை தெரியுமா?
Can she who is pounding rice examine precious stones? 670.

THE WORTHLESS CANNOT BE IMPROVED.

675. அழுக்கைத் துடைத்து மடியில் வைத்தாலும், புழுக்கைக் குணம் போகாது.
Though you wipe off the dirt and place her in your lap, the (mean) disposition of a slave girl will not leave her.

"*A crow is never the whiter for washing herself often.*"

676. எத்தனைதான் துலக்கினுலும், பித்தளை நாற்றம் போகாது.
However much you may polish brass, its bad smell won't leave it. 650.

677. கங்கையிலே முழுகினுலும், காக்காய் அன்னம் ஆகுமா?
Even if a crow bathe in the *Ganges*, it will not become a swan. 686, 2654.

678. கழுதைக்கு ஜீனி கட்டினுலும் குதிரை ஆகுமா?
If a saddle is put on an ass, will it become a horse? 687.

"*Fine feathers do not make fine birds.*"

679. கழுவிக் கழுவி ஊற்றினுலும், கவிச்சு நாற்றம் போகாது.
However much you may wash bad food, its bad smell won't go.

680. கழுத்து வெளுத்தாலும், காக்காய் கருடனுகுமா?
Though its neck is made white, a crow won't become a sacred kite (*Garudan*).

"*The wolf changes his hair, but not his nature.*"

681. கறுப்புநாய் வெள்ளைநாய் ஆகாது.
A black dog won't become a white dog.

"*What's bred in the bone, will never be out of the flesh.*"

682. கோழியின் காலில் கச்சையைக் கட்டினுலும், குப்பையைச் சீக்கும்.
Though a fowl's legs are adorned with bells, it will go and scratch on a dunghill. 695.

"*An ape's an ape, a varlet's a varlet, though they be clad in silk and scarlet.*"

683. நாயைக் குளிப்பாட்டி நடுவீட்டிலே வைத்தாலும், வாலைக் கிளப்பிக் கொண்டு பீ தின்னப் போகும்.

Though you wash a dog and put it in the household shrine, it will raise its tail and go and eat filth.

There is a little shrine or a room where the domestic images, &c., are kept, in every Hindu house.

"*Wash a dog, comb a dog, still a dog is but a dog.*"

684. நாய் வாலைக் குணக்கு எடுக்கலாமா?

Can you get the curl out of a dog's tail?

"*Crooked by nature is never made straight by education.*"

685. பறைச்சி பிள்ளையைப் பள்ளிக்கு வைத்தாலும், பேச்சிலே அய்யே என்னுமாம்.

Although a Paria woman's child is sent to school, it will still say '*Ayyé*'!

Ayyé is vulgar Tamil for *Ayar* or *Appar* meaning 'father.' The proverb, means that education will not eradicate vulgarity, and that modern science will not overcome the old science of the Sacred Books.

"*Nature overcomes nurture.*"—"*Dogs bark as they are bred.*"

"*As the old cock crows, so crows the young.*"

686. முக்காலும் காகம் முழுகி குளித்தாலும், கொக்கு ஆகுமா?

Even if a crow is washed and bathed thrice a day, it will not become a white crane. 677.

"*Set a frog on a golden stool, and off it hops again into the pool.*"

687. முட்டிக்கால் கழுதை பட்டவர்த்தன பரியாமா?

An ass with knock-knees will never become a royal steed. 678.

He who is born in an inferior position is not fit for a superior position.

Cf. 514 *ff.*

THE WORTHLESS ARE CONTEMPTIBLE.

688. அகத்தி ஆயிரம் காய்த்தாலும் புறத்தி புறத்தியே.

However many fruits the *akatti* tree (*coronilla*) yields, they are only fit to throw away.

689. அருமை பெருமை அறியாதவன் ஆண்டு என்ன, மாண்டு என்ன.

It does not matter whether a person who does not appreciate what is rare and noble, rules or dies.

690. உடைந்த (or ஓட்டை) சங்கில் ஊதை (or காற்று) பறியுமா?

Can you get a sound out of a broken conch?

Or Can wind play on a broken conch?

The conch shell is frequently used by Hindus, especially at funerals.

"*A cracked bell can never sound well.*"

691. எலி புழுக்கை இறப்பில் இருந்து என்ன, வரப்பில் இருந்து என்ன.

It does not matter whether rat's dung is on the beam or on the ridge in the field.

692. சுரைப்பூவுக்கும் பறைப்பாட்டுக்கும் வாசனையில்லை.
The flower of a gourd and a Paria's song have no savour.

693. முட்டுக்கு முட்டுமல்ல, மூடக் கதவுமல்ல, சன்னிதிவாசலுக்குச் சாத்தக் கதவுமல்ல.
You are neither a support to a support, nor a door to shut, nor a door in a temple gate.

Utterly useless for all purposes.

N.B.—*The above are but a few out of many proverbs on this subject, many of which are but slight variations of the above.*

THE UNWORTHY NOT TO BE HONOURED.

694. ஓட்டை நாழிக்குப் பூண் கட்டினதுபோல.
Like fastening a silver ring round a broken measure.
"*A leaden sword in an ivory scabbard.*"

695. கருடன் காலில் சதங்கை கட்டினதுபோல.
Like tying little bells to the leg of a sacred kite. 682.

696. கருங்காலி உலக்கைக்கு வெள்ளிப் பூண் கட்டினதுபோல.
Like fastening a silver ferrule on a rice pounder made of ebony.

To make a rice pounder of ebony and then adorn it with a silver ferrule would be the height of folly. To honour fools is folly.

697. கள்ளிக்கொம்புக்கு வெள்ளிப் பூண் கட்டினதுபோல.
Like fastening a silver ferrule on a staff (cut from) the *Kalli* plant.

Wasting valuables on the worthless.

698. துப்பற்ற நாரிக்குக் கொப்பு அழகைப்பார்.
Look at the beauty of the ornament in the ear of that worthless woman.
"*Garlands are not for every brow.*"

699. பங்கறை (*i.e.*, பதங்குறைந்த, without beauty) சாவானுக்குப் பல் அழகைப் பார்.
Look at the beauty of the teeth of that worthless scamp.

Both these proverbs refer to privileges being enjoyed by those unworthy of them.

700. புழுக்கைக்குப் பொன்முடி பொறுக்குமா?
Can a slave sustain a crown of gold?
"*As meet as a sow to bear a saddle.*"

701. மூக்குத்தூள் போடாத முண்டத்துக்கு முப்பதுபணத்தில் வெள்ளி டப்பி.
(As useless as) a silver snuff-box costing thirty coins (*i.e.*, very expensive) to a fool who does not use snuff!

ON INFERIOR PEOPLE WHO ARE RAISED ABOVE THEIR STATION.

"Give promotion to the rude,
They will chase away the good.
Can the dog that eats old shoes
Taste the sugarcane he chews?"

CH. E. GOVER: *The Folk-songs of Southern India.*

702. அம்பட்டனை மந்திரித்தனத்துக்கு வைத்துக்கொண்டதுபோல.
Like a barber who was made a minister. 708, 1363, 1364, 1365.

The proverb refers to a story that tells about three men, a barber, a potter and a washerman, who were all raised to a high position by a king. They were equally little-minded, and also equally anxious to show off their dignity and authority, so they fared very badly.

703. அறுப்புக்காலத்தில் எலிக்கு ஐந்து பெண்சாதி.
In harvest time a rat keeps five wives.

When the poor prosper they live extravagantly.

704. அற்பனுக்குப் பவுஷு வந்தால், அர்த்தராத்திரியில் குடைபிடிப்பான்.
If a low-bred man obtains wealth (*or* authority) he will carry an umbrella at midnight. 709, 712.

In India an umbrella is a sign of affluence and authority.

"*Set a beggar on horseback and he will ride to the devil.*"
"*The higher the ape goes the more he shows his tail.*"

705. எருது கொழுத்தால் தொழுவத்தில் இராது, பறையன் கொழுத்தால் பாயில் இரான்.
If an ox grow fat, it will not remain in its stall; if a *Pariah* become fat, he will not stay on his mat! 711.

706. கண்டறிந்த நாயுமல்ல, கனமறிந்த கப்பறையுமல்ல.
He is not an experienced dog, neither is he a pot that knows politeness.

Said of upstarts who do not know their work, but are too proud to ask advice from others.

707. காக்கையின் கழுத்தில் பனங்காயைக் கட்டினதுபோல்.
Like tying a palmyra fruit to the neck of a crow. 708*a*, 1999.

Giving a heavy burden to a weak person.

707*a*. காறிப்போன கருணைக்கிழங்கு பழம் புளியால் பதம் பெற்றது.
The white yam that tasted rancid has been made tasty by the use of last year's tamarind.

Said of worthless people who attain prosperity through the gratuitous aid of others.

708. குடிமக்கள் துரைத்தனம் செய்ததுபோல.
Like menials set in authority. 702.

708*a*. குருவிக் கழுத்தில் தேங்காயைக் கட்டினதுபோல்.
Like tying a cocoanut to the neck of a bird. 707.

Said when a weak person is given work beyond his strength; or when such a person attempts to do work beyond his strength; or about afflictions which he has no strength to bear.

709. கோவணத்தில் ஒரு காசு இருந்தால், கோழி கூப்பிட (or கூவ) ஒரு பாட்டுவரும்.

If he has a coin in his rags, he will sing a song when the cock crows. 704, 712.

710. சிட்டுக்குருவிக்குப் பட்டம் கட்டினால், சட்டிப்பானை எல்லாம் லொட லொடவென்று தத்தும்.

If you honour a sparrow, it will hop on all the pots and pans, and make them bang against each other.

711. நண்டு கொழுத்தால் வளையில் இராது, பள்ளி கொழுத்தால் பாயில் இரான்.

If a crab gets fat, it won't remain in its hole; if a *Palli* gets fat, he won't remain on his mat. 705.

If mean people prosper they will become impudent.

"*The priest when he begins the mass, forgets that ever clerk he was.*"

712. பள்ளி கையில் பணமிருந்தால், பாதிராத்திரியில் பாடுவான்.

If a *Palli*-man gets money into his hand, he will sing at midnight. 709.

The *Pallis* are a low Sudra caste. They now claim to be of the warrior (Kshatreya) high caste.

713. ராங்கி (rank) மிஞ்சிரூம் (room) தேடுகிறது, ஆக்கிப்போட ஆள் தேடுகிறது.

His rank is exalted and he seeks a room, and he also seeks a person to cook for him.

Said of one who is too proud to do petty necessary work for himself. A vulgar proverb in mongrel Tamil.

"*Beggars mounted run their horses to death.*"

Cf. 591 *ff.* 1357 *ff.*

DECEPTION, RUIN.

மோசம், நாசம்.

SELF-DECEPTION AND SELF-DESTRUCTION.

714. அதிகாரி வீட்டிலே திருடி, தலையாரி வீட்டிலே வைத்ததுபோல்.

Like stealing from the headman's house, and hiding the stolen goods in the house of the village watchman. 723.

"*To break the constable's head and take refuge with the sheriff.*"

715. அவன் தன்னாலே தான் கெட்டால், அண்ணாவி என்னசெய்வான்?

If he ruins himself, what can his teacher do?

Said of a person, who through presumption rushes into ruin; and of a meddlesome man who undertakes work for which he has no ability, and thus loses his living.

716. அழகுக்கு மூக்கை அறுப்பான் உண்டா?
Will any one cut off his nose to increase his beauty?
" *Like cutting off your nose to spite your face.*"

717. ஆப்பைப்பிடுங்கின குரங்கு நாசம் அடைந்ததுபோல்.
As a monkey perished by drawing out a wedge.
The story is that of the monkey who sat on a tree that some wood-cutters were trying to split and pulled out the wedge they had driven in. The wood at once closed on the monkey and he was killed.
"*He brings a staff to break his own head.*"

718. ஆரால் கெட்டேன், நோரால் கெட்டேன்.
By whom was I ruined? By my mouth! 2506.
" *A fool's tongue is long enough to cut his own throat.*"
" *Evil that cometh out of thy mouth flieth into thy bosom.*"

719. ஆனை தன் தலையில் தானே மண்ணைப் போட்டுக்கொள்ளும்.
An elephant will put earth on its own head.
" *To put one's elbow into one's eye.*"

720. இடையன் கரடிமேல் ஆசைப்பட்டதுபோல.
Like the shepherd who lusted after a bear! 733.
To seek one's own destruction.
" *He makes a rod for his own breech.*"

721. உண்கிற சோற்றிலே நஞ்சைக் கலக்கிறதா? (or கல்லைப்போடுகிறதா?)
Who will mix poison with the rice he is eating? (*or* Who will put stones into the rice he eats?)
Who will destroy his own livelihood?

722. எள்ளை நீக்கிக்கொண்டுவரப்போன பேய், எண்ணெய்க் கொண்டுவர இசைந்ததுபோல.
Like tho devil that went to relieve his friends from bringing *oilseed*, but agreed that they should bring *oil*. 314.
He brought worse trouble over his friends whom he came to set free, for after his interference they had to crush the oil out of the seed and bring it to their master.

723. ஒளிக்கப் போயும் தலையாரி வீட்டிலா?
Though you go and hide yourself, should you do so in the house of the village watchman? 714.
" *To run into the lion's mouth.*"

724. கம்பளியிலே சோற்றைப்போட்டு, மயிர் மயிர் என்கிறதுபோல்.
Like putting boiled rice in a blanket, and then grumbling because it is full of hair.

725. கழுத்து அறுக்கக் கத்தி கையில் கொடுத்தாற்போல.
Like giving another man a knife to cut your own throat. 731.

726. கிணற்றைத் தூர்த்தால், வயிற்றைத் தூர்க்கும்.
If you fill up the well, your stomach will be filled up (as no meal can be prepared without water).
Folly will come back to its author.
"*Birds come home to roost.*"

727. சணப்பன் வீட்டுக்கோழி தானே விலங்கு பூட்டிக்கொண்டதுபோல.
As the hempdresser's fowl entangled itself in the hemp.
Said of a person who involves himself in difficulties through his own folly.

728. செடியிலிருக்கிற ஓணானை மடியில் விட்டுக்கொண்டு, குடைகிறது குடைகிறது என்கிறான்.
She takes a lizard from the hedge and puts it in her own lap, and then complains because it tickles her. 186, 735.
Said of self-inflicted evil. Also used in an obscene sense.
"*Fly the pleasure that bites to-morrow.*"

729. சேணியனுக்கு ஏன் குரங்கு?
Why should a weaver keep a monkey?
It will only damage his work. Why should a man cherish bad habits?

730. தன் வாய்க்கஞ்சியை கவிழ்த்துப்போட்டான்.
He spilt his own soup.
i.e., He destroyed his own livelihood.

731. தன்னைக் கட்ட கயிறு தானே கொடுத்தாற்போல.
Like giving a rope to bind yourself. 725.
"*I gave you a stick to break my own head with.*"

732. தான் சாக மருந்து தின்பானா?
Will any one eat medicine to kill himself?
"*Life is sweet.*"

733. தூங்குகிற புலியைத் தட்டி எழுப்பினதுபோல.
Like striking a sleeping tiger to wake him up! 720.
"*Let sleeping dogs lie.*"

734. நெருப்பிலே ஈ மொய்க்குமா?
Will flies fly into fire?

735. நெருப்பை மடியிலே முடிகிறதா?
Shall I put fire in my own lap? 728.
The two last proverbs are said by women, when blamed for being too free with men; or said by others in defence of such a woman; or by a chaste woman to a rude person who seeks her with evil intentions.

736. பிடாரியைப் பெண்டு வைத்துக்கொண்டதுபோல.
Like taking a vixen as a wife. 3572.
A *Pidâri* is a haughty, obstinate, and bad woman.
"*To make a halter to one's own neck.*"

737. மடியிலே பூனைக்குட்டியைக் கட்டிக்கொண்டு சகுனம் பார்க்கிறதுபோல.
Like tying up a kitten in one's lap, and looking for a good omen.
The cat is considered an ill-omened animal by Tamils.
" *Don't take an ill-wisher along with you, when you start for something good.*"

Cf. 3251 *ff.*

ON HELPING TO RUIN THOSE WHO ARE ON THEIR WAY TO RUIN.

738. இளைத்தவன் தலையில் சொட்டு.
A tap on the head for an impoverished man. 892, 3502.
" *All the world will beat the man whom fortune buffets.*"

739. ஏழை என்றால் எவர்க்கும் எளிது.
If he is poor he is slighted by everyone. 894.
" *A low hedge is easily leaped over.*" " *Every poor man is counted a fool.*"

740. ஏழையைக் கண்டால், மோழையும் பாயும்.
If it sees a poor man, even a beast without horns will butt at him. 894, 3372.
" *Even a child may beat a man that's bound.*"

741. ஒருவன் குழியிலே விழுந்தால், எல்லாரும் கூடி அவன் தலையிலே கல்லைப் போடுகிறதா?
If a person fall into a pit, should all join and throw stones on his head? 744.
" *Him that falls, all the world runs over.*"

742. கருவாட்டுக்காரி சந்துவிட்டால், நான் வந்துவிட்டேன்.
If the fish-wife gives me a chance, I'll take it. 194.
Used by one who wants a pretext to enter into a dispute or quarrel with somebody who is already in trouble.

743. சேற்றிலே புதைந்த ஆனையைக் காக்கையும் குட்டும்.
Even a crow will peck an elephant that has stuck in the mud.
" *All bite the bitten dog.*" " *Hares may pull dead lions by the beard.*"
" *Little birds may peck a dead lion.*"

744. நரி (or குள்ளப்பார்ப்பான்) கிணற்றில் விழுந்தால், தண்டு எடு, தடி எடு என்பார்கள்.
When a fox (*or* a dwarf Brahmin, *i.e.*, a mischievous Brahmin) falls into a well, all will cry: Bring clubs and sticks! 741.
" *He that is down, down with him, cries the world.*"

Cf. 887 *ff.* 1369 *ff.* 1694 *ff.*

MISCELLANEOUS PROVERBS ABOUT DECEIT AND RUIN.

745. அடுக்குசட்டி பூனைபோல இடுக்கிலே ஒளிக்கிறது.
He hides himself in a corner like a cat near a pile of pots.
Said of one who is cunning in all he does and says.

746. அடுத்த கூரை வேகும்போது, தன் கூரைக்கு மோசம்.
When a neighbour's thatch is burning, one's own thatch is in danger.
The evil that happens to your neighbour may come home to you.
"*When the neighbour's house doth burn, be careful of thine own.*"

747. அந்தப் பருப்பு இங்கே வேகாது.
Those beans will not be cooked here. 748, 776.
i.e., You will not take me in, however cunning you may be!

748. அவன் அண்டை அந்தப் பருப்பு வேகாது.
Those beans will not be cooked in his house. 747.
He is not to be deceived.

749. அவன் என் தலைக்கு உலை வைக்கிறான்.
He is getting the rice-pot ready for my head. 750, 1875.
He is preparing to cook my head; *i.e.*, he is bent on ruining me.

750. அவன் கழுத்துக்குக் கத்தி தீட்டுகிறான்.
He sharpens a knife for that man's throat. 749.
Said of a deceitful person who does harm to one who least expects it from him.

751. அவன் தலையில் ஒட்டை கவிழ்ப்பாள்.
She has upset a pot on his head.
Said of a wife who has ruined her husband by her extravagance.

752. ஆட்டுக் கிடையிலே கோனாய் புகுந்ததுபோல.
Like a wolf in a sheep-fold!

753. ஆணையும் வேண்டாம், சத்தியமும் வேண்டாம், துணியைப் போட்டுத் தாண்டு.
Neither swear nor take an oath. Spread the cloth and jump over it. 759.
To spread a cloth and leap over it is a most emphatic oath.

754. ஆழும் பாழும் அரைக் கீரை பாத்தியும்.
(As badly off as) a crop of *areikkeerei* on the bed of a dry lake.
The *areikkeerei* grows wild, and nobody looks after it, and the lake may rise any day and destroy it all. Said of a family that is totally ruined. Sometimes more briefly ஆழும் பாழும் போச்சுது.

755. அம்பட்டன் மாப்பிள்ளைக்கு மீசை ஒதுக்கினதுபோல.
Like the barber's son-in-law who had his moustaches shaved away at the marriage.
Each of his barber friends tried to make some improvement in the bridegroom's moustaches till there was not a hair left on his lip.
"*Too many cooks spoil the broth.*"
"*Many dressers put the bride's dress out of order.*"

756. இடையன் கெடுத்தது பாதி, மடையன் கெடுத்தது பாதி.
The shepherd destroyed half, and the fool half. 788.
In India a shepherd is considered an incarnation of stupidity.

757. இரண்டு கையும் போதாது என்று அகப்பையும் கட்டிக்கொண்டான்.
Finding his two hands were not enough, he tied on a ladle (to serve as a third hand). 524.

Said about a cunning person. This proverb is used of officials open to bribery.

758. இருந்தும் கெடுத்தான், செத்தும் கெடுத்தான்.
He destroyed while alive, and also after his death.
Tennalarama the Jester, ordered his body to be buried across the boundary line of his village. The people in the next village objected to any part of the grave being in their village. Hence strife arose and so though he had done harm while alive he did more after his death. Used when things go from bad to worse.

759. எண்பது வேண்டாம், ஐம்பதும் முப்பதும் கொடு.
I don't want eighty, give me fifty and thirty. 753.
The debtor offers terms to the creditor. The creditor veils his eagerness for the money by putting his demands in other terms.
"*It's six of one, and half a dozen of the other.*"

760. எலித் தலையில் கோடாலி விழுந்ததுபோல.
As the axe fell on the head of the rat.
Complete destruction.

761. எல்லாரும் கூடி, எனக்குக் குல்லா (or நாமம்) போட்டார்கள்.
All have joined to put a cap (*or* Námam) on me (*i.e.*, to deceive me).

762. ஒரு கண்ணிலே புகுந்து, ஒரு கண்ணிலே வருகிறான்.
He goes in at one eye, and comes out of the other. 594.
"*He has as many tricks as a lawyer.*"

763. கட்டினான் தாலி, காட்டினான் கோலம்.
He tied the *thali*, and then showed his own character. 773.
Having married the girl, he showed his real disposition. Said of those who gain their ends by false pretences.

764. கண் கட்டி வித்தை காட்ட வந்தாயா?
Have you come to tie up our eyes and show off your skill? 776, 781.

765. கம்மாளன் பசுவைக் காது அறுத்துக்கொள்ள வேண்டும்.
You must only buy a *Kammalan's* cow after cutting its ears.
This caste is considered so full of deceit, that one cannot be sure that the cow a *Kammalan* wants to sell is not a wooden cow till its ears have been cut and the blood has flowed.

765*a*. கம்மாளன் பசுவைக் காதறுத்து கொண்டாலும், உள்ளே செவ்வரக்கு பாய்ச்சியிருப்பான்.

Though you buy a *Kammalan's* cow only after cutting its ears, he will have put red wax in its ears.

This proverb is a sequel to the former. The *Kammalan* knows the trick there referred to and is so cunning that he will put red wax into his wooden cow's ears so that if they are cut into they will look like red flesh. Used of a perfect rogue.

766. கழுத்துக்குமேல் கத்தி வந்திருக்கச்சே செய்யவேண்டியது என்ன?
When the knife is on the neck, what can be done?

767. காலைப் பிடித்த சனியன் ஊரைச் சுற்றி அடிக்கும்.
If the baneful influence of the star Saturn attack your legs, it will make you wander all over the village.

Some times a Hindu wife scolds a husband so much that he leaves home and wanders about.

768. காளித் தோட்டத்துக் கற்பக விருக்ஷம் ஆருக்கும் உதவாது.
The *Kalpaka* tree in *Kâli's* garden is of no use to any one.

The goddess *Kali* is so revengeful, that if anyone eat the fruits of her wonderful tree, she will kill him.—What is the good of property in the hands of those who will not make a generous use of it?

769. கிணற்றில் தள்ளி, கல்லையும் போட்டான்.
He pushed him into the well and threw stones upon him.
i.e., He betrayed and ruined him.

770. குடலைப் பிடுங்கி ஜஞ்சம் (or பூணூல்) போட்டுக்கொள்ளுவேன்.
I will tear out your entrails and wear them as my sacred cord! 768.

This proverb refers to a *Kali* or Pidari festival. Her priests go in the dead of the night to the burning-ground, where they kill an infant and bring its entrails in order to hang them round the neck of *Kali*, who delights in cruelty.

Said of one who boasts of his inhuman actions.

"*He could eat my heart with garlic.*"

771. கும்பிட்ட கோவில் தலைமேல் இடிந்து விழுந்ததுபோல.
Like the temple that fell on the head of him who revered it.

Spoken of a man who has been ruined by a person whom he respected and trusted.

772. குருவுக்கும் நாமந் தடவி (or போட்டு), கோபால பெட்டியில் கை போட்டதுபோல.

Like putting a *Nâmam* on a priest's forehead, and putting your hand into the vessel in which he receives alms. 238.

Clever and daring cheating.

773. கைத்தாலி கழுத்தின்மேல் ஏறட்டும்.
Let the *thali* first be tied on the neck. 763.

i.e., Only when I am actually married to her shall I believe you mean to let me have your daughter. The proverb expresses fear of deceit.

774. கொடுத்தாற்போல் கொடுத்து வாங்கிக்கொள்ளுகிறது.
He took it back again just when he had given it. 917.

775. சிவ சொத்து குல நாசம்.
Siva's property destroys a family.
He who steals what is sacred or what belongs to a temple will be ruined.

776. ஜால் (or காக்காய்) வித்தை காட்டுகிறேன் பராக்கில்லாமல் பார்.
I will show you magic, watch attentively! 764, 781.
i.e., I am up to your tricks. A hint to a cheat who is trying to deceive. "*Stuffing is good for geese, but not for me.*"

777. தரை தட்டின கப்பல் போல.
Like a ship which has run ashore.

778. தலைக்குமேல் கை காட்டுகிறது.
To show one's hand over one's head. 260.
i.e., To revoke with the hand what has been promised by the lips. The proverb is often used in condemnation of a crafty person in power who plays a double part.

779. தலையில் கை வைத்தான்.
He put his hand on my head.
Said of one who has taken advantage of trust reposed in him to deceive and ruin those who have trusted him.

780. துஷ்ட நிக்கிரகம், சிஷ்ட பரிபாலனம்.
To destroy the wicked, and protect the good.
This Sanskrit phrase appears often in the Sastras in connection with the incarnations of the Divinity, who appeared on earth to protect the good and destroy the wicked.

781. நீ படித்த பள்ளியிலேதான், நானும் படித்தேன்.
I have studied in the very school in which you studied. 764, 776, 1324, 1811.
i.e., I am as smart as you are.

782. பழிபோட்டுத் தலை வாங்குகிற ஜாதி.
A race that blames innocent people and cuts their throats. 234.
Said of those who are unscrupulous in their treachery.

783. பாட்டி பைத்தியகாரி, பதக்கைபோட்டு முக்குறுணி என்பாள்.
Grandmamma is silly! When she gives one a small measure (of something) she says it is a big one.
Said ironically of one who is full of tricks and dodges but cannot hide her true character.

784. பின்னாலே இருந்து கூண்டு முடைகிறான்.
He keeps behind me to weave wicker-work (to bury me in).
The proverb refers to a practice of the Thuggs, the sect of religious murderers.

785. மண்ணுக்கு இரையாய்ப் போகிறது.
It becomes food for the earth.
Said, for instance, about something destroyed by white ants; or by a person who is pleading for help, but sees his request refused.

786. முக்காட்டுக்குள்ளே மூடு மந்திரமா?
What! Are there secret incantations inside your veil?
This proverb is used when one finds a secret plot against oneself in an apparently guileless person.—The veil is often used to signify *modesty*.

786*a*. முக்காட்டுக்குள் சமுதாடா?
What! (Did you conceal) a dagger inside your veil?

787. மேய்கிற கோழி மூக்கை ஒடித்தாற்போல.
Like breaking the beak of a fowl. 558.
If its beak is broken, it must die of starvation.—Used when the chief supporter of a family dies.

788. வாதி கெடுத்தது பாதி, வண்ணான் கெடுத்தது பாதி.
The alchemist spoiled half, and the washerman spoiled half. 756.
Neither knew his own business.

789. வேரைக்கல்லி வெந்நீர் வார்த்தான்.
He digged up the roots and poured hot water on them.
Utter destruction.

790. அவன் என்னை ஊதிப் பறக்க அடிக்கப் பார்க்கிறான்.
He tries to blow me off and make me fly away.
Tries to ruin me.

"IT IS EASIER TO PULL DOWN THAN TO BUILD UP."

790*a*. அடுக்கிற அருமை உடைக்கிற நாய்க்குத் தெரியுமா?
Does the dog that breaks the pots understand how difficult it is to pile them up?
In the potter's house and verandah pots of all sizes are placed in great piles. It takes much time to pile them up, but it is easy to knock them down and smash them all.

791. குசவனுக்குப் பல நாள்வேலை, தடிக்காரனுக்கு ஒரு நிமிஷவேலை.
What is many day's work for the potter, is but a few moment's work for him who breaks pots.
"*An hour may destroy what an age has built up.*"

LOSS.

நஷ்டம்.

LOSS UPON LOSS.

792. கலம் போனதுமல்லாமல், கண்ணுக்கும் மூக்குக்கும் வந்தது கேடு.
I have not only lost my pot, but I have also lost my eyes and my nose.
"*After one loss come many.*"

793. கழுதை கடித்ததுமல்லாமல், காலையும் மிதித்ததாம் (com. மெரித்ததாம்).
Not only did the ass bite him, but it also trampled on him.

794. குதிரை செத்ததுமல்லாமல், குழிதோண்டப் பத்து பணம்.
Not only has his horse died, but it has also cost ten coins to bury it.

795. கோழி போனதுமல்லாமல், குரலும் போச்சுது.
Not only has she lost her fowl, but her voice is gone also.
She has lost her fowl, and her voice in screaming for it.

796. சாப்பிள்ளை பெற்றாலும், மருத்துவச்சி கூலி தப்பாது.
Though the child was still-born, the midwife did not miss her fee.

797. பிள்ளைக்காரன் பிள்ளைக்கு அழுகிறான், பணிசெய்வோன் (com. பணிச்சன்) காசுக்கு அழுகிறான்.
The father weeps for the (dead) child, the people who arrange the funeral weep for hire.
In India there are classes of low caste people whose business it to perform last rites for the corpse.

798. முடிச்சு அவிழ்க்கக் கொடுத்ததுமல்லாமல், இளித்தவாய்ப் பட்டமும் கூடக் கிடைத்தது.
Besides losing the money he had tied up in his cloth, he has also been called a grinning fool!

799. விளக்கெண்ணெய்க்குக் கேடே தவிர, பிள்ளை பிழைப்பது இல்லை.
Besides losing the oil, the child did not live.
Oil is often used as medicine in India.

Cf. 301 *ff.*

MISCELLANEOUS PROVERBS ABOUT LOSSES.

800. அடுப்பும் நெருப்பும் போய், வாய்த் தவிடும் போச்சுது.
After losing both the hearth and the fire, the bran (*i.e.*, the food) in my mouth was lost too. 809.
"*All is lost: both labour and cost.*"

801. ஆயிரம் மாட்டில் ஒரு மாடு உதைத்துக்கொண்டால் என்ன?
If one cow out of a thousand kicks, what does it matter?

802. உழக்கு நெல்லுக்கு உழைக்கப்போய், பதக்கு நெல்லைப் பன்றி தின்றதுபோல.
Like the man who toiled for a small measure of rice, while the pig (at home) ate up a big measure. 806.

803. கட்டிவைத்த பணத்தைத் தட்டிப் பறித்தாற்போல.
As the money tied up for safety was snatched away!
Spoken of the sudden loss of what was carefully protected.

804. கப்பல் ஏறிக் கடலில் கவிழ்ந்ததுபோல.
Like embarking on a vessel and being shipwrecked at sea.

805. குளத்தோடு கோபித்துக் கால் கழுவாதவன்போல.

Like the man who was angry with the pool and so would not wash his feet in it!

"*When a man grows angry, his reason rides out.*" (II. Kings 5, 11.)

806. ஜாண் ஏற, முழம் சறுக்குகிறதா?

While rising a span, should one slip back a cubit? 802.

"*One step forward and two steps back.*"

807. தண்ணீர்க்குடம் உடைந்தாலும் ஐயோ, தயிர்க்குடம் உடைந்தாலும் ஐயோ!

If a water pot (a worthless thing) breaks, they exclaim 'Alas'! and if a pot of curds (a valuable thing) breaks they say the same!

808. பிடித்த கிளையும் மிதித்த (com. மெரித்த) கொம்பும் முறிந்து போச்சுது.

The branch I had seized and the branch on which I was standing both broke!

809. புது வெள்ளம் வந்து பழைய வெள்ளத்தையும் அடித்துக்கொண்டுபோகிறது.

A new flood came and carried off the old flood! 925, 1241, 3153.

The loss of what one possesses together with the loss of what one is seeking.

810. மலையைப் பார்த்து நாய் குலைத்தால், மலைக்குக் கேடோ நாய்க்குக் கேடோ?

If a dog look at a mountain and bark, will the mountain or the dog suffer?

"*What does the moon care, if the dog bark at her.*"

"*To bark against the moon.*"

THEFT, THIEVES.

திருட்டு, திருடன்.

ACCOMPLICES IN THEFT.

811. அதிகாரியும் தலையாரியும் கூடி, விடியுமட்டும் திருடலாம்.

If the head-man and the village watch-man are in league, they can steal till daybreak. 814.

812. உளவில்லாமல் களவு இல்லை.

No robbery takes place without the help of an inmate of the house.

813. உளவனில்லாமல், ஊர் அழியாது.

A town will not be destroyed without a traitor.

814. உள்ளனும் கள்ளனும் கூடினல், விடிகிறமட்டும் திருடலாம்.
If the inmate of a house and a thief are in league, they can steal till day-break. 811.

815. கள்ளனும் தோட்டக்காரனும் ஒன்று கூடினல், விடியுமட்டும் திருடலாம்.
If the thief and the gardener are in league, they can steal till day-break.

THIEVES.

816. அவன் கை மெத்த கூராச்சே.
His hand is very sharp!
i.e., He is a thief.

817. ஐந்து விரலும், ஐந்து கன்னங்கோல்.
His five fingers are five crow-bars.
Said of a clever thief.

818. கட்டி அழுகிறபோது, கையும் துழாவுகிறது.
While embracing and weeping she gropes with her hand. 2311.
After a death in a house while the women sit weeping in a circle with their hands on one another's shoulders, a thievish woman will try to steal the jewels of the woman next her. Nothing is sacred to a thief.

819. தட்டான் தாய்ப் பொன்னிலும் மாப்பொன் திருடுவான்.
A goldsmith will pilfer a little gold-dust even from his mother's gold!

820. தோலிருக்க, சுளே விழுங்கி (com. முழுங்கி).
He swallowed the pulp, but left the peel intact.
Said of a thief who steals without being found out.

THEFT.

821. அள்ளிக்கொண்டே போகச்சே, கிள்ளிக்கொண்டு வருகிறன்.
While I was going away with what I had stolen, he came and pilfered from it.

822. இந்த வீட்டிலே வைத்தது மாயமாயிருக்கிறது.
What is kept in the house becomes an illusion. 830, 831.
Said when little things disappear from one's house without anybody knowing how they disappear. The allusion is to the doctrine of illusion (*Maya*) according to which everything is phenomenal and nothing real.

823. ஊசிக்குக் கள்ளன் உடனே இருப்பான்.
There will be a thief for a needle immediately.
Little things, if not looked after, will be stolen at once.

824. கள்ளன் பெரிதோ, காப்பான் பெரிதோ?
Is the thief great, or the watchman? 415.
The thief is more alert than the watchman.

825. கிள்ளுகிறவனிடத்தில் இருந்தாலும், அள்ளுகிறவனிடத்தில் இருக்கலாகாது.

Though he who pilfers may be endured, he who steals in quantities cannot be endured.

826. கொள்ளைக்குப் போனாலும், கூட்டு ஆகாது.

When a thief goes to plunder, he should go without a partner.

827. சம்பந்தி கிரகஸ்தன் வருகிறான், செம்பு (com. சொம்பு) தவலை உள்ளே (or ironically: வெளியே) வை.

Our honest relative is coming, put all the brass pots inside (*or* ironically, outside)!

Used ironically about a friend in whom one has no confidence, implying that even one's relatives may be thieves.

828. கண்ட இடத்திலே திருடன் கண்போகிறது.

The eyes of a thief run over the place he sees. 972.

While he is in a place he will stealthily study it well, with intent to use his knowledge ill.

829. நரி நாலு கால் திருடன், இடையன் இரண்டு கால் திருடன்.

The jackal is a thief with four legs, the shepherd a thief with two legs.

830. நின்றுகொண்டே இருந்தவன் எப்படியோ கண்ணில் மண்ணைப் போட்டு, அதை எடுத்துக்கொண்டுபோனான்.

He who just stood here has somehow managed to throw dust into your eyes and run off with something! 822, 831.

831. வைத்து வைத்தவன்போல எடுத்துக்கொண்டான்.

He carried it off as though he had placed it ready to hand. 822, 830.

THE END JUSTIFIES THE MEANS.

832. ஆயிரம் பொய் சொல்லிக் கோவிலைக் கட்டிவை.

Tell a thousand lies in order to build a temple.

Or, ஆயிரம் பொய் சொல்லி ஒரு விளக்கு ஏற்றிவை, Tell a thousand lies to light a lamp: Or, ஆயிரம் பொய் சொல்லி ஒரு தாலி கட்டிவை, *and* ஆயிரம் பொய் சொல்லி ஒரு கலியாணஞ் செய்துவை, Tell a thousand lies and marry.

The latter forms of the saying refer to the lies told by the bridegroom's friends to the bride's relatives about his character, person, habits and wealth, in order to make them eager to complete the arrangements for the marriage.

GENEROSITY.

GENEROSITY AT ANOTHER'S EXPENSE.

833. கடைத்தேங்காய் எடுத்து, வழிப்பிள்ளையாருக்கு உடைத்தாற்போல.

Like stealing a cocoanut in the market and breaking it as an offering to *Ganesa*. 360.

Ganesa is the popular god of learning and remover of obstacles.

834. பசுவைக் கொன்று செருப்பு தானஞ் செய்ததுபோல.

Like killing a cow and making its hide into shoes as a gift to a Brahmin.

The cow is sacred, and the gift of shoes made from its hide to a Brahmin cannot expiate the crime of killing it. One cannot buy merit with wealth made unrighteously.

"*Robbing Peter to pay Paul.*"

835. வெல்லப்பிள்ளையாரைக் கிள்ளி, அதற்கு நைவேத்தியஞ் செய்கிறது.

Pinching off a little sugar from an image of *Ganesa* (that is made of sugar) and offering that sugar to the image (from which it has been stolen)!

"*Broad thongs are cut from other men's leather.*"

CHEAP GENEROSITY.

836. ஆற்றிலே போகிற தண்ணீரை, அப்பா குடி, ஆத்தாள் குடி.

O, father, O mother! drink of the water that runs in the river.

Often used of shameless claims on public money, especially public charities.

837. ஆற்றிலே ஆயிரம் காணி தானம் பண்ணினாற்போல.

Like making you a gift of a thousand acres of land in a sandy river!

A worthless gift. Sometimes used of a master who assigns much work on little pay.

838. கடிக்கமாட்டாத பாக்கு உத்தம தானம்.

The areca-nut which one cannot bite, is an excellent gift to others!

Besides being a sarcasm on a mean gift this saying is also used of the gift of a miser, which is a great thing to him however small others may think it. There is a Telugu song that tells how a miser mourned because he had to pay a few cash for the wood for the funeral pyre of some one who died in his house.

HABIT.

வழக்கம்.

THE NATURAL DISPOSITION CANNOT BE CHANGED.

839. ஊத்தை போகக் குளித்தவனுமில்லை, பசி போகத் தின்றவனுமில்லை.
No one gets rid of dirt by bathing, and no one has his hunger satisfied by eating.

The dirt and the hunger will soon return ; the washing and the eating must be repeated.

840. எத்தனை புடம் இட்டாலும், இரும்பு பசும்பொன்னாகுமா?
Will iron become fine gold, however often refined?

841. குணத்தை மாற்ற குரு இல்லை.
There is no priest who can change the natural disposition. 122.

842. ஜென்மத்தில் பிறந்தது செருப்பால் அடித்தாலும் போகாது.
What is born with you will not leave you even if beaten with slippers. 850.

" *He who is born a fool is never cured.*

843. தண்ணீர் வெந்நீரானாலும் நெருப்பை அவிக்கும்.
Though cold water is made hot, it will put out fire. 2372.

"*Foul water as soon as fair, will quench hot fire.*"

844. வெங்காயத்துக்கு (or வெள்ளைப்பூண்டுக்கு) எத்தனை வாசனை கட்டினாலும், துர்க்கந்தத்தையே வீசும்.
However many perfumes you put on an onion it will still emit a bad smell.

Cf. 514 *ff.* 852, 858-860, 873 *ff.*

THE POWER OF HABIT.

845. அங்காடிக்காரியைச் சங்கீதம் பாடச்சொன்னால், வெங்காயம் கருவேப்பிலை என்பாள்.
If you ask a woman, who goes about the street selling vegetables to sing a song, she will only go on crying, ' Onions and greens ' !

846. அம்மணத்தேசத்தில் கோமணம் கட்டினவன் பைத்தியக்காரன்.
He who ties on a rag in a country where all go naked will be considered a mad man.

" *You must do in Rome as Rome does.*".

847. அருமை மருமகன் தலைபோனாலும் போகட்டும், ஆதிகாலத்து உரல் போகலாகாது.
Although the head of your dear son-in-law comes to grief, it does not matter ; but see that the rice-mortar you have inherited comes to no harm.

Said about overvaluing that which is old because it is old, and undervaluing that which is recent or new because it is not ancient.

" *Custom is the plague of wise men and the idol of fools.*"

848. ஊருக்கு எல்லாம் ஒரு வழி, உனக்கு ஒரு வழியா?
The whole village has one way (of doing things); do you want a different one? 2828.
Said as a rebuke to one who makes innovations.

849. கந்தப்பொடிக் கடைக்காரனுக்கு வாசனை தெரியுமா?
Is a merchant who sells scented powder, able to smell it? 395, 639.
He has got so used to it, that he does not perceive it. Constant association with anything, good or evil, is apt to give rise to indifference to its moral worth.

850. தொட்டில்பழக்கம் சுடுகாடுமட்டும்.
Habits acquired in the cradle last to the grave. 842.
"*What belongs to nature lasts to the grave.*"

CASTE.

ஜாதி, குலம்.

851. அசலிலே பிறந்த கஸ்மாலம்.
He is dross born from pure metal! 252, 545*a*.
Said sarcastically to a worthless person who prides himself on belonging to a high caste.

852. அவன் ஜாதி எந்தப் புத்தி, குலம் எந்த ஆசாரமோ, அதுதான் வரும்.
A man will inherit the intellect and the rites of his caste. 856.
The characteristics of a man's caste will show themselves in him, however much he tries to hide them.
"*Nature will out.*"

853. கலம் கலந்தால், குலம் கலக்கும்.
If we mix our pots (*i.e.*, If we take food together), our castes will get mixed.
People of different castes and sub-castes cannot eat together without contracting ceremonial defilement.

854. கன்மத்தினால் ஜாதியேயன்றி, ஜென்மத்தினால் ஜாதியில்லை.
One does not belong to a caste by birth, but by reason of actions done in a former existence.
Explained in the Mahabharata :—நன்னெறி நல்ல நடக்கையுடையவர்கள் எவர்களோ, அவர்களே நல்ல ஜெனனம், only those who walk in the right way with good conduct are of good birth.

855. குணம் பெரிதேயன்றி, குலம் பெரிதல்ல.
Not caste, but virtue is great.

856. குலம் எப்படியோ, குணம் அப்படியே.
As his caste is, so is his character. 852, 1392.

857. குலம் குப்பையிலே, பணம் பந்தியிலே.
High caste lies on a dunghill, wealth has the feast.
"*Worth has been underrated ever since wealth was overvalued.*"

858. சந்நியாசிக்கும் ஜாதிமானம் போகாது.
Even an ascetic (who has renounced all) has not lost pride in his caste.

859. ஜாதிவாக்கு ஜங்கிடவாக்கு, இலுப்பைப்பூ தொளை வாக்கு.
The caste's custom is common to every village, just as there are holes in every *Iluppai* flower.

The faults and shortcomings of a caste mark the caste wherever it is found. Low caste people often attempt to mingle with the higher castes, but they find it difficult, as their mannerisms of speech betray them.

860. வம்சத்து (com. வங்குசம்) வாடிகைக்கு ஒரு குடுவை பொங்கலிட்டாலும் போகாது.
The habit of your caste will not leave you even if you boil a vessel full of rice as an offering to it.
A man can never lose the sentiments of his caste.

Cf. 839 *ff.*

ABSTINENCE FROM MEAT.

861. ஆடு தின்பாளாம், இரண்டு ஆடு தின்பாளாம், ஆட்டைக் கண்டால், சீச்சீ என்பாளாம்.

She will *eat* a sheep, yea even two, but if she *sees* one, she exclaims: "fie, fie"!

Used ironically of those who profess not to eat flesh, but who really enjoy it.

862. உப்புக் கண்டம் பறிகொடுத்த பார்ப்பாத்திபோல்.

Like the Brahmin woman who had lost her salted mutton! 1025.

Used when something is lost, that the owner dare not enquire after for fear of public disgrace. Brahmins are not allowed to eat flesh in any form. By the rules of her caste the Brahmin woman ought not to have had any salted mutton to lose; and when it was lost she dare not inquire about it, lest she should be turned out of her caste and disgraced for breaking caste rules.

863. ஒருபொழுது (or ஆசாரப் பூசை)ச் சட்டி, அதின்மேல் கவுச்சிச் சட்டி (or மீன்கறி).

The pots used daily by flesh eaters are put on the top of the pots kept for sacred purposes! 2281.

The two ought never to come in contact as the former defile the latter. Said in sarcasm about those who make great professions of ceremonial piety but do not carry them out.

864. சிற்றிலே (com. சீத்திலே) வேண்டாம், சாற்றிலே வாரு.
Do not give me any piece of meat. Give me the broth only.

865. கொன்றால் பாவம், தின்றால் தீரும்.
If you kill an animal, it is sin; but if you eat it, you will get rid of the sin!

Killing is a sin, but among many Sudra sub-castes the eating of flesh is allowed.

866. சாற்றிலே பீ இறுத்தாற்போல வாரு.
Strain the filth from the soup and let me have the soup.

867. சாற்றிலே வேண்டாம், தெளிவிலே வாரு.
I don't want the soup (with the meat in it), give me the clear soup only!

864, 866, 867 and 869 all mean the same. What the person says he does not want, is exactly what he wants. These proverbs are sarcasms on the growing disregard for Shastraic rules against flesh eating.

868. சுத்த சைவம், மரக்கறி எல்லாம் தள்ளுபடி.
He is a pure vegetarian, so throw all vegetables away.

Said ironically to one, or about one, who pretends to be a strict vegetarian.

868*a*. சைவத்துக்கு ஆசைப்பட்டு மரக்கறி தள்ளிவிட்டேன்!
I wish to become a vegetarian, and so I have given up vegetables!

869. ஞாயிற்றுக்கிழமை ஒருபொழுது நண்டு வேண்டாம், சாறு விடு.
I don't want crabs as it is a fast day; pour out the soup only for me. 867.

"*As good eat the devil, as the broth he is boiled in.*"

870. நாலாம் தலைமுறையைப் பார்த்தால், நாவிதனும் சிற்றப்பனுவான்.
If you look back four generations you may find that a barber is your uncle.

871. சைவ முத்தையா (a name) முதலியாருக்குப் சமைத்துப்போட வள்ளுவப் பண்டாரம்.
A Pariah priest cooked for the vegetarian, Muttaiya Muthaliyar!

The Muthaliyar's professions of vegetarianism, which is counted a virtue in India, were overthrown by the fact that his cook was a flesh-eating Pariah.

872. சைவம் முற்றி, எலும்பு எலும்பாய்க் கழியுது.
Pretending to severe vegetarianism he excretes bones.

An ironical and rather vulgar proverb denoting that the professed vegetarian is really a flesh eater.

Cf. 386.

WHAT IS DONE CANNOT BE UNDONE.

திருப்புதல், மாற்றல்.

873. அணை கடந்த வெள்ளம் அழுதாலும் வராது.
Will the flood that has leaped over its banks go back if you weep?

874. உறியிலே கட்டித் தூக்கினாலும், அழுகற் பூசனிக்காய் அழுகலே.
Though a rotten gourd is hung up in a net (*uri*), it is still a rotten one.

875. ஒரு பணம் கொடுத்து அழச்சொல்லி ஒன்பது பணம் கொடுத்து ஓயச் சொன்னால் ஓயுமா?
If you have paid him one small coin to weep, will he cease weeping if you give him nine coins?
Easy to do evil, hard to remedy it. See 884 *N.B.*
"*Give the piper a penny, and two pence to leave off.*"

876. கறந்த பால் முலைக்கு ஏறுமா?
Can milk that has been drawn, enter the udder again?
"*Can a man be born again.*"

877. காய்ந்த இரும்பு குடித்த நீரை வாராது.
The water the hot iron has drunk, will not come back!

878. கோபம் வந்து கிணற்றில் விழுந்தால், சந்தோஷம் வந்தால் எழுந்திருக்கலாமா?
If you get augry and fall into a well, will you get out by trying to feel happy?
"*Anger begins with folly, and ends with repentance.*"

879. கோபத்தில் அறுத்த மூக்கு சந்தோஷத்தில் வருமா?
Will happiness restore a nose that has been cut off in anger?
A jealous husband in India sometimes cuts off his wife's nose in his anger. If the quarrel is made up and he lives happily with his wife again, he would like to undo what he has done, but, of course, cannot.

880. சுடுகாடு போன பிணம் திரும்பாது.
A corpse that has gone to the burning ground will not come back.

881. சோறு சிந்தினால் பொறுக்கலாம், மானம் சிந்தினால் பொறுக்கலாமா?
If boiled rice be spilt, it may be picked up; but if honour be lost, can it be had back?

882. தோண்டக் குறுணி, தூர்க்க முக்குறுணி.
One measure for digging, but three for filling up again.

883. சுண்டைக்காய் கால் பணம், சுமைக் கூலி முக்கால் பணம்.
The price of the *sundakai* (a vegetable) is a quarter of a *panam*, the charge for carrying it is three times as much!

884. செத்த ஆடு கால் பணம், சுமைக் கூலி முக்கால் பணம்.

The price of the dead sheep is a quarter of a *panam*, the charge for carrying it is three times as much !

N. B.—Nos. 875, 883 and 884 scarcely come in this section, but it is difficult to class them more accurately. The idea in them seems to be that what is begun without thought, must be completed, though it involves much labour and loss.

885. மறந்து செத்தேன், பிராணன் வா என்றால் வருமா?

I forgot myself and died ; if I call my life back, will it come ?

Used of one who thoughtlessly does something wicked ; which he cannot rectify.

" *Evil comes to us by ells, and goes away by inches.*"

886. முப்பது பணம் கொடுத்தாலும், மூளிப் பட்டம் போகாது.

Though you give thirty *panams*, a bad name will not forsake you.

" *Give a dog an ill name, and you may as well hang him.*"

Cf. 514 *ff.* 839 *ff.* 994 *ff.* 1288 *ff.*

FORBEARANCE, LENIENCY, PLIABILITY.

இளக்காரம், இளப்பம், தாக்ஷிணியம்.

887. அறிந்த பார்ப்பான் சிநேகிதன் ஆறு காசுக்கு மூன்று தோசையா?

The Brahmin he knew as his friend, gave him only three cakes for six *cash*.

He ought to have given him six.

888. அறிந்தவன் என்று கும்பிட அடிமை வழக்கிட்ட கதை.

The story of the man who bowed down to his friend, and was claimed by this friend as his slave !

889. ஆள் இளப்பமாயிருந்தால், (or ஏமாந்தவனானால்) எமனையும் நமனையும் பலகாரம் பண்ணுவாள்.

If Death present himself without his terrors, she will take advantage of it and cook him in a cake. 2649.

A shrew will take advantage of the least indulgence to get the upper hand over her husband or master.

889*a*. இளைப்பு ஓட்டினால் எமனையும் நமனையும் பலகாரம் பண்ணுவாள்.

If you allow her leaness to be cured by with good eating, she will make Death into a cake.

890. ஆளைப் பார்த்தான், வாயில் எய்த்தான்.

He saw him, and deceived him in his own mouth. 3372.

" *He did him in the eye.*"

891. ஆளைக் கண்டு ஏமாத்துமாம் (or ஏய்க்கும் or மிரட்டுமாம்) ஆலங்காட்டு பேய் (or நரி).

The devil (*or* jackal) that lives in the banyan grove, sees a man and cheats him (*or* intimidates him).

They will harm no one who turns a bold face to them.

Cf. ஏமாந்தவனை ஏமாத்துகிறது, to deceive him who can be deceived.

"*An easy fool is a knave's tool.*"

892. உழுகிற மாட்டை நுகத்தால் அடித்ததுபோல்.

Like beating the ploughing ox with the yoke. 738, 3502.

Said about the ill-treatment of an inferior who has done good service; or about over-severe punishments.

893. எதிரி இளப்பமானால், கோபம் சண்டப் பிரசண்டம்.

If your opponent betrays weakness, then your rage will be overwhelming.

894. எதிர்த்தவன் ஏழை என்றால், கோபம் சண்டாளம்.

If your opponent is a poor man, your rage will be savage. 739.

895. என் இளக்காரம் விளக்காய் எரிகிறது (com. எரியுது).

My good nature burns like a lamp.

i.e., All in the house know my good nature or my submissiveness and I suffer, just as a lamp wastes by burning. Said by an overworked daughter-in-law or by a servant.

"*The least boy always carries the greatest fiddle.*"

"*A candle lights others and consumes itself.*"

896. ஏர் உழுகிறவன் இளப்பமானால், எருது மச்சான் முறை (or மைத்துனன்) கொண்டாடும்.

If the ploughman is yielding, the bullock will treat him like a brother-in-law!

If the superior is weak, the inferior will get his own way.

897. ஏனவாயனைக் கண்டாளாம், ஏணிப்பந்தம் பிடித்தாளாம்.

Seeing that her husband was a simpleton, she carried the torches very high.

i.e., Knowing his easy-going foolishly kind nature, she did what she liked without regard to his wishes.

"*She wears the breeches.*"

898. ஏமாந்தால் நாமம் போடுவான், இளைப்பு ஒட்டவில்லை.

If I am yielding he will put a *Namam* on me (*i.e.*, cheat me), but he is too weak to try (*or* he has no chance). 910.

899. ஓடுகிறவனைக் கண்டால், துரத்துகிறவனுக்கு இளக்காரம்.

Seeing the pursued man run away, makes (pursuit) easy to the pursuer.

900. கண்குத்திப் பாம்புபோல் கண்ணிலே மண்ணைப் போடுகிறான்.

He throws earth into your eyes with the malice of a whip-snake.

The green whip-snake is said to hide itself in the tops of palms and wait for the drawer of palm juice to climb up. When he nears the top the snake darts forth and strikes out his eyes. Here it is used as an emblem of malice.

901. கொட்டினால் தேள், கொட்டாவிட்டால் பிள்ளைப்பூச்சி.

If it sting it is a scorpion; if not, it is only a mud-gryllus.

902. கொல்லன் எளிமை (or பேதமை) கண்டு, குரங்கு காலுக்குப் பூண் கட்டச் சொன்னதாம்.

It is said, that a monkey seeing the good nature of the blacksmith, asked him to adorn its legs with anklets!

Said of one who is so good natured, that every one takes advantage of him.

903. தாங்கித் தாங்கிப் பார்த்தால், தலைமேல் ஏறுகிறான்.

If you treat a person too leniently, he will jump on your head.

If a servant says he will leave, but is coaxed to stay, he will treat his employer with contempt.

904. தாக்ஷிணியம் தன நாசம்.

Over complacency is the ruin of wealth. 1085.

i.e., The inability to say 'No.' (*Tākshinyam*) is ruinous to all material prosperity.

" *Foolish pity spoils a city.*"

905. தாய் தூற்றினால் ஊர் தூற்றும், கொண்டவன் தூற்றினால் கண்டவன் தூற்றுவான்.

If a mother slanders her daughter, the village will slander her also; if the husband slanders his wife, every body else will slander her. 3200.

906. பூச்சி பூச்சி என்றால், புழுக்கை தலைமேல் ஏறும்.

If you speak kindly to a maid-servant, she will jump on your head.

If servants be treated too kindly, they will take advantage of their employer.

" *He that handles a nettle tenderly is soonest stung.*"

Cf. 738 *ff.* 3334 *ff.*

DESIRE.

ஆசை.

VAIN WISHES.

907. ஆசையிருக்கிறது தாசில்பண்ண, அமிசை (prop. அமிசம்) இருக்கிறது கழுதை மேய்க்க.

He has the desire to rule over a district, but his lot is to herd asses.

" *The wolf loses his teeth, but not his inclination.*"

" *If wishes were thrushes, beggars would eat birds.*"

908. எழுந்திருப்பாள் காலில்லை.
She would like to stand up, but has no legs.
Said of one who wants to do mischief, but lacks the power.

909. குருட்டுக்கோழி தவிட்டுக்கு வீங்கினதுபோல.
The blind bird had a great desire for bran.
Its blindness prevented it from finding any.

910. தம்பி கவர்னர் (Governor) ஆவான், இளைப்பு ஒட்டவில்லை.
The younger brother wants to be the governor, but his feebleness prevents him. 898.
"*If you cannot bite, don't show your teeth.*"

911. தம்பி உழுவான், மேழி எட்டாது.
The younger brother would plough, but he cannot reach the handle of the plough.
"*If wishes might prevail, shepherds would be kings.*"

912. முடவன் கொம்புத்தேனுக்கு ஆசைப்பட்டதுபோல.
Like the lame man who wanted the honey up in the tree. 1017.
Said of a person who craves for something beyond his reach.
"*The grapes are sour.*"

Cf. 1669 *ff.* 2670 *ff.*

DISAPPOINTED DESIRES.

913. அழுகிற பிள்ளைக்கு வாழைப்பழம் காட்டுகிறதுபோல.
Like showing a plantain (*or* banana) to a crying child.
The sight of the fruit only makes the child cry more.

914. ஆசை சொல்லிக்காட்டி, மோசம் செய்கிறது.
To excite desires and then deceive. 2363.
To give hopes either by promises, ambiguous words or invitations, but finally to disappoint the hopes formed.

915. என்னை நம்பாதே, தாலி வாங்காதே.
Do not trust in me and take off your *thâli!*
Said about one who disappoints the faith that others have in him. The saying is, literally, a warning to a married woman not to forget her marriage vows. It is also explained as follows:—In the *Woddar* (navvy) caste a widow is allowed to remarry, and may wear the *thâli* given to her by her first husband up to the day of her second marriage. There was a lazy *Woddar* who wanted to marry a certain hard-working widow so that he might live on the profits of her work. One day he found out that she had the same idea in her mind about him, so he uttered the above words, meaning, If you want to remarry in order to live an idle life, don't marry me.

916. ஏறவிட்டு, ஏணியை வாங்குகிறது.
What! make me mount (a tree) and then remove the ladder!
Do not excite hopes only to deceive them.

917. கலத்தில் சோற்றை இட்டுக் கையைப் பிடித்தாற்போல.
Like serving up rice in a vessel and then laying hold of your hand (to prevent you from eating it). 774.
To promise and afterwards disappoint.
"*Give a thing and take again, and you shall ride in hell's wain.*"

918. கிளியை வளர்த்துப் பூனை கையில் கொடுக்கிறதா?
Is it right to rear a parrot and then leave it to the claws of a cat?

919. கொடுக்கிறேன் என்றால் ஆசை, அடிக்கிறேன் என்றால் பயம்.
If I say I will bestow, I give hope; if I say I will beat, I cause fear. 1095
Promises and threats should be carried out.

Cf. 219 *ff.* 239 *ff.* 913 *ff.* 2328 *ff.* 2373 *ff.*

UNGRATEFUL GREEDINESS.

920. இடம் கொடுத்தால், மடம் பிடுங்குவான்.
If you give him a place (to lie down in), he will take the whole hermitage.
"*Give a rogue an inch and he'll take an ell.*"

921. இடுப்பு வைத்த இடம் எல்லாம் அடுப்பு வைத்தான்.
Wherever he got a place to lie on, he made a hearth.
"*Give me a seat, and I will make myself room to lie down.*"

922. ஈனருக்கு இடங்கொடுத்தால், இல்லிடம் கைகொள்வான்.
If you make room for a mean person, he will take your whole house.
"*He that takes the devil into his boat, must carry him over the sound.*"

923. உம் (com. உ) என்கிறாளாம் காமாக்ஷி, ஒட்டிக்கொண்டாளாம் மீனாக்ஷி.
Kamakshee (Siva's wife Parvati) only said 'um,' but *Meenakshee* (Kuberan's daughter) stuck to her. 963, 980, 1934.
After the former had promised a thing, the latter did not leave her till she got it. Siva and Kubera are popular deities.

924. எறும்பு ஊர இடங்கொடுத்தால், எருதும் பொதியும் உள்ளே செலுத்துவான்.
If you leave sufficient room for an ant to creep in, he will drive in his bullock and its load!
"*Give a clown your finger and he will take your whole hand.*"

925. ஒண்ட வந்த பிடாரி ஊர் பிடாரியைத் துரத்தினதுபோல.
Like the goddess that came and asked for a place to rest, and then expelled the goddess of the village. 809.

Hindu applications of this proverb would be:—The Brahmins came to India for shelter in ancient times; but made themselves the priests and masters of the land: the English came to trade, but have taken all authority out of the hands of the Brahmins.

"*I gave the mouse a hole, and she is become my heir.*"

926. இட்டவா நாயே என்றால், மூஞ்சியை (prop. முகத்தை) நக்குகிறது.
If you say, Come here, dog! it will lick its face and come (cringing).

If spoken to kindly it will beg for something to eat. If low people are encouraged at all they will try to make profit of the kindness shown to them.

"*The dog wags its tail, not for love of you, but of your bread.*"

927. தாதன் ஆட்டம் திருப்பதியிலே தெரியும்.
The tricks of a Vaishnava mendicant are known in Tirupathi.

These mendicants will come to villagers and promise to help them to perform religious rites at the sacred shrine at Tirupathi, but when they have persuaded the villagers to make a pilgrimage to the shrine and have got them to the place they refuse to do anything unless handsomely rewarded, at the same time threatening these ignorant people with the anger of the deity unless they conform to their demands. A man's greed is best known in the place where he has most influence.

928. நரிக்கு இடங்கொடுத்தால், கிடைக்கு இரண்டு ஆடு பிடிக்கும்.
If you give any room to a jackal, it will take two sheep from your flock.

929. விரல் நுழைய இடங்கொடுத்தால், உரலை (or தலையை) நுழைக்கிறான்.
If you give room for him to push in a finger, he will push in a rice-mortar (*or* his head).

930. வெள்ளைக்காரனுக்கு ஆட்டுத்தோல் இடங்கொடுத்தார்கள், அது அறுத்து, ஊர் முழுதும் அடித்து, இது எனது என்றான்.
(Our ancestors) gave as much room as a sheep-skin can cover to a European, but he cut it into bits, conquered the whole place, and said, "This is mine."

Cf. 2172 *ff*.

"GRASP ALL, LOSE ALL."

931. அறச்செட்டு முழுநஷ்டம்.
Over niggardliness is utter loss.
"*Much would have more, and lost all.*"

932. கஞ்செட்டுக் கண்ணை (or தயவை)க் கெடுக்கும்.
Stinginess ruins the eyes (*or* one's sense of sympathy).
"*A covetous man is good to none, but worst to himself.*"

933. கன ஆசை, கன நஷ்டம்.
Great desire, great loss.
"*Avarice bursts the bag.*" "*All covet, all lose.*"

934. பேராசை தீராத் தரித்திரம்.
Much greed is endless poverty.

935. வட்டி ஆசை முதலுக்குக் கேடு.
Greed of high interest is loss of capital.

COVETOUSNESS.

936. அசலார் (or ஊரார்) உடமைக்குப் பேயாய்ப் பறக்கிறது.
He flies like a devil after a neighbour's property.
"*No one is content with his lot.*"

937. அரிசி அள்ளின காக்காய்ப்போல.
Like the crow that plundered the rice.
A crow that has once eaten rice, always seeks more.
"*As greedy as a dog.*"

938. குட்டிபோட்ட நாய்போல அலைகிறது.
To be as anxious as a dog that has pups.
A mother-in-law often applies this to a daughter-in-law who covets some luxury: but it is also applied to all kinds of desires.

939. பிடிபிடியாய் நட்டால், பொதிபொதியாய் விளையுமா?
If you plant rice by the handful only, will it grow up in sheaves? 933.
Said sarcastically to children who fill their mouths greedily when eating.
"*He that grasps at too much holds nothing fast.*"

940. பொன் காப்புக்கு ஆசைப்பட்டுப் புலி கையில் அகப்பட்டதுபோல.
He longed for the gold bracelets and was caught by the tiger!
The story is told in the *Panchatantra*. A certain tiger grew too old to hunt and was dying of hunger, when he thought of a device for securing a meal, and wove a bracelet of yellow grass round his paw. A Brahman who, came that way saw the bracelet and believing it to be gold, coveted it. The tiger, who professed intense penitence for all his former sins, declared that he would give the bracelet to the Brahman, if he would take it. The Brahman led by his avarice approached to take the gift, and was killed and eaten by the tiger.

941. மந்தையிலும் பால், வீட்டிலும் தயிரா?
If (you take) the milk when with the herd, can you have curds at home?
"*The first cut and all the loaf besides.*"

Cf. 1205 *ff.*

CONFLICTING DESIRES.

942. ஆசை அவள்மேல், ஆதரவு பாய்மேல்.
He wants the woman, but he loves his mat!
Parsimony *versus* lust.

942*a*. ஆற்றிலே ஒருகாலும், சேற்றிலே ஒருகாலுமாயிருக்கிறான்.
He stands with one leg in the river, and one in the mud.

943. இரண்டு வீட்டிலும் கலியாணம், இடையில் செத்ததாம் நாய்க்குட்டி.
A wedding was going on in two houses; the pup died between them. 951.

"*He that hunts two hares oft loseth both.*"
"*Between two stools he falls to the bottom.*"
Kashmiri: "*The washerman's dog is not of the house, nor of the ghât.*"

944. இரண்டு ஆட்டிலே ஊட்டின குட்டி ஆனான்.
He has become a lamb that sucks two sheep.

Said of one who tries to take advantage of the favour of several persons instead of cleaving to one patron, and finds that the end of all his scheming is failure and disappointment.

"*No man can serve two masters.*"

945. இரண்டு ஓடத்திலே கால் வைக்கிறதா?
Can you keep your legs in two different boats?

946. ஏறச்சொன்னால் எருதுக்குக் கோபம், இறங்கச்சொன்னால் நொண்டிக்குக் கோபம்.
If a lame man is told to mount a bull, the bull gets angry; if he is told to dismount, he gets angry.

Said for example, when a mother-in-law and her daughter-in-law quarrel and the girl's husband does not know what to do, for if he sides with either party, he offends the other.

947. கம்புக்குக் களை வெட்டினாற்போலும் இருக்கவேண்டும், தம்பிக்குப் பெண் பேசினாற்போலும் இருக்கவேண்டும்.
Appear as if you were weeding the corn, and as if you were arranging the marriage of your younger brother! 220.

"*Killing two birds with one stone.*"

948. காசுக்கு ஒரு குதிரையும் வேண்டும், காற்றைப்போல பறக்கவும் வேண்டும்.
He wants (to buy) a horse for a few *cash*, but it must run as swiftly as the wind.

949. கூழுக்கும் ஆசை, மாவுக்கும் (or மீசைக்கும்) ஆசை.
He is fond of gruel, and of flour (*or* of his moustache).

950. சொன்னாள் ஆய் (தாய்) செத்துப்போவாள், சொல்லாவிட்டால் அப்பன் செத்துப்போவான்.
If I tell it, the mother will die; if I don't tell it, the father will die.

A man caught a hare and gave it to his wife to cook. The hare ran away, and the wife to avoid her husband's anger killed their cat and prepared it for dinner. The son who happened to know this, to save his father from eating the cat, came running in and threw one of his slippers into the rice and the other into the curry and ran off.—Used when one servant knows something bad of another and desires to inform their master but fears his fellow-servant's vengeance.

951. துக்கல் ஊரிலும் கலியாணம், துடியல் ஊரிலும் கலியாணம், நாய் அங்கே ஓடியும் கெட்டது, இங்கே ஓடியும் கெட்டது.

There was a wedding in the villages of Tukkal and Tudiyal, the dog ran to one, but got nothing, and to the other but got nothing. 943.

952. பணமும் பத்தாயிருக்கவேண்டும், பெண்ணும் முத்தாயிருக்கவேண்டும், முறையிலேயும் அத்தைமகளாயிருக்கவேண்டும்.

The money (that has to be paid for my bride) must be ten *panams* only, the girl herself must be a pearl, and she must also be the daughter of my father's sister.

The bridegroom wants to give a very small dowry for his bride, but is very exacting in his requirements.

953. பாம்பு சாகாமல், பாம்பு அடித்த கோலும் முறிக்காமல் இருக்கவேண்டும்.

It must be done without killing the snake, and without breaking the stick that strikes the snake.

Said of one who wants to force something from another, but without injuring him.

954. மதில்மேல் பூனைபோல.

Like a cat upon the wall.

No one can say which side it will jump. Used about cases in the law courts of which the result is not certain.

955. மெல்லவும் மாட்டாமல், முழுங்கவும் மாட்டாமலிருக்கிறான்

He will not chew it, nor will he swallow it.

He will not tell his secret or sorrow, nor have done with it.

"COUNTING THE CHICKENS BEFORE THEY ARE HATCHED."

956. அக்காடு வெட்டி பருத்தி விதைக்கிறேன் என்றால், அப்பா எனக்கு ஒரு துப்பட்டி என்கிறான் பிள்ளை. அதற்கு அப்பன் கைகால் பட்டுக் கிழியப்போகிறது, மடித்துப் பெட்டியிலே வை என்கிறான்.

If the father says, I will cut down that forest and sow cotton seed; the son replies, Father give me a new cloth. On this the father remarks. It is too long for your legs and hands; it will be torn; fold it up; and put it away in the box! 960, 1282.

A variation of the last clause is: அதற்கு அப்பன் காலிலே மாட்டி கிழிக்கவா என்று கன்னத்தில் அடித்தான். On this the father remarks, What! will you tear it with your feet? and boxes his ears.

The boy takes for granted that the cotton has grown up and been woven. The father takes for granted that the boy has got the cloth. Used of premature and unreasonable requests and hopes.

957. ஊர் உண்டாகியல்லவோ கிழக்கே மேற்கே உண்டாகவேண்டும்.

When you have built the village, then talk of East and West.

"*Don't holloa till you are out of the wood.*"

958. எருமை இருந்தால் அல்லவோ பால் கறக்கவேண்டும்.

When you own a buffalo, then milk it.

959. எருமை வாங்குமுன் நெய்விலை கூறுகிறதா?
Should *ghee* (clarified butter) be offered for sale, before a single buffalo is bought?

"*Don't reckon your eggs before they are laid.*"

960. பருத்திக்கு உழும் முன்னே, தம்பி எட்டுமுழம் என்கிறான்.
Before ploughing in order to plant cotton, the younger brother asks for eight cubits of cotton-cloth. 956, 1269, 1282.

961. பிள்ளை பெற்றுப் பேரிடவேண்டும்.
A name must be given to a child after its birth.

"*Never buy the cradle, till the baby comes.*"

962. மரத்தை வைத்துக்கொண்டு, பழத்தைக் கோரவேண்டும்.
You must plant the tree, before you long for the fruit.

Cf. 2530 *ff.* 2882 *ff.*

MISCELLANEOUS PROVERBS ON DESIRE.

963. அசைவு இருந்தால் விட்டுப் போகமாட்டான்.
As long as there is a bustle, he won't leave. 923, 975, 978, 981.

Thus children keep near when cakes are baking, in hope of getting one. *Cf.* அங்கே அசைவில்லை, There is nothing going on there, I can get nothing there.

964. ஆசை நோவுக்கு அவிழ்தம் ஏது.
There is no antidote for the disease called Desire! 2520.

965. ஆசை பெரிதோ, மலை பெரிதோ?
Is Desire or a mountain the greater? 982.

The *Vishnu Purana* says:—"There is no end of my desires. Though all I hope should come to pass for ten thousand or a hundred thousand years, still new wishes would spring up."

966. ஆசைக்கு அளவில்லை.
Desire has no limits. 965.

"*Ever drunk, ever dry.*"

967. ஆடப் பாடத் தெரியாது, இரண்டு பங்கு உண்டு.
He can neither dance nor sing (*i.e.*, can do nothing), but wants a double share (of the rewards). 977.

968. ஆவல்மாத்திரம் இருந்தால் என்ன, அன்னம் இறங்கினால் அல்லோ பிழைப்பான்.
What avails mere desire? If he swallows rice, he will live.

969. உண்டால் தீருமோ பசி, கண்டால் தீருமோ பசி?
Will seeing food, or eating food, satisfy your hunger? 968.

970. எட்டிப்பழத்தை இச்சிக்கிறதுபோல.
Like wishing to eat poison (*nux vomica*)!

971. கத்தரிக்காய் வாங்கி பூசணிக்காய்க் கொசுறா?
When you buy a brinjal (a small vegetable), will they give you a pumpkin (a big vegetable) into the bargain?

" *The calf is bought and the buffalo demanded into the bargain.*"

972. காமனுக்குக் கண்ட இடத்தில் கண்.
Wherever *Kâman* goes, there is his eye. 828.

The God of love always makes good use of his eyes. Said of one who desires every woman he sees.

973. காமத்துக்குக் கண் இல்லை.
Lust has no eyes.

This means that lust lacks discrimination.

" *Love is blind.*"

974. கால் அணா கொடுக்கிறேன் என்றால், காதவழி நடப்பான்.
If you say, I will give you a quarter-anna coin, he will walk ten miles (to get it).

A quarter-anna is worth about a farthing.

975. சதையுள்ள இடத்தில் கத்தி நாடும்.
The knife seeks the fleshy parts. 963, 978, 981.

Said of avaricious or lustful or even merely greedy persons who know their best friends and get out of them all they can.

976. சந்நியாசி கோவணத்துக்கு இச்சித்துச் சமுசாரம் மேலிட்டதுபோல.
Like the ascetic who was anxious to protect his loin cloth and got a big family!

The story goes that a Sannyâsi bought a cat to protect his clothes from rats; to feed the cat he got a cow; to graze the cow he hired a cowherd; the cowherd soon married and had a number of children; then a famine came, and the Sannyâsi had to keep them all. The story shows how one desire leads to many, each greater than the other.

" *No one is content with his lot.*"

977. துப்புக்கெட்டவளுக்கு (or கெட்டக்கேட்டுக்கு) இரட்டை பரியம்.
A worthless woman demands a double wedding present. 967.

The worthless are often the most importunate.

978. பச்சை கண்டால், ஒட்டு அடி மகளே!
O daughter, if you see green places keep to them! 963, 975, 981.

Stay where there is something to be got. Said also of children, when one of them has some sweets, and the others surround it to get some.

979. பங்கில்லாப் பங்கை விழுந்து அள்ளலாமா?
Should you fall on a share which is not yours and plunder from it?

980. பார்ப்பானுக்கு வாய் போக்காதே, ஆண்டிக்கு அதுதானும் சொல்லாதே.
Do not promise a Brahmin anything, and still less a mendicant. 923, 1934.

Both are proverbially importunate until they get what they think their due. Hence never promise them anything. அவர்களுக்கு வாய் விற்றுப்போடாதே, Don't sell your mouth to them.

" *Three things are insatiable: priests, monks, and the sea.*"

981. பானையில் அரிசி இருந்தால், பார்ப்பான் கண் உறங்காது.
As long as there is rice in the pot, the Brahmin will not sleep. 963, 975, 978.

Said of covetous people who are always trying to get something out of the rich.

982. பிள்ளை பெறப் பெறப் ஆசை, பணம் சேரச் சேர் ஆசை.
The wish is for more and more children, and for more and more money. 965.

Desire increases by being satisfied.

"*The more one has, the more one wants.*"

983. பூனை கொன்ற பாவம் உன்னோடே, வெல்லம் தின்ற பாவம் என்னோடே.
Let the sin of killing the cat be with you, and the sin of eating the sugar with me.

Said by a greedy merchant to a Brahmin priest to whom he brought the cheapest offering that would expiate the sin he had committed in killing a cat, *viz.*, a little image of a cat made of sugar, which he himself swallowed, saying the above words.

984. மன்மதன் அவனை பம்பரம்போல ஆட்டுகிறான்.
The God of Love (*or* Lust) plays with him as with a top.

985. வாணியன் ஆசை கோணியும் கொள்ளாது.
No sack is big enough to hold an oilmonger's avarice!

Cf. 1205 *ff.*

FAT PEOPLE.

தடியன், திடக்காத்திரன், கெண்டன், புஷ்டியுள்ளவன்.

986. அடியும் நுனியும் தரித்த கட்டைபோல.
He is like the trunk of a tree from which the root and top have been cut off.

987. ஆனைபோல மெலிசாயிருக்கிறாய்.
You are as thin an an elephant. (*Ironical.*)

988. எனடி (or என் அடி) பெண்ணே! இளைத்தாய் குதிர்போல.
Why my dear woman! you are as thin as a rice-bin! 987.

Ironical. A rice-bin is a huge clay receptacle for grain.

989. ஐயா கதிர்போல, அம்மாள் குதிர்போல.
The husband is as thin as a spike of corn, the wife is as plump as a rice-bin!

990. கதிர்போல இளைத்துக் குதிர்போல ஆச்சுது.
He was as thin as a spike of corn, but is now like a rice-bin!

991. கழுக்கு மொழுக்கு (prop. மெழுகு) என்று இருக்கிறான்.
He shines like fat and grease.

992. பொத்தைப் பூசணிக்காய்போலிருக்கிறான்.
He is like a big pumpkin.

993. மணலிலே பிடுங்கின வள்ளிக் கிழங்குபோலிருக்கிறான்.
He is round and nice like a white potato (the sweet potato) just pulled up from a sandy soil.
Said of a sleek lazy person.

993a. தலையணைக்கு உறைபோட்டதுபோலிருக்கிறான்.
He is like a well stuffed pillow in a cover.

ON BEING INVOLVED IN TROUBLE FROM WHICH THERE IS NO ESCAPE.

அகப்படுதல், மாட்டப்படுதல், சிக்கப்படுதல், தப்பிப்போகுதல்.

994. உரலிலே தலை மாட்டிக்கொண்டு, உலக்கைக்குப் பயப்பட்டால் தீருமா?
If you fear the rice-pounder after putting your head into the mortar, is that enough to save you?

995. எலி அழுதால் பூனை விடுமா?
If the rat weeps, will the cat let it go?
"*Too late repents the rat, when caught by the cat.*"

996. எமன்கையில் அகப்பட்ட உயிர்போல.
Like a soul fallen into the hands of Death.
i.e., In difficulties from which there is no escape.

997. கழுதைக்கு வாழ்க்கைப்பட்டு, உதைக்கு அஞ்சினால், தீருமா?
If you marry an ass, and then fear its kicking, will that be enough to save you? 3540.
"*To be tied to a sour apple tree.*"

998. காட்டுக்கோழிக்கு உரல் குழியே கைலாசம்.
The inside of a rice-mortar is heaven to a wild-fowl. 1747, 3371.
The fowl that once gets into the rice-mortar can never get out again.

999. தலையை நனைத்து ஆச்சுது, கத்தியும் வைத்து ஆச்சுது.
The head is made wet and the razor is ready. 1028.
Said of a difficulty in which one is caught and from which there is no escape. *e.g.*, If anything is found wrong with the child-bride after the betrothal (நித்திய தாம்பூலம்), the betrothal cannot be undone.

1000. தூண்டிலில் அகப்பட்ட மீன் துள்ளி நத்தினால் விடுவார்களா?
If the fish caught on the hook longs to wriggle off it, will (the fishermen) let it go?

1001. பாம்பின்வாய்த் தேரைபோல.
Like a frog in the mouth of a snake.
"*Like a lump of butter in a dog's mouth.*"

Cf. 873 *ff.*

THE PITCHER THAT GOES OFTEN TO THE WELL WILL BE BROKEN AT LAST.

அகப்படுதல்.

1002. அங்கும் தப்பி, இங்கும் தப்பி, அகப்பட்டுக்கொண்டான் தும்மட்டிப் பட்டன்.
The rogue *Tummattipattan*, who had escaped here and escaped there, was caught after all. 1004.

1003. கெட்டிக்காரன் புளுகு எட்டுநாளையில் தெரியும்.
A cunning man's falsehood will be found out within eight days. 20.
"*Punishment though lame, yet overtakes the sinner at last.*"

1004. பலநாள் திருடன் ஒருநாளைக்கு அகப்படுவான்.
He who has been a thief many days will be caught some day.
"*The old fox is caught at last.*"

NARROW ESCAPES.

தப்பிப்போகுதல்.

1005. எமன் வாயிலிருந்து வந்தது (or மீண்டது) போல.
Like returning from the mouth of Death.
Said of a thing which had been lost, but was recovered, or of an unexpected recovery from sickness.

1006. தாய் வயிற்றில் இரண்டாவது பிறந்ததுபோல.
Like being born a second time in one's own mother's womb. 1007.
Said of a marvellous recovery from a very dangerous illness.

1007. நரி (or எமன்) வாயிலே மண் போட்டாயா?
Did you throw earth into the mouth of the jackals (*or* Death)? 1006.
i.e., Did you disappoint the Jackals? Jackals wait in the burial ground to eat the corpses.

1008. பாம்பு வாயில் புகுந்து தப்பினதுபோல.
Like escaping after getting into the mouth of a snake. 3408.
A marvellous escape.

DECEIVED HOPES, PERPLEXITY.

ஏமாந்துபோகுதல், விழித்தல்.

1009. அணில் ஏறவிட்ட நாய்போல்.
Like the dog that let the squirrel run up a tree.
He could never catch it again.

1010. ஆசைபட்டேன், ஊசிப்போச்சுது.
I wanted it; now it has gone bad. 1178

1011. ஆந்தைபோல் விழிக்கிறது.
To stare like an owl, (*i.e.*, to be perplexed).
Said of one who begins a thing without being able to accomplish it.

1012. ஆனை குட்டி போடும் என்று நம்பி லத்தைப்போட்டதுபோல.
Like expecting an elephant to bring forth a young one, when it only dropped dung. 1014.
Said when one's expectations of some great man's kindness are disappointed.

1013. இஞ்சி தின்ற குரங்கைப்போல.
Like the monkey that had eaten ginger!
i.e., மூஞ்சி சுளித்துக்கொண்டு திரியும், It will go about with a twisted face.

1014. இடுவாள் இடுவாள் என்று எக்கமுற்று இருந்தாளாம்; நாழி கொடுத்து நாலு ஆசையும் தீர்த்தாளாம்.
She was obsequious to her mistress saying 'she will give, she will give.' The mistress satisfied her four desires with a measure of rice. 1012, 1026.
i.e., She got little for all her trouble. The four desires of a Hindu girl are:— ஊண், உடை, பூ, மஞ்சள். Food, dress, flowers and saffron.

1015. இலவு காத்த கிளிபோல.
Like the parrot waiting for the ripening of the pods of the cotton tree.
These pods burst when ripe, and the cotton flies away on the wind, so the parrot gains nothing by waiting for them to mature.

1016. எண்ணின எண்ணம் என்ன அடி, அண்ணு என்று அழைத்த முறை என்ன அடி?
What! My girl, why did you call me your elder brother?
A man was making evil advances to a woman, and she seemed about to yield, but suddenly called him 'elder brother,' which made him say this, meaning that to be her elder brother, was just what he did *not* wish to be. The proverb is used of persons who disappoint one's expectations of them.

1017. ஏறப்படாத மரத்திலே எண்ணுயிரம் காய்.

On the tree that one cannot climb, there are eight thousand fruits. 912, 2128.

Said also as a riddle about the *ragi* (Cynosurus). It is a kind of corn, very short, but with numberless seeds on each head.

"'*Fie upon hens,' quoth the fox, because he could not reach them.*"

1018. ஒருநாளும் சிரிக்காதவன் திருநாளில் சிரித்தான், திருநாளும் வெறு நாளாச்சுது.

One who had never smiled, smiled on a sacred day, and then the sacred day became a common day. *Or better :—*

ஒருநாளுமில்லாமல் திருநாளுக்குப் போனல், திருநாளும் வெறுநாளா ச்சுது.

If a man, who never attended a festival, attends one, the festival day becomes a common day.

Used when something happens at the last moment to prevent one from enjoying what he had expected to enjoy, or when one goes to a show or festival and is disappointed with what he sees.

1019. ஓடி ஓடி உள்ளங்காலும் வெளுத்தது.

I have been running after it so much that the skin has come off my feet.

Great efforts to get something, but disappointment at last.

1020. கம்பளி மூட்டை என்று கரடி மூட்டையை அவிழ்த்தானும்.

It is said that he opened the bundle thinking it was a wool-pack, but it was a bear !

Said of a servant, who thinks his master is careless and lenient, but finds himself disappointed.

"*He has caught a Tartar.*"

1021. கானலை நீர் என்று எண்ணி, மான் ஓடி இளைத்ததுபோல.

Like the deer that was wearied with running after a mirage which it thought was water. 2439.

Thus most people seek satisfaction in things that will only increase their desires. (Luke 12, 16—19.)

1022. கைக்கு எட்டினது, வாய்க்கு எட்டவில்லை.

It reached the hand, but not the mouth.

"*Many a slip t'wixt the cup and the lip.*"

"*A miss is as good as a mile.*"

"*Near dead never helps the kirkyard.*"

1023. கொல்லைக்காட்டு நரி பல்லைக் காட்டினதுபோல.

As a jackal in a grove showed its teeth.

Said of one who is asked to do work, which he knows he is unable to do, and yet will not admit his inability. The jackal in the grove can do no harm, though it appears ready to bite.

1024. திகைப்பூண்டு மிதித்து (com. மொரித்து) திக்குக்கெட்டாற்போல.

He has lost his bearings like one who has trodden on the "*tigai pundu.*"

This plant is said to have the property of confusing the senses of any one who treads on it.

1025. திருடனைத் தேள் கொட்டினதுபோல.

Like the scorpion stinging the thief. 862.

He came to steal, but he trod on a scorpion as he entered the house and had to suffer the terrible agony in silence, lest the household should be aroused and catch him.

1026. பெரிய இடம் என்று பிச்சைக்குப் போனாளாம், கரியை வழித்து முகத்திலே தேய்த்தாளாம் (or தடவினாளாம்).

They say, she went there for alms, thinking it was a rich house, but the mistress of that house blackened her face with charcoal! 388, 1014.

Used of great expectations rudely disappointed.

1027. போனதுபோல வந்தானாம் புது மாப்பிள்ளை.

The new son-in-law came back as he went.

The son-in-law went to the mother-in-law's house for presents after the wedding, but he returned empty-handed. Said of one who begins a work in hope of profit, but is disappointed.

1028. மூன்று அடி அடித்துப் போர்மேல் போட்டு ஆச்சுது.

The corn has been threshed thrice and thrown on the straw-stack. 999.

i.e., The matter is done with. In threshing corn it is supposed that all the corn will be got out of the straw in three beatings. Said of one or by one, who has done everything in his power to bring a law-suit to a successful ending; but has not succeeded.

1029. வெண்ணெய் திரளச்சே தாழி உடைந்ததுபோல.

Like breaking the churn just as the butter was forming.

N B.—*The following eight proverbs differ a little from the above. Their meaning is:—*

THOUGH ONE DOES WHAT ONE OUGHT TO DO, OR PAYS WHAT ONE OUGHT TO PAY, YET THE RESULT IS DISAPPOINTMENT.

1030. அஞ்சு பணம் கொடுத்து, கஞ்சித்தண்ணீர் குடிப்பானேன்?

Why should he pay five coins to get rice-water to drink?

Why pay so much and get so little for it?

1031. உழக்கு மிளகு கொடுப்பானேன், ஒளித்திருந்து மிளகு சாறு குடிப்பானேன்?

Why should he give a measure of pepper and drink the pepper-broth in secret?

A measure (urakku) is a great deal and should supply a great feast with pepper-broth (mulligatanny). If a man supplies so much for a feast he ought to be well served. But if after he has made great preparations, he gets no pleasure for his pains, he may use this proverb. Or, a Hindu lady may save up money secretly, and buy some sovereigns, and take them to the goldsmith to have a jewel made. He may steal some of the gold, and when she gets the jewel and finds out his theft, she may say this proverb meaning that she has got no pleasure in return for all her pains.

1032. கடன் பட்டும் பட்டினியா?

After borrowing money, am I to starve? 1033.

1033. *கலியாணம் செய்தும் சந்நியாசியா?*
Am I to live a bachelor life after getting married? 1032.
Used generally of privileges of which one cannot fully avail himself.

1034. *குத்தக் கூலியும் கொடுத்து, எதிர் மூச்சுப் போடுகிறதா?*
Besides giving wages for pounding, should I also assist in the pounding?
" *What, keep a dog and bark myself.*"

1035. *கொடுக்கிறது கொடுத்து, குஷ்டரோகி காலிலே விழுவானேன்?*
Besides giving him what I can give, shall I fall at the feet of the leper?
e.g., If a good doctor can be had for ten rupees, why pay my ten rupees to a quack?

1036. *கொடுத்தும், கொல்லை வழியாய்ப் போகிறதா?*
If one pays (like others) why should one go away through the back door.

1037. *சீரங்கத்துக்குப் போயும், சொறிதாசன் காலிலே விழுகிறதா?*
Why go to *Sreerangam* and fall at the feet of a man who has skin disease?
Much toil and no profit. *Sreerangam* is a sacred place of the Vaishnava sect near Trichinopoly.

INDIFFERENCE AND CARELESSNESS.

ஏனோதானோ என்றிருத்தல், அக்கறையில்லாமை.

1038. *அதெல்லாம் உண்டிட்டு, வா என்பாள்* (or *ஏப்பம் கொள்வாள்*).
Having taken it all in, she says, Come on again (*or* hiccups). 1041.
Said of a bad wife who has become callous to threats and punishments.

1039. *அரக்கன் ஆண்டால் என்ன, மனிதன் ஆண்டால் என்ன?*
It does not matter who rules, whether a demon or a man.

1040. *அன்று கண்டதை அடுப்பில் போட்டு, ஆக்கின பானையைத் தோளில் போட்டுக்கொண்டு திரிகிறதுபோல்.*
What he gets daily he cooks (and eats) and then puts his pot on his shoulder and wanders about (begging again).

1041. *ஆயிரம் அரைக்கால் பணம்.*
A thousand (kicks) are only one-eighth of a small coin to him. 1038.
Said of a person so hardened to punishment that he thinks nothing of any threats, and of one who is so clever that he fears no task. 'A thousand' means a large number of kicks or some other kind of punishment.

1042. ஆருக்கு வந்ததோ, எவருக்கு வந்ததோ?
To whom did it come, to which person did it come?
This phrase is used by people about matters concerning which they are quite indifferent.

1043. ஆரோ செத்தான், எவனோ அழுதான்?
Some one died, some one else cried.
Said to one or about one who is careless about his duties.

1044. இழவுக்கு வந்தவள் தாலி அறுப்பாளா?
Will a woman take off her *tháli* when she goes to a funeral?
i.e., So long as she is not made a widow, she is indifferent to the sorrow of others.
"*The comforter's head never aches.*"

1045. ஊராரே வாருங்கள், முதுகுநீர் குத்துங்கள்.
Come, village people, and pour water on the back of this woman!
Refers to a family ceremony connected with the first pregnancy of a woman (*seemantham*) performed by the woman's husband's elder or younger sister. The pregnant woman stands bending over a rice mortar, and woman's milk is poured on her back, and some rupees are given for jewelry for the still unborn child. Strangers, of course, have no interest in the ceremony. The saying is used when outsiders are called in to do for a person what his own family should do for him.

1046. எழுத்துக்குப் பால்மாறின கணக்கனும், உடுக்கைக்குப் பால்மாறின (or பல் காட்டின) தாசியும் வருத்தம் அடைவார்கள்.
The accountant who neglects his account, and the prostitute who neglects her dresses (*or* who shows her teeth) will suffer.

1047. காற்றுக்கா மழைக்கா போர்த்துக்கொள்ளத் துணிக்கா?
Is that a cloth to be put on against rain and wind?
Said of the indifference of a man who cares nothing about the blame or abuse he gets; and also about money or goods that are insufficient for some given purpose.

1048. செத்தபின் எப்படி போனாலும் என்ன?
Does it matter how things go after death?

1049. நின்றவரையில் நெடும் சுவர், விழுந்த அன்று குட்டிச் சுவர்.
While it stands, it is a high wall; the day it falls, it is a ruin. 2916.
Said about one who is careless and indifferent as to how he gets on in life. Also said of what has only a temporary value.

1050. பீச்சைகை வாட்டமாய் வைத்திருக்கிறான்.
He has laid it down at his left hand.
Said when one has carelessly forgotten where he left something.

1051. பெண்ணுக்கு ஒரு கும்பிடு, வில்லுக்கு ஒரு கும்பிடு.
One obeisance to the girl and one obeisance to the bow.
Both a girl and a bow are easily bent, but who can trust either? Very little respect should be shown to either.

1052. போன மாட்டைத் தேடுவாருமில்லை, வந்த மாட்டைக் கட்டுவாருமில்லை.

There is no one to seek for the lost cow, and no one to tie it up after its return. 3171.

Said of people who are heedless and careless about their possessions.

1053. வாங்கின கடனைக் கொடுக்கிறதில்லை, கொடுத்த கடனைக் கேட்கிறதில்லை.

He does not give back what he has borrowed, and he does not ask for what others have borrowed from him.

Utterly indifferent concerning all his affairs.

LOVE OF GAIN.

லாபம்.

1054. அற்பத்துக்கு அழகு குலைகிறதா?

Who will let her beauty be destroyed for a trifle?

Only great profit can be a temptation.

1055. ஒன்றுக்கு வாங்கி, எட்டுக்கு விற்றால் லாபமே லாபம்.

If we buy a thing for one rupee and sell it for eight, that will be profit indeed! 1062.

" *He bought the fox-skin for three pence, and sold the tail for a shilling.*"

1056. கணபதி பூசை கைமேலே.

To worship Ganesa is immediate (gain).

1057. கலியாண வீட்டுக்குக் கறி அகப்பை, சாவு வீட்டுக்குச் சோற்று அகப்பை.

He is a ladle for food in the house where there is a wedding, and a ladle for rice in the house where there is a funeral. 1545.

Said of a person who is seen everywhere where something is to be gained.

1058. கூத்தாடி கிழக்கே பார்த்தான், கூலிக்காரன் மேற்கே பார்த்தான்.

The dancer watched the east (to see if the sun was rising so that he might get his pay and go home); the labourer looked towards the west (to see when the sun would set, that he might get his pay and go home).

1059. கூலிப் படை வெட்டுமோ?

Will a hired army fight? 1077.

Mercenaries are indifferent to their work, and care only for their pay.

1060. கெண்டையைப் போட்டு விராலை இழுக்கிறது.

To use a small fish to hook a big one. 2734.

Used about the custom, so common in India, of making presents to influential people in order to secure their patronage. For the converse see 2003.

" *Throw in a sprat and catch a salmon.*"

1061. கைமேலே கண்ட பலன்.

Profit seen on your hand.

Sure profit.

1062. கொண்டபடி விற்றால், கோடி லாபம்.

If you sell things at the price you bought them, you will make ten millions. 1055.

Honesty is the best policy.

1063. பந்திக்கு முந்திக்கொள், படைக்குப் பிந்திக்கொள்.

Be first for food and be last for war.

Be the first to seek profit, and the last to incur loss.

1064. பார்ப்பாத்தி அம்மா, மாடு வந்தது, பார்த்துக்கொள்.

O! Brahmin woman, the cow has come; look after it now! 1067.

The cow-herd shouts this when, after herding the village cows on the grazing grounds during the day, he brings them back in the evening and leaves each cow at its owner's house. Said of one who has no interest in his work, and only wants to get his wages.

1065. பையனுக்கு என்ன வரும்? எனக்கு மாசம் இரண்டு சின்ன பணம் வரும்!

(I don't care) what happens to the boy so long as I get my monthly fees (*lit.* two little *panams*).

Put into the mouth of the typical village-schoolmaster whose one aim is to keep his own body and soul together.

1066. பொதி அளக்கிறதற்கு முன்னே, சத்தத்திற்கு அளக்கிறதா?

Is the hire to be paid before the load has been measured out?

Is the cooly's hire to be paid before the load that he has to carry is determined?

1067. மாடு மேய்த்தானும், கோலைப் போட்டானும்.

They say he herded the cows, and then threw down his stick. 1064.

i.e., He minded his work only just as long as he was forced to, but took no interest in it, and left it as soon as he could.

1068. மார் அடித்த கூலி மடிமேலே.

Their hire for beating their breasts is in their laps.

Or கூலிக்கு மார் அடிக்கிறது.

To beat one's breast for hire.

The reference is to mourners who come to the house of mourning for what they can get.

1069. முப்பது நாளே போ, பூ வராகனே வா!

Let the thirty days of the month go, and let my gold *varâkan* come.

Said of one who does his work for money's sake only. A *varâkan* is a coin worth three and a half rupees.

Cf. 341 *ff.* 2732 *ff.*

WEALTH.

பணம்.

1070. *ஈட்டி எட்டு முழம் பாயும், பணம் பாதாளம்வரைக்கும் பாயும்.*
A spear will reach for eight cubits, but money will reach down to Hades (*Pâtâla*).
"*An ass laden with gold overtakes anything.*"

1071. *உறவுக்கும் பகைக்கும் பொருளே காரணம்.*
Wealth is the cause of both friendship and hatred.

1072. *எட்டினமட்டும் வெட்டும் கத்தி, எட்டாத மட்டும் வெட்டும் பணம்.*
A knife will cut as far as it can reach, but money cuts where it cannot reach.
The power of money has no limit.

1073. *கம்பளி விற்ற பணத்துக்கு மயிர் முளைத்திருக்கிறதா?*
Has hair grown on the money made by selling blankets?
As blankets are made of animal hair Hindus think the trade contemptible. But no one thinks the profits mado in the trade contemptible. Money is good no matter how it is gained; the great thing is to get it. This proverb and 1074, 1075, 1076 and 1082 are alike.

1074. *கரி விற்ற பணம் கறுப்பாயிருக்குமா?*
Will the money acquired by selling charcoal be black?

1075. *கிழவன் கொடுத்த பணத்துக்கு நரை உண்டா?*
Will the money given by an old man have grey hair?

1076. *நாய் விற்ற காசு குலைக்குமா?*
Will the money got by selling a dog bark?
"*Money is welcome though it comes in a dirty cloth.*"

1077. *பணம் உண்டானால், படையையும் வெல்லுவான்.*
If one has money, one can conquer an army. 1059.
"*All things are obedient to money.*"

1078. *பணக்காரன் பின்னும் பத்துப்பேர், பைத்தியக்காரன் பின்னும் பத்துப் பேர்.*
Ten persons run after a rich man, and ten after a mad man.

1079. *பணமில்லாதவன் பிணம்.*
He who has no money is a corpse.
"*A man without money is a bow without an arrow.*"

1080. *பணம் என்றால், பிணமும் வாய் திறக்கும்.*
If you say 'money,' even a corpse will open its mouth!
A sarcastic description of the power of money.

1081. பணம் என்றால், பேயாய்ப் பறக்கிறது.
If you say 'money', he will fly like the devil.

1082. வேப்பெண்ணெய் விற்ற காசு கசக்குமா?
Will the money acquired by selling *Margosa* oil be bitter?

The oil of the *Margosa* or *Neem* tree is very bitter, but that does not affect the acceptability of the profits made by selling it.

Cf. 2732 *ff.*

DEBT.

கடன்.

INDIFFERENCE TO DEBT.

1083. ஆறும் கடன், நூறும் கடன் பெருக்கச், சுடு அடா, பணிகாரத்தை.
Let the debt increase six fold or a hundred fold, but fry the cakes, fellow!

" *He has a hole under his nose that all his money runs into.*"

1084. கடனோடு கடன் (or செலவோடு செலவு) கந்தப்பொடி காற்பணம்.
Though the debt increase, I must have a quarter of a *panam's* worth of scented powder.

1085. கடனோடு கடனாகிறது, அண்டைவீட்டின்மேலே சீட்டு ஆகிறது, பிள்ளைக்குக் கலியாணம் பண்ணு.
Though the debt increase and you give a promissory note on your neighbour's house (which is not yours), your son must be married! 3514.

When parents are considering about the expenses of their son's wedding, this is their decision. Debts of this kind are one of the great curses of Indian thrift. 904.

1086. நூறோடு நூறாகிறது, நெய்யிலே சுடு அடி பணிகாரம்.
Let the debt increase by hundreds, but let me have my cake baked in *ghee*.

Ghee is clarified butter. Oil made from sesamum seed is generally used. *Ghee* is an extravagance for the poor and poorer middle classes.

BORROWING AND LENDING EASY; REPAYMENT DIFFICULT.

1087. ஆட்டுக்கறியும் நெல்லுச்சோறும் தம்மா கும்மா, அந்தக் கடன் கேட்கப் போனால் இயா மிய்யா!
They enjoy the mutton and rice (obtained with borrowed money), but if you ask them to pay what they owe, they blink their eyes.

" *He that doth lend, doth lose his friend.*"

1088. *ஆர் கடன் வைத்தாலும், மாரி கடன் வைக்கக்கூடாது.*

Though you do not pay your debt to others, you must pay your debt to the goddess *Mâri.*

Mâri is a form of the goddess Durga who sends small-pox. The meaning is that a powerful creditor is not to be trifled with.

1089. இருந்து பணம் கொடுத்து நடந்து வாங்கவேண்டியது.

He who sits down to lend money, will have to walk to get it back again.

" *Scrape and pare, and thou shalt have ; lend and trust, and thou shalt crave.*"

1090. இரவல் உடைமை இசைவாயிருக்கிறது, என் பிள்ளை ஆணை, நான் கொடுக்கமாட்டேன்.

Borrowed property is pleasant, therefore I swear on my child, I will not return it.

"*Trust nor contend, nor lay wagers, nor lend; and you'll have peace to your end.*"

1091. உடைமையும் கொடுத்து, அருமையும் குலைகிறது.

To lend your property is to have your name ruined.

"*When I lent I was a friend ; when I asked I was unkind.*"

1092. உரலும் கொடுத்து, குரலும் போகவேண்டும்.

If you lend your rice-mortar, you will lose your voice (in asking for its return).

1093. உறிப்பணம் (or மடிப்பணம்) போய் தெருச சண்டையை இழுக்கிறது.

My savings have gone and brought on a street quarrel.

Lending money is easy : getting it back is often the cause of much strife.

" *Money lent, an enemy made.*"

1094. கொடுத்ததுக் கேட்டால், அடுத்ததும் பகை.

If you ask for what you have lent, your neighbour will hate you.

" *If you would make an enemy, lend a man money, and ask it of him again.*"

1095. கொடுத்து நிஷ்டூரம் படுவதைவிட, கொடாமல் நிஷ்டூரம் படுவதே மேல்.

Better suffer the pain of refusing to lend, than suffer the pain of lending. 919.

" *He that trusteth not is not deceived.*"

1096. பட்டுப்புடவை இரவல் கொடுத்து, மணை தூக்கிக்கொண்டு அலைய வேண்டியாச்சுது.

After lending a silk cloth (*pattuppudurei*) you must follow the borrower everywhere with a seat.

The *pattuppuduvei* is a long piece of silk worn by women as an outer dress. If the lender does not watch, the borrower will soil the garment she has borrowed by sitting on the ground while wearing it. The proverb is a warning against lending to persons who neglect their liabilities.

1097. பணத்தைக் கொடுக்கச் சொல்லி உயிரை வாங்குகிறது.
He kills me by asking me to return the money. 2714.

"He that fast spendeth must needs borrow; but when he must pay again, it is all sorrow."

1098. முள்ளுமேல் சீலை போட்டால், மெள்ள மெள்ள வாங்குகிற வழியா யல்லவோ? (or வாங்கவேண்டும்).
If a cloth be spread on a thorny bush, it must be taken off very carefully. 3133.

If anything is lent to a mean person, it can only be recovered by great forbearance. The proverb is also a warning against friendship with mean people.

1099. வாங்கிறபோது ஒரு பிள்ளை பெற்றதுபோல, கொடுக்கிறபோது ஒரு பிள்ளை செத்ததுபோல.
Borrowing is like the birth of a son, returning what has been borrowed is like the death of a son.

In India the birth of a son is welcomed with the highest possible joy, and the death of a son is the most terrible loss that an Indian father can experience.

1100. வாங்கிறதைப்போலிருக்கவேண்டும் கொடுக்கிறதும்.
Returning what has been borrowed should be like borrowing it!

In both cases cheerfulness is desirable.

"He that goes a borrowing, goes a sorrowing."

MISCELLANEOUS PROVERBS ON DEBT.

1101. அண்டைவீட்டுக் கடனும் பிட்டத்துச் சிரங்கும் (or அரையிலே புண்ணும் or இடுப்பிலே புண்ணும்) ஆகாது.
Being in debt to a neighbour and itch on one's breech ought not to be. 1106, 2310.

1102. அவன் உள்ளெல்லாம் புண், உடம்பெல்லாம் கொப்புளம்.
His inside is full of sores and his body is covered with blisters.

"He is head and ears in debt."

1103. இரவல் துணியாம், இரவல் துட்டாம், இழுத்துக்கொட்டு மேளத்தை, இறுக்கிக்கட்டு தாலியை.
They say the wedding-dress and the money (to perform the wedding) were borrowed; beat the drum loudly and tie the *thāli* securely!

1104. இரவற் சோறு பஞ்சம் தாங்குமா?
Can borrowed rice ward off famine?

1105. உப்புசட்டி வறையோடும் விற்றுக் கடனைக் கொடுத்துவிட்டான்.
He has sold his salt-pot and potsherds to clear his debt.

He has had to sell all he had. A very common proverb.

1106. உள்வீட்டுக் கடனும், உள்ளங்கைச் சிரங்கும் கெட்டது.
A debt at home, and itch in your palm are alike bad. 1101.

1107. எழுதாக் கடனுக்கு அழுதால் தீருமா?

If one weeps about what has been lent without a receipt, will that do any good? 1111.

1108. கன்றுக்குட்டிக் கிட்டவும், கடன்காரன் கிட்டவும் இருக்கப்படாது.

Do not stay near a calf or a creditor.

If you go near them the calf will lick you and the creditor will ask for his money.

"*Creditors have better memories than debtors.*"

1109. கடனில்லாத கஞ்சி கால்வயிறு.

To be without debt fills a quarter of the stomach.

"*Without debt, without care.*"

"*Rather go to bed supperless, than rise in debt.*"

"*Poverty without debt is independence.*"

1110. சில்லறைக் கடன் சீர் அழிக்கும்.

Small debts destroy dignity (*or* honour).

1111. சீட்டு நாட்டில்லாத கடனுக்கு அழுதாலும் தீருமா?

If you weep for what you have lent without getting the borrower's mark to the receipt, will that do any good? 1107.

1112. தேய்ந்த அம்மாள் தெய்வயானை, தெய்வத்துக்கு இட்டாலும் ஏறாது.

The woman who is afraid of her things wearing out is called a god-elephant, but if she offers gifts to the gods, they will not accept her gifts.

Said by women chiefly about a well-to-do woman, who is so stingy, that she is afraid to lend her jewels to anybody, lest they should suffer a little by being handled.

1113. நான் சாப்பிட்டது சாப்பாடல்ல, பீ!

The food I have eaten is not food, it is filth! 1114.

So says a man who regrets that he has not been able to pay off his debts.

"*Debt is the worst poverty.*"

1114. நான் உங்கள் கடன் தீர்க்கிறவரையில், நான் சாப்பிடுகிற சாப்பாடு சாப்பாடல்ல, பீ!

Until I have cleared off my debts to you, what I eat will not be food, but filth. 1113.

"*A pound of care will not pay an ounce of debt.*"

1115. பாகை சொந்தம், மற்றதெல்லாம் இரவல்.

The turban is his own, the rest is borrowed.

Said of a bridegroom who had borrowed all his clothes, except his turban. In India even rich people will borrow jewels, &c., for great occasions.

1116. வெட்கத்துக்கு அஞ்சினவன், கடனுக்கு அஞ்சுவான்.

He who fears shame, will fear debt.

1117. கடன்வாங்கிச் செலவு செய்தவனும், மரம் ஏறிக் கைவிட்டவனும் சரி.

He who borrows and spends, and he who climbs a tree and lets go his hold, are alike.

LAZY PEOPLE.

சோம்பேறி.

1118. அசைப்புக்கு (or அடிக்கு) ஆயிரம் பொன் வாங்குவாளா? (or வேண்டுமா?)

Will she get a thousand gold-pieces for each movement (*or* step)? 1133.

Applied to a lazy and unreasonable man, or to a dancing-girl who will not dance unless well paid.

1119. அம்பலம் வேகுது (வேகுகிறது).

The rest-house is on fire!

1120. அதைத்தான் சொல்லுவானேன்? வாயைத்தான் நோவானேன்.

Why should he say so? Why pain his mouth by saying so? 3084.

1121. சந்தை இரைச்சலிலே குடியிருந்து கெட்டேனே.

I lived in the midst of the market-noise and was ruined.

The story runs that three exceedingly lazy fellows permanently took up their abode in a public rest-house. The owner of the *chattiram* was anxious to get rid of them, but seeing them disinclined to go, he set fire to the *chattiram.* When the men perceived this, the one who was a "half lazy" said the first of the above three sayings. The one who was "three quarters lazy" did not like the remark and quoted the second, and the third man, who was "fully lazy" got very angry over the disturbance caused by the remarks of his two companions and used the third saying. The sayings are used as striking examples of laziness.

"*As lazy as Ludlam's dog, that leaned his head against the wall to bark.*"

1122. அவளுக்கு இவள் எழுந்திருந்து உண்பாள்.

Compared with her, this woman sits up eating!

The story is that the first wife of a certain man was so lazy that she would lie down to eat her food; and his second wife was a little better than the first, for she sat up to eat.

Used of improved circumstances as well as of laziness.

1123. அறுக்கமாட்டாதவன் இடுப்பிலே ஐம்பத்தெட்டு அரிவாள்.

He who is unable to reap, carries fifty-eight sickles at his side.

1124. இராப்பட்டினி கிடந்தவன் உரித்த வாழைப்பழம் விற்கிறதா என்று விசாரித்தானாம்?

The man who had starved all night asked, if *peeled* plantains (bananas) were for sale? 1137.

Though very hungry, he was too lazy to peel the fruit.

1125. இருந்த கால் மூதேவி, நடந்த கால் சீதேவி.

Mu Devi is in the legs of an inactive person, and *Sree Devi* in the legs of an active man. 1126, 1141.

Mu Devi is the goddess of ill-luck, the elder sister of *Sree Devi* (Lakshmi) the goddess of good fortune.

1126. இருந்தவன் எழுந்திருக்கிறதற்குள்ளே, நின்றவன் நெடும் தூரம்.
While the lazy man was getting up; the man on his feet had already walked a long distance. 1125, 1141.

" *Lost time is never found again.*"

1127. உத்தியோகம் தடபுடல், சேவிக்கிறவர்கள் இன்னாரினியார் என்றில்லை, சம்பளம் கணக்கு வழக்கில்லை, குண்டையை விற்று நாலு வராகன் அனுப்பச்சொல்லு.
My employment gives me no rest; I am unable to say who my masters are (for I have many); my salary is unsettled; tell our people to sell their bullocks and to send me about fifteen rupees.

Thus writes a self-important young man, one of the many who leave their villages and go to Madras to try their luck and find that hard work is essential.

1128. உழுகிற நாளில் ஊருக்குப் போய், அறுக்கிற நாளில் அரிவாள் கொண்டு வந்ததுபோல.
During the ploughing season he went about paying visits, but returned at harvest time with his sickle (ready to reap the harvest for which he had not toiled). 1322.

1129. உனக்கு முதுகு வளைகிறதா?
Will your back bend?

i.e., Are you willing to work? Said to a lazy person, உடம்பு வளையாதவன், one who will not bend his body.

1130. உன்னை அடித்துப்போட்டால், பத்து காணிக்கு எருவு போடலாம்.
If I kill you, you may make manure for ten acres of land.

Said sarcastically to a strong healthy man, who goes about begging.

1131. எனக்குக் கொடுக்கிறதைக் கொடுத்தால், நான் போகிறேன்.
If you give me what you usually give, then I will go! 1911.

Put into the mouth of a lazy person who has got so used to rebukes and blows that he will do nothing unless they are first applied. e.g. Used of children who will not go to school unless compelled.

1131*a*. கஞ்சி கண்ட இடம் கைலாசம், சோறு கண்ட இடம் சுவர்க்கம்.
Whatever place gives him rice-gruel is his *Kailasa*, and whatever place gives him rice and curry is his *Swerga*.

Kailasa is Siva's heaven, and *Swerga* is Indra's.

1132. கண்ட இடம் கைலாசம்.
Whatever place he goes to, is heaven (*Kailasa*) to him. 1135, 1136, 1138.

i.e., He will make himself at home anywhere.

1133. கால் நடைக்கு இரண்டு காசு, கை வீச்சுக்கு ஐந்து காசு.
Two copper coins for walking on foot, and five for swinging the arms! 1118.

Said in ridicule of a lazy and unreasonable person.

1134. குந்தி (or இருந்து) தின்றால், குன்றும் மாளும்.
If one sits eating, a mountain will be destroyed. 1887.

A man who will not work because he is rich, will soon see his property lessened.

"*His thrift waxeth thin that spendeth more than he doth win.*"

1135. சத்திரத்திலே சாப்பாடு, மண்டபத்திலே படுக்கை.
He gets his food in a *Chattram*, and sleeps in a *Mantapam*. 1132, 1136, 1138.

A *Chattram* or *Choultry* is a public rest-house. Food is often given away freely at such places by pious Hindus. A *Mantapam* is a sort of portico to a temple. The proverb describes a lazy vagabond.

1136. சோறு அகப்பட்ட இடம் சுகம்.
There is comfort where there is rice. 1132, 1135, 1138.

Applied to people, who attend weddings and festivals to get something at the feasts.

1137. சோம்பேறிக்கு வாழைப்பழம் தோலோடே.
A lazy man eats plantains (bananas) with their skins on. 1124.

He won't take the trouble to peel them, though it is so easily done.

1138. பொழுதுபட்ட இடம், விடுதி (or தங்கும் இடம்) விட்ட இடம்.
Where the sun sets, there is his lodging. 1132, 1135, 1136.

Said of a person full of excuses for remaining where he finds comforts.

1138*a*. பட்ட (விழுந்த) இடம்பொழுது, விட்ட இடம் விடுதி.
Where he fell down he remains lying the whole day, and the place given him for rest, he claims as his permanent place.

A more common form of 1138.

1139. மாதம் காதவழி மானாகப் பறப்பான்.
He will fly ten miles like a deer—in one month!

An ironical description of a lazy man's activity.

1140. மூலை வீட்டிலே முட்டை இடுகிறான்.
He is laying eggs in a corner of the house!

Sarcastic description of a lazy man's sloth.

1141. நடந்தால் நாடு எல்லாம் உறவு, படுத்தால் பாயும் பகை.
If you walk, the whole country is your friend; if you lie down, even your mat (bed) will hate you. 1125, 1126.

A lazy man has few friends; an active man can get on any where.

1142. வெந்த சோற்றைத் தின்று, விதி வந்தால் சாகிறது.
Eating his food when it is cooked, dying when his fate arrives.

1143. வெந்ததைத் தின்று, வந்ததை உளறுகிறது.
Eating what is cooked, and clamouring about what happens.

Said by the wage-earner about those who sit at home doing nothing beyond eating, chatting and sleeping,—the women inside the house, the men on the verandah.

FOOD, EATING.

சாப்பாடு.

SLOW TO WORK, QUICK TO EAT.

1144. உண்ணப் படை உண்டு, வெல்லப் படையில்லை.

There is an army of people to eat, but no army to conquer with. 1402.

There is no one to work and earn anything for the support of the family.

1145. உழவுக்கு ஒரு சுற்றும் வராது, ஊணுக்குப் பம்பரம்.

At ploughing he will not plough a furrow, but he will dance like a top for food.

" *He eats till he sweats, and works till he freezes.*"

1146. கப்பி (or கொள்ளு) என்றால் வாய் திறக்கும், கடிவாளம் என்றால் வாய் மூடிக்கொள்ளும்.

If you say 'Grain,' his mouth opens; if you say 'Bridle,' his mouth is shut.

" *He deserves not sweet, that will not taste of sour.*"

1147. கொட்டிக் கிழங்கு பறிக்கச்சொன்னால் கோபித்துக்கொள்வார் பண்டாரம், அவித்து உரித்து முன்னே வைத்தால் அமுதுகொள்வார் பண்டாரம்.

If they say 'Go and dig up potatoes,' the mendicant is angry; but if the potatoes are boiled and peeled and set before him, he will devour them. 2736.

" *Spread the table and contention will cease.*"

1148. தீண்டிக்கு அவசரம், வேலைக்கு ஒளிப்பு (or சாக்கு).

There is haste to eat, but an excuse (for escaping) work.

1149. தெண்டச் சோற்றுக்காரா, குண்டு போட்டு வா அடா! (or தின்று போட்டுப் போ!)

O, Thou sluggard, come for food when the gun is fired.

The evening gun is fired in Madras at eight o'clock in the evening. Said of a lazy fellow in a family who earns nothing, but never forgets the meal-time and is impatient for his meals.

1150. பருப்பு சோற்றுக்குப் பத்து (com. பதிங்) காதம் போவான்.

He will go a hundred miles to get *dhall*!

Dhall is a luxurious dish.

HUNGER IS THE BEST SAUCE.

1151. குடல் காய்ந்தால், குதிரையும் வைக்கோல் தின்னும்.
When its bowels are dry with hunger, a horse will eat straw.
"*A hungry ass eats any straw.*"

1152. பசி ருசி அறியாது, நித்திரை சுகம் அறியாது.
Hunger is indifferent to flavour, sleep is indifferent to comforts.
Hunger and weariness make a man indifferent to trifles.

1153. பசிக்குக் கறி வேண்டாம், தூக்கத்துக்குப் பாய் வேண்டாம்.
Hunger needs not spices, sleep needs not a mat. 1152.

GOOD FOOD.

1154. இந்தச் சிற்றுண்டி எனக்குத் தெவிட்டிப்போச்சுது.
This pastry nauseates me.
"*He digs his grave with his teeth.*"
"*That is not always good in the man, that is sweet in the mouth.*"

1155. அன்று சாப்பிட்ட சாப்பாடு, இன்னம் ஆறு மாசத்துக்குத் தாங்கும்.
The food I ate that day will help me over six months. 1914.
Said in praise of a lady for the good food she prepares. If it is used interrogatively it means, 'Will what you gave me help me for six months?' *i.e.*, It will be of little use to me! It is also used ironically.

1156. ஆடி (மாசம்) பழஞ்சோறும், ஆதண்டங்காய் வற்றலும் தேடித் தின்றவனுக்குத் தெய்வலோகம் கிடைக்கும்.
He who seeks and eats cold rice with dried *áthandan* fruit in the hot weather (*lit.* the month *Adi*) will gain heaven.
This dish is a very suitable one for the hot season, and also very palatable.

1157. இறுக்கறியோ, புறுக்கறியோ?
Is it prawn curry, or is it pigeon curry? 1160.
Prawn curry and pigeon curry are both rich.

1158. நித்தியம் கிடைக்குமா அமாவாசைப் பருக்கை?
Will rice (such as is eaten) at the New Moon Festival come every day?
Hindus eat only one meal on the day of the New Moon, and it is therefore a good one.
"*Angels visits, few and far between.*"

1159. பொன்னங்கண்ணிக்குப் புளிவிட்டு ஆக்கினால், உண்ணாப் பெண்ணும் ஒரு உழக்கு உண்ணும்.
If tamarind is added in cooking the *Ponnang kanni* vegetable, even a woman who eats nothing will eat very much.
Tamarind is a favourite condiment and the vegetable is pleasant. The two together make a very rich dish.

1160. மீன் குழம்போ, தேன் குழம்போ?
Is it fish sauce, or is it honey sauce? 1157.

GLUTTONY.

1161. இருக்கிற அன்றைக்கு எருமை மாடு தின்றாற்போல.
The day he has something to eat, it is as if a buffalo was feeding.

1162. இரை முழுங்கின பாம்புபோல.
Like a snake that has just swallowed its food.

1163. உப்பில்லாமல் ஒரு மிடாக் கஞ்சி குடிப்பான் (or எனதல்லவென்று குடிப்பான்).
He will swallow a huge pot full of rice, without any salt (*or* saying, It is not mine)!

1164. உப்பைத் தொட்டுக்கொண்டு உரலை முழுங்குவான்.
He touches his lips with salt and swallows a big rice-mortar!

A great glutton. Also said of one who wants to make great profits with slight exertion.

1165. ஊசிபோல தொண்டையும், சாலுபோல வயிறும்.
He has a throat like a needle, and a stomach as big as a washerman's pot.

Said of one who pretends to be able to eat a little only, but is found to have an enormous appetite.

1166. ஊறுகாயைக் கடித்துக்கொண்டு ஒரு பானைச் சோற்றை எனதல்ல என்பான்.
He will swallow a pot full of rice with a little chutney, saying, It is not mine!

1167. காய்ந்த மாடு கம்பிலே விழுந்தாற்போல.
Like a starving cow getting into a corn-field.

A glutton's appetite.

1168. கோட்டுச் சம்பா ஆக்கிவைத்தால், போட்டுச் சாப்பிட வருவார்கள்.
If I prepare rice and set it before them, they will come and swallow it up. 2736.

Said in sarcasm on those who are ready to eat, but unwilling to work. The கோட்டுச்சம்பா is fresh threashed rice, which has a sweet taste.

1169. சலிப்போடு சம்மந்தி இழுத்தால், ஏழு இலை.
If a man who feigns unwillingness to join in a meal, is induced to partake of it, he will eat seven helpings (*lit.* leaf-plates full) of rice. 1177.

" *Do as the maids do, say no, and take it!* "
" *I don't want it, I don't want it, but put it into my hood.*"

1170. சோற்றுக்குக் கேடு, பூமிக்குப் பாரம்!
He is the ruin of food, and a burden to the earth!

A useless person who is a burden to all.
" *He is not worth his salt.*"

1171. நீக்குப் போக்குக் கெட்டவனுக்குத் தொண்டைமட்டும் வாயும் வயிறும்.
A person that is without modesty has a stomach and mouth that meet at his throat.

" *To have a belly up to one's mouth.*"

WHERE THERE IS MUCH TO TAKE CARE OF, A LITTLE IS NOT MISSED.

1172. கிணற்றுத் தவளை தண்ணீர் குடித்ததைக் கண்டது யார், குடியாததைக் கண்டது யார்?

Who has seen a frog in a well drink water, and who has seen it not drinking?

Often said of a man and a woman who live by themselves in the same house. Everybody believes that they treat each other as man and wife, though no one has any proof.

1173. குளம் காக்கிறவன் தண்ணீரைக் குடியானோ?

Will not he who guards the tank drink from it?

"*He who manages other people's wealth, does not go supperless to bed.*"

1174. தேனை வழிக்கிறவன் புறங்கையை நக்கமாட்டானோ?

Will not he who gathers honey lick the back of his hand?

"*He guides the honey ill, that may not lick his fill.*"

1175. பசு உழுதாலும், பயிரைத் தின்ன ஒட்டான்.

Though the cow plough, its owner will not allow it to eat the crop.

The cow is held sacred by the Hindus, and should never be used for ploughing; bnt this man yokes it and gives it nothing to eat.

1176. போர் மெரிக்கிற மாடு, வைக்கோல் தின்னாதா?

Will not the bullock that treads the stack eat the straw?

"*He is a poor cook who cannot lick his own fingers.*"

MISCELLANEOUS PROVERBS ABOUT FOOD AND EATING.

சாப்பாடு.

1177. உண்ணும் வயிற்றை ஒளிக்கிறதா?

Why hide a stomach which wants food? 1169.

Applied to one who, from a false feeling of modesty, refuses to take what he is longing for.

"*Never be ashamed to eat your meat.*"

1178. ஆசைப்பட்ட பண்டம் ஊசிப்போச்சுது.

The cakes I had hoped to enjoy have been spoiled. 1010.

1179. என்ன தின்றாலும், அதற்குமேலே நாலு பேரீச்சம் பழம் தின்ன, எல்லாம் அடிபடும் (or செரிக்கும்).

Whatever you eat, if you also eat four dates, all will be digested.

1180. என்ன அடா, ஒன்று ஒன்றாய் குருவிபோல கொறிக்கிறாய்.

Why, you pick up your food like a bird, a grain at a time.

i.e., You take too little in your hand at a time; fill your hand with rice and eat well. Food is eaten in India without the aid of knives, forks, and spoons.

1181. குத்துப்பட்டுப் பொறுத்தாலும், குறை வயிறு பொறுக்குமா?

Though you may bear a blow, can you endure a stomach only half filled? 1189.

1182. கூழுக்குக் கொறடா மிளகாய்.

Chillies (*Capsicum frutescens*,) serve as whips to make one eat gruel.

The hot taste of the chilli is a stimulus to the appetite.

1183. கூழ் என்றாலும், குடிக்கிறவன் பிழைப்பான்.

Although it is called 'gruel,' he who drinks it will live. 1725.

A person can at least sustain life on the poorest food.

"*Half a loaf is better than no bread.*"

1184. சோற்றால் அடித்த சுவர்.

(Man's body) is a wall built of rice.

The body cannot exist without food.

1185. ஜாணோ வயிறு, சரீரம் எல்லாம் வயிறா?

Is not the stomach only one span? Is the whole body stomach?

Why is there so much falsehood and deceit in this world merely to provide the stomach with good things?

1186. ஞானமும் கல்வியும் நாழி அரிசியிலே.

Wisdom and learning are both in a measure of rice.

Food is essential if knowledge is to be gained.

1187. தின்ற சோறு உடம்பிலே ஒட்டவில்லை.

The food I eat does not stick to me.

Said when sickness or sorrow makes food loathsome.

1188. தின்கிறதைத் தின்றும், தேவாங்கு ஆட்டமாயிருக்கிறான்.

Though he eats well, he is still like the thin sloth.

"*He is nothing but skin and bones.*"

1189. முதுகிலே அடித்தால் ஆறும், வயிற்றில் அடித்தால் ஆறுமா?

If one is beaten on his back, it will heal; if beaten on the stomach, it will not heal. 1181.

Said when too little to eat or too little salary is given.

1190. மறு சாதம் போட்டுக்கொள்ளாதவன் மாட்டுப் பிறப்பு.

He who will not receive rice the second time it is passed round, is born a bullock.

The distributer says this to the guests. It is thought to be bad manners not to take a second helping.

COMFORT, EASE, LUXURY.

சுகம், வாழ்வு.

1191. உத்தியோகத்துக்கு தக்க சுகம்.

One's comforts must be suited to one's business in life.

1192. எடுப்பாரும் பிடிப்பாரும் உண்டானால், இளைப்பும் தவிர்ப்பும் உண்டாகும்.

If you have servants to take and fetch, you will be weary and fatigued.

Luxury leads to enervation.

1193. என்ன அடா, தாதா? புரட்டாசி மாசம் முப்பதும் ஒரு கந்தாயம் (or லாபம்).

(If you say) O, Vaishnava mendicant what is the matter? (He says) The thirty days of *Purattasi* are days of profit to me! 258.

Purattasi is the month August—September in which Vaishnavas are specially liberal to all mendicants.

1194. குதிரை குருடானாலும், கொள்ளு தின்கிறதில் குறையா?

Though the horse be blind, will it eat less gram?

Though a person be worthless, he will expect his food and comforts like anybody else.

"*A bad horse eats as much as a good one.*"

1195. சுகம் கெட்டால் விரதம் தக்கவேண்டும், விரதம் கெட்டால் சுகம் தக்கவேண்டும்.

If your worldly comfort fails, asceticism is the right thing (to seek to attain); if asceticism is of no avail, worldly comfort is to be sought.

Speaking generally, Hinduism rejects the idea of the possibility of combining the pursuit of temporal and spiritual prosperity.

"*If you can be happy without health, you may be happy without virtue.*"

1196. ஜெகத்தைக் கொடுத்தும் சுகத்தை வாங்கிக்கொள்.

Even if you have to give the world for it, acquire prosperity. 2251, 2449.

Here 'prosperity' may be translated 'spiritual welfare.'

1197. திருநாளுக்குப் போகிறாயா என்றால் ஆம், ஆம் (*said quickly and joyfully*), திரும்பி வருகிறாயா என்றால் உம், உம்! (*said slowly and sadly*).

If we ask anyone if he is going to a festival, he will say, "yes, yes" (with joy). If we ask if he is returning, he will say, "um, um" (with sorrow).

People are happy when entering on a new delight but after enjoying it disgust arises.

1198. நாய் கெட்ட கேட்டுக்குத் தேங்காய்ப் பாலும் சோறுமா?
Does the wretch of a dog crave for cocoanut milk and rice? 636.
Hankering after comforts above one's position.

1199. நோவற்ற வாழ்வே வாழ்வு, குறைவற்ற செல்வமே செல்வம்.
Prosperity without pain is prosperity, and wealth without lack is wealth.
"*It is a fortunate head that never ached.*"

1200. பசியில்லாதவனுக்குக் கருப்பு மயிருக்குச் சமானம்.
To a person never hungry, famine is like hair.
i.e., It is not worth his notice.

1201. பள்ளத்திலே இருக்கிறவன், பள்ளத்திலே இருப்பானா?
Will a person in a valley always remain there? 87.
"*After a storm comes a calm.*"

1202. பாலுக்கு மிஞ்சின சுவையில்லை, பல்லக்குக்கு மிஞ்சின சொகுசுமில்லை.
In taste nothing surpasses milk, in comfort nothing excels a palanquin.

1203. பிள்ளை பிறக்கிறதற்கு முன்னே தின்றுபார், மருமகள் வருகிறதற்கு முன்னே கட்டிப்பார் (or போட்டுப்பார்).
Eat and enjoy before you get a child; put on your jewelry and enjoy it before a daughter-in-law comes to your house.
After a child is born the mother will have to regulate her diet for the child's sake. And after the daughter-in-law comes to the mother-in-law's house, it is not considered becoming in the mother-in-law to wear as much jewelry as before; she must give her jewels to the daughter-in-law, however much the girl may have brought with her from her own home. The meaning of the proverb is therefore: use your chances of enjoyment.
"*Make hay while the sun shines.*"

1204. வந்தது கப்பல், மலர்ந்தது தொப்பை.
That which came was a ship, the outcome of it was a big belly.
Said of a family that suddenly becomes prosperous. Wealth and corpulence often go together in India.

CONTENT, DISCONTENT.
திருப்தி, திருப்தியில்லாமை.

1205. இட்டதெல்லாம் கொள்ளும் பட்டிமகன் கப்பறை.
A wretch who has a vessel for alms that can hold whatever is put into it. 1211, 1220.
Never satisfied.
"*A beggar's purse is bottomless.*"

1206. உண்ட வயிற்றுக்குச் சோறும், மொட்டைத்தலைக்கு எண்ணெயும்போல.
Like food to a satisfied stomach, and oil to a bald head!
Applied to one who shows indifference to a gift, because he is already well off.

1207. உண்ட வயிறு கேட்கும், தின்ற பாக்கு சிவக்கும்.

The stomach that has eaten will ask for more; the areca-nut one has eaten will make (the mouth) red. 2178.

Said of people who have received much help but are not satisfied, and will certainly seek more assistance.

1208. உண்பது நாழி, உடுப்பது நாலு முழம், எண்பதுகோடி நினைந்து எண்ணும் மனம்.

Man needs a measure of rice for food, and four feet of cloth for dress, but the mind thinks of eight hundred millions of things. 1215, 2708.

"*Had you the world on your chessboard, you could not fit all to your mind.*"

1209. உன்னைப் பிடி, என்னைப் பிடி, உலகாத்தாள் தலையைப்பிடி.

Catch you, catch me, and catch the head of the goddess.

Said by one who has already exerted himself to the utmost for some one when he is asked to do yet another kindness, implying that there is no end to the demands made on him. *e.g.*, Draupadi made a vow when the Pandavas were conquered at gambling, that she would not tie up her hair till their enemies the Kauravas were killed. When this had been accomplished by Krishna's favour, she again declared that she would not tie up her hair till Aswathama, who had killed her children, was slain. Then Krishna said this proverb to her.

1210. காலத்துக்கு ஏற்ற கோலம்.

The appearance (*or* The ornaments, *or* The costume) must be adapted to the occasion. 2310, 3058.

"*Cut your coat according to your cloth.*"

1211. கூடை கூடையாய்க் கொடுத்தாலும் குறை நீங்காது.

Though you give him baskets full, his wants will not be satisfied. 1205, 1220.

1212. சாஸ்திரத்தைச் சுட்டு, சதுமறையைப் பொய்யாக்கி, சூத்திரத்தைக் கண்டு, சுகம் பெறுவது எக்காலம்?

When shall I, having burnt the Shastras, having proved the four Vedas false, and having seen the mystery, obtain spiritual happiness? 131.

"When may I know the hidden things of life,
And thus attain perfection? I would show
How false the Vedas are, with error rife,
And burn the Shasters, so the truth might grow."

From Pattanattu's songs, in GOVER'S "*The Folk-songs of Southern India.*"

1213. சிணுங்குகிறது எல்லாம் பூசைக்கு அடையாளம்.

All grumbling is a signal for punishment.

Children that whine for things they cannot have get punished.

1214. புல்லு இருக்கிற இடத்தில் மேயவிடாது, சோறு இருக்கிற இடத்தில் தின்ன ஒட்டாது.

Where there is grass the cow will not graze, and where there is rice you will not eat. 1208.

Discontentedness makes people change from one thing to another "to improve their circumstances." Give a man half the world in the one hand, and he will soon ask for the other half, says Carlyle.

1215. போதும் என்கிற மனமே பொன் செய்யும் மருந்து.

A heart that is satisfied is a medicine (*or* philtre) that will make gold. 1208.

"*A contented mind is a continual feast.*"

1216. மூன்று முழமும் ஒரு சுற்று, முப்பது முழமும் ஒரு சுற்று.

If you have three cubits of cloth, you can only wind it round yourself once; if you have thirty cubits of cloth, you can only wind it round yourself once. 562.

Said of one who is never satisfied.

1217. ருசி கண்ட பூனை உறியை உறியைத் தாவுகிறது.

The cat that has tasted nice things will continually jump at the *uri*.

He who has got a taste for pleasure will not be satisfied easily. The *uri* is the loop in which a vessel to hold food, &c., is hung from the roof.

"*The escaped mouse ever feels the taste of the bait.*"
"*Stolen waters are sweet.*"

1218. வயிறு நிரம்பினாலும், கண் நிரம்பாது.

Though the stomach is filled, the eye is never filled.

"*The eye is bigger than the belly.*"

1219. வாயுவும் புள்ளுமாக அலைகிறான்.

He wanders about like the wind and birds.

Said of one who has too much to do, or about a person who seeks wealth in all sorts of ways, but is never satisfied.

1220. வந்ததெல்லாம் கொள்ளும் மகாராஜன் கப்பலிலே.

A king's ship will hold everything that comes. 1205, 1211.

Cf. 963 *ff.* 1669 *ff.*

STUPIDITY AND IGNORANCE.

முட்டாள், பேதை.

1221. ஆலை இலை புளிபோல இருக்கும்.

The leaves of a banyan tree are like tamarind!

"*He knows not a pig from a dog.*" "*Very like a whale.*"

1222. இஞ்சி என்றால் தெரியாதா? எலுமிச்சம்பழம் போலிருக்கும்.

What, don't you know ginger? It is as sweet as a lime!

"*He does not know A from a goose's foot.*"

1223. நாகசுரம் என்ன, தெரியாதா? மத்தளம்போல கல கல என்னும்.
What, don't you know a horn? It sounds like a drum!

"*As like a dock as a daisy.*"

1224. பூசணிக்காய்க்கும் புடலங்காய்க்கும் வித்தியாசம் தெரியாமல் பேசுகிறாய்.
You speak as though you don't know the difference between the gourd and the snake-vegetable.

The *pudalangkai (Trichosanthes anguina)* is a long snake-like vegetable.

"*As like as an apple is to a lobster.*"

1225. பாண்டவாள் தெரியாதா? கட்டில் காலுபோல மூன்றுபேர் என்று வாயால் சொல்லி, இரண்டு விரலைக் காட்டி, நிலத்தில் ஒரு கோடு எழுதினானும்.
"Don't you know how many Pandava princes there were? They were as many as the legs of a bed—three" So said a fool, and held up two fingers, and made a single mark on the ground!

Every Hindu school-boy and every Hindu woman knows that the Pandavas were *five* brothers, the heroes of the Mahabharata.

"*He speaks one word nonsense, and two that have nothing in them.*"

1226. ஆற்றுக்குப் போனதுமில்லை, செருப்பு கழற்றினதுமில்லை.
He neither went to the river nor did he take off his shoes.

1227. ஈனவும் தெரியாது, நக்கவும் தெரியாது.
(A cow that) understands neither how to bring forth (a calf) nor how to lick it!

A simpleton.

1228. எட்டும் இரண்டும் தெரியாத பேதை.
A stupid fellow who cannot add eight and two together!

1229. கலியாண வீட்டில் போய் அறியான், மேளச் சத்தமும் கேட்டு அறியான்.
He knows nothing about going to a wedding, and he does not understand the sound of the drum.

Said of a man who acts foolishly because he lacks experience.

1230. கொடுத்ததும் அறியான், கொடுத்தவர்களைக் கண்டும் அறியான்.
He has never known what giving is, nor has he ever seen people who give!

He has not a charitable disposition naturally, and is too stupid to acquire such a disposition.

1231. நகை போட்டதுமில்லை, போட்டவர்களைப் பார்த்ததுமில்லை.
She has neither worn jewels herself, nor has she seen people who wear them!

Innocent; knows nothing of the world.

1232. பொன்னும் தெரியாது, பொன் முடிந்த துணியும் தெரியாது.
He neither knows gold, nor does he know a cloth in which gold is tied up! 2547.

A fool.

1233. வைக்கவும் தெரியாது, வைத்துப் படைக்கவும் தெரியாது.

He does not understand how to keep it, and he does not understand how to make use of it.

Said about those who do not know how to manage wealth or fortune or business; especially about servants, daughters-in-law, and wives.

1234. வைக்கத் தெரியாமல், வைக்கோல் போரில் வைத்தாளாம்.

She did not understand how to keep her property, so she placed it in a stack of straw. 1261, &c., &c.

Said when women or servants entrust their little savings to untrustworthy persons.

1235. அடித்த இடம் கண்டுபிடித்து அழ, ஆறுமாசம் செல்லும்.

To find the spot on his body where he was beaten, and to cry about it, will take him six months.

Dullness, stupidity.

1236. அரிவாள் சூட்டைப்போல காய்ச்சல் மாற்றவோ?

Can fever be removed as (easily as) the heat from a sickle?

The story goes that a sickle had become hot in the sun, and a passer by thought it had fever, so he put it in water and found that it grew cool again. At another time he found his mother in a burning fever, and put her into water also, where she was drowned.

"*A fool will laugh when he is drowning.*"

1237. அவன் வாயில்லாத பூச்சி.

He is a worm without a mouth.

He won't bite; is innocent; does not meddle with others. Also used ironically.

1238. இடையனும் பள்ளியும் இறைத்த புலம் சாவி.

The land cultivated by a shepherd and a *Palli* proved a failure. 1245, 3317.

These two castes are proverbially stupid.

1239. இட்டுவைத்தால் தின்னவும், எடுத்துவைத்தால் சுமக்கவும் தெரியும்.

What you place before him he will eat, and what you put upon him he will carry.

He can eat and work, but in other things he is a simpleton.

1239*a*. Or வைத்ததைத் தின்று, போட்டதைச் சுமக்கும்.

He will eat what is given him and carry what is laid on him.

Said of an ass or a stupid man.

1240. இராமுழுதும் ராமாயணம் கேட்டு, சீதைக்கு ராமன் என்னவேண்டும் என்பதுபோல.

After having heard the *Ramayana* read (and explained) all night, he asked how Rama was related to Sita?

He listened so stupidly as to miss the chief point, *i.e.*, that Sita was Rama's devoted wife. Of such a person it can be said, இவன் புத்தி உலக்கை கொழுந்து, his wit is as blunt as a rice-pounder.

"*John has been to school to learn to be a fool.*"

1241. உள்ளதையும் கெடுத்தான் நொள்ளைக்கண்ணன்.

The one eyed (*or* angry-eyed) man ruined what existed. 809.

To make bad worse. Said also of one who destroys what is in good order by his incapacity.

1242. எட்டுவருஷம் எருமைக்கடா ஏரிக்குப் போக வழி தேடுமாம்.

The buffalo-bull that had been used to go to a lake to drink for eight years, was still doubtful about the way.

The buffalo is proverbial for its stupidity.

" *Send a fool to the market, and a fool he will return.*"

1243. எருது ஈன்றது என்றால், தொழுத்தில் கட்டு என்கிறதுபோல.

If he is told that a bull is in calf, he will say 'Tie it in the stall'!

" *As wise as Waltham's calf, that ran nine miles to suck a bull.*"

1244. எருமுட்டைப் புராணம் வாசிக்கிறான்.

He is reading the *Purâna* written on cow-dung cakes.

Said of a very stupid fellow. The *Purânas* are the scriptures of later Hinduism and are largely mythological.

1245. கடா மேய்க்கிறவன் அறிவானோ கொழு போன இடம்.

Does a shepherd know where the plough-share is? 1238.

It is not his business. An Indian shepherd is always counted a fool.

1246. கழுதைபால் குடித்தவன்போலிருக்கிறான்.

He is like one who has drunk asses' milk.

i.e., Very stupid.

1247. கள்ளுக் குடியனுக்கு வாய் என்றும் சூத்து என்றும் தெரியாது.

A person who drinks toddy does not know the mouth of the cup from the bottom of it. 3085*a*.

1248. காண ஒருதரம், கும்பிட ஒருதரமா?

Do you come at one time to see me and at another to salute me? 1254.

Labour in vain; both might be done at the same time. Said to one who, when ordered to do two small tasks, which might be done at once, arranges to do one now and the other another time.

" *Lazy folks take the most pains.*"

1249. கீழே பாம்பு என்றால், மேலே பார்க்கிறதுபோல.

If you say there is a snake on the ground, he will look up.

" *He cannot say " bo" to a goose.*"

1250. குருடும் செவிடும் கூத்துப் பார்த்தாற்போல் செய்கிறாய்.

You do your work like the blind man and the deaf man at the show.

The blind man criticised the dancing, and the deaf the singing as though each had understood what had taken place on the stage.

1251. கையில் எடுக்குமுன்னே கோழி மோசம் என்று அறியாது.
He does not know that he may lose the fowl till it is stolen out of his hands.

The innocent man believes the deceiver till the deceit is flagrant.

"*A fool loseth his estate before he finds his folly.*"

1252. கொக்குத் தலையில் வெண்ணெய் வைத்துப் பிடிக்கிறதுபோல்.
Like putting butter on a crane's head and catching it.

Said of a stupid undertaking about which one is ignorant of the steps to be taken.

1252*a*. Or நெல்லுக் காய்க்கிறமரம் கேட்டவன்போல.
Like the man who asked: "Which is the tree on which rice grows?"

1253. ஞாபகமில்லை என்று எவனும் சொல்லுவான், ஞானமில்லை என்று எவனும் சொல்லான்.
Any one will say, I have forgotten it; but no one will say, I am without sense.

"*All complain of want of memory, but none of want of judgment.*"

1254. நடக்கமாட்டாத லவாடிக்கு நாலுபக்கமும் சவாரி.
The old horse that is unable to work gets work on all sides. 1248.

Said of a fool who, instead of finishing the work he has on hand, turns to some other work, toils at that for a while, and then seeks something else.

1255. நுனி மரத்தில் ஏறி, அடி மரத்தை வெட்டினதுபோல்.
Like climbing to the top of the tree, and cutting it off by the root.

"*The fool hunts for misfortune.*"

1256. நான் கொக்கோ? கொங்கு நாட்டானே!
Am I a crane? O man from the *Konkân* country!

Cf. நான் ஏமாந்த சோகிரியா? Do you take me to be a fool?

When a Rishi (a saint) was doing penance, a crane let its droppings fall upon him from a tree. The angry glance he gave the bird slew it. This made the Rishi believe himself to be a great wonder-worker, and when he met the wife of the Tamil saint Tiruvalluvar, who did not at once obey his orders, he looked at her, thinking that she also would fall dead; but instead of doing so, she looked at him and uttered this proverb.

1257. பகலில் பசுவும் தெரியவில்லை, இரவில் எருமை தெரியுமா?
During the day he does not know what a cow is; will he know a buffalo at night?

If one cannot understand simple matters, how about what is difficult?

1258. பன்றிக்குத் தவிடு வைக்கப்போனாலும் உர் என்கிறது, கழுத்து அறுக்கப்போனாலும் உர் என்கிறது.
If you lay bran before a pig, it will say 'ur'; if you cut its throat, it will say 'ur.'

It cannot distinguish between good and evil, and it does not understand how to be polite.

1259. புட்டுக்கூடை முண்டத்தில் பொறுக்கி எடுத்த முண்டம்.
He is a fool picked out of a basket of fools. 1261.
Said of a great fool.

1260. பூனை பானையில் தலையை இட்டுக்கொண்டு எல்லாம் இருண்டுபோச்சுது என்று நினைக்குமாம்.
After the cat has put its head into a pot, it thinks that all is darkness.
" *He is a fool that thinks not that another thinks.*"
" *As a fool sings, so he thinks the bell rings.*"

1261. மட்டியிலும் மட்டி மகா மட்டி.
He is a greater blockhead than all blockheads. 1259.

1262. முட்டாளுக்கு என்ன சொன்னாலும் கட்டோடே கேளான்.
Though you give a fool advice, he will not listen with any attention.
" *Fools are pleased with their own blunders.*"

HASTE AND RASHNESS.

ஆத்திரம்.

1263. அவசரத்திலே குண்டுசெட்டியில் கை நுழையாது.
The hand won't go into the round pot in a hurry. 1276.
The mouth of this pot is very large, but a man in a hurry will fail to get his hand into it.
" *More haste, less speed.*"

1264. அவசரத்துக்கு (or ஆபத்துக்கு or ஆத்திரத்துக்கு)ப் பாவமில்லை.
Necessity (knows) no sin.
" *Necessity knows no law.*"

1265. ஆத்திரக்காரனுக்கு (or அவசரக்காரனுக்கு)ப் புத்தி மட்டு.
A hasty person's judgment is limited.
" *He that is hasty of spirit exalteth folly.*" (Prov. 14, 29.)
" *A hasty man never wants woe.*"

1266. ஆறு காதம் என்கிறபோதே கோவணத்தை அவிழ்த்துக் குடுமியிலே கட்டிக்கொண்டானாம்.
When the river was still sixty miles off, he untied his loin-cloth and put it on his head.
He ought not to have taken it off till he was crossing the river. Inopportune haste.
" *Do not strip before bed-time.*"

1267. இரிஷி பிண்டம் இராத் தங்காது.

The embryo of a Rishi will not stay (in the womb) a single night. 1272.

i. e., A Rishi will be born before the dawn after the night in which his mother has conceived him!—Said if people are over hasty in getting back things that they have lent; and also if things lent are returned sooner than is expected. A Rishi is a Hindu sage.

1268. உட்கார்ந்திருக்கச்சே அடித்தால் பொன்னாகும், ஓடச்சே அடித்தால் செம்பானாலும் ஆகும், இரும்பானாலும் ஆகும்.

If one strikes while sitting down, it may become gold; if while running, it may either become copper or iron.

"*The admonition Nothing rashly, is everywhere useful.*"
"*Haste and wisdom are things far different.*"
"*He that can stay, obtains.*"

1269. எள்ளு என்கிறதற்குமுன்னே, எண்ணெய் எங்கே என்கிறான்?

Before one says, Sesamum seed, he says, Where is the oil? 956, 960, 1282.

Too hasty to wait for something expected.

1270. ஒரு சுற்று சுற்றி வயிற்றைத் தடவிப்பார்த்துக்கொண்டதுபோல.

Like the woman who rubbed her stomach (to know if she was pregnant) after going round (the sacred fig-tree) only once! 2677.

She was worshipping the god in the tree to obtain its favour and bear a child. Walking round a sacred place from left to right is a very common form of adoration.

1271. காசியில் இருந்தவன் கண்ணைக் குத்தக் காஞ்சிபுரத்திலிருந்து கை நீட்டிக்கொண்டு போனான்.

While in Conjeevaram he stretched out his arm to strike the eye of a man in Benares!

The two places are twelve hundred miles apart.

"*Make not the sauce till you have caught the fish.*"

1272. காட்டேரி (or இருசி) உடைமை இராத்தங்காது.

The property of a demoness will not remain till the next morning. 1267.

1273. காணி கவிழ்ந்துபோகிறதா?

Will your land capsize?

i.e., Take things quietly. Why toil and struggle as if defeat and ruin are about to befall you?

1274. குளம் உடைந்து போகும்போது முறைவீதமா?

When a tank bursts, is there time to ask whose turn it is (to repair its banks)?

In a time of calamity every one must do his best to stop the evil.

1275. *க்ஷணச் சித்தம், க்ஷணப் பித்தம்.*
At one moment it is his will; at another it is bile to him. 1285, 2905.
Or *வேளைக்கு ஒரு குணம்,* an ever changing mind.
"*Women, wind and fortune are ever changing.*"

1276. *தீப்பட்ட வீட்டுக்குப் பீக்குட்டை தண்ணீர்.*
Water from a cess-pool is of use to a house on fire. 1263.
"*Foul water will quench fire.*" "*Good and quickly seldom meet.*"

1277. *நாய்க்கு வேலையுமில்லை, நிற்க நேரமுமில்லை.*
The dog has nothing to do, and yet has no time to be quiet.
Said when one is in a hurry about nothing.
"*He has more business than English ovens at Christmas.*"
"*Idle folks have the least leisure.*"

1278. *நினைத்தபோது பிள்ளை பிறக்குமா?*
Will a child be born at the time expected?
One must not be in a hurry to gain the fulfilment of a wish, but must work and wait for it.

1279. *பதினாயிரம் கொடுத்தாலும், பதைப்பு ஆகாது.*
Even if you give ten thousand rupees, anxiety is of no avail.

1280. *பஞ்சத்தில் பிள்ளை விற்கிறதுபோல.*
Like selling a child during a famine.
Said when one is compelled to sell a thing cheap in order to live. The proverb is founded on fact. Cases were known during the Great Famine of 1876-8 and during the famine in the north of India at the end of 1896.

1281. *பயணக்காரன்* (prop. *பிரயாணக்காரன்*) *பைத்தியக்காரன்.*
A man going a journey is mad.
He is so hurried and worried, that he appears to be mad. Making a journey is an anxious undertaking to most Hindus.

1282. *பருத்தி புடவையாய்க் காய்த்ததுபோல.*
Like the cotton tree that yielded a woman's dress ready-made! 956, 960, 1269.
The cotton after being gathered has many processes to go through before it become cloth. Said sarcastically of one in great haste.
"*All is not butter that comes from the cow.*"

1283. *பார்ப்பானுக்குப் பறப்பு, கோவிலிலேயும் சிறப்பு.*
The Brahmin is in haste for the temple must be adorned.

1284. *பறப்பான் பயிர் இழந்தான்.*
The hasty man lost his crop.
"*Haste makes waste.*"

1285. *மூத்திரம் பெய்கிறதுக்குள்ளே முப்பத்தெட்டு குணம்.*
While easing himself he had thirty-eight minds. 1275.
Said of one who is very fickle.
"*A woman's mind and winter wind change oft.*"

1286. விடியற்காலத்தில் கலியாணம் பிடி பாக்கு.
To-morrow morning the wedding will be performed; take betel!
Said when one receives notice at the eleventh hour of an important matter. It is customary when inviting people to a wedding to send them betel-leaves and areca-nut.
"*Haste trips up its own heels.*"

1287. வெந்தது போதும் முன்றானையில் கொட்டு.
It is boiled enough; throw it into my lap. 218.
"*Too hasty burned his lips.*"

PROCRASTINATION.

தாமிசம்.

SLOWNESS TO LEARN.

1288. ஆம்புடையான் செத்தபிறகு அறுதலிக்குப் புத்தி வந்ததுபோல.
As the widow only got sense after her husband's death. 1439. 2679.
"*Experience is a dear school but fools learn in no other.*"
"*Misfortunes tell us what fortune is.*"

1289. ஒரு தரம் விழுந்தால் தெரியாதா?
If you fall once only, don't you perceive it?
"*Bought wit is best.*" "*Beware of the stone thou stumbledst at before.*"

1290. கண் கெட்டபிறகா சூரிய நமஸ்காரம் செய்கிறது?
Is it only after you have lost your sight that you will worship the sun? 1293.
"*The night cometh, when no man can work.*" (Joh. 9, 4.)
"*Blessings are not valued, till they are gone.*"
"*When the sun shines, nobody minds him; but when he is eclipsed, all consider him.*"

1291. காலிலே பட்ட பிறகா, கிரகசாரம் (or சனி) போதாது.
Is the influence of planets of no account when you have hurt your foot? 1295.

1292. கிணற்றில் விழுந்தவன் மறுபடியும் விழுவானா?
Will the man who has fallen into a well once, fall into it again?
"*Experience is the mistress of fools.*" "*To-day is yesterday's pupil.*"

1293. செத்தபிறகு, செய்தவனுக்குச் செய்கிறதா?
Is it after his death that you should recompense him who does (evil) to you? 1290.
"*Know your opportunity.*"

1294. சூடுகண்ட பூனை அடுப்பங்கரையில் சேராது.
The cat that has been burnt will not go near the fire-place.
"*A burnt child dreads the fire.*"
"*Adversity makes a man wise, not rich.*"

1295. தலையில் இடித்த பிறகா, தாழக்குனிகிறது?
Is it only after knocking your head, that you bend it? 1291, 1297.
"*When the head is broken, the helmet is put on.*"

1296. பத்து இறுத்த பின்பு பாரச் சந்தேகம் தீர்ந்தது.
After paying a fine of ten (rupees), my grave doubt was removed.
"*Wisdom rides upon the ruins of folly.*"

1297. வாசல்படி தலையில் பட்டபிறகா, குனிகிறது?
"Will you only bend your head after having knocked it against the door frame? 1295, 1331.

Cf. 873 *ff.* 1439 *ff.* 2975 *ff.*

MISCELLANEOUS PROVERBS ABOUT PROCRASTINATION AND DELAY.

1298. ஆகட்டும் போகட்டும், அவரைக்காய்க் காய்க்கட்டும், தம்பி பிறக்கட்டும், அவனுக்குக் கலியாணம் ஆகட்டும், உன்னைக் கூப்பிடப்போகிறேனோ?
Let it be or let it go, let the vegetable grow up, let a boy be born, and let him be married, but do you think I am going to invite you to the wedding? 2377.

1299. கார் அறுக்கட்டும், கத்திரி பூக்கட்டும்.
Let the harvest come, and let the briujal-plant blossom.
Said to put off one who asks for help.

1300. தலை இருக்கிற இடத்தில் கழுத்து வரட்டும்.
Let your neck grow up to where your head is now. 3329.
i.e., Wait till you are a little older.
"*You must eat another yard of pudding first.*"

1301. மூன்று முடிச்சு கழுத்தில் விழட்டும், முப்பது இலை குப்பையில் விழட்டும்.
Let the three knots be tied on your neck, and let thirty leaf-plates be thrown on the dunghill.
i.e., You feel very happy that an excellent offer for your daughter has been made; but the wedding has not been performed yet. Let the three knots of the *thâli* be tied, and let Brahma, Vishnu and Rudra's names be pronounced over each knot; and after that, let the family be present for the grand final feast before you make sure that the wedding is really to take place. *Cf.* Solon to Croesus :—
"*Do not feel happy till you are in your grave.*"

1302. மேலைக்குத் தாலிகட்டுகிறேன், கழுத்தே சுகமே இரு என்பதுபோல.

Like saying, Be happy, O neck! some day I shall tie a *thâli* on thee! 2377.

Said of one who promises help, but delays in giving it.

" *He loses his thanks who promiseth and delayeth.*"

" *Hell is paved with good intentions.*"

N.B.—*The above five proverbs are put together here not only on account of their meaning, but also on account of the peculiar expressions in them.*

1303. ஆயோதன முகத்தில் ஆயுதம் தேடுகிறதுபோல.

To seek for weapons while the battle is going on. 619, 625, 1332.

1304. ஆலசியம் அமிர்த விஷம்.

Sloth turns nectar into poison. 1409.

" *Delay is dangerous.*"

1305. ஆறின கஞ்சி பழங் கஞ்சி.

Cold food is (soon) old food.

Delay in doing duty makes the duty irksome.

" *The purpose of to-day to-morrow wrests away.*"

1306. இன்றைக்கு ஆகிறது நாளைக்கு ஆகட்டும்.

To-day it is done; to-morrow it may be done.

" *From to-morrow till tomorrow time goes a long journey.*"

" *Don't put off till to-morrow what can be done to-day.*"

1307. இன்றை என்பதும், நாளை என்பதும், இல்லை என்பதற்கு அடையாளம்.

To say "to-day" or "to-morrow" means "no!"

" *One 'take it' is better than two 'you shall have it.'* "

1308. எரிகிற வீட்டை அவிக்கக் கிணறுவெட்ட, நாள் பார்த்ததுபோல.

Like looking out for an auspicious day to dig a well to quench a burning house!

" *In haste like a snail.*"

1309. கடல் வற்றிக் கருவாடு தின்னலாம் என்று உடல் வற்றிச் செத்ததாம் கொக்கு.

The body of the bird who said 'After the sea is dried up I can eat salted fish,' dried up and died (while it was waiting).

" *He that doth not what he ought, that haps to him which he never thought.*"

1310. கண்ணுள்ளபோதே காக்ஷி.

While you have your eyes you have sight.

" *Take time while time is, for time will away.*"

" *Take time by the forelock.*"

1311. கண்ணும் கருத்தும் உள்ளபோதே காணோம், அதின் பின்பு என்ன கிடைக்கும்?

While there is sight and sense, we do not perceive what will happen to us afterwards?

"*After death the doctor?*"

1312. காற்றுள்ளபோதே தூற்றிக்கொள்.

Winnow while the wind blows.

"*Make hay while the sun shines.*"

1313. கிணறு வெட்டித் தாகம் தீர்க்கலாமா?

Can't you wait to quench your thirst until you have dug a well?

"*Don't have your cloak to make when it begins to rain.*"

1314. சமுத்திர அலை ஓயப் போகிறதுமில்லை, தம்பிதலை முழுகி தர்ப்பணம் பண்ணப்போகிறதுமில்லை.

The waves of the sea will not stop, and the young man will not finish washing his head and performing the rites for his deceased father. 1871.

"*He who will not sail till he has a full fair wind will lose many a voyage.*"

"*He who will not sail till the dangers are over must never put to sea.*"

1315. செட்டி சிங்காரிக்கிறதுக்குள்ளே, பட்டணம் பறிபோகிறது.

While the merchant was adorning himself the city was looted.

"*He brings his machines after the war is over.*"

1316. திருடன் புகுந்து ஆறுமாதம் நாய் குலைத்ததுபோல.

Like a dog barking six months after a thief had entered the house.

"*To lock the stable door when the steed is stolen.*"

1317. தேவடியாள் சிங்காரிக்குமுன்னே, தேர் ஓடித் தெருவிலே நிற்கிறது.

Before the dancing-girl had adorned herself, the car ran on and came to a standstill in the street.

The procession was over before she was ready to join in it. It is part of the duty of the dancing-girls attached to a temple to dance before the sacred car when the God of the temple is taken out on festival-days.

1318. நனைத்து சுமக்கிறதா?

Will any one wet his burden (and so make it heavier)? 402.

Said of him who puts off moral improvement till evil increases, or postpones repairs while decay increases, and thus double the cost of repairing.

1319. பத்தியத்துக்கு முருங்கைக்காய் வாங்கிவா என்றால், பால் தெளிக்கு அவத்திக்கீரை கொண்டுவருவான்.

If you say, Go buy the *murungei* fruit for the patient's diet, (he delays, and then) brings *aratti* vegetables (*coronilla grandiflora*) for the milk-sprinkling (funeral) ceremony.

i.e., The sick man is allowed to die because the person in charge of him will not trouble to get him medicine. The milk-sprinkling ceremony is an offering of milk to the *manes* of the dead person on the third day after death. Used, for instance, when a loan of ten rupees which would have preserved a sick man's life, comes only in time for his funeral.

1320. பதறாத காரியம் சிதறாது.
A thing done without haste does not fail.
Cf. பதறின காரியம் பாழ்.
An affair that is hurried is all in vain.

1321. மஞ்சள் குளித்து மணைமேலே இருக்கும்போது மாட்டேன் என்றீரே, பிள்ளை பெற்று நொந்திருக்கச்சே வேண்ட (or கோண்ட) வந்தீரே.
While I was adorned with saffron and was ready for you, you refused to come to me; now that I have borne a child and am weak, you want me.
Literally a wife's complaint against a phlegmatic husband. Also used about any privilege that is neglected too long.
"*He that will not when he may, when he would he shall have nay.*"

1322. மேலைக்கு உழுவார், கூழுக்கு அழுவார்.
They who delay ploughing will have to cry for food. 1128.

1323. வேகிற வீட்டுக்கு வெட்டுகிற கிணறு.
A well that is being dug for a house on fire!
"*To cover the well when the child is drowned.*"
N.B.—*Some of the above may be compared with* 873 *ff.*

WATCHFULNESS.

ஜாக்கிரதை.

1324. ஆளைச் சுற்றிப் பார்க்காமல் அளக்கிறதா?
Do you gossip without looking (at your hearers)? 781, 2585.
Be careful when you try to deceive.

1325. ஆற்றிலே கணுக்கால் தண்ணீரிலும் அஞ்சி நடக்கவேண்டும்.
Though the water in a river is not more than ankle-deep one should walk carefully.

1326. உச்சந்தலையில் செருப்பால் அடித்ததுபோல.
(His influence is) like striking the crown of the head with a slipper.
In ancient times a Tamil man might take a woman as a wife of inferior degree by putting his slipper on her head. This signified that the woman became his slave for life, and was to have nothing more to do with other men. The position of such a woman was less honourable than that of a legal wife and her children had no right to inherit family property; but on the other hand it was far higher than that of an ordinary prostitute. The proverb is often used to one who allows himself to be subjected to the influence of others.

1327. கண்டும் காணவில்லை, கேட்டும் கேட்கவில்லை என்று இருக்கவேண்டும்.
You should be like one who seems not to have seen what he has seen, and not to have heard what he has heard.
i.e., Be wary.
"*There is a time to wink as well as to see.*"

1328. கண்ணோ புண்ணோ?
Is it an eye, or a wound?
Said as a warning to one who is treating a delicate matter carelessly.

1329. குடி வைத்துக்கொண்டாயோ, கொள்ளி வைத்துக்கொண்டாயோ?
Did you receive a family into your house (as tenants) or did you receive a firebrand?
i.e., Be careful as to whom you admit into your house or into your employment.

1330. பத்திரம், என் வாசலில் அடி வைக்காதே.
Be careful, don't put your foot inside my threshold! 2243, 2394.

1331. முட்டுமுன் குனியவேண்டும்.
Stoop before you get into difficulties. 1297, 1337.
"*Look before you leap, for snakes among sweet flowers do creep.*"

1332. வெள்ளம் வருகிறதற்கு முன்னே, அணை போடவேண்டும்.
The dam must be built before the flood comes. 1303.
"*A stitch in time, saves nine.*"
"*Prevention is better than cure.*"

PRUDENCE.

நினைப்பு, யோசனை.

1333. ஆரை நம்பி, தோழா, காருக்கு எற்றம் போட்டாய்?
From whom did you expect (help), my friend, when you put up a water-lift (to irrigate) the *kar* rice.
Don't begin an undertaking without being sure of the necessary assistance.

1334. ஆழம் தெரியாமல் காலை இட்டுக்கொண்டதுபோல.
Like stepping into the water without knowing its depth.
Used about beginning operations without fully understanding their cost. (*Cf.* Luc. 14, 28.) Also about evil deeds that are done in the belief that they will never be found out.
"*A danger foreseen is half avoided.*"

1335. உடும்பு போனால் போகிறது, கை வந்தால் போதும்.
Let the iguana go. If I can only get my hand (out of its mouth) it is enough.
The story runs that a man had foolishly put his hand into a hole to catch an iguana, but it seized his hand with such strength that he could not extricate it. Said of a person who has involved himself in great difficulties, out of which he is glad to get at any price.
"*Catching a Tartar.*" "*To burn one's fingers.*" "*Do as little as you can to repent of.*"

1336. எண்ணிச் செய்கிறவன் செட்டி, எண்ணாமல் செய்கிறவன் மட்டி.

He that thinks before he acts is a *Chetty*, but he who acts without thinking is a fool.

The *Chetty* caste is a class of merchants renowned for their business ability.

"*Consideration is the parent of wisdom.*"

"*Consideration is half conversion.*"

1337. எண்ணித் துணிவது கருமம், துணிந்தபின் எண்ணுவது இழுக்கு.

It is a deed to think and then venture; but to think after venturing is a disgrace. 1331.

"*Think of the end ere you begin, and you will never be thrall to sin.*"

"*Some do first, think afterwards, and repent for ever.*"

1338. கிணற்று ஆழமும், கயிற்று நீளமும் பார்க்கவேண்டும்.

One must consider the depth of the well and the length of the rope.

"*Look before you leap.*"

1339. சமாசாரம் தெரியாமல், அமாவாசைக்குப் போகிறான்.

Without knowing any particulars about it, he goes to the New Moon festival. 1009.

i.e., He went to the house expecting a meal, but found that he had come on a fast-day and so was disappointed. High caste Hindus fast on the day of the New Moon festival. Said of one who commences an undertaking without understanding it.

1340. வாய் புளித்ததோ, மாங்காய் புளித்ததோ?

Which is sour, the mouth or the mango?

Said to one who draws hasty conclusions, or judges from superficial knowledge. Thus Europeans often draw too hasty conclusions about Hindus and *vice-versa*. Or said to one who says it is easy to lead a religious life, or, to gain a university degree.

"*A hard thing it is, I wiss, to judge a thing that unknown is.*"

KINGS.

அரசன்.

N.B.—It should be remembered that in India each king or prince was a despot, and that each subordinate ruler was in his degree a despotic ruler. This is true to-day of the rulers of dependent native states—more than six hundred in number—save that they are subordinate to the British supremacy.

1341. அரசனில்லாத நாடு அச்சில்லாத தேர்.

A country without a king is like a car without a linch-pin. 1380.

Or அரசனில்லாத நாடு அலைகழித்தாற்போல. As a country without a king is harrassed.

1342. அரசனுக்கில்லை சிறுமையும் பெருமையும்.
To a king there is neither low nor high.
An oriental potentate treats his people as he likes.

1343. அரசன் நாவு அசைய, நாடு அசையும்.
If the king moves his tongue, the country will be stirred up.
The power of a king's words.

1344. அரசனில்லாப் படை வெல்லுவது அரிது.
An army without king (a head) will hardly conquer. 1379.

1345. ஒருவனைக் கொன்றவன் உடனே சாவான், பலபேரைக் கொன்றவன் பட்டம் ஆளுவான்.
He who kills one person will die at once, he who kills many will become a king.
Many an eastern king has waded to the throne through blood.

1346. கோவுக்கு அழகு செங்கோல் முறைமை.
A sceptre of justice is the beauty of a king.

1347. துறவிக்கு வேந்தன் துரும்பு.
The king is a mere straw to the ascetic.
In this saying the result of the long struggle in India between the priest-caste (Brahmans) and the warrior-caste (Kshattriyas) is epitomised. The social life of modern India is priest-ridden, and the priests are the pillars of all the old customs and prejudices. Said of one who in righteous indignation against tyranny has resolved to sacrifice himself for his country or for his family.

AUTHORITY.

அதிகாரம்.

ARBITRARY AUTHORITY.

1348. அவன் சொன்னதே சட்டம், அவன் இட்டதே பிச்சை.
Whatever he says is law, whatever he gives is alms.
His words and deeds are to be accepted as law.

1349. உடையவன் சொல்படி உரலைச்சுற்றிக் குழிபறி.
Dig a ditch round the rice-mortar according to the owner's words.
Said of a man whose will must be done though it be to his own disadvantage.
" *All that he says is law.*"

1350. அரைத்து மீந்தது அம்மி, சிரைத்து மீந்தது குடுமி.
After the grinding is finished the stone remains, after the shaving the tuft of hair (*Kudumi*) remains.
i.e., However much grinding is done on it the stone is not worn out, and however carelessly the barber shaves he is sure to leave the *Kudumi*. Said of a proud master, who cares nothing for the privileges of others. The *Kudumi* is the tuft of hair on the back of the head worn by all Hindus except certain ascetics and never touched by the razor.

1351. எமன் நினைக்கவும், பிள்ளை பிழைக்கவுமா?
When Death thinks the child must die, will it live? 2939.

Said of rich people and of people of authority who do what they like, not minding what others think of them.

1352. ஏற்றப் பாட்டுக்கு எதிர்ப் பாட்டில்லை.
There is no chorus to the song of the worker on the water-lift.

The songs sung by workers on the water-lift are sung at random, and are often only strings of phrases sung to a monotonous cadence while the worker performs his solitary work. The proverb is applied to a man who will allow no voice to criticise his doings.

1353. கடல் மீனுக்கு நுளையன் இட்டது சட்டம்.
The name the fisherman gives to the seafish is law. 1595.
"*If a jury say it is a cat, it must be so.*"

1354. நம்பியான் விட்டதே தீர்த்தம்.
Whatever the Vaishnava Brahmin pours out to people is holy water.

What the great do is above common people's criticism.
"*Must; is a king's word.*"

1355. வலியான் எடுத்ததே வாய்கால், வலவான் ஆடினதே பம்பரம்.
What the strong man dug was a channel, and what the clever man spun was a top.
"*Might is right.*"

1356. வைத்தியன் சொன்னதெல்லாம் மருந்து.
Whatever the doctor says is medicine, that is medicine. 1602.

Hindu physicians are said to give their vegetarian patients all sorts of meat broths, but the patients must obey the doctor's word even if they break the rules of their castes.

TYRANNY.

1357. அழுத பிள்ளையும் வாய்மூடும் அதிகாரம்.
Authority that shuts the mouth of a crying child!
A description of tyranny.

1358. அவன் அதிகாரம் கொடிகட்டிப் பறக்கிறது.
His authority is a hoisted flag fluttering in the wind.

The daughter-in-law applies this to her mother-in-law when the latter acts unjustly towards her. It is also applied to one who acts according to the prompting of others.

1358*a*. கண்மூடித் துரைத்தனமாச்சே.
It is a government that shuts its eyes!
All is done blindly and unfairly.

1359. *கண்டறியாதவன் பெண்படைத்தால், காடுமேடு எல்லாம் இழுத்துத் திரிவானாம்.*

It is said, that if a man without experience of women marries (*or* gets a girl into his possession) he will drag her through every jungle and over every hill. 1367, 1368.

The novelty of the thing makes the silly fellow anxious to show off his authority to his wife and before his neighbours. Domestic tyranny.

1360. *கழுதை வளையற்காரன் கிட்டபோயும் கெட்டது, வண்ணான் கிட்ட போயும் கெட்டது.*

The ass suffered much when the bangle-seller was its owner and when the washerman was its owner. 3371.

Both gave it much work and little food.

1361. *கிழிஞ்சாப்பிள்ளை மணியத்திலே நீட்டின விரல் அற்றுப்போம்.*

The finger that is pointed at the authority of Kirinjapillei will be lost.

Said of officials who will not allow their doings to be criticised.

"*Might is right.*"

"*Accusing is proving, where malice and force sit judges.*"

1362. *குத்திக்கொண்டு வா என்றால், வெட்டிக்கொண்டு வருகிறான்.*

Though you tell him only to reprimand that man, he brings him cut up in little pieces. 2650.

Said of a person who arrogantly exceeds the limits of the authority that has been delegated to him.

1363. *சாலாய் வைத்தாலும் சரி, சட்டியாய் வைத்தாலும் சரி.*

Whether you make it a big pot or a small pot, it is all the same.

See explanation appended to No. 1365.

1364. *சிரைத்தால் மொட்டை, வைத்தால் குடுமி.*

If you shave me, my head will be bald; if you don't, the tuft (*Kudumi*) will remain.

See explanation appended to No. 1365.

1365. *வெளுத்து விட்டாலும் சரி, சும்மா விட்டாலும் சரி.*

Whether you wash it or not, it is all the same. 702, 2718.

Each of the above three means that whatever the person addressed does, is right. There is a story that a king gave high offices to a potter, a barber and a washerman. While they were in authority, a rogue beat a poor farmer, who complained to the potter, and closed his complaint with the first of the above three proverbs. He meant to say, "It is in your power to do good, I therefore leave it all to you." The potter, fool that he was, took the proverb as a sneer at *himself*; and ordered the farmer to be beaten and sent away. The poor farmer then went to the barber magistrate and complained, ending his complaint with the second proverb. The barber took this as a personal insult and the farmer was again beaten. Finally the farmer went to the washerman-judge, recited his wrongs and closed his appeal for justice with the third proverb. He was again beaten for his pains. The story is a satire on the hypersensitiveness of upstarts about their humble origin.

1366. தேளுக்கு மணியம் கொடுத்தால், ஜாம ஜாமத்துக்குக் (or பொழுதுவிடுகிற மட்டும் or நிமிஷத்துக்கு நிமிஷம்) கொட்டும்.

If you give office to a scorpion, it will sting all the time.

Said about the abuse of authority by wicked persons.

"*Men of cruelty are birds of the devil's hatching.*"

1367. படையாத படைத்த மாமியாரே, உன்னைப் பறையன் அறுக்கக் கனவு கண்டேன்.

O, mother-in-law, who possessest what you ought not to possess! I dreamed that a Pariah had cut you up. 704, 1359.

Said in disgust of ono who is not accustomed to dignity and power, and therefore tyranises over servants or relations when he gets into authority.

1368. போலைக்கு ஒரு பொன்மணி கிடைத்ததாம், அதைப் பொழுது விடியளவும் தொட்டுத் தொட்டுப் பார்த்ததாம்.

They say that when a vain woman got a golden ornament, she handled it the whole night. 1359.

Cf. 591 *ff.* 702 *ff.* 1374 *ff.* 1694 *ff.*

HAVING ANOTHER PERSON IN ONE'S POWER.

1369. அவனுக்குள்ளே அகப்பட்டிருக்கிறது என் பிழைப்பு எல்லாம்.

What is in his hands is my whole livelihood. 1372.

1370. உன் வண்டவாளம் எல்லாம் எனக்குத் தெரியும்.

I know your character, (*i.e.*, all your wickedness).

1371. ஊர் இளக்காரம் வண்ணானுக்குத் தெரியும்.

The washermen knows the defects of the village.

When getting the clothes to wash he learns a great deal about the private affairs of the different families.

1372. என் குடுமி அவன் கையில் அகப்பட்டுக்கொண்டது.

My hair-tuft is in his hands. 1369.

i.e., I am in his power. For 'hair-tuft' (*Kudumi*) see 1350.

1373. நீட்டி நீட்டிப் பேசுகிற வெள்ளாளப்பையா, உங்கள் துரைசானி எங்கள் சிறைச்சாலையில் இருக்கிறாள்.

O, thou Vellâla fellow, why spin such a long yarn? Your mistress is in our jail.

i.e., We know all about you and your affairs too.

THE OVERBEARING SUBORDINATE.

'Dressed in a little brief authority.'

1374. அண்ணாமலையாருக்கு அறுபத்துநாலு பூசை, ஆண்டிகளுக்கு எழுபத்து நாலு பூசை.

The god Annamalaiyar is worshipped sixty-four times, while his priests are worshipped seventy-four times. 1377.

One must spend more in bribes on small officials than on big ones. Or, subordinates are more punctilious in exacting homage than great officials.

"*The servant of a king is a king.*"

1375. அதிகாரி வீட்டுக் கோழிமுட்டை குடியானவன் வீட்டு அம்மியை உடைத்ததாம்.

It is said that an egg laid in a great man's house smashed a farmer's grinding stone!

The servants of a great man can ruin humble folks. Servants in India arrogate to themselves at least two thirds of their master's authority.

1376. அவன் மூத்திரம் விளக்காய் எரியுது (or எரிகிறது).

His urine shines like a lamp!

Servants say this of one of themselves who has paramount influence with his master.

1377. சுவாமி வரம் கொடுத்தாலும், பூசாரி இடம் கொடுக்க மாட்டான்.

Though the god may grant a gift, his priest will not. 1374.

Priests (*pujari*) are proverbially extortionate and ungenerous.

1378. பிடாரி வரம் கொடுத்தாலும், ஒச்சன் வரம் கொடுக்கிறதில்லை.

Though Pidâri (a village goddess) may grant a gift, it will be difficult to get a gift from her priest!

Cf. 1357 *ff.*

A MASTER NECESSARY EVERYWHERE.

1379. அரசன் இல்லாத படை வெட்டுமோ?

Will an army without a king fight? 1344, 1381.

1380. அரசனில்லாத நாடு, புருஷனில்லாத வீடு.

A country without a king is a house without a man in it. 1341. 3168.

1381. ஆளில்லாமல் ஆயுதம் வெட்டுமோ?

Will a sword cut without a person to wield it? 1377.

1382. கடிவாளமில்லாத குதிரை.

A horse without a bridle.

1383. கயிறு இல்லாத பம்பரம்.

A top without a string.

1384. *கூத்தியார் பிள்ளைக்குத் தகப்பன் யார்?*
Who is the father of the harlot's child?

Her children have no legal father. The proverb is used on occasions when a head or master is wanting to an affair.

1385. *தலை இருக்க வால் ஆடுமோ?*
While the head is still, will the tail wag?

The servant can do nothing except on the initiative of his master.

MISCELLANEOUS PROVERBS ON AUTHORITY.

1386. எசமான் வெளியே போனால் பசங்கள் எல்லாம் கும்மாளம் போடுவார்கள்.
When the master is out all the children and servants romp about.

" *When the cat's away, the mice will play.*"

1387. எருது (or ஆடு) நினைத்த இடத்தில் தொழும் (or பட்டி) கட்டுகிறதா?
Are we to build the stall (*or* fold) where the bullock (*or* sheep) thinks proper?

" *An ass must be tied where the master will have him.*"

1389. *தலைக்குமேல் குடை இருக்கிறது.*
There is an umbrella over my head. 299, 300.

There is authority over me to protect me. The umbrella always signifies *dignity* and *authority* in India.

1390. வாத்தியாரை மெச்சின பிள்ளை இல்லை.
There is no child that praises its teacher. 3640.

No servant is satisfied with his master.

1390*a*. பாழ் ஊருக்கு நரி ராஜா.
A jackal is the king in a deserted village.

To rule over something worthless.

" *King among cobblers.*"

LIKE MASTER, LIKE SERVANT.

1391. குருவுக்கு ஏற்ற சிஷன்.
A disciple suited to his spiritual teacher (*guru*). 475, 2286

1392. *தான் அடங்க, தன் குலம் விளங்க.*
If he be humble, his caste will be notable. 856.

" *A good Jack makes a good Jill.*"

1393. பாரதம் எப்படி பக்தர்கள் அப்படி.
As is the Mahâbhârata, so are its devotees.

" *Water never rises above its level.*"

1394. ராஜன் எவ்வழி, குடிகள் அவ்வழி.

As is the king, so are his subjects.

The masses will behave like their superiors.

1395. ராமனைப்போல் ராஜா இருந்தால். அனுமானைப்போல் சேவகனுமிருப்பான்.

If the King is like *Rama*, his servant will be like *Hanuman*.

A good master makes a good servant. The Râmâyana tells of the faithful service that the monkey-god *Hanuman* rendered to *Rama*.

Cf. 2259 *ff*.

MANY MASTERS.

1396. ஆர் ஆருக்கு ஆளானேன், ஆகாத உடம்பையும் புண்ணாக்கிக்கொண்டு?

To whom am I to submit? My worthless body is all ulcerated.

Said in disgust by one who has too many masters.

"*The ass of many owners is eaten by the wolf.*"

1397. ஆளுக்கு ஒரு குட்டுக் குட்டினால், அடியேன் தலை மொட்டை.

Being buffeted by every one, miserable creature that I am, my head has become bald!

Said by one who is ill-treated by everybody, or by one who has a small income and out of it lends various little sums to different persons, till he is helpless himself.

"*A pot that belongs to many is ill stirred and worse boiled.*"

1398. ஊருக்கு ஒரு தேவடியாள் ஆருக்கு என்று ஆடுவாள்?

The village has only one dancing-girl; for whom is she to dance?

As all want her services, she is not only in doubt where to go, but also suffers from being overworked. Very commonly said by a daughter-in-law who comes from a poor home and who is therefore despised and overworked by her mother-in-law's household.

1399. ஊருக்கு இளைத்தவன் பிள்ளையார் கோவில் ஆண்டி?

One who is a cripple in a village becomes a mendicant at *Ganesa's* temple. 3351.

Ganesa's temple is not highly esteemed, and there is no money to be had there, so the case of the mendicant who takes up his abode there is likely to be a hard one. A member of a family or a servant who is despised by all and required to do all sorts of work says this about himself, or another says it about him.

1400. ஒரு கூடைகல்லும் தெய்வமானால், கும்பிடுகிறது எந்தக் கல்லை?

If all the stones in a basket are gods, which stone am I to worship?

If all are masters, who is to be obeyed?

1401. ஓட்டைக் கப்பலுக்கு ஒன்பது மாலுமி.

For a leaky ship there are nine captains.

Said when there are many heads to a profitless undertaking.

1402. கஞ்சி வார்க்க ஆளில்லாமல்போனாலும், கச்சை கட்ட ஆளிருக்கிறது.
Though there is no man to pour out the gruel, there will be somebody to tie the girdle (*i. e.*, to quarrel). 1144.

If a woman has no protector, and yet manages to provide for herself, everything that she does will be criticised, and she will get all sorts of contrary orders.

1404. பிடித்தவர்களுக்கு எல்லாம் பெண்டு?
(I am a) woman that everybody can take hold of!

Said by a woman who is disgusted by having too many masters in the house. If her husband is too easy going and his brothers begin to order her about, a woman will say this. It is also said of a woman of light virtue.

" *Better master one than engage with ten.*"

EXAGGERATION.

அதிகமாக்குதல்.

1405. ஈரைப் பேனாக்கிப், பேனைப் பெருமாள் ஆக்குகிறான்.
He makes a nit a louse, and a louse into the God Vishnu.
" *To make a mountain of a mole hill.*"

1406. ஒன்றைப் பத்தாகவும், பத்தை ஒன்றாகவும் சாதிக்கிறான்.
He maintains that one is ten, and ten is one.

1407. கண்ணாரக் காணாதது மூன்று பங்கு.
What he has not seen is three times what he has seen.

1408. துரும்பைத் தூணாக்கிறதா?
Do you make a straw into a pillar?

EXCESS AND DEFICIENCY.

அதிகம்.

"TOO LITTLE AND TOO MUCH SPOILS EVERYTHING."

1409. அளவுக்கு மிஞ்சினால் அமிர்தமும் விஷம்.
If taken in excess even nectar is poisonous. 1304.

1410. அறக்குழைத்தாலும் குழைப்பாள், அரிசியாய் இறக்கினாலும் இறக்குவாள்.
She will either boil the rice too much, or not boil it at all.

Said of a person who goes to extremes.

1411. கரும்பை விரும்ப விரும்ப வேம்பு.
If you constantly long for (and eat) sugarcane, it will become bitter *margosa* (to you).

The leaves and the oil of the *Margosa (Azadirachta Indica)* are very bitter.

" *More than enough breaks the cover.*"

1412. சேரச் சேரச் செடியும் பகை.
If you draw too near, even a plant will hate you. 2773.
" *You can have too much of a good thing.*"

1413. நித்தம் போனால் முற்றம் சலிக்கும்.
If you go daily (to see the same people), the entrance of their house will be disgusted. 2744, 2755.
" *Familiarity breeds contempt.*"

1414. படுக்கப் படுக்கப் பாயும் பகை.
If you lie down too often, your bed (mat) will hate you.

1415. பழகப் பழகப் பாலும் புளிக்கும்.
If you constantly drink milk, it will become sour to you.
A constant guest is never welcome.

1416. பெய்தும் கெடுத்தது, காய்ந்தும் கெடுத்தது.
If it rains, the crop is spoiled; if there is a drought, it is also spoiled.

1417. வைத்தியன் பிள்ளை நோவு தீராது, உவாத்தியர் பிள்ளைக்குப் படிப்பு வராது.
The sickness of a doctor's child will not be cured, and a teacher's child will not learn.
The doctor gives too much medicine, and the teacher overdoes his teaching.

ABUNDANCE.

அளவு.

1418. இத்தனை அத்தனையானால், அத்தனை எத்தனையாகும்?
If this amounts to that, how much will that be?

1419. கழுதைப் புட்டை கை நிரம்பினால் போதும்.
He is satisfied if he gets his hands full of asses' dung! 3076.
Said of one who looks to the quantity rather than the quality of his profits.
" *A bellyful is a bellyful whether it be meat or drink.*"

1420. கொசுவு மூத்திரம் குறுணி.
The urine of a mosquito is plentiful!
No want of worthless things.

1421. மலிந்த சரக்கு (or பண்டம்) கடைத்தெருவுக்கு வரும்.
When there is plenty of grain (*or* provision), it will come to the bazaar-street for sale. 2582.
If sin abounds, or is not kept with in limits, it will come to the knowledge of the public.

1422. விரல் உரல் ஆனால், உரல் என்ன ஆகும்?
If a finger becomes as big as a rice-mortar, how big will the rice-mortar become? 2048.

RARITY, SCARCITY.

அருமை.

1423. அத்திப் பூ கண்டதுபோல.
Like seeing the flower of a fig tree. 1427, 1428.
The blossom of the fig is not to be distinguished from the fruit itself. Said in joy on seeing a friend whom one has not seen for a long time.

1424. அன்னப்பிடி வெல்லப்பிடி ஆச்சுது.
A handful of rice has become (as dear) as a handful of sugar. 1429, 1430.

1425. உத்தியோகம் குதிரைக் கொம்பாயிருக்கிறது.
Employment has become like the horns of a horse.
"*It is as rare as hen's teeth.*"

1426. ஒரு துட்டு ஒரு ரூபாயாயிருக்கிறது.
A small copper coin is now a rupee!

1427. கார்த்திகைப் பிறை கண்டவன்போல.
Like the man who saw the new moon in November (*Kârttikei*).
A rare sight, as the sky is overcast with clouds in this rainy month.

1428. காற்றிலே கருப்பிலே கண்டதில்லை (or நினைக்கவில்லை).
I have not seen him either in storm or in famine.
These two are rare, so the proverb is used of rare visitors.

1429. சோறு வெல்லமாய்ப் போச்சுது.
Boiled rice has become sugar. 1424, 1739.
i.e., Rice has become as dear as sugar.

1430. பிண்டம் பெருங்காயம், அன்னம் கஸ்தூரி.
Food has become (as dear as) assafœtida, and rice (as rare as) musk.
"*In ill years straw is corn.*"

SUPERABUNDANCE.

அருமையில்லாமை.

1431. அணிற்பிள்ளைக்கு நுங்கு அரிதோ, ஆண்டிச்சி பிள்ளைக்குச் சோறு அரிதோ?
Is palmyra fruit a rarity to a squirrel? Is rice a rarity to a beggar-woman's child?
A sarcasm on the 'poverty' of religious mendicants.

1432. இருளன் பிள்ளைக்கு எலிக்குஞ்சு கருப்பா?
Does a hunter's son ever find a scarcity of young rats.
This caste eats rats, and rats are never scarce.

1433. உரல் பஞ்சம் அறியுமா?
Does the rice-mortar experience the famine?
Nearly all food stuffs are pounded in it before being cooked, and even in famine times there is something to be pounded.

1434. கலியாணத்திலும் பஞ்சமில்லை, களத்திலும் பஞ்சமில்லை.
At a wedding and on the threshing-floor there is no scarcity.
No one need be hungry at the one or on the other.

1435. கொண்ட கடையிலேயா விற்கிறது?
Should you sell things in the very shop where you bought them?

1436. கொல்லன் தெருவிலே ஊசி விற்கிறதா?
Why sell needles in a blacksmith's street?
"Carrying coals to Newcastle."

1437. தீப்பட்ட வீட்டிலே கரிக்கட்டை பஞ்சமா?
Is there any lack of charcoal in a house that has been burnt down.

1438. வேடனுக்குத் தேன் பஞ்சமா? மூடனுக்கு அடி பஞ்சமா?
Is a hunter ever in want of honey; does a fool ever lack a beating.

EXPERIENCE.

அனுபோகம்.

LEARNING BY EXPERIENCE.

1439. அப்பன் அருமை அப்பன் செத்தால் தெரியும், உப்பின் அருமை உப்பில்லாதேபோனால் தெரியும்.
The worth of a father is only known at his death, and the worth of salt is only known when it is lacking. 1288.
"You never miss the water till the well goes dry."

1440. காவடிப்பாரம் சுமக்கிறவனுக்குத் தெரியும்.
He who bears the yoke knows its weight. 1447.
The yoke or *Kavadi* here referred to is that used when anything dedicated to a deity is carried to the temple by the person who has offered it.
"No one knows the weight of another's burden."

1441. தலைநோவும் காய்ச்சலும் தனக்கு வந்தால் தெரியும்.
If one gets head-ache and fever himself he will know what they are.
"He laughs at scars who never felt a wound."

1442. நிழல் அருமை வெயிலில் போனால் தெரியும்.
If you walk in the sun, you will know the blessedness of (being in the) shade.
"Health is not valued till sickness comes."

1443. பட்டால் தெரியும் பறையனுக்கு.
A Pariah will learn if he suffers.

"*Adversity makes a man wise, not rich.*"

1443*a*. பட்டால் தெரியும் பார்ப்பானுக்கு, கெட்டால் தெரியும் கோமுட்டிக்கு.
A Brahmin will learn if he suffers, and a *Komutti* will learn if he is ruined!

A Brahmin will only behave well after suffering, and a *Komutti* will be brought to his senses by losing the capital he has invested. The *Komutti* caste is a class of rich merchants.

1444. பார்த்தால் தெரியுமா, பட்டால் தெரியுமா வருத்தம்?
Is it by beholding pain or by suffering pain yourself that you learn to understand it?

"*Experience teaches.*" "*Need makes the old wife trot.*"

Cf. 1288 *ff.*

"EVERY MAN KNOWS BEST WHERE HIS OWN SHOE PINCHES."

1445. எருது நோய் காக்கைக்குத் தெரியுமா?
Does a crow know what pain it causes a bullock?

Crows frequently get on the back of bullocks and peck at any sores they may find.

1446. கண்ணுக்குப் புண்ணுமல்ல, காண்பார்க்கு நோவுமல்ல.
(Mine is) a disease which the eye cannot see; and lookers-on do not notice it.

i.e., The pain is real, but secret.

"*Every heart knows its own bitterness.*"

1447. சுமை எடுப்பவனுக்குச் சுமை பளுவு தெரியும்.
He who carries the burden knows the weight of it. 1440.

1448. நோயாளிக்குத் தெரியும் நோயின் வருத்தம்.
The sick person knows the pain of his malady.

"*I know best where the shoe wringeth me.*"

1449. முட்டை இடுகிற கோழிக்கு வருத்தம் தெரியும்.
The hen that lays the egg knows the pain.

MISCELLANEOUS PROVERBS ABOUT EXPERIENCE.

1450. இடைச்சன் பிள்ளைக்காரிக்குத் தலைச்சன் பிள்ளைக்காரி மருத்துவம் பார்த்தாற்போல.
Like the woman who had only borne one child, but wanted to be midwife to one who was going to have her second child. 3325.

1451. இறைச்சி தின்கிறவன் கடுப்புக்கு மருந்து அறிவான்.
A flesh-eater knows the medicines for (stomach) complaints.

Flesh-eating is considered abominable by large sections of Hindus.

1452. கலப்பணத்தைவிட, ஒரு கிழப்பிணம் நல்லது.
An old corpse is better than a big measure full of money. 3628.

The experience of the aged is worth more than money.

1453. காதவழி போய் அறியாதவன் மாதம் எல்லாம் நடந்தானும்.
He who had never walked ten miles, is said to have walked the whole month (before he had advanced ten miles).

Having no experience in walking, he was unable to make progress quickly.

1454. குடியிருந்து பார், கூட்டுப்பயிர் இட்டுப்பார்.
Learn to know people by living with them, and by farming with them. 1713.

Know people by mingling with them in daily life.

1455. தேவடியாள் பீ எடுத்தாற்போல.
Like a dancing-girl wiping a child.

A dancing girl is supposed to have no children, so she does not know how to keep them clean. Said of one who tries to mend a matter, but lacks experience and makes things worse than they were before.

1456. தொட்டுக் காட்டாத வித்தைச் சுட்டுப்போட்டாலும் வராது.
Learning not acquired from practical example will never become your own, even if it is branded on you. 3566.

The teacher must exemplify his teaching if the disciple is really to grasp it.

"*Practice not your art, and it will soon depart.*"

"*Precepts may lead, but examples draw.*"

"*The example of good men is visible philosophy.*"

"*Religion is best understood when most practiced.*" (*Cf.* John 7, 17.)

1457. நேற்று வெட்டின கிணற்றிலே முந்தாநாள் வந்த முதலேபோல.
Like the crocodile that came the day before yesterday into the well that was only dug yesterday.

Said sarcastically about some one who professes long acquaintance with what he has only recently learned.

1458. பட்டா உன் பேரில், சாகுபடி ஊரிலே (or என்மேலே).
The deed is in your name, the fruits of the cultivation are enjoyed by the village (*or* by me).

One has the right, another the profit. Said when a married woman lives with a man who is not her husband.

"*Wealth is not his who gets it, but his who enjoys it.*"

1459. புதிய வண்ணானும், பழைய அம்பட்டனும் தேடு.
Get a new washerman and an old barber! 1461.

With the former muscular exertion is all that is wanted; with the latter, skill.

"*A barber learns to shave by shaving fools.*"

1460. மலடிக்குத் தெரியுமா பிள்ளையைப் பெற்ற அருமை?
Does a barren woman understand the joy of motherhood?

"*He who has no children knows not what is love.*"

1461. வால ஜோசியனும், விருத்த வைத்தியனும் நன்று.
A young astrologer and an aged doctor are best. 1459.
" *An old physician, a young lawyer.*"

1462. வீட்டைக் கட்டிப்பார், கலியாணம் செய்துபார்.
Build a house and see what happens, marry and see what happens. 3514.
Only actual experience will reveal the cost of a house and the expense of a wedding.
" *Building and marrying of children are great wasters.*

PRACTICE, EXPERTNESS.

பழக்கம், அப்பியாசம்.

1463. அப்பியாசம் கூசா வித்தை.
Practice is the science that gives confidence.
" *Practice makes perfect.*"

1464. அப்பியாசம் குல விருது.
Expertness in an art is the glory (*lit.* trophy) of a caste.

1465. அரைச்சொற்கொண்டு அம்பலம் ஏறினால், அரைச்சொல் முழுச்சொல்லாமா?
If one attempts to gain popularity with half a word (*i.e.*, with little learning) will his half word ever become a whole word? 1466.

1466. அறையில் ஆடியல்லவோ அம்பலத்தில் ஆடவேண்டும்.
It is only after practising in a room, that one may perform in public. 1465.
" *By working we become workmen.*"

1466*a*. ஊமையன் பேச்சு பழகின பேருக்குத் தெரியும்.
Those who are used to the signs (*lit.* speech) of the dumb, understand them.
" *Custom makes everything easy.*"

1467. எந்த ஆயுதமும் தீட்டத் தீட்டக் கூர்.
The more any weapon is whetted, the sharper (it becomes). 2083.
Every one needs continual discipline to become good.

1468. ஒரு கூண்டு முடைந்தவன் ஒன்பது கூண்டு முடைவான்.
He who can plait one basket will plait nine.
" *He that makes one basket may make a hundred.*"

1469. சித்திரமும் கைப்பழக்கம், செந்தமிழும் நாப்பழக்கம்.
By practising the hand you learn how to draw pictures, by practising the tongue you learn to speak classical Tamil.
" *All things are difficult before they are easy.*"

Cf. 1881 *ff.*

KNOWLEDGE.

அறிவு.

TO KNOW ONE'S SELF.

1470. *கணக்கன் கணக்கு அறிவான், தன் கணக்கைத் தான் அறியான்.*
An accountant knows others' accounts, but not his own.
People can adviso others but do not apply their knowledge to themselves.

1471. *கல்வி கற்கிறதைவிட, தன் கருத்து ஆராய்கிறது நன்மை.*
It is better to investigate one's own thoughts than to study science.
"A handful of good life is better than a bushel of learning."
"Self-examination is a good medicine for the soul."

1472. *தன்னை அறிந்தவன், தலைவனை அறிவான்.*
He who knows himself will know the Ruler (*i.e.*, God).
"A disease known is half cured."
"It is a great point of wisdom to find out one's own folly."

MAN'S KNOWLEDGE LIMITED.

அறிவு, கல்வி.

1473. *எத்தனை வித்தை கற்றாலும், செத்தவனைப் பிழைப்பிக்க அறியான்.*
However much you learn, you do not know how to raise the dead. 1502.
Hindus sometimes say this about Europeans.

1474. *எல்லாம் அறிந்தவனுமில்லை, ஒன்றும் அறியாதவனுமில்லை.*
No one knows everything, nor is there anyone who does not know something.
"No living man all things can."

1475. *கண்ணில் கண்டது கோடி, காணாதது அனந்தம் கோடி.*
What we have seen with our eyes is very much, but what we have not seen is infinite.
"Half the world knows not how the other half lives."

1476. *கற்றது கையளவு, கல்லாதது உலகளவு.*
What we have learned is a handful, what we have not learned is a world in quantity.

1477. *காசிமுதல் ராமேஸ்வரம்வரையில் தெரிந்தவன்.*
He knows everything from Benâres to Râmêsvaram. 1805.
i.e., He knows everything in the land of India. Ironical.
"Jack of all trades and master of none."

1478. காட்டில் புதைத்த கனதனமும், பாட்டில் புதைத்த பழம்பொருளும், வீட்டின் மனையாள் மனமும், அறிவது அரிது.

In the country it is difficult to know these three things: the treasure buried in the forest, the old meaning buried in a song, and the heart of the mistress of a house.

1479. குறை அறக் கற்றவன் கோடியில் ஒருவன்.
A learned man without defects is one among ten millions.

A LEARNED FOOL.

1480. அறக்கூர்மை முழுமொட்டை.
A sharp blade (gives) a good shave.

Said of a man who gets himself into trouble through his own over-cleverness.

"*A mere scholar is a mere ass.*"

1481. கற்றறி மோழை.
Though learned yet stupid.

1482. கெட்டிக்கார முட்டாள்.
Clever, but a fool.

"*Folly and learning often dwell together.*"

1483. சொன்னதைச் சொல்லும் கிளிப்பிள்ளை.
A parrot will only say what it is taught. 510*a*, 1539.

This is explained in the Mahâbhârata thus:—கிளி எவ்வளவு கற்றுக் கொண்டாலும், பூனை பிடித்தால், "அம்மா, பூனை பிடிக்கிறது" என்று சொல்லாது, However much a parrot may learn, it is unable to cry out: "Mother, the cat is laying hold of me," if the cat seizes it.

"*All is but lip wisdom that wanteth experience.*"

1484. படித்து முட்டாளாயிருக்கிறான்.
He has studied, but is a fool.

1485. மெத்தப் படித்தவன் பைத்தியக்காரன்.
He who has much learning is mad.

"*Thy much learning doth turn thee to madness.*" (Act. 26, 24.)

Cf. 1221 *ff.*

MISCELLANEOUS SAYINGS ON LEARNING AND LEARNED MEN.

1486. அவிவேகி உறவிலும், விவேகி பகையே நன்று.
Better is the hatred of a learned man than the friendship of a fool.

"*A friend's frown is better than a fool's smile.*"

1487. அறப்படித்தவன் அங்காடிபோனால், விற்கவுமாட்டான், கொள்ளவுமாட்டான்.

If a very learned man goes to the market he will neither sell nor buy. 1507.

A sneer at learning as having nothing to do with matters of common life.

"*Experience without learning is better than learning without experience.*"

1488. அறிய அறிய கெடுவார் உண்டா?

Will any one suffer by constantly exerting himself to learn?

1489. அறிவு ஆர் அறிவார்? ஆய்ந்தவர் அறிவார்.

Who comprehends knowledge? He who reflects.

1490. அறிவு பெருத்தோன் நோய் பெருத்தோன்.

He who increases knowledge, increases sorrow.

"*For in much wisdom is much grief.*" (Ecclesiastes 1, 18.)

1491. உடைமை என்பது கல்வியுடைமை.

Wealth of learning is (true) wealth.

1492. எழுத வழங்காத வாழ்வு கழுதை புரண்ட களம்.

The life of one who cannot write is like the threshing-floor where an ass has been rolling.

"*Better unborn than untaught.*"

1493. கசடான கல்வியினும் கல்வியீனம் நலம்.

Ignorance is better than imperfect learning.

"*Better untaught than ill taught.*"

1494. கண்டதைக் கற்கப் பண்டிதன் ஆவான்.

He who studies what he sees will become a learned man.

1495. கல்லாதவரே கண்ணில்லாதவர்.

A man without learning is a man without eyes.

1496. கல்லாதார் செல்வத்திலும் கற்றார் வறுமை நலம்.

The poverty of the learned is better than the wealth of the unlearned.

1497. கல்வி அழகே அழகு.

The beauty of learning is (true) beauty.

1498. கல்வி என்ற பயிருக்குக் கண்ணீர் என்ற மழை வேண்டும்.

The rain of tears is necessary to the harvest of learning.

"*There is no royal road to learning.*"

1499. கற்பித்தவன் கண்ணைக் கொடுத்தவன்.

He who teaches is a giver of eyes.

1500. கற்றதைக் காய்ச்சியா குடிக்கப்போகிறாய்.

Do you boil and drink your own learning?

Refers to many learned pundits in India who keep their wisdom to themselves.

1501. கெடுக்கினும், கல்வி கேடுப்படாது.
Whatever else may be destroyed, learning will not be destroyed.

1502. கை உண்டாவது கற்றவர்களுக்கு ஆமே.
Only the learned possess hands (*i.e.*, ability).

1502*a*. சாவாமல் கற்பதே கல்வி, பிறர் இடத்தில் ஏகாமல் உண்பதே உணவு.
That is learning which teaches you to escape death, and that is food which is eaten without your going to others (to beg it). 1473.

1502*b*. நீட்டு வித்தை ஏறுமா ?
Will learning long drawn out be worth much ?

1503. நுனியில் மேய்கிறது.
To graze on the tops (of herbs).

Said of one who has superficial knowledge only ; or of one who, though he possesses only superficial knowledge, talks as if he knew everything.

1504. பழிப்பான கல்வி பாவத்தின் ஊற்று.
Faulty knowledge is the source of sin.

1505. வித்துவானுக்கு ஏது பரதேசம்.
What land is foreign to a learned man ?

His learning fits him to live in any country.

1506. வைத்தியம், ஜோசியம், சங்கீதம், மந்திரம் தெரியாதவர்களில்லை.
Everyone knows something of doctoring, astrology, music and exorcisms.

1507. வைத்தியன் காய்கறிக்குப் போனதுபோல.
Like the doctor who went to buy vegetables. 1487.

His learning made him criticise everything and buy nothing.

" *Gentry sent to market will not buy one bushel of corn.*"

N.B.—As these aphorisms (for very few of them are *proverbs*) on learning abound in Hindu literature, a few only are given. They might be multiplied indefinitely.

BLESSINGS.

ஆசீர்வாதம்.

1508. ஆல்போல் விழுது விட்டு, அறுகுபோல வேர் ஓடி, மூங்கில்போல சுற்றும் முசியாமல் வாழ்ந்திருப்பீர்கள்.

May you prosper without fail, sending down fresh stems like a Banyan tree, taking root like the spreading *Arugu* grass, and surrounded (by friends) like a Bamboo (surrounded by other Bamboos). 2595.

" Happy man and beauteous bride,
Be this place your home of pride !
Loving man and dutious wife,
In peaceful union pass your life !
May prattling children fill your home with peace,
And lisping babes their grand-sire's bliss increase !"

DUTT : " *Lays of Ancient India.*"

1509. என் வயசு போட்டுக்கொண்டிரு.
May you take my age upon you.
i.e., May you live to be as old as I am! Said by an old man to young people.

1510. கெடுப்பதும் வாயால், படிப்பதும் வாயால்.
With the mouth you injure others, and with the mouth you read (the Vedas). 1511.

1511. சீச்சீ என்கிறதும் இந்த வாய்தான், சிவ சிவா என்கிறதும் இந்த வாய் தான்.
With the same mouth you say 'Fie, Fie,' and 'Siva, Siva.' 2443, 2501, 2689.
"*With the tongue bless we God, and therewith curse we men.*" (James 4, 9.)

1512. திட்டிக் கெட்டாருமில்லை, வாழ்த்தி வாழ்ந்தாருமில்லை.
No man was ever ruined by being cursed, and no one ever prospered because he was blessed. 3125.
"*No one dies of threats.*"

1513. பதினாறும் பெற்று, பெருவாழ்வும் வாழ்கிறது.
May you have sixteen children and live most prosperously.
"*One year of joy, another of comfort, and all the rest of content.*"

1514. மார்க்கண்டாயுசாயிரு.
May you always be of the age of *Markandeya* (*i.e.*, always be a youth). 2216.
Markandeya was the sage who was the author of the sacred book called the Markandeya Purana, he was fated to die in his 16th year; but through severe penance and invocation of Siva secured everlasting youth.
"*So that thy youth is renewed like the eagle's.*" (Psalm 123, 5.)

CURSES.

சாபம்.

N.B.—"There are four measures of good, but nine of filth in this world." (3014.) So says a proverb and it is emphatically true that Tamil curses are more numerous than Tamil blessings. A few common curses are subjoined.

1515. இடி விழுவான்.
May he be struck dead!

1516. உன் இழவு எடுக்க.
May your funeral take place!

1517. உன் வாயிலே மண் விழ.
May earth fall into your mouth!
i.e., May you die!

1518. உன்னைப் பாடையிலே வைத்துப் பிரயாணம் (com. பயணம்) இட.
May you be laid on the bier, and take your journey!
i.e., May you be carried to the burning-ground!

1519. உன் தாலி அறுந்து தண்ணீர் பானையில் விழ.
May your *thâli* be cut off and fall into a water pot!

1520. உன் பெண்சாதி தாலி பிணத்தின்பேரில் விழ.
May your wife's *thâli* fall on your corpse!
May you die and your wife be left a widow!

1521. உன் பிள்ளையைத் தின்று, தண்ணீர் குடிக்க.
May you have to eat your own child, and drink water after it (*i.e.*, digest it)!

1522. உன் எண்ணத்தில் எமன் பூர.
May *Death* blight your prospects!

1523. உன் கொண்டை குலைய.
May your hair be dishevelled!
i.e., May you have to mourn for the death of your husband! In India a widow is condemned to a life of wretchedness.

1524. உன்னை வெட்டி பலிபோட.
May you be cut down and sacrificed!

1525. உன்னை அள்ளத்துள்ள கொண்டுபோக.
May you be taken away while you struggle for life!

1526. உன் பொங்கு குங்க.
May your pride be brought down!

1527. உன் மதம் மண்ணாய்ப்போக.
May your pride become dust!

1528. உன்னை ஒண்டிப் பாடை கட்ட.
May you go to the grave alone!
Hindus believe that when one man dies, another one also dies somewhere else. In using this saying the speaker expresses a wish that the person addressed may not have any such comrade at the hour of death.

1529. ஓரம் வெளுத்து, ஒரு பக்கம் செல்லு அரிக்க.
May your lips be bleached white, and white ants gnaw one of your sides!

1530. கட்டையிலே வைப்பான்.
He will be laid on his funeral pile!

1531. தொண்டையிலே கண்டமாலை புறப்பட.
May scrofula come out on your neck!

1532. மாரியாத்தாள் குழியில் மறைத்துவைக்க.
May you be hidden in the pit of the goddess of small-pox!

1533. பல்லிலே பச்சரிசி வைக்க.
May raw rice be put into your mouth!

Rico is put into the mouth of a corpse during tho funeral ceremonies.

1534. வஞ்சனை நெஞ்சு அடைக்க.
May your deceit choke you!

IMITATION.

1535. அன்ன நடை நடக்கப்போய், தன் நடையும் கெட்டதுபோல.
Like the man who tried to walk like a swan, and thereby lost his own way of walking. 3325.

This proverb has a wide range of application all over the world. It is especially applicable to India where the transition from an old civilization to a new is so marked. Tamils describe a person who follows the new fashions as இரண்டாம் கெட்டான், 'He is spoiled a second time,' or திரிசங்கு ராஜா போல 'He is like king Trisanku.' Trisanku did much good to the Rishi Viswamitra, in return for which Viswamitra tried to elevate Trisanku in his mortal body to heaven. But the Gods were unwilling to receive him and a compromise had to be made between the Gods and Viswamitra, by which Trisanku was left suspended between heaven and earth. (*Vishnu Purana*, Book 4, Chap.3.)

"*Apes are never more beasts, than when they wear men's clothes.*"

1536. ஆமையுடன் முசல் முட்டை இடப்போய் கண் பிதுங்கி செத்ததாம்.
It is said that when a hare went with a turtle to lay eggs, its eyes bulged out and it died.

Cf. The story in "Aesop's Fables" about the frog that tried to make itself as big as an ox, but burst in the effort.

1537. ஊர் ஒக்க ஓடவேண்டும்.
Agree with the village and go on your way!

Do as others do, and you will be safe!

"*You must do at Rome as Rome does.*"

1538. கண்ட பாவனையாய்க் கொண்டை முடிக்கிறது.
Arranging her hair in imitation of others.

Also said of a person who takes undue liberties with strangers, as if he were an old friend.

1539. தாயில்லாதவனுக்கு ஊர் எல்லாம் தாய்.
The whole village will be a mother to a motherless child. 1483.

The story goes that a certain man who was headman or judge in his village quoted this proverb in order to console his younger brother after the death of their mother. The younger brother, who was a great fool, succeeded his brother in the office of headman or judge in due time, and as it was his principle to imitate the doings and sayings of his brother matters went on well for a time. But one day a man whose wife had died came to him for consolation and he, mindful of the way in which his elder brother had comforted him when their mother died, quoted the above saying adapting it to circumstances thus:—

1539*a*. உன் பெண்சாதி ஊருக்கும் எல்லாம் பெண்சாதி, எனக்கும் பெண் சாதி அல்லவா?

Was not your wife the wife of the whole village, and was not she my wife?

It need hardly be said that this was no consolation to the bereaved husband. The whole story is a satire of senseless imitation.

1540. நீர் ஓட்டத்தில் தெப்பம் செல்லும் தன்மைபோல.

Like a raft that goes with the current.

"*It is hard striving against a stream.*"

1541. பங்காளத்து நாய் சிங்காசனம்மேல் ஏறினது என்று வண்ணான் கழுதை வெள்ளாவி பானையில் ஏறினதாம்.

It is said, that a washerman's ass having seen a Bengali dog ascending a throne mounted it's master's washing pot (and broke it).

When inferiors ape their betters, ruin is the result.

1542. பார்ப்பாரைப் பார்த்துப் பரதேசம் போகிறதுபோல.

Like looking at others and going a pilgrimage.

Primarily used of imitation of a good example, but also used of those who follow a bad example, and sometimes applied to young Hindus who imitate European customs and habits.

"*He that for the new way leaveth the old way, is often times found to go astray.*"

1543. புலியைப் பார்த்துப் பூனை சூடு போட்டுக்கொண்டதுபோல.

Like the cat who saw a tiger and branded itself (so as to be striped like the tiger)!

Persons in inferior stations in life should not try to imitate the great lest they hurt themselves.

"*Borrowed garments never fit well.*"

1544. மயிலைக் கண்டு வான்கோழி ஆடினதுபோல.

Like the turkey who saw a peacock and danced!

"*An ape is ne'er so like an ape as when he wears a doctor's cap.*"

Cf. 2324 *ff.*

FLATTERY.

மெச்சல்.

1545. அங்கும் இருப்பான், இங்கும் இருப்பான், ஆக்கின சோற்றுக்குப் பங்கும் இருப்பான்.

He is there and he is here, and he is sure to come for his share of food. 606, 1057.

Some persons by carrying tales of different people to their enemies, gain favour from both parties. This proverb is said sarcastically about such busy-bodies.

"*Like a dog in a fair: here, there, everywhere.*"

1546. *அம்பாத்தூர் வேளாண்மை யானை கட்டத்தாள், வானமுட்டும் போர்; ஆறுகொண்டது பாதி, தூறுகொண்டது பாதி.*

In the harvest at Ambattur (village) the stubble (was strong enough) to tie up an elephant, and the stacks reached the sky; but a flood carried off half, and the jungle took half.

The story goes that when the tax-collector came to assess the village crops, the village headman uttered the first part of this proverb as a description of the good harvest. But a farmer held up his hand in such a way as to show the village headman his golden ring, signifying that a heavy bribe would be paid to him if the taxes were remitted, so the headman added the second part of the proverb—for it was more important to please the farmers of the village than to give an exact return to the collector.

"*He hath a conscience like a cheverel's skin, that will stretch.*"

1547. *அரசன் ஒன்றை இகழ்ந்தால் ஒக்க இகழவேண்டும், ஒன்றைப் புகழ்ந்தால் ஒக்கப் புகழவேண்டும்.*

If a king speaks and contemns anything, you must contemn it likewise; if he praises anything, you must praise it likewise.

"*Like a miller, he can set to every wind.*"

1548. *அரசன் கல்லின்மேலே கத்திரி காய்க்கும் என்றால், கொத்து ஆயிரம் குலை ஆயிரம் என்பார்கள்.*

If the king says, the *brinjal* (vegetable) will grow on stones; the people will say, in thousands of bunches, in thousands of clusters.

"*A flatterer's throat is an open sepulchre.*"

1549. *அவன் நடைக்குப் பத்துப்பேர் வருவார்கள், கைவீச்சுக்குப் பத்துப் பேர் வருவார்கள்.*

Ten people will imitate his style of walking, and ten others will swing their hands like him. 3439.

Said in flattery of or irony about an ugly person.

1550. *உற்றார் தின்றால் புற்றாய் விளையும், ஊரார் தின்றால் பேராய் விளையும்.*

If one's own people are fed, an anthill grows up; but if the villagers are fed, your reputation will grow. 1553, 1565, 3196.

1551. *அவன் சூத்தைத் தாங்குகிறான்.*

He supports that man's breech.

Said of one who flatters to please, or *காக்காய்ப் பிடிக்கிறது*, he is catching crows.

1552. *இலுப்பை சக்கரை கொடையாம், துரைகள் மெச்சின நடையாம்.*

Flattery of gentlemen is the way to get common sugar as a gift.

Said in ridicule of one who takes pains to please a great person, and gets little by it.

1553. உடல் மெச்சப் பால் குடிக்கிறாயா? ஊர் மெச்சப் பால் குடிக்கிறாயா?
Do you drink milk to please your body or to please the village? 1550, 1565, 1583, 2146, 2147, 3193.
"He that doth good for praise only, meriteth but a puff of wind."

1554. உனக்கு உட்பட்டுப் பின்பாட்டுப் பாடுகிற மனிதர்கள்போல்.
Like people who depend on you, and therefore sing after you.
"To dance to every man's pipe."

1555. எச்சிற்கல்லைக்கு இச்சகம் பேசுகிறது.
To flatter for a leaf-plate! 1562, 1563.
Flattery for something worth nothing!
"The coin most common is flattery."

1556. எடுப்பார் கை குழந்தை.
He is a baby (who goes) to anyone who will take him!
One who yields to everybody.
"To turn with the wind and tide."

1557. கூத்துக்கு ஏற்ற பந்தம் பிடிக்கிறது.
Holding the torch according to the movements of the dancer.
"He has a saddle for every horse."

1558. கொடுத்தால் ஒரு பேச்சு, கொடுக்காதேபோனால் ஒரு பேச்சு.
If you give to him, he will speak one word (favourably); if you refuse him, he will speak one word (contrarily). 260.

1559. குந்து இல்லாத குடுவை.
A gourd without a bottom to stand on!
The bottle gourd has no flat end to stand on, and rolls this side and that without any steadiness. People who spend their lives in seeking the favour of others have to yield in all things to all whom they want to please, and are thus like the unsteady gourd.
"An empty bag cannot stand upright."

1560. குந்துக்குத் தடுக்குப் போட்டுச் சுற்றிக்கொண்டு திரிகிறது.
Going round (a great man) to push his mat under him. 1561.
Obsequiousness.

1561. தடுக்குத் தள்ளி பேச்சுப் பேசுகிறது.
Pushing the mat under him and speaking (to him). 1560.
Hindus often sit on a little square mat. One who wants a great man's favour, will wait to place this mat wherever it is required to get the chance of a word with him.
"To dance attendance on one."

1562. மெச்சிக்கொள்ள, எச்சிலை எடுக்கிறது.
To get praise he will remove the leaf-plates that have been used. 1555, 1563.
Said of one who will do the most menial acts to earn the favour of the great.
"Set your sail according to the wind."
"You have a handsome head of hair; pray give me a tester."

1563. மொத்தை சோற்றுக்கு மேளம் அடிக்கிறான்.

He beats a drum to get a mouthful of boiled rice. 1555, 1562.

" *Cringing is a gainful accomplishment.*"

1564. வாழைப்பழம் கொண்டுபோனவள் வாசலில் இருந்தாள், வாயைக் கொண்டு போனவள் நடுவீட்டில் இருந்தாள்.

She who brought a plantain (banana) sat at the entrance; she who brought her mouth sat in the middle of the house. 2776.

The first woman brought a gift but she was left outside. The second was a false friend but she could flatter and she therefore got a seat of honour.

" *Flattery sits in the parlour, when plain dealing is kicked out of doors.*"

" *All doors open to courtesy.*" " *They love most who are least valued.*"

1565. வீட்டுக்குப் புகழ்ச்சியோ, நாட்டுக்குப் புகழ்ச்சியோ?

(Is one to seek) praise at home or abroad? 1550, 1553.

SELF-PRAISE.

தற்புகழ்ச்சி.

1566. அவன் கையைக்கொண்டே அவன் கண்ணில் குத்தினான்.

He struck his own eyes with his own hand!

i.e., He cleverly managed to do harm to his opponent by the means on which he depended. Also said of a person who ruins an enemy, but does it so cleverly that no blame attaches to himself.

1567. ஆகாசத்தை வடுப்படாமல் கடிப்பேன் என்கிறான்.

He says he can bite the sky without leaving a scar in it. 1808, 2556.

" *Your trumpeter's dead, and so you blow your trumpet yourself.*"

1568. உள்ளங்கையில் வைகுண்டம் காட்டுகிறேன்.

He will show you heaven (*Vaikuntham*) in the palm of his hand!

" *Great boast and small roast.*"

1569. எனக்கு எதிரில்லை, நெல்லுக்குப் பதரில்லை.

No adversary for me, and no chaff in my rice!

i.e., I am not afraid of foes or misfortune.

1569*a*. உன் காரியம் முப்பத்திரண்டிலே!

Your case lies in thirty-two! 1573.

Said to one who praises himself, signifying that he is worthless; after his death all his affairs will come to light, the *Karmantiram* funeral ceremony for him will be performed on the thirty-second day after his death. This ceremony should be performed on the tenth day after the death of a Brahmin, on the twelfth day after the death of a Kshattriya or Vaisya, on the sixteenth day after the death Sudra. The saying is therefore a wish that a man's affairs may all be in confusion at his death, or that dishonour may put an end to all his self-complacency.

1570. என்னைப்போலக் குரலும், என் அக்காளைப்போல ஒயிலும் இல்லை என்கிறதாம் கழுதை.

The ass says that no one has a voice (for singing) like his, and no one has gait like that of his eldest-sister!

" *Did you ever before hear an ass play upon a lute?* "

" *Every ass loves to hear himself bray.*"

1571. குப்புற விழுந்தாலும், மீசையிலே மண் படவில்லை என்கிறான்.

Though he fell flat on his face, he says that his moustache was not soiled!

Even at the moment of defeat he finds a reason for self-complacency.

" *There is no such flatterer as a man's self.*"

1572. குலைக்கிற நாய் வேட்டைப் பிடிக்காது.

A barking dog is not fit for hunting. 1576.

Said of one who is too full of brag to succeed in anything.

" *A barking dog seldom bites.*"

1573. கோழி கூவி விடிகிறதா?

Does day dawn because the cock crows? 489, 1565, 2559.

Said of one who thinks himself very important.

" *Daylight will come, though the cock do not crow.*"

1574. செத்தால் பிழைக்கமாட்டான்.

If he dies (it is because) he is determined not to live.

Applied sarcastically of one who boasts of the great deeds he can do.

" *When you die, your trumpeter will be buried.*"

1575. செல்வப்பெண் சீரங்கநாயகிக்குச் சீதனம் வந்ததாம் வறையோடு.

A potsherd was sent as dowry to the petted goddess of Srirangam.

Said to one who boasts about riches he has not got. Instead of வறையோடு the common people insert a very obscene word.

1576. துள்ளுகிற மாடு பொதி சுமக்காது.

A frisky bullock will carry no burden. 1572.

1577. துள்ளாதே துள்ளாதே குள்ளா! பக்கத்தில் பள்ளம் அடா!

Oh dwarf, don't jump for joy; there is a ditch close by!

Don't boast too much; some one may accept your challenge.

1578. துள்ளித் துள்ளித் தொப்பென்று விழுகிறாய்.

If you frisk about too much you will fall headlong.

Do not abuse people too much; you may fare badly yourself.

1579. நான் வாழ்ந்த வாழ்வைச் சொல்லுகிறேன், அண்டை வீட்டுக்காரனிருக்கிறானா, பார்?

I will tell you the story of my life; but go and see if my neighbour is at home.

Said of one who is willing to speak about himself, but he wants to make sure that his neighbour is not at hand to check his self-glorification, by the recital of facts.

" *He dwells far from neighbours who is fain to praise himself.*"
" *Every man's tale is gude till another's be tauld.*"

1580. பொரிமாவை மெச்சினான் பொக்கைவாயன்.

A toothless person praises the flour made from parched rice.

Every man praises what he himself is ablo to enjoy or master or which suits him.

Cf. 1794 *ff.* 2108 *ff.*

DIGNITY, SOCIAL IMPORTANCE.

பெருமை, கனம், மானம், பேர்.

1581. அக்கிராரத்து நாய் பிரதிஷ்டைக்கு அழுததுபோல.

Like a dog belonging to a Brahmin street weeping for (*or* hankering after) honour. 858.

A dog in a Pariah village used to visit a dog in a Brahmin village, and enticed it to enter the Pariah village by saying:—"You can get neither meat nor bones from vegetarian Brahmins; come to my place and you shall have both." The other replied:—"I prefer this place, for here I have the great honour of being called the father of Brahmins. For when the Brahmins quarrel they call each other Son of a dog, நாய் மகன்!" A sarcasm on those who have false ideas of dignity.

" *Desire of glory is the last garment that even wise men put off.*"

1582. அரைப்பணம் சேவகமானாலும், அரண்மனை சேவகம் போலாகுமா?

Is there any service like service in a palace, though the wages there be only half a *fanam?*

The honour of serving a king is great though the pay may be small.

1583. ஆண்டிக்குக் கொடுக்கிறாயோ? சுரைக்குடுக்கைக்குக் கொடுக்கிறாயோ?

Do you give to the mendicant or to the gourd? 1553.

i.e., Give in order to do good, and not to get praise for your charity. The 'gourd' is a vessel in which alms are received by a mendicant.

1584. என் மூக்கை முன்னுக்குக் கொண்டுவா.

Bring my nose forward! 879.

A curious phrase. The allusion is to the mutilation of a faithless wife by her husband. Sometimes the adulteress' mother was mutilated also. Hence when a girl was leaving home for her husband's house after marriage, her mother would use this saying meaning 'Be careful to bring credit to me; don't do anything that will make your husband cut my nose off.' It is now used by a superior to an inferior as an warning to behave himself, lest he bring disgrace on his master.

1585. என் பறையா! என்கிறதை விட, வள்ளுவ பறையா என்கிறது மேல்.

Instead of saying simply "*Pariah*," why not say "*Valluva Pariah*"? 678.

A *Valluvan* is a Pariah-priest, but both live in the Pariah village and both are Pariahs. A title does not raise a low man.

"*Vain glory blossoms but never bears.*"

"*What good can it do to an ass to be called a lion.*"

"*Fame is a magnifying glass.*"

1586. ஒன்றுமற்ற நாரிக்கு ஒன்பதுநாள் சடங்கு, அதுவுமற்ற நாரிக்கு ஐம்பதுநாள் சடங்கு.

A ceremony lasting nine days for a worthless woman, and a ceremony lasting fifty days for one still worse.

The allusion is to the long festivals that the parents of a deformed girl will hold in order to get her married. The lamplight and bustle of the festival prevent anyone from noticing her defects, and a marriage may be arranged before anyone knows that there is anything wrong with her. The proverb is said of people who seek honour and respect, but do not deserve it.

1587. கட்டோடே போனால், கனத்தோடே வரலாம்.

If you go with a load, you may return with honour. 347.

i.e., If you take presents with you you will be well received.

"*He that bringeth a present findeth the door open.*"

1588. கம்மனாட்டி (கைம்பெண்டாட்டி) பிள்ளையானாலும் செய்யும் சடங்கு செய்யவேண்டும்.

Though the son of a widow, all the proper rites should be performed for him.

Even an illegitimate child, when a bridegroom, should be fully honoured. This saying is often quoted in reply to a man who urges caution in some expenditure.

1589. கனத்திற்கு நற்குணம் சுமைதாங்கி.

Virtue is the support of dignity.

The 'support' referred to in the proverb is the erection of stone, brick or wood, by the road-side upon which coolies, and others who carry loads on their heads, may rest their burdens.

"*From our ancestors come our names, but from our virtues our honours.*"

1590. காலிலே கட்டினால் விருது, குப்பையில் கிடந்தால் துணி.

If tied round the leg it is a trophy, if lying on a dunghill it is only a rag. 1595, 1602.

A man is honoured according to the work he does, or according to his position, and not according to his intrinsic worth.

1591. காறி உமிழ்ந்தவர்களைக் (com. காறி முழிந்தவர்களை) கண்டீர்களா? அங்கே ஒரு தட்டு வைத்தீர்களா?

Did you see those persons who were spued out, or did you place a tray before them?

Said of one who is of low caste, or is very poor, or has a bad character yet wants to be honoured; or said to one who wants to honour such a person. Also said of two persons who blame each other for the faults common to both. The tray referred to is the tray of betel leaves, sandal-paste, rose water, &c., placed before a guest as a mark of honour.

1592. கும்பிடு கொடுத்து, கும்பிடு வாங்குகிறதா?

Do you make a bow to get a bow?

Said of those who cringe in order to get into the society of their superiors.

1593. குன்றுமேலிட்ட விளக்கைப்போல்.

Like a lamp on a hill. 2624.

Said of one who is widely honoured.

1594. கோவில் மணியம் என்கிற பேர் இருந்தால் போதும்.

If I can only get the title of Manager of the temple, I shall be satisfied.

Said of a person who longs for honours and titles.

"*A rose called by any other name would smell as sweet.*"

1595. சங்கிலே விட்டால் தீர்த்தம், மொந்தையிலே விட்டால் தண்ணீர்.

If water is poured into a conch, it is sacred water; if poured into an earthen pot, it is common water. 1353, 1590, 1602.

1595a. நாட்டான் பெண்சாதி என்றால் ஏன் என்பாள், நாலுபேருக்குச் சோறு என்றால் ஊம் என்பாள்.

When they say she is the headman's wife, she is pleased; but when they say, she must give her four labourers their wages, she is glum.

Said of one who magnifies his authority to the utmost, but will not give just wages to those who work for him.

1596. பத்துப்பேரிலே பதினோராம்பேராய் இருக்கவேண்டும்.

Be the eleventh person among ten.

i.e., Do not seek to be honoured; or if you require special notice, separate yourself from the rest.

1597. புழுக்கைச்சிமேல் சன்னதம் (தெய்வம்) வந்தால், பூ இட்டுக் கும்பிட வேண்டும்.

If an oracle inspires a slave girl, you should present flowers to her and worship her. 1601.

People of low birth are not to be despised if they obtain greatness.

1598. போலை நாரி வாடி (வா அடி), காடிமேல் ஏறடி!

Come shameless lassie! Climb into the cart!

Said sarcastically to one who seeks the place of honour everywhere without being invited.

1599. வாதுக்கு ஆடின தம்பன் (or தேவடியாள்) வயசு சென்றால் கழுதை மேய்ப்பான் (or மேய்ப்பாள்).
When the acrobat (*or* dancing-girl) who acts to the admiration of all becomes old, he (*or* she) will herd asses!

1600. விருதுக்கா வேட்டை ஆடுகிறது?
Do you hunt for the sake of the trophy?

1601. வெள்ளாட்டிக்குச் சன்னதம் வந்தால், விழுந்துதான் கும்பிடவேண்டும்.
If an oracle inspires a maid-servant, you should fall at her feet and worship her. 1597.

When God works through a person look at the good in him, and not at his former social position.

1602. வைத்தியன் கொடுத்தால் மருந்து, இல்லாவிட்டால் மண்ணு.
If the doctor gives it, it is medicine; if not, it is only earth. 1356, 1590, 1595.

SHAME, CONTEMPT, DEPRECIATION.

வெட்கம், அவமானம், அசட்டை.

1603. அவன் கொஞ்சப் புலியா?
Is he an insignificant tiger?

Don't despise anyone for his apparent insignificance.

1604. அவன் உனக்குக் கிள்ளுக்கீரையோ?
Do you take him to be a soft vegetable?

1605. ஆயிரம் குதிரையை அறவெட்டின சிப்பாய்தானு இப்போது பறைச் சேரி நாயோடே பங்கமழிகிறான்.
The soldier who cut down a thousand horsemen is now living in disgrace along with the dogs of the Pariah village!

1606. குளம் (or ஆறு, or ஏரி, or கடல்) எத்தனை சூத்தைக் கண்டதோ? சூத்து எத்தனை குளத்தைக் கண்டதோ?
How many breeches has the pool (*or* river, *or* sea) seen? How many pools has your breech seen?

Refers to the Hindu practice of washing in rivers or tanks after obeying the calls of nature. A servant uses this, meaning that he has had many masters, and many masters have had him.

1607. என் ஜாண் உடம்பு ஒரு ஜாண் ஆனேன்.
My eight span body became one span.

i.e., I was put to shame.

1608. என் பிழைப்பு (or பேச்சு or பவிஷு) சிரிப்பாய்ச் சிரிக்கிறது (or காறி முழிக்கிறது) தெருவிலே.
My livelihood (*or* my word, *or* my respect) is ridiculed (*or* has been spat out) in the street.

All laugh at me; all despise me.

1609. கண்டவர்களுக்குக் கனம் குறைந்தேன், பார்ப்பவர்களுக்குப் பதம் குறைந்தேன்.

I have lost my respect before the public, and my honour has decreased before spectators.

1610. கந்தையை அவிழ்த்தால், சிந்தை கலங்கும்.

If he unties his rags you will pity him. 1613.

If a man's inner character or the secret history of any family or policy is revealed, there is always something to be pitied in it.

"*There is a skeleton in every man's cupboard.*"

1611. காய்ந்த சுண்ணாம்பையும், வதங்கின வெற்றிலையையும், இளைத்த ராஜாவையும் விடக்கூடாது.

Don't give up a bit of dried lime (used in chewing betel), nor withered betel leaves, nor a reduced king.

Any of these may afterwards be of great advantage.

1612. சுவர்க்கீரையை வழித்துப்போடடி, சுணைகெட்ட வெள்ளாட்டி.

Oh, you shameless woman, scrape the vegetables off from the wall and give them to me!

A husband was displeased with the vegetables his wife had prepared for his meal, and he threw them away against the wall. But after a little while, seeing that there was nothing else for him to eat, he asked his wife (but in abusive language) to scrape them off and give them to him. 1614.

"*To swallow the bitter pill.*"—"*To make a virtue of necessity.*"

1613. சொன்னால் வெட்கக்கேடு, அழுதால் துக்கக்கேடு.

If I tell it, it is shameful to me; and if I weep over it, it is painful to me. 1610.

1614. தின்று துப்பின (or கக்கிவிட்ட) தாம்பூலத்தைத் தின்ன நினைப்பார்களா?

Who will think of chewing again the betel that he has chewed and spat out.

A friend or a mistress once despised will not be restored again. This saying is the reverse of 1612.

1615. நான் என்றால், உனக்குக் கடைவாயில் பீ.

As far as I am concerned, you do not esteem me more than the dirt in the corners of your mouth!

1616. மயிர் சிக்கினால், உயிரை வைக்குமா கவரிமான்?

If the yak is caught by its hair, will it keep its life?

The long hair of the yak is its pride. Rather than lose this, it would give up its life.

1617. மானம் பெரிதோ? பிராணன் பெரிதோ?

Is honour or life the more valuable? 1616.

"*Either live or die with honour.*"

1618. விட்டேச் சொன்னால் கட்டுக் (or குட்டு) குலையும், விரித்து உடுத்தினால் அழுக்குப்படும்.

If I let go my hold of it the knot will come untied; if I spread my cloth out it will become dirty. 1728.

The cloth is old and worn and has some holes in it. In order that others shall not observe these defects, the wearer knots it together, and refuses to spread it out, and gives as an excuse, that if she does so it will touch the floor and get dirty. This saying is used of genteel poverty.

"*Decency and decorum are not pride.*"

1619. வெட்டிக்குப் பெற்று வேலியில் எறிந்துவிட்டார்கள்.

I have been born for nought, and have be thrown into a hedge (of thorns).

A poor daughter-in-law has often to serve a rich daughter-in-law; and she may quote this proverb when bemoaning her lot in the joint-family.

Cf. 376 *ff.*

OSTENTATION.

டம்பம்.

"O man, why boastest thou in pride,
The smallness of thy mind to screen?
Go, bathe thy vile polluted hide
In meditation's sacred stream."

CH. E. GOVER: *The Folk Songs of Southern India.*

1620. அக்கியானம் பிடித்த முண்டைக்குச் சிவக்கியானம் என்று பேர்.

The widow is seized with stupidity, but her name is "The Wisdom of Siva"!

1621. அண்ட நிழலில்லாமல்போனாலும், பேர் ஆலால விருக்ஷம்.

Though he gives no shade for you to resort to, his name is 'Banyan tree.'

The Banyan, *Ficus Indica*, is a very shady tree.

1622. அமுர்தம் பூச்சியம், ஆடம்பரம் அதிகம்.

The nectar is lacking, the pomp is great.

"*A proud heart and a beggar's purse were never loving companions.*"

1623. அள்ளிக் குடிக்கத் தண்ணீரில்லை, பேர் கங்காதேவி.

She has not water enough to fill her hand for a drink but her name is "The goddess Ganges." 1658.

"*Where you think there are flitches of bacon, there are not even hooks to hang them on.*"

1624. ஆட்டில் ஆயிரம், மாட்டில் ஆயிரம், வீட்டிலே கரண்டி பாலில்லை.

He has a thousand sheep, and a thousand cows, but not a spoonful of milk at home.

1625. அப்பன் சோற்றுக்கு அழுகிறான், பிள்ளை கும்பகோணத்தில் கோதானம் செய்கிறான்.

The father is crying for rice, while his son is giving cows (to the Brahmins) at Kumbakonam. 1626, 1657.

The gift of cows to Brahmans is one of the highest forms of Hindu charity. Kumbakonam is a very holy place in the Tanjore District.

"*Be just before you are generous.*"

1626. ஆத்தாள் அம்மணம், கும்பகோணத்தில் கோதானம்.

While the mother goes naked, her son gives cows (to the Brahmins) at Kumbakonam.

"*Charity begins at home.*"

1627. ஆழாக்கு அரிசி, மூவாழாக்குப் பானை, முதலியார் வருகிற வீறுப்பைப் பார்.

The Mudaliyar has only a small measure of rice, but keeps a pot that can hold three such measures. Behold the pomp of the Mudaliyar! 1648, 2261, 2284.

1628. ஆளைப்பார்த்தால் அழகுமலை, வேலையைப் பார்த்தால் இழவுமலை.

If we look at his person he seems to be a mountain of beauty, but if we look at his actions he seems to be a mountain of worthlessness. 545*a*.

1629. இந்தச் சளுக்கனுக்கு இரண்டு பெண்சாதி, வந்தவாசிமட்டும் வல்லவாட்டு (or அங்கவஸ்திரம்).

This foppish fellow has two wives, and his scarf reaches to the village of Vandavasi!

1630. உயிரோடு இருக்கும்போது ஒரு கரண்டி நெய்க்கு வழியில்லை, ஓமத்துக்கு ஒன்பது கரண்டி நெய் விட்டதுபோல.

While he was alive they did not give him one spoonful of *ghee*, but after his death they spent nine spoonfuls of *ghee* at the funeral ceremony to please the public.

The funeral ceremony referred to is the *Karmantiram*, usually performed by Brahmans on the tenth day after death, and by Sudras on or after the sixteenth day after death.

1631. உள்ளே பார்த்தால் ஒக்காளம், வெளியே பார்த்தால் டம்பம் (or மிம்மிணும் பூச்சி).

If you look inside, there is retching; if you look outside, there is pomp (*or* it is like a fire-fly).

"*He is like a silvered pan, fair without, but foul within.*"

1632. ஊர் எங்கும் பேர், வீடு பட்டினி.

His fame is all over the village, but there is starvation in his house.

1633. எங்கள் ஆத்துக்காரனும் கச்சேரிக்குப் போய்வந்தான்.

My husband has returned from court.

A bombastic way of announcing that the husband is connected in some menial capacity with the court-house and has returned from his daily duty.

1634. எச்சிலைத் தின்று, ஏப்பம் இட்டாற்போல்.
Like belching after eating the (defiled) refuse of food.

Said in contempt of one who gets very poor food at home, but belches in the public as if his stomach were full of good things. Belching is not thought rude; on the contrary, it is rather complimentary to a Tamil host to belch after eating the meal he has provided, for that is supposed to show that the stomach is replete, *i.e.* that the food was rich and plentiful.

1635. எடுக்கிறது சந்தை கோபாலம், ஏறுகிறது தந்த பல்லக்கா?
What! Is his occupation begging, and his conveyance an ivory palanquin? 1273.

"*A proud mind and a poor purse are ill met.*"

1636. ஒய்யாரக்கொண்டையாம், தாழம்பூவாம், உள்ளே இருக்குமாம் ஈரும் பேனும்.
Her hair is gracefully done up, and (adorned) with *Pandanus* flowers, but there are nits and lice in it!

"*A fair exterior with a foul interior.*"

1637. கட்டக் கரிமணியில்லாமல்போனாலும், பேர் பொன்னம்மாள் (or முத்துமாலை).
Though she does not possess even a black bead (a very cheap ornament) her name is 'Mother of gold' (*or* 'Wreath of Pearl').

1638. கறிக்கு இல்லாத வாழைக்காய் பந்தலிலே கட்டித் தொங்கவோ?
What, are the plantains (bananas) to hang (as ornaments) at the front of the house, while we have nothing to eat?

Sometimes said of a person who will not help his poor relatives.

1639. காசில்லாதவனுக்கு வராகன் பேச்சு என்ன?
Why should he who is without a cash speak of a big gold coin?

1640. குடல் கூழுக்கு அழுகிறது, கொண்டை பூவுக்கு அழுகிறது.
While the stomach is crying for gruel, the hair is crying for flowers. 1671.

1641 குடிக்கிறது கூழ், கொப்பளிக்கிறது பன்னீர்.
He drinks only gruel, but washes his mouth with rosewater!

1642. சக்கு சக்கு என்று பாக்குத் தின்பான் சபை மெச்ச, வீட்டிலே வந்து கடைவாயை நக்குவான் பெண்டுகள் மெச்ச.
To be praised by the public he chews areca-nut when abroad; to be praised by the women of his household he licks his lips at home. 2352.

1643. சம்பளம் அரைப்பணமானாலும், சளுக்கு முக்கால்பணம்.
Though his salary is half a *panam*, three-quarters of a *panam* goes to keep up appearances. 473.

"*The devil wipes his tail with the poor man's pride.*"

1644. செவக்க முற்றின வாழைக்காய் (sarcastic) புளியில்லாமல் இனிக்கிறது.

The ripe plantain (banana) craves some tamarind.

The ripe plantain is too sweet for use in the kitchen, and a good deal of sour tamarind is needed to correct its flavour. Hence the proverb is used about those who have been over indulged, and need to have their fine airs severely corrected.

1645. சூத்திலே கட்டத் துணியில்லை, கூத்தியார் இரண்டு.

He has not a scrap of clothes, but he keeps two concubines!

Some Hindus keep concubines simply to exhibit their own wealth.

1646. ஜாண் பண்டாரத்துக்கு முழம் விபூதி (or லிங்கம், or தாடி).

A religious mendicant a span long daubs a cubit of holy ashes on his forehead (*or* wears a beard a cubit in length).

Said of one who seeks honour that he does not deserve.

1647. தம்பி கால்நடை, பேச்சு பல்லக்கிலே.

The young fellow has to walk, but he speaks (as if he had) a palanquin (to ride in).

" *Great cry and little wool.*"

1648. தான் தின்னத் தவிடு இல்லை, சம்பா நெல்லுக்குத் தொம்பை (or கூண்டு) வைத்திருக்கிறான்.

He has not even bran to eat, but he keeps a (huge) basket for good rice! 1627.

" *Penniless, but bragging of having a plum.*"

1649. தான் குடிக்கக் கூழ் இல்லை, வாரத்துக்கு (பங்கு) இரண்டு பன்றிக்குட்டி வளர்க்கிறான்.

He has not even gruel to drink, and yet he undertakes to bring up two pigs for hire.

The gruel referred to is pig-meal. When one has not even pig-meal for his own table, it is only vain ostentation to undertake the rearing of two pigs for hire.

1650. தான் தின்னத் தவிடில்லை, தங்கத்தாலே தாலி தொங்கத் தொங்கப் போடச்சொன்னாளாம்.

He has not even bran to eat, but his wife asks for a *thâli* of pure gold to hang on her neck!

1651. தான் போனால் தாகத்துக்குக் கிடையாது, எழுதடா ஓலை நூறுகுடம் தயிருக்கு என்றான்.

If he goes himself he won't get anything to drink, so he says (to his clerk) "Order (*lit.* write on a palm-leaf for) one hundred pots of curds."

1652. தான் போய் மோரில்லாமல்வந்தவன், தயிருக்குச் சீட்டு எழுதினனும்.

He went himself for buttermilk but got none; he then wrote an order for curds.

1653. பிள்ளை புழுக்கை, பேர் முத்து மாணிக்கம்.

The boy is a slave, but his name is 'Pearl-jewel.'

1654. பெருமை பீதக்கலம், இருக்கிறது ஓட்டைக்கலம்.

His boast (is that he eats from) a golden vessel; but it is only a broken pot.

1655. பெருமைக்கு ஆட்டை அடித்துப், பிள்ளைகையில் காதைச் சுட்டுக்கொடுத்தான்.

He killed a sheep (to appear wealthy) but he only fries the ears of it for his son.

1656. பெருமை ஒரு முறம், புடைத்து எடுத்தால் ஒன்றுமில்லை.

He has a sieve full of grandeur, but if it be sifted nothing remains.

"*Sift him grain by grain and you will find him all chaff.*"

1657. பெற்ற தாய் பசித்திருக்க, பிராமணப்போஜனம் செய்வித்ததுபோல்.

While his own mother starves, he feeds Brahmins. 1625, 1626. (Math. 15, 5.)

1658. பேர் செல்லப்பிள்ளைராயர், நாமமற்றுப்போச்சுது.

His name is Sellapilleirayan, but he has no *nâmam* (on his forehead).

The *nâmam* is a trident shaped mark worn by Vaishnavites on the fore-head and other parts of the body, painted on the forehead, at least, before taking food. Sellapilleirayan is one of the names of Vishnu. A Sellapilleirayan without a *nâmam* cannot be the real Sellapilleirayan. Said of a man who makes great professions, but has nothing to support them with.

1658*a*. பேர் கங்காபவானி, குடிக்கத் தண்ணீரில்லை.

Though her name is Ganga Bavâne she has no water to drink. 1623.

Ganga is the holy river Ganges. Bavâne is a name of one of the tributaries of the Cauveri River.

1659. மடப் பெருமைதான் நீச்சுதண்ணீருக்கு வழியில்லை.

The hermitage (Sanscr. *mat'ha*) is a grand one, but there is no way of getting even rice-water in it! 2126.

1660. தரம் தரமாய் மொட்டை, அவள் பேர் கூந்தல் அழகி.

She has inherited a bald head but her name is 'The woman with beautiful hair.'

1661. *தாராளம் தண்ணீர்ப்பந்தல், நீச்சுதண்ணீர் நெய் பட்டபாடு.*
He says he has plenty of sheds where water (is given away in charity); but rice-water is as rare (in his house) as *ghee*. 1659, 1792.

1662. *முதலியார் டம்பம் விளக்கெண்ணெய்க்குக் கேடு.*
The Mudalyar's ostentation causes the loss of lamp-oil.

After taking a wretched meal, he rubs his hands and the leaf-plates that are thrown into the street with oil, that it may appear as if he were living in high style; for according to Hindu ideas food that is cooked with oil or *ghee* is very rich.

" *Reputation is the darling of human affection.*"

1663. *முடக்கப் பாயில்லாதேபோனாலும், சடக்குக்குக் குறைச்சலில்லை.*
Though he has not a mat to lie on there is no lack of bustle.

1664. *வரப்பு எறித் தாண்டமாட்டாள், அவள்பேர் தாண்டாய் (i.e. தண்டு+ ஆய்).*
Though her name is 'She who leaps and dances,' she is unable to get over a *varappu*.

A *varappu* is the earthen ridge that separates one rice-field from another. They are usually only a foot or so high, and a few inches broad. Prop. *தாண்டாய* means *தாண்டவ—ஆய்* a name for *Kâli*, referring to her dancing with Siva at Chidambaram.

1665. *வாழுகிறான் வாழுகிறான் என்று மதுரை எல்லாம் பேராம், ஆற்றில் இறங்கினால் ஐம்பத்தெட்டுத் தொல்லையாம்.*
He was famed over all Madura for being well off, but when he descended into the river (*i.e.* at his death) there were fifty-eight difficulties (*i.e.* debts). 1569*a*, 1573.

1666. *வீட்டுக்குச் சோறில்லை சிவன் அறிவான், நாட்டுக்குச் செல்லப்பிள்ளை நானல்லவா?*
Siva knows there is no rice in my house, but am I not called 'The darling of the country.'

1667. *வீடு வெறும் வீடு, வேலூர் அதிகாரம்.*
His house is only an empty house, but his rule (over it is as exacting as that of) the Nawab of Vellore.

Said by a wife to a husband who demands dainties, but gives her very little money for household expenses.

1668. *வைத்ததற்குமேல் வழியில்லை, பிச்சைக்குப் போகச் சுரைக்குடுவையில்லை.*
He boasts of having no more room in his house to keep things, but he has not even a gourd shell to take with him when begging.

Cf. 2396 *ff.*

DISCONTENTED POVERTY.

ஏழை.

1669. *அன்று குடிக்கத் தண்ணீரில்லை, ஆனைமேலே அம்பாரிவேண்டுமோம்.*

He had not even water to drink that day, but he wanted (to ride in) a howdah on an elephant.

1670. *உள்ள பிள்ளை உரலை நக்கிக்கொண்டிருக்க, மற்றொரு பிள்ளைக்குத் திருப்பதிக்கு நடக்கிறாள்.*

While the child she has is licking a stone mortar, she goes to Tripati to beg the God for another child.

Though she has no food to give to the child she already has, she wishes to bear another. Improvidence.

" *Better have one plough going than two cradles.*"

1671. *கிடக்கிறது ஒட்டுத்திண்ணை, கனாக்* (or *கனவு*) *காண்கிறது மச்சுவீடு* (or *மாளிகை*).

What he has is only a miserable verandah, but he dreams of a palace. 1640, 1670.

" *Hope and expectation are a fool's income.*"

" *He lives in a hut, but dreams of a palace.*"

1672. *கையால் ஆகாத சிறுக்கி வர்ணப்புடவைக்கு ஆசைப்பட்டதுபோல.*

Like a servant girl fit for nothing longing for a coloured cloth. 1687.

A long 'cloth', *pudavei*, is the ordinary dress of Tamil women.

1673. *செய்கிறது சிரைக்கிற வேலை, நினைக்கிறது சிரஸ்ததார் வேலை.*

He is doing the work of a barber, but aspires to become Sheristadar. 1635, 1677.

A Sheristadar is a petty official.

" *Every ass thinks itself worthy to stand with the king's horse.*"

1674. *தொங்குகிறது குட்டிச்சுவர், கனாக் காண்கிறது மாளிகை.*

That which he owns is a ruined wall but what he sees in his dream is a palace.

" *Too much hope deceiveth.*"

1675. *நீச்சுதண்ணீருக்கு கெஞ்சினவள், பசும்பாலுக்குச் சர்க்கரை தேடுகிறாள்.*

She who begs for rice water is seeking sugar to sweeten her cow's milk.

Said of a poor man who will not be contented with any but the best of food.

1676. பிறந்த பிள்ளை பிடி சோற்றுக்கு அழுகிறது, பிறக்கப்போகிற பிள்ளைக்குத் தண்டை சதங்கை தேடுகிறார்களாம்.

The child is crying for a handful of rice but (its parents) are seeking anklets with bells on them for a child yet unborn.

1677. பூமி ஆளலாம் என்று மனப்பால் குடிக்கிறதுபோல்.

He drinks mind-milk (*i.e.* nourishes a foolish hope) thinking that he can rule the world. 1673.

"*It is good fish, if it were but caught.*"

Cf. 997 *ff.* 1205 *ff.* 2670 *ff.*

UNREASONABLE IMPORTUNITY.

பெருமை, ஏழை.

1678. அப்பச்சி குதம்பையைச் சூப்ப, பிள்ளை முற்றின தேங்காய்க்கு அழுகிறதுபோல.

While the father is sucking cocoanut fibre, his child is crying for a ripe cocoanut.

"*He can give little to his servants who licks his own trencher.*"

1679. ஆண்டியே அன்னத்துக்கு அலையச்சே, தன் லிங்கம் பால்சோற்றுக்கு அழுகிறது.

While the mendicant is praying for rice, his *Linga* cries for milk and rice. 1686.

1680. ஆத்தை படுகிற பாடுக்குள்ளே, மகன் மோருக்கு அழுகிறான்.

While the mother is distressed (for want of food) her son cries for buttermilk.

1681. ஆவுடையாரையும் (நந்தி) லிங்கத்தையும் ஆறு கொண்டுபோகவே, சுற்றுக்கோவில் சுவாமி எல்லாம் சர்க்கரை பொங்கலுக்கு அழுதது போல.

Like all the (little) gods of the surrounding temples crying for sweetmeats, while the river carries off the sacred stone bull and the *Linga*. 3075.

The stone bull (Nandi) and the *Linga* are both emblems of the great God Siva.

1682. ஆளான ஆட்களுக்கு அவிழ் அகப்படாத காலத்தில், காக்கா பிசாசு கஞ்சிக்கு அழுததுபோல்.

Like crow-devils crying for rice-soup while respectable people cannot get a single grain of boiled rice.

1683. ஆன தெய்வத்தை ஆறு கொண்டுபோகிறது, காவற்காரனுக்குத் தெப்பத் திருவிழாவா?

Is it a floating-festival for the watchman when the river carries off the gods ?

At certain festival times the idols in some temples are taken on rafts for a sail on the temple lake.

1684. ஏழாயிரம் பொன்பெற்ற குதிரை இறப்பைப் பிடுங்கையில், குருட்டுக் குதிரை கோதுமை ரொட்டிக்கு வீங்கினதாம்.

While the horse worth seven thousand gold coins was feeding on straw from the eaves, the blind (worthless) horse was hankering after wheat bread.

1685. ஒன்றான தெய்வம் ஒதுங்கி கிடக்கச்சே, மூலைவீட்டுத் தெய்வம் குங்கிலியம் கேட்குமாம்.

While the chief god is badly off, the little gods in the corners are asking for perfume.

i.e. Though the head of the family is in difficulties, his dependents will never cease to ask for all sorts of luxuries.

1686. சடைத்தம்பிரான் சாற்றுக்கு அழுகிறானாம், லிங்கம் பஞ்ச அமிர்தத்துக்கு அழுகிறதாம்.

It is said that the chief priest of a Saivite temple was crying for pepper-water, and that the *Linga* was crying for a dish consisting of five kinds of nectar. 1679.

The priest was in want, but the symbol of the deity wanted luxuries just as much as in times of prosperity.

1687. தகப்பனுக்கு ஒட்டு கோவணமாம், மகன் எழுத்துபோட்டது வேண்டும் என்கிறான்.

The father wears a loin-cloth made of rags stitched together, but the son wants print-cloth. 1672.

1688. தகப்பனுக்குக் கட்டக் கோவணமில்லை, மகன் தஞ்சாவூர்மட்டும் நடைப் பாவாடை போடச்சொன்னானாம்.

It is said that the father had not even a loin-cloth, but the son asked for cloth to spread (on the road) as far as Tanjore (for a procession to walk on).

1689. தங்கமும் பொன்னும் தரையிலே, ஒருகாசு நார்த்தங்காய் உறியிலே.

Pure gold and common gold are buried in the ground, but a cash-worth of lemons is kept in a swinging tray (*uri*).

In times of distress servants or inferiors will complain if they lack little comforts, although their betters suffer great anxieties and losses with fortitude.

1690. பஞ்சைநாரி பணிகாரம் சுட்டாள், வீங்கினாரி விசாரப்பட்டாள்.

A poor beggar woman was cooking cakes; a starving woman yearned for them.

1691. பெருமாள் புளிச்ச தண்ணீருக்கு அலைகிறான், அனுமார் தத்தியோதனம் கேட்கிறார்.

While Vishnu is wandering about to get tamarind-water, the Monkey-God is demanding boiled rice and curds.

1692. முதல் பிள்ளை மூத்திரத்துக்கு அழும்போது, இரண்டாம் பிள்ளை பாலுக்கு அழுகிறதாம்.
While the first born child cries for urine, the second cries for milk.

1693. வண்ணக்குதிரை மண்ணைத் தின்கையில், தட்டுவாணிக்குதிரை கொள்ளுக்கு அழுகிறதாம்.
While a beautiful horse eats earth, the country pony neighs for gram (a kind of lentil).

RICH AND POOR.

பணக்காரன், ஏழை.

1694. அரசனுக்கு ஒரு சொல், அடிமைக்குத் தலை சுமை.
The king's command is but a word, but it lays a burden on the head of his slave. 1699.

Easy to command, hard to obey.

1695. அரண்மனைக்கு அயிரம் செல்லும், குடியானவன் என்ன சொல்வான்.
Thousands of rupees go to the royal palace; what can the (poor) farmer do? 1711.

1696. ஆண்டியை அடித்தானும், குவோவையை (or ஜோளியை)ப் போட்டு உடைத்தானும்.
It seems that he beat the poor beggar, and threw his vessel down and smashed it! 1709, 1718.

1697. ஆற்றில் பெருவெள்ளம், நாய்க்கு என்ன? சளப்புத்தண்ணீர்.
What is it to the dog, that the river is in full flood? It can only swallow one draught. 1706.

However plentiful good things may be, it is the poor man's lot to get but little.

1698. ஆனைமேல் போகிறவனைச் சுண்ணாம்பு கேட்டால் அகப்படுமோ?
If you ask lime to chew with betel leaves from one who rides on an elephant, will you get it?

A poor man is too insignificant to receive favours from a great personage.

1699. உனக்கு ஒரு பேச்சு, எனக்கு ஒரு மூச்சு.
Your order is but a word to you, it cost me my breath. 1694.

"*Saying and doing are two things.*"

1700. எல்லாரும் பல்லக்கு ஏறினால், பல்லக்கு யார் தூக்குகிறது?
If all should sit in palanquins, who would carry them?

A palanquin is a litter carried by a number of men. This seems to be a Telugu proverb, but it is used in Tamil.

"*You a lady, I a lady; who is to drive out the sow?*"

"*I proud, thou proud, who shall bear the ashes out?*"

1701. ஏழைபேச்சு அம்பலம் ஏறாது.
The words of the poor will not reach the assembly.

"*Poor men's words have little weight.*"

1702. ஏழை அழுத கண்ணீர் கூறிய வாளை ஒக்கும்.
The tears of poor people are like sharp swords (against the rich).

"*Tread on a worm, and it will turn.*"

1703. கழைமேல் ஏறி ஆடினாலும், கீழே வந்துதான் பிச்சை கேட்கவேண்டும்.
Though he plays on the top of the pole, he will have to come down to ask for gifts.

In spite of his seeming superiority the acrobat must come down among the crowd to beg for the rewards of his skill. So a poor man though engaged in an important piece of work must bear himself humbly or he will get no wages. This is especially true in India where every petty official expects the utmost obsequiousness in every one who is under his orders.

1704. கன்னத்தில் அடித்தாலும், கதறி அழ சீவனில்லை.
Even though they beat me on my cheek, I have no strength (*lit.* life) to scream out.

Poverty is powerless to oppose oppressors.

1705. காசுக்கு ஒரு சேலை விற்றாலும், நாயின் சூத்து அம்மணம்.
Though a cloth were sold for a *cash* only, yet a dog's breech would be bare.

The poor must go without what others consider to be essentials.

1706. காவேரி கஞ்சியாய்ப்போனாலும், நாய் நக்கித்தான் குடிக்கவேண்டும்.
Even if the river Kâvêri were turned into gruel, a dog could only lick up (a little).

1697, 1705 and 1706 contain the Hindu idea of the unchangeableness of the lot of the poor. 92.

1707. குண்டி எத்தனை கோணற்கோணினாலும், சுமை வீட்டில் போய்ச் சேர்ந்தாலே சரி.
It does not matter into how many contortions the body is bent, if the burden is carried home. 2642.

"*He serves the poor with a thump on the back with a stone.*"

1708. சிறுமீன் எல்லாம் பெருமீனுக்கு இரை.
All small fish are food for big ones.

1709. ஜோளியைப் பிடுங்கிகொண்டா பிச்சை போடுகிறது.
Should you snatch a beggar's bag with its contents, and then give him an alms? 1696, 1718.

1710. நரிக்குக் கொண்டாட்டம், நண்டுக்குத் திண்டாட்டம்.
Fun to the jackal, but agony to the crab. 1711, 1717, 1719.

1711. நரி கலியாணத்துக்கு, நண்டு பிராணார்த்தம்.

A fox's marriage costs many crabs their lives. 1695.

This might be said of a Viceroy's visit to a Native Prince, whose subjects will have to find the funds squandered by their lord in doing honour to the Viceroy.

1712. நனைந்த கிழவன் வந்தால், உலர்ந்த விறகுக்குச் சேதம்.

If a wet old man comes, dry firewood will suffer.

Said for instance by a poor man to a rich man, who has invited him to a feast, meaning:—You will gain nothing from me though you will have to send me away with a gift. A polite refusal from an inferior to a superior who invites him to a feast or ceremony.

1713. பசி ஏப்பக்காரனும் புளி ஏப்பக்காரனும் கூட்டுப்பயிர் இட்டதுபோல்.

As two persons, one belching from hunger and one from eating tamarind, cultivated a field jointly! 1454, 1861.

The poor man will be the sufferer, if he deals with the rich.

"*Those who eat cherries with great persons shall have their eyes squirted out with the stones.*"

1714. பணக்காரனுடன் பந்தயம் போடலாமா?

Can you lay a wager with a rich man? 1722.

"*Contend not with thy betters.*"

1715. பல்லக்குக்கு மேல்மூடியில்லாதவனுக்கும், காலுக்குச் செருப்பில்லாதவனுக்கும் விசாரம் ஒன்றே.

The sorrow of one who has no cover over his palanquin, and that of one who has no shoes for his feet are the same.

Both the rich and the poor have sorrows.

"*A country man may be as warm in kersey as a king in velvet.*"

1716. பாடகக்காரியிடம் பாரதம் சொன்னால், பாடகத்தைப் பார்ப்பாளா? பாரதத்தைக் கேட்பாளா?

If you recite the Mahâbhârata to a richly bejewelled woman, will she look at her ornaments or will she listen to the poem? 2102.

It is useless to make complaints to an unsympathetic hearer.

"*Little knows the fat sow what the lean doth mean.*"

"*The full belly does not believe in hunger.*"

1717. பாம்பு தன் பசியை நினைக்கும், தேரை தன் விதியை நினைக்கும்.

The snake (when catching a frog) thinks of its own hunger, the frog thinks of its fate. 1710, 1711.

1718. பிச்சை எடுக்கிறதாம் பெருமாள் (கருடன்), அதைப் பிடுங்கிறதாம் அனுமார்.

It seems that Vishnu begged an alms and that the Monkey God snatched the alms away from him.

Said when some one attempts to deprive another of what the latter has won with difficulty. Used even by children. 1696, 1709, 1980.

"*The poor man turns his cake, and another comes and takes it away.*"

1719. பூனைக்குக் கொண்டாட்டம், எலிக்குத் திண்டாட்டம்.

What is sport to the cat, is death to the rat. 1710.

1720. மகாராஜன் மண்ணை (or பீ) தின்றால், மருந்துக்குத் தின்றான் என்பார்கள், பிச்சைக்காரன் மண்ணைத் தின்றால், வயிற்றுக்கில்லாமல் தின்றான் என்பார்கள்.

If the king eats dust (*or* filth), people will say he takes it for medicine; but if a poor man eats dust they will say it is because his stomach lacks food.

Excuses are easily found for the whims of great people, but the poor man is never excused. 1736.

"*Rich men have no faults.*"

1721. மகா லக்ஷ்மி பரதேசம்போனாற்போல்.

As the goddess of wealth went to a far country.

Used of rich men who are 'not at home' or are unsympathetic to their needy friends.

1722. மகாராஜனோடு சொக்கட்டான் போடலாமா?

Can you play at draughts with a king.

Applied to comparatively poor people who borrow money in order to imitate rich people or who waste their time in paying court to rich men, instead of working. 1714.

"*Acquaintance of the great will I nought, for first or last dear it will be bought.*"

1723. மச்சு இருக்க, மாளிகை இருக்க, ஓட்டன் குடிசைக்கு வேலைவந்தது.

Whether it is a terraced-roof, or a palace (that has to be built) the toil comes to the hut of the navy.

A terraced-roof is a flat roof made of bricks and cement and polished. It is more expensive than a tiled roof. The proverb means that the poor have to bear 'the burden and heat of the day.'

Cf. 738 *ff.* 1369 *ff.*

KEEPING UP APPEARANCES.

1724. இரக்கப்போனாலும், சிறக்கப்போ!

Though you have to beg, do so decently clad.

"*He bears poverty very ill who is ashamed of it.*"

1725. கந்தையானாலும் கசக்கிக்கட்டு, கூழானாலும் குளித்துக்குடி.

Though you dress in rags, wash and then dress; and though you drink gruel, bathe and then drink it. 1183.

1726. காலக்ஷேபத்துக்குக் கூலிக்குக் குத்தினாலும், கமுக்கட்டு (or அக்குள்) மயிர் வெளியே தெரியப்போகாதாம்.

Though you have to pound rice for your living, do not let the hair of your armpit be seen. 2572.

It is not thought seemly for a woman to raise her arm so that her armpit can be seen. The proverb means that however humble the work may be that one has to do, one must never allow poverty to destroy his sense of self-respect.

"*He is a wise man that can wear poverty decently.*"

"*A broken sleeve holdeth the arm back.*"

1727. கூழ் குடித்தாலும், குட்டாய்க் குடிக்கவேண்டும்.

Though you have only gruel, drink it in a respectable fashion.

"*Poverty is not a shame, but the being ashamed of it.*"

1728. கை மூடிக்கொண்டிருந்தால் கமுக்கம், திறந்தால் வெட்டவெளி (or விட்டால் ஒன்றுமில்லை).

If one keeps the fist closed, what may be inside is a secret; but if one opens the hand, all is clear. 1618, 2572, 3158.

This refers to secrets, and also to all family affairs, that should be hushed up.

"*It is an ill bird that fouls it own nest.*"

1729. மண்ணைத் தின்றாலும், மறையத் தின்னு.

If you eat dust, do so secretly.

Let not others know your poverty.

Cf. 3156 *ff.*

MISCELLANEOUS PROVERBS ABOUT THE POOR.

ஏழை, பிச்சைக்காரன்.

1730. அங்காடி விலையை அதிர அடிக்காதே.

Do not lower the market rate too much.

Do not curtail the wages of the poor. Dr. Percival explains this as an injunction not to contravene the established opinions and practices of one's associates.

1731. அடித்த ஏருக்கும், குடித்த கூழுக்கும் சரி.

His ploughing and the gruel he drank were equal. 1732, 1741, 2259.

What he earned was just enough to live on.

"*From hand to mouth.*"

1732. அம்மையார் நூற்கிற நூலுக்கும், பேரன் அரைஞாண் கயிற்றுக்கும், சரி.

The thread the woman spun, was just enough to make a string to tie round her grandson's waist. 1731.

1733. அறங்கையும் புறங்கையும் நக்குகிறதே.
(I am so poor as to have) to lick my hand on both sides. 1765, 1769.

1735. இல்லாத பிள்ளைக்கு இலுப்பைப் பூ சக்கரை.
An orphan must take the Iluppai-flower (*Bassia*) for sugar. 2057.

It must take what it can get.

"*Something is better than nothing.*"

1736. இல்லாதவன் பொல்லாதவன்.
He who has nothing is wicked. 1720, 1745.

1737. இவன் வீட்டிலாவது சாப்பாடாவது, இவன் பரம்பரையாய்ப் (or தரம் தரமாய்) பிச்சைக்காரனுச்சே.
Do not speak of food in his house, for he is a beggar by heredity.

The professional beggar is by no means badly off in India; some are even rich. 1786.

1738. உடம்பு எடுத்தவன் எல்லாம் ஓடு எடுத்தான்.
Every one who has carried a body has carried a potsherd.

Every one has begged in one way or another.

1739. உண்கிற சோறு வெல்லம்.
The rice he eats is sugar (to him).

He is so poor as to value a little rice as if it were sugar. 1429.

1740. உயிர் போகாமல் தண்ணீர் குடித்துக்கொண்டிருக்கிறோம்.
We go on drinking water without being able to die. 3397.

i.e. The lot of the poor is hard; scanty food and hard work, they can neither live nor die.

1741. உழுகிறவன் கணக்கு பார்த்தால், உழக்கோலும் மிஞ்சாது.
If the cultivator looks into his accounts, not even a plough-tail will be left as clear profit. 1731.

The lot of the agriculturist is hard.

1742. ஊண் அற்றபோதே, உறவு அற்றது.
When there is no food, there is no relationship. 1761, 1745, 2527, 2732 and 3555.

"*Want makes strife betwixt man and wife.*"

1743. எச்சிலைத்தின்று பசி தீருமோ?
Can a man satisfy his hunger by eating (old) leaf-plates?

1743*a*. எச்சிற்கலைக்கு மண்ணுங்கட்டி ஆதாரம்.
A clod of earth is a support to a leaf-plate. 1765, 1773, 2293.

The poor supports the poor. In India food is eaten from plates made of leaves.

1744. எத்தனை ஏழையானாலும், எலுமிச்சங்காய் அத்தனை பொன் இல்லாமல் போமா?

However poor a man may be, will he lack a piece of gold the size of a lime?

Said by a barber who had just so much gold himself. People are apt to think that others are as well off as themselves.

"*He that is warm thinks all so.*"

1745. எண்டா, பட்டப்பகலிலே திருடுகிறாய்! என் அவசரம் உனக்குத் தெரியுமா?

(If you say) What! do you steal in broad day-light? (The thief-replies) Do you know my need? 1736, 1761, 1742.

"*Poverty has no shame.*"

"*Necessity has no law.*"

1746. கச்சல் கருவாடு மோக்ஷத்துக்குப் போனாலும், பிச்சைக்காரன் மோக்ஷத்துக்குப் போகமாட்டான்.

Though salt fish obtains heaven, a beggar will not.

Contemptibleness of beggary.

1747. கழனியில் (or அகழியில்) விழுந்த கழுதைக்கு அதுவே கைலாசம்.

The field (*or* The ditch) in which the ass falls becomes its heaven (*Kailasa*).

i.e. The ass will die where it falls as no one will help it. This proverb as well as 1748 and 1770 may be applied to poor people, who have to suffer because they have neither the means nor the time to look after their own comfort. 998, 2512, 3371. It must die there, as no one pities and helps it. கைலாசம்போகிறது = to go to Kailasa, is a euphemism meaning 'to die.'

1748. கழுதைப்புண்ணுக்குத் தெருப்புழுதி மருந்து.

The dust of the street is the only medicine for the wound of an ass. 1747, 1770.

1749. குதித்துக் குதித்து மாவு இடித்தாலும், புழுக்கைக்கு ஒரு கொழுக்கட்டை.

Though a slave pounds rice most actively (*lit.* leaping, leaping) he (*or* she) only gets a cake of bread.

Though the poor toil hard, they get little pay and honour for their work.

1750. குபேரன் பட்டணத்திலேயும் விறகுதலையன் உண்டு.

Even in the city of Kubera (the god of riches) fuel-carriers are found. 92.

"*The poor ye have always with you.*" John 12, 8.

1751. கூலிக்காரன் பெண்சாதி குளிகுளிக்கப்போகிறாளாம், குப்பையிலே ஆமணக்கு முளைக்கப்போகிறதாம்.

It seems that the labourer's wife went to be confined, and the castor oil plant (*Ricinus*) started growing on the dunghill.

i.e. No one has any forethought for a poor man's troubles, and a poor woman must do without what every one else looks on as necessaries. The oil of the castor-oil plant is much used by Hindus at confinements and ought to be ready for use, but according to the proverb the plant from which the oil is to be obtained only begins to grow on the day that the woman who needs it is confined. Hence the application.

1752. கையிலே காசுமில்லை, முகத்திலே களையுமில்லை (or பவுசுமில்லை).
No money in my hand and no beauty in my face.

1753. சுற்றத் துணியுமில்லை, நக்கத் தவிடுமில்லை.
He has no cloth to wear, and no bran to lick.
Utterly destitute.

1754. சோற்றுக்குக் காற்றாய்ப் பறக்கிறது.
He flies after rice like the wind.
Said of one who tries hard to get work.

1755. சோற்றுப்பானை உடைந்தால், மாற்றுப்பானை இல்லை.
If his rice-pot breaks, there is no pot to replace it. 1767.
Said of those who are without resources.

1756. சோறும் துணியும் தவிர, மற்றத்துக்கு எல்லாம் குறைவில்லை.
There is no lack of anything but food and clothing. 1771, 3322.
A sarcastic description of poverty.

1757. தொட்டுக்கோ துடைத்துக்கோ என்று இருக்கிறது.
There is just enough to touch or to wipe off.
There is nothing to eat. Said of a poverty-stricken home. Often கடித்துக்கொள்ளுகிறதற்கு ஒன்றுமில்லை: there is nothing to bite.

1758. நடுத்தெருப் பிச்சைக்கு நாணயம் பார்க்கிறதா?
Should one be shy when going out to beg in the middle of the street? 1763, 1766.
"*Hungry dogs will eat dirty puddings.*"

1759. நவாப் அத்தனை ஏழை, புலி அத்தனை சாது.
He is as poor as a Nawâb, and as gentle as a tiger!
An ironical description of a rich man who pretends to be poor. A Nawâb is a Musalman prince. A Rájá is a Hindu prince.

1760. நானும் ஒட்டை, என் நடுவீடும் பொத்தல்.
I am cracked and my home is a hole!
Said of one in a miserable condition.

1761. பசிவந்தால் பத்தும் பறக்கும்.
When one is hungry, the ten fly away. 1742, 1742*a*, 1745, 2903.
The 'ten' are: மானம், self-respect; குலம், caste; கல்வி, learning; வண்மை, good manners; அறிவுடைமை, knowledge; தானம், charity; தவம், self-control; முயற்சி, perseverance in the good; தாளாண்மை, energy; தேனின் கசிந்த சொல்லியர்மேல் காமுறுதல், the love of women whose words are as honey drops.
"*Bashfulness is an enemy to poverty.*"

1761*a*. பசி வந்தால் பக்தி பறக்கும்.
If hunger comes, virtue flies away.

1762. *பறையன் பொங்கலிட்டால், பகவானுக்கு ஏறாதா?*
If a Pariah boils rice as an offering (to a god) will not the god notice it? 2285.

God will notice the piety of the poor, however despised they may be.

1763. *பிச்சை எடுக்கிறதிலும் பிகுவா?*
(Should one feel) embarrassment while receiving alms? 1758.

"*He that is too proud to ask, is too good to receive.*"

1764. *பிச்சைச்சோற்றிலும் எச்சில் சோறா?*
What! Do you object to the rice left on a leaf-plate, after going out to beg? 1950, 1994.

If one has stooped to do a mean thing, he should go through with it.

"*Beggars must not be choosers.*"

1765. *பிச்சைச்சோற்றிலும் குழந்தை சோறா?*
(What! am I to give) food to children out of the food I have got by begging? 1733, 1743*a*, 1769, 1773, 1920.

Said by a poor man when others are troubling him for a help.

Or *பிச்சைச்சோற்றிலும் குழைந்த சோறா?*
Will there be over-boiled rice in the rice that is got by begging?

Beggars ought not to be over-scrupulous.

1766. *பீ தின்கிறதிலேயும் ஒய்யாரமா?*
Should one put on airs when eating filth? 1758, 1824.

1767. *மறைத்துக் கட்ட மாற்றுப் புடவையில்லை.*
She has not a change of dress to hide her shame. 1755.

i.e. She is so poor as only to have one 'cloth' (*puduvei*).

1768. *முகத்திலே மூதேவி வாசம்.*
The goddess of ill luck lives in his face!

1769. *மூக்கை பிடித்தால், சீவன் போகிறது.*
If one lays hold of my nose, I shall lose my life. 1733, 1765.

A poor man will say this when asked to help others.

1770. *வண்ணானுக்கு நோவு வந்தால் கல்லோடே.*
When a washerman gets sick, his sickness must leave him at the stone. 1747, 1748, 2512.

The Indian washerman cleans clothes by soaking them in the water of some tank or river and beating them against a large stone. The proverb means that however sick a washerman may be, his work must be done; or, more generally, that no one makes any allowances for the pains and troubles of the poor. 1747, 1748, 2512.

1771. *வயிறாற போஜனமுமில்லை, இடுப்பாறப் புடவையுமில்லை.*
She has no food to satisfy her stomach, and no cloth to satisfy her hips. 1756.

Said of one who has no food and no clothes.

1772. வாளுக்கு ஆயிரம், தோளுக்கு ஆயிரம் சம்பாதிக்கிறாயோ ?

Do you earn a thousand by your sword and another thousand by your shoulders ?

In the old days of Hindu rule a high military officer would receive a thousand gold pieces for his sword and another thousand for wielding it. The saying is a way of reminding the person addressed that his salary is *not* a large one, and is used by a wife to a husband who wants many luxuries but earns little, or to a young Hindu who demands Western comforts.

1773. வௌவால் வீட்டுக்கு வௌவால் வந்தால், நீயும் தொங்கு நானும் தொங்கு.

When bats visit one another, they say, You hung yourself up and I will hang myself up ! 1743*a*, 1765.

This is said by one who is destitute to another who comes and asks for help, and means, You had better go to those who can help you, for I have nothing. The bat referred to is of a large species sometimes called the 'flying-fox.'

STINGINESS—AVARICIOUSNESS.

பிசினாறி—சிக்கனக்காரன்.

1774. அரைத்துட்டுக்குப் பீ தின்னுகிறவன்.

One who buys filth for a few *cash* and eats it !

1775. அறுத்த விரலுக்குச் சுண்ணாம்பு இடமாட்டான், ஆண்டி வந்தாலும் பிச்சை இடமாட்டான்.

He will not give lime for a cut finger (to stop the bleeding) and he will not give alms to a mendicant !

" *Ye'll break your neck as soon as your fast in his house.*"

1776. உலுத்தன் விருந்துக்கு ஒப்பானது ஒன்றுமில்லை.

Nothing can be compared to the feast of a stingy man ! (*Ironical*)

1777. உலோபிக்கு இருசெலவு.

A miser has double expenses.

" *A stingy man is always poor.*"

1778. எச்சில் கையால் காக்கை ஓட்டமாட்டான்.

He will not drive off a crow with the hand, (with which he is eating rice), lest he should lose some grains of rice (that stick to his hand).

Rice is eaten with the right hand from off leaf plates, and naturally some grains stick to the outside of the hand. A miserly man will not wave his hand to drive off the crows that come to watch for and if possible steal a meal from him, lest these few grains should be dropped.

1779. எட்டி பழுத்து என்ன, ஈயாதார் வாழ்ந்து என்ன?
What good is it if the strychnus fruit ripens, and a miser prospers?

Both are harmful. The Nux vomica is poisonous.

1780. கட்டாணித்தனமாய்க் கலியாணம் செய்தான்.
He performed the marriage in a very stingy way.

1781. கொடாகெண்டன், விடாகெண்டன்.
This man is determined not to give anything and that man is determined not to leave till he gets something!

1782. கொடுக்கமாட்டாதவன் கூத்தைப் பழித்தான், இடமாட்டாதவன் எச்சில் என்று சொன்னான்.
He who would not give money blamed the dancing, and he who would not give rice, said it was defiled!

The first would not pay enough money to hire a well-trained dancing-girl, but he put the blame for his stinginess on her dancing; the other pretended that the food he should have given had gone bad.

1783. கொடுக்கமாட்டாத இடையன் சினை ஆட்டைக் காட்டினதுபோல்.
Like a shepherd who would not give anything, but showed an ewe big with young.

1784. செம்பால் அடித்த காசும் கொடான்.
He will not even give copper coins.

"*His money comes from him like drops of blood.*"

1785. தானும் இடாள், இட்டவர்களைப் பார்த்தறியாள்.
She herself does not give and she does not know people who do give.

Charity and the charitable are foreign to her.

1786. தேடிப் புதைத்துத் தெருவில் இரக்கிறதா?
Should one acquire wealth and bury it, and go about begging in the streets? 1737, 1791.

Much wealth is acquired and hidden in this way by professional mendicants in India.

1787. நாறவாயன் (or ஊத்தைவாயன்) தேட, நல்லவாயன் தின்ன.
While the man with evil breath (*i.e.* the miser) acquired the property, the man with sweet breath (*i.e.* his son) enjoyed it.

"*After a great getter, comes a great spender.*"

1788. படுக்கப் பாயும் கொடான், தூங்க இடமும் கொடான்.
He won't give a mat to sleep on, and he won't give a place to sleep in.

1789. பரியத்துக்கு அஞ்சி குருட்டுக் கன்னியைக் கொண்டாற்போல.
Like him who feared (that he would have to give a great) nuptial present for a nice girl, and so married a blind virgin.

"*Covetousness often starves other vices.*"

1790. பீ தின்கிறவன் வீட்டுக்குப் போனால், பொழுது விடிகிறமட்டும் பேலச் சொல்லி அடித்தானும்.

A vulgar proverb meaning that if you go to a miser's house, he will trouble you all night to give him something.

1791. பொதியை வைத்துவிட்டுப் பிச்சைக்குப் போனான், அதையும் வைத்து விட்டுச் செத்துக்கிடந்தான்.

He left his bundle at home and went to beg; what he got he also left (at home), and he now lies dead. 1786.

"*A covetous man does nothing that he should till he dies.*"

1792. மகாராஜன் கலியாணத்தில் நீராகாரம் நெய் பட்டபாடு.

At a great king's wedding (plain) water and (poor) food are treated as if they are *ghee*.

Shabby food is given sparingly as if it were as rare or as dear as *ghee*. 1661.

"*He is not fit for riches, who is afraid to use them.*"

1793. வடித்தால் காணுமா? பொங்கினால் காணுமா?

Shall I get more by straining or by boiling it?

Said of one, who is anxious to get as much out of a thing as possible.

Cf. 2119 *ff.*

CLEVERNESS AND DEXTERITY.

கெட்டிக்காரத்தனம்.

1794. ஆகிறவன் அரைக்காசிலும் ஆவான், ஆகாதவனுக்கு ஆயிரம் கொடுத்தாலும் ஆகமாட்டான்.

A skilful man will become (what he ought to be) with half a *cash*, but though you give the worthless man a thousand (coins) he will not prosper. 3473.

1795. ஆயிரம் கப்பியில் நழுவின கப்பி.

He is the little grain that has slipped out from among a thousand grains.

He knows how to get out of a difficulty.

"*He is like a cat, he always falls on his feet.*"

1796. ஆளான ஆள் புகுந்தால் (com. பூண்டால்) ஆமணக்கும் விளக்கு எண்ணெய்யாம்.

If the right man enters, castor-seed will turn into lamp-oil. 1802, 1818.

1797. ஆனால் அச்சிலே வார், ஆகாவிட்டால் மிடாவிலே வார்.

If successful, pour it into a mould, if not pour it into the melting pot.

The goldsmith examines the gold after melting it. If it is free from dross he pours it into the mould; if it is still impure, it goes back into the pot. By one method or other he accomplishes the task he has undertaken. 1798, 2847.

"*Good riding on two anchors men have told, for if one break, the other may hold.*"

1798. ஆனால் ஆதிவாரம், ஆகாவிட்டால் சோமவாரம்.

If successful, it is Sunday; if not, it is Monday. 1797.

Sunday is a fortunate day. Monday is an ordinary day.

"*To have two strings to one's bow.*"

1799. இராஜ முகத்துக்கு எலுமிச்சம்பழம்.

As a lime to a king!

The lime is a formal gift given to procure an audience with a great man. Just as a lime procures an audience so a skilful man accomplishes the purpose that he has formed, with little cost or trouble.

1800. உள்ளங்கையில் அஞ்சுகொண்டை முடிக்கிறான்.

He can tie the hair of five women in the palm of one hand!

Great cleverness.

1801. ஊரை உழக்கால் அளக்கிறாள், நாட்டை நாழியால் அளக்கிறாள்.

She measures the village with a small measure and the country with a bigger one.

Said of a clever woman who has studied the weakness of everyone around her, and uses it for her profit, and so benefits by the faults of others.

1802. கரைப்பார் கரைத்தால் கல்லும் கரையும்.

If the right man grind, even a stone will turn to dust. 1796, 1818.

1803. கல்லிலே நார் உரிக்கிறதுபோல.

Like stripping off bark from a stone. 1817, 2622.

Said of one who knows how to get money from a stingy man.

"*He'll flay a flint.*"

1804. காலால் முடிந்ததைக் கையால் அவிழ்க்கமுடியாது.

What he has tied with his foot, others cannot untie with their hands.

Said of a clever and skilful person.

1805. கீழ் ஏழுலகமும், மேல் ஏழுலகமும் பார்த்தவன்போல பேசுகிறான்.

He speaks like one who has seen both the seven lower and the seven upper worlds. 1477.

Said ironically of one who makes great professions of cleverness.

1806. கெட்டிக்காரன் கொல்லையிலே கழுதை மேய்கிறது.
The ass is grazing in the clever man's garden. 207.
Even a clever man may be deceived.

1807. சமர்த்துள்ள சேவகனுக்குப் புல்லும் ஆயுதம்.
Even a blade of grass is a weapon in the hands of a skilful warrior.
" *A wise man will make tools of what comes to hand.*"

1808. தண்ணீரில் அடிபிடிக்கிறது.
Tracing footsteps on water. 1567, 1813.
An ironical description of somebody's cleverness.

1809. நீண்டது தச்சன், குறைந்தது கருமான்.
The carpenter wants (his wood) too long, and the blacksmith wants (his iron) too short.
Both are knowing. A carpenter can easily shorten a piece of wood, and a blacksmith can easily hammer out a piece of iron.

1810. பதுமைபோல் நடிக்கிறான்.
He dances like a puppet.
Said of one who is an adept in his art and never wearies in it.
" *He moves like a machine.*" " *He goes like clock-work.*"

1811. புளித்த காய்க்குப் புளி புகுத்துவாயோ?
Do you want to put acid into sour fruit. 781.
" *Don't try to teach your grand-mother how to suck eggs.*"

1812. மகனே வல்லாண்மை!
You are very clever, my girl!
Said to a person who maintains that he can do for a small sum, what others think will cost a great deal. Used with or without sarcasm.

1813. மணலை கயிறாய்த் திரிக்கிறது, வானத்தை வில்லாய் வளைக்கிறது.
Twisting a rope from sand, and bending the sky into a bow! 1808.

1814. மழைக்கால் இருட்டானாலும், மந்திகொம்பு இழந்து பாயுமா?
Will a monkey miss a branch it has jumped at, even in the gloom of the rainy season?
A man will give this as a reply, when warned that he may be deceived.

1815. முறிந்து ஓடும் விமானத்தற்குப் பறந்து ஓடி ஒட்டப்போடுகிறவன்.
He is a man who will fly along and repair a damaged car while it is in motion!

1816. மொட்டைத்தலையும், முழங்காலும் முடிபோடுகிறவன்.
He can tie together a bald head and a knee. 2567.
A clever and deceitful man.

1817. வறட்டு மாடானாலும் ஒரு பீர் பால் கொடுக்காதா?
Though it is a barren cow, won't it give one drop of milk? 1803, 1920,1967.
" *If you squeeze a cork, you will get but little juice.*"

1818. வல்லவன் ஆட்டின பம்பரம் மணலிலும் ஆடும்

A top spun by a clever man will spin even in sand. 1796,1802.

1819. வாயிருந்தால் மகளே, வாழ்ந்துவிட்டு வருவாய்.

If you have a mouth, my daughter, you will contrive to prosper. 1949, 2615.

Said of a woman guilty of some fault, who defends her case so well that she escapes. Generally said by another person who may be quite as guilty, but has not the ability to defend herself, and hence has to suffer.

"*An ill plea should be well pleaded.*"

"*A dumb man never gets land.*"

1820. வித்தை அடிக்கிற கோழிக்கு (corruption from கோள்) விளாவில் (corruption from வாய்) இருக்கிறதாம் பித்து (or பிச்சு.)

A cunning backbiter has bile in her mouth.

Cunning people know how to hide their cunning.

Cf. 1566 *ff.* 3480 *ff.*

EXCUSES, PRETEXTS.

சாக்கு.

1821. ஆடமாட்டாத தேவடியாள் கூடம் போதாது என்றாளாம்.

The dancing girl, who could not dance, said that the hall was not big enough. 1782.

"*When the devil could not swim, he laid the blame on water.*"

1822. ஆடாதான் மத்தளத்தைப் பழித்தானும்.

He who could not dance, blamed the drum (*or* music).

"*An ill shearer never got a good hook.*"

1823. ஆண்மையற்ற வீரன் ஆயுதத்தின்மேல் குறை சொல்லுவான்.

A warrior without courage blamed his weapons.

"*A bad workman complains of his tools.*"

1824. அவள் சாட்டிலே (or மறைப்பு) திரைசாட்டா?

Is the screen (mentioned) in her excuse any excuse (for her wrong doing)? 1766.

It is no excuse for wrong doing that it was done secretly.

1825. ஆகாத பஞ்சாங்கத்துக்கு அறுபது நாழியும் தியாச்சியம்.

In a bad almanac the whole day is unlucky (*Tyajya*).

i. e., No time in the day is the right time to begin work. *Tyajya* is a period following the asterism that rules the day and is considered an inauspicious time for beginning any undertaking, called in Tamil *Irâkhukâlam*. It varies with the different days of the week.

1826. இரும்புத்தூணை செல் அரிக்குமா?
Can white ants eat an iron pillar?
A reply to a foolish excuse.

1827. உதட்டிலே புண்ணானால், பால் கறக்காதா?
Though the cow have sore lips, will it not yield milk? 1834.
Said of a lame excuse.

1828. உப்பு மிஞ்சினால் தண்ணீர் போடு, தண்ணீர் மிஞ்சினால் உப்பு போடு.
If there is too much salt, pour water; if too much water, put salt.
The meals of the poor consist of rice boiled in salt and water with some condiments. Said of one who knows how to adapt excuses to occasions and so extricates himself from difficulties.

1829. உழுகிறதை விட்டு நழுவுகிறவன் தெய்வம் ஆடினாற்போல.
Like one who left his ploughing and slipped away to dance as if he were possessed (by a god or devil).

1830. ஏண்டா, தென்னமரத்திலே ஏறினாய் என்றால், கன்றுக்குட்டிக்குப் புல் பிடுங்க என்கிறான்.
If you say: O fellow, why did you climb the cocoanut tree? he replies, I went to get grass for the calf.
A lame and vain excuse.

1831. கொரடி கற்றவன் இடறிவிழுந்தால், அதுவும் ஒரு வரிசை என்பான்.
If the fencer slips and falls, he will say that even that was part of his art.
"*All things that great men do are well done.*"

1832. சட்டி சுட்டதும், கை விட்டதும்.
The pot burnt him, and was dropped.
Said of a poor excuse for leaving work that has turned out to be unprofitable.

1833. சாக்கும் போக்கும் ஏற்காது ஐயன் முன்.
Excuses will not be accepted before God.
"*It is always term-time in the Court of Conscience.*"

1834. குத்திலே அடித்தான், பல்லுபோச்சுது.
He beat him on his breech, and his teeth fell out. 1827, 2833.

1835. தேவரைக்காட்டி பூதம் தின்றதுபோல.
Like the goblin who pointed to the gods, and swallowed (the offering.) 1838.
Used of people, who make profit for themselves while professing to be disinterested.

1836. நொண்டி குதிரைக்குச் சறுக்கினது சாக்கு.
To the lame horse stumbling is an excuse (for idleness).
Said of a lazy person glad of any excuse to get off work.

1837. பார்க்கக்கொடுத்த பணத்துக்கு வெள்ளிக்கிழமையா?

Is Friday (a sufficient excuse for keeping) money that was lent for you to look at?

Friday is an unlucky day to undertake any enterprise and there is a superstition that money returned on a Friday will involve loss of property or of life. No Hindu will be willing to give or return money on a Friday. Friday is also the day for Hindus to visit their temples.

1838. பிள்ளையைச் சாக்கிட்டு, பூதம் முழுங்குகிறது.

Making the child an excuse for asking for food the goblin swallowed the food itself. 1835.

Said of a beggar woman with a child who asks for some food for her child with the intention of eating it herself.

1839. பிள்ளைக்காரி குசுவிட்டால், பிள்ளைமேல் சாக்கு.

If a woman who has a child breaks wind, she will lay the blame on the child. 1841.

"*Better a bad excuse than none at all.*"

1840. ரெட்டியாரே ரெட்டியாரே என்றால், கலப்பையை பளிச்சென்று போட்டதுபோல்.

Like the man who left his plough the moment you said 'Reddi, Reddi'!

Reddis are a class of Telugu farmers. The word 'Reddi' specifies no particular farmer, and the man who professes to think that he is being called when some one calls out 'Reddi', and leaves his ploughing, must be a very lazy and careless man.

"*Idle folks lack no excuse.*"
"*Don't let the plough stand to kill a mouse.*"

1841. வேலைக்கள்ளிக்குப் பிள்ளைமேல் சாக்கு.

Her child is an excuse to a lazy woman. 1839.

"*When the maid leaves the door open, the cat's in fault.*"

INVESTIGATION, CRITICISM, INQUISITIVENESS.

சோதனை, நோட்டம், தேடுதல்.

1842. அம்பட்டன் குப்பையிலே கிளறினால், மயிர் மயிராய்ப் புறப்படும்.

If you stir up the rubbish heap in a barber's dust heap you will find hair only.

Leave mean people's affairs alone.

1843. இது சொத்தை, அது புளியங்காய்போல்.

This is worm-eaten, and that is (sour) like tamarind.

Said to one who criticizes and rejects everything.

"*He lives unsafely that looks too near on things.*"

1844. *இந்தப் பூராயத்தில் (பூர்—ஆய்) குறைச்சலில்லை.*
There is no failing in this inquisitiveness (of yours).

1845. *ஈச்சம் முள்ளாலே இருவாயும் தைத்தாலும், தேங்காய்க்கு மஞ்சளில்லை பூவுக்கும் மணமில்லை என்கிறாள்.*
If you tie her mouth up with the thorns of the date-palm she will still say, "There is no saffron on the cocoanut, and the flowers have no perfume." 2588.
Said of a woman who insists on talking about everything.

1846. *ஈர வெங்காயத்திற்கு இருபத்து நாலு புரை எடுக்கிறது.*
To peal twenty-four skins off a fresh onion (is very difficult.)
Said of one clever in criticisms. Old people say this about young people who are hypercritical.

1847. *உன் நெஞ்சில் தட்டிப்பார்* (or *தொட்டுப்பார்*).
Knock at your own breast (*or* heart).
i.e., What does your own conscience say about you?

1848. *ஊசி கொள்ளப்போய்த் துலாக் கணக்குப் பார்த்ததுபோல.*
Like inquiring about its weight when going to buy a needle!
Silly inquisitiveness about trifles.

1849. *எச்சில் எடுக்கச் சொன்னார்களா? எத்தனைபேர் என்று எண்ணச்சொன் னார்களா?*
Did they tell you to remove the fragments left or to count how many people there had been for dinner? 2844.
Don't be inquisitive about what is not your business.

1850. *எருமை மாட்டைத் தண்ணீரில் போட்டுக்கொண்டு விலைபார்க்கிறது.*
To estimate the price of a buffalo while it is lying in the water.
Buffaloes lie in ponds with all but their heads covered by the water.
"*To buy a pig in a poke.*"

1851. *ஒரு பானை சோற்றுக்கு ஒரு சோறு பதம்.*
One grain is sufficient as a sample of a jar full of boiled rice. 1863, 2692.
"*From one circumstance judge of all.*"

1852. *கட்டின வீட்டுக்கு நோட்டம்* (or *பழுது* or *கருத்து* or *சொத்தை* or *பணிக்கை*) *சொல்லுவார் அநேகர்.*
Many will criticize a finished building.
"*Every fool can find faults that a great many wise men can't remedy.*"
"*Of judgment every one has a stock for sale.*"

1853. *கிணற்றுத் தவளைக்கு நாட்டு வளப்பம் ஏன்?*
What has a frog in a well to do with the affairs of the country? 1855.
e.g., What has a woman to do with what is published in a newspaper—an application which will appeal to every Hindu man.

1854. *குதிரை நல்லதுதான் சுழி கெட்டது.*
The horse is good, no doubt, but its marks are faulty. 1864.

The marks in the mane and hair of a horse are supposed to be signs of fortune or misfortune to its owner. Many a good horse fetches a low price because its 'marks' are not lucky.

1855. *கொட்டை நூற்கிற அம்மாளுக்குப் பட்டணம் விசாரிக்கிறது என்?*
Why should a woman who spins cotton thread inquire about the affairs of the town? 1853.

1856. *கொண்டு குலம் பேசுகிறதா?*
Should a woman criticize the caste into which she is married?

1857. *தாதுமில்லை, பிராதுமில்லை.*
There is neither indifference to nor complaint about it.

Said about a matter which nobody looks after.

1858. *தண்ணீரையும் தாயையும் பழிக்கலாமா?*
Are water and one's mother to be criticized?

1859. *நதிமூலத்தையும், ரிஷிமூலத்தையும் விசாரிக்கப்படாது.*
It is not right to investigate the origin of a river or of a *Rishi*.

Do not think of their possibly insignificant origin, rather admire their excellent qualities. *Rishis* are the highest order of saints in Hindu hagiology.

1860. *நாறல்சோற்றுக்குப் பதம் பார்க்கிறது என்?*
Why examine spoiled rice? 1866.

"*There is but bad choice where the whole stock is bad.*"

1861. *பங்காளியையும் பனங்காயையும் பதம் பார்த்து வெட்டவேண்டும்.*
Cut into your partner and a palmyra fruit only after testing them (*i.e.*, when you can make gain out of them).

When a partner is in difficulties then is the time to give him up, and the palmyra fruit must be cut when it is tender.

"*When two persons have a common purse, one sings and the other weeps.*"

1862. *பல மரம் கண்ட தச்சன் ஒருமரம் வெட்டமாட்டான்.*
The carpenter who has seen many trees, will cut down none.

He finds fault with them all, criticizes them and leaves them alone.

1863. *பிள்ளை திறத்தைப் பேலவிட்டுப் பார்.*
If you wish to ascertain a child's health, send it to stool. 1851.

Investigate everything so as to secure the knowledge you need.

1864. *பிள்ளை நல்லதுதான், பொழுதுபோனால் கண் தெரியாது.*
The child, to be sure, is a nice child; but when the sun sets it cannot see? 1154, 1867.

Said of a person with one glaring fault.

1865. புண்ணியத்துக்கு உழுத குண்டையைப் பல்லைப் பிடித்துப் பதம் பார்த்ததுபோல.

Like examining the teeth of the plough-bullock that has been lent as a favour.

Do not be so ungrateful as to criticize the kindness of others.

"*Look not a gift horse in the mouth.*"

1866. மணற்சோற்றிலே கல் ஆய்கிறதுபோல்.

Like searching for the grit in sand. 1860.

Said of something that cannot be set right, because it is radically wrong. *e.g.*, What is the use of correcting an essay that is completely wrong in matter, style and grammar?

1867. நிழல் நல்லது தான் முசுறு கெட்டது (or பொல்லாதது).

The shade is certainly good, but the red ants are bad. 1880.

People seek shelter from the sun under shady trees, but the red ants that often live in such places, give nasty bites to those who sit or lie down where they are away.—Good people surrounded by wicked and selfish ones are hindered in doing good to the public.

1868. முடி வைத்த தலைக்குச் சுழிக் குற்றம் பார்க்கிறதா?

After the head has been crowned, why look at the cure of the hair?

Mistaken criticism. The crown puts the wearer above criticism.

1869. வலிய பெண் கொடுக்கிறோம் என்றால், குலம் என்ன, கோத்திரம் என்ன என்பார்கள்.

If you say that you will give your daughter in marriage willingly, the bridegroom's friends will ask what is your caste and what is your family?

"*Give neither counsel nor salt till you are asked for it.*"

1870. வீடுவீடாய்ப் பதம் பார்க்கிறான்.

He goes from house to house examining everything, (and finds satisfaction nowhere).

Cf. 192.

OBSTACLES.

தடை, தடங்கள்.

1871. ஆற்றைத் தாண்டியல்லவோ கரை ஏறவேண்டும்.

Only by crossing the river can one reach the other shore. 1314.

No success without effort to overcome difficulties.

"*No gains without pains.*"

1872. இடுவோர் பிச்சையைக் கெடுக்கிறதா?

Should one prevent the giver from giving? 1877.

1873. இராஜன் ஏறின குதிரைக்கு மேடு ஏது, பள்ளம் ஏது?

What are hills and valleys to a king's horse?

1874. இராஜீகம் தெய்வீகம் எப்படியோ?
How shall we know what is the King's will and God's will?

God works his will, and a king does what he likes. What man can oppose either?

1875. எனக்குப் பாக்கு பிடிக்கப் பார்க்கிறான்.
He tries to make me accept betel and areca-nut. 749.

After a work has been completed the employer gives betel-leaf and areca-nut to the workmen when dismissing them. Hence 'to give betel and areca-nut' means 'to dismiss,' and the above saying is used about an enemy who is trying to oust the speaker out of some employment.

1876. ஓடுகிற வெள்ளம் அணையில் நிற்குமா?
Will a rushing flood stop at a dam?

1877. கூலிக்குப் பாவி குறுக்கே வந்தான்.
That sinner came between me and my wages. 1872.

1879. பிச்சை இட்டது போதும், நாயைப் பிடித்துக் கட்டு.
I am satisfied with what you have given me. Seize the dog and tie it up. 1880.

Said by a beggar to the elders in a family when the younger members of it have vexed and ridiculed him, and by a mother-in-law about her daughter-in-law, implying that though her son is dutiful, his wife frightens and worries her as a fierce dog would.

1880. மாளிகை கட்டி வன்குரங்கு (or மரநாய்) கட்டினதுபோல.
Like building a palace and keeping a monkey (*or* pole-cat) in it. 1867.

The 'monkey' is the stingy person in a family, who prevents others from being liberal to beggars.

"*Like the gardener's dog, that neither eats cabbage itself, nor lets anybody else.*"

"*Like a dog in a manger.*"

PERSEVERANCE.

தாளாண்மை ; கடைப்பிடி.

"LITTLE STROKES FELL GREAT OAKS."

1881. அடிமேல் அடி அடித்தால், அம்மியும் நகரும்.
Stroke upon stroke will make even a grinding-stone creep. 1822.

A grinding-stone is the slab used in grinding curry-stuff and is so heavy that two men are required to lift it.

1882. அடிக்க அடிக்கப் பந்து அதிக விசை கொள்ளும்.
The harder the blow, the faster the *ball flies.*

Now used of one who becomes worse by neglecting repeated advice and chastisement.

1883. உட்கார்ந்து அல்லவோ படுக்கவேண்டும்.
You must sit down before you lie down. 1888.
Said to a man inclined to do things hastily.
"*First creep, then go.*"

1884. ஒரு முழுக்கிலே மண் எடுக்கிறதா?
Can you clean out a well at one dive?
The reference is to getting out the mud or dirt in a well by diving.
"*Rome was not built in a day.*"
"*An inch in an hour is a foot in a day's work.*"

1885. ஒன்று ஒன்றாய் நூறு? ஒருமிக்க நூறு?
Does it become a hundred by adding one and one? Does it become a hundred in a moment?
"*Drop by drop the lake is drained.*"
"*An oak is not felled at one chop.*"

1886. குச்சுவீடு கட்டியல்லவா மச்சுவீடு கட்டவேண்டும்?
Must we not first build a hut, and afterwards a big house?

1887. கொஞ்சங் கொஞ்சந் தின்றால், பனையும் தின்றுவிடலாம்.
If you eat it little by little, you can devour a palmyra tree. 1134.
"*Constant application overcomes the greatest difficulties.*"

1888. நின்றாற்போல் விழுந்தால், தலை உடையும்.
If you fall suddenly you will break your head. 1883.

Cf. 1463 *ff.* 1889 *ff.* 2005 *ff.*

PERSISTENCE.

உறுதி, பிடிவாதம்.

1889. அடுத்து அடுத்துச் சொன்னால் தொடுத்த காரியம் முடியும்.
If you speak to him over and over again, the work he has undertaken will be completed.

1890. அது நான் செய்யாதேபோனால், என் மீசை எடுத்துவிடுகிறேன் (or இது மீசையா?)
If I do not accomplish that work, I will take off my mustache.
This proverb is used by Sudras to express the determination to succeed in an enterprised named or else to renounce all secular things. Hindus generally wear only a mustache. But Brahmins generally do not wear even a mustache as the mustache is looked on as a sign of pride, and they profess to be without pride. Some ascetics however, wear both beard and mustache and Mahratta Brahmins wear mustaches.

1891. ஊக்கமது கைவிடேல்.
Never give up persevering.

1892. எறும்பு ஊரக் கல் தேயும் (or குழியும்).

A stone will be worn away by the creeping of ants. 1881.

"*Constant dropping wears the stone.*"

1893. ஒரே காலிலே இருக்கிறான்.

He is on one leg.

The reference is to the story of Arjunas's penance as told in the Mahâbhârata. He stood on one leg for a fabulous space of time and by this perseverance in penance gained a magic arrow that could destroy anything it was aimed at.

1894. தனம் இழந்தாலும், கன்னத்திலே கை விடுகிறதா?

Even if you lose your property, don't rest your head on your hand. 1896.

Don't appear to lose courage in adversity.

"*Set hard heart against hard hap.*"

"*Fortune lost, nothing lost; courage lost, much lost; honour lost, more lost; soul lost, all lost.*"

1895. குரங்குப்பிடிபோல் பிடிக்கவேண்டும்.

Lay hold of a thing as firmly as a monkey does.

i.e., Be firm! *or* Be obstinate!

1896. கேட்டில் உறுதி, கூட்டும் உடைமை.

Perseverance in time of adversity, will bring back lost property. 1894.

"*Fortune favours the brave.*"

"*Calamity is the touchstone of a brave mind.*"

1897. தான் பிடித்த முசலுக்கு மூன்றே கால்.

The hare he caught had only three feet!

Said of a self-opinionated person who is obstinate in his own view in spite of all argument.

1898. நெற்றியிலே மூன்று கண் படைத்தவன் வரவேண்டும்.

Let the destroyer with the three eyes in his forehead come!

According to popular mythology Siva, the god of destruction, has three eyes, and his appearance is always described as most terrifying. The proverb is used by an obstinate man who is not to be moved from his purpose even by the fear of the wrath of Siva. Said, for instance, by a man who refuses to give back a borrowed article, or by one who is subjected to threats but will not give way, or reveal a secret.

1899. மேய்த்தால் கழுதை மேய்ப்பேன், இல்லாதேபோனால் பரதேசம் போவேன்.

I prefer tending asses to tending other animals; if I am not allowed to do so I shall go on a pilgrimage. 491, 2843.

Said ironically to one who persists in what is low and mean, when honourable and profitable employment is open to him.

Cf. 1881 *ff.*

COERCION.

பலவந்தம், வலக்கட்டாயம்.

1900. *அடி உதவுகிறதுபோல, அண்ணன் தம்பி உதவுவார்களா?*
Can an elder brother and a younger brother give help like the help a stick gives? 3302.
"*Spare the rod and spoil the child.*"
"*It is the bridle and spur that make a good horse.*"

1901. *உடம்பிலே பயமிருந்தால், நன்றாய்ச் செய்வான்.*
If a person has fear in his body (*or* mind), he will do his work well.

1901*a*. *எரிச்சல் வந்து அல்லவோ கடிக்கும், எழுப்பிவிட்டா கடிக்கும்?*
When it gets enraged it is sure to bite, but will it do so at another's instigation? 2065.
Whatever a person does, he should do of his own accord, not because he is compelled by outside influences.

1902*a*. *எழுபது சென்றாலும், பறை ஏவினால்தான் செய்யும்.*
Though a Pariah be seventy years old, he will only work if ordered.

1902*b*. *கடையச்சே வராத வெண்ணெய், குடையச்சே வரப்போகிறதா?*
Is the butter that did not come during churning, likely to come when one stirs gently? 3132, 3210.
e.g. A son who did not love his mother and father before he married is not likely to love them after he marries and gets children of his own.

1903. *கண்ணைக் காட்டி அழைத்தால் வராதவள், கையைப் பிடித்து அழைத்தால் வருவாளா?*
Will she who does not come when called by loving glances, come if you lay hold of her hands?
"*You may force a man to shut his eyes, but not to sleep.*"

1904. *குரங்கின் பீயை மருந்துக்குக் கேட்டால் கொடுக்குமா? அடித்து வாங்க வேண்டாமா?*
If you ask a monkey (an inferior being) for its excrement for medicine, will it give it? Must you not beat it to get it?
Very many other things quite as unpleasant as the excrement of monkeys are found in the Hindu pharmacopoea.
"*The bird that can sing, and will not sing, must be made to sing.*"

1905. *கோல் ஆட, குரங்கு ஆடும்.*
If the stick dances (beats), the monkey will also dance.
"*It is the raised stick that makes the dog obey.*"
"*A whip for a fool, and a rod for a school, is always in good season.*"

1906. சடையைப் பிடித்து இழுத்தால், சந்நியாசி கிட்ட வருவான்.

Only when you lay hold of an ascetic's (*Sanniyasi*) long hair and pull him, will he come.

" *He's an ill boy that goes like a top only when he is whipt.*"

1907. தானாய்க் கனியாதது, தடிகொண்டு அடித்தால்கனியுமா?

Will that which does not ripen by itself, ripen if you take a stick and beat it?

Nature will have its course in spite of education.

1908. மயிலே மயிலே இறகு கொடு என்றால், கொடுக்குமா?

If you say, 'O peacock! O peacock! give me a feather,' will it give you one?

" *There is no argument like that of the stick.*"

1909. முறையோ (com. மொறை) என்கிறவன் கழுத்திலே லிங்கம் கட்டினால், மறைவிலே அறுத்துப் போட்டுவிடுவான்.

If you tie a *linga* round the neck of a person who objects to it, he will secretly untie it and throw it away. 2763, 3097.

Applicable to many marriages in India, when the girl-bride or the young bridegroom, is forced to marry unwillingly—with sad results.

" *One man may lead a horse to the water, but ten men cannot make him drink.*"

1910. வாயாலே கேட்டால் வாழைப்பிஞ்சும் கொடான், தண்டித்துக் கேட்டால் தாறோடே கொடுப்பான்.

If entreated he will not give you even one unripe plantain, but if compelled by force he will give the whole bunch.

1911. வெளுப்பானுக்கு (or உதைப்பானுக்கு) வெளுப்பான் ஜாதி (or அசல்) வண்ணான்.

For a master who beats (*or* kicks), the good (*ironical*) washerman will wash well. 1131.

A pun on the word வெளுக்க, to wash, which is also the slang for 'giving, a sound thrashing.'

" *Fear keeps the garden better than the gardener.*"

Cf. 2064 *ff.* 3299 *ff.* 2763 *ff.*

PUNISHMENT, WORRY.

சிக்ஷை, தொந்தரவு.

1912. அது அதற்கு ஒரு கவலை, எனக்கு எட்டுக் கவலை.

Others have only one anxiety, but I have eight anxieties.

1913. அழுகிற வீட்டில் இருந்தாலும், ஒழுகிற வீட்டில் இருக்கப்படாது.

One can stay in a house where there is sorrow, but not in one that leaks!

A sharp quarrel that is soon over can be endured but who can endure constant quarrels.

1914. அன்றைக்கு அடித்த அடி ஆறுமாசம் தாங்கும்.
The thrashing he got that day (was so severe that it) will do him good for six months. 1155, 2784.

1915. ஆசையெல்லாம் தீர அடித்தாள் முறத்தாலே.
She beat her husband with a winnowing-fan to her heart's content! 3578.

1916. ஆளை நீட்டிப்போடு.
Stretch that person on the ground (and thrash him)!

1917. உங்கள் உறவிலே வேகிறதைவிட, ஒருகட்டு விறகிலே வேகிறது மேல்.
It is better to be burned in a bundle of firewood (in the cemetery) than in one's relationships.

Said in reproof of a relative or friend who takes liberties and is a great expense and worry.

1918. உன்னைப் பிழிந்து எடுத்துப்போடுவேன்.
I will squeeze you and turn you out.

i.e. I will give you endless trouble.

1919. எல்லாரும் ஏறி இளைத்த குதிரைமேலே தம்பி பொன் பட்டம் கட்டிப் புறப்பட்டான்.
The younger brother tied a gold piece (on the forehead) of the jaded horse that all had ridden, and started out.

Said by a master, who has been worried by a number of people and is tired out, when one more comes to vex him.

"*A man may bear till his back break.*"

1920. ஒட்டினாலும், ஒழக்குப் பீர்க்கும் என்கிறதா?
Is it right to say (to a cow), Though your skin sticks to your bones give me a measure of milk? 1765, 1817, 1967.

Said of the importunity that tries to exact work from a person who is already exhausted.

1921. ஒரு இழவு என்றால், உள்ளபடி ஆகும்.
If you say there is a funeral, things will go on properly.

i.e. If a funeral takes place in his house, even an unjust tyrant will come to terms. Used by the oppressed against tyrants who act lawlessly. Also used of one who has too many irons in the fire. Also: இது என்ன இழவு! Why this constant trouble!

1922. ஒரு அடி அடித்தாலும் பட்டுக்கொள்ளலாம், ஒரு சொல் கேட்க முடியாது.
One may endure a beating, but one cannot endure a word. 1931, 1933, 1935.

"*A word hurts more than a wound.*"

"*Many words hurt more than swords.*"

1923. *கடா கடா என்றாலும், மருந்துக்கு ஒரு பீர் என்கிறான்.*

Though he said the goat was a he-goat. he asks for a drop of its milk for medicine!

Said of one who worries incessantly in order to get something.

1924. *காலைச் சுற்றின பாம்பு கடித்தால் ஒழிய விடாது.*

A snake that has coiled round your leg will not leave without biting you.

An importunate man will worry till he gets what he wants.

1925. *குட்டுப்பட்டாலும் மோதிரக்கையால் குட்டுப்படவேண்டும்.*

If I have to suffer a beating let it be with a jewelled hand. 1926.

Better to suffer at the hands of a worthy man than at the hands of a base person.

" *Be it better or be it worse, be ruled by him that bears the purse.*"

1926. *குதிரை உதைத்தாலும் உதைக்கலாம், கழுதையா உதைக்கிறது.*

A horse may kick me; but may an ass kick me? 1925.

1927. *கூலிக்குக் கழுவிருப்பார்களா?*

Will any one (allow himself to) be impaled for hire?

1928. *குலைக்கிற நாய்க்கு எலும்பைப் போட்டதுபோல.*

Like throwing a bone to a barking dog.

i.e. Satisfying the momentary worry caused by a child or an importunate person.

1929. *கொள்ளிக்கட்டையால் சுட்டால் கொப்பளிக்கும் என்று வாழைப்பழங் கொண்டு வடுவெடுவாய்ச் சுடுகிறான்.*

He thinks, that if he were to burn him with a firebrand, it would blister him, and so he brands him with a plantain fruit. 233.

Said of one who takes his revenge by indirect means.

1930. *சாகிறவரையில் வைத்தியன் விடான், செத்தாலும் விடான் பஞ்சாங்கக்காரன்.*

The doctor won't leave, till you die, but the Brahmin (who determines auspicious days) won't leave after your death. 980.

When one is dead the care of the doctor ends, but the Brahmin will worry for money for the various funeral ceremonies.

1931. *சாட்டை அடியும் சவுக்கு அடியும் பொறுக்கலாம், மூட்டைப்பூச்சி கடியும், முணமுணப்பும் ஆகாது.*

One may bear blows from a rope and a whip, but the bites of bugs, and grumbling tones are unbearable. 1935.

" *No cut like unkindness.*"

1932. சீக்கிரான் கறிப்பிலே (கறிவேப்பிலே) இழுத்துக்கொண்டு திரிப்பிள்ளை.
Shickiran leaves drag one about. 3396.

These leaves are used by poor people as soap, and are very sticky. Used by a person already worried and troubled, when some one comes and increases his worry. Also said in ridicule of a person who is in hot haste to dispose of a daughter in marriage.

1933. தீப்புண் ஆறும், வாய்ப்புண் ஆறாது.
A wound caused by fire will heal, but a wound caused by words will not heal. 1922, 2789.

1934. நெய்வார்த்த பணம் முழுகிபோகிறதா?
Is the money for pouring out *ghee* irrecoverably lost? 923, 980.

Said to one to whom some small gift has been promised and who is as urgent for it as if the promised gift were a debt.

One "take it" is better than two "you shall have it."

1935. முறத்தடி பட்டாலும், முகத்தடி படலாகாது.
One may endure the blows of a sieve, but not frowns. 1931.

1936. வடக்கத்தி யானையை அடித்தால், தெற்கத்தி யானைக்குப் புத்திவரும்.
If you beat an elephant from the North (*i.e.* a strong elephant), the elephant from the South (*i.e.* a weak elephant) will get sense. 163.

The punishment of one offender is a warning to others.

OVER-HARSHNESS SUCCEEDED BY OVER-INDULGENCE.

சிக்ஷை, தாக்ஷிணியம்.

1937. கொழுக்கட்டை தின்ற நாய்க்குக் குறுணி மோர் குருதக்ஷிணையா?
Should one give a measure of buttermilk as an offering to a dog that has (stolen and) eaten one's cakes?

Ought a man who deserves punishment to be favoured?

1938. செருப்பால் அடித்து, பட்டுப் புடவை கொடுத்தாற்போல.
Like beating a woman with your shoe, and afterwards giving her a silk cloth.

To strike anyone with the slipper is the utmost insult among Hindus.

1939. பாப்பாச்சாலே அடித்து, பருப்பும் சோறும் போட்டதுபோல.
Like beating a person with your slipper and then serving him nice food!

1940. விளக்குமாற்றால் அடித்து, குதிரையோடு தீவட்டி கொடுத்தாற்போல.
Like beating one with a broom-stick, and afterwards giving him a horse and a torch.

To punish or disgrace a person, and afterwards to repent of it, and to give him large gifts as compensation.

ANGER.

கோபம்.

1941. கோபம் சண்டாளம்.
Anger (ends in) baseness.
"*Anger is a sworn enemy.*"

1942. சாது மிரண்டால் காடு இடங் கொள்ளாது.
When a gentle person gets angry, a forest will not hold (his wrath). 3055.
"*In the coldest flint there is hot fire.*"
"*Nothing turns sourer than milk.*"

1943. நெருப்பு பந்தம் கட்டிக்கொண்டு நிற்கிறான்.
He stands, holding a torch.
An idiomatic phrase meaning that his face flames with anger.

1945. மூஞ்சி (or முகம்) காட்டுகிறான்.
He shows his face.
i.e. He is discontented or angry and his face shows it.
"*He has eaten sparrow-dumpling.*"

EXERTION.

கஷ்டம், முயற்சி.

EFFORT REWARDED.

1946. அத்தை மகளானாலும், சும்மா வருமா?
Though she is your paternal aunt's daughter she cannot be obtained for nothing. 1955.
By custom a man must marry his paternal aunt's daughter, but though he has a right to demand such a girl, he will have the same expenses for the wedding, and must perform the same ceremonies as if she were a more distant relation. He must persevere.
"*No sweet without sweat.*"
"*Think of ease, but work on.*"

1947 அழுத பிள்ளை பால் குடிக்கும்.
A crying child will get milk. 1961.

1948. உண்ட உடம்புக்கு உறுதி, உழுத கழனி நெல்லு.
To the body that eats, strength comes; the ploughed field (will yield) grain.

1949. ஊர் இருக்கிறது, வாயிருக்கிறது.
The village is there, and you have a mouth. 1819, 1961.
Make use of your tongue and you will find what you want.
"*Asking costs nothing.*" "*Lose nothing for want of asking.*"

1950. எச்சில் தின்றாலும் வயிறு நிறையத் தின்னவேண்டும், எச்சுக்கேட்டாலும் பொழுது விடிகிறமட்டும் கேட்கவேண்டும்.

If you eat offal, you must do it till your stomach is full; if you listen to bad language, continue to do so till day break. 1764, 1952, 1994.

Persevere in what you undertake, though it may be ever so insignificant, or unpleasant, and you will gain something by it.

1951. ஏழை அடித்தேனோ, கூழை அடித்தேனோ?

Did I beat the poor beggar, and thereby strike a blow at my fortune? 1962.

The deity that rewards virtue is supposed to inflict poverty on the oppressor of the poor.

1951*a*. ஏரை அடித்தேனோ, கூழை அடித்தேனோ?

Did I diminish the number of my ploughs? Did I diminish my own food?

i.e. He that stints labour will find food lacking.

1952. ஒடியமாகிலும் ஊடுருவக் கேள்.

Though the language be obscene, listen to it attentively. 1950.

1953. கை காய்த்தால், கமுகு (பாக்கு) காய்க்கும்.

If the hand becomes hard (by watering the areca palm) the areca will bear fruit.

Constant application will produce the required result.

1954. சிரைத்தால் கூலி, சேவித்தால் சம்பளம்.

If you shave you will get pay, if you serve you will be paid for it. 1962.

1955. சும்மா கிடைக்குமா சோணாசலன் பாதம்?

Can Siva's feet (*i.e.* God's mercy) be obtained for nothing? 1946.

"*The Gods sell us everything for our labours.*"

"*The best things are worst to come by.*"

1956. நாடின பொருள் கைகூடும்.

What we seek, we shall obtain.

"*Seek and ye shall find.*"

1957. நீண்ட கை நெருப்பு அள்ளும்.

The stretched-out hand will take up fire. 1004, 2420.

Thieves will come to grief. This proverb refers to the old custom by which a suspected person had to prove his innocence by taking red-hot iron in his hand without being burnt.

கை நீட்டக்காரன் கழு ஏறுவான்.

The person who has long arms (*i.e.* has thieving propensities) will one day be impaled.

"*Be sure your sins will find you out.*"

1958. பள்ளம் இறைத்தவன் பங்கு கொண்டுபோகிறான்.
He who irrigates low-lying land will get his sharo.
"*He who will have the fruit must climb the tree.*"

1959. பாடுமில்லை, பலனுமில்லை.
No exertion, no fruit.
"*No pains, no gains.*"

1960. மந்திரத்தால் மாங்காய் விழுமா?
Will the saying of an incantation cause mangoes (a fruit) to fall from a tree? 2041, 2349.

Nothing can be done by words; exertion is needed.

1961. வாய் உண்டானால், பிள்ளைபிழைக்கும்.
If the child has a mouth, it will live. 1947, 1949.

If it cries for milk, it will get it.

1962. வேலை செய்தால் கூலி, வேஷம் போட்டால் காசு.
If you work you will be paid, and if you mount the stage as a player you will get your wages. 1951, 1954, 2642.

Cf. 2699 *ff.*

MUCH EXERTION AND LITTLE GAIN.

1963. அடியும் பட்டுப் புளித்த மாங்காயும் தின்னவேண்டுமோ?
Am I to take a beating and also to eat sour mangoes?
"*Great pain and little gain will make a man soon weary.*"

1964. அதிலே குறைச்சலில்லை, ஆட்டடா மணியை பூசாரி.
There is no fault to find in you, O, poojâri (priest of Kâli), only be punctual in ringing the bell before the image.

Used of any rogue who pretends to honesty.

1965. இந்தக் கூழுக்கா இத்தனை திருநாமம் (or இருபத்தெட்டு நாமம்).
Is it for this little gruel that I have put on so many *nâmams*. 1970.

Used by a Siva mendicant forced by hunger to assume the Vishnuvite *nâmam* (mark on the forehead) in a Vishnuvite village.
i.e. Is it for nought that I have made these great professions of piety?
"*To have nothing for one's labour but one's pains.*"

1966. ஊரார்வீட்டுக் கலியாணமே, என் அவிழ்ந்தாய்க் கோமணமே.
It is the wedding of another villager, why have you loosened your loin-cloth for it?

Said by an outsider to one who is so very busy at a wedding; that even his loin-cloth is loosened, and he is put to shame. Used of those who take much pains in affairs that do not concern them and get no good by their exertions.

1967. எருமை கடா என்றாலும், குழந்தைக்குப் பால் ஒரு பீர் இல்லையா என்கிறான்.

Though told that it is a male buffalo, he asks if there is not a drop of milk to be had for the child. 1817, 1920.

Said of one who tries to get something out of what seems hopeless.

"*To milk a he-goat.*"

1968. காலுக்குக் கடுப்பே தவிர, கண்ட பலன் ஒன்றுமில்லை.

Besides wearying my legs, the profit I anticipated was lacking.

1969. குண்டாக்கரணம் போட்டாலும், பிண்டாச்சோற்றுக்கு வழியில்லை.

Though he turns a somersault in a pot (*i.e.* does the impossible) there is no way (for him to get) a mouthful of rice.

1970. ஒரு நாள் கூத்துக்கு மீசை சிரைக்கவா?

Why shave off the mustache to go and dance for one day? 1965.

In India female characters are represented by male actors in female garb. Said to one who tells a number of lies to get a trifle.

"*The game is not worth the candle.*"

1971. கொடுக்கிறது உழக்குப்பால், உதைக்கிறது பல்லுப்போக.

(The cow) yields only a small measure of milk, but it kicks out (the milkman's) teeth.

Said of a severe master, who pays small wages but demands much work.

1972. தச்சன் அடித்த தலைவாசல் எல்லாம் உச்சி இடிக்க உலாவி திரிந்தேன்.

I wandered about knocking my head against all the door-lintels which the carpenter had put up.

I have exerted myself to the uttermost but achieved nothing.

1973. பட்டும் பாழ், நட்டும் சாவி.

My exertions are fruitless; what I planted is blighted.

1974. பறந்து பறந்து பாடுபட்டாலும், பகலுக்குச் சோறில்லை.

However much I exert myself, I get no rice to eat all day.

1975. வரவு கொஞ்சம், வலிப்பு மெத்த.

The income is little, the pain (to earn it) is great.

1976. வீண் இழவுக்கு மார் அடிக்கிறதா?

Why beat your breast at a funeral where you get nothing?

Even at the humblest Hindu funerals the guests receive betel leaves and areca nut. The proverb is used to express contempt for an enterprise that yields no profit. A very common proverb.

Cf. 1995 *ff.* 2616 *ff.*

ONE HAS THE TOIL, ANOTHER THE PROFIT.

1977. அப்பாசுவாமிக்குக் கலியாணம், அவர் அவர் வீட்டிலே சாப்பாடு, கொட்டுமேளம் கோவிலிலே, வெற்றிலைபாக்கு கடையிலே, சுண்ணாம்பு சூளையிலே.

Appâswâmy's wedding is being performed. The guests have to dine in their own houses; the drum is beaten in the temple; betel leaf and areca nut are to be had at the shops; and at the kiln they can get lime (to chew with the betel)!

Said of a miser, or more commonly of a person who has the knack of getting what he wants at the expense of others.

1978. ஆக்கி அரைத்துப் போட்டவள் கெட்டவள், வழிகூட்டி அனுப்பினவள் நல்லவள்.

She who prepared the food and served it, is taken no notice of; she who was sent to start you on your journey is praised.

The one who does the work is often overlooked.

" *Another threshed what I reaped.*"

1979. இட்டவர்கள் தொட்டவர்கள் கெட்டவர்கள், இப்போது வந்தவர்கள் நல்லவர்கள்.

Those who give and those who help are despised, new-comers are honored.

Said, for instance, by old servants, when a new-comer is favoured or promoted.

1980. இடித்தவள் புடைத்தவள் இங்கே இருக்க, எட்டிப் பார்த்தவள் கொட்டிக்கொண்டுபோனாள்.

While the woman who pounded and sifted the rice is left here, she who only looked on has gone off with it all. 1718.

Said by a mother-in-law about a daughter-in-law who gets the benefit of all her economy and thrift.

" *One man knocks in the nail, and another hangs his hat on it.*"

1981. ஊர் கூடி செக்கு தள்ள, வாணியன் எண்ணெய் கொண்டுபோக.

The whole village helped to work the oil mill, but the oil merchant took the oil away.

" *Little dogs start the hare, the great get her.*"

1982. எலி கட்ட, பாம்பு குடிகொள்ள.

The rat makes (the hole); the snake inhabits it. 1987.

" *Fools build houses, and wise men live in them.*"

1983. ஒரு குருவி இரை எடுக்க, ஒன்பது குருவி வாய் திறக்க.

One bird brings the food, and nine open their mouths for it.

The head of a family does not enjoy what he earns.

1984. கடன்பட்டு உடன்பட்டு அம்மை கும்பிட, நீ யார் கூத்தி விழுந்து கும்பிட.

In order to worship the Goddess, I have borrowed money and given bonds ; but whose concubine are you, to bow down here and worship the Goddess? 1988.

One profits by another's labour.

Used by a selfish mother-in-law against a disliked daughter-in-law, when the latter attempts to profit by the former's economy.

" *One soweth and another reapeth.*"

1985. காத்திருந்தவன் பெண்சாதியை, நேற்று வந்தவன் அடித்துக்கொண்டு போனானாம்.

He took care of the girl (in the hope of marrying her) but a stranger who arrived yesterday came and took her away for himself.

1986. கலமாவு இடித்தவள் பாவி, கப்பி இடித்தவள் புண்ணியவதியா?

Is she who pounded a *kalam* of flour a sinner, while she who pounded the grit is virtuous?

Used when one person gets credit for a piece of work, nearly all of which has been done by another. *e.g.* A daughter-in-law has had all the hard labour of preparing for an approaching wedding, but just at the last the daughter of the house gives a finishing stroke to the preparations, and her mother honours her as if she had done all the work.

" *God heals and the physician hath the thanks.*"

1987. கறையான் புற்றில் பாம்பு குடிகொண்டதுபோல்.

Like a snake making its home in the ant-hill of the white ants. 1982.

" *The sparrow builds in the martin's nest.*"

1988. நான் தேடிப் பச்சைபோட, நாரிகள் எல்லாம் வந்தார்கள் தெய்வம் ஆட.

I have procured and arranged these plants and trees, and then all these women come to dance for the goddess! 1984.

The allusion is to the ceremony (*pacchei poda*) performed by a woman who has been possessed by a spirit (*piddri*), in which a great pot is taken and ornamented with a nose, and eyes, &c., made by streaks of saffron, which she then worships under a shed made of green leaves. While she is worshipping, others naturally come to watch. If they also join in the worship, and dance before the goddess Paccheiyammâl in the pot, the woman who performs the ceremony must present half a cocoanut and some flour to the Goddess for each worshipper. This is a great expense and no benefit to her. She has the trouble, they have the advantage. The proverb is commonly used when the efforts of a good man to do his duty are turned to their own advantage by unscrupulous persons.

" *Fools lade out all the water, and wise men take the fish.*"

1989. வெல்லம் தின்கிறவன் ஒருவன், விரலைச் சூப்புகிறவன் ஒருவன்.

One eats the sugar ; another licks his fingers.

1989*a*. உண்பான் தின்பான் பைராகி, குத்துக்கு நிற்பான் வீரமுஷ்டி.

The mendicant fares sumptuously at my master's table, but it is I, *Veeramusti*, that must bear his blows and hard treatment.

Used by a hard working day labourer against an indulged fellow labourer.

1990. அகல உழுகிறதைவிட, ஆழ உழுகிறதுமேல்.

Better to plough deep than wide.

If you begin a work, do it thoroughly and not superficially.

1991. உளை (or சேறு) வழியும், அடை மழையும், பொதி எருதும் தனியுமாய் அலைகிறதுபோல்.

Like going single-handed in a road full of quagmires in unceasing rain with pack-bullocks.

A simile expressing the very highest degree of discomfort for very small profit. The driver of pack-bullocks gets small wages for all the pains he takes.

1992. எள்ளுத்தான் எண்ணெய்க்கு உலருகிறது (or காய்கிறது) எலிப் புழுக்கை என்னத்துக்கு உலருகிறது?

Sesamum-seed is dried for oil, but why dry rats' dung.

Said about a person who loiters about with others who are hard at work.

1993. ஒண்டிக்காரன் பிழைப்பும், வண்டிக்காரன் பிழைப்பும் ஒன்று.

A single man's life and a cart-driver's are alike.

Both are ever on the move and have no comforts.

1994. நாய்வேஷம் போட்டால், குலைக்கவேண்டும்.

If you agree to personate a dog, you must bark. 1764, 1950.

Anything once begun should be done thoroughly. (The proverb implies that the work in question was begun with some unwillingness.)

GREAT EXERTIONS OVER TRIFLES.

காரியம் சிறிது, பிரயத்தினம் பெரிது.

1995. அகாரியத்தில் பகீரதப் பிரயத்தனமா செய்கிறது?

Should one make the efforts of Bhagiratha over a trifle?

King Bhagiratha by his austerities brought the Ganges from heaven. Many people take great pains for no adequate purpose.

1996. ஆட்டுக்குட்டிக்கு ஆனையைக் காவு கொடுக்கிறதா?

Should an elephant be sacrificed to save a sheep? 2002.

1997. ஆனையை விற்று, பூனைக்கு வைத்தியம் பார்க்கிறதா?

Should one sell an elephant to get medicine for a cat?

1998. இரும்பு கதவு இடித்து, தவிட்டுக் கொழுக்கட்டை எடுக்கிறதா?

Should one knock down an iron door in order to take a bran-cake?

1999. ஊர்க் குருவிமேல் ராமபாணம் தொடுக்கிறதா?
Is a good arrow to be shot at a sparrow? 707.

1999*a*. எலி வேட்டைக்குத் தவிலடிப்பா?
Should you beat the drum when catching rats?
Unimportant people make much noise about their unimportant deeds.

2000. கீரைத்தண்டு பிடுங்க, ஏலேலப்பாட்டா?
Why should a number of persons sing a chorus when rooting up a small vegetable?
Coolies when lifting a great burden together or carrying a load, shout or sing in unison so that all shall lift or step together.

2001. கோழி அடிக்கிறதற்குக் குறுந்தடியா?
Is a club needed to kill a fowl?

2002. கோழி முடத்துக்குக் கடா வெட்டிக் காவு கொடுக்கிறதா?
Should a sheep be sacrificed to cure a lame fowl. 1996.

2003. சுடு கெண்டைக்கு ஏரியை உடைக்கிறதா?
What! Make a breach in a lake in order to catch a small fish!
This proverb is the converse of 1060.

2004. மலையை நோண்டி (or கல்லி) எலியைப் பிடிக்கிறதா?
Should you dig up a mountain to catch a rat.
"*Sue a beggar and catch a louse.*"

Cf. 1963 *ff.* 2616 *ff.*

LITTLE THINGS.

சிறியதை அசட்டைபண்ணுதே.

THE IMPORTANCE OF LITTLE THINGS.

2005. அச்சாணி (or தேராணி, or சுள்ளாணி, or கடையாணி) இல்லாத தேர் முச்சாணும் ஓடாது.
A car without a linch-pin will not move three span.

2006. அறுகம் கட்டையும் ஆபத்துக்கும் உதவும்.
Even bundles of grass may be of use in adversity.

2007. அற்பத் துடைப்பமானாலும் உள் தூசியை அடக்கும்.
A worn broom will serve to lessen the dust.
"*Small rain lays great dust.*"

2008. ஆயிரம் மாகாணி அறுபத்திரண்டரை.
A thousand sixteenths make sixty-two and a half.
"*Little and often fills the purse.*"
"*One grain fills not the sack, but helps his fellows.*"

2009. ஆனை வேகம் அடங்கும் அங்குசத்தினால்.

The swiftness (*or* impetuosity) of an elephant is subdued by a goad. 2049.

"*A great wind is laid with a little rain.*"

2010. நீரைச் சிந்தினையோ, சீரைச் சிந்தினையோ?

Did you spill water or did you spill your fortune? 3171.

If you do not mind unimportant things, you will not mind important things. Economic use of water is supposed to lead to fortune: waste of water is superstitiously dreaded as the sure way to misfortune. Water is the element dear to the Goddesses Lakshmi and Sarasvati.

"*Of saving cometh having.*"

2010*a*. உப்பை சிந்தினையோ துப்பை சிந்தினையோ?

Did you spill your salt or did you spill your food.

If trifles are not attended to, misery will arise. Salt is an emblem of food. If one spills a single grain of it, this the loss is superstitiously taken to forebode of food, or employment, in the near future.

2011. கொஞ்சத்தில் உண்மையில்லாதவன், கோடியிலும் இருக்கமாட்டான்.

He who is not faithful in little things, will not be so in great ones.

2012. பல துளி பெரு வெள்ளம்.

Many drops make a great flood. 2029.

"*Many drops make a shower.*"

Cf. 660 *ff.* 1881 *ff.*

LITTLE EVILS DESTROY MUCH GOOD.

2013. அற்ப ஆசை கோடி தவத்தைக் கெடுக்கும்.

A little desire destroys a penance carried on for a long time.

The great aim of the penances (*Tapas*) of Hindu ascetics is the complete suppression of all desires and passions. The attainment of this state of passionless peace is supposed to confer supernatural power.

2014. ஆயிரம் குணம் ஒரு லோபக்குணத்தால் தட்டும்.

A thousand good qualities will be thwarted by avarice.

"*One ill weed mars the whole pot of pottage.*"

2015. எல்லாம் நன்றாய்ச் செய்து (or பேசி) கொஞ்ச பீ தடவினான்.

He did it all right, but (just at the last) he smeared it over with a little filth.

2016. கடுகு அத்தனை நெருப்பானாலும் போரைக் கொளுத்திவிடும்.

Though there be only as much fire as a grain of mustard, it will burn a stack. 2021.

"*A little fire burns up a great deal of corn.*"

2017. கலப் பாலுக்குத் துளிப் பிரை.
A drop of curd is enough for a *Kalam* (measure) of milk.
"*A little leaven leaveneth the whole lump.*"

2018. காணிக்குச் சோம்பல், கோடிக்கு வருத்தம்.
To be lazy in little things (will lead) to countless sufferings.
"*A little neglect may breed endless mischief.*"

2019. காணி ஆசை, கோடி கேடு.
A little desire (will lead to) immense loss.
"*A man is not so easily healed as hurt.*"

2020. நூற்றைக் கெடுத்தது குறுணி.
One measure (of chaff) has spoiled a hundred (of corn).

2021. நெருப்பு சிறிது என்று முன்றானையில் முடியலாமா?
Can you cover up fire in your lap because you say 'There is but little fire.'
Avoid the wicked though their company seems almost harmless. 2016.

Cf. 424 *ff.*

GREAT THINGS CANNOT BE DONE BY SMALL MEANS.

2022. ஆனைவாலைப் பிடித்துக் கரை ஏறலாம், ஆட்டின் வாலைப் பிடித்துக் கரை ஏறலாமா?
If you catch hold of the tail of an elephant you may reach the other bank (of the river); if you catch hold of the tail of a sheep how can you reach the bank?
Seek great people for help and protection, not the feeble. 2028, 2006.

2023. கப்பல் ஓடிப் பட்ட கடன் கொட்டை நூற்று விடியும்?
Will the debt incurred by sending out a ship be cleared by spinning cotton?
"*A drop in the ocean.*"

2024. குள்ளனைக்கொண்டு கடல் ஆழம் பார்க்கிறான்.
He wants to fathom the depth of the sea with the aid of a dwarf! 2026, 2028.
Used when a man wants to do something for a small sum that requires an expenditure of much money.

2025. சீப்பு எடுத்து ஒளித்தால், கலியாணம் நிற்குமா?
Can you stop a wedding by hiding the comb?
The bridegroom gives the bride certain presents on the eve of the wedding; among these there is always a comb, but a wedding would not be stopped if the comb were not forthcoming.

2026. நரி வாலைக்கொண்டு, கடல் ஆழம் பார்க்கிறதுபோல.
Like sounding the depth of the sea with the tail of a jackal! 2024, 2028.
Little people cannot do great things.

2027. நாய் குலைத்து நத்தம் பாழாகுமா?
Will a village be ruined by the barking of a dog?

2028. நாய் வாலைப்பற்றி, ஆற்றில் இறங்குகிறதா?
Can you lay hold of a dog's tail and go into a river (safely)? 2024, 2026.

It is not safe to rely on the help of mean people when face to face with great difficulties.

"*Trust not to a broken staff.*"

2029. மயிர் சுட்டுக் கரியாகுமா?
Can charcoal be made by burning hair?

If one is in need he should not waste his time over vain devices to help himself but should go to those who are able to help him.—For the converse see. 2012.

2030. மினிமினிப் பூச்சி வெளிச்சத்துக்கு இருள்போமா?
Will darkness disappear before the shining of fire-flies?

2031. மூக்குமயிர் பிடுங்கினால் பாரம் குறையுமா?
Will one's weight be lessened by pulling out the hair from the nostrils?

LITTLE THINGS WILL NOT BECOME BIG THINGS.

2032. ஆயிரம் நட்சத்திரம் கூடினாலும் ஒரு சந்திரன் ஆகாது.
A thousand stars though joined together will not make a moon.

"*Better one virtuous son than even a hundred fools.*" (*Hitopadesa*).

2033. எட்டுக் குஞ்சு அடித்தாலும், சட்டிக் கறி ஆகாது.
Even if you kill eight tiny chickens, they won't make a meal.

2034. கொட்டிக் கொட்டி அளந்தாலும், குறுணி பதக்கு ஆகாது.
Though measured a thousand times over, a small measure of grain will not become a big one. 106.

2034*a*. பனி பெய்து குளம் ரொம்புமா? மழை பெய்து குளம் ரொம்புமா?
Will a lake be filled by the falling of dew, or by the falling of rain?

"HE WHO CAN DO GREAT THINGS CAN EASILY DO LITTLE THINGS."

2035. அண்டத்தைச் சுமக்கிறவனுக்கு சுண்டைக்காய்ப் பாரமா?
What is the burden of a small fruit to him who bears the universe?

2036. ஆறு (or கடல், or சமுத்திரம்) நீந்தினவனுக்கு வாய்க்கால் எம்மாத்திரம்?
What is a water-channel to him, who can swim across a river (*or*, a sea). 2046.

2037. ஆனையைக் கொன்றவன், பூனையை வெல்லமாட்டானா?
Cannot he who has killed an elephant conquer a cat?

2038. ஆனையை (or மலையை) முழுங்கின அம்மையாருக்குப் பூனை சுண்டாங்கி.

To a woman who has swallowed an elephant (*or* mountain) a cat is but a trifle.

2039. ஆனைக்குத் தீனி இடும் வீட்டில், ஆட்டுக்குட்டிக்குப் பஞ்சமா?

Will a lamb find a famine in a house where an elephant is fed?

2040. ஆனை மேயும் காட்டில், ஆடு மேய இடம் இல்லையா?

Is there not space for a sheep to graze in a forest where elephants feed?

2041. உலக்கைப் பூசைக்கு அசையாதது, திருப்பாட்டுக்கு அசையுமா?

Will he who does not yield to a sound thrashing with a rice-pounder yield on hearing a sacred song. 1960, 2790, 3151.

2042. பிய்த்துவிட்டாலும் போச்சுது, பிடுங்கிவிட்டாலும் போச்சுது.

If you tear it off it is gone, if you pull it off it is gone. 2049.

i.e. It is a matter of no importance at all, *e.g.* After spending 1000, rupees in building a house, the builder thinks nothing of spending fifty more on an improvement in it.

Cf. 424 *ff.* 2013 *ff.*

THE MAN UNABLE TO ACCOMPLISH SMALL DEEDS CANNOT DO GREAT THINGS.

2043. ஆடு கொடுக்காத இடையன், பசுவு கொடுப்பானா?

Will the shepherd who refuses to give a sheep, give a cow?

2044. உட்கார்ந்தவனைக் கட்டமாட்டாதவன், ஓடுகிறவனைக் கட்டுவானா?

Can he who is unable to bind a person who is sitting down bind a man that is running?

2045. உள்ளூரில் ஓணான் பிடிக்காதவன், உடையார்பாளையம் போய் உடும்பு பிடிப்பானா?

Will the man who cannot catch a lizard in his own village be able to go to a foreign place and catch an iguana?

2046. கால்வாயைத் தாண்டாதவன், கடலைத் தாண்டுவானா?

Can one who is unable to cross a water-channel, cross the sea? 2036.

"*He that can't ride a gentle horse must not attempt to back a mad colt.*"

2047. சோற்றில் கிடக்கிற கல்லை எடுக்கமாட்டாதவன் ஞானத்தை எப்படி அறிவான்.

If he cannot pick the bits of grit out of his rice, how will he understand wisdom?

"*He may ill run, that cannot go.*"

2048. மொந்தை தண்ணீரிலே வீடு வெந்துபோனால், மிடாத் தண்ணீருக்கு எப்படி?

If a house is scalded by a small pot of water, how will it be affected by a large pot of water. 1422.

If you cannot overcome little difficulties, how are you to get over great ones?

Cf. 2059 *ff.*

"PENNY WISE AND POUND FOOLISH."

2049. ஆயிரம் பொன்போட்டு ஆனை வாங்கி, அரைப்பணத்து அங்குசத்துக்குப் பால்மாறுகிறதா?

After paying one thousand gold coins for an elephant, why hesitate to pay half a cash for a goad? 2009, 2042.

2050. ஊசி போகிற கணக்குப் பார்ப்பான், பூசினிக்காய்ப் போகிறது தெரியாது.

He makes a note of a lost needle, but he does not perceive the loss of a pumpkin!

2051. கடுகு போகிற இடத்தில் தடி எடுத்துக்கொண்டு திரிவான், பூசினிக்காய்ப் போகிற இடத்தில் தெரியாது.

He will wander about with a stick (in his hand searching) the place where a mustard-seed was lost but he does not know where he lost a pumpkin!

"*They drink their water by measure, but eat their cakes without.*"

2052. குதிரை கொண்டால், லகானுக்கு வழக்கா?

After buying the horse, why dispute about the bridle? 2053.

2053. பசுவை விற்றால், கன்றுக்கு வழக்கா?

If you have sold the cow, why dispute about the calf? 2052.

"*If you buy the cow take the tail into the bargain.*"

"ANYTHING IS BETTER THAN NOTHING."

2054. கழுதைக்குப் பரதேசம் குட்டிச்சுவர்.

To go to a ruined wall for grazing is an ass's pilgrimage.

2055. வந்ததை வரப்படுத்தடா வலக்காட்டு ராமா?

Take what you can get, O Valakkâtturâma?

Said to the creditors of an insolvent or stingy person who cannot get their demands satisfied.

"*When you can't get bread, oat-cakes are not amiss.*"

2056. வந்த காசுக்கு வட்டமில்லை.

There is no interest on the money you received!

Be satisfied with what you can get from an insolvent debtor.

"*A bad bush better than an open field.*"

2057. வெறும் காதுக்கு ஓலைக்காது மேல்.

Ears (ornamented) with palmyra leaf are better than ears with no ornaments. 1735.

When Tamil woman are unable to buy jewels to put in their ears they frequently roll up a strip of palmyra leaf and insert it in the hole that is always pierced in the lobe of the ear. This is done to prevent the hole from contracting and so becoming too small to hold the *Kammal* ear ornament.

"*Better a bare foot than no foot at all.*"

"*Half a loaf is better than no bread.*"

2058. வெறும் சூத்தை நக்குகிறதைவிட, பீ சூத்தை நக்குகிறது மேல்.

It is better to lick a dirty breech than a clean one!

HE WHO CANNOT BEAR A LITTLE SUFFERING CANNOT BEAR GREAT DISASTERS.

2059. எறும்பு கடிக்கப் பொறுக்காதா?

Can you not bear an ant's bite?

2060. கழுவேறத் துணிந்த நீலி கண்ணில் மை இட்டதற்குக் கரிக்கிறது என்கிறாளாம்.

The woman (who professes to be) ready to be impaled, says that her eyes smart when she blackens her eyelids!

Hindu women blacken their eyelids with certain pigments, thinking that they beautify themselves.

2061. காது குத்தப் பொறுக்காதா?

Can you not bear to have your ears bored?

If such a slight pain is unbearable, how can you bear greater pain?

2062. சிந்தி அறுந்துபோகிற மூக்கு, எந்தமட்டும் இருக்கும்?

How long will a nose last that breaks off when blown?

Also said of a person who gets unreasonably angry over trifles.

2063. வெடவெடவென்று தண்ணீர் குளிக்காதவளா உடன்கட்டை ஏறப் போகிறாள்?

Will she who refuses to bathe in tepid water ascend the funeral pyre?

The reference is to the rite of *sati* or *suttee*, by which a widow immolated herself on the funeral pyre of her husband. The practice was abolished by Lord William Bentinck about 1830.

Cf. 2043 *ff.*

HEREDITARY CHARACTERISTICS AND NATURAL INSTINCTS.

இயல்பு.

2064. அக்காளைக் கொண்டால், தங்கையை முறை கேட்பானேன்?
Having married the elder sister why does he ask what is his relationship to the younger? 2071.

2065. ஆண்டி மகன் ஆண்டியானால், நேரம் அறிந்து சங்கு ஊதுவான்.
If a son of a mendicant becomes a mendicant, he will blow the conch at the proper time. 279, 1901*a*, 2499, 2852 f. f; 3085.

" *As natural to him as milk to a calf.*"

2066. ஆலமரம் பழுத்தது என்று பறவைக்கு ஆர் சீட்டு அனுப்பினது?
Who sent letters to the birds that the banyan tree was in fruit? 2070, 2072, 2074..

They know that by their own natural instinct.

2067. இயற்கை வாசனையோ, செயற்கை வாசனையோ? or எற்கை வாசனையோ, சேற்கை வாசனையோ?
Is the smell natural or artificial?

i.e. Is the habit natural or acquired?

2068. ஏற ஆசைப்பட்டால், சாணாரப் பிறவி வேண்டும்.
If you desire to climb trees, you must be born a *Shanar.*

The Shanar caste who draw the juice from palms to make the intoxicating toddy are necessarily skilful climbers of trees.

2069. கம்பன் வீட்டு வெள்ளாட்டியும் (or கட்டுத் தறியும்) கவிபாடும்.
Even the servant woman (*or* the peg to which a cow is tied) in (the poet) Kamban's house will sing. 2331.

A great man's influence on others.

" *In a fiddler's house all are dancers.*"

2070. கரும்புக் கட்டுக்கு எறும்பு தானே வரும்.
Ants will come of themselves (to devour) sugar cane. 2066, 2072, 2074.

" *Wheresoever the carcase is, there will the eagles be gathered together.*"

2071. கிழவியைப் பாட்டி என்பதற்குக் கேட்கவேண்டுமா?
Why ask if you may call an old woman 'grand-mother'? 2064.

2072. குளம் தோண்டி தவளை கூப்பிடவேண்டுமா?
Need you send for frogs after digging a pool? 2066, 2070, 2074.

2073. சிதம்பரத்தில் பிறந்த பிள்ளைக்குத் திருவெண்பாவைக் கற்றுக்கொடுக்க வேண்டுமோ?

No one need teach a child born at Sithambaram to sing a sacred song.

Sithambaram (Chillumbram) is a very holy place about one hundred and fifty miles south of Madras near the East coast containing a famous temple dedicated to Siva.

"*Teach your grand-mother to suck eggs.*"

2074. தேனுக்கு ஈயைப் பிடித்து விடவேண்டுமோ?

Is it necessary to catch flies to bring them to honey? 2066, 2070, 2074.

2075. நட்டுவன் பிள்ளைக்குக் கொட்டிக்காட்டவேண்டுமோ?

Do you need to show the child of a musician (*nattuvan*) how to beat a drum?

The *Nattuvan* is the person who trains dancing girls and directs their performances.

2076. கடல் மீனுக்கு நீச்சுப் பழக்கவேண்டுமோ?

Is there any need to teach sea-fish to swim?

The son follows in his fathers profession. This is especially true in India where so many trades are hereditary.

"*Don't teach fish to swim.*"

2077. வௌவாலுக்கு யார் தாம்பூலம் வைத்தார்கள்?

Who has offered *Tâmboola* to the flying foxes?

Tâmboola is betel leaf enclosing areca-nut and lime ready for chewing, given when inviting people to feasts. The flying fox is a large bat. It goes where its instincts lead it without needing any invitation.

Cf. 1900 *ff.* 2852 *ff.*

NEGLECT.

உபயோகம், உபயோகமில்லாமை.

2078. உடையவன் பாராப் பயிர் உருப்படுமோ?

If the owner does not look after it, will the crop thrive? 3227.

"*Tis the farmer's care that makes the field bear.*"

2079. உடுக்காத புடவை பூச்சிக்கு இரை (or செல்லு அரிக்கும்).

A woman's cloth that is not worn will be food for insects (*or* will be eaten by white-ants).

Paper, cloth, serge, &c., is attacked by many different kinds of grubs and small insects in India. If any books or any clothes are put away and neglected they are soon riddled through and through by these pests.

2080. உடையவன் கண் ஓடாத பயிர் உடனே அழியும்.

The crop over which the owner's eyes do not run will be spoiled immediately.

Said of anything the owner ought to protect, as his children, his house, etc.

2081. உண்ணுச் சொத்து மண்ணுய்ப் போகும்.

Property not enjoyed goes to dust.

2082. உறவு போகாமல் கெட்டது, கடன் கேட்காமல் கெட்டது.

If you do not visit your friends and relations, relationship will be destroyed; if you do not ask for what you have lent out, it will be destroyed.

2082*a*. சம்பா விளைந்து சாய்ந்து கிடக்குது (கிடக்கிறது), உண்பாரில்லாமல் ஊர்க்குருவி மேயுது (மேய்கிறது).

The *sambâ* crop is over-ripe, but since those who should eat it do not come for it, the sparrows devour it.

Sambâ is a superior sort of rice.

2083. துலக்காத ஆயுதம் துருப்பிடிக்கும்.

A weapon not polished will gather rust. 1467.

"*The used key is always bright.*"

2084. பார்க்காத உடைமை பாழ்.

Property not looked after will decay.

PROTECTION, CARE, SUPPORT.

காப்பாற்றுதல்.

2086. ஆலை விழுது தாங்குகிறதுபோல.

As the aerial roots of the banyan support it.

Children ought to support their parents as the aerial roots of the banyan support the parent tree.

2087. எங்கே திருடினாலும், கன்னக்கோல் வைக்க ஒரு இடம் வேண்டும்.

Though you steal everywhere, there must be one place where you keep your implements.

i.e. There must be one place where even a thief won't steal, *viz.*, his home. Even the worst people reverence something.

2088. எள்ளு விழுந்தால், எடுக்க மகா சேனை, இடறி விழுந்தால் எடுக்க ஆள் இல்லை.

If a sesamum seed fall, there are hosts of people to pick it up, but if (a man) slip and fall there is no one to help him. 741, 3348.

People are eager for profit, but they have little desire to help their fellows.

2089. கண்ணை இமை காத்ததுபோல.

As the eye-lash protects the eye. 151, 3214.

Tender and unselfish care.

2090. கல்லுக்குள் இருக்கிற தேரையையும், முட்டைக்குள் இருக்கிற பறவை குஞ்சையும் ஊட்டி வளர்க்கிறது யார்?

Who is it that nourishes the frog inside the stone, and the chicken inside the egg, and makes them grow? 3387.

An afflicted woman may use this proverb, indicating her trust in God, as the one who will protect her, even if all forsake her.

> "The true and living God knows all griefs
> He nourishes the egg ere 'tis begot:
> He feeds the frog before its rock it leaves:
> If thus he cares for unborn things. will not
> He make them grow, when He new life doth add?"
>
> CH. E. GOVER: *The Folk-Songs of Southern India.*

2091. கற்பித்தவனுக்குக் காக்க வல்லமை இல்லையா?

Has not the creator the power to protect? 3387.

2092. காட்டுக்குப் புலி ஆதரவு, புலிக்குக் காடு ஆதரவு.

The tiger is the protection of the woods, and the woods of the tiger. 2094.

2093. கால்படி (or உழக்கு) அரிசிக்காரன் உள்ளமட்டும்தான்.

It exists only as long as the man lives who earns. 2098, 2099, 2105.

When the head of the family dies, the family fares badly. Said also of the responsible head of an institution or office.

2094. காலுக்குக் கை உதவி, கைக்குக் கால் உதவி.

The hand is a help to the leg and the leg to the hand. 2092.

2095. குறும்பைத் தவிர்க்கும் குடிதாங்கி.

One who removes inhumanity and saves people!

A description of a protector.

2096. சுக்குத் தின்று முக்கிப் பெற்ற பிள்ளையைப்போல் காப்பாற்றுகிறான்.

He protects the child as if he had borne it in sorrow and eaten ginger for it! 2100.

Said of a step-mother or of a woman who takes tender care of a child that is not her own. Ginger is given to women at the time of their confinement. 'To eat ginger' is a phrase meaning 'to bear a child.'

2097. தன் உயிரைப்போல், மன் உயிரையும் காக்கவேண்டும்.

Protect others' lives as you protect your own. 2180.

"*Do as you would be done by.*" "*Live and let live.*" (Mark. 12, 33.)

2098. *தேர் இருக்கிறமட்டும் சிங்காரம், தேர் போனபிறகு என்ன?*

As long as the temple-car moves it is ornamented; but what ornament is left after it has gone back (to the temple)? 2093, 2099, 2105.

Temple-cars on which images of the gods ride out at festivals are marvellously adorned for the occasion. When the festival is over, the car is stripped of all its ornaments and covered up with mats.

2099. *தேரோடே போச்சுது திருநாள், தாயோடே போச்சுது பிறந்தகம்* (or *பிறந்த அகம்*).

The festival ends with the procession of the car, and all help and support from home ceases when the mother dies. 2093, 2098, 2105.

The daughters of the deceased are then left to the mercy of their stepmother, or mother-in-law, and they are often not kind to them. Said of one who has lost his chief supporter.

2100. *நெருப்பை மடியில் கட்டிக்கொண்டிருக்கிறாப்போல்.*

It is as if she had tied up fire in her lap. 2096.

Said of one who protects with the greatest care something he has charge of.

2101. *பறந்துபோகிற எச்சிற்கலைமேல், கல்லைத் தூக்கிவைத்தாப்போல.*

Like placing a stone on a leaf-plate that is going to fly away.

Protecting a person who would otherwise go to ruin.

2102. *பாடகக்காரி வாழ்ந்தால், பத்தெட்டு ஜனம் பிழைக்கும்.*

If a woman with anklets (*Pâdakam*) prospers, eight or ten of her relations will be supported by her. 1716.

They will get help for nothing.

2103. *பிடித்தால் சுமை, விட்டால் கூளம்.*

If I hold you, you are my bundle (*i.e.* are safe); if I let you go, you are bits of straw (*i.e.* are uncared for). 1027, 1369 *ff*.

2104. *பெருமரத்தைச் சுற்றின வள்ளிக்கொடிபோல.*

Like a convolvulus (a creeper) that encircles a big tree. 2334.

A weak person with a strong protector.

2105. *பெருமாள் இருந்தாலல்லவோ, திருநாள் நடக்கப்போகிறது.*

As long as Perumâl lives there will be festival days. 2093, 2098, 2099.

Perumâl is another name for Vishnu. The proverb means that while the protector or the head of a family is alive the members of the family will live in happiness.

2106. *வேலி தானே பயிரை மேய்ந்தால், விளைவது எப்படி?*

If the hedge graze on the crop, how will the crop thrive? 3236, 3256.

If the gardener robs the garden, or the police the people, how can the garden or the people prosper.

2107. *வைத்தால் பிள்ளையார், வழித்து எறிந்தால் சாணி.*

If I keep thee, thou art Ganesa, if I scrape thee off (*i.e.* discard thee) thou art but cowdung! 2103.

i.e. You are in my power; I have helped you on; but if you get proud I can bring you down again. Ganesa (Tam. Pillaiyar) is the God of Good Luck, whose image is made of cow dung for household worship, the cowdung-ganesa is scraped off when the worship is over.

BRAGGING, GREAT PROFESSIONS.

2108. *ஆகாசத்தில் பறக்க உபதேசிப்பேன், என்னைத் தூக்கி ஆற்றுக்கு அப்பால் விடு என்கிறான் குரு.*

The spiritual teacher says, I will teach you to fly in the sky. but first lift me up, and drop me on the other side of the river.

2109. *கூரை எறிக் கோழி பிடிக்கமாட்டாத குருக்களா, வானம் கீறி வைகுண்டம் காட்டுவார்.*

Can spiritual teachers who are unable to climb a roof to catch a fowl, rend the skies and show people Vishnu's heaven (*Vaikuntha*).

"*Physician heal thyself.*"

2110. *கையைப்பிடித்துத் தூக்கிவிடு, பிணக்காடாய்க் குவிக்கிறேன் என்கிறானும்.*

He says: Lay hold of my hands and raise me up, and I will heap the whole of them in the burial ground!

Said in scorn of a feeble braggart.

"*Make me a diviner and I will make thee rich.*"

2111. *பசியாமல் வரந்தருகிறேன், பழங்கஞ்சி இருந்தால் வாரு.*

I will give you a boon to save you from hunger; but if you have stale gruel, give me some.

"*His wit got wings and would have flown, but poverty still kept him down.*"

2112. *மலையைத் தூக்கிவைத்தால் (என் தலைமேல்), நான் அதை எடுத்துக் கொண்டுபோகிறேன் என்கிறான்.*

If you will lift up the hill and place it on my head, I will carry it away.

Cf. 1566 *ff.*

HELP AND CHARITY.

உதவி, தர்மம்.

"You see the tall grain in the field of the man
Who lived to his God and did right in the world.
Who tilled his own land, and then cheerfully helped
His neighbour or friend. He gave alms to the poor,
The hungry he fed, to the cold he brought fire.
The naked he clothed, and the poor he relieved."

CH. E. GOVER: *The Folk-songs of Southern India.*

2113. இட்டதில் ஒன்றும் குறையாது.
Nothing will be diminished by charity.
"*To a good spender God is a treasurer.*"
"*Alms-giving never made any man poor, nor robbery rich, nor prosperity wise.*"

2114. இட்டாருக்கு இட்ட பலன்.
To those who give a reward is given!
"*Give, and it shall be given unto you.*" (Luc. 6, 38.)

2115. இறைக்க இறைக்கக் கிணறு சுரக்கும்.
Water will spring up in the well that is constantly used.
"*Give and spend and god will send.*"

2116. இறைத்த கிணறு ஊறும், இறையாத கிணறு நாறும்.
The well from which water is drawn will flow; the well not used will stink!
"*Drawn wells are seldom dry.*"

2117. உதாரிக்கு (com. ஊதாரி, *Udâri*) பொன் துரும்பு.
To a charitable mind, gold is but straw.
"*The charitable give out of the door, and God puts it in at the window.*"

2118. கறக்கக் கறக்க ஊறும் பசுவின்பால், படிக்கப் படிக்க ஊறும் மெய்ஞ் ஞானம்.
The more you milk, the more a cow will give; and the more you read, the more true wisdom will spring up (in your mind).
"*The hand that gives gathers.*"

MISCELLANEOUS PROVERBS ON HELP AND CHARITY.

2119. ஆசரித்த தெய்வம் எல்லாம் கட்டோடே மாண்டது.
All the gods whom I worshiped have entirely perished.
Those on whom I depended have left me helpless.

2120. ஆனையை வித்வானுக்கும், பூனையைக் குறவனுக்கும் கொடு.

Give an elephant to a pandit, and a cat to a *Kuravan.* 2278, 2298.

Let your gifts correspond to the rank of the recipients. Pandits and other learned men are venerated throughout all India. A *Kuravan* is a man of one of the tribes that live by the chase, and are despised by Hindus because they kill animals and eat the flesh of various animals especially cats.

2121. இட்டதின்பேரில் ஏறுசைப்பட்டால் கிடைக்குமோ?

If you want more than what is given to you, will you get it? 965, 2179.

2122. இட்டோர் பெரியோர், இடாதோர் இழிகுலத்தோர்.

Those who give are the great, those who do not give are of low-caste.

2123. இரந்தும், பருந்துக்கு (com. பிராந்து) இடு.

Even if you beg, give to the kites.

However poor be charitable. Some Hindus, as an act of piety, occasionally buy flesh and toss it into the air to the Brahmany kite, which is considered the vehicle of Vishnu (*garuda, Falco Pondicherianus*).

2124. இல்லை என்கிற வீட்டில் பல்லியும் சேராது.

Even a lizard will not live in a house that says 'No' (to a beggar). 2141, 2393, 2768.

The lizard, *Lacerta gecko*, is very common in India, and is much reverenced as a fortune-teller by its chirps. Every Hindu consults the lizard's chirps before commencing any domestic business.

2125. உயிர் உதவிக்கு மிஞ்சின உதவி வேறில்லை.

No charity surpasses the charity of giving one's life. 2143.

"*Greater love hath no man than this, that a man lay down his life for his friends.*" (Joh. 15, 13.)

2126. எங்கும் மடமாயிருக்கிறது, இருக்கத்தான் இடமில்லை.

There are *Choultries* (rest houses for travellers) everywhere, and yet no place to stay in. 1659, 2147.

Said by one who has many acquaintances but who finds that none of them will give him real help.

2127. எடுப்பார் மழுவை, தடுப்பார் புலியை, கொடுப்பார் அருமை.

There are some who will take up a hot iron (in trial by ordeal), and there are others who will stop tigers, but the generous are scarce. 2147.

2128. எட்டாப் பூ தேவர்களுக்கு, எட்டும் பூ தங்களுக்கு.

Flowers beyond reach belong to the gods, but those we can pluck are our own. 1017.

"*What the Abbot of Bamba cannot eat, he gives away for the good of his soul.*"

2129. என்றைக்கும் போடாத லட்சுமி இன்றும் போடவில்லை, தினம் போடு கிற தேவடியாளுக்கு இன்றைக்கு என்ன கேடு வந்தது?

Lakshmi who never gives alms, did not give to-day; but what evil has befallen the dancing-girl who always gives, but did not do so to-day?

A sarcasm on the stinginess of a well-to-do person, and a lament over the forgetfulness of a true friend.

2130. கார்த்திகைக்குப் பின் மழையில்லை, கர்ணனுக்குப் பின் கொடையில்லை.

There is no rain after *Karthikei*; there is no generosity surpassing Karnan's! 2137, 2149, 3120.

Karthikei is a festival in honour of the Pleiades who, in the form of nymphs, nursed the infant God Skanda. It is held in the Tamil month *Karthikei* (Nov.-Dec.), and it is commonly believed that if the annual heavy rains have not begun before the festival they will not come at all. Karnan is one of the heroes of the Mahabharata renowned for his charitable disposition.

2131. கலப்பாலை ஒருமிக்கக் குடித்த பூனையை உழக்காகிலும் கறக்கச்சொன்னால் கறக்குமா?

Will the cat that drank a big measure of milk without stopping, yield any milk if you milk it.

Said of those who are ready to enjoy benefits, but unwilling to confer them.

2132. கன்றுள்ளபோதே காணோம், கன்று செத்தபிறகா சொட்டப்போகிறது?

While the calf was alive the cow gave no milk; is it likely to give a drop after the death of the calf? 2154, 3210.

e.g. If he did not give you anything while his wife, who was your sister, was alive, is he likely to help you after her death?

2133. காட்டுப்புறாவுக்கு பக்ஷமாகச் சதை அரிந்த மன்னன் கதைபோல.

Like the story of the king who cut off some of his own flesh for the benefit of a pigeon!

The story which is told in the *Râmâyana* says that King Sivichakkiravertti was performing a sacrifice when a pigeon escaping from a hunter flew to him for safety. The king ransomed the pigeon by giving his own flesh for it. This phrase is quoted in "Râmakirthanai."

"*If you oblige those who can never pay you, you make Providence your debtor.*"

2134. குருடனுக்குக் குருடன் கோல் பிடிக்க முடியுமா?

Can a blind man take hold of another blind man's stick (*i.e.* to guide him)? 2108, 2112.

The helpless can help no one.

"*If the blind lead the blind both will fall into the ditch.*"

2135. குருடனுக்குக் கண் வேண்டும் என்றுதானே சொல்லுவான்; வேண்டாம் என்று சொல்லுவானா?

The blind man is sure to say that he wants eyes; will he ever say that he does not want them? 323.

i.e. There are always people who need help and are ready to accept it.

2136. கேட்காமல் கொடுக்கிறது உத்தமம், கேட்டுக் கொடுக்கிறது மத்திமம், கேட்டும் கொடுக்காதிருப்பது அதமம்.

To give without being asked is excellent; to give after being asked is moderately good; not to give when asked is baseness!

2137. கையில் இருந்தால் கர்ணன்.

If he has something in his hand, he will be (charitable like) Karnan. (See 2130 note.)

Said of one ready to help others; also ironically of a stingy person.

2138. கொடுக்கிறவன் கன்னத்தில் அடித்துக் கொடுப்பான்.

He who is anxious to give will strike people on the cheek and give (*i.e.* compel them to receive). 108.

2139. கொடுத்துக் கொடுத்துக் கையும் காய்ப்பு ஏறிப்போய்விட்டது.

His hand has become hard through his constant giving.

2140. கோவில் விளங்க, குடி விளங்கும்.

If the temple shines (*i.e.*, prospers through your gifts) your families will shine (*i.e.* become renowned).

2141. சீ என்கிற வீட்டிலே பேயும் நுழையாது.

Even a devil will not enter a house in which the word "fie, fie" is heard. 2124.

A devil will avoid a house where beggars are driven from the door without alms.

2142. சுமைதாங்கி ஆயம் தீர்க்காது.

The roadside resting-block pays no toll. 2150.

This block is a small brick or plaster platform on which coolies and others may rest the loads they carry on their heads.

2143. செத்தும் சாகாதவன், தியாகம் கொடுப்போன்.

He who makes an offering will live though he be dead. 2125.

2143*a*. தனக்கு மிஞ்சினது தர்மம்.

What has been left over is for charity.

2144. தீயும் பயிருக்குப் பேயும் மழைபோல்.

Like rain on a scorched crop.

Opportune help.

2145. துரை கையில் எலும்பு இல்லை.

There is no bone in a gentleman's hand. 2505, 2130.

Said of one who gives lavishly.

2146. தெண்டத்துக்குப் பணமும், திவசத்துக்குக் கறியும் அகப்படும்.

You can always find the money for vain charity and food at the feasts on the anniversary of a relative's death. 2147.

2147. தெண்டத்துக்கு அகப்படும், பிண்டத்துக்கு அகப்படாது.
One can get money for vain charity but not for food! 1553, 2126, 2127.

A wife may say this to her husband meaning "you help all sorts of people; you give charity to people to enable them to perform ceremonies; you helped your fellow caste-man to escape justice, &c. &c., but you hesitate to give me a new cloth." 2126, 2127, 2151.

Both 2146 and 2147 are sarcasms on the indiscriminate alms-giving that is so marked a feature of Hindu social life.

2148. நொந்த கண் இருக்க, நோகாத கண்ணுக்கு மருந்து.
While the suffering eye is left to suffer, he applies medicine to the eye that does not suffer.

Instead of helping the poor and needy, he helps those who are well off. 2517.

2149. படைக்கும் ஒருவன், கொடைக்கும் ஒருவன்.
Only one for the army, and only one for charity. 2130, 2137, 3120.

Referring to the rarity of great and charitable men.

2150. பனைமரம் ஏறுகிறவனை எத்தனைதூரம் தாங்கலாம்.
How far can one support a man, who is climbing a palmyra-tree? 2142, 2152.

One can only help according to one's ability. Or, one cannot teach more than one knows.

2151. பாத்திரம் அறிந்து பிச்சை போடு.
Give alms only when you know the begging bowl. 2137.

Against indiscriminate alms-giving.

2152. பாலை ஊட்டுவோர்கள், பாக்கியத்தை ஊட்டமாட்டார்கள்.
People will deal out milk to others, but they cannot deal out happiness. 2142, 2150.

People may help each other in little things, but only God is able to give men lasting happiness (*bhagya*).

2153. பிச்சை இட்டால் மோக்ஷம்.
By giving alms we obtain heavenly bliss.

2154. நல்ல நாளையில் நாழிப்பால் கறவாதது, கன்று செத்துக் கலப்பால் கறக்குமோ?
Will a cow that does not yield a small measure of milk in its happy days (*i.e.* when its calf is alive) yield a big measure after the death of its calf. 2132, 3210.

2155. பிச்சை இட்டுக் கெட்டவனும் உண்டா?
Has any one ever been ruined by giving alms?

"*He who lends to the poor gets his interest from God.*"

2156. பிடித்து ஒரு பிடியும், கிழித்து ஒரு கிழியும் கொடுத்ததுண்டா?
Have you ever given me one handful of rice, or torn off a rag for me to wear?

This may be used to an unkind friend or relation.

"*I thank you for nothing.*"

2157. பிர்மா நினைத்தால், ஆயுசு குறையா?
Will his life be shortened if Brahma thinks of him?
Said about a friend or relation who is as able and willing to help as God is.

2158. வந்தவனுக்குச் சோறு, வராதவனுக்கு உலை வைக்கிறது.
To those who come rice is given, and for those who do not come the cooking-pot is kept ready. 3208.
Said of a very charitable family that is always ready to feed any stranger.

2159. வாயில் போகிறதைக் கக்கிக் கொடுக்கிறது.
To vomit out and give away what ought to go into one's own mouth! 3261.
To deny oneself for the sake of others.

2160. வானம் சுரக்க, தானம் சிறக்கும்.
If the sky pours down (rain) charity will be abundant.

Cf. 1774 *ff.*

UNTRUSTWORTHY GUARDIANSHIP.

காவற்காக்குதல்.

2161. கட்டுச்சாதத்தில் எலிக்குஞ்சை வைத்துக் கட்டினதுபோல்.
Like fastening up a young rat in one's bundle of food and keeping it there. 1234.
Entrusting a thing to an unsuitable guardian.

2162. கள்ளனை உள்ளே வைத்துக் கதவைச் சாத்தினாப்போல்.
Like putting the thief inside (your house) and shutting the door on him.

2163. தொம்பைகூண்டிலே எலி காவற்வைத்துக் கட்டினதுபோல்.
Like fastening a rat inside a corn-bin to guard it.

2164. நண்டைச் சுட்டு நரிகாவற்வைத்ததுபோல்.
Like keeping a jackal to guard a roasted crab. 2166.
"*You give the wolf the wether to keep.*"
"*A fox should not be of the jury at a goose's trial.*"

2165. பாலுக்குக் காவல், பூனைக்கும் தோழன்.
(He is kept) to guard the milk, (but he is also) a friend of the cat.
"*To hold with the hare and run with the hounds.*"

2166. பால் சட்டிக்குப் பூனை காவல் வைக்கிறதுபோல்.
Like keeping a cat to watch a pot of milk. 2164.
"*To entrust the sheep to the wolf.*"

GRATITUDE AND INGRATITUDE.

நன்றி மறவேல்.

THANKFULNESS FOR BENEFITS RECEIVED.

2167. இட்ட வீட்டுக்குப் பிட்டிட்டுக்கொண்டு, இடிந்த வீட்டுக்கு மண்ணிட்டுக்கொண்டு திரிகிறதுபோல்.

Like dividing your food with the household that has helped you, and going about repairing broken down houses.

Gratitude to those who have been kind.

" *He is my friend that grindeth at my mill.*"
" *For if you love them that love you, what reward have ye?*"

2168. என் தோலைச் செருப்பாய்த் தைத்துப்போடுவேன்.

I will take off my skin and give it to make slippers for you.

" *He that requites a benefit pays a great debt.*"

2169. நான் செத்து எழு பிறப்பு பிறந்தாலும், அவன் செய்த நன்மை மறக்க மாட்டேன்.

Even if I die and pass through seven births, I shall not forget the good he has done me.

" *One kindness is the price of another.*"

2170. மலை அத்தனை சுவாமிக்குக் கடுகு அத்தனை கர்ப்பூரம் (or சம்பிராணி).

A piece of camphor as big as a mustard-seed is given to a god as big as a mountain. 2171.

Said in deep gratitnde by one who has been largely helped and who is unable to show his gratitude adequately. Camphor is burned before the images of the gods in every sacred place.

2171. மிளகு அத்தனை பிள்ளையாருக்குக் கடுகு அளவு நைவேத்தியம்.

(Give) an offering as big as a mustard-seed to a Ganesa as big as a chilly.

Images of Ganesa, the god of luck, are made of all sizes, some of them are very large.

INGRATITUDE CONDEMNED. UNGRATEFULNESS.

2172. அன்னம் இட்டாரைக் கன்னம் இடலாமா?

Should we break through the walls of those who have supported us?

" *I taught you to swim and now you would drown me.*"

2173. உண்ட வீட்டுக்கு இரண்டு நினைக்கிறவன் உண்டா?

Is there a person who has two opinions abont the home that has nurtured him?

" *Mud not the fountain that gave drink to thee.*"

2174. உபகாரத்துக்கு அபகாரம் வருகிறது துரதிஷ்டம்.

To receive evil for good is bad luck.

" *Hell is full of the ungrateful.*"

2175. உப்பு இட்டவரை உள்ளளவும் நினை.

Think of your benefactor as long as you live.

"*Let every man praise the bridge he goes over.*"

2176. உள்ளங்கையில் லக்கிரி (இலை, கறி, கீரை) இட்டவர்களை உள்ளளவும் நினை.

As long as you live think of those who put food in your hand.

2177. எந்த நன்றியை மறந்த பாவத்திற்கும் பிராயச்சித்தம் உண்டு, ஒருவர் செய்த நன்றியை மறந்த பாவத்திற்கு மாத்திரம் பிராயச்சித்தமில்லை, நரகமே!

There is an atonement for the sin of forgetting any good thing received (providentially) but no atonement for the sin of forgetting the good received from others; hell is the only punishment of that sin!

2178. கசக்கி மோரலாமா?

Are you to crush a flower to smell it? 1207, 2179.

Be satisfied with the perfume it gives naturally.

"*Much would have more.*"

2179. கரும்பு ருசி என்று வேரோடு பிடுங்கலாமா?

Because the sugar cane is sweet, is it right to pull it up by the root? 2121, 2178.

"*Milk the cow but don't pull off the udder.*"

2180. பரோபகாரமே பெரிது.

To be kind to others is a great thing. 2097.

Cf. 920 *ff.*

MISCELLANEOUS PROVERBS ON GRATITUDE AND INGRATITUDE.

2181. ஆறு கடக்கிறவரையில் அண்ணன் தம்பி, ஆறு கடந்தால் நீயார் நானார்.

As long as people are crossing a river together, they call each other 'Brother;' but after crossing they say, Who are you? and Who am I? (*i. e.* they treat each other as strangers).

When the object is attained, those who assisted in its attainment are forgotten.

"*Danger past, God forgotten.*"

2182. ஆற்றைக் கடந்தால், ஓடக்காரனுக்கு ஒரு சொட்டு.

After crossing the river the boatman gets a blow.

"*The river passed, the saint forgotten.*"

"*The nurse is valued till the child has done sucking.*"

2183. இட்டவன் இடாவிட்டால், வெட்டுப்பகை.

If the giver, who used to give, ceases to give, (he incurs) mortal hatred.

"*All is lost that is put in a riven dish.*"

2184. உண்ண வா என்றால், குத்த வருகிறான்.

When I invite him to a meal, he comes to strike me.

"*Do good to a knave and pray God he requite thee not.*"

2185. ஊன்றக் கொடுத்த தடி மண்டையைப் பிளந்தது.
With the staff I gave him to support himself, he broke my skull.
"*Save a thief from the gallows, and he will be the first to cut your throat.*"

2186. காரியம் ஆகுமட்டும் காலைப்பிடி, காரியமானபிறகு குடுமியைப் பிடி.
Embrace his feet till you gain your case; after gaining your case take him by the hair. 356.
Obsequiousness should be used till what is desired is obtained. Embracing a teacher's or great man's feet is a sign of the greatest possible respect.

2187. குடியிருந்த வீட்டிலே கொள்ளி வைக்கிறவன்.
One who sets fire to the house which sheltered him!
Said of one who betrays his benefactors.
"*Anoint a clown, and he will grip you.*"

2188. கூடக் குடியிருந்துகொண்டு, கொள்ளி சொருகலாமா?
Is it right to put a firebrand to the house of the people with whom you are living? 226.
"*Ingratitude is the daughter of pride.*"

2189. கைக்குக் கை நெய் வார்த்தாலும், கணக்கு தப்பாது.
Though you give him handful after handful of *ghee* he will not forget his accounts with you.
However much good you do to an ungrateful person, he will not forget what little you may owe him, or what little good he may have done to you.

2190. கொடுக்கிறவனைக் கண்டால், வாங்குகிறவனுக்கு இளக்காரம் (or ஏய்ப்பான்).
When he sees his benefactor, the recipient will seek (*lit.* take) favours.
An ungrateful person, who never earns, but only receives, will constantly trouble his benefactor to give him more.
"*A good man will request a gift; an ill man will ask more.*"

2191. கொண்டானும் கொடுத்தானும் ஒன்று, இந்தக் கலியாணத்தைக் கூட்டி வைத்தவன் வாயில் பிடிமண்.
He who married her and he who gave the girl have become great friends, but let a handful of dust be thrown into the mouth of him who brought about the wedding!
The man who arranges the wedding has all the trouble, but after the wedding is over his kindness is quite forgotten by all parties.
"*A favour ill placed is great waste.*"

2192. சாரத்தை உட்கொண்டு சக்கையை உமிழ்ந்துவிடுவதுபோல.
Like drinking the juice and spitting out the pulp.
Said of one who is friendly only as long as he is helped.
"*He that gets, forgets; but he that wants, thinks on.*"

2193. தேள் நெருப்பிலே விழுந்தால், எடுத்துவிட்டவனைக் கொட்டும்.
A scorpion, that has fallen into the fire, will sting him who takes it out. 2196.
Wicked people always return evil for good.
"*Foster a raven and it will peck out your eyes.*"

2194. நன்றிசெய்த கீரிப்பிள்ளையைக் கொன்றதுபோல.

Like killing the mongoose that had done good!

The story occurs in the *Panchatantra* of a mongoose that lived in a house and destroyed a snake which approached a sleeping child. The mother who had been to the well, met the mongoose at the door covered with the blood of the snake, and thinking the mongoose had killed her child, she killed it, and so unthinkingly rewarded its bravery with death.

2195. பழைய குருடி, கதவைத்திறவடி.

O blind woman, open the door.

A saint met some blind women in a certain house, and had compassion on them, and gave them their sight, for which they were very grateful. After some time he happened to visit the house again and found the women so proud and ungrateful that they would not open the door for him though he addressed them as above to remind them of their former condition and the blessing he had given them.

" *The peril past the saint mocked.*"

2196. பாம்புக்குப் பால் வார்த்து வளர்த்தாலும், விஷத்தைக் கொடுக்கும்.

Though you give milk to a snake and bring it up, it will give you a deadly bite. 2193.

It is a common practice to put milk near the holes inhabited by cobras. Indeed the cobra is looked upon as a sacred being and is always spoken of euphemistically as 'the good snake'—*nalla pâmbu*—in Tamil, in spite of its venomousness.

" *Put a snake into your bosom, and when it is warm it will sting you.*"
" *He hath brought up a bird to pick out his own eyes.*"

N.B.—Mahabharata (சாந்திபர்வம்) criticizes the ungratefulness of mean people in the following terms:—"சின்ன மனிதரைச் சேர்க்கலாகாது. அவர்களால் பெரிய காரியம் ஆகமாட்டாது. தீமை முளையுமல்லது நன்மை விளையாது. அவர்களுக்கு என்ன உபகாரஞ் செய்தபோதிலும், எவ்வளவு சகாயம் பண்ணினபோதிலும், இவர்களாலே செவ்வைப்பட்டோம் என்று ஒருக்காலுஞ் சொல்லமாட்டார்கள். பலநாள் உதவிசெய்து ஒருநாள் உதவாவிட்டால், பலநாளுஞ் செய்த உதவி பாழாய்ப்போய், பாக்குமரம் நித்தியந் தண்ணீர் விடாமற்போனால் எப்படி வாடுமோ, அப்படிப்போல் முகம் வாடி, வம்பு வார்த்தைகளாடி அபகாரம்பண்ணுவார்கள். நமக்குப் பகையாயிருப்பவர்களுடன் உறவாடி நமது உண்மைகளை வெளியிட்டுவிடுவார்கள்." The passage may be translated as follows:—"You must not associate with inferiors. They can accomplish no great deeds. Evil flourishes in their actions, good will not thrive. Whatever benefit we render to them, however much help we give them, they will never admit that they have been made the better for it. If we aid them for many days but omit to help on any future day, all the help that we have given will be in vain, and just as the areca-palm will wither if its daily supply of water fails, so with angry face and with much abuse, they will injure us. Making friends with our enemies, they will reveal our secrets to them." From this it will be seen that ingratitude is in Hindu eyes a very grave sin, and though it must be confessed that gratitude is somewhat lacking to-day in India, and that the sneer that some people make about the absence of a word for 'thanks' or 'gratitude' in Tamil is not altogether unjustified, the sweeping assertion that the Hindus are ungrateful is however as false as it is sweeping!

CAUSE AND EFFECT.

காரணம், காரியம்.

2197. அக்காள் இருக்கிறவரையில் மச்சான் உறவு.
The relationship of a brother-in-law lasts as long as his sister lives. 3210.

2198. அடியற்றால், நுனி விழாமலிருக்குமா?
Will not the top fall if there is no root?
A proverb of wide application.

2199. அவனிடத்தில் எல்லாரும் பிச்சை வாங்கவேண்டும்.
From him all must receive alms. 2202, 2208, 3438.
Applied to anyone who is the embodiment of goodness, justice, beauty, &c.

2200. அள்ளாது குறையாது, சொல்லாது பிறவாது.
If nothing be taken, nothing will be wanting; if nothing be spoken, nothing will be rumoured.
"*Every why has a wherefore.*"

2201. ஆறின புண்ணிலும் அசடு நிற்கும்.
The scar will last when the wound is healed. 3418.

2202. எல்லா தேசத்துக்கும் இந்தியா பார்த்து இட்டதே பிச்சை.
India has bestowed alms on all other countries. 1671, 2199.
It is a common idea in India that Europe owes its civilization, its science, and its religion, to India.

2203. எங்கே புகை உண்டோ, அங்கே நெருப்பும் உண்டு.
Where there is smoke, there is fire.
"*No smoke without fire.*"

2204. எரிகிறதைப் பிடுங்கினால், கொதிக்கிறது அடங்கும்.
If the burning fuel be removed, the boiling will cease.
"*Take away fuel, take away flame.*"

2205. கலகம் என்னும் செடிக்குக் கிழங்காய் (or ஊற்றாய்) இருக்கிறான்.
He is the root (*or* source) of the plant called 'strife.'

2206. காற்றில்லாமல் தூசிப் பறக்குமா?
Will dust fly about without wind?
"*There is a cause for all things.*"

2207. சகல தீர்த்தங்களுக்கும் சமுத்திரமே காரணம்.
The sea is the cause of all sacred rivers and waters.
Thus God is the cause of all holiness in the human heart.

2208. மோக்ஷத்துக்கு அவன் பார்த்து இட்டதே பிச்சை.
He is the only person who gives alms (to support us) to heaven. 2199, 2202.
Said of a person who has unique authority.

2209. வித்து இல்லா சம்பிரதாயம் மேலுமில்லைக் கீழுமில்லை.
No growth of life without seed either up in heaven or down on earth.

TIME.

காலம்.

2210. அவப்பொழுதிலும், தவப்பொழுது நல்லது.
Better is time spent in penance than time spent in vain.

2211. ஆர் ஆற்றுவார்? நாள் ஆற்றும்.
Who will comfort us? Time will do it. 95.
" *In the end things will mend.*"
" *Time is a file that wears and makes no noise.*"

2212. ஐயர் வருகிறவரையில் அமாவாசை நிற்குமா?
Will the new moon wait for the Brahmin's arrival? 2923.
" *Time and tide wait for no man.*"

2213. காலம் கலிகாலம் அல்லவா?
Is not this time the Kaliyuga?
Hindus divide time into four ages, the Kreta, Treta, Duvâpara and Kali-Yugams or ages. The last or present age is an 'iron age.'

2214. கலிக்குப் புதுமையான காரியமிருக்கிறது.
In this last age (*kali*) strange things happen!
Generally used about the European habits and customs that are creeping into Hindu society and upsetting the old order of things.

2215. பொங்கும் காலம் புளியங்காய், மங்கும் காலம் மாங்காய்.
When times of plenty are coming the tamarind is fruitful; when famine is coming the mango is fruitful.

2216. நாற்பதுக்குமேல் சென்றால் நாய்க் குணம்.
When a person is above forty years of age, he gets the disposition of a dog. 1514.
He has seen too much and tried too much, and feels more or less disgusted with all.

2217. பழம் பழுத்தால், கொம்பிலே தங்காது.
When a fruit is ripe it will not remain on the branch. 3160.
Events will take place at the proper time. *e.g.* When children come of age, they will marry.

2217*a*. போனது போச்சுது, பொழுது விடிந்தது.
What is gone is gone, the dawn has come. 195.
" *Let by-gones be by-gones.*"

SIGNS AND OMENS.

குறி, சகுனம்.

2218. *ஆரக்கழுத்தி அரண்மனைக்கு ஆகாது.*

A woman who is born with an inauspicious mark on her neck must not be in a palace.

The marks referred to are lines in the skin of the neck.

2219. *ஏறுநெற்றி சூறுதலை எதிர்க்கவந்தால் ஆகாது.*

If one with a high forehead and curly hair meets you, it is a bad omen.

2220. *ஏறும் தேமல், இறங்கும் படர் தாமரை, கூடும் புருவம், குடியைக் கெடுக்கும்.*

Ascending spots on the skin, descending ring-worms, and the eyebrows grown together, will destroy a family.

2221. *கட்டி இடமானால், வெட்டி அரசாளலாம்.*

If the *katti*-bird fly to your left hand side, you will triumph and reign as a king.

The *katti* is the black Swallow.

2222. *கட்டுக்காடை இடமானால், குட்டிச்சுவரும் பொன்னாகும்.*

If the quail passes on the left side, even an old wall becomes gold.

2223. *கருடன் இடமானால் எவன் கையில் பொருளும் தன்கையில் சேரும்.*

If a kite passes you on the left, other's property will become yours.

2224. *காகம் வலமானால், ஆயுசு விர்த்தியாகும்.*

If a crow passes you on the right, you will attain old age.

2225. *காடை இடமானால், நாட்டை ஆளலாம்.*

If a quail pass you on the left, you may rule a country.

2226. *காலமே எழுந்திருந்து காக்கை பார்க்கிறது ஆகாது.*

It is a bad sign to see a crow, on rising in the morning.

On the other hand it is lucky to see two crows.

Cf. the English rhyme about crows:—One for sorrow, two for mirth, three for wedding, four for a birth, five for a letter, six for something better, seven for silver, eight for gold, nine for a secret, never to be told.

2227. *காடை கட்டினால், பாடை கட்டும்.*

If a quail appears before you, your bier must be made (*i.e.* you must die).

2228. *கொடி சுற்றிப் பிறந்த பிள்ளை குலத்திற்கு ஆகாது.*

A child born with its navel string round its body, will be a curse to its caste.

2229. சாகிற நாய் வீட்டிலே ஏறினதுபோல.
Like a dying dog climbing a roof. 321, 463, 2947.

Said of a person, who is getting more and more wicked, and is approaching his ruin. A dog seldom climbs a roof, but if it does so, the omen is thought to signify the death of several members of the family, so its ears and tail are cut off, and the blood sprinkled on the roof.

2230. சுருட்டை சோறு இடும், பம்பை பால் வார்க்கும், கோரை குடிகெடுக்கும்.
Curly hair gives food, thick hair brings milk, and very stiff hair destroys a family.

These different kinds of hair are to be noted when selecting a girl for a wife. (*Ruthusastram*).

2231. செம்போத்து வலமானால், சம்பத்து உண்டாகும்.
If the Indian red cuckoo passes on your right side, you will get a fortune.

2232. மாலைசுற்றிப் பெண் பிறந்தால், மாமனுக்கு ஆகாது.
If a girl is born with her navel string round her neck, she causes death to her mother's brother.

2233. விச்சுளி வலமானால், நிச்சயம் வாழ்வு உண்டாம்.
If the *Vichuli*-bird passes on your right hand, happiness is certain to come to you.

The *Vichuli*-bird is the fowler's hawk:

THE MALIGNANT INFLUENCES OF THE PLANET SATURN.

சனி.

2234. அகப்பட்டவனுக்கு அஷ்டமத்துச் சனி, ஓடிப்போனவனுக்கு ஒன்பதாம் இடத்து இராஜா.
He who was caught was under the influence of Saturn in the eighth sign; and he who escaped, was under the influence of Saturn in the ninth.

Saturn situated in the eighth sign from that of one's birth is supposed to exercise a most malignant influence. (Percival, *Tamil Proverbs*).

2235. அஷ்டமத்துச் சனி பிடித்தது, புட்டத்துத் துணியும் உரிந்துகொண்டது.
Saturn in the eighth sign seized him, and stripped off even his loin-cloth.

Said of a person who has ruined another.

2236. அவன் எனக்கு அஷ்டமத்துச் சனி.
To me he is Saturn in the eighth sign. 2235.
i.e. He is my enemy.

2237. ஆறுமாசத்துக்குச் சனியன் பிடித்ததுபோல.
The evil he has done to me is like Saturn's seizing me for six months.

2238. சனி பிடித்ததோ, சனி பிடித்ததோ?

Have you caught a cold, or has Saturn caught you?

The unpleasantness of a cold compared with the trouble caused by the evil influences of the planet Saturn.

2239. சூரியனைக் கிரகணம் (com. கிராணம் or ராகு) பிடித்ததுபோல என்னைச் சனி பிடித்தது.

As an eclipse (*or* the dragon Rahu) seizes the sun, so has Saturn seized me.

Said when some disaster has occurred that cannot be accounted for. Rahu and Kethu are the dragons that are said to devour the sun at an eclipse.

2240. பொங்கு சனி போய், மங்கு சனி வந்தது, மங்கு சனி போய் குங்கு சனி வந்தது.

The favouring Saturn left, and Saturn that causes decline came; when it left, Saturn that causes final decay came. 30, 301 ff.

Said of youth, manhood and old age.

2241. போன சனியன் போச்சுது என்று இருந்தேன், மயிருக்குள் இருந்து கீச்சு கீச்சு என்கிறது.

I believed that Saturn was gone, but he squeaks in my hair. 842.

This reminds one of a European story about a hobgoblin which had been the torment of a family for a long time. At last the householder decided to remove to another house, hoping that the hobgoblin would remain where it was but as he was going along the road to the new house with the last cart-load of his things rejoicing that he had left the goblin behind, it poked its head out of a bushel measure on the cart and said: "It seems that we two are moving to-day!" And this again reminds one of the Tamil proverb: "Even if you go to Benares, your sin will follow you." 320.

ABANDONMENT, REJECTION, DONATION, ADOPTION.

கைவிடுதல், நீங்குதல், தத்தம்பண்ணுதல்.

2242. அதைக் கை கழுவவேண்டியதுதான்.

You must wash your hands of it. 2243.

Give up hopes of getting that money; you will never get it; he is unable to pay you.

2243. உன்னைக் கடலிலே கை கழுவினேன்.

I have washed my hands of you in the sea. 1330, 2245, 2255.

I will have nothing more to do with you.

32

2244. எள்ளும் தண்ணீரும் விட்டு, தத்தம்பண்ணிவிட்டேன் (or கை கழுவினேன்).

I poured out sesamum and water and gave it over (*or*, and washed my hands of it). 2256.

A solemn ceremony when a person hands over a gift to another, that is to be his for ever. If it is a daughter he hands over to the bridegroom, the father of the bride keeps the sesamum and water in his hands and says three times: தாரவார்த்துக் கொடுக்கிறேன் = I pour her out and give her to you as your wife.

2245. ஒரு முழுக்காய் முழுகிவிடவேண்டும்.

Leave it all while dipping once under the water.

Wash it all off with one dip. Forget all about that affair, or offence, completely.

2246. கட்டைக் கோணல் அடுப்பில் நிமிர்ந்தது.

The crookedness of the firewood became straight in the fire. 2248.

i. e. The strength of humble folk is of no avail against that of the great. Also, affliction removes blemishes. Also, a bad man may become great.

2247. கண்ணைக் கட்டிக் காட்டிலே விட்டதுபோல.

Like covering his eyes and leaving him in the forest. 2252.

Abandoning a man completely.

2248. கூண்டோடே போச்சுது குளிரும் காய்ச்சலும்.

Both the cold and the fever left with the body (*lit.* nest). 2246.

Said when an evil, a sin, a wicked person, a sickness or a trouble is got rid of. Said in the Maha Bharata by Duryodhana and his party, when they had set fire to the house in which they thought the five Pandavas were sleeping soundly.

2249. சக்கரை தின்று பித்தம் போகுமானால், கசப்பான மருந்தை ஏன் தின்னவேண்டும்?

If one can get rid of biliousness by eating sugar, why take bitter medicine?

If one can get rid of an evil easily, why incur trouble to get rid of it. 2513.

2250. சூரியனைக் கண்ட பனி (or இருள்) போல் நீங்கினது.

It vanished like the dew (*or* darkness) that has seen the sun.

2251. தன் கண்ணைக் கொடுத்து, வெங்கண்ணை வாங்கவேண்டும்.

Give away your eyes and buy *vankan*-fish. 1196.

This fish is said to have such an excellent flavour that too much cannot be paid for it. One cannot pay too much for a good thing.

2252. நட்டாற்றிலே கை விட்டாற்போல.

Like abandoning (a trusting person) in the middle of a river. 2247, 2253.

Said of one who deceives or betrays him who has trusted him.

2253. நம்பினபேரை நட்டாற்றிலே கை விடலாமா?
If a person trusts you, is it right to forsake him in the middle of a river? 2252, 3251.

2254. நிலை விட்டால், நீச்சு.
If you get out of your depth, swim!
Don't give up your appointment in order to go about searching for the uncertain.

2255. பாலை வார்த்துத் தலையை முழுகிவிடு.
Pour out milk and bathe your head.
i.e. Free yourself entirely from the companionship of a person previously mentioned.

2256. புல்லும் பூமியும் உள்ளமட்டும், என் நிலத்தை அனுபோகம்பண்ணு.
As long as grass and the earth exist you shall enjoy my land. 2244.
Said in handing over property in perpetuity.

2257. விட்டது அடி, உன் ஆசை விளாம்பழத்து ஓட்டோடே.
O woman, I am cured of my desire for you as completely as the ripe fruit of a wood-apple is separated from its shell. 272, 2835.
Give up friendship or connection with one who has proved himself to be a bad character.

2258. வைத்தியன் கைவிட்டதுபோல.
Like the doctor who gave up his patient.
Said of the abandonment of a hopeless case or project.

LIKE SEEKS LIKE, LIKE SUITS LIKE, "TIT FOR TAT."

சரிக்குச்சரி, ஒப்பு.

2259. அடிக்கும் பிடிக்கும் சரி.
The beating and the clutching were equal. 2262, 2266, 2282, 2292, 1731.
"*To give one tit for tat.*"

2260. அடிப்பானேன் பிடிப்பானேன், அடக்குகிறபடியே அடக்குவேன்.
Why does he beat and why does he lay hold of him? I will subdue him by means that will subdue him. 2264, 2265.
"*Different sores must have different salves.*"
"*A boisterous horse must have a boisterous bridle.*"

2261. அரிசிக்குத் தக்க உலையும், ஆம்புடையானுக்குத் தக்க வீறாப்பும்.
A pot sufficient for the rice (that is to be boiled) and pride that suits her husband's position. 1627, 2271, 2272, 2273.

2262. அவன் வம்புக்கும் இவன் தும்புக்கும் சரி.
This man's brutal language is equal to that man's insolent language. 2259, 2266.
"*I will give him a kick for a cuff.*"

2264. ஆடிக் கறக்கிற மாட்டை ஆடிக் கறக்கவேண்டும், பாடிக் கறக்கிற மாட்டைப் பாடிக் கறக்கவேண்டும்.
A dancing cow must be milked dancing, and a singing cow must be milked singing. 2260, 2265, 2285, 3463.
Conform to the nature of those with whom you have to do.
"*A bird may be caught by a snare that will not be shot.*"

2265. ஆடு கெட்டவன் ஆடித் திரிவான், கோழி கெட்டவன் கூவித் திரிவான்.
He who has lost a sheep will wander about (seeking it); and he who has lost a fowl will wander about calling for it. 2260, 2264.

2266. ஆனைக்கும் பானைக்கும் சரி.
The elephant and the pot are equal. 2259, 2262. 2282.
The allusion is to the story of a man who would not be consoled on the death of his elephant although much money was offered to him to buy a new one, but was put to shame by a man who pretended to be equally inconsolable about the breaking of an old pot. The saying is used when people by their stupidity refuse satisfactory compensation for losses.
"*To return like for like.*"

2267. இனத்தை இனம் தழுவும்.
Kindred will embrace kindred. 2274, 2277, 3205.
"*Birds of a feather flock together.*"

2268. ஈடு ஜோடு எங்குமில்லை.
Like and like are nowhere. 2997.
Two persons quite alike do not exist.

2269. ஒரு ஊருக்கு ஒரு வழியா?
Is there only one way to a village? 2828.
There are many ways of doing things and of treating people.
"*There are more ways to the woods than one.*"

2270. ஒன்றே குதிரை, ஒன்றே ராவுத்தன்.
The horse for the rider, and the rider for the horse. 2996.
Said of two people who suit each other. This is not a pure Tamil proverb.

2271. ஓட்டைத் தோண்டிக்கு அறுந்தபோன கயிறு சரி.
A broken rope will suit a broken pot. 2261, 2272, 2273.
"*Like pot, like cover.*"

2272. கதிகெட்ட மாப்பிள்ளைக்கு எருமுட்டைப்பணிகாரம்.
Cakes of cow-dung will be given to a worthless son-in-law. 2271, 2293.

2273. கந்தைக்குத் தகுந்த பொந்தை.

A shred suited to a rag. 2271.

Said of a poor, miserable man who has a wife to suit him.

2274. கனத்தைக் கனம் பார்க்கும், கருவாட்டுப் பானையை பூனை பார்க்கும்.

Dignity looks for dignity, and a cat will look out for the pot containing salt fish. 2267, 2277, 2296.

The great seek the great, and the low the low. Often said by one relative to another, who is better off and apt to overlook him.

"*The wise and the fool have their fellows.*"
"*Every lamb knows its own dam.*"
"*A thief knows a thief, and a wolf knows a wolf.*"

2275. காலுக்குத் தக்க செருப்பும், கூலிக்குத் தக்க உழைப்பும்.

Shoes that fit the feet, and toil that suits the labourer (*or* the wage).

2276. காலுக்கு ஆகிற செருப்பு தலைக்கு ஆகுமா?

Will shoes that fit the feet, fit the head? 2281.

2277. குலம் குலத்தோடே, வெள்ளம் ஆற்றோடே.

Caste joins with caste, and the flood goes along with the river. 2267, 2274.

2277*a*. குருவிக்குத் தகுந்த இராமேஸ்வரம்.

The bird should be suited to Râmêswaram.

The task a man attempts should be suited to his ability. A small bird is not able to fly away to distant Râmêswaram.

2278. கெட்டுப்போன பார்ப்பானுக்குச் செத்துப்போன பசு தானம்.

A dead cow is given as a gift to a degenerate Brahmin. 2120, 2298.

Treat everyone as he deserves.

"*A thistle is a fat salad for an ass's mouth.*"

2279. கைக்குருவியைக் கொண்டு, காட்டுக் குருவியைப் பிடிக்கவேண்டும்.

You must catch a wild bird by the help of a tame bird.

Trained birds are used as decoys.

2280. கொண்டைக்குத் தக்க பூ.

Flowers fit for women's hair. 2295.

2281. சாணிச் சட்டி வைக்கிற இடத்தில் சாணிச் சட்டி வைக்கவேண்டும்.
சரிகைச்சட்டி வைக்கிற இடத்தில் சரிகைச்சட்டி வைக்கவேண்டும்.

Let the pot for cow-dung be put in its place, and the pot for gold-thread in its place. 863, 2276.

Show politeness according to the worth of people; what is due to one, is not due to another. Cow-dung is universally used in India as a purifier. The cow and all its products are regarded as holy.

2282. *செட்டி பணத்தைக் குறைத்தான், சேணியன் நூலைக் குறைத்தான்.*

The merchant gave less money (to the weaver than he had promised) and the weaver put less thread into the cloth (than he had promised). 2259, 2262, 2266.

"*Tit for tat.*"

2283. *செருப்புக்குக் காலைத் தறிக்கிறதா?*

Are we to shorten the feet to (make) the shoes (fit)?

Is religious teaching to be suited to men's wishes, or are men to conform to religious teaching?

2284. *ஜாண் பண்டாரத்துக்கு முழம் விபூதி* (or *லிங்கம்* or *தாடி*).

A mendicant only a span high wears a Siva mark (*or linga or* beard) a foot long. 1627.

2285*a*. *தங்க செருப்பு ஆனாலும் தலைக்கு ஏறாது.*

Though the shoes be of the finest gold they will not be put on the head.

e.g. Though a Pariah may become rich, he remains a Pariah. 1762.

2285*b*. *தண்ணீரிலே விளைந்த உப்புத் தண்ணீரில் கரையவேண்டும்.*

Salt that has been formed in water must be dissolved in water. 299, 2264.

2286. *திருட்டுப் பயலுக்குப் பிரட்டுக் குருக்கள்.*

A rogue has deceitful priests. 292*a*, 475, 1391.

"*To a rogue a rogue and a half.*"

2287. *நான் செருப்பு விடுகிற இடத்திலேகூட அவன் நிற்க யோக்கியனல்ல.*

He is not fit to stand where I have left my shoes. 3022.

On entering a house a Hindu leaves his shoes outside. The proverb expresses utter contempt.

2288. *நூலுக்கு ஏற்ற சரடு.*

Yarn fit to make a cord.

2289. *பச்சைப் பாண்டத்தில் பாலை வைத்தால், பாலும் உதவாது பாண்டமும் உதவாது.*

Don't keep milk in a new earthen pot, for both the milk and the pot will be spoiled. Matt. 9, 17.

A new earthen pot gives a pungent and unpleasant taste to any liquid put into it, and it also retains the taste of the liquid in its pores after being emptied.

2290. *பரிக்கு இடும் கடிவாளத்தை நரிக்கு இடுகிறது.*

Putting the horse's bridle on a jackal. 678.

If a second wife receives the jewels that belonged to a first wife, this proverb may be quoted.

2291. பள்ளிக்குப்பத்துக்கு அம்பட்டன் உவாத்தியார்.

A barber is the teacher in a Palli village.

Pallis are a low Sudra caste.

"*A mad parish must have a mad priest.*"

2292. பெய்ந்த மழைக்கும் சரி, காய்ந்த வெயிலுக்கும் சரி.

The rain that fell and the heat that dried it up are alike. 2259.

2293. மண்ணாங்கட்டி மாப்பிள்ளைக்கு எருமுட்டை பணிகாரம்.

A son-in-law who is like a clod will get nothing but cow-dung cakes. 1743*a*, 2272.

"*A lean fee is fit for a lazy clerk.*"

2294. மண் காசுக்குச் சாம்பல் கொழுக்கட்டை.

For coins made of clay you will get cakes made of ashes.

2295. மண்டைக்கு ஏற்ற கொண்டை.

The right sort of hair for a woman's head. 2280.

2296. மாமரம் பழுத்தால் கிளிக்கு ஆகும், வேம்பு பழுத்தால் காக்கைக்கு ஆகும்.

When the mango tree bears fruit the parrot will get food, when the margosa tree bears fruit the crow will get food. 2274.

The noble seek what is noble, and the low what is mean.

2297. மாவுக்குத் தக்க பணிகாரம்.

The number of the cakes will depend on the quantity of the flour. 2611.

2298. மூப்புக்குச் சோறும், முறத்துக்குச் சாணியும்.

Food for old people and cow-dung for a winnowing basket. 2278, 2110.

Cow-dung, which is thought to be very holy in India, is used to plaster over the wicker-work of the broad shallow basket, like an elephant's ear, in which grain is winnowed. The saying means, treat every one according to his worth.

2299. விரலுக்குத் தக்க வீக்கம்.

The swelling will be according to the size of the finger.

Let your expenditure fit your income.

2300. வரவுக்குத் தகுந்த செலவு, மாப்பிள்ளைக்குத் தகுந்த மஞ்சள்.

The expenses must be proportioned to the income, and the amount of the saffron to the station of the bridegroom. 1210, 2314.

"*Cut your coat according to your cloth.*"

Cf. 1391 *ff*, 2605 *ff*, 3582 *ff*.

HAPPINESS.

சந்தோஷம்.

2301. உன்பாடு கொள்ளைதானே.
Your lot is a lucky one.
Said to a man who has got just what he wants.

2302. காணாதது கண்டாற்போல.
Like seeing the unseen.

2 03. சூரியனைக் கண்ட தாமரைபோல்.
Like the lotus flower that has seen the sun.
A simile describing happiness.

2304. ஜென்மக் (or பிறவி) குருடனுக்குக் கண் கிடைத்ததுபோல்.
Like a man born blind getting sight.

2305. பசித்தவனுக்குப் பால் அமிர்தம் கொடுத்தாற்போல.
Like giving milk and nectar to a hungry person.

2306. பருப்பிலே நெய் விட்டதுபோல.
Like pouring *ghee* into *dhall*.
Ghee and *dhall* together make a most savoury dish.
"*His bread fell into the honey.*"

2307. பழம் நழுவிப் பாலில் விழுந்ததுபோல.
Like fruit slipping into milk.

2308. புதையல் எடுத்தவனைப்போல்.
Like a man who has found hidden treasure.

2309. வயிற்றிலே பாலை வார்த்ததுபோல.
Like filling your stomach with milk.

Cf. 1205 *ff.*

RESTLESSNESS.

2310. இரும்பு பிடித்த கையும், சிரங்கு பிடித்த கையும் சும்மா இராது.
A hand that has laid hold of iron and a hand that has itch will not keep quiet. 1101, 2715.
"*Itch and ease can no man please.*"

2311. சூதுகாரன் கையும், கோள்காரன் வாயும் சும்மா இராது.
The hand of a deceitful person and the mouth of a slanderer will not keep quiet. 818.

2312. திருட்டுக் கை நிற்காது.
A thievish hand will not be still.

2313. பிய்ந்த (or கிழிந்த) சீலையும், பேச்சுக்கற்ற வாயும் சும்மா இராது.
A torn cloth and a mouth that has learnt to speak will not be quiet.

A rent will get bigger and a fool will talk.

" *An old sack asketh much patching.*"

SPENDING.

செலவு.

2314. அளகேசன் (or குபேரன்) ஆனாலும், அளவு அறிந்து செலவு செய்ய வேண்டும்.

Though as rich as Kubera (the god of riches), know how much you have and then lay out your money. 2300.

2315. ஆடிக்காலத்தில் இலவம்பஞ்சு பறக்கிறதுபோல.
It flies away like cotton-down in (the wind of) July.

" *Money has wings.*"

2316. செல்லும் செல்லாததுக்குச் செட்டியார் இருக்கிறார்.
Whether the coin is current or not the merchant is here to tell you.

Said by women when a quantity of food is prepared for some guests who do not come, and the question arises what is to be done with it. One of the family quotes this phrase referring to some glutton in the house who is able to eat it all up as easily as a merchant can tell whether a coin is good or not.

2317. ஐயர் கொண்டுவருகிற பிச்சைக்கு அறுபத்தாறு பை.
There are sixty-six purses to hold the alms a man gets.

All a man's earnings do not suffice to meet the expenses of his family.

" *Ask thy purse what thou shouldest buy.*"

Cf. 533 *ff.*

COMPANIONSHIP.

சேர்க்கை, கூட்டுறவு.

ONE MUST SUFFER WITH ONE'S ASSOCIATES

2318. ஊரைப் பிடித்த சனி பிள்ளையாரையும் பிடித்தது.
Saturn that had bewitched the village, also bewitched (the god) Ganesa.

As Ganesa was the village god he had to suffer with the villagers.

2319. எட்டியுடனே சேர்ந்த இலவும் தீப்பட்டது.
The silk-cotton tree that grew with the strychnus tree took fire.

The useful tree was burned along with the poisonous, when the latter took fire simply because of its proximity. i. e. A good man who associates with evil companions will suffer with them when they get into trouble

2320. ஓடுகிற கழுதை வாலைப் பிடித்தால், உடனே கொடுக்கும் பலன் (உதை).

If you lay hold of the tail of an ass that is running, you will be paid for your trouble immediately (*i.e.* you will be kicked).

Avoid low companions (அவான் ஜோலிக்குப் போகாதே).

" *Beware of the hind part of a mule, and all sides of a priest.*"

2321. காடு வெந்தால் சந்தன மரமும் வேகாதா?

If the forest burns, will not the sandal-tree burn with it?

2322. பிள்ளையாரைப் பிடித்த சனி, அரசமரத்தையும் பிடித்தது.

Saturn that bewitched Ganesa also bewitched the fig-tree *(Ficus religiosa)*.

The image of Ganesa is kept under this holy tree. Ganesa is the god of luck.

2323. முண்டையைப் பிடித்த கண்டமாலை, முருங்கையையும் பிடித்தது.

When the tumor seized the widow's neck it also seized the drumstick-tree.

Cf. 3083 *ff.*

THE INFLUENCE OF COMPANIONS.

2324. இந்தப் பையனுக்கு இந்த வீட்டு ஓதம் உறைத்துப்போய்விட்டது.

The dampness of this house (family) has got right into this boy. 2325.

Used of the effect of evil influences, surroundings or companions.

2325. உப்பு தண்ணீரும், கப்பு மஞ்சளும் ஊறிப்போச்சுது.

The salt water and the sticky saffron have soaked well into her. 2324.

She begins to overstep the bounds of modesty and to imitate women of character.

2326. ஐயனார் கோவில் மண்ணை மொரித்தவர்கள், அத்தனைபேரும் பத்திரக் காளி.

All those who tread on the soil of Ayanâr's temple are wicked people.

Ayanâr is an inferior tutelary god, whose temple Brahmins will not enter.

" *Meddle with dirt and some of it will stick to you.*"

2327. சேற்றிலே கல் விட்டு எறிந்தால், மேலே தெறிக்கும்.

If you throw stones into mud it will splash over yourself.

" *If you will stir up the mire, you must bear the smell.*"
" *He who blows in the dust fills his eyes with it.*"
" *Do not throw clods into dung to spatter your own clothes.*"

2328. பன்றிக்குப்பின் போகிற கன்றும் பீ தின்னும்.

A calf that goes after a pig will eat filth.

" *He who touches pitch defiles himself.*"
" *One scabbed sheep will mar a whole flock.*"
" *A wicked companion invites us all to hell.*"

2329. பனைமரத்தின் கீழே பாலைக் குடித்தாலும், கள்ளு என்பார்கள்.
Though you drink milk under a palmyra-palm people will say that you drink toddy.

The juice of the palmyra-palm is made into the intoxicating drink called toddy, hence the inference. People are judged by the company they keep.

2330. வீட்டுப் பாம்பு காட்டுக்குப் போனால், அதுவும் காட்டுப் பாம்பு ஆகும்.
If a tame snake goes to the woods, it will become wild.

Cf. 1535 *ff.*

ASSOCIATE WITH THE GREAT.

"There is nought better than to be with noble souls in company;
There is naught dearer than to wend with good friends faithful to the end.
This is the love whose fruit is sweet, therefore to bide therein is meet."

E. Arnold: *Indian Idylls.*

2331. கற்பக விருக்ஷத்தைச் சேர்ந்த காகமும் அமிர்தம் உண்ணும்.
Even the crow that seeks the *Kalpa* tree in *Swerga* (the heaven of Indra) will feed on nectar. 2069, 2337.

If the meanest seek the highest ideal he may attain it.

"*He hath no mean portion of virtue that loveth it in another.*"

2332. குட்டி ஆடு கொழுத்தாலும் வழுவழுப்பு தீராது.
Though a kid fattens, its flesh will always be clammy.

2334. கொல்லையில் குற்றியை அடைந்த புல்லு உழவன் உழுபடைக்குக் கெடுமோ?
Will the grass that has grown round a stump in the field be destroyed by the plough-share? 2104.

The stump saves the grass from being ploughed down and the great will protect their dependants.

2335. நெருப்பைச் சேர்ந்த யாவும் அதன் நிறமாகும்.
Whatever is put into fire will be of the colour of fire.

"*He that walked with the virtuous is one of them.*"

2336. பூவுடன் கூடின நாரும் மணம் பெற்றாற்போல்.
The strings with which the flowers are bound get the perfume of the flowers.

2337. மேருவைச் சேர்ந்த காக்காயும் பொன்னிறம்.
If the black crow keep near Mount Meru it will shine like gold. 2331.

Mount Meru is a fabulous mountain of pure gold.

N.B.—Except 2332, the above are aphorisms, not proverbs.

Cf. 3075 *ff.*

WORDS WITHOUT DEEDS.

சொல், பேச்சு.

2338. அச்சி என்றால் உச்சி குளிருமா? அழுவணம் (or ஐவணம்) என்றால் கை சிவக்குமா?

Will the crown of your head feel cool if you simply say *Achi?* Will your nails become red if you say *Aruvanam?*

Achi is the legendary capital of *Kuveran* (the god of wealth). The *Aruvanam* (Lawsonia) plant is used in India, as it was in Egypt also by women as a dye to colour their nails red.

"*Good words and no deeds, are rushes and reeds.*"

2339. அடா என்பான், வெளியே புறப்படான்.

He will say '*Addâ*' but he will not set out.

His words are forcible but he does nothing.

2340. அப்பா என்றால் உச்சி குளிருமா?

If you only say '*Appâ*' will the crown of his head become cool?

Mere speech will effect nothing.

2341. அர அர என்பது பெரிதோ? ஆண்டிக்கு இடுவது பெரிதோ?

Which is greater, to say '*Hara, Hara*' or to give alms to the mendicant?

Hara is a name of Siva.

"*All talk and no go.*"

2342. குறை குடம் தளும்பும், நிறை குடம் தளும்பாது.

A pot half full of water splashes, a full pot does not splash.

Either part of this proverb may be used separately.

"*The deepest streams flow with least noise.*"
"*Deep rivers move in silence, shallow brooks are noisy.*"
"*Still waters run deep.*"

2343. அவசாரிக்கு வாய் பெரிது, அஞ்சு ஆறு அரிசிக்குக் கொதி பெரிது.

A prostitute has a big mouth; five or six grains of rice make a noise when boiling.

A prostitute will deny her faults with much talk. Women often use this saying about a person who tries to hide a fault by repeated denials.

"*Empty barrels make most noise.*"

2344. ஆண்டிகள் மடம் கட்டுகிறதுபோல.

Like mendicants building a rest-house for travellers! 2358.

When these worthies meet together at night after begging all day they take opium and other drugs and chat and criticise persons and things, and in their imagination build all sorts of castles in the air till they sleep. Next morning they start out again begging.

"*A deluge of words and a drop of sense.*"

2345. ஆயிரம் கோவிந்தம் போட்டாலும், அமுது படைக்கிறவனுக்குத் தெரியும்.

Though a beggar cries out *Govinda*! (Krishna) a thousand times, it is the man who cooks the food that has the trouble. 1440.

The householder who gives to the religious mendicant has all the trouble.

2346. ஆயிரம் சொல்லுக்கு அரை எழுத்து மேல்.

Better a half-formed letter than a thousand (spoken) words.

A written receipt, however imperfect it may be, is better than mere words.

2347. உபசார வார்த்தை காசாகுமா? உண்டால் ஒழிய தீருமா?

Polite words will not become coins; will (your hunger) be satisfied unless you eat?

"*Words do not fill the belly.*"

2348. எச்சிலும் பேச்சிலும் வல்லவனே.

He is quite a hero in talk and abuse.

"*A man of words and not of deeds, is like a garden full of weeds.*
For when the weeds begin to grow, then doth the garden overflow."

2349. எட்டுச் சுரக்காய் கறிக்கு ஆகுமா?

Will the word pumpkin serve for a meal? 1960, 2376, 3230.

"*Bare words buy no barley.*"
"*The wine in the bottle doth not quench thirst.*"

2350. ஓடவும்மாட்டான், பிடிக்கவும்மாட்டான், ஓயாமல் பேசுவான்.

He will neither move nor take hold of anything but he will talk without ceasing.

"*The noisiest drum has nothing in it but air.*"

2351. காசி இரண்டு எழுத்துத்தானே, அதைக் காண எத்தனை நாள் செல்லும்?

The name *Kâsi* (Benares) has two syllables only; but how many days will it take to get there?

Kâsi is the most sacred place in India. It is the Hindu's Jerusalem.

2352. காரியம் பெரிதோ, வீரியம் பெரிதோ?

Which is the greater, deeds or boasting? 2365.

2352*a*. குண்டு சட்டியில் குதிரை ஓட்டுகிறான் (or கரணம்போடுகிறான்).

He drives horses (*or* turns a summersault) in an earthen pot. 1642.

Said of one who talks boastfully about his own deeds when at home, but does nothing to match with his great professions.

"*It is not the hen which cackles most, that lays most eggs.*"

2353. குதி குதி என்பார்கள் எல்லாரும் கூடக் குதிப்பார்களா?

All will say: "jump, jump," but will they join in jumping? 2357.

All are ready with encouragement, but no one will do anything.

2354. கொஞ்சப்பொருளை மந்திரம் பண்ணுகிறதுபோல கைகாட்டுகிறான்.

He speaks the charm to make the little he gives to appear much.

Said of a parsimonious man who makes a great show on small means.

2355. கோவிந்தா என்றால் கோடிஸ்நானம் என்று குளிக்காமல் முழுகாமல் இருக்கிறதா?

Is it right to think that to say *Govinda* (*Krishna*) once is as good as bathing a thousand times, and therefore to neglect all washing? 2411, 3030.

2356. சக்கரை என்றால் தித்திக்குமா?

Will your food be sweetened if you only say 'sugar'?

2357. சொல்வார் எல்லாரும், துணிவார்களா தீப்பாய?

All will encourage the deed, but who will dare to leap into the fire? 2353.

" *Deeds are fruits, words are leaves.*"

" *Deeds are males, words are females.*"

2358. தத்தனூர் ஆண்டி கதைபோல்.

Like the talk of the mendicants at Tattanûr. 234.

After they had been well fed at the monastery (*Madam, matt*) they forgot that they were beggars and began to build castles in the air.

" *It is better to do well than to say well.*"

2359. தம்பி வார்த்தையை வண்டியிலே வைத்துதான் இழுக்கவேண்டும்.

The words of the younger brother must be placed in a carriage and paraded.

An ironical estimate of the value of a younger brother's judgment.

" *The greatest talkers are always the least doers.*"

2360. நான் நீட்டின விரலை மடக்கமாட்டான், நீட்டி நீட்டிப்பேசுவான்.

He is unable to bend the finger I stretch out, but he is able to speak at great length.

" *A long tongue has a short hand.*"

2361. நீர் என்று சொன்னால் நெருப்பு அவியுமா?

Will fire be put out by saying 'water'?

2362. நெருப்பு என்றால் வாய் வெந்துபோமா?

Will one's mouth be burnt by saying 'fire'?

2363. நோயாளிக்கு ஆசைவார்த்தை சொல்லுகிறதுபோல்.

Like speaking words of hope to a sick person (without trying to help him). 914.

2364. படிக்கிறது திருவாசகம், இடிக்கிறது சிவன் ஆலயம் (கோவில்).

He reads a poem in Siva's praise, and then breaks down Siva's temple. 3566.

" *Much praying but no piety.*"

2365. போதனை பெரிதோ, சாதனை பெரிதோ?

Which is greater, teaching or practice? 2352, 3566.

2366. மனோராச்சியம் பண்ணுகிறதுபோல்.

Like making a kingdom in the imagination. 2370.

" *Castles in the air.*"

2367. முருங்கைக் காய் என்கிறதும் (உம்= உடனே), முறிந்ததாம் பத்தியம்.

It seems, that as soon as one uttered the name of the *murunga* vegetable his diet-prescription was broken.

Murungai-kai, Moringa Pterogospermum, is also called the drumstick-tree, and the fruit, leaves and roots of this plant are all used in cookery.

" *Good words fill not a sack.*"

2368. ரூபாய் என்றால் வயிறு நிறைந்துபோகுமா?

Can one's stomach be filled by saying the word 'Rupee.'

The rupee is the standard coin of India, made of silver, about the size of an English florin, and worth (at the time of publishing) about one shilling and three pence.

" *Fair words make me look to my purse.*"

2369. வாய் வாழைப்பழம், கை கருணைக் கிழங்கு.

His words are (as sweet as) plantains, his deeds are like the burning taste of the *karunei*-root. 254.

" *Fair words do not fill the pocket.*"

2370. வாயால் பந்தல் போடுகிறதுபோல.

Like building a booth with your mouth! 2366.

2371. வார்த்தைக்குத் தரித்திரமா?

Is there any scarcity of words?

" *A deluge of words and a drop of sense.*"

" *Much smoke and little roast.*"

2372. வெந்நீரிலே வீடு வேகுமா?

Will a house be burned down by hot water? 843. 1512.

Words will do you no harm. Said to comfort one who feels distressed at being abused.

Cf. 239 *ff.* 913 *ff.* 2373 *ff.* 2783 *ff.* 2792 *ff.* 2801 *ff.*

POLITENESS.

மரியாதை, உபசாரம்.

HYPOCRITICAL POLITENESS.

2373. அன்றில்லை இன்றில்லை அழுகல் பலாக்காய்! கலியாண வாசலிலே கலந்து உண்ண வந்தாயே!

Oh rotten jack-fruit! you did not come to see me yesterday or to-day, and now you come to my house to eat at my wedding feast!

Said about a man who refuses help to those who are in need, but is always ready to put in a claim on their kindness when they happen to be in better circumstances.

2374. உபசார வார்த்தை வாய்க்குக் கேடு, தூற்றுப் பருக்கை வயிற்றுக்குக் கேடு.

Polite words are the ruin of the mouth, thinly served boiled rice is the ruin of the stomach.

Said of stingy politeness that does not mean hospitality. A stingy host will so spread out the rice that is put on the leaf-plates for the guests that it shall seem to be more than it is. 2365.

"*There is not always good cheer where the chimney smokes.*"

2375. கடித்த பாக்கும் கொடாத சிற்றப்பன் காதவழி வந்தானும்.

It seems that his uncle, who would not even give him a nut once chewed, accompanied him ten miles on his road!

"*Fair words and foul play cheat both young and old.*"

2376. சக்கரையும் தேனும் சிற்றப்பா! ஏட்டில் எழுதி நக்கப்பா!

Oh uncle, write the words 'sugar' and 'honey' on a leaf and lick it. 2349.

A sarcasm on the kindness that means nothing. The 'leaf' referred to (*Yēdu*) is a strip of palm leaf. The palm leaf was much used by Hindus as the material on which books and documents might be written with a style. Paper is now largely used in towns, but elsewhere it is no uncommon thing to find strips of palm leaf used for notes and accounts. They are commonly called *ōlei*.

"*Less of your courtesy and more of your purse.*"

2377. சாவளவும் இருந்தால், கலியாணஞ் செய்துவைக்கிறேன்.

If you remain with me till you die, I will bear your marriage expenses. 1298, 1302.

"*Fair words butter no parsnips.*"

2378. சோறும் துணியும் கேளாமலிருந்தால், என் பெற்ற பிள்ளையைவிட பத்துமடங்கு அதிகமாய்க் காப்பாற்றுவேன்.

If you don't ask me for rice and clothes, I will cherish you ten times more dearly than my own dear child.

"*Good words and no deeds are rushes and reeds.*"

2379. சோற்றுக்கு வீங்கின நாயே! மாட்டுப்பொங்கல் கழித்த மற்றநாள் வாயே!

O starving dog, come the day after the Ox Pongal Feast is over. 3217.

The Pongal feast is held in the Tamil month Tay (Jan. Feb.) for three days. It is really a thanksgiving when the earth begins to come nearer to the sun at the time of the winter solstice. On the first day new rice is boiled in honour of the sun and dedicated to him and eaten with much rejoicing. On the second day the horns of cattle are painted and sometimes gilded, and their bodies are decorated in honour of the God Indra. This is the Ox Pongal. No strangers or servants are fed in any household on this or the previous day. But on the third day visits are exchanged and all comers are fed. The proverb is used about a person who is unwilling to help the needy in their distress.

2380. தின்னவேண்டாம், உண்ணவேண்டாம் மகளே, மூஞ்சியாவது (or முகமாவது) கழுவி பொட்டு வைத்துக்கொண்டுபோ!

Don't eat and don't drink in my house, my dear daughter, but wash your face and put the spot (of vermilion) on your forehead and go home.

Said to a married daughter by her stingy father when he will not help her but only pretends to do so. Sudra women who are living with their husbands wear a spot of vermilion (*Kunkuma*) on their foreheads. The mark has no sectarian significance, though Vaishnavas sometimes say that it represents Vishnu's wife Lakshmi, and Saivas that it represents Parvati the wife of Siva.

"*All is not gospel that comes out of his mouth.*"

2381. தேன் ஒழுக பேசி, தெருவழியே விடுகிறது.

Speaking honeyed words and accompanying him across the street.

Said of one who speaks kindly to his friends or relations, but gets rid of them without helping them.

"*Sugared words generally prove bitter.*"

2382. காஞ்சீவரம் உபசாரம் (or தெற்கே, or நாகூர்).

The politeness of *Conjevaram* (*or* the South, *or* Negapatam).

A phrase signifying insincere politeness.

"*He who gives fair words feeds you with an empty spoon.*"

2383. படிக்குப் படி நமஸ்காரம்.

Prostrations over and over again (to a long train of officials from the lowest till you reach the highest).

Said by those who can only reach a great person by cringing to, and even bribing many minor officials. The prostration (*Namaskâra*) is a most respectful salutation. But it is also the common salutation of all Hindus.

2384. வைப்பு வரப்பு வைத்துப் பேசவேண்டும்.

One ought to observe decorum (*lit.* to set bounds to what one says) when speaking.

A mother-in-law may say this when her daughter-in-law forgets to speak respectfully to her.

34

2385. பச்சைச் சிரிப்புப் பல்லுக்குக் கேடு, தூற்றுப் பருக்கை வயிற்றுக்குக் கேடு.

Feigned laughter ruins the teeth, and loosely spread boiled rice is a loss to the stomach. 2374.

Cf. 239 *ff.* 913 *ff.* 2338 *ff.*

HONOURING ONE'S SELF.

2386. அரைச்சீலை கட்டக் கைக்கு உபசாரமா?

Should one compliment one's own hand for tying one's waist-cloth?

2387. உண்ட வயிற்றுக்கு உபசாரமா?

Should one's stomach be honoured for digesting food?

2388. எக்கு (or அவிழ) புடவை சேர்ந்தால், கைக்கு உபசாரமா?

(If a woman's hand) fasten her cloth when it is loosened, will that hand be praised?

2389. கைக்கு வாய் உபசாரமா?

Is the mouth to honour the hand (because the hand puts food into the mouth)?

MISCELLANEOUS PROVERBS ON POLITENESS.

2390. அண்ணன் பெரியவர், அப்பா, காலைப் பிடி.

(He admits that) his elder brother is his superior but calls out to him '*appâ*! shampoo my feet!'

Used of an inferior who demands respect from his betters. *Appâ* is a familiar term for *Aiya*, Sir.

2391. அதிக கரிசனம் (or பக்ஷம்) ஆனாலும், ஆம்புடையானை அப்பா என்று அழைக்கிறதா?

Should you ever call your husband '*appâ*,' however much you may like him?

A husband should always be treated respectfully.

2392. உண்ட வீட்டிலே உட்கார்ந்துகொள்ளாதேபோனால், கண்டவர்கள் எல்லாம் கடு கடு என்பார்கள்.

If you do not sit down a little while in the house where you have eaten food (in courtesy to the host) all who see you will be angry with you. 3208.

2393. சுங்கா (prop. சுருங்காத) மூஞ்சி (or முகம்) காட்டாதே, வந்த விருந்தாளியை ஓட்டாதே.

Don't show a cross face and don't drive away a guest from your house. 2124, 2766, 3208.

"*It is a sin against hospitality to open your doors and shut up your countenance.*"

2394. மதியாத வாசலிலே மிதியாதிருப்பதே உத்தமம்.
It is best not to set your foot in the house of those who do not respect you. 1330.

"*Welcome is the best cheer.*"

2395. மரியாதை தப்பினால் (or கெட்டால்) மாலவாடு.
He who fails in politeness is a *Mâla*.

Mâla is the Telugu name for the Pariah non-caste class.

DON'T JUDGE ACCORDING TO APPEARANCES.

தோற்றம்.

2396. பசு கறுப்பு என்று பாலும் கறுப்பா?
Though the cow's skin is black, will its milk also be black? 2403, 2412, 2863.

Though the mother be wicked, the daughter may be good.

2397. இது அனுமானுச்சே.
This boy is a *Hanumân*.

You take him to be a good boy because he behaves well when you see him, but he is really very bad. Hanumân is the Monkey-God.

2398. எல்லாரும் மனிதரா? கல் எல்லாம் மாணிக்கமா?
Are all men men? are all stones rubies? 656.

"*A white glove often conceals a dirty hand.*"

2399 கணக்கப்பிள்ளை எல்லாம் எழுத்துப்பிள்ளையா?
Can all who belong to the accountants' caste write? 2065.

By birth they belong to the accountant-caste (*Kanakkan*), but they may be fools at figures.

2400. கறுத்ததெல்லாம் தண்ணீர், வெளுத்ததெல்லாம் பால் என்கிறான்.
He says that everything black is water and everything white is milk.

He takes things according to their outward appearance. He believes things to be what he sees them to be, without making inquiries. Said of an innocent simple fellow (பேதை).

"*At ease he is that seldom thinketh.*"

2401. கற்கண்டால் செய்த எட்டிக்கனியும் கசக்குமா?
Will a Strychnus (Nux vomica) fruit made of sugar-candy be bitter?

Though it has the appearance of the bitter strychnus fruit, it will be sweet. Appearances are deceptive.

2402. குரு வேஷம் கொண்டவன் எல்லாம் குரு ஆவானா?
Are all priests who dress like priests?

"*You can't judge a horse from the harness.*"

2403. கோழி கறுப்பானாலும், அதின் முட்டையும் கறுப்பா?
Though a fowl be black, are its eggs also black? 2396, 2412.
"*A black plum is as sweet as a white.*"

2404. தடி எடுத்தவன் எல்லாம் தண்டற்காரனா?
Are all who carry staves rent-collectors?
The staff of office does not make them rent-collectors.
"*All are not hunters that blow the horn.*"

2405. நரைத்தவன் எல்லாம் கிழவனா?
Are all who have grey hair old men?

2406. நாமம் போட்டவன் எல்லாம் தாதனா? விபூதி பூசினவன் எல்லாம் ஆண்டியா?
Not every one who puts on a *Nâmam* is a Vaishnava mendicant, and not every one who smears himself with holy ashes is a Siva mendicant.
"*It is not the beard that makes the philosopher.*"

2407. நீறு பூத்த நெருப்புபோல.
Like fire covered with ashes. 660, 2681, 3057.
Said of a virtue not discovered at first sight. This phrase is often used in the Mahâbhâratha about men of secret virtue. Real virtue works humility, and this humility is like ashes that hide true greatness. "Said of a very learned and humble man." (CARR, *Telugu Proverbs.*)
"*A good name keeps its lustre in the dark.*"

2408. பித்தளை துலக்கினாலும் பொன்குணம் வருமா?
Will the nature of gold belong to brass although it shines. 676.
"*All is not gold that glitters.*"

2409. பெற்றதெல்லாம் பிள்ளையா, இட்டதெல்லாம் பயிரா?
Are all who are born, true children? Does every field that is sown yield a crop?
A child may look like its father and yet not have its father's characteristics. This commonly means that all that is temporal is uncertain; the children may die, and the corn may fail.
"*Birth is much, but breeding more.*"

2410. பை எடுத்தவன் எல்லாம் வைத்தியனா?
Are all who carry bags (of medicines) doctors?
"*An old goat is never the more reverend for his beard.*"

2411. மஞ்சளும் மலரும் கொண்டு துதிக்காவிட்டாலும், நெஞ்சில் நினைப்பதே போதும்.
Though you do not worship God with offerings of saffron and flowers, to think of him in your heart is enough. 2355.
Inward worship compared with outward ceremony.

2412. மாடு கிழமானாலும், பாலின் ருசி போகுமா?
Though the cow be old, its milk will not lose its good taste. 2396, 2403.

Cf. 1620 *ff.*

REFERRING TO WHAT IS SELF-EVIDENT.

தெளிவு, வெளிச்சம்.

2413. அப்பம் என்றால் பிட்டுக் காட்டவேண்டுமோ?
If you say it is a pancake, is it necessary to break it in two to show that it is one? 2071.

2414. ஆனையைப் பார்க்க வெள்ளெழுத்தா?
Do you think me so purblind as not to be able to see an elephant?

2415. உள்ளங்கையில் நெல்லிக்கனிபோல.
Like a *nelli*-berry in the palm of the hand.

The *nelli* (Phyllanthus) bears a bright yellow transparent fruit.

"*As plain as the nose on a man's face.*"
"*As clear as crystal.*" "*As plain as a pikestaff.*"

2416. கண்ணாரக் கண்டதற்கு என் அகப்பைக் குறி?
Why require the mark of the ladle (in the food) to prove a theft that you have seen with your own eyes?

2417. கண்கொண்டு அல்லவோ, வழி நடக்கவேண்டும்.
Must you not walk on the road by the help of your eyes?

2418. கண்ணாலே கண்டதற்குச் சாட்சியா?
Do you need a witness of what you have seen with your own eyes?

2419. கைப்புண்ணுக்குக் கண்ணாடியா?
Do you want a mirror to see a wound in your hand?

2420. கையில் இருக்க, நெய்யிலே கை இடுவானேன்.
While the stolen thing is in her hand, why should she put her hand in (hot) ghee (butter) to prove her innocence? 1957.

Putting the hand in hot oil to prove one's innocence of a crime is one of the many ordeals practiced in India. I have met with this even among Native Christians.

2421. நாடு (or ஊர்) அறிந்த பார்ப்பானுக்குப் பூணூல் என்?
Why is a sacred thread necessary to a Brahmin who is known to the whole country side (*or* village)?

What is well known need not be published.

2422. பட்டபகல்போல்.
As clear as broad daylight.

"*As clear as the sun.*"

2423. வெட்டவெளிச்சம் பட்டபகலாய்ப் போச்சுது.
It has become as clear as broad daylight.

Said of something that was hidden or unperceived before, *e. g.*, the poverty of a man who was believed to be wealthy.

DARKNESS.

இருட்டு.

2424. இருட்டுக்கு எல்லாம் சரி.

In darkness all things are alike.

" *All cats are grey in the dark.*"

" *When candles be out, all cats be grey.*"

2425. இருட்டு வேலையோ, குருட்டு வேலையோ?

Was the work done in darkness, or by a blind man?

Said of something done clumsily.

2426. திருடன் வீட்டு விளக்குபோல் எரிகிறது.

It burns like the lamp in a thief's house (*i.e.* very dimly).

2427. விளக்கில்லாத வீட்டிலே பேய் குடியிருக்கும்.

A demon will live in a house where there is no light.

Evil thrives best in darkness.

SEEKING.

TO SEARCH FOR THAT WHICH ONE ALREADY HAS.

2428. ஆட்டுக்குட்டியைத் தோளிலே வைத்துக் காடு எங்கும் தேடினது போல.

Like searching through a forest for a lamb that is on your shoulders.

" *The butcher looked for his knife when he had it in his mouth.*"

2429. உள்ளங்கையில் போட்டுப் புறங்கையை நக்கலாமா?

Why lick the back of your hand, when you have (food) in your palm?

i.e., When a man is already well off why should he seek money in dishonest ways.

2430. உள்வீட்டிலே (or தன் கொல்லையில்) கீரை வைத்துக்கொண்டு, அசல் வீட்டுக்குப் போவானேன்.

Why should he go to his neighbour's house for vegetables, when he has them in his own house (*or* garden)?

2431. உறியிலே வெண்ணெய் இருக்க, நெய்க்கு அலைவானேன்!

Why should one wander about for *ghee*, when there is butter in the hanging pot (*uri*) at home?

2432. கிணறு இருக்க மலை தோண்டாதே.
Do not dig through a mountain for a well when you have one already.

2433. கையில் காசிருக்க, கறிக்கு அலைவானேன்.
Why go wandering about seeking vegetables when you have money in your hand (to buy them)?

2434. சாதுரியப்பூனை மீன் இருக்க, புளியங்காயைத் தின்கிறதாம்.
The artful cat ate tamarind when there was fish (in the house so that the owner should leave the fish exposed without suspicion).

Said of one who pretends to be satisfied with what he has, while he is bent on getting something better.

2435. விளக்கு இருக்க, நெருப்புக்கு அலைவானேன்.
Why wander about seeking for a light while the lamp is burning.
"*He looks for his ass, and sits on its back.*"

TO SEEK FOR SOMETHING IN A WRONG PLACE.

2436. ஆனை காணாமல்போனால், குண்டுச் சட்டியில் தேடினாற்போல.
Like seeking a lost elephant in an earthen pot.
"*To seek a hare in a hen's nest.*"

2437. கடலிலே போட்டு, சாக்கடையில் தேடுகிறதா?
Why seek in a gutter for what you have thrown into the sea?

2438. குளத்தில் போட்டுக் கிணற்றில் தேடலாமா?
Why search in a well for what you have thrown into a pool?

2439. வண்ணானிடத்தில் துணியைப் போட்டுக் கொக்கின்பிறகே அலைந்தது போல.
Like wandering after a paddy-bird (to get back) a cloth sent to the washerman. 2021.

The story is that a man who had lost his clothes thought these white birds were his own white cotton garments and ran after them!

A THING SOUGHT FOR COMES TO HAND.

2440. ஆடப்போன கங்கை அண்டையில் வந்தாற்போல.
Like the Ganges which came (to meet) the bather.

2441. கும்பிடப்போன தெய்வம் குறுக்கே வந்தாப்போல.
Like the deity that came (to meet) the *guru* who worshipped him.

2442. தேடப்போன மருந்து, காலிலே தட்டினதுபோல.
Like the medicinal herb striking the foot of him who is seeking it.

MISCELLANEOUS PROVERBS ON SEEKING.

2443. ஆனை கேட்ட வாயால், ஆட்டுக்குட்டிக் கேட்கிறதா?

Will the mouth that asked for an elephant ask for a lamb? 1510, 1511, 3441.

Those who seek great things will not centre their thoughts on the insignificant.

2444. எரிந்த பசியில் இழந்த மணியைத் தேடப்போனதுபோல்.

Like seeking a lost gem to satisfy raging hunger. 2447.

To search for what is urgently needed.

2445. சந்திரன் குளிர்ச்சியாய்க் காய்ந்தாலும், சூரியனையே உலகத்தார் நாடுவார்கள்.

However much the cool moon shines, the whole world seeks the sun.

It is well to have heard the great *Rishis* (Prophets), but it is far better to have heard God himself.

2446. தட்டானிடத்தில் இருந்தால் இருக்கும், குமிட்டிச் சட்டியில் இருந்தால் இருக்கும்.

It must either be with the goldsmith or in the pot in which he melts gold.

It will be found somewhere in the house. Said to one who is in search of something that cannot be found.

2447. பசித்தவன் பழங்கணக்கைப் பார்த்ததுபோல்.

Like a hungry man looking at his old accounts. 2444.

Said of one who tries to console himself for past folly. The proverb always refers to something lost or spent carelessly.

2448. பட்டுக்கு அழுவார், பணிக்கு அழுவார் வையகத்தில், பாக்குக்கு அழுத பாரதத்தை கண்டதில்லை.

In this world people weep for silk and for jewelry, but no one has ever heard any elaborate description (*lit.* Mahâbhârata) of anyone crying for areca-nuts.

People do not trouble about little things.

2449. பரபோகந்தேடி, இகபோகம் நாடி வாழ்கை பெறவேண்டும்.

One must get happiness by seeking both heavenly and earthly enjoyment. 1196.

COURAGE, TRUE AND FALSE.

தைரியம்.

2450. ஆண் கேடு அரசு கேடு இல்லை.
Men and the sacred fig-tree are never destroyed.

In comparison with women men will persevere in their purposes and the sacred tree will send its roots deeper and deeper into the ground.

2451. ஆருக்கும் அஞ்சான், ஆர் படைக்கும் தோலான்.
He fears no one and is not defeated by any one's army.

Enterprise is the first, the second, and the third thing in commercial success.

2452. ஆள் ஆளை இடிக்கும் (or குத்தும்), ஆள் முடுக்குப் பத்துபேரை இடிக்கும்.
One man can strike another but the show of might will strike ten.

2453. உருவின வாளை உறையில் இடாத வீரன்.
A hero who does not sheath his drawn sword.

2454. எதிர்த்தவன் மாருக்கு ஆணியாயிரு.
Be a nail in the breast of your enemy.

2455. எரிகிற விளக்கானாலும், தூண்டுகோல் ஒன்று வேண்டும்.
Though the lamp burns brightly, a splinter is necessary to raise the wick.

A good man needs encouragement.

2456. ஒருத்தன் ஜோலிக்குப் போகவுமாட்டேன், என் காலை மெரித்தால் விடவுமாட்டேன்.
I will not meddle with other people's affairs, but if anyone treads on my toe I will not let him go! 2468.

2457. ஒளிக்கும் சேவகனுக்கு முகத்தில் மீசை ஏன்?
Why should a soldier who hides himself have a moustache on his face?

"*An excellent soldier: he lacks nothing but a heart and a feather.*"

2458. கடலைத் தூர்த்தும் காரியம் முடிக்கவேண்டும்.
Though you have to fill up the sea, complete your work.

2459. சாகத் துணிந்தவனுக்குச் சமுத்திரம் முழங்கால் ஆழம்.
To a man who dares to die, the sea is only knee-deep.

2460. சுத்த வீரனுக்கு உயிர் துரும்பு.
To a perfect hero life is but a straw.

"*A stout heart crushes ill-luck.*"

2461. சூரனுக்குத் துரைமக்கள் துரும்பு.
Princes are only straw before a hero.

2462. ஜெயமுள்ளமட்டும் பயமில்லை.
There is no fear as long as there is victory.

2462a. திக்கு விஜெயம் கொள்பவனுக்கு ஜெய அபஜெயக் காலம் தெரியாது.
He who is bent on conquering the whole world knows not times of victory or of defeat.
All times are alike to brave men.

2463. தைரிய லக்ஷ்மி, தன லக்ஷ்மி.
The goddess of bravery is the goddess of wealth.
"*Faint heart never won fair lady.*"
"*Nought venture, nought win.*"

2464. பகுத்தறிவில்லாத துணிவு பாரமில்லாத கப்பல்.
Bravery without discernment is like a ship without cargo.

2465. பக்கச்சொல் பதினாயிரம்.
A word of encouragement is worth ten thousand (coins).

2466. முசலை எழுப்பிவிட்டு நாய் பதுங்கினதுபோல்.
Like the dog, that started the hare and then stopped. 2469.
Sham valour.

2467. முன்வைத்த கால், பின்வைக்கமாட்டேன்.
I will not withdraw the foot I have put forward.

2468. வலிய சண்டைக்குப் போகிறதுமில்லை, வந்த சண்டையை விடுகிறது மில்லை.
There is no seeking for quarrels but there is no slackness in quarrels that arise. 2456, 3086, 3099.
Said of a quiet man who knows how to bear himself well if quarrels arise.

2469. விருது கூறிவந்து, செடியிலே நுழைகிறதுபோல்.
Like creeping into a bush after proclaiming your valour. 2466.

2470. வைத்தியன் தலைமாட்டிலிருந்து அழுததுபோல.
Like the doctor weeping at the head of the bed.

FEAR AND COWARDICE.

பயம், கிலி.

2471. அஞ்சினவன் கண்ணுக்கு ஆகாசம் எல்லாம் பேய்.
To the eye of the coward the sky is full of devils. 2491, 2492.

2472. அஞ்சினவனைப் பேய் அடிக்கும்.
A devil will strike a coward.

2473. அஞ்சினவனைக் குஞ்சும் வெருட்டும்.
Even a young bird may terrify a coward.

2474. அடி வயிற்றில் இடி விழுந்தாப்போல.

As if lightening struck the lower part of his stomach.

Description of sudden terror.

2475. ஆடு கடிக்கிறது என்று இடையன் உறி ஏறிப் பதுங்கினதுபோல.

Like the shepherd saying that the sheep would bite him, and climbing into a pot hanging from the roof (*uri*) and hiding himself.

" *The worst ills are those that never happen.*"

2476. ஆயிரம் காக்கைக்கு ஒரு கல்லே போதும்.

One stone will frighten a thousand crows.

It is easy to frighten cowards.

2477. ஆறுமாசப் பிரயாணம் (or பயணம்) அஞ்சி நடந்தால் முடியுமா?

Will a person who walks in fear ever accomplish a six month's journey?

" *He that dares not venture must not complain of ill luck.*"

2478. இடி ஓசை கேட்ட பாம்புபோல்.

Like the snake that heard the sound of thunder.

2479. உங்கள் அப்பன் பூச்சிக்குப் பயப்பட்டேனு? உன் பூச்சிக்குப் பயப் பட.

Did I fear the threats of your father? Shall I fear your threats? 493.

2480. எலியைக் கண்டு பூனை ஏக்கம் அடையுமா?

Will a cat be alarmed at seeing a rat? 2561, 3064.

2481. கட்டிப் பீ எல்லாம் தண்ணீர்ப் பீ ஆச்சுது.

His constipation became diarrhoea. 2492*a*.

2482. கண்டது பாம்பு, கடித்தது மாங்கொட்டை.

What bit him was the kernel of a mango and what he saw was a snake.

After the mangoes are eaten the kernels are thrown away. These are sometimes two inches long. When lying about and dried up, some of them open at one end, and fancy may make them resemble a snake's mouth. Should a man strike his toe against one of them, and at the same time see a snake, the conclusion that the snake bit him is easily drawn. Fear has a great deal to do with the number of deaths which are recorded as the results of the bites of snakes in India. A case occurred in 1896 in South India when an educated Native Christian gentleman died, as his medical attendant declared, almost entirely because he was overcome with terror though the snake that bit him was not venomous. 2489.

Also:—பாம்பு கடித்ததோ, மாங்கொட்டை கடித்ததோ?

Did a snake or a mango kernel bite him? 2486, 2491, 2670.

2483. கயிற்றைப் பாம்பு என்று எண்ணிக் கலங்கினதுபோல்.

Like taking a rope for a snake and trembling.

A common example of *Mâyâ*, Illusion, in the Vedânta philosophy.

2484. கரடிகையில் உதைப்பட்டவனுக்குக் கம்பளிக்காரனைக் கண்டால் பயம்.

If he who was once struck by the paw of a bear sees a person wrapped up in a (hairy) blanket he will be frightened.

This proverb sometimes occurs with other phrasing, but always contains the same simile.

2485. கருடனைக் கண்ட பாம்புபோல.

Like a snake that sees a kite.

Sudden fear. Kites are great enemies of small snakes.

2486. கிலி பிடித்ததோ, புலி பிடித்ததோ?

Did fear or a tiger lay hold of you? 2482.

"*A man surprised is half beaten.*"

2487. குளிர் விட்டுப்போச்சுது.

The shivering has left him.

Said of servants or wives who are forward.

2488. நாயைக் கண்டோ நான் காயம் கூட்டுகிறது.

Was it after seeing the dog that I mixed the assafœtida?

e.g. You think I treat my wife (*or* anyone else) kindly because some one makes me, but I do so because I like to do so.

2489. பாம்பு என்றால், படையும் நடுங்கும்.

The word "snake" will make even an army tremble. 2482.

2490. புலிக்குப் பயப்பட்டவர்கள் எல்லாம் வந்து என்பேரில் படுத்துக்கொள்ளுங்கள்.

All of you who are afraid of the tiger come and lie on the top of me!

Said of one who gets into the safest place when danger comes.

2491. மனப் பேயே ஒழிய, மற்றப் பேய் இல்லை.

Except imaginary devils there are no others. 2471.

2492. மிரண்டவன் கண்ணுக்கு இருண்டதெல்லாம் பேய்.

To a coward every dark thing is a devil. 2471.

"*Foolish fear doubleth danger.*"

2492*a*. பேச்சுப் பேசும்போதே, பீச்சிப் புடவையில் கட்டிக்கொள்ளுகிறாள்.

She is so timid that she gets diarrhoea at the mere mention (of something dreadful). 2481.

"NEW BROOMS SWEEP CLEAN!"

புதியது.

2493. ஆரம்பத்தில் சூரத்துவம்.

Heroism at the beginning.

2494. புதிய வண்ணான் பொந்துகட்டி வெளுப்பான்.

A new washerman will knot up the cloth before he washes it.

The common cotton cloths often have silk ends and edges. These would be damaged if they were boiled along with the rest of the garment, and ought to be knotted up in another piece of cloth so as not to be injured. A new washerman will do this very carefully because he wishes to get the praise of his customer.

2495. புதிதாய் வந்த மணியக்காரன் நெருப்பாயிருக்கிறான்.

The new village officer is all fire. 336.

2496. புதுப்பெண்ணே, புதுப்பெண்ணே நெருப்பு எடுத்துவா! உனக்குப் பின்னாலே இருக்கிறது செருப்பு அடி.

O new girl, bring fire! in future you will be beaten with a slipper!

Said to a servant who rejoices over good treatment received from a new master not knowing that it will not last.—Or a mother-in-law says the first part to her daughter-in-law and the latter thinks the second part.

2497. வந்தாற்போல் சிறுக்கி பந்து அடித்தாள், வர வரச் சிறுக்கி நொண்டிப் போனாள்.

In the beginning the girl played at ball but she became lame by degrees.

Said of one who begins an enterprise with much zeal, but soon wearies of it.

"*He that doth most at once, doth least.*"

2498. வந்தாற்போல் மாமி பந்து அடித்தாள், வர வர மாமி கழுதை மேய்க்கிறாள்.

When the daughter-in-law came to her husband's house her mother-in-law played at ball but by and by the mother-in-law herded asses.

The daughter-in-law found her mother-in-law pleasant at first but her true nature soon came out. Said of one who professes sorrow for wrong doing but soon forgets his repentance.

THE TONGUE.

நாக்கு.

2499. உடல் ஒருவனுக்குப் பிறந்தது, நாக்கு பலருக்குப் பிறந்தது.

One's body was born for one's own benefit, but one's tongue for (the benefit *or* ruin) of many.

"*Birds are entangled by their feet, and men by their tongues.*"

2500. உடும்புக்கு இரண்டு நாக்கு, உனக்கும் இரண்டு நாக்கா?

The iguana has two tongues, have you also two?

"*A sinner that hath a double tongue.*" Ecclesiasticus 6, 1.

2501. எதை அடக்காவிட்டாலும் நாக்கை அடக்கவேண்டும்.

Whatever else you do not subdue, subdue your tongue! 1511.

"*A bridle for the tongue is a necessary piece of furniture.*"

"*Put to your tongue a bridle, that it talks not idle.*"

2502. எலும்பில்லா நாக்கு எல்லாம் பேசும்.

A tongue that has no bones says everything.

"*The tongue breaketh bone, and itself hath none.*"

2503. நடக்கும் கால் தவறுகிறதிலும், நாக்கு தவறுகிறது கெட்டது.

A slip of the tongue is worse than a slip of the foot that walks. 212.

"*Better a slip of the foot than of the tongue.*"

2504. நாவு அசைய, நாடு அசையும்.

If the tongue move, the country will move.

"*A good tongue is a good weapon.*" Or, this phrase may mean:— "*A tyrant's breath is another's death.*"

2505. நாக்குக்கு எலும்பில்லை.

There are no bones in the tongue. 2145.

"*Your tongue is made of very loose leather.*"

"*He lies as fast as a dog can trot.*"

2506. பேசப்போனாயோ, சாகப்போனாயோ?

Did you go to speak or to die? 718, 2907.

Take care what you say; the mouth may say things that lead to ruin.

"*A fool's tongue is long enough to cut his own throat.*"

"*A word and a stone once let go cannot be recalled.*"

"*Rule thy word while thou art young, for life and death lie in thy tongue.*"

Cf. 2684 *ff.*

DOCTORS, MEDICINE, HEALING.

வைத்தியன், மருந்து, சௌஷதம்.

2507. அனுபோகம் தொலைந்தால், அவிழ்தம் பலிக்கும்.
When I have experienced my appointed lot the medicine will take effect.

Said by a sick man. All Tamils believe that fate has allotted a certain amount of suffering to a man which he must endure.

2508. ஆயிரம்பேரைக் கொன்றவன் அரை வைத்தியன்.
He who has killed a thousand people is half a doctor. 2518.

2509. ஆனை கொழுத்தால் வாழைத்தண்டு, ஆண்பிள்ளை கொழுத்தால் கீரைத்தண்டு.
If an elephant becomes fat, give it the inside of the banana tree to eat; if a man become fat, give him the stalk of a (big) vegetable.

2510. இலங்கனம் பரம ஔஷதம்.
When sick, fasting is the supreme remedy.
"*Diet cures more than the lancet.*"
"*Feed sparingly and defy the physician.*"
"*The best physicians are Dr. Diet, Dr. Quiet and Dr. Merryman.*"

2511. ஊழிக் (or விடா) காய்ச்சல் அதிகமானால், சூனியக்காரன் கொள்ளை.
Much chronic fever (among the people) will be spoil to the sorcerer.

2512. எருதின் புண்ணுக்குச் சாம்பல் மருந்து.
Ashes are the medicine for the wound of a bullock. 1747, 1770, 3371.

The poor can neither afford to call in a doctor nor to spend time away from their work.

2513. கட்டைப்பாறையை முழுங்கிப்போட்டு (prop. விழுங்கி), சுக்கு கஷாயம் குடித்தால் தீருமா?
If one swallows a crowbar and takes ginger as medicine, will he be cured? 2249.

Great evils will not yield to small remedies.
"*He who will not bear the itch must endure the smart.*"

2514. கால்மாடு தலைமாடு வைத்தியன் வந்தான்.
The doctor that offered to bear to the cemetery the head-side and not the foot-side of the patient he had killed is come.

Said of one who does not understand his occupation.

2515. கூரைக்காய் வைத்தியம், (or சில்லறை வைத்தியம், or பெண்டுகள் வைத்தியம்).
Vegetable medicines (*or* Little medicines *or* Women's medicines). 2523.

Different terms for 'domestic medicines.'

2516. *தாது (or நாடி) அறியாத பேதை வைத்தியன்.*
A simpleton of a doctor who does not understand the pulse.

2517. *நோவு ஒன்று இருக்க, மருந்து ஒன்று கொடுத்தது.*
The disease is one thing and giving medicine is another. 2148.
This proverb is also used generally; *e.g.* a young Hindu wife often wishes to go home to her mother, and to prevent her from doing so her husband buys fruits, sweets and even jewels and gives them to her but without result.

2518. *பழம் புண்ணாளி பாதி வைத்தியன்.*
He who has had many sores is half a surgeon. 2508.
Experience is as important as skill.

2519. *பிறக்கிறபொழுதே முடமானால், தெய்வத்துக்குப் படைத்தால் தீருமா?*
If one is born a cripple, will healing come by making an offering to a God?

2520. *பொல்லாத குணத்துக்கு மருந்து உண்டோ?*
Is there any remedy that will cure an evil disposition? 964, 544 *ff*; 2521.

2521. *மனோவியாதிக்கு மருந்து உண்டா?*
Is there any remedy for the sickness of the heart? 964, 2520.

2522. *வெள்ளை கொடுத்தால் வினை தீரும், பச்சை கொடுத்தால் பாவம் தீரும்?*
If you offer silver (money) the effects of sins you committed in a former birth will be removed; if you offer betel your present sin will go.
A doctor says this to his patient meaning that he can effect a cure for money.

2523. *வைத்தியன் மருந்துக்குக் கைமருந்து நல்லது.*
Domestic medicines are preferable to doctors' medicines. 2515.

ON RAIN.

மழை.

2524. *ஆய்ச்சலாய்ச்சலாய் மழை பெய்கிறது.*
It rains shower after shower.

2525. *ஈசெல் பறந்தால் மழை.*
When white ants swarm, it will rain.

2526. *எறும்பு முட்டை கொண்டு, திட்டை எறினால் மழை பெய்யும்.*
If ants remove their eggs, and ascend a hillock (with them), rain is coming.
Ants do this in order to save their eggs from the effects of rain.

2527. ஐப்பசிக்கும் (or அற்பசிக்கும்) கார்த்திகைக்கும் மழை பெய்யாவிட்டால், அண்ணனுக்கும் சரி, தம்பிக்கும் சரி.

If there is no rain in October and November the elder brother and the younger brother will be alike. 1742.

The 'elder brother' is the upper lip; the 'younger brother' is the lower lip, and the whole proverb means that the mouth will have no work if the rain does not come in the rainy season.

2528. கார்த்திகை மாசத்து மழை கலம் கழுவுகிறதற்குள்ளே வந்துபோகும்.

The rain of November comes and goes while a pot is being washed.

In this month it rains frequently.

2529. கார்த்திகை மாசத்தில் கடுமழை பெய்தால், கல்லின்கீழ் இருக்கிற புல்லும் கதிர்விடும்.

If it rain well in November even the grass under the stones will shoot.

THE ESSENTIAL:

OR, THAT WHICH IS THE MOST IMPORTANT IN A TRANSACTION.

முக்கியமான காரியம்.

2530. அடி என்று அழைக்கப் பெண்சாதியில்லை, பிள்ளை எத்தனை, பெண் எத்தனை என்கிறான்.

I have not got a wife to call me "my dear," and yet he asks me how many sons and daughters I have?

Do not ask for the result of a work before the work has commenced.

2530*a*. அம்மை குத்தினாலும், பொம்மை குத்தினாலும் வேண்டியது அரிசி.

Whether a woman or a puppet pound the rice is of no consequence, if only we get rice (to eat). 2535.

2531. ஆரியக் கூத்தாடினாலும், காரியத்தில் கண்ணாயிரு.

Though they are dancing ever so cleverly, keep your eye on your own affairs. 2545.

"*To have an eye on the main chance.*"

2532. ஆர் குத்தினாலும் அரிசியானால் சரி.

It does not matter who pounds the rice so long as the husks are got off.

2533. உட்சுவர் இருக்க, புறச்சுவர் பூசலாமா?

Is it right to neglect the inner and to whitewash the outer wall?

Outward morality and inward depravity. Also an advice to regard the welfare of one's own family before taking thought for that of strangers.

2534. எல்லாம் இருக்கிறது பெட்டியிலே, இலைக்கறி கடையச் சட்டியில்லை.
We have everything needed in the box, but we have no pot in which to mash the vegetables.

Said when the essential is absent, though all sorts of unnecessary things abound; also said of vain excuses.

2534a. எல்லாம் தெரிந்த நாரி, திரிட்டி ஏற்று அடி விளக்கை.
O woman, you know everything, trim the wick and light the lamp.

A thief went into a house at night to steal; the woman in the house heard him, and got up. She tried to light the lamp, but as she had not trimmed the wick, it took her such a time that the thief finished his business, and while running away uttered this saying, which is now used of a person who in spite of his cleverness forgets what is essential to the accomplishment of his purpose.

2535. ஓட்டை (or மூளி) சட்டியானாலும், கொழுக்கட்டை வேகிறது ஒன்று.
Though the pan may be a cracked one it does not matter so long as the cakes are fried. 2548.

"*All's well, that ends well.*"

2536. கலியாணச் சந்தடியில் தாலி கட்ட மறந்தாற்போல.
As if they had forgotten to tie the *thâli* in the bustle of the wedding!

2537. கோணல் கோணல் கோவிந்தா.
Though everything is crooked. God will put all right. 832, 3317.

Now said with the meaning that it is not present circumstances but the end attained that is important.

2538. சங்கு ஊதாமல், தாலி கட்டுவது உண்டா?
Can the *thâli* be tied without the blowing of the conch? 2536.

The blowing of a conch celebrates this part of a Hindu wedding.

2539. சுக்கு அறியாத கஷாயம் உண்டா?
Is there any decoction without dry ginger in it?

2540. சுண்ணாம்பிலே இருக்கிறது சூக்ஷம்.
(In chewing betel leaves) the essential thing is the lime.

Betel leaves are chewed with areca nut and lime.

2541. சுவரை வைத்துக்கொண்டு அல்லவோ சித்திரம் எழுதவேண்டும்.
Build the wall first, and then draw the pictures on it.

Sometimes used in an obscene sense.

2542. செட்டி முடுக்கோ, சரக்கு முடுக்கோ?
Which is the more important, the merchant or his wares?

2543. தலை சுற்றிக் கவளம் வாயில்தான் வரவேண்டும்.
Though you pass your handful of rice round your head it must come to your mouth at last. 2549.

Said of one in a family who has run away from home on account of quarrels or for some other reason; he is sure at some time to return home.—Or, an old servant may say this when dismissed, meaning that he is sure he will be re-engaged.

2544. துட்டு வந்து பெட்டியிலே விழுந்ததோ, திட்டு வந்து பெட்டியிலே விழுந்ததோ?

Did the money I earned or the abuse I got go into my money box?

Why care for a little abuse, the chief thing is to get money.

"*Account not that work-slavery that brings in penny savory.*"

2545. தூண்டில் போட்டவனுக்குத் தக்கை (or மெதப்பு) மேல் கண்.

The fisherman keeps his eyes on the float. 2531.

2546. பருப்பு இல்லாத கலியாணம் உண்டா?

Is there a wedding (feast) in which there is no pulse?

i.e., We could not possibly celebrate our festival without your presence. Said either as a sneer or in earnest.

2547. பொன் அகப்பட்டால் பொன் முடிய துணி அகப்படாதா?

If one gets gold, won't one find a bit of cloth to tie it in? 1232.

2548. மண் பூனையானாலும், எலி பிடித்தால் சரி.

Though the cat be made of clay, it is all right, if it catch rats. 2535.

2549. மலையில் விளைந்தாலும், உரலில்தான் மசியவேண்டும்.

Though (the grain) grew on the hills, it must be bruised in a mortar (at home). 2543, 3435.

E.g., Though a girl is born in a rich family, if she marries into a poor family she must submit to her lot.

2550. மாவு உண்டானால், பணிகாரம் சுடலாம்.

If you have flour, you will be able to make cakes.

2551. மாவு மறந்த கூழுக்கு உப்பு ஒரு கேடா? (or குறையா?)

Is the omission of salt the chief defect in gruel made without flour?

This proverb has many applications. *E.g.*, If a woman dressed in rags expresses a desire for some fine jewelry this may be said to her.

2552. வட்டுவத்தின்மேல் சொட்டுப்போட்டால், வட்டுவத்துக்கு மாத்திரமா படும்?

If you knock the bag (in which betel and other things are kept) will the bag only suffer? (Every thing inside will be bruised).

If the head of a family suffers in any way, all the family will suffer. 1 Cor. 12, 26; Matt. 10, 25.

THE IMPROBABLE AND IMPOSSIBLE.

முடியாத காரியம்.

2553. அடங்கின பிடி பிடிக்கவேண்டும், அடங்காத பிடி பிடிக்கப்பார்க்காதே.
Grasp what you can reach, and do not try to grasp what is beyond your reach.
"*He that takes too great a leap falls into the ditch.*"

2554. அதிக்கிரமமான ஊரில் கொதிக்கிற மீனும் சிரிக்குமாம்.
Even a fish that is being boiled laughs in a very wicked village.
Said to one who relates something very doubtful.

2555. ஆகாசத்தைப் பருந்து எடுத்துக்கொண்டுபோமா?
Can a kite fly away with the sky? 2558.
"*That is as likely as to see a hog fly.*"

2556. ஆகாசத்தை வடுப்படக் கடிக்கிறதா?
Can you bite the sky so as to leave a scar in it? 1567.
"*He is teaching iron to swim.*"

2557. ஆகாசத்துக்கு மையம் காட்டுகிறதா?
Can you point out the middle of the sky?

2559. ஊதுகிற சங்கு ஊதினால், விடிகிற பொழுது விடிகிறதா?
Will the dawn come at the blowing of the conch? 1573.
Human efforts cannot change natural laws. Do what you have to do and leave the rest to God.

2560. ஊமை பிரசங்கம்பண்ண, செவிடன் கேட்டதுபோல.
Like a dumb man preaching and a deaf man listening.
"*He holds a looking-glass to a mole.*"

2561. எலி பூனையை வெல்லுமா?
Can a rat conquer a cat? 2480.
"*Can a mouse fall in love with a cat?*"

2562. ஏணியைத் தள்ளிப் பரண்மேல் ஏறலாமா?
Can you get up to a loft (*paran*), if you push the ladder aside?
Paran may also be the platform on which watchmen sit in the fields at night to guard the crops from thieves.

2563. ஏறுமடைக்கு நீர் பாய்ச்சுகிறதுபோல.
Like conducting water into channels that are above its level. 531.
It is useless to give advice to a fool.

2564. காய்ந்த மரம் தளிர்க்குமா?
Can a withered tree sprout again? 2570.

2565. *கைம்பெண்சாதி தாலியைக் கூழைக்கையன் அறுத்தானும்.*
The man whose hands had been cut off, cut off the *thâli* of a widow. 2567.

As he had no hands, he could not do it, and a widow wears no *thâli*. Said about an improbable story.

2566. *சமுத்திரத்திலே ஏற்றம் போட்டதுபோல.*
Like erecting water-lifts (to draw the water) out of the sea.

" *He is building a bridge over the sea.*"

2567. *சாத்தானி குடுமிக்கும், சந்நியாசி பூணூலுக்கும் முடிபோடு.*
Tie a knot on the *Sâttâni's* tuft of hair and on the ascetic's holy thread. 1816, 2565.

The *Sâttâni* shave the whole head and the *sannyâsi* have no sacred thread. The *Sâttâni* are a low Vaishnava caste of flower gatherers, mendicants and minstrels.

2568. *திருப்பதியில் மொட்டைத்தாதனைக் கண்டாயா?*
Have you seen the bald-headed Vaishnava mendicant at Tripaty?

As these mendicants are found there by hundreds it is impossible to distinguish a particular one.

2569. *மலடியைப் பிள்ளை பெறச்சொன்னால் பெறுவாளா?*
Can a barren woman give birth to a child if you tell her to do so?

Said to one who demands the impossible.

2570. *வறுத்த பயறு முளைத்தாப்போல.*
Like parched pulse germinating. 2564.

SECRETS.

ON KEEPING SECRETS.

இரகசியம், ஒளிப்பு.

2571. *இது பெரிய இடத்துப் பேச்சு.*
This is talk about high places.

This may be said by a servant, who is asked the secrets of the family he serves, meaning that he intends to keep what he knows to himself.

" *It is wise not to seek a secret, and honest not to reveal it.*"

2572. *இலை மறைவு காய் மறைவு வேண்டாமா?*
Should not the leaves give shade to the fruit? 1726, 1728, 3158.

Everything that goes on in a family does not concern the public.

" *Thy secret is thy prisoner.*"

" *To tell our secrets is folly; to divulge the secrets of others is treachery.*"

2573. உள்ளுக்குள்ளே கொட்டின தேளே, ஒரு மந்திரம் சொல்லுகிறேன், கேளே.

The scorpion has stung a private part; I will say an incantation (to cure it). Listen!

Said when something scandalous or unpleasant happens in a family which must be kept secret. 3207.

2574. ஒருவன் அறிந்தால் ரகசியம், இரண்டுபேர் அறிந்தால் அம்பலம்.

If only one person knows it, it is a secret; if two know it, it is public.

"*Three may keep counsel, if two be away.*"

2575. கடலிலே துரும்பு கிடந்தாலும், மனதிலே ஒரு சொல் கிடவாது.

Though a little straw may remain on the sea, a secret will not remain in the heart.

2576. கடித்த வாய் துடைத்தாற்போல்.

Like wiping your mouth after eating anything obnoxious to others.

This act is done quickly and is unnoticed. In communicating a secret the communication should be brief so as to be unnoticed by others.

2577. காதும் காதும் வைத்தாற்போல, வைக்கவேண்டும்.

Keep it (as a secret) between my ear and yours.

"*Two eyes, two ears, only one mouth.*"

2578. கிணற்றிலே கல் போட்டதுபோல்.

Like throwing a stone into a well.

Telling secrets to one who knows how to keep them.

2579. கூட்டத்தில் கட்டுச்சோறு அவிழ்த்தாற்போல.

Like untying the food prepared for a journey in a public gathering.

No Hindu likes his food to be seen by persons of other castes.

2580. சாராயத்தை வார்த்துப் பூராயத்தைக் கேள்.

Give him intoxicating drink, and then hear the secrets of his mind.

"*When ale is in, wit is out.*"

2581. சின்ன வீட்டுச் சேதி அம்பலத்திலே வரும் (or சீமந்தத்திலே தெரியும்).

What takes place inside the bed-room will reach the public, (*or* will be known when the *Seemantha* ceremony is performed after the conception of the child). 2589 *ff*.

2582. தண்ணீர் கீழ் குசு விட்டால், தலைக்குமேல்.

All bad secrets will come out.

This proverb is too vulgar to be literally translated. 1421.

2583. தொடையில் புண்ணை நடையில் காட்டுகிறதா?

Should you show a wound on your thigh when walking about?

Keep your secrets to yourself.

2583*a*. நாலு பேருக்குச் சொல்லி, மனதிலே போட்டு வைக்கிறவன்.
He is a person who keeps secrets in his heart after having told them to four persons.
Said sarcastically of one who cannot keep secrets.

2584. நெல்லுக்குள்ளே அரிசி.
There is rice within the husk.
A truth uttered to one who is overanxious to get a secret out of you.

2585. பகலில் பக்கம் பார்த்துப் பேசவேண்டும், ராத்திரியில் அதுதானும் பேசவேண்டாம்.
At day-time one should look round before speaking, at night one should not speak even after taking that precaution. 1324.
"*Hills see, walls hear.*"

2586. பீ தின்னும் வாய் துடைத்ததுபோல.
Like wiping a mouth that has eaten filth.
Seek to hide your faults quickly.

2587. மனதில் இருக்கும் ரகசியம் மதிகேடனுக்கு வாயிலே.
The secrets of a fool's heart will be on his lips.

2588. மூடிவைத்தாலும் முணு முணு என்னும், தைத்து வைத்தாலும் டம டம என்னும்.
Though I cover it up, they whisper; though I stitch it together, they will announce it by beating a drum. 1845, 2805.
Used of secrets which one part of a family desires to keep from the other, but which get out.

Cf. 2589 *ff.*

SECRETS OR TRUTH WILL COME OUT AT LAST.

2589. ஆர் ஆத்தாள் செத்ததும், பொழுது விடிந்தால் தெரியும்.
When it dawns, it will be known whose mother is dead. 2581.
Said by a man to his wife at whose instigation he had agreed to kill his own mother. His own mother and his wife's mother slept together, and the wife's mother was murdered instead of the husband's, with the latter's knowledge. The wife, having an inkling of the truth, endeavoured to persuade her husband to go and see which of the two they had spared, and he replied as above. (CAPTAIN CARR'S *Telugu Proverbs.*)
"*Truth is the daughter of time.*"

2590. என் குடி கெட்டதும், உன் குடி கெட்டதும், பொழுது விடிந்தால் தெரியும்.
Whether my household or thine is ruined will be known at daybreak.
"*What is done by night, appears by day.*"

2591. *செத்தால் தெரியும், செட்டியார்* (or *சீமாட்டி*) *வாழ்வு.*
When the Chetty (merchant) dies, his affairs will become public.

2592. *நீள நீள* (or *போகப் போக* or *வர வர*) *தெரியும் மெய்யும் பொய்யும்.*
What is true and what is false will be understood as time goes on.

2593. *மூன்றும் கட்டு அவிழ்த்தால் தெரியும்.*
On untying the third knot we shall know (his character).

A man always wears a thread round his waist, and as soon as he is dead the thumbs of his two hands, and great toes of his two feet are also tied together, and the three knots are cut by the relatives when the corpse is to be buried or burnt. The proverb means that a man's real character will be known after his death.

2594. *விடிந்தால் தெரியும் மாப்பிள்ளைக் குருடும், பெண் குருடும்.*
The dawn will reveal the bridegroom's and the bride's blindness.

" *Truth will out at last.*"

Cf. 2571 *ff.*

GROWTH, PROGRESS, DECAY.

சீர், விர்த்தி.

2595. *அறுகம் கட்டைபோல அடி வேர் துளிர்க்கிறது* (com. *துளுக்கிறது*).
It will spread out its roots like the *aruga* grass. 1508.

2596. *ஆமை புகுந்த வீடும், அமினா நுழைந்த வீடும் உருப்படாது.*
A house in which a tortoise has entered (a bad omen), and a house in which officials have entered (to take the taxes that people have neglected to pay) will not prosper.

2597. *எழுதுகிறது பெரிதல்ல, இன்னம் அறிந்து சேர்க்கிறது பெரிது.*
It is no great thing to be able to write; developing the knowledge that has been acquired is the great thing.

2598. *காலாலே நடந்தால் காத வழி, தலையாலே நடந்தால் எவ்வளவு தூரம்?*
If you walk on your legs you can walk ten miles; but how much progress will you make if you walk on your head?

2599. *கெட்டான் வாழ்ந்தால் கிளை கிளையாய்த் துளிர்ப்பான், வாழ்ந்தான் கெட்டால் வறையோட்டுக்கும் ஆகான்.*
If he who was ruined begins to prosper, he will put forth branch after branch; but if he who prospered is ruined, he is not worth a potsherd. 569.

2600. *கெட்டுக் கெட்டுக் குடி ஆகிறதா?*
Will a family that is constantly ruined continue to exist?

2601. தீராச் செய்கை சீராகாது.

If what ought to be done is not accomplished, there is no prosperity.

2602. வடகோடு உயர்ந்து என்ன, தென்கோடு சாய்ந்து என்ன, வளர் பிறைக்கே.

What does it matter whether the Northern cusp of the new moon point upward and the Southern point downward; in either case it is the waxing new moon. 3124.

2603. நல்ல எழுத்து நடுவே இருக்க, கோணல் எழுத்து குறுக்கே வந்தது.

While there was a good letter (*i.e.* good luck) in the midst, a crooked letter, (*i.e.* ill luck) came across it.

e. g. A family was living prosperously but the folly or crime of one of its members brought shame or disgrace on it.

2604. பண்ணைப் பூ (or பாவட்டம்) ப் போல நரைத்தும், புத்தியில்லை.

Though your hair is as white as the *celosia*-flower, you have no sense.

"*The head grey, and no brains yet.*"

"AS YE WOULD THAT MEN SHOULD DO TO YOU, DO YE ALSO TO THEM LIKEWISE."

2605. அளந்த நாழிகொண்டு அளப்பான்.

He will give back according to the measure he received from you. 2612.

"*What bread men break is broken to them again.*"

2606. ஆமணக்கு விதைத்தால், ஆச்சா முளைக்குமா?

If you sow castor seed, will ebony grow up? 2872.

As is the cause, so is the effect.

2607. இருக்கிறவன் செவ்வையாயிருந்தால், சிரைக்கிறவன் செவ்வையாய்ச் செய்வான்.

If the person (who is being shaved) sit properly, the barber will shave him properly.

2608. ஊதினால் போகும், உறிஞ்சினால் வரும்.

If blown it will fly off, if sucked it will come near.

If you are unkind to people, they will desert you; if you are kind they will associate with you.

"*As you salute, you will be saluted.*"

2609. பண்ணின பயிரில் அல்லவா புண்ணியம் தெரியும்.

Is it not through the crop the worth is known of those who cultivate?

A virtuous man will get a good wife; he will have good children; his fields will yield rich crops. The converse of 2987 ff; 3308, 3573, 3576.

"*The tree is known by its fruits.*"

"*If virtue keep court within, honour will attend without.*"

2610. பால் தொட்டுப் பால் கறக்கவேண்டும்.
You must touch (the udder) with milk, to draw the milk.
" *Love to be loved.*"—" *As you give, so you will get.*"

2611. மாவு இருக்கிற மணத்தைப்போல, கூழில் இருக்கும் குணம்.
As the savour of the flour is, so will the nature of the gruel be. 2297.

As you are, so you will be treated.—As the tree, so its fruits.—If a daughter-in-law complains to her husband, that his mother ill-treats her, and the husband knows his wife to be a quarrelsome woman, he may quote this proverb. While 2613 has a general application, this is limited to the family or household and always refers to the inner disposition.

2612. முன் அளந்த நாழி பின் அளக்குமே.
As you measure unto others, so will it be measured to you. 2605.
" *As you sow, so you shall reap.*"

2613. முன் கை நீண்டால், முழங்கை நீளும்.
If you stretch out your hand, others will stretch out the arm. 2611.
" *One never loses by doing a good turn.*"

2614. வணங்கின முள் தைக்கும்.
The thorn that bends will pierce.

If you are proud and take airs, you will have no friends. Humility often gains more than pride.—If a child shows more love to its father than to its mother, and the mother feels a little jealous, and makes remarks about it to the father, he may answer by quoting this proverb.

2615. வாய் நல்லதானால், ஊர் நல்லது.
If your mouth is good, the village will be good. 1819.
If you speak kindly to others, you will receive kindness from others.

Or ஊர் நல்லதோ. வாய் நல்லதோ?
Is the village good, or is your mouth good?
" *To him that soweth righteousness shall be a sure reward.*" Proverbs. 11, 18.
" *He that any good will win, at his mouth must first begin.*"
" *Good language cures great sores.*"

Cf. 197 *ff.* 2259 *ff.*

VAIN EXERTION.

வீண், விருதா.

2616. ஆற்றிலே கரைத்த புளிபோல.
Like dissolving tamarind in a river. 2620.

Useless waste. The tamarind will not affect the taste of the volume of water found in a river.

2617. உமியைக் குத்தி கை சலித்ததுபோல.
Like wearying one's arm with pounding chaff. 2622.
" *To beat the air.*"

2618. எருமை மாட்டின்மேல் மழை பெய்ததுபோல.
Like rain on a buffalo.
"*Like pouring water on a duck's back.*"

2619. ஓட்டைப் பானையில் விட்ட தண்ணீர்போல்.
Like pouring water into a cracked pot. 2626.
"*All is lost that is put into a riven dish.*"
"*Torn sacks will hold no corn.*"

2620. கடலில் பெருங்காயம் கரைத்ததுபோல்.
Like dissolving assafœtida in the sea. 2616.

2621. கமரில் ஊற்றின பால்.
It is milk poured into a crevice in the dry soil. 357.

2622. கலம் பதரைக் குத்தினாலும், அரிசி ஆகாது.
Though you pound a big quantity of husks, you will not get rice-flour. 2617.
The converse of 1803.
"*You cannot get blood out of a stone.*"

2623. காட்டிலே எறிந்த நிலா (நெலா com.)
Moonshine thrown on a forest.

2624. (*a*) குடத்தில் ஏற்றின விளக்கு (*b*) விளக்கு ஏற்றிக் கூடையால் மறைக்கிறது.
(*a*) A lighted lamp in a pot. (*b*) Lighting a lamp and covering it with a basket. Matt. 5, 15.—1593.

2625. கோழிமுட்டைக்கு மயிர் பிடுங்கிறது.
Plucking the feathers off a hen's egg. 2629.
Said about a lazy person or about one who spends his time uselessly. This has also an obscene meaning and should not be quoted.

2626. புதுக் குடத்தில் வார்த்த தண்ணீர்போல்.
Like pouring water into a new earthen pot. 2619.
The water will percolate through the sides of the pot and be lost. Don't speak confidentially with strangers.

2627. வீணுக்கு உழைக்கிறவன் வீணன்.
He who spends his energy in useless work is a nonentity.
"*He is teaching a pig to play on a flute.*"

2628. விழலுக்கு இறைத்த நீர்போல.
Like irrigating useless grass.

2629. வேலை யில்லாக்கெட்ட அம்பட்டன் தன் மகளை (or பூனையை)ச் சிரைத்தானும்.
The barber who had nothing to do shaved his daughter's head (*or* his cat).

"SERVANTS DEMAND SERVANTS."

வேலை, வேலைக்காரன்.

2630. அடுப்பு கட்டிக்குத் துடைப்பக்கட்டை.

A hearthstone demands a broomstick (to help it to hold the pot). 2631.

2631. ஆட்டாளுக்கு ஒரு மோட்டாள்.

The shepherd can get some fool to serve him. 2630.

Indian shepherds are proverbially stupid, but even a shepherd can find some one more stupid to serve him. Said when a servant is told to do a thing, and sends someone else to do it, or when a child is asked to fetch something, and the child sends a younger brother or sister.

"*The master orders the man; the man orders the cat; and the cat orders her tail.*"

2632. ஆட்டாளுக்கு ஒரு சிட்டாள் (or மாட்டாள்), அடப்பக்காரனுக்கு ஒரு துடைப்பக்கட்டை.

A shepherd has a servant, and the bearer of the wallet (adappakkâran) has a broomstick (a lower helper).

The *adappakkâran* is one who does all sorts of menial services for his master.

2633. சிறை கீழ் சிறை, அதின் கீழ் அம்பட்டன்.

A slave under a slave, and under him a barber.

The barber caste is held in very low esteem although all classes of Hindus use the barber.

2634. சிட்டாளுக்கு ஒரு முட்டாள், செருப்புத் தூக்கிக்கு ஒரு அடப்பக்காரன்.

The servant has an assistant, and the shoe-bearer has a wallet-bearer (adappakkâran). 2632.

2635. தலை சிரைக்கிற அம்பட்டனுக்கு அடப்பம் தாங்க ஒரு ஆள்.

A man to carry the bag for the barber who shaves people's head.

WORK AND WORKERS.

வேலை, வேலைக்காரன்.

2636. அமிஞ்சி உண்டோ, குப்பு நாயக்கரே.

Oh, *Kuppu Naikâr*, have you some work for me?

அமிஞ்சி வேலை is also used of forced labour.

2637. அரைவேலையைச் சபையிலே கொண்டுவருகிறதா?

Should you bring half-finished work before the assembly?

2638. அவசரக் கோலம் அள்ளித் தெளித்ததுபோல் சொல்லுகிறாய்.
You speak like the woman, who hurridly takes a handful of powder and strews it instead of working the Kolam pattern carefully.

Said of one who takes people in by shuffling excuses, or by hasty and worthless work.

2639. என்டி சிறுக்கி, புல்லு ஆச்சா? ஒரு நொடிக்குமுன் கட்டாச்சே!
If you say, "Well, woman, did you cut the grass?" she says, "It was tied up in bundles a little while ago!" 502, 2640, 2650.

Said of a hard-working and willing servant. 502, 2640, 2650.

2640. காலால் நடக்காமல், காற்றாய்ப் பறக்கிறது.
He does not walk, he flies like the wind. 2639.

2641. குருடி தண்ணீருக்குப்போனால், எட்டாள் மினக்கெடு.
If a blind woman goes for water, eight persons have to forego work. 2648.

As she can't find her way, one is sent to find her, and another to find these two, and so on.

"*Work ill done must be twice done.*"

2642. கூனியானாலும் கூடை சுமந்துதான் கூலி பெறவேண்டும்.
Though she is a hump-backed woman she must carry her burden home before she gets her hire. 1962, 1707.

"*If a man will not work, neither shall he eat.*"

2643. தான்போகாத காரியத்துக்கு ஆள்போனால் ஒரு சொட்டு.
If a servant goes about business that his master won't go for, there will be defects (in the way it is done). 2644, 2649.

"*And he that by the plough would thrive, himself must either hold or drive.*"

"*If you wish a thing done, go; if not, send.*"

2644. தினவு எடுத்தவன் சொறிந்துகொள்ளவேண்டும்.
"*Let him that is itchy scratch himself.*" 2643.

Let the thing be done by one interested in it.

2645. திருப்பதி அம்பட்டன் சவரஞ் செய்கிறதுபோல.
Like the Tirupathi barber shaving.

Tirupathi is a most sacred place, and on festival days at Tirupathi there are numbers of people to be shaved. It is considered meritorious to get shaved and to present the hair to the temple. To make them wait, the barber shaves a little hair off each person, so that they may be ashamed to go and wait till he has finished his work properly. The proverb is said about work that is half done, அரையும் குறையுமான வேலை, or about work that is done hastily, or about clever devices for securing one's own advantage.

2646. பண்ணிப் பதித்தாற்போல்.
Like a piece of filagree work well fitted together.

2647. பூராயமாய் வேலை கற்றுக்கொள்ளவேண்டும்.
Learn to do thoroughly the work you have to do.

2648. முட்டாளுக்கு இரண்டு ஆள்.
A fool must have two helpers. 2641.

He will do things so badly, that two persons will be wanted to set things right again.

2649. மூஞ்சை (*or* ஆளை) பார், முகத்தைப் பார்.
Meet persons face to face, meet them directly. 889, 2643.

Go yourself for what you require that people may see you know what you are about and they will fear to cheat you.

"*If you will have a thing well done, do it yourself.*"

2650. வெட்டிக்கொண்டு வரச்சொன்னால், கட்டிக்கொண்டு வருகிறான்.
If you tell him to cut firewood, he brings it tied up. 1362, 2639.

"*All things are easy that are done willingly.*"

2651. வேலையில் நல்ல அடி அடிக்கிறான்.
He strikes a good blow in his work.

i. e. He works hard, and earns much.

ANXIETY AND TROUBLE.

கவலை, அலைச்சல்.

2652. அக்குத்தொக்கு இல்லாதவனுக்குத் துக்கம் ஏது?
What sorrow has he, who has no family and no wealth?

2653. ஆசையுள்ளளவும் அலைச்சல் உண்டு.
As long as there is desire, there is anxiety.

2654. ஆண்டிவேஷம் போட்டும், அலைச்சல் தீரவில்லை.
Though you assume the guise of a religious mendicant, the anxieties of life will not cease. 1033.

Outward religious devotion is no remedy for the evils of life. 677.

2655. உடல் உள்ள வரைக்கும், கடல் கொள்ளாத கவலை.
Even the ocean cannot contain the anxieties of mortal life. 3388.

2656. உப்பு இருந்தால் பருப்பு இராது, பருப்பு இருந்தால் உப்பு இராது.
If there is salt there are no beans, if there are beans there is no salt. 2658, 2659.

Always something wanting.

2657. கப்பிடாவு மில்லை, வெட்டுக்கத்தியு மில்லை.
He has neither cloth nor scissors.

Said in blame of him who does not care for what he ought to care for.

2658. கல்லைக் கண்டால் நாயைக் காணோம், நாயைக் கண்டால், கல்லைக் காணோம்.

If you see a stone there is no dog (at which to throw it); if you see a dog there is no stone to throw at it. 2656, 2659.

Said when something cannot be found that is needed.

"*All is not at hand that helps.*"

2659. பிள்ளையாரைக் கண்டால் தேங்காயைக் காணோம், தேங்காயைக் கண்டால், பிள்ளையாரைக் காணோம்.

If we see an image of Ganesa (the god of luck), we do not see a cocoanut (to offer to him); if we see a cocoanut, we do not see Ganesa. 2656, 2658.

2660. மனக் கவலை, பலக் குறைவு.

Mental worry is loss of strength.

"*Care killed the cat.*"

Cf. 1205 *ff.*

DISTRESS, PERPLEXITY.

கலக்கம், தவிப்பு.

2661. ஆயிரம் பாம்பில் அகப்பட்ட தேரைபோல் தவிக்கிறான்.

He pants like a toad caught among a thousand snakes.

2662. ஆற்றிலே விட்ட தெர்ப்பை போல் தவிக்கிறது.

To be harrassed like a straw (*lit.* Kusa-grass) let afloat in a river.

2663. கண்ணியில் (or வலையில்) அகப்பட்ட (or சிக்கிக்கொண்ட) மான்போல் கலங்குகிறான்.

He is confused like a stag caught in a trap (*or* net).

2664. கரை காணாத தோணி போல் தவிக்கிறது.

To be distressed like a boat that cannot find the way to the shore.

2665. கன்றைத் தேடிப் பசு தவிக்கிறது போல்.

Like the distress of a cow seeking her calf. 3151.

2666. காற்றிலே அகப்பட்ட கப்பல் போல் அலைகிறது மனம்.

The mind is agitated like a ship caught in a (storm of) wind.

2667. தாமரை இலையில் தண்ணீர் போல் தவிக்கிறான்.

He is in distress like water (quivering) on a lotus-leaf.

2668. தேனில் விழுந்த ஈ போல் தவிக்கிறான்.

He is struggling like a fly that has fallen into honey.

Said of a person who is in great trouble and does not know what to do to get out of it.

2669. மலை கலங்கினாலும், மனம் கலங்கப் போகாது.

Though mountains shake, the mind should not be troubled.

REALITIES, FANCIES AND DREAMS.

கனவு.

2670. இராக் கண்ட கனவு மிடாப்போல் வீங்கினது.

What one saw at night in a dream swelled to the size of a huge pot.

Said of hopes not likely to be realized.

2671. ஊமை கண்ட கனவு (com. கனா) போல்.

Like the dream of a dumb man.

He is unable to communicate it to anyone.

2672. எண்ணம் எல்லாம் பொய், எமன் ஓலை மெய் (or ஏனிதம் மெய்).

Hopes and plans are all vanity but Death's decree is the one thing true.

2673. கனவில் கண்ட பணம் செலவுக்கு உதவுமா?

Money seen in a dream will not pay your bills.

"*He who lives on hope has but a slender diet.*"

2674. கனவில் கண்ட பொருள் கைக்கு எட்டுமோ?

Will wealth seen in a dream reach your hands?

"*If wishes were horses, beggars would ride.*"

2675. கனவில் உண்ட சோறு பசி தீர்க்குமா?

Will rice eaten in a dream satisfy hunger?

"*Golden dreams make men wake hungry.*"

2676. கனவில் கண்டவனுக்குப் பெண் கொடுத்ததுபோல்.

Like giving one's daughter in marriage to a man seen in a dream.

2677. பெரு வயிறு கொண்டது அறியாமல், சீமந்தத்தற்கு நாள் இட்டுக் கொண்டானும்.

Not knowing that his wife had dropsy, he appointed a day for the *Seemanta* ceremony. 1270, 2698.

The *Seemanta* is a ceremony performed during the first pregnancy of a woman.

"*That which has its value from fancy is not very valuable.*"

2678. மருவில் உண்ட சாப்பாட்டை இலங்கணத்தில் நினைத்துக் கொண்டது போல்.

Like thinking, during one's fast, of the food eaten by him at the feast given in his honour by his bride's family.

To dream of past glory in the midst of present distress.

"*The memory of happiness makes misery woeful.*"

2679. மெய் என்று இருந்தேன், முழித்தேன், கனவு ஆச்சுது.

I believed it all to be real; I awoke, and found it only a dream.

e. g. A widow may use this proverb meaning that she was happy till her husband's death, and had foolishly thought her happiness permanent till then. 1288, 2024.

2680. கரட்டு ஓணான் புகுந்து கொண்டதுபோல், or அவன் வயற்றில் கரட்டு ஓணான் இருக்கிறது.

Like a blood-sucker (a lizard) entering into him; *or* There is a blood-sucker in his stomach.

The story runs that a man was taking water in his palms to drink under a tree; a lizard that was up in the tree was reflected in the water in his hands and the man saw the reflection of the lizard as the water ran into his mouth. He at once felt pain, and thought himself fatally sick. —Said of imaginary sicknesses and imaginary conclusions; or said of one who may be right in being suspicious of a certain person, but thinks himself right in suspecting everyone.

Cf. 907 *ff.* 1669 *ff.* 2882, 2486, 2491, 2695 *ff.* 2907 *ff.*

THE MIND OR HEART.

மனம், நெஞ்சு.

2681. எந்தப் புற்றிலே எந்தப் பாம்பு இருக்குமோ?

Who knows what snake is found in a particular hole? 2407.

Said of a person whose capabilities are not yet known.

2682. நீர் ஆழம் கண்டாலும், நெஞ்சு ஆழம் காணப்படாது.

Though you fathom the depth of water, you cannot fathom the depths of a heart.

Generally said about women.

"*No one can see into another further than his teeth.*"

2683. மணலை அளவிட்டாலும், மனதை அளவிடப்படாது.

Though you measure grains of sand, you cannot measure a heart.

"OUT OF THE ABUNDANCE OF THE HEART THE MOUTH SPEAKETH."

2684. உட்புறத்துக்கு வெளிப்புறம் கண்ணாடி.

The outer man is the mirror of the inner man. 2702.

"*A bird is known by its note, and a man by his talk.*"

2685. உண்டதுதானே ஏப்பம் வரும்.

What has been eaten will be (perceived by) the belching.

"*What the heart thinketh the tongue speaketh.*"

2685a. மனதில் இருக்கிறது, வாக்கிலே வருகிறது.
What is in the heart will come into the mouth.

2686. குலத்துக்கு ஏற்ற பேச்சு.
Each man's speech accords with his caste. 685.
"*Good horses cannot be of bad colour.*"

2687. சோற்றுக்கு ஏற்ற மலம் (or பீ).
The excrement varies with the food.
A mother-in-law sometimes says this to her daughter-in-law, implying that her words and her deeds are alike vulgar.
"*Every tub smells of the wine it holds.*"
"*Muddy springs will have muddy streams.*"

2688. நல்லார் பொல்லார் நாவிலேதான்.
The good and the bad (are known) by their tongues.

2689. நாக்கிலே இருக்கிறது நன்மையும் தீமையும்.
Good and evil are in the tongue. 1510, 1511.

2690. நல்லதும் பொல்லாதும் நாக்கிலே.
In the tongue is good and evil.

2691. நல்லாரை நாவில் உரை, பொன்னைக் கல்லில் உரை.
Find out the good by their tongue, and pure gold by the touchstone.
"*Speech is the picture of the mind.*"

2692. பறக்கச்சே தெரியாதா காக்காயின் முடுக்கு?
Don't you know the strength of the crow when it flies? 1851.
People are known by their deeds and words.

2693. பாலைக் குடித்தவனுக்குப் பால் ஏப்பம் வரும், கள்ளைக் குடித்தவனுக்குக் கள் ஏப்பம் வரும்.
He who has drunk milk will belch milk, and he who has drunk toddy will belch toddy.
"*From a clear spring clear water flows.*"

2694. பெருமையும் சிறுமையும் வாயால் வரும்.
Greatness and littleness come by the mouth, *or* is known by words

Cf. 2499 *ff*; 282 *ff*. 5.

OVER-ESTIMATION OF WHAT IS DESIRED.

மனம், நெஞ்சு, நாட்டம்.

2695. இராஜன் மெச்சினது ரம்பை.
Whomsoever the Raja has praised becomes Ramba. 3436.

Ramba was a beautiful celestial nymph. The ugliest creature in the world becomes as beautiful as Ramba if the king takes a fancy to her and praises her.

"*Fair is not fair, but that which pleaseth.*"
"*Fancy surpasses beauty.*"
"*An incensed lover shuts his eyes, and tells himself many lies.*"

2696. காடும் செடியும் அவளாகவே தோன்றுகிறது.
Trees, forest and all seem to be she.

Because she is so dear, she seems to be in everything.

"*A lover's soul lives in the body of his mistress.*"

2697. திருநாளைக் கண்கொண்டு பார்க்கக் கூடவில்லை.
I had not eyes enough to see all the splendour of that festival day. 3451.

2698. மனம் கொண்டது மாளிகை (or கொள்கை).
What the heart is set on seems (as grand as) a palace. 2677.

"*A good hope is better than a bad possession.*"
"*Fancy may bolt bran and think it flour.*"
"*A black plum is as sweet as a white.*"

Cf. 2670 *ff*; 3145 *ff*.

"WHERE THERE IS A WILL, THERE IS A WAY."

மனம், நெஞ்சு, நாட்டம்.

2699. ஒட்டினால் தொட்டிலும் கொள்ளும், ஒட்டாவிட்டால் கட்டிலும் கொள்ளாது.
When there is agreement between the two, the very cradle can hold it! when there is no agreement, even a cot cannot hold it. 2771.

2700. வேண்டும் என்றால் எதுதான் செய்யக்கூடாது.
If one really will, what is impossible? 3146.

"*The will is everything.*"

2701. வேண்டும் என்று நூற்றால் வெண்ணெய் மொத்தைபோல் நூற்கலாம்.
Thread may be spun as (soft as) a ball of butter, if while spinning one says it must be so.

"*The will is the soul of work.*"

Cf. 1946 *ff*.

MISCELLANEOUS PROVERBS REFERRING TO THE MIND AND HEART.

மனம், நெஞ்சு.

2702. அகத்தில் அழகு முகத்தில் தெரியும்.
The beauty of the soul is known in the face. 2684.
"*'Tis the stainless soul within, that outshines the fairest skin.*"
"*The countenance is the index of the mind.*"
"*In the forehead and the eye, the lecture of the mind doth lie.*"

2703. இரக்கமில்லாதவன் நெஞ்சும் இரும்பிலும் கொடியது.
A merciless man's heart is harder than iron. 3287.

2704. உப்பிருந்த பாண்டமும், உபாயமிருந்த நெஞ்சமும் தட்டுண்டுபோகும்.
A vessel containing salt, and a heart containing deceit will be broken and ruined. 202.

2705. கல்லையாகிலும் கரைக்கலாம், மனதைக் கரைக்க முடியாது.
Though you may dissolve a rock, you may fail in melting the heart. 3287.

2706. துறவறம் இல்லறம் மனதிலே.
Asceticism and domestic life are matters of the heart.
i. e. Whether one is an ascetic or lives with his family, piety in the heart is the chief thing.

2707. பொல்லாத மனம் கேளாது.
An evil heart will not hearken. 531, 3287.

2708. பஞ்சு பறந்தால் படியும் ஒரு தேசம், நெஞ்சு பறப்பதற்கு நிலைகாணேம்.
Though cotton flies off by the wind it will settle down in some land, but we find no resting place for the flight (restlessness) of the heart.

2709. தினம் தவநிலையில் மனதை நிறுத்து.
Keep the mind daily in a state of devotion.

2710. மாமியார் தலையில் கையும், மாப்பிள்ளைமேல் சிந்தையும்.
Her hands are busied with her mother-in-law's head, but her thoughts are with her husband.
"*Her hands are on the wheel, but her eyes are in the street.*"

CONSCIENCE, WITNESS, AND WITNESS OF CONSCIENCE.

மனம், சாக்ஷி.

2711. அரசன் உடைமைக்கு ஆகாயவாணி சாக்ஷி.
The sky is the witness to a king's property.
A higher power protects a king's property.

2712. அவன் அவன் மனசே, அவன் அவனுக்குச் சாக்ஷி.
Each person's heart is his own witness. 76.

2713. அறிவு மனதை அரிக்கும்.
Conscience will gnaw the heart.
" *A wicked man is his own hell.*"

2714. கடன் பட்டார் நெஞ்சம்போல் கலங்குகிறது.
As confounded as the mind of a debtor. 1097.

2715. கள்ள மனம் துள்ளும்.
The deceitful heart is ever restless. 2310.
" *A wicked man is afraid of his own memory.*"

2716. குறும்பியுள்ள காது தினவு தின்னும்.
An ear full of wax will itch. 2718.
A guilty conscience is restless.

2717. குற்ற மனச்சாட்க்ஷி கூடிவாழும் சத்துரு.
The guilty conscience is a foe that lives with us.
" *A guilty conscience needs no accuser.*"

2718. குற்றமுள்ள நெஞ்சு குறு குறு என்னும், குறும்பியுள்ள காது தினவு கொள்ளும்.
A guilty conscience murmurs; an ear full of wax itches. 2716.
The three persons mentioned in 1363, 1364 and 1365 are clear examples of the statement in this proverb.

2719. கோமட்டி சாக்ஷி.
A Komati's evidence.
A Komati (merchant) was asked to identify a horse about which a Musalman and a Hindu were quarrelling. He said the fore quarters of it seemed to belong to the Musalman, and the hind quarters to the Hindu. —He was indifferent to the truth, and was afraid to offend either party.

2720. தன் நெஞ்சு அறியாத பொய் இல்லை.
There is no deceit without the doer's mind being conscious of it.

2721. தன்னை ஒளித்து ஒரு வஞ்சனை இல்லை.
There is no dodge by which one can hide one's way of concealing one's self.

2722. தான் அறியாத ஆவேசம் உண்டா?
Can anyone be possessed by a spirit without knowing it?

2723. தீரா நெஞ்சுக்குத் தெய்வமே சாக்ஷி.
God is the only witness to the doubting heart.
Said to comfort one's self or others in great sorrows.

2724. தீரா வழக்குக்குத் தெய்வமே சாக்ஷி.
God is the only witness in an unsettled law-suit. 3036.

2725. நெஞ்சு அறியப், பொய் சொல்லுகிறதா?
What! to tell a lie, while your heart knows the truth?

2726. மடியில் கனம் இருந்தால் வழியிலே பயம்.
If there is money in the pocket, there is fear in the road. 2729.
He who has sinned fears.

2727. மனதுக்கு மனதே சாக்ஷி.
The heart is its own witness.

2728. மனதே மனதுக்குப் பந்து, மனதே மனதுக்குச் சத்துரு.
The heart is its own friend or enemy. (Bhagavat-gita 6, 5.)

"Soul is self's friend when self doth rule over self,
But self turns enemy if Soul's own self hates Self as not itself.'
E. Arnold : The Song Celestial.

"*Their thoughts accusing or else excusing one another.*" Rom. 2, 15.

"*A good conscience is the best divinity.*"

2729. முதுகிலே புண் உண்டானால், செடியிலே நுழையப் பயம்.
With wounds on one's back one fears to enter into a bush. 2726.

"*Conscience makes cowards of us all.*"

2730. மோருக்குப் போய் மொந்தையை ஒளிப்பானேன்?
When going to buy buttermilk, why hide the vessel?

"A *good conscience need never sneak.*"
"*Truth seeks no corners.*"

2731. வேலிக்கு ஓணான் சாக்ஷி.
A lizard is witness to (what goes on in) the hedge (where it lives).

Dependents will support their protector's case.

Most of the above proverbs go to show that the Hindus as well as other nations have a conscience. I have often been told that the Hindus have no conscience, and that before anything can be done for them a conscience will have to be created in them. Apart from the Bible, is there any nation that has said more and said it so well about good and evil (நன்மை, தீமை) as the Hindus? Do they not know the difference between knowing the good and not realizing it? (Cf. 3566.) Cf. also the proverbs from 139 to 218 and Rom. 2, 14—15.

FRIENDSHIP FOR GAIN.

உறவு, சிநேகம்.

2732. இட்ட உறவு எட்டு நாளைக்கு, நக்கின உறவு நாலு நாளைக்கு.
Friendship gained by giving lasts for eight days, platter friendship, only for four. 356.

"*He that is won with a nut may be lost with an apple.*"
"*A friend that you buy with presents will be bought from you.*"
"*With provision in store, we have friends by the score.*"
கைநட்பு சேவகன் is a common phrase for this thought.
"*If you would have the dog to follow you, feed him.*"

2733. இட்ட கையை நத்துமோ, இடாத கையை நத்துமோ?
Is the hand that gives, loved or the hand that does not give? 370.

2734a. நீர் நிறைந்த குளத்தில் சேர்ந்திருக்கும் பக்ஷிகள் நீர் வறண்டால் நெடுந் தூரம் பறக்கும், அதில் இருந்த தாமரைகளோ நீருடன் இறக்கும்.

The birds that live in a lake full of water fly away when the lake dries up, but the lotus flowers that grow in the same lake will (remain) die with the drying up of the water.

2734. கொழுக்கட்டை சுட்டு உறவாடுகிறதா?

Is friendship to be kept up by baking cakes? 1060.

"*While the pot boils friendship blooms.*"

2735. பானையிலே பதக்கு நெல் இருந்தால், மூலையிலே முக்குறுணி தெய்வம் கூத்தாடும்.

If there is grain in the pot, many gods will dance in the corners of the house.

"*Let us have florins and we shall find cousins.*"

"*I wot well how the world ways: he is most loved that has most bags.*"

"*Now I have got an ewe and a lamb, everyone cries, Welcome, Peter!*"

2736. மாவு இடித்தால் மண்டி கொள்ளுகிறது, கூழ் கொதித்தால் கூடிக் கொள்ளுகிறது.

If the rice is being pounded they draw near, if the gruel is being boiled they come as friends to eat. 1168, 1147.

Said of one who does not care for others unless he can profit by them.

"*Daub yourself with honey, and you will have plenty of flies.*"

2737. கூரைமேலே சோறுபோட்டால், ஆயிரம் காக்காய்.

If you put rice on the top of your houses, a thousand crows will gather. 351.

"*A full purse never lacked friends.*"

"*Money is the best bait to fish for man with.*"

"*In time of prosperity friends will be plenty, in time of adversity not one among twenty.*"

Cf. 1070 *ff.*; 1054 *ff.*; 1742; 3136 *ff.*

FRIENDSHIP AT A DISTANCE AND NEAR BY.

உறவு, சிநேகம்.

2738. அகல இருந்தால் நிகள உறவு, கிட்ட இருந்தால் முட்டப் பகை.

If separated by a long distance, there will be long-lived friendship, but if they are near each other, there will be perfect hatred.

"*Friends agree best at a distance.*"

2739. *அகல இருந்தால், பகையும் உறவாம்.*
If (two people) live at a distance, their hatred will turn into friendship.
" *A hedge between keeps friendship green.*"

2740. *அக்கரை மாட்டுக்கு இக்கரை பச்சை.*
The cow on one side of the river (thinks) the other side green.
" *Distance lends enchantment to the view.*"

2741. *சேர இருந்தால் செடியும் பகை, தூர இருந்தால் தோட்டியும் உறவு.*
If you live together the slightest thing will cause enmity, but if you are far apart you may be friends with a scavenger.

2742. *தூர மிருந்தால் சேர உறவு.*
If friends live apart their friendship is close.

2743. *தூரத்துப் பச்சை கண்ணுக்குக் குளிர்ச்சி.*
Green at a distance is cool (pleasant) to the eyes.

FAMILIARITY BREEDS CONTEMPT.

2744. *கம்மாளன் நாய் சம்மட்டித் தொனிக்கு அஞ்சுமா?*
Will the blacksmith's dog fear the sound (of the hammer)?

2745. *பனங் காட்டு நரி சல சலப்புக்கு அஞ்சுமா?*
Will the fox that lives in a palmyra-grove fear the rattling of the palm leaves?
The leaves of the palmyra-palm make a rattling and creaking sound which sounds very weird in the dark.

2746. *கோவில் பூனை தேவருக்கு அஞ்சுமா?*
Will the temple-cat fear the gods? 1412, 1413, 1414, 1415.
" *The nearer the church the further from God.*"

CLOSE FRIENDSHIP.

உறவு, சிநேகம்.

2747. *இராம லட்சுமணரை போல் இசைந்திருக்கிறது.*
To be friends like Rama and (his younger brother) Latchmanan. 2818.
Like David and Jonathan, or Damon and Pythias, or Pylades and Orestes.

2748. *உடல் இரண்டு, உயிர் ஒன்று.*
Two bodies, but one soul.

2749. *உயிரும் உடலும் போல.*
Like soul and body.

2750. உற்ற சிநேகிதன், உயிருக்கு அமிர்தம்.
A close friend is nectar to one's life.

2751. நகமும் சதையும் போல்.
As close as nail and flesh.
"*They are hand and glove.*"

2752. பாலும் நீரும் போல்.
(They are as closely united) as milk and water.

2753. பூவும் மணமும் போல்.
As inseparable as the flower and its scent.

2754. மலரில் மணமும், எள்ளில் எண்ணெய்யும், உடலில் உயிரும் கலந்தது போல.
To be one like the scent in the flower, like the oil in the oil-seed, and like the soul in the body.
Sayings of this kind might be multiplied indefinitely from Indian literature.

DANGERS OF TOO CLOSE INTIMACY.

உறவு, சிநேகம்.

2755. உறவு உறவு தான் பறியிலே கை வைக்காதே.
No doubt, we are friends (*or* relatives), but do not put your hand into my basket (*or* pot).
"*I love you well, but touch not my pocket.*"

2756. கடுஞ் சிநேகம் கண்ணுக்குப் பொல்லாப்பு.
Too close a friendship is offensive to the eye.
"*Hot love is soon cold.*"
"*Friends are like fiddle strings, they must not be screwed too tight.*"

2757. மயிர் ஊடாடாதவர்கள் நட்பு, பொருள் ஊடாடக் கெடும்.
Friendship that is so intimate, that there is no room to insert a hair (between the friends), will be ruined if money-matters occur (between the friends).

2758. மார் மட்டும் உறவு இருந்தாலும், மார் மேல் கை போடாதே.
Though your friendship reach her bosom, don't put your hand on her bosom.
Though very much in love with her, don't take any liberty with her.

Cf. 1413, 2773 *ff*; 2777*ff*.

"TO AGREE LIKE CATS AND DOGS."

உறவு, சிநேகம்.

2759. இவனுக்கு அவனுக்கும் எழு பொருத்தம்.
There are seven points of agreement between the pair. 3577.
When a Brahmin examines astrologically, whether persons, between whom a marriage is proposed, are adapted to each other, and finds that there are seven points of agreement in their horoscopes, they are considered unfit for marriage.
"*They agree like bells; they want nothing but hanging.*"

2760. எலியும் பூனையும் போல் வாழ்கிறது.
Living together like rat and cat. 2762, 2846, 3622.
"*Two cats and a mouse, two wives in one house, two dogs and a bone, never agree in one.*"

2761. காட்டுக் கிளாக்காயும், கண் கெட்ட தயவில்லாத ஒணானும் கோர்த்துக் குலாவுது போல.
Like the wild *Kilâ*-fruit and the blind unmerciful blood-sucker embracing each other and playing.
Said of people who after quarrelling come to be very friendly.

2762. பாம்பும் கீரியும் போல்.
To live like a snake and a mongoose.
A mongoose is said to attack the most venomons snake and kill it.
"*At daggers drawn.*"

LIKE AND DISLIKE.

விருப்பு, வெறுப்பு.

2763. அமிஞ்சிக்கு உழுதால் சரியாய் விளையுமா?
If you plough because you are compelled (*i.e.*, unwillingly), will the crop grow well? 1907, 1909.
No good result can be expected from forced work.

2764. அருவருப்புச் சோறும், அசங்கிதக் கறியும்.
The rice was disgusting, and the curry was filthy.

2765. இஷ்டமற்ற முனியன், அஷ்டமத்துச் சனியன்.
Munian whom nobody likes is to every one the malignant planet Saturn (*sani*). 179, 2234 *ff*.

2766. கோணி கோடி கொடுப்பதிலும், கோணாமல் காணி கொடுப்பது நல்லது.
Instead of giving much with a wry face, it is better to give a little willingly. 2393.
"*God loveth a cheerful giver.*" 2 Cor. 9, 7.
"*A gift with a kind countenance is a double present.*"

2767. சொறிந்து தேய்க்காத எண்ணெய்யும், பரிந்து இடாத சோறும் பாழ்.

Oil not rubbed into the body properly, and food given without affection are worthless.

When Hindus take an oil-bath, the oil is rubbed into the skin by the friction of another person's hands.

"*Dry bread is better with love, than a fat capon with fear.*"

2768. பிரியமில்லாத சோறு, பிண்டா சோறு.

Rice given without love is but a morsel. 2124, 2393.

"*Better is a dinner of herbs where love is, than a stalled ox and hatred therewith.*" Proverbs 15, 17.

"*Better a friendly denial than an unwilling compliance.*"

2769. பரிவு இல்லாப் போசனத்திற் பட்டினி நன்று, பிரியமில்லா பெண்டீரிற் பேய் நன்று.

Hunger is preferable to (receiving) food (given) unkindly; a demon is preferable to an unkind wife.

2770. வேண்டா வெறுப்பாய், ஏண்டா கொடுப்பாய்?

Why do you give it with such an air of disgust? 180, 185.

2771. வேண்டும் என்றால் வீடு, வேண்டாம் என்றால் காடு.

If I like it, it is my home; if I dislike it, it is a wilderness. 2699.

A right disposition of the mind overlooks inconveniences.

2772. வேம்பும் கரும்பாச்சே, வெற்றிலையும் விஷமாச்சே.

The bitter *Margosa*-tree has become a sugar-cane, and the *betel*-leaf has become poison.

Said of broken friendship; they have become நெடி நாற்றம், a pungent unpleasant smell, to each other.

Cf. 1900 *ff.* *Cf.* 3145 *ff.*

REJECTED FRIENDSHIP.

REFERRING TO PEOPLE WHO DESIRE TO BE TRUE FRIENDS, BUT WHOSE FRIENDSHIP IS NOT APPRECIATED.

தானாக வருகிறவர்கள்.

2773. ஒட்டிக்கொண்டு வந்தாலும், தட்டிக் கழிக்கிறான்.

Though I cleave to him, he repels me. 1412.

2774. கிட்டக் கிட்ட வந்தாலும், எட்ட எட்டப் போகிறான்.

Though I constantly try to get near him, he goes further away.

2775. வலிய வந்த சீதேவியைக் காலால் உதைத்துத் தள்ளுகிறது.

He kicks ont with his foot the goddess of good fortune (Lakshmi) who has come to him of her own accord.

Wilful rejection of kindly help.

2776. வலிய உறவாடி வாசலிலே வந்தாலும், பொய் உறவாடி போய்வா என்று சொல்லுகிறான்.

Though you enter his doorway as his friend of your own accord, he says hypocritically, 'Come some other day!' 1564.

True friendship rewarded with indifference.

Cf. 2755 *ff*.

INTRUSION.

2777. அழையா வீட்டுக்கு நுழையாச் சம்பந்தி (com. சம்மந்தி).

A relative who invites himself to a house from which he has received no invitation.

The proverb is a sarcasm on all those unavoidable parasites, who come nninvited to all weddings and feasts in Hindu houses.

"*Fiddlers, dogs and flees come to a feast unca'd* (*uncalled*)."
"*He who comes uncalled, unserved should sit.*"

2778. ஊரிலே கலியாணம், மாரிலே சந்தனம்.

There is a wedding in the village, and there is sandalwood paste on his breast.

Said of an impertinent intruder, who puts his nose into what does not concern him.

2779. தள்ளிப்பேசினாலும், தழுவிக் குழைகிறது.

Though I order him off, he tenderly embraces me (with some selfish object in his mind). 2782.

2780. பந்தியிலே வேண்டாம் வேண்டாம் என்றால், இலை பொத்தல் இலை பொத்தல் என்கிறான்.

Though I constantly refuse to take him to dinner, he constantly says that the leaf-plates are full of holes.

Said of people who are told many times that they are not wanted, but, having no sense of modesty (ரோசம் or சொரணையில்லை), do not take the hint, but criticise everything and make themselves quite at home.

"*Forbid a fool a thing, and that he will do.*"

2781. பிடரியைப் பிடித்துத் தள்ளத் தள்ளப், பெண்ணுடைய சிற்றப்பன் என்று நுழைகிறானாம்.

Though taken by the neck and turned out over and over again, he slips in, saying that he is my wife's sister's husband.

"*Follow love and it will flee : flee love and it will follow thee.*"

2782. விட்டுவிட்டாலும், ஒட்டிக்கொண்டு வருகிறான்.

Though you let him go, he sticks to you. 2779.

Cf. 2755 *ff*.

THE POWER OF WORDS, KIND OR HARSH.

சொல், பேச்சு.

2783. *அம்பு ஆணி தைத்ததுபோல பேசுகிறது.*
Speech pierces like arrows and nails.

2784. *அன்றைக்குச் சொன்ன சொல் ஜென்ம ஜென்மத்துக்கு உறைக்கும்.*
The words spoken that day have effect for generations. 1914.

2785. *இராமபாணம் பட்டு உருவினதுபோல்.*
As if hit and cut through by the arrow of Rama.
So sharp were his words.

2786. *உண்மை நன்மொழி, தின்மை உறுத்தம்.*
A kind word is a blessing, but a harsh word will pain.

2787. *கடுஞ்சொல் கேட்டால், காதுக்குக் கொப்பளம்.*
If you hear a harsh word, your ears will blister.

2788. *காதிலே நாராசம் காய்ச்சிவிட்டதுபோல்.*
Like heating an iron rod, and putting it into the ear.
Hearing bad words, or receiving sad information is very painful.

2789. *காலம் போகும், வார்த்தை நிற்கும்.*
Time passes, but words remain. 1933.
Said to a person who uses abuse.

2790. *நயமொழியினால் ஜெயம் உண்டு.*
Kind words conquer. (For the reverse see 2041).

2791. *பசு மரத்தில் தைத்த ஆணிபோல்.*
Like a nail entering (*Or*, as a nail enters) into fresh timber.
His words cut to the quick.

Cf. 2338 *ff.*

TO SPEAK DECISIVELY AND CLEARLY.

சொல், பேச்சு.

2792. *அவன் பூராயமாய்ப் பேசுகிறான்.*
He speaks without modesty.

2793. *என்னடா, சவுக்கம் கட்டிப் பேசுகிறாய்.*
Sir! your speech is clever.
Said to one who speaks so clearly and decisively that he leaves no room for being attacked.

2794. காசிக்குப் போனேன், காவடி கொண்டுவந்தேன்.
I went to Benares, and brought back the *Kâvadi*.

The *Kâvadi* is the pole put across the shoulders at each end of which jars of holy Ganges water are slung and so brought by the pilgrim from Benares to Râmeswaram to be poured on the idol there as an offering. *Cf.* note to 1440.

Said to one who spin yarns, when wanted to be brief. By this proverb he is asked to be brief, or to state only the essentials of what has happened or has been done.

2795. தேங்காய் உடைத்தாப்போல பேசுகிறான்.
His speech is like the breaking of cocoanuts. 593.

i.e. Terse, emphatic, clear speech, like the hard blows which break a cocoa-nut.

2796. தொடுத்தாப்போல பேசுகிறது.
To speak logically.

2797. நூற்றுக்கு ஒரு பேச்சு.
A word (of sense) is worth a hundred (of nonsense).
"*Deliver your words not by number, but by weight.*"
"*To hit the nail on the head.*"

2798. பட்டுக் கத்தரித்ததுபோல பேசுகிறது.
Speaking like cutting silk cloth.

Decisive speech.

2799. வெட்டு ஒன்று, துண்டு இரண்டு.
One cut, two pieces.

Said chiefly of the right word that decides a matter.

2800. வெள்ளையாய்ச் சொல்லிவிட்டான்.
He said it in clear words.

Cf. 2338 *ff.*

NONSENSE AND EMPTY BABBLE.

சொல், பேச்சு.

2801. அவன் பேச்சு தண்ணீர் மேல் எழுதி வைக்கவேண்டும்.
His talk must be recorded on water (*i.e.* it is not worth writing on paper).

2802. அவன் பேச்சு விளக்கெண்ணெய் (or, வெண்டைக்காய்) சமாச்சாரம்.
His speech is a matter of lamp oil, *or* His speech is like the vendeikai vegetable (*i.e.* very greasy).

2803. உன் சொல்லிலே உப்புமில்லை, புளியு மில்லை, பசையு மில்லை.
There is neither salt, tamarind, nor juice in your words. Empty talk.

2804. உன் வாயிலே ஸ்ரீதேவி.
The goddess of good fortune (Lakshmi) dwells on your lips.
Used ironically of a petitioner who does not know how to ask gracefully and so fails to gain what he requests.

2805. உலை வாயை மூடினாலும், ஊர் வாயை மூடலாமா?
Although you cover the mouth of a rice-pot, can you cover the mouth of the village? 2588.
No one can prevent people from slandering and backbiting.

2806. கதைக்குக் காலு மில்லை தலையு மில்லை.
The story you tell has neither head nor tail.
A story may be spun out to any length, when it is a story without facts or reason.
"A *story without a head.*"

2807. கத்துமட்டும் கத்திப்போட்டுக் கதவு சாத்திவிட்டுப்போ!
When you have chattered as much as you like, shut the door and be off!
Said to one who comes and talks a lot of rubbish.

2808. கலவைக் கீரை பறிப்பது போல பேசுகிறான்.
He speaks like one gathering mixed vegetables.
i.e. He talks inconsistently, holds all sorts of opinions.

2809. தொண்டையைக் கிழித்துக் கொண்டுபேசுகிறான்.
He speaks so as to tear his own throat.
Said of beggars, preachers and children who talk very loud.

2810. பன்னிச் சொன்னால் பாரதமாகும்.
If he goes on speaking, a Mahabharata will be produced. 1502*c*.
"*Great talkers are like leaky pitchers, everything runs out of them.*"

2811. பன்னிப் பன்னிப் பழங் கதை படியாதே.
Do not tell the old story again and again.

2812. முற்ற கல்வி பேசாதே.
Don't tell us your high wisdom.
An ironical way of expressing contempt for the feeble nonsense of some pretentious talker.

2813. மெத்த அத்து மிஞ்சின பேச்சுக்காரன்.
A talker who is transgressing all proper limits.
He speaks haughtily.

2814. மை மை சுந்தரி, கதவை ஒஞ்சரி.
My pretty maid, leave the door ajar.
Said in sarcasm to a servant or child, who, when relating something, goes too much into details.—A mother may say it to her child, when the child cannot get what it wants from her, and threatens to ask its father.

2815. வழி வாய்க் காலில்லாமல் பேசுகிறாய்.
There is no way or channel in your speech.
There is nothing in what you say; it is all against reason.

2816. வாக்கு வயணம் தெரியாமல் பேசுகிறான்.
or நீக்கு போக்கு தெரியாமல் பேசுகிறான்.
He speaks regardless of persons.

2817. வெறும் கை முழம்போடுமா?
Will an empty hand bestow a cubit's length (of cloth)?
He who has nothing, can only talk.
"*No flying without wings.*"

Cf. 2338 *ff.*

UNION.

ஒருமைபாடு, சம்பந்தம்.

2818. அடம்பங் கொடியும் திரண்டால் மிடுக்கு.
If tender creepers cling together there will be strength. 2005 &; 2747.
"*Weak things united become strong.*"

2819. அவன் எங்கே இருந்தான், நான் எங்கே இருந்தேன்.
Where was he, and where was I?
There was no connection between us before; we have been brought together by wonder, as it were. Eph. 2, 12—13.

2820. உள்ளும் புறம்பும் ஒத்திருக்கவேண்டும்.
Man's inner self must agree with his outward life.

2821. எத்தால் வாழலாம், ஒத்தால் வாழலாம்!
How can we live together? By agreeing!

2822. எருதும் வண்டியும் ஒத்தால், மேடு பள்ளம் ஏது?
If the bullocks and carriage agree, what are hills and valleys to them?

2823. ஒரு கை தட்டினால், ஓசை எழும்புமா?
If one hand only is moved (*lit.* struck), will the sound (of clapping) be produced?
"*Hand washes hand, and finger finger.*"
"*One flower makes no garland.*"

2824. கடலிலே பிறக்கும் உப்புக்கும், மலையிலே விளையும் நாரத்தங்காய்க்கும் தொந்தம்.
There is union between the salt born in the sea, and the lemon that grows on the hills.
These two are united in pickles (ஊறுகாய்). The saying is applied to two people, who, though born in different countries, meet and act in unison.

2825. பத்துப்பேருக்குப் பல்குச்சி, ஒருவனுக்குத் தலை சுமை.

For ten persons it is as light as a tooth-brush; if one has to carry it, it will be a heavy burden.

The word translated 'tooth-brush' means, literally, a small twig with which the teeth are cleaned. No Hindu would defile himself by putting a brush made with an animal's bristles into his mouth, nor would he think it cleanly to use the same brush twice.

"*Company in distress makes trouble less.*"

2826. முக்கூட்டுச் சிக்கு ஆறாது.

The dispute in an assembly of three persons cannot be appeased.

A dispute between two persons may be settled, but not one between many. Or, it is difficult to unite many people in one opinion.

"*So many men, so many minds.*"

DISUNITY, DISAGREEMENT.

ஒருமைப்பாடில்லாமை.

2827. இரண்டு பட்ட ஊரிலே குரங்கு குடியிராது.

In a village divided against itself even a monkey will not abide. Matt. 12, 25. 2831, 2841.

2828. உலகம் பலவிதம்.

The world has many ways. 848, 2269.

Every one acts according to his own will.

"*No gale can equally serve all passengers.*"

2829. உன் பாடு உனக்கு, என் பாடு எனக்கு.

You have your sufferings: I have mine.

i.e. We have nothing to do with each other; we will not help each other.

2830. ஒரு மரத்துப் பட்டை ஒரு மரத்திலே ஒட்டுமோ ?

Will the bark of one tree stick to another tree? 2832.

2831. ஒருமை பாடில்லாத குடி ஒருமிக்கக் கெடும்.

A disunited family will suffer destruction together. 2827.

2832. சுட்ட மண்ணும், பச்சை மண்ணும் ஒட்டுமோ?

Will burnt earth and fresh earth stick together? 2830.

2833. திண்ணைக்கு தேள் கொட்ட, மிடாவுக்கு நெறி கட்ட.

The scorpion stung the veranda-floor, and the swelling (caused by its poison) arose on a pot. 1834.

A sarcasm on irrelevant reasoning.

2834. நார் அறுந்தால் முடியலாம், நரம்பு அறுந்தால் முடியலாம், மனம் அறுந்தால் (or, முறிந்தால்) முடியாது.

If a fibre breaks it may be joined again, if a vein breaks, it may be joined together, but if the heart breaks (*i.e.* if friendship is broken) it cannot be (joined). 3205.

"*Broken friendship may be soldered, but never made sound.*"

2835. புளியும் ஓடும் போல் ஒட்டாமலிருக்கிறது.

The ripe fruit of the tamarind and the shell that covers it do not stick together.

As the tamarind fruit and its shell do not stick together, so the argument does not stick together.

In Hindu Philosophy the same as 272, 2257.

2836. வண்ணானுக்கும் நீர் வாணிக்கும் உறவு என்ன?

What relation is there between a washerman and a naked man?

ENMITY, OPPOSITION, CONTRARIETY.

விரோதம்.

2837. அரி அரி என்றால், ராமா ராமா என்கிறான்.

If I say "Vishnu," he says "Rama." 488.

2838. அரி என்றால் ஆண்டிக்குக் கோபம், அர என்றால் தாதனுக்குக் கோபம்.

If I say "Vishnu" the Saiva mendicant gets angry, if I say "Siva" the Vaishnava mendicant gets angry. 179, 248.

The Vaishnavas and Saivas are the two great divisions of modern popular Hinduism, and no love is lost between them.

2839. ஆண்டிக்கு இடச்சொன்னால், தாதனுக்கு இடச் சொல்லுகிறான்.

If I say, "Give alms to the Saiva mendicant," he says, "Give alms to the Vaishnava mendicant."

2840. உலகத்துக்கு ஞானம் பேய், ஞானத்துக்கு உலகம் பேய்.

Wisdom is the world's demon, and the world is Wisdom's demon.

i.e., The world and Wisdom (*Gnana*) are opposed.

2841. ஊர் இரண்டுபட்டால், கூத்தாடிக்குக் கொண்டாட்டம்.

If the village be divided into two parties, a show-man is happy. 2827.

He make profit out of the feuds of the rival factions.

2842. காலுக்குப் போட்டால், தலைக்குப் போடுகிறான்.

If I put it at his feet, he puts it on his head. 2845.

2843. கீரைக் கட்டை வெட்டச் சொன்னால், தோரணங் கட்டுகிறதா?

When I order him to cut vegetables, he ties garlands. 503, 1897, 1899, 2844.

"*He calls for a shoe-horn to help on his gloves.*"

2844. சொன்னது இருக்க, சுரை பிடுங்குகிறாய்.

While that which you were ordered to do is left undone, you are pulling up gourd-plants. 2843.

Said of one who is told to do one thing, but does something else. 1849.

2845. தலைக்குப் போட்டால் காலுக்கு, காலுக்குப் போட்டால் தலைக்கு.

If put at the head it is removed to the feet, if put at the feet it is removed to the head. 2842.

Said by a servant about a master who gives all sorts of irregular orders.

2845a. நெல் விளைகிற நிலமுந்தெரியாது, நிலாகாய்கிற இடமுந் தெரியாது.

He does not know a field in which rice is growing, and he does not know a place on which the moon is shining.

These two things everybody knows. Said ironically to a person who in any given case which he knows well, wilfully speaks as if he did not know it. Also applicable to a stupid person. 1232.

2846. பஞ்சும் நெருப்பும் போல்.

Like cotton and fire.

Said of two things that cannot be brought into connection without mutually destroying each other. 2760.

2847. பட்டால் பகல் கறி, படாவிட்டால் இராக் கறி.

If I get it, I will have it for my dinner, if not for my supper. 1797.

The Hindu's dinner is at twelve o'clock noon, their supper is at eight o'clock at night. The former is the chief meal.

2848. முன்னாலே போனால் முட்டுகிறது, பின்னாலே போனால் உதைக்குறது.

If you go before he will butt you, if after he will kick you. 2851..

Said of a cross-grained man.

2849. ராப்பிறந்த பிள்ளையும் ஆகாது, பகல் பிறந்த பிள்ளையும் ஆகாது.

Whether the child is born at night or in day-time it is disliked. 2851.

2850. வெண்கலம் வெண்கலம் என்றால், ஓட்டை ஓட்டை என்கிறான்.

When I say, it is bell-metal, he keeps saying that it is a cracked pot. 488.

Said of a person, who, through spite, wilfully depreciates what deserves praise.

2851. வெய்யிலிலே போட்டாலும் காய மாட்டான், தண்ணீரிலே போட்டாலும் நனைய மாட்டான்.

If put in the sun, he will not dry, if put into water, he will not get wet. 2848, 2849.

Said of one who wilfully puts himself at cross purposes with everybody and everything.

"*We piped unto you, and ye did not dance; we wailed, and ye did not mourn.*" Matt. 11, 17.

SIMILARITY, LIKENESS.

CHIEFLY IN THE SENSE OF INHERITED LIKENESS.

ஒப்பாயிருத்தல்.

2852. *அஞ்சு எழுத்தும் பாவனையும் அப்பனைப்போலிருக்கிறது.*
He is like his father both in the five senses and in his appearance.

2853. *அண்டத்துக்கு ஒத்தது பிண்டத்துக்கு.*
That which is like the whole is like its parts.
Like father like son; like master like servant.

2854. *அவனை உரித்துவைத்தாற்போலிருக்கிறான்.*
This man resembles that, as if he had skinned him and put on his skin.

2855. *அள்ளிப் பால் வார்க்கையில், சொல்லிப் பால் வார்த்திருக்கிறது.*
When feeding the child with milk-food, they have also poured the milk of words into it.
Parents, by their talk to, and by their behaviour before a child infuse their own good or evil nature into it. The proverb is generally said of the evil influences.

2856. *ஆட்டுக்கு ஒத்தது குட்டிக்கு.*
The lamb is like its mother.
"*She hath a mark after her mother.*"

2857. *ஒரு அச்சிலே உருக்கி வார்த்தாற்போல்.*
As if melted and poured into one mould.
Said about men or things that exactly resemble each other.

2858. *கள்ளன் பிள்ளைக்கும் கள்ளப் புத்தி.*
A thief's son has the disposition of a thief.
"*We may not expect a good whelp from an ill dog.*"

2859. *குதிரை எட்டு அடி பாய்ந்தால், குட்டிப் பதினாறு அடி பாயும்.*
If the horse leap eight feet, the colt will leap sixteen. 2863.

2860. *குரங்கு மூஞ்சி (முகம்) எல்லாம் ஒரு மூஞ்சி.*
The face of one monkey is like all the rest.
Said by a person to another who will not help him, meaning that he is a worthless comrade. It is also said by Hindus about Europeans, implying that they all keep together as one against foreign nations.

2861. *செட்டிப்பிள்ளையோ, கெட்டிப்பிள்ளையோ?*
If he is a merchant's son, he is a clever lad.
The merchant caste is naturally expert in figures.
"*A chip of the old block.*"

2862. தாயைப்போல் பிள்ளை, நூலைப்போல் சீலை.
As the mother so the child, as the yarn so the cloth. 3275, 3495.
"*As is the mother, so is her daughter.*" Ezekiel, 16, 44.

2863. தாய் எழ் அடி பாய்ந்தால், மகள் எட்டு அடி பாய்வாள்.
If the mother leaps seven feet, her daughter will leap eight feet. 2396, 2859.

2864. தாய்க்கு உள்ளது மகளுக்கு.
The daughter will inherit her mother's nature.
"*Bad crow, bad eggs.*"—"*Like mother, like daughter.*"

2865. துபாக்கி வயிற்றில் பீரங்கி பிறந்ததுபோல்.
Like a cannon being born from the womb of a musket.

2866. துப்பட்டியிலே கிழித்த கோமணம்தானே.
It is only a rag torn off from a piece (of cotton cloth).
Said of the bad son of a bad father.
"*He is his father's son.*"

2867. புலிக்குப் பிறந்து நகமில்லாமல் போகுமா?
Being born of a tiger, will it lack claws? 3063.
A soldier's child will not be a timid child.
"*That which comes of a cat will catch mice.*"

2868. மாதா செய்தது மக்களைக் கார்க்கும்.
A mother's deeds will stick as a stigma on her children.
"*Visiting the iniquity of the fathers upon the children.*" Exodus 20, 5.

2869. முண்டைச்சி பெற்றது மூன்றும் அப்படியே.
The three children the widow bore (while a widow) were all alike bad.
i.e. The children of a vicious woman will be vicious.
Among Hindus illegitimate children can only be the children of widows or dancing girls, as girls are married as soon as they attain puberty. 481, 3495.
"*He is the son of a bachelor.*"
"*A vicious man's son has a good title to vice.*"

2870. வசநாபியிலே புழுத்த புழு.
He is a worm sprung from deadly poison.

2871. வாழை அடி வாழை.
The (shoots springing from the) roots of the banana-tree will be banana-trees.

2872. விரை ஒன்று போட்டால், சுரை ஒன்று முளைக்குமா?
Will a gourd grow up from seed that is not gourd-seed? 2606.

Cf. 279. 2064 *ff.* 2684 *ff.*

PATIENCE, FORGIVENESS.

பொறுமை, மன்னிப்பு.

2873. ஆக்கப் பொறுத்தவன், ஆறப் பொறுக்கமாட்டானோ?
Will not he who has waited till the food is cooked, also wait till it cools?

2874. ஓடும் மீன் ஓடி ஒரு மீன் வருமளவும் வாடியிருக்குமாம் கொக்கு.
The crane will stand hungry and let fish after fish pass, till the proper one turns up.

Great people overlook things not worth notice. 252*a*.

2875. தண்ணீரும் மூன்று பிழை பொறுக்கும்.
Water forgives three offences.

Referring to the three times a man is said to rise to the surface before drowning.

2876. நல்லோருக்குப் பொறுமையே துணை.
Patience is the support of good men.

"*He that can quietly endure overcometh.*"

2877. நூறு குற்றம் ஆறு பிழைகொண்டு பொறுக்கவேண்டும்.
A hundred offences must be considered as six faults only and forgiven. *Cf.* Matt. 18, 22.

2878. நொய் அரிசி கொதி பொறுக்குமா?
Will pounded rice endure boiling?

Mean people possess no real patience; there is nothing noble in them. Winslow says this proverb means that the poor cannot bear sudden wealth.

2879. பெற்ற தாய் ஆனாலும், குற்றம் எத்தனை பொறுப்பாள்.
Though she is your own mother, how many offences will she forgive? 3212.

There is a limit even to her patience.

2880. பூமியைப்போல பொறுமைவேண்டும்.
One should have patience like the earth.

The earth bears the sins of one generation after another, but according to the Puranas, in ancient times the goddess Earth (*Bhumi Dêvi*) sometimes lost her patience and applied to the gods for help against the sins of men.

2881. பொறுத்தார் பூமி ஆள்வார்.
The patient will rule the world.

பொங்கினார் காடுகொள்வார்.
The passionate will inherit the burning or burial ground.

Said in allusion to the Pandavas and the Kauravas in the Mahabharata.

"*Command yourself and you will command all things.*"

ON QUITTING CERTAINTY FOR HOPE.

நம்பிக்கை, நிச்சயம்.

2882. அரசனை நம்பிப் புருஷனைக் கைவிட்டதுபோல்.

Like believing in the king and giving up one's husband.

Said of one who gives up a post with a small but certain salary, for the sake of a better post which he fails to get.

" *Never quit certainty for hope.*"

2883. அன்றைக்குக் கிடைக்கிற ஆயிரம் பொன்னைவிட, இன்றைக்குக் கிடைக்கிற அரைக்காசு நல்லது.

A little copper coin obtained to-day is better than a thousand gold coins that you may get some day. 2889.

" *One to-day is better than ten to-morrows.*"

2884. ஆனைமேலிருக்கிற அரசன் சோற்றைவிட, பிச்சை எடுக்கிற பார்ப்பான் சோறு மேல்.

Better is the rice of a mendicant Brahmin, than the rice of a king riding on an elephant.

A king may lose his kingdom but a mendicant Brahmin is welcome everywhere.

2885. இரவல் சீலையை நம்பி, இடுப்புக் கந்தையை எறிந்தாளாம்.

Trusting to the borrowed cloth, she threw away the rags she had round her waist.

The folly of forsaking certainties. The woman who threw away her own ragged clothes because she was dressed in a borrowed cloth, found that when she had to return the borrowed dress she was left quite naked.

2886. கலையும் மப்பை நம்பி, கரைத்த மாவை வட்டிக்கு விட்டதுபோல்.

Believing in the dispersing clouds (*i.e.* that it was going to rain, and she would soon get a fresh harvest), she lent the flour she had ground (to her neighbour).

" *Although in rain, throw not away thy watering-pot.*"

2887. கைப்பழத்தைப் போட்டுவிட்டு, துறட்டுப் பழத்துக்கு ஆசைப்பட்டது போல்.

Like dropping the fruit in your hand, and longing for the fruit that has to be got down from the tree.

2888. கொண்டவன் இருக்க, கண்டவனோடு போவானேன்.

While I have my husband, why commit adultery with a stranger?

2889. நாளைக்குத் தின்கிற பலாக்காயைவிட, இன்றைக்குத் தின்கிற களாக் காய் மேல்.

Better to eat *Kála*-fruit (an inferior fruit) to-day, than to eat jack-fruit (a favourite Indian fruit) to-morrow. 2883.

" *A bird in the hand is worth two in the bush.*"

2890. நெய்கிறதை விட்டு நினைத்துக்கொண்டாலும் கைகோளன்.
The weaver thought of abandoning weaving.
"*The cobbler should stick to his last.*"

2891. வந்தது போய்விடும், இருக்கிறது போகாது.
That which comes will go again, but what one has will not go.

2892. வயிற்றுப் பிள்ளையை நம்பி, கைப்பிள்ளையை விட்டதுபோல்.
Like a mother believing that she will bring forth the child in her womb, and giving away the child in her arms.

Cf. 956 *ff.*

BELIEF, TRUST.

நம்பிக்கை.

HE WHO WILL NOT BELIEVE CANNOT BE MADE TO BELIEVE.

2893. கண்ணைப் பிடுங்கி முன்னே எறிந்தும், கண்கட்டி வித்தை என்கிறான்.
Though one pulls out one's eyes and throws them before him, he will only say it is jugglery.
Wilful stupidity.
"*None so blind as those who won't see.*"

2894. வயிற்றுக் குடலைக் காட்டினாலும், வாழைநார் என்கிறான்.
Although you show him the entrails of your body, he will say that they are the fibres of a banana-tree (*Musa*).

2895. வயிற்றைக் கீறிக் காண்பித்தாலும், இந்திர ஜாலம் என்பான்.
Even if I cut open my stomach and show it to him, he will only say that it is jugglery.

THE UNTRUSTWORTHY.

2896. அசல்வீட்டான் பிள்ளை ஆபத்துக்கு உதவுவானா?
Will a neighbour's child give help in times of adversity? 3537.

2897. அடி ஒட்டி அல்லவோ மேற்கரணம் போடவேண்டும்.
Rest on something solid and then make your somersault. 1333.
Do not enter into any undertaking without having something to depend on.

2898. உனக்கு ஒட்டுத் திண்ணைபோலிருக்கிறான்.
He is like a narrow veranda to you.
One cannot sleep comfortably on a narrow veranda for fear of rolling off. One cannot be comfortable if one has a doubtful or untrustworthy partner or benefactor.

2899. சூத்துத்துணியை நம்புகிறதில்லே.
He is afraid of trusting the cloth he has tied round his waist.

He is afraid that somebody will steal it. Said of a very suspicious person who suspects everyone, even his own wife. 365.

2900. சேற்றிலே நட்ட கம்பம்போல்.
Like a pole stuck in the mud.

A pole stuck in the mud may fall at any time any way. Applied to an untrustworthy person; or, to an unsettled law-suit.

2901. நடக்கிறது நடக்கட்டும், தெய்வம் இருக்கிறது.
Come what may, God remains. 2090.

2902. பசு சாதும், பார்ப்பான் ஏழையும் நம்பப்படாது.
One should not trust a gentle cow or a poor Brahmin. 2903.

The cow may gore, and the Brahmin may prove a cheat.

2903. பசித்தவன்மேல் நம்பிக்கை வைக்காதே.
Do not trust a hungry man. 1761.

"*Trust not a broken staff.*"
"*Hunger and cold deliver a man up to his enemy.*"

2904. பத்துவிதத்திலும் பறையனை நம்பலாம், பார்ப்பானை நம்பக்கூடாது.
In ten cases you may believe a Pariah, but not a Brahmin.

2905. பேன் பார்த்தாலும் பார்க்கும், காதைக் கடித்தாலும் கடிக்கும் (or பிய்த்தாலும் பிய்க்கும்).
It may hunt lice in the hair, but it may also bite the ear (said of a monkey).

Said of a person who is not uniform in his treament of others; he may do good and may also do harm; not a noble character. வேளைக்கு ஒரு குணம். 1275.

2906. மண் குதிரையை நம்பி, ஆற்றிலே இறங்கலாமா?
Should one mount a horse made of mud to get across a river? 2022, 2028.

Don't trust mean people, though their outward appearance be ever so grand.

CERTAINTY AND UNCERTAINTY, STEADFASTNESS AND UNSTEADFASTNESS.

நிச்சயம், நிச்சயமில்லாமை, நிலை, நிலையில்லாமை.

2907. அங்கே போனேனே செத்தேனே?
If I go there, I shall be killed. 2506, 2915.

In colloquial: அங்கேபோனால் செத்தேன். The past for the future denotes certainty.

2908. ஆருக்கு ஆர் சதம்?
Are we eternal to one another?

Death's approach is uncertain. Consequently we do not know how long we shall have our dear ones and friends or protectors.

2909. ஆர் வாழ்வு ஆருக்கு நின்றது?

Whose prosperity will remain with him for ever? *or*, who can depend on his present prosperity?

"*To-day stately and brave, to-morrow in the grave.*

2910. இடைச்சி சம்பத்தும், சாணாத்தி வாழ்வும் சரி.

The prosperity of a shepherd woman, and that of a woman of the toddy-drawer's caste are equal.

Sometimes there is no grass for the sheep; and the juice of the palmyra trees is not to be had at all seasons. 87.

"*Danger is next door to security.*"

2911. இந்த உலக வாழ்வு சதமா?

Does worldly prosperity last for ever? 87.

"*No morning sun lasts a whole day*" (in England.)

"*No gain on earth without its loss; no back of ours without a cross;*
No pleasure here without its pains; thus earth and earthly things are vain."

2912. இது எல்லாம் பொம்மல் ஆட்டம்.

All this (*i.e.* world) is a puppet show.

All is illusory, and lasts only for a short time. This is the doctrine of *Maya.*

2913. இரவல் சதமா, திருடன் உறவா?

Do borrowed things remain with you for ever? will a thief be a friend?

2914. இன்றைக்கு இருக்கிறவன் நாளைக்கு இல்லை.

He who is to-day, is not to-morrow.

This may be illustrated by the saying of Pattanathâr Pillei, இருப்பது பொய், போவது மெய். 'Existence in this world is falsehood, leaving this world is truth.' 2936.

2915. ஊரைப் பகைத்தேனோ ஒரு நொடியில் கெட்டேனோ?

If I hate the village, I shall be ruined in a moment. 2907.

2916. எந்த மடத்துக்கு எந்த ஆண்டி சதம்?

What mendicant occupies any lodging-house permanently? 1049.

He moves to a new rest-house every day.

2917. கண் கணிசமாய்ச் சொல்லுவான்.

His estimate of it will be but a guess.

2918. கல்மேல் எழுத்து கலையுமா?

Will a letter written on a stone be obliterated?

2919. குமரிக்கு ஒரு பிள்ளை, கோடிக்கு ஒரு வெள்ளை.

One child for a young woman, and one wash for a new cloth.

The beauty of both soon fades. The cares of maternity destroy the beauty of Hindu girls very early. It is no uncommon thing for a child-wife of fourteen to bear a child. One washing is enough to dim the gorgeousness of the colours in a new cloth.

2920. சொன்ன சொல்லுக்கு இரண்டில்லாமல் வருவான்.

There are no two opinions about his words; he will surely come.

He has said it, and he will act accordingly.

2921. தோட்டக்காரன் (or, கப்பற்காரன்) வாழ்வு காற்றுஅடித்தால்போச்சுது.

A gardener's prosperity may end any day, if a storm comes.

A man's worldly prosperity may be upset any day by unforeseen events.

"*A merchant's happiness hangs upon chance, winds and waves.*"

2922. நாய் வாய் வைத்ததுபோல் வேலைசெய்கிறது (or படிக்கிறது).

Working like a dog that runs about putting its mouth to everything.

Describes unsteadiness of purpose.

2923. பஞ்சாங்கம் போனாலும், நக்ஷத்திரம் போகுமா.

If the almanac is lost, will the stars be lost? 2212.

That which is derived may fail or be lost, but the original of all does not fail. Even if the Vedas were lost, God would not be affected by it.

2924. பொங்கின பால் பொய்ப்பால்.

Boiling milk is deceptive.

When milk is being boiled, it may rise very high and seem much, but it subsides as soon as the pot in which it is being boiled is removed from the fire. Said of people who are proud and conceited on account of their position or of a little money they have. Also said when some one's pride and conceit are seen to be founded on purely temporary prosperity.

2925. மழை பெய்கிறதும், பிள்ளை பெறுகிறதும் மகா தேவருக்கும் தெரியாது.

Even the great gods do not know when it will rain, and when a child is to be brought forth.

2926. வாழைக்கு ஒரு குலை.

A banana-tree yields only one bunch of fruit (and then it dies).

2927. வெந்தயம் (or, வெங்காயம்) இட்ட கறிக்குச் சந்தேகமில்லை.

There can be no doubt about a curry with fenugreek seed in it.

The smell of the fenugreek or onion at once settles all doubt.

Said of a person who has done some evil, or betrayed a secret and then denies it, though it is evident that he and no one else is the sinner.

Cf. 2670 *ff.*

"ONE'S DEATH ANOTHER'S BREAD."

சாவு.

2928. ஆண்டி எப்போ சாவான்? மடம் எப்போ ஒழியும்.
When will the mendicant die, and when will his place in the rest-house (Matt, *Matha*) become vacant? 3642.

" *He pulls with a long rope that waits for another's death.*"

2929. இடைக் (or தாய்) கிழவி எப்போ சாவாளோ? இடம் (or தாழ்வாழம்) எப்போ ஒழியுமோ?
When will the old shepherd woman die, and when will her place (*or* shed) be empty?

" *He that waits for dead men's shoes, may go long enough barefoot.*"

2930. செத்தவன் உடைமை இருந்தவனுக்கு அடைக்கலம்.
The property of the dead is the refuge of the living.

2931. மச்சான் செத்தால் மயிராச்சு, கம்பளி மெத்தை நமக்காச்சு.
I care a hair for the death of my brother-in-law, for his blanket and mat will become mine.

REFERRING TO DEATH.

சாவு.

2932. அவன் சோற்றை மறந்துவிட்டான்.
He forgot to eat his rice (*i.e.* he died).

2933. அழுவார் அற்ற பிணமும், ஆற்றுவார் அற்ற சுடலையும்.
A corpse that has no one to weep over it, and a funeral pyre that has no one to quench it.

Said of one who dies in a foreign place away from his own people.

2934. அங்காலம் எல்லாம் அவசாரி ஆடி, சாங்காலம் சங்கரா சங்கரா என்கிறாள்!
Throughout life she was a harlot, but at the time of death she cried 'Siva, Siva!'

When nearing death all cry to God for help.—Death-bed repentance.

2935. ஆறிலும் சாவு, நூறிலும் சாவு.
A person may die when six or when a hundred years old.

" *Of young men die many, of old escape not any.*"

" *Death does not blow a trumpet.*"

2936. இருப்பது பொய், போவது மெய்.
To remain here is a lie, to depart to another world is the truth. 3124.

i.e. Not earthly life, but life after death is the true life.

2937. இருந்தவன் இருப்பவனுக்கு வழிகாட்டி.

The dead is the guide of the living.

The dead are witnesses that the living must also die.

2938. ஈசல் மடிந்தாற்போல் மடிந்ததே சேனை.

The army died like swarms of ants. *i. e.* in heaps or by thousands.

2939. என் சீட்டுக் கிழிந்துபோனால் அல்லவோ சாவு வரும்.

I shall die only after my fate-leaf is torn. 1351, 2948.

In allusion to the Hindu belief that the fate of every person is written on a cadjan-leaf by Brahma and left in the custody of Yama's clerk, Chittraputra. This latter is supposed to tear the leaf of everyone whose term of life is out and to hand the torn leaf over to Yama's messengers who execute death.

This is sometimes said by people, who, in great illness or intense suffering, long to die, as follows: இன்னம் என் சீட்டுக் கிழியவில்லையே. My fate-leaf is not yet torn! The proverb may also mean: Nothing can be done in any sphere of life without the will of the person in authority.

> "Mrityu! thou art created unto this,
> To make an end to all that lives, go, child!
> Make them to end, each at his time; spare none!
> Such is my will, and never otherwise;
> Thou shalt be blameless, doing Brahma's will."
>
> E. ARNOLD: *Indian Idylls.*

2940. ஓடிப்போன முசல் பெரிய முசல்.

The hare that ran away was a big one. 2949.

The loss of anything makes it precious. Matt. xxiii. 29.

"*He that boasted of his ancestors confesseth he hath no virtue of his own.*"

2941. கட்டை போனால் அடுப்போடே.

When this body goes (dies), there is no more.

2942. காடு வா என்கிறது, வீடு போ என்கிறது.

The burial place says: "Come," and the house says "Go!"

Said about or by old people, who on account of age must soon die.

"*He is burnt to the socket.*"

2943. காது அறுந்த ஊசியும் வாராது காண் (ஐயா) கடைவழிக்கே.

On your last journey (*i.e.* to the burning ground) you will not carry even an eyeless needle with you. 136, 3361.

"*A thousand pounds and a bottle of hay are just the same at doomsday.*"

2944. கூடு இருக்கக் குயில் (or குருவி) போன மாயம் என்ன?

How wonderful, that I, the cage, am left behind, while the cuckoo, its inhabitant, has flown away without my knowledge!

The bereft wife considers herself the cage, and her husband the bird that lived in it. Said by a widow over her husband's corpse.

2945. சனிப்பிணம் துணை தேடும்.

A man who dies on a Saturday will seek help. 2953.

Saturday is an inauspicious day. Hence if one dies on that day another must die and follow him.

2946. சாகவேண்டும் என்கிற சதுரியை விட்டுவிட்டுவா, வாழவேண்டும் என்கிற வலதியை அழைத்துவா.

Leave the wise woman who wants to die, and bring the bold woman who wants to live.

So says *Death* to his servant. Those who seek death, cannot find it (as *Damayanti* in the forest after *Nala* had left her), and those who fear death are called away.

2947. சாகிற நாய் வீரத்தைக் காட்டினதுபோல.

Like a dying dog showing courage. 2229.

Said of one, who in despair at Death's approach, does as much evil as he can.

2948. சித்திரப்புத்திரனுக்குத் தெரியாமல் சீட்டுக் கிழியுமா?

Will the label (with one's name) be destroyed without the knowledge of the accountant of *Death*.

No one dies without the will of *Death*. 2939.

2949. செத்தவன் கண் கடா கண், இருந்தவன் கண் இல்லி கண்.

The dead man's eyes are very big, those of the living very small. 2940.

Lavishing praise on the dead which is not bestowed on the living.

2950. செத்த இடம் புல்லு முளைத்துப்போம்.

Grass will grow on the place of his death.

Said to signify that the person referred to died long ago. Or:—Had he not helped that family, it would have been ruined long ago.

2951. செத்துத் தெய்வமாய் நிற்கிறான்.

Though dead, he stands like a god.

Women often say this about a deceased person meaning: Do not speak ill of him for he can hear what you say.

"*Speak well of the dead.*"

"*Of the dead nothing but what is good.*"

2952. செத்தவன் சூத்து கிழக்கே இருந்தால் என்ன, மேற்கே இருந்தால் என்ன!

What does it matter whether a dead man's body is turned to the East or the West?

Whatever ceremonies the Brahmins perform after a man's death are of no avail, if they have not taught him the right path in this life.—Or, a man should be treated properly while he is alive.—Or, said of a man who is ruined morally, for whom there is no help.

2953. தங்கின வியாழன் தன்னுடன் மூன்று.

A person who dies on a Thursday will take three with him. 2945.

Death on a Thursday is even more inauspicious than death on a Saturday. In India we meet with the idea, that he who dies on Thursday must have, as companions, a chicken, some cocoanuts and a bolt; while he who dies on a Saturday needs only a chicken.

2954. *நூற்றுக்கு இருந்தாலும், கூற்றுக்கு (யமன்) அறைக்கீரைதான்.*

Even if one lives a hundred years, he is but a vegetable to Death.

" *Death is the common lot of all.*"

2955. *பிணத்தை மூடி மணத்தைச் செய்.*

Cover up the corpse and attend to the marriage. 2957.

Postpone the former for the latter.

2956. *வரப்போ தலையணை* (com. *தலைக்காணி*), *வாய்க்காலோ பஞ்சுமெத்தை.*

After death an earthen ridge is the pillow for the head, and a water-channel is the cotton mattress.

This is the last comfort provided for the human body.

The Lingáyat Sivites bury their dead. The corpse is placed in a sitting position in the grave. The artisans (Kammalar) also bury.

2957. *வாழ்வைத் தள்ளினாலும், சாவைத் தள்ளப்படாது.*

Though you reject prosperity, you cannot reject death.

Though you stay away from a wedding, you should not stay away from a funeral. The reverse of 2955.

A GOOD ENTERPRISE THAT ENDS UNLUCKILY.

2958. *அலுத்துப் பொலுத்து அக்காளண்டை போனால், அக்காள் இழுத்து மச்சானிடத்தில் விட்டாளாம்.*

If weary and fatigued she (left her husband and) went to her elder sister's house (hoping to rest a while from worry), her elder sister dragged her back to her brother-in-law.

2959. *கற்பக விருக்ஷமண்டை போய், எட்டிக்காய் வாங்கினதுபோல்.*

He went to the *Kalpaka*-tree, but got poisonons fruit.

The *Kalpaka*-tree is one of the five magic trees of Indra's heaven, supposed to yield whatever is desired.

2960. *கிணறு வெட்டப் பூதம் புறப்பட்டதுபோல்.*

When digging a well, a devil came out.

2961. *குடித்தனம் மேலிடவேண்டி, பிடாரியைப் பெண்டு வைத்துக்கொண்டான்.*

Being anxious to have a family, he married a vixenish woman. 3558.

" *A man has choice to begin love, but not to end it.*"

" *He has a great fancy to marry that goes to the devil for a wife.*"

2962. *குளிக்கப்போய், சேற்றைப் பூசிக்கொண்டதுபோல.*

Like smearing yourself with mud after bathing.

Said of one who tries to make money, but loses what little capital he had instead.

2963. *குளிசங்கட்டக் குட்டி இரட்டித்தது.*

After tying on a charm against having too many children, and then bearing twins.

2964. கூத்துப் பார்க்கப்போன இடத்தில், பேய் பிடித்ததுபோல்.
Like going to see a play, and being seized by a devil.

2965. கொண்டாட்டம் போய், திண்டாட்டம் ஆச்சுது.
After the pleasure, sorrow comes. 3514.

When the wedding festival is over, the debts incurred in performing the ceremonies have to be paid.

2966. பிள்ளை வரத்துக்குப் போன இடத்தில், புருஷனைப் பறி கொடுத்தது போல்.
Like the woman who lost her husband at the place where she went to perform ceremonies in order to have a child.

Hindu woman frequently make pilgrimages to shrines in order to worship idols that are supposed to have power to remove barrenness.

" *The camel seeking horns lost its ears.*"

2967. பிள்ளையார் பிடிக்கப்போய், குரங்காய் முடிந்ததுபோல்.
Like attempting to make an image of Ganesa, and ending by making an image of the monkey-god.

2968. பெருமாள் என்கிற பேரை மாற்றப் பெரிய பெருமாள் ஆச்சுது.
He went to have his name Perumâl (Vishnu) changed, but had it changed to "great Perumâl."

A Hindu had a Pariah Servant of this name. Being a Vaishnava he did not like his servant to have the name of the god he worshipped; he therefore sent him home to change his name and paid all the expenses of the ceremony. The servant however returned with the above name, which was even more sacred than his former name.

2968*a*. விளையாட்டாயிருந்தது, வினையாய் முடிந்தது.
The beginning was play, the end was serious.
" *Play's gude while it is play.*"

Cf. 301 *ff*.

BEGINNING.

2969. இறங்கச்சே நீச்சானால், கரை ஏறுகிறது எப்படி.
If on entering the river one has to swim, how is one to get to the other side?

How is one to accomplish a task that is hard at the very beginning.

" *All beginning is hard, said the thief: he began by stealing an anvil.*"

2970. எடுக்குமுன்னே கழுதை இடுப்பு ஒடிந்து விழுந்ததாம்.
Before the ass had moved its load, it broke its hip and fell down.
" *Getting out well is a quarter of the journey.*"

2971. எடுத்தாப்போல் தப்பட்டைக்காரன் பட்டான் (or செத்தான்).
Just when about to start, the drummer died.

2972. ஏற்றக்கோலுக்குப் பிடித்தால், அரிவாள் பிடிக்கு வரும்.

If you take (a bamboo pole long enough) for a water-lift it may by and by be shortened.

Let the beginning be grand, you can easily be brought down. Many *bazaar*-men and peddlers act according to this proverb, when they ask ten times more for their things than they want, and gradually come down to the proper price.

2973. முதல் கோணல், முற்றும் கோணல்.

If the beginning is crooked, the whole will be crooked. 3308.

"*He who begins ill, finishes worse.*"

2974. முதல் பிறந்த பிள்ளை முத்து பிள்ளை, பின்னே பிறந்த பிள்ளை பீ பிள்ளை.

The first-born is a pearl, the next child is filth. 3529.

Used to signify that first thoughts and impressions are best.

SUFFERING BENEFICIAL TO MEN.

2975. அட்டாலும், பால் சுவையில் குன்றாது.
Though milk be boiled, its flavour does not diminish.

2976. அரைக்கினும் (or தேய்ந்தாலும்) சந்தனம், அதன் மணம் அறாது.

Though sandal-wood be ground, its fragrance will not vanish.

Or, சந்தனக்கட்டை தேய்ந்து, கந்தம் குறையுமா?

Will the fragrance of a piece of sandal-wood lessen, if it is rubbed?

2977. இழுக்கான (or மட்ட) பொன்னைப் புடத்தில் வைத்து எடுப்பார்கள்.
(Goldsmiths) put inferior gold into the refining-pot.

2978. கரும்பும் எள்ளும் கசக்கினால் (or இறுக்கினால்) பலனாகும்.

Only when sugar-cane and oil-seed are crushed do they yield profit. 3351.

Men must go through hardships and trial.

"*Crosses are ladders to heaven.*" "*No cross, no crown.*"

2979. குத்தி வடித்தாலும் சம்பா, குப்பையில் போட்டாலும் தங்கம்.

Though pounded and cleaned, *Samba* rice is still *Samba* rice, and pure gold, though thrown on a dunghill, is still pure gold.

2980. குப்பையில் போட்டாலும், குன்றிமணி மங்காது (or குன்றிமணிதான்).

Though *kunri* seed be cast on a dunghill, it loses not its lustre (*or*, it is still *kunri* seed).

Though one of high rank mingles with the lowly, he will not lose his dignity.

2981. கெட்டாலும் செட்டி செட்டியே, கிழிந்தாலும் பட்டுப் பட்டே.
A reduced merchant is still a merchant, torn silk is still silk. 2984, 3054.

What was originally good and noble will never lose its worth entirely.

"*A myrtle among thorns is a myrtle still.*"

"*Good blood cannot lie.*"

2982. தங்கம் புடத்தில் வைத்தாலும், தன் நிறம் போகாது.
Though gold be put into the melting-pot, it will not lose its colour.

2983. பட்டவளுக்குப் பதவி, படாதவளுக்கு நரகம்.
She who suffers attains heaven (*Padavi*), she who does not suffer will go to hell.

"*Well thriveth that well suffereth.*"

2984. பட்டு மக்கினாலும் பெட்டியிலே.
Though a silk-cloth rots, it will be kept in a box. 2981, 3061.

Rare and valuable things are not easily given up.

2985.´ புடம் போட்டால், பொன் வேறு களிம்பு வேறு.
If gold is put into the melting-pot, it will be separated from its dross.

Adversity tries men and forms their character.

"*Bitter pills may have sweet effect.*"

2986. பெருமை கண்டவர், சிறுமை கண்டாலல்லது தேறார்.
He who attains honour will not thrive unless he endures humiliation.

Cf. 1288 *ff.*

It is said in a Tamil song, (நீதிவெண்பா) that gold, sugar-cane, sandal-wood and milk only improve by suffering. Cf. 2975, 2976, 2978, 2985.

THE GOOD SUFFER AND THE WICKED PROSPER.

2987. அஞ்சினாரைக் கெஞ்சுவிக்கும், அடித்தாரை வாழ்விக்கும்.
(God) makes the timid to cringe, and the violent to prosper.

A master will often bully an obedient servant while he yields to an insolent one.—God keeps the good from prospering in a worldly sense, and allows the wicked to prosper. 2609.

"*The more rogue, the more luck.*"

2988. அஞ்சி நடக்கிறவர்களுக்குக் காலமல்ல.
(The present age) is not (favourable) to God-fearing people. 3117.

2989. அஞ்சுவோரைக் கெஞ்ச அடிக்க (or, பறக்க அடிக்க)ப் பார்க்கிறான்.
He tries to make honest people cringe before him, or tyrannizes over them.

2990. அதிர அடித்தால், உதிர விளையும்.
He who is severe in his treatment of others will prosper.

2991. இறுப்பானுக்குப் பணமும் கிடையாது, உழைப்பானுக்குப் பெண்ணும் கிடையாது.
The honest man who pays his debt has no money, and he who toils cannot get a wife.
The irony of fortune.
"*Better God than gold.*"

2992. தாட்டோட்டக்காரனுக்குத் தயிருஞ்சோறும், விசுவாசக்காரனுக்கு வெந்நீரும் பருக்கையும்.
A deceitful man gets rice and curds, while a faithful man gets only warm water and a grain of rice.
"*The devil's children have the devil's luck.*"

2993. காய்த்த மரத்தில் கல் எறிபடும், காய்க்காத மரத்தில் எறிபடுமோ.
Stones will be thrown at a fruitful tree, but not at a barren tree.
Generally meaning: The good-natured are worried by beggars and not the hard-hearted. 887 ff.

2994. பொய்யிருந்து புலம்பும், மெய்யிருந்து முழிக்கும்.
Falsehood is noisy, truth stands perplexed.
Lying and hypocrisy succeed in this world; honest people are disheartened.
"*Knaves are in such repute, that honest men are accounted fools.*"

2995. மெத்தப் படித்தவருக்குச் சோறு வெல்லம்.
To a very learned men daily food is (as rare as) sugar.

2996. வைதாரை வாழவைக்கும், வாழ்ந்தாரைத் தாழவைக்கும்.
God makes revilers to prosper, and humbles those who are prosperous.

GOOD AND EVIL.

நன்மை, தீமை.

2997. ஆனதுக்கு ஒரு ஆகாதது, ஆகாததற்கு ஒரு ஆனது.
With the worthy the unworthy, and with the unworthy the worthy are linked. 2268, 2270, 3013.
"*Every couple is not a pair.*"

2998. ஆனவன் ஆகாதவன் எங்கும் உண்டு.
Good and bad people are found everywhere. 139, 142.

2999. உதட்டிலே வாழைப்பழம் உள்ளே தள்ளுகிறதா?
Are you to force a banana into a man's mouth? 3008.
Are we to compel a lazy or wicked person to enjoy a good thing?

3000. கரும்பிலே தேன் இருக்கும், கள்ளியிலும் பால் இருக்கும்.
There is honey in sugar-cane, and sap (*lit.* milk) in the (useless) tree-spurge.
The sap of the Euphorbia tirucalli is white like milk.

3001. கரும்புக்குக் கணு இருந்தாலும் கசக்குமா?
Though there be joints in a sugar-cane, will it be bitter?
Though a man has faults, his real goodness need not necessarily be affected by them.

3002. கரும்பு தின்னக் கூலியா?
Do you want to pay for eating sugar-cane?

3003. கல உமி தின்றால், ஒரு அவிழ் (com. அவில்) தட்டாதா?
If you eat a big measure of chaff, will you not come across a grain of rice?

3004. கறந்த பாலைக் காக்காயும் தொடாது.
Even a crow will not touch fresh drawn milk. 146.
Hindus do not drink milk till it has been boiled.

3005. காட்டுத் தேனை விட்டு, கள்ளைக் குடித்ததுபோல.
Like giving up eating honey, and drinking toddy. 3007.
Choosing evil instead of good.

3006. குடியில்லாத வீட்டில், குண்டுப்பெருச்சாளி உலாவும்.
Fat bandicoots (a kind of big rat) will occupy an empty house.
If piety ceases in a home, evil will take possession of it.
"*Hell is wherever heaven is not.*"

3007. கையில் இருக்கிற சோற்றைப் போட்டுவிட்டு, எச்சில் சோற்றுக்குக் கை ஏந்ினதுபோல்.
Like throwing away the good food in his hand, and begging for defiled food. 3005.

3008. கொஞ்சத்தில் இருக்கிறதா குரங்கு மிளகு நீர் குடிக்கிறது.
It is no easy task to make a monkey drink pepper-water. 2999.
It is difficult to do that which is good, for it requires great exertion. It is hard to make men admit the good and to accept it.—It is ever difficult for parents to make children understand that it is good to keep themselves neat and clean, good to take medicine when sick, good to go to school, &c.

"*One may lead a horse to the water, but four an' twenty cannot make him drink.*"

3009. கோவில் இடிக்கத் துணிந்தவனா, குளம் வெட்டப்போகிறான்.
Is he who dares to break down a temple likely to dig a tank?
He who is wicked, will not do virtuous deeds. Constructing tanks in the precincts of temples is an act of piety.

3010. சாஸ்திரம் பாராத வீடு சமுத்திரம்.
A household that does not respect astrology is an ocean (of wealth).

3011. சிதேவியுடன் கூட மூதேவி பிறந்தாற்போல்.
As the goddess of ill-luck was born along with the goddess of good-luck.
Wherever good is found, evil will also be found.

3012. தொன்மை நாடி, நன்மை விடாதே.
In loving what is ancient (*i.e.* traditional), do not forsake what is good at present.

"*The olden age was never the present age.*"

3013. நல்லதுக்கு ஒரு பொல்லாதது, பொல்லாததுக்கு ஒரு நல்லது.
With a good there is evil, with an evil there is good.

It is rarely that both husband and wife are good. If one is good, the other is bad. The more usual form is given in No. 2997.

3014. நல்லது நால் கலம், ஊத்தை ஒன்பது கலம்.
There are four measures of good to nine of filth.

3015. நல்லது செய்து நடுவழியே போனால், பொல்லாது போகிற வழியே போகிறது.
If one does good and walks in the middle of the road, evil will go its own way.

Evil will not be able to do any harm to such a person.

"*A good cause makes a stout heart and a strong arm.*"

3016. நெய்க்குடம் உடைந்தால், நாய்க்கு விருந்து.
If the pot of *ghee* breaks, there will be a feast for the dog.

"*It is an ill wind that blows nobody good.*"

3017. பெரும் வெள்ளம் பாயும் கடலிலே, பீ வாய்க்காலும் பாயும்.
It is to the sea to which the big floods flow that the sewers also flow. 2537.

Both good and evil end at last in heaven.

3018. முந்நாழி கறக்கிற பசுவானாலும், முன் இறப்பைப் பிடுங்கிற பசு ஆகாது.
Though a cow give three measures of milk, she must not pull out straw from the eaves.

A good character is not an excuse for ill-doing.

3019. விஷத்தைக் குடித்தவன், மிளகு நீர் குடிக்கவேண்டும்.
He who has taken poison, must drink pepper water.

He who has done evil, must seek good as an antidote.

3020. விறகு கோணலானாலும் நெருப்புப் பற்றாதா?
Though firewood be crooked, will it not burn?

If it is firewood, the shape is of no account. Though a woman is ugly, if she is good, she will fill her place in the house.

"*A crooked log makes a straight fire.*"

3021. வீணை கோணினாலும், நாதம் கோணுமா (or குறையுமா)?
Though the instrument (*veena*) is crooked, will the music be crooked (*or* faulty)?

GOOD MEN.

நல்லவன்.

3022. அவன் மிதித்த (com. மெரித்த) இடத்தில் புல்லும் சாகாது.
Where he treads, grass will not die. 2287.

3023. உத்தமனுக்கு எத்தாலும் (எதினாலும்) கேடு இல்லை.
Nothing can injure an excellent man. 3065.

3024. உழுகிற மாடு பரதேசம் போனால், அங்கு ஒருவன் கட்டி உழுவான் இங்கு ஒருவன் கட்டி உழுவான்.
If a plough-bullock goes to a foreign country, some people will yoke it to do their ploughing.

A good man is always made to toil.

3025. உழுகிற குண்டையானால், உள்ளூரில் விலையாகாதா?
If the plough-bullock be a good one, will it not sell in its own village?

Good people will always be appreciated in their own place and need not go abroad for work or for game.

"*Good ware makes quick markets.*"

"*Good ware will sell itself.*"

3026. ஏலேலசிங்கன் பொருள் ஏழு கடலில் போனாலும் திரும்பும்.
Though the property of Elêlasingan (a certain honest man) go over the seven seas it will return to him.

An honest man's property is always under God's protection. Elêlasingan was a faithful disciple of the Tamil Pariah Sage Tiruvalluvar.

3027. கபடு சூது கடுகாகிலும் தெரியாது.
There is not as much as a mustard seed of deceit or guile in him. 3043.

3028. களைபிடுங்காத பயிர் கால் பயிர்.
A cornfield not weeded will produce only a quarter of a harvest.

If a man's faults are not removed he can do little good in the world.

3029. கீரை நல்லதானால், கழுவின தண்ணீரே போதாதா வேக.
If the vegetables are good, will not the water in which they were washed do to boil them?

A clever and good man will get on without artificial precautions.

3030. குருட்டுக் கண் தூங்கி என்ன, தூங்காது என்ன?
What does it matter whether a blind eye sleeps or wakes? 2355.

If one has no true piety, it matters little whether he performs ceremonies or not.

3031. கெட்டவனுக்குக் கெட்டதுதான் கிடைக்கும், நல்லவனுக்கு நன்மையே கிடைக்கும்.
An evil person will obtain evil, a good person will obtain good. 3113.

"*As you sow so you will reap.*"

3032. சுத்திக்காரனுக்கு மூன்று இடத்திலே பீ.

A person careful about cleanliness will get filth in three places.

If he treads on something he thinks dirty, he will touch it with a finger and then smell it. Thus foot, hand and nose are defiled. A refined person has much more need to be careful than a pig.

"*Dirt is dirtiest upon the fairest spots.*"

"*A spot is most seen upon the finest cloth.*"

3033. தான் பத்தினியானால், தேவடியாள் தெருவிலும் குடியிருக்கலாம்.

If a matron is chaste, she may live in the dancing-girls' street.

"*To the pure all things are pure.*"

3034. நல்ல உயிர் நாற்பதுநாள் இருக்கும்.

A good life will last for forty days.

Said to an angry person who refuses to take his food, implying that his obstinacy does not matter as a good man can go for forty days without food. Said ironically.

3035. நல்ல பெண்டுக்கு ஒரு சொல், நல்ல மாட்டுக்கு ஒரு அடி.

One word to good woman, and one beating to a good bullock. 8042.

"*A nod for a wise man, and a rod for a fool.*"

3036. நல்லவன் ஒருத்தன் நடுவே நிற்க, ஆறாத வழக்கும் அற்றுப்போகும்.

If a good man is mediator, an unsettled quarrel will be settled. 2724.

3037. நல்லவன் உறவை நாலு பணம் கொடுத்துச் சம்பாதிக்கவேண்டும், கெட்டவன் உறவைப் பத்துப் பணம் கொடுத்து நீக்கவேண்டும்.

You may acquire a good man's friendship for four cash, but you should get rid of a bad man's friendship though you pay ten cash to be rid of him.

3038. நல்லோர் நடத்தை தீயோருக்குத் திகில்.

The life of the good is a terror to the wicked. 3106.

"*He that follows truth too near the heels shall have dirt thrown in his face.*"

3039. நீதியற்ற பட்டணத்தில் நிறை மழை பெய்யுமா?

Will plentiful rain fall in a city without righteousness?

3040. நெல்லுக்குப் பாய்ந்த நீர், புல்லுக்கும் பாயும்.

The water that waters the rice field, waters the grass too.

"*For he sendeth rain on the just and on the unjust.*" Matt. 5 ; 45.

"Do rain and wind avoid some men among the rest,
Because their caste is low?
When such men tread the earth hast seen it quake with rage?
Or does the brilliant sun refuse to them its rays?"

Ch. E. Gover : *The Folk Songs of Southern India.*

3041. புண்ணியம் ஒருவன் பங்கல்ல.

Virtue is not assigned to anyone (one must struggle to get it.)

"*Virtue is tied to no degrees of men.*"

3042. வம்சம் (com. வங்கிசம்) வார்த்தைக்கு அஞ்சும், புழுக்கை உதைக்கு அஞ்சாது.

A respectable man fears a word, but a slave does not fear a kicking. 3035.

3043. வெள்ளைக்கு இல்லை கள்ளச் சிந்தை.

The pure of heart are without fraud. 3027.

They will neither deceive nor be deceived.

EVEN THE GREAT MAY ERR.

3044. ஆனைக்கும் அடி சறுக்கும்.
Even an elephant's foot will slip.

" *Good Homer sometimes nods.*"

" *He that stumbles and falls not, mends his pace.*"

3045. ஊருக்கு எல்லாம் சாஸ்திரம் சொல்லுகிற பல்லி, கழுநீர் (or காடிப் பானையில், or கூழ்பானையில்) விழுகிறதுபோல.

Like the lizard that was the religious adviser of the whole village falling into a tub of dirty water.

The sound of the "speaking" lizard is believed by Hindus to be an omen according to the point from which it is heard, the number of times it is heard, &c.

" *He rode sure indeed that never caught a fall.*"

3046. எல்லாம் சொல்லுமாம் பல்லி, கழுநீர்ப்பானையில் விழுமாம் பல்லி.

They say that a lizard will tell us everything, but it may also fall into a dirty pot.

" *Let him that thinketh he standeth take heed lest he fall.*"

3046*a*. பார்க்கிற கண்ணுக்குக் கேட்கிற காது மேல்.

The ear that hears is above (is more important than) the eye that sees. 192.

Said in the Mahabharata to a king by a minister (*Mantri*) whom the king wants to employ. Implying, you may lend your ears to such persons, who are slandering me. You may take what you hear from such persons to be true, and without investigating matters and seeing things with your own eyes, punish me. Big people often blame their inferiors unjustly.

DIFFERENT SIGNS OF GREATNESS.

3047. அடக்கமுடையார் அறிஞர், அடங்காதார் கல்லார்.
The humble are wise, the haughty are ignorant.

3048. ஆட்டுக்குத் தோற்குமா கிழப்புலி.
Will an old tiger be defeated by a lamb? 3064.

3049. ஆயிரம் உடையார் அமர்ந்திருப்பார், கந்தை பொறுக்கி 'தொந்தோம் தொந்தோம்' என்று கூத்தாடுவாள்.

The owners of thousands are quiet people, while one who goes about in search of rags is presumptuous and noisy. 3057, 3061, 3068.

3050. ஆயிரம் காக்கைக்குள் ஒரு அன்னப்பட்சி அகப்படுகிறதுபோல்.

Like a swan among a thousand crows.

The great and excellent are rare. Most men are like crows, greedy and noisy.

" *Wise men in the world are like timber-trees in a hedge, here and there one.*"

3051. ஆனை செத்தாலும் ஆயிரம் பொன்.

Even when dead an elephant is worth a thousand gold pieces.

" *A lion's skin is never cheap.*"

3052. ஆனை தழுவின கையால் ஆட்டுக்குட்டி தழுவுகிறதா?

Should the arm that embraced an elephant embrace a lamb? 3441.

3053. ஆனை ஏறித் திட்டிவாசலில் நுழைவதுபோல.

Like entering a wicket while riding an elephant.

" *Can a camel go through a needle's eye?*"

3054. ஆனை விழுந்தாலும் குதிரைமட்டம்.

Though an elephant falls down it is still as high as a horse. 2981, 3051.

The grandeur of the great is not quite lost when they come down in the world.

3055. கடல் கொதித்தால், விளாவ நீர் ஏது.

If the sea boils, how can water be had to cool it? 1942.

If a great man gets angry, what will pacify him? Also: If a great man fall who shall set him right?

3056. கலக்கினும் கடல் சேறுகாது.

Though you stir up the sea, it will not turn to mud.

Nothing can disturb the equilibrium of a great mind.

3057. கெட்டித் தங்கமானால் கலீரென்று ஒலிக்குமா?

If the gold is solid gold, will it give a tinkling sound? 2407, 3049, 3061, 3068.

3058. பங்குனி என்று பருக்கிறதுமில்லை, சித்திரை என்றும் சிறுக்கிறதுமில்லை.

He does not expend more in March; he does not lessen his expenses in April.

March (Punguni) is the plentiful month of harvest. April (Sittarei) is a month when one can make little profit. The proverb is used of a man who pursues the even tenor of his way in all seasons. "A wise man is he who knows that prosperity and adversity are alike" (Bhagavat Gita II. 15 Tamil version).

" *He swells not in prosperity, and shrinks not in adversity.*"

3059. சிறியோர் செய்த சிறு பிழை, பெரியோர் பொறுப்பது கடனே.
It is the duty of the great to forgive the little faults of lesser folk.

"*To forgive a wrong is the best revenge.*"

3060. பனிப் பெருக்கிலே கப்பல் ஓடுமோ?
A ship cannot sail in a flood of dew.

"*Great ships require deep waters.*"

3061. பட்டும் பட்டாடையும் பெட்டியில் இருக்கும், கால்காசுக்கந்தை ஓடி உலாவும்.
Silk and silk cloths are kept in a box, while rags not worth a quarter of a cash run about the street. 2984, 3049, 3057, 3068.

3062. புலி பசித்தால் புல்லுத் தின்னுமா?
Will a hungry tiger eat grass?

Great or good people will never stoop to what is mean.

3063. புலிக்குப் பிறந்து பூனையாய்ப் போகுமா?
Will the cub of a tiger ever become a cat? 2867.

3064. பூனையைக் கண்டு, புலி அஞ்சுமா?
Will a tiger be frightened at seeing a cat? 2480, 3045.

3065. பெரு நெருப்புக்கு ஈரமுண்டா?
Will dampness extinguish a great fire? 3023.

3065*a*. பெருங்காயம் (or இங்கு) இருந்த பாண்டம்போல (or பாண்டம் வாசனை போகாது.)
Like the pot that had contained assafœtida.

The traces of former greatness are never quite forgotten, as the smell of assafœtida never leaves the vessel that has held it.

"*Every tub smells of the wine it holds.*"

3065*b*. மங்கை தீட்டானால் கங்கையிலே முழுகுவாள், கங்கை தீட்டானால் எங்கே முழுகுவாள்.
If a woman is unclean she can bathe in the Ganges, but if the Ganges itself (the goddess, the chief of waters) is unclean, whither can it go?

The humble can get pardon from the great; but if the great commit faults where can they get absolution for their sins?

3066. மலையின் உயரம் மலைக்குத் தெரியுமா?
Does a hill know its own height? 2407.

The great are so great in humility, that they do not know their own greatness. Said of God, kings and the wise.

3067. மாணிக்கக் காலுக்கு மாற்றுக்கால் இருக்கிறதா?
How can a pillar of rubies be replaced?

It is difficult to replace the great when they die.

3068. வெள்ளி மோதிரம் ஓசை பெறும், பொன் மோதிரம் ஓசை கொடுக்காது.
A silver ring will ring, but not a gold one. 3049, 3057, 3061.

COMPARATIVE GREATNESS.

3069. ஆலையில்லா ஊரிலே இலுப்பைப்பூ சர்க்கரை.
In a village without a sugar-mill the flower of the Bassia tree serves as sugar.

An ignorant professor must serve in the absence of the learned.
"*Among the blind the one-eyed man is king.*"

3070. ஊமைக்கு உளறுவாயன் (or தெத்துவாயன்) உற்பாதபிண்டம்.
The dumb look up to a stammerer as a person of great wit.

Both worthless, yet the one a bit better than the other.

3071. குதிரையில்லாத ஊருக்குக் கழுதை தம்பிரான்.
In a village without a horse an ass is a king.

3071*a*. தட்டிப் பேச ஆளில்லாவிட்டால், தம்பி சண்டப்பிரசண்டன்.
When there is no one to check him, a young fellow is very boisterous.

"*When the cat is away the mice will play.*"

3072. தொட்டில் பிள்ளைக்கு நடக்கிற பிள்ளை யமன்.
To a child in a cradle a walking child is like the God of Death.

The child in the cradle is so weak that the toddling child can do what he likes with him.
"*A coward's fear may make a coward valiant.*"

3073. நின்ற மரத்திலே நெடுமரம் போனால், நின்ற மரமே நெடுமரம்.
When the tallest tree in a forest is cut down, the trees left will appear tall trees.

Applied to the head of a family; if he dies, the one next to him will become the head.

3074. முடவனுக்கு (or சப்பாணிக்கு) நொண்டி சண்டப்பிரசண்டன் (or சடுகுடுப்பை).
A lame man is very boisterous before a (complete) cripple (*or*, a man without legs).

"*There could be no great ones were there not little ones.*"

MISCELLANEOUS PROVERBS ON GREATNESS.

3075. ஆடிக்காற்றிலே அம்மி பறக்கச்சே இலவம் பஞ்சுக்கு எங்கே கதி?
While the grinding stone is flying about in the wind of July, where will the silk-cotton go? 1681, 3079.

When the great meet with adversity, what will be the fate of common people?

3076. ஆனை ஒரு குட்டிபோட்டும் பலன், பன்றி (com. பண்ணி) பலகுட்டிபோட்டும் பலனில்லை.
Though the elephant brings forth only one young one, it is of value; though a pig bring forth many young ones, they are of no value. 1419.

"*Better a handful of gold, than a sack full of mould.*"

3077. இரும்பு அடிக்கிற இடத்தில் நாய்க்கு என்ன வேலை?
What has a dog to do in a blacksmith's workshop?
If a man attempts to do work he is not fitted for, this saying is quoted.

3078. ஊர் ஆளுகிறவன் பெண்டு பிடித்தால், ஆருடன் சொல்லி முறையிடு கிறது?
If the ruler in a village commits adultery, to whom should complaint be made?

3079. கட்டைப்பாறை பறக்கச்சே, எச்சில்கல்லை எனக்கு என்னகதி என் கிறது?
When the crowbar flies about, the leaf-plate says, what will my fate be? 3075.

3080. குதிரையும் கழுதையும் ஒன்று?
Are the horse and the ass the same? 678.
Low caste and high caste must not be thought equal.
"*A sceptre is one thing, and a ladle another.*"

3081. தம்பிரான் தயவு இருந்தால், சந்நியாசம் என்னத்திற்கு?
If we have the favour of the head of the monastery, what need is there of asceticism?

3082. மூன்று மாதத்திற்குமுன்னே பல் போனவளுக்கு முறுக்குக் கடையில் என்ன வேலை.
What has she who lost her teeth three months ago to do in the bazaar where *murukku* (a very hard cake) is sold?

Cf. 2331 *ff.*

MEDDLESOMENESS.

USELESS INTERFERENCE THAT RECOILS ON THE PERSON WHO INTERFERES.

தலையிடுதல்.

3083. எலும்பைக் கடிப்பானேன் சொந்த பல்லுப் போவானேன்?
Why should he bite bones and lose his teeth?

3084. கல்லைக் குத்துவானேன், கை நோவானேன்.
Why beat a stone with your hand and why hurt your hand? 1120.
"*Do not trust nor contend, nor borrow nor lend, and you'll gain in the end.*"

3085. குத்தாத காதுக்கு ஊனமில்லை.
There is no defect in ears that have not been pierced.
Said by one who does not wish to involve himself in another's quarrels because of the trouble that will come on him if he does so.

3085a. சங்கு சூத்தாகிறது, ஆண்டி வாயாகிறது.

The mendicant put the wrong end of the conch into his mouth. 1247, 2065.

i.e. A mendicant is familiar with the conch shell, which he has to blow at so many ceremonies; for him to make a mistake in its use is most reprehensible, but it is not my business to blame him.

"*A wise head makes a close mouth.*"

3086. தூக்குணங்குருவி குரங்குக்குப் புத்திச் சொன்னதுபோல.

Like the loxia bird that taught the monkey wisdom. 623, 2468, 3099.

This bird makes large hanging nests for itself. One rainy day while well sheltered in its nest one of these birds saw a monkey shivering in the rain, and advised him to make a shelter for himself. The monkey instead of taking the advice, became very angry and tore the bird's nest to pieces. Bad people do not like good advice.

"*Good reasons said, and ill understood, are roses thrown to hogs, and not so good.*"

"*A wise man may look ridiculous in the company of fools.*"

3087. நாறல் பீயை மெரிப்பானேன், நல்ல தண்ணீரை வார்த்துக் கழுவானேன்.

Why should I tread in filth, and then use good water to wash it off?

3088. நெல்லால் அடித்தால், கல்லால் அடிப்பான்.

If I hit him with rice, he hits me with stones.

3089. பிய்ப்பானேன், தைப்பானேன்.

Why tear a cloth to pieces, only to stitch it together again?

3090. பேலச்சொன்னவன் யார், வாரச்சொன்னவன் யார்.

A vulgar proverb.

Said of one who goes wilfully into some evil and has to suffer the consequences; or who involves himself in an undertaking that leads to great loss; or who makes friendship with a wicked person to the loss of his reputation.

3091. போகாத இடத்துக்குப் போனால், வராத சொட்டு வரும்.

If you go where you ought not to go, you will suffer what you ought not to suffer. 198, 2643.

"*Pry not into the affairs of others.*"

3092. வெட்டியானும் பிணமும் கட்டிப் புரளட்டும்.

Let the grave-digger and the corpse struggle as they like.

When fire is applied to the pyre at the burning ground, it sometimes happens that the muscles of the corpse contract in such a fashion that the body moves, and the grave-digger has to beat it down into the fire. It looks as if the two were engaged in a struggle. But no one else should interfere. The grave-digger knows his own work best.

Cf. 2318 *ff.*

WANTON INTERFERENCE WITH QUIET PEOPLE.

தலையிடுதல்.

3093. அறையில் இருந்த பேர்களை அம்பலம் எற்றுகிறான்.

He publicly exposes people who stay in their own rooms.

Said of a person who wantonly worries quiet folk.

3094. உண்ணுமல் தின்னுமல் ஊர் அம்பலமானேன் (or வயிறு உப்புசம் கொண்டேன்).

Though I have never eaten another's food (*i.e.* have kept myself) I have been dragged into publicity (*or*, I have become pregnant.)

A language of a widow, who blames herself for having gone astray. Said also by a dishonest person who has lost his situation but tries to cover over it.

3095. சிவப்பூசையில் கரடி புகுந்ததுபோல.

Like the bear that joined in the worship of Siva.

Said of an intruder who is a source of annoyance.

3096. சிவனே என்று இருந்தாலும் தீவினை விடவில்லை.

Though I do my own duty without meddling in the affairs of others, people will not leave me alone.

"*You must ask your neighbour if you shall live in peace.*"

3097. சும்மா கிடக்கிற சங்கை ஊதிக் கெடுத்தான் ஆண்டி.

The mendicant blew the unused conch and spoiled it. 1909.

Said when a person does not want to marry, but his relations will not leave him alone till he unwillingly agrees to a marriage which turns out unhappily. Or, when somebody mentions *fruits*, while children are playing merrily, and the children at once begin to ask for some.

3098. சும்மா இருக்கிறவன் சூத்திலே சுப்பல் எடுத்துக் குத்தினதுபோல்.

Like taking a straw and pricking a quiet man's breech.

3099. பேச்சைக் கொடுத்து, எச்சை வாங்கிறது.

Giving a word, and getting abuse. 2468, 3086.

Why trouble to advise a bad man to improve ; he will only get angry with you.

3100. வாயுள்ளார் பேசவும் வலதுள்ளார் கொழிக்கவும் ஆச்சுதே (*or*, எனக்கு வந்தது).

It is my fate to be at the mercy of talkers and the fool of those who have power over me.

"*When I did well I heard it never; when I did ill I heard it ever.*"

3101. வாய்ப்பேச்சைப் பிடுங்கி, வயிற்றெரிச்சலைக் கொட்டிக்கொள்ளுகிறது.

Getting words out of somebody, and then throwing them at him to cause him remorse. 228.

To fish out secrets from a person, and afterwards to make a bad use of the information gained.

TRUTH.

TRUTH IS BITTER FOOD.

உண்மை.

3102. உள்ளதைச் சொன்னால், உடம்பு எரிச்சல்.

If the truth is told, the body (is full of) anger.

i.e. Speaking the truth is often disastrous to ease and comfort.

"*Truth may be blamed but not shamed.*"

3103. உள்ளதைச் சொன்னால், நொள்ளைக் கண்ணிக்கு நோப்பாளம்.

If I speak the truth, I shall offend those with defective eyesight.

"*Truth finds foes, where it makes none.*"

3104. உள்ளதைச் சொன்னால், ஊருக்குப் பகை (or பொல்லாதவன்).

If a man tell the truth, the village will hate him (*or*, he will be an enemy of the village.)

"*Follow truth too close at the heels, it will strike out your teeth.*"

3105. உள்ளதைச் சொல்லி மெலிந்தேன், நொள்ளைக் கண்ணச்சி, பிச்சை போடு.

I have become thin by speaking the truth, but give me alms, thou blind woman!

"*He that scoffs at the crooked had need go very upright himself.*"

3106. யதார்த்தவாதி வெகுஜன விரோதி.

He who speaks the truth will have many enemies. 3038.

TRUTH, FRANKNESS, CONFESSION.

3107. உற்றது சொல்ல, அற்றது பொருந்தும்.

By telling the truth, defects will be adjusted.

"*Confession of a fault makes half amends.*"
"*A sin confessed is half redressed.*"

3108. கண்ணோடே பிறந்த காவேரியானாலும் உதட்டைச் சுட்டு உறவாடுவேன்.

Though he be as precious as the river *Kâvêri* that was born with my eyes (*i.e.* as dear as my eyes to me) I shall only become his friend when I have scarred his lips with hot iron.

Though he be my relative there shall be no false leniency in my treatment of him. 3112*a*.

3109. கீறி ஆற்றினல் புண் ஆறும்.

If you lance a sore it will be relieved.

When misunderstandings arise between friends, frank speech however painful is the best remedy.

3110. துக்கத்தைச் சொல்லி ஆற்றவேண்டும், கட்டியைக் கீறி ஆற்றவேண்டும்.

To get relief in a trouble tell it; to get relief for a boil lance it.

3111. மூடிவைத்த புண் ஆருது.

A wound kept covered will not heal.

3112. வெந்த புண் வினை செய்யாது.

If you cauterise a sore it will do no harm (but heal up). 3109.

Radical remedies must be used for radical evils.

3112*a*. தாயைச் சேர்ந்த உறவானலும், அறுத்துத்தான் உறவாடவேண்டும்.

Distinct understandings must be maintained even with your relations on your mother's side. 3108, 3220.

Relation on the father's side become dire enemies in India on account of innumerable feuds arising from property claims.

Cf. 3217 *ff.*

MISCELLANEOUS PROVERBS ABOUT TRUTH.

உண்மை.

3113. உண்மை சொன்னல் உண்மை பலிக்கும், நன்மை சொன்னல் நன்மை பலிக்கும்.

Speak truth and it will produce truth, speak goodness and it will produce goodness. 3031.

3114. உண்மைப்படு, உறுதிப்படு.

Be true and be firm.

3115. உண்மையில்லாத பட்சம் கரையில்லாத குளத்தில் தண்ணீர் நிற்பது போல்.

Love without truth is like water in a pool without banks.

3116. உருக்கின நெய் வார்த்தாலும், கண்ட நியாயந்தான் சொல்லுவான் (or, கண்ணுரைக் கண்டதைச் சொல்லுவான்).

Though they deal out clarified *ghee* to him, he will only say what he has seen. 598, 3126.

A thoroughly honest man.

3117. உள்ளது சொல்ல ஊருமல்ல, நல்லது சொல்ல நாடுமல்ல.

This is not a village in which to speak truth, nor is this a country in which one can speak good words. 2988.

Said in blame of the people of a place. Or, implying that no one speaks in favour of the user of the proverb.

3118. கறந்த பால் கறந்தபடியே பேசு.
Speak like milk just drawn (from the cow). 265.
To speak the pure truth.
"*Craft must have clothes, but truth loves to go naked.*"
"*Truth's best ornament is nakedness.*

3119. குறையச் சொல்லி, நிறைய அள.
You may ask a high price, but measure honestly.
It frequently happens that when rice is only nine measures for a rupee people will not buy. The *bazaar*-man therefore says he will sell ten measures for a rupee, and steals a little out of each measure, so that the customer actually gets only nine measures. Or, you may demand a high salary, but must do honest work.
"*Cheat me in the price, but not in the goods.*"
"*It is not a sin to sell dear, but it is to make ill measure.*"

3120. சத்தியத்துக்கு ஹரிச்சந்திரன்.
In speaking the truth he is a Harichandra.
Harichandra was a Hindu king who never told a lie. This phrase is also used sarcastically about an inveterate liar. Harichandra is renowned in Indian history for truthfulness; Karna for charity (*cf.* 2130); Arjuna for heroism (*cf.* 2149); and Narada for quarrelling and double-dealing.

3120*a*. உனக்கு அரிச்சந்திரன் வீட்டுக்கு அடுத்த வீடா?
Do you live next door to Harichandra?
Said to a pretender to truthfulness.

3121. சத்தியமே வெல்லும், அசத்தியமே கொல்லும்.
Truth conquers, falsehood is defeated.

3122. சத்தியவாசகன் சமஸ்த நற்குணன்.
He who speaks the truth, possesses all good qualities.

3123. பொய் மெய்யை வெல்லுமா?
Can falsehood conquer truth?
"*Truth is God's daughter.*"

3124. பொய் பூரண சந்திரன், மெய் மூன்றாம் பிறை.
Falsehood is like the full moon, truth is like the crescent new moon three days old.
2602, 2936. Falsehood will come to nought just as the full moon wanes. Truth will increase just as the new moon waxes.

3125. மெய் சொல்லிக் கெட்டவனுமில்லை, பொய் சொல்லி வாழ்ந்தவனுமில்லை.
No one has been ruined by speaking the truth, and no one has prospered by lying. 1512.
"*Oil and truth will get uppermost at last.*"
"*A man never surfeits of too much honesty.*"

3126. தலைமேலே அம்பு பறந்தாலும், சொன்ன சொல் தவறாதே.
Even if arrows fly over your head, do not swerve in your words. 3116.

FALSEHOOD.

பொய்.

3127. அவன் பேசுகிறதெல்லாம் தில்லும் பில்லும் திருவாதிரை.
All that he says is lies and tricks.

தில்லும் பில்லும் திருவாதிரை is a colloquial expression commonly used by women and girls meaning 'tricks, deceptions.'

"*He lies as fast as a horse can trot.*"

"*There is as much hold of his words as of a wet eel by the tail.*"

3127*a*. அவனுக்குப் பொய்ச் சத்தியம் பாலும் சோறும்.
To swear or give false statements is as pleasant to him as milk and rice.

Said of a very wicked person. 458.

3128. ஒரு பொய்க்கு ஒன்பது பொய்.
(To establish) one falsehood nine (must be told.)

"*One lie makes many.*"—"*One lie draws ten after it.*"

3129. கலகத்தில் புளுகாதவன் நரகத்திலே போவான்.
He who does not tell a lie in a quarrel will go to hell.

One must tell a lie to get out of a scrape. The term 'hell' is not to be taken too literally.

"*He who hath shipped the devil must make the best of him.*"

3130. திசைப் புரட்டனுக்குப் புளுகுக்குத் தாழ்ச்சியில்லை.
To him who reverses the cardinal points there is no scarcity of lies.

He who dares to tell a big lie will not shrink from fibs.

3131. நீலங் கட்டுப்படப் பேசுகிறான்.
He talks so that the indigo shall be tied up.

i.e. He makes all sorts of false promises in order to get his workmen to finish the work. Said of a liar.

"*That is a lie with a witness.*"

3132. புளுகினாலும் பொருந்த புளுகவேண்டும்.
If you lie, do it so as to be believed.

3133. பேராசைக்காரனை பெரும் புளுகு சொல்லி வெல்லவேண்டும்.
A man of much avarice must be conquered by great lies. 1098.

One must always hold out hopes of great profit to him.

3134. மக்காவுக்குப் போய்க் கொக்கு பிடித்ததுபோல.
Like going to Mecca and catching a crane.

Said of one who wilfully tells all sorts of lies.

"*He may lie boldly who comes from afar.*"

"*He has been as far as Delhi and says all men there walk on their heads.*" (Hindi or Hindustani Proverb).

3135. மூட்டைக்காரச் சுவாமி.
The big man with the big bundle of lies.
The 'bundle' is a pack of lies.
Also :—மூட்டை அளக்கிறவன், he measures bundles.
" *He lies as fast as a dog can lick a dish.*"

REFERRING TO FRIENDSHIP.

உறவு, சிநேகம்.

3136. ஆடு பகையும், குட்டி உறவுமா?
Will he hate the sheep and love the lamb? 3141.
Said of one who is on bad terms with the parents, but professes to love their children.

3137. ஆபத்திலே சிநேகிதனை அறி.
Know a friend when you are in adversity.
" *A friend in need is a friend indeed.*"
" *Prosperity is no just scale, adversity is the only balance to weigh friends in.*"

3138. இருவர் நட்புக்கு ஒருவர் பொறுமை.
The friendship of two depends on the forbearance of one.

3139. உழக்கிலே கிழக்கு மேற்கா?
Will there be East and West in a little round vessel?
i. e. There should be no differences between members of one family.

3140. ஐங்காதம் போனாலும் அறிமுகம் வேண்டும்.
Ensure a known face before you undertake a journey of fifteen miles. 3143.
The Hindu is miserably homesick when he has to live among strangers.

3141. தலை பகை, வால் உறவா?
Will it hate the head and love the tail? 3136.

3142. பதமாய்ச் சிநேகம்பண்ணவேண்டும்.
Make friendship with moderation. 1413.
" *Friendship increases in visiting friends, but more in visiting them seldom.*"

3143. பத்து (com. பதிங்) காதம் போனாலும், பழக்கம் வேண்டும்.
Though you go fifty miles for it you must have society. 3140.

3144. வைத்தியன் உறவு தெருவாசல்மட்டும்.
The doctor's friendship lasts only to the door.

Cf. 1409 *ff*; 2732 *ff*; 2738 *ff*; 2744 *ff*; 2747 *ff*; 2755 *ff*; 2759*ff*; 2763*ff*; 2773; 2777.

LOVE.

அன்பு, பக்ஷம்.

3145. அன்புள்ள குணம் அலையில்லாத நதி.
A character full of love is like a river without a wave.

3146. அன்பு இருந்தால், ஆகாததும் ஆகும்.
If there is love the impossible becomes possible. 2700.
"*He that hath love in his breast hath spurs at his heels.*"
"*Kind will creep where it cannot go.*"

3147. அன்பே பிரதானம், அதுவே வெகுமானம்.
Love is all important, and it is its own reward.

3148. ஆசை உண்டானால், பூசை உண்டு.
If there is desire (of gods or men) there will be worship (of them).
i.e. Men honour those whom they love.

3149. எட்டிமரமானாலும் பச்சென்று இருக்கவேண்டும்.
Though it is a (poisonous) nux-vomica tree, we ought to wish that it may be green.
Hate no one, wish evil to no one; love all, however wicked they may be.

3150. எதுக்கும் உருகாதவன், இச்சைக்கு உருகுவான்.
He who is not melted by anything else may be melted by love. 2041.
The 'love' referred to is passionate desire, rather than 'love' as it is understood in Europe.

3151. கன்றைக் கண்டு, ஓடிவரும் பசுவைப்போல.
Like the cow that ran to its calf immediately on seeing it. 6665.
A simile frequently used to describe tender affection.

3152. காந்தம் இழுத்த ஊசியைப்போல்.
Like the needle that was attracted by the magnet.
Said of the attractive power of love.

3153. கிணற்றுத் தண்ணீரை வெள்ளம் கொண்டுபோகுமா?
Can the flood carry off the well-water? 809.
No outside force can destroy the love of those who are united in heart. Used also about well protected property.

3154. தெவிட்டாக் கனி, பிள்ளை; தெவிட்டாப் பானம், தண்ணீர்.
A child is a fruit, and water is a drink, that one never tires of.

3155. பார்த்துப் பார்த்துக் கண்ணும் பூத்துப்போச்சுது.
By looking and looking my eyes have grown dim.
Said by one who has long been waiting for a person he loves.

Cf. 2695 *ff*; 2763 *ff*.

FAMILY LIFE.

REFERRING TO HOME AND DOMESTIC LIFE.

குடித்தனம்.

3156. அஞ்சும் மூன்றும் உண்டானால், அறியாப்பெண்ணும் சமைக்கும்.

If the five and the three are at hand, even a young girl may make curry.

It is easy to do a thing when one has all the help required.

The 'five' are pepper, salt, mustard, cumin and tamarind. The 'three' are water, fire and fuel.

3157. அரைக்கவும் மாயம், கரைக்கவும் மாயம்.

It is an illusion to grind it and an illusion to dissolve it.

May be said by a daughter-in-law to a mother-in-law, when the latter gives the former too little of the rice, &c., required in preparing a meal.

3158. அவன் குடித்தனத்தை கமுக்கமாய்க் கொண்டுபோகிறான் (or, சமுசாரத்தைக் குட்டாய் நடத்துகிறான்).

He manages domestic affairs with great reserve (*i.e.* he hides his poverty). 1726—1729, 2572.

3159. அறுபது நாளைக்கு எழுபது கந்தை.

For sixty days seventy rags.

Said of children when they wear out their clothes very soon (*or* tear up their school-books); and of the expenses of a family that are incurred through want of economy.

3160. இறகு முற்றிப் பறவையானால், எல்லாம் தன் வயிற்றைத் தான் பார்க்கும்.

When its wings are fully developed and it is fully grown, every bird must look after its own stomach, *i.e.* must feed itself. 2217.

3161. உற்ற கணவனும் ஒரு நெல்லும் உண்டானால், சித்திரம்போல் குடிவாழ்க்கை செய்யலாம்.

If a woman has a faithful husband and a little rice, she may make her domestic happiness (as beautiful) as a picture. 3165, 3167, 3183.

"*I live and lords do no more.*"

3162. ஊசி ஒரு முழத் துணியையாவது கொடுக்கும், அதுதானும் (com. அதானும்) உற்றார் கொடுக்கார்கள்.

A needle will give at least a cubit of cloth, but relatives will not. 3239.

Trust to your own efforts rather than to the good offices of friends.

"*Help yourself and your friends will bless you.*"

3163. எச்சில் இரக்க அடிக்கும், பற்றுப் பறக்க அடிக்கும்.

Dirtiness will make you beg, uncleanliness will make you fly away. 3164, 3172.

Here எச்சில் means அஞ்சாரம், ceremonial defilement. Used to children who suck their fingers. It is commonly thought that children who suck their fingers will not get on in life.

" *Want of care admits despair.*"

3164. எச்சில் இரக்கும், தூமை (or தீட்டு) துடைக்கும்.

Dirty habits will drive a family to beggary, and ceremonial defilement will sweep (all property) out of the house.

The defilement referred to is that caused by catamenia, child birth or contact with a dead body. It is most commonly used with the first meaning.

3165. ஒரு முருங்கையும் ஒரு எருமையும் உண்டானால், வருகிற விருந்துக்கு மனங்களிக்கச்செய்வேன்.

If I have a *murungei*-tree and a buffalo, I can make people happy at the coming feast. 3161, 3167, 3183.

The *murungei*-tree yields a tasty fruit.

" *A little house well filled, a little land well tilled, and a little wife well willed, are great riches.*"

3166. ஒற்றைக் காலும் ஓரியுமாய்ச் சமுசாரஞ் செய்கிறான்.

He lives the life of an old one legged jackal (*or*, the monkey).

i.e. He will associate with no one.

" *Like a snail in the shell.*"

3166*a*. கம்மாளன் குடித்தனம் பண்ணாதே, கடைகெட்ட வெள்ளாட்டி.

Don't keep house like a Kammâlan (an artisan), thou wretched maid-servant! 547.

Said to one in a family who is not economical. The reverse of: செட்டி குடித்தனம் பண்ணுகிறாள். She keeps house like a merchant-caste woman, *i.e.* very economically.

3166*b*. கம்மாளன் துணி வாங்கினால், கால் மயிர் தெரிய வாங்குவான், அதைச் சலவைக்குப் போடும் போதும், அடுப்பிலேபோட்டாலும் வேகாது.

When a Kammâlan buys cloth, the stuff he buys is so thin that it does not hide the hair on his legs and when sent to be washed or bleached, (it will be so dirty that), if put on a fire, it will not burn. 547.

Great desire for ostentation (டம்பம்), but dirty habits spoil everything. ரவைச் சல்லாதுணி, muslin; thin transparent cloth.

3167. கறவையுள்ளான் விருந்துக்கு அஞ்சான்.

He who has a milk cow will not fear to give a feast. 3161, 3165, 3183.

He has milk, and from it he gets curds, buttermilk and ghee (butter).

" *Enough is as good as a feast.*"

" *He who desires but little has no need of much.*

3168. குடித்தனமோ துரைத்தனமோ ?

Is it a household or a kingdom ? 1380, 3170, 3479.

A family must be governed as carefully as a state. This proverb asserts in strong terms social reform as the basis of political reform.

3169. கை பட்டால் கண்ணாடி.

If the hand touches it, it will be like a glass.

Only used about feminine tidiness.

3170. சமுசாரம், சாகரம்.

Family life is an ocean (of trouble). 3168.

3171. சிந்தின வீட்டிலே சேராது, மங்கின வீட்டிலே வாராது.

(Nothing) accrues in a household of squandering people, and (nobody) comes to a gloomy house. 1052, 2010*a*.

Used about a family that is lazy, dirty and wasteful.

"*There is but an hour in a day between a good housewife and a bad.*"

3172. சுத்தம் சோறு போடும், எச்சில் இரக்க வைக்கும்.

Cleanliness will give you food, and dirty habits will make you beg. 3163.

"*Cleanliness is both decent and advantageous.*"

3173. திறந்த வீடு செல்லாத்தாள் கோவில் போலிருக்கிறது.

An open house is like Sellâttâl's temple.

The temple of this goddess is always open ; worshippers go in and out as they please. Said about those who are careless about their own possessions.

"*At open doors dogs come in.*"

3174. நாளைக்கும் சீர் நடக்கத்தான் போகிறது, இன்றைக்கும் சீர் இருக்கத் தான் போகிறது.

To-morrow we are sure to prosper and to-day we are certainly prospering.

Said by a young wife when her husband grumbles at the dowry she has brought : meaning that they have done very well so far, and that if her relatives do not help him, he will have no money at all.

3175. பாழாய்ப் போகிறது பசுவின் வாயிலே.

That which is waste (left after the meal is finished) goes into the cow's mouth.

Let nothing be wasted ; whatever is left after a meal, should be given to the cow or to the poor.

3176. மட்டாய் இருந்தது மதனி (அண்ணி) குடி வாழ்க்கை.

His brother's wife's management of the house was frugal.

3177. மரியாள் குடித்தனம் சரியாய்ப் போச்சுது.

Mary's household management went on well.

A Roman Catholic proverb used ironically about a woman who manages some household matter badly. The Mary referred to, is the Holy Virgin Mary.

3178. வடக்கே பார்த்த மச்சு வீட்டைவிட, தெற்கே பார்த்த குச்சு வீடு மேல்.
A hut facing the South is better than a palace facing the North.
A house facing the North gets more sunshine in the hot weather, and more rain during the rainy season than a house facing the South.

3179. வயிறு நிரம்பினால், பானை மூடாள்.
After filling her stomach, she does not cover up the pot.
Said of a wasteful, improvident house wife.

3180. விருந்து இல்லாச் சோறு மருந்து.
Food taken without company is like physic.
Said by the women in the house of a very hospitable man, who have to cook food for his many guests, either in admiration or in sarcasm because of his hospitality.

3181. விளைவது அரிசியானாலும் மேல் உமி போனால் விளையாது.
Though it is rice, if it is without husks, it will not grow.
No one can get on without the help of others.

3182. வீட்டுக்கு அலங்காரம் பெரிய குடி.
The beauty of a house is a large family.
The opposite of 3166.

3183. வீட்டுச் செல்வம் மாடு, தோட்டச் செல்வம் முருங்கை.
The wealth of a house is a cow; the wealth of a garden is the *Murungei*-tree.
The milk, dung, and urine of the cow are used in every Hindu house, and all parts of the *Murungei*-tree (Hyperanthera moringa) are used as food or medicine. 3161, 3165, 3167.

3184. வெல்லப்பானையை எறும்பு மொய்த்துக்கொண்டதுபோல்.
Like ants swarming round a pot of sugar.
Said when there are many in a family who are greedy to get a share in the prosperity of the family.

1724 *ff*, 2373-2395, 3473 *ff*.

REFERRING TO DISTINCTIONS MADE IN FAMILY LIFE BETWEEN NEAR RELATIVES, DISTANT RELATIVES AND STRANGERS AND BETWEEN HOME AND ABROAD.

குடித்தனம்.

3185. இடுகிறவள் தன்னவளானால், அடிப்பந்தியில் இருந்தால் என்ன, கடைப்பந்தியில் இருந்தால் என்ன?
If she who serves out the food to the guests be one's own friend (*or* relation) what matters it whether one has the first or last seat. 345.
"*A friend in court makes a process short.*"

3186. *அஷ்டத் தரித்திரம் பிடித்தவள் அமராவதியில் வாழ்கிறாள் என்று நித்தியத் தரித்திரம் பிடித்தவன் நின்ற நிலையிலே இட்டுக்கொண்டு வந்தான்.*

Though he knew that she who had suffered the eight kinds of poverty (*i.e.* want of wealth, children, jewels, &c.,) was enjoying married happiness in the heaven of Indra, he (her brother or father) who suffered eternal poverty came and persisted in taking her away. 3298.

It frequently happens that the relations of a woman insist on fetching her from her husband's house, because they think she is not happy, though they themselves are too poor to give her the comforts she had in her husband's house. The above proverb is quoted about such foolish fondness.

3187. *அண்ணன் சேனையில் அள்ளி உண்ணப்போகிறாள்.*

She goes to eat food by handfuls in her elder brother's great household.

A sneer at the harshness of the girl's mother-in-law. It is only in her own mother's house that the girl can enjoy herself and feel at liberty to feast as she likes.

3188. *அண்ணன்தான் கூடப் பிறந்தான், அண்ணி கூடப் பிறந்தாளா?*

Your elder brother was born to your own mother, but was his wife also? 3212.

Your brother may help you, but his wife, a stranger, will not.

3189. *ஆடுவதே மணியமாயிருக்கிறான், ஊருக்கு வேலை செய்வதே மணியமாயிருக்கிறான்.*

He makes it his business to play, and to do work for the village.

Said of one who neglects home duties. 3101, 4195.

3190. *ஆற்று நீர் ஊற்றி அலசக் கழுவினாலும், வேற்று நீர் வேற்று நீர்தான்.*

Though you pour river water and wash it with it, the river water will be foreign water, *i.e.* will not cleanse.

Said by a step-mother, implying that all that she does for a step-son cannot get her his affection.

3191. *இவன் ஊருக்குப் பிள்ளை.*

He is a child of the village.

He does nothing at home, but is always in the village. 3189.

3192. *உருக்கமுள்ள சிற்றாத்தை (சிறிய தாய்) ஒதுக்கில் வாடி (வா அடி கட்டி அழ).*

Oh, come, my gentle step-mother, to a retired place and let us embrace each other and weep.

Said sarcastically to the step-mother who shows her love for her step children only in public. 3193.

3193. *உழக்கு உள்ளூருக்குப், பதக்கு பரதேசிக்கு.*

A small measure of rice as a helping for the people of one's own village, but a big one for a stranger. 1553, 3196.

Said of one who seeks honour from outsiders and is careless about the opinions of his own people.

3194. உள்ளூர் மருமகனும் உழுகிற கடாவும் சரி.

A son-in-law from your own village and a plough buffalo are esteemed alike. 3205.

"*A prophet is not without honour, save in his own country.*"

3195. தனக்குத் தவிடு இடிக்கத் தள்ளாது, அசலுக்கு (*or*, தம்பிரானுக்கு *or*, ஊருக்கு) இரும்பு இடிக்கத் தள்ளும்.

She is unable to pound bran for herself, but she can beat iron for strangers.

Said of women who dislike to do their home duties, but delight in going to friend's houses and helping them. 3189, 3603, 3612.

"*Charity begins at home.*"

3196. உறவுக்கு ஒன்பதுபடி, ஊருக்குப் பத்துப்படி.

Nine measures of grain for relations, but ten for strangers. 1550, 3193.

3197. உன்னோடே பிறந்ததில், மண்ணோடே பிறக்கலாம்.

Being born with you (as my brother), I might as well be born with a clod of earth (for a brother):

Said by a sister to an unsympathetic brother.

3198. ஒக்கப் பிறந்த தங்கை ஓலமிட்டு அழச்சே, ஒப்பாரித் தங்கைக்குச் சிற்றாடையாம்.

While one's own sister is screaming for a cloth (*i.e.* a new dress), it is given to her who is only a sister by manner of speech. 3202.

It is usual for Tamil men and women when talking together to address each other as 'Brother' 'Sister' 'Mother' 'Father' although they may not be related.

3199. ஓடி ஒரு கோடி தேடுவதிலும், இருந்து (or உட்கார்ந்து) ஒரு காசு தேடுவது நல்லது.

Better to remain (where one was born) to earn one cash, than to roam about (in foreign places) to earn great wealth. 1268.

3200. கொண்டவன் இல்லாத வெட்கம், கண்டவனுக்கு உண்டா?

If the husband is not ashamed (of his wife's bad life), will an on-looker (*i.e.* stranger) be ashamed? 905.

3201. தச்சன் கருமான் தள்ளுபடி, மற்றதெல்லாம் ஏறுப்படி.

He spurns the carpenter and blacksmith, and treats the rest well. 2147.

Said of a farmer who refuses their dues to the useful craftsmen, who make his implements for him, and wastes his money on the idle and useless.

3202. தனக்குப் பிறந்த பிள்ளை தவிட்டுக்கு அழுகிறதாம், ஊரார் பிள்ளையை ஊட்டி வளர்க்கிறான்.

While his own child is crying for bran, he feeds and nurtures the child of strangers. 3198.

3203. தன் பிள்ளைக்குப் பதைக்காதவள், சக்களத்திப் பிள்ளைக்குப் பதைப்பாளா?

If her heart does not beat for her own child, will it beat for that of a rival wife? 3564.

Some Hindus marry a second wife while the first is still alive, and the quarrels in such a household are proverbial. The proverb is used generally about heartless friends and relatives.

3204. தான் ஆடாவிட்டாலும் தன் சதை ஆடும்.

Though he does not dance, his flesh does. 3211.

Refers to enmity between near relatives.—Though a brother may say that he will have nothing to do with his brother, or sister or parents, yet he cannot keep to this position; he cannot but feel for the misfortunes of his own family.

3205. நீரை அடித்தால் வேறாகுமா?

If we strike water, will it divide into two parts? 2267, 2834.

It is impossible to separate relations.

"*They are finger and thumb.*"

3205*a*. புறக்கடை மருந்து கவைக்கு உதவாது.

Medicinal plants from one's own back-yard are not valued. 3194.

Children obey their teacher and his rod more readily than they obey their parents. Or, the natural tendency of all people is to value what i strange.

"*Far fetch'd and dear bought is good for ladies.*"

3206. பாலைப் பார்க்கிறதா? பானையைப் பார்க்கிறதா?

Should one look at the milk, or at the pot that holds it? 3569.

If one's child does harm to others, and someone wants the child punished for it, another quotes this proverb: meaning thereby:—Think of his good father who is like milk and overlook the faults of the child who is only like an earthen pot. In some Hindu philosophy it means:—We should look at the good in man, and not at his defects.

"*Do not look upon the vessel but upon that which it contains.*"

"*The jewel is not to be valued for the cabinet.*"

3207. பொங்கியும் பால் புறம்போகவில்லை.

Though the milk boiled, it did not boil over. 2573.

Said of something unpleasant or shameful that has happened within a family but which the family tries to keep secret.

3208. மருந்தும் விருந்தும் மூன்று பொழுது (or நாள்).

For medicine and for feasting three days. 2158, 2392, 2393.

The effect of medicine will be known within three days, and one relative should not stay more than three days with another lest his host be tired of him.

"*Fresh fish and guests smell at three days old.*"

3209. மருமகனுக்கு என்று வைத்த நெய்யை மகனுக்கு ஊற்றி வயிறு எரிந்தாள்.

The ghee (butter) which she had kept for her son-in-law, she poured out to her son, and then envied him.

Ghee being thick flows out of the pot very slowly. The story is that the son, knowing his mother's partiality for her son-in-law, had managed to melt the ghee without her knowledge. When she came at his meal time to pour out a little ghee for him, she turned the pot quickly, expecting the ghee to be stiff, but it all ran out into her son's vessel, and the son-in-law had none.

3210. மாவும் போச்சுது, மாவு கட்டின துணியும் போச்சுது, இனி என்ன உறவு?

The flour is gone and the cloth in which it was kept: what friendship will there be in the future? 1902*b*, 2132, 2154, 2197.

Said when he dies through whom two families were related.

3211. ரத்தபாசம் விடாது.

The ties of blood do not give way. 2267, 3204.

"*Blood is thicker than water.*"

3212. அரிசிகொண்டு அக்காள் வீட்டுக்குப் போவானேன்.

Why should I bring rice with me, when I go to my elder sister's house? 3188.

She is my sister and has natural love for me. She is sure to give me food.

3213. கண்ணில் பட்டால் கரிக்குமா, புருவத்தில் பட்டால் கரிக்குமா?

Will the smart be produced when the eye is hit, or the eyebrow?

It pains one most when his near relatives are suffering; also:—one's own relatives will take an interest in one, and not strangers.

3214. கண்ணுக்கு இமை காதமா?

Are the eyelids ten miles away from the eye? 151, 2089.

A family will protect its members.

3215. காலில் பட்டது, கண்ணில் பட்டதுபோல்.

The hurting of your foot (pained me) as if my eye had been hurt.

3216. விரல் கண்ணிலே குத்தினது என்று வெட்டிப்போடுகிறதா?

Do you cut off your finger because it poked into your eye?

One does not disown a member of the family on account of a fault done within the family circle.

TAKING UNFAIR ADVANTAGE OF THE TIES OF RELATIONSHIP AND SACRED PRIVILEGES.

3217. *உத்தராயணம் என்று உரியைக் கட்டிக்கொண்டு சாகிறதா?*

One should not hang himself because it is Uttarayanam. 2379.

Uttarayana is the time when the sun moves northward, *i.e.* from January till June. Dakshanayana is the time when the sun moves southward, *i.e.* tho rest of the year. The former is the daytime of the heavenly years, the latter the night time. Whatever is good is done in the day-time. Thus Brahmins solemnize weddings only during Uttarayana. Just as the doors of houses in this world are kept open in the daytime so are the doors of heaven kept open during Uttarayana and all who die during Uttarayana enter heaven at once; while those who die during Dakshanayana have to wait outside heaven till Uttarayana begins again.

3218. *ஏகாதசி விரதம் என்று நாக்கைப் பிடுங்கிக்கொண்டு சாவார்களா?*

Though it be the *Ekâdasi* fast, should you pull out your tonguo (*i.e.* in order to die and get to heaven) ?

3219. *தகப்பன் வெட்டின கிணறு என்று தலை கீழாய் விழலாமா?*

Will anyone throw himself headlong into a well because his father dug it ?

Whatovor is handod down by our ancestors, should be used and not abnsod.

3220. *தன் வீட்டு விளக்கு என்று முத்தம் இட்டுக்கொள்ளலாமா?*

Should one kiss a lamp because it belongs to his house ? 2879, 3112*a*.

The lamp will not be partial, but burn him. One should not offend his near relations, thinking that they will forbear to blame or punish him.

" *A man may love his house well, though he ride not on the ridge.*"

3221. *தன் பிள்ளை என்று தலைமேல் வைத்துக்கொள்ளலாமா?*

Though it be your own child, should you carry it on your head ?

Parents should not be partial to their own children.

3222. *சகுனம் நன்றாயிருக்கிறது என்று பொழுதுவிடிகிறவரைக்கும் கன்னம் வைக்கலாமா?*

Though a thief meets a good omen while on his way to steal, will it be right for him to steal till day-break ? 2179.

Though your superior is kind to you and overlooks your faults, his kindness must not be strained too much.

3223. *தான் கும்பிடும் தெய்வமானாலும், பொய்ச்சத்தியம் செய்தால் பொறுக்குமா?*

If I speak falsehood as truth, will God bear with me, even if I worship him ?

3224. *பொன் கத்தி என்று கழுத்து அறுத்துக்கொள்ளலாமா?*

Ought you to cut your throat with a knife, because it is made of gold ?

This is an injunction againt that obsequiousness which leads a man to pander to the faults of a superior or friend.

Cf. 3107.

OWNERSHIP, POSSESSION.

சொந்தம்.

3225. அம்மான்வீட்டு வெள்ளாட்டியை அடிக்க, அதிகாரியைக் கேட்கவேண்டுமோ?

Is it necessary to ask the headman for permission to punish a maid-servant in an uncle's house. 3232, 3563.

3225*a*. அவனுக்கு ஜெயில் (or, ஆஸ்பத்திரி) தாய் வீடு.

The jail (*or*, hospital) has become his home. 395, 3438.

Said of one who is put into jail time after time or of a person who is so often sick, that he is found more often in the hospital than at home. In both cases the person is ridiculed for behaving like a young married girl who, instead of staying permanently with her mother-in-law, too often goes home and makes a long stay with her mother.

3226. அற்பன் கை ஆயிரம் பொன்னிலும், சற்புத்திரன் கைத் தவிடே நன்று.

Bran in a good man's hand is better than a thousand gold pieces in a mean man's hand. 3239.

3227. உடையவன் இல்லாச் சேலை ஒரு முழக்கட்டை.

A cloth without an owner (to look after it) will be a short cloth (*i.e.* destroyed). 2078, &c.

3228. உடையார் வீட்டு மோருக்கு அகப்பைக் கணக்கு என்ன?

Why keep an account of the butter-milk enjoyed by the owner himself?

If he chooses to waste it, that is his own affair.

3229. எலி வளையானாலும் தனி வளை வேண்டும்.

Though only a rat hole, it should be one's own. 3240.

"*East or West, home is best.*"

"*Home is home be it ever so homely.*"

3230. கடையில் அரிசி கஞ்சிக்கு உதவுமா? அண்டைவீட்டுக்காரிப் (*or*, அபிசாரி) புருஷன் ஆபத்துக்கு உதவானு?

Is the (unpounded) rice in the *bazaar* ready to be eaten? Is a neighbour's husband (*or*, harlot's paramour) any help in trouble? 2349.

3231. கேட்பார் சொல்லைக் கேட்டுக் கெடாதே.

Do not be ruined by listening to hearsay (*or*, everybody's advice). 3234.

3232. சத்திரத்துக் கூழுக்குத் தாதஜயன்கார் உத்தரவா?

Is it necessary to get the sanction of the custodian of the *Chattiram* in order to get the free meal bestowed on all comers. 3225.

3233. *சித்தி பெருத மருந்தும் மருந்தோ? பெற்றுப் படையாத பிள்ளையும் பிள்ளையோ?*
Is that a medicine that does not cure? Is that your child that you have not borne and brought up yourself?

3234. *சொல்லுவார் சொன்னுல், கேட்பாருக்கு மதியில்லையா?*
If talkers talk, have not those who hear got discrimination? 3231.
Judge for yourself.

3235. *தனக்கு என்று இருந்தால், சமயத்துக்கு உதவும்.*
If a thing is one's own, it will be of use at the (right) time.

3236. *தன் இனம் தன்னைக் காக்கும், வேலி பயிரைக் காக்கும்.*
His kindred will protect him; the hedge will protect the crop. 2106.

3237. *தன் ஊருக்கு ஆனை, அசல் ஊருக்குப் பூனை.*
In his own village he is an elephant, in a neighbouring village only a cat. 3238.
"*Every one is a king in his own house.*"

3238. *தன் ஊருக்கு அன்னம், பிற ஊருக்குக் காகம்.*
He is a swan in his own village; in another village only a crow. 3237.
"*Every dog is a lion at home.*"

3239. *தாய்க்கைப் பசும் பொன்னிலும், தன் கைத்தவிடே மேல்.*
Better to depend on your own bran, than to depend on your mother's fine gold.
It is better to depend on one's own property, though small, than to depend on that belonging to others. 3162, 3226.
"*A little in one's own pocket, is better than much in another man's purse.*"
"*Dry bread at home is better than roast meat abroad.*"

3240. *மண் பிள்ளையானுலும், தன் பிள்ளையாயிருக்கவேண்டும்.*
Though a child be only dust, it should be one's own. 3229, 3319.

WHAT ONE HAS NOT LABOURED FOR IS LITTLE VALUED.

சொந்தம்.

3241. *தான் தேடாப் பொன்னுக்கு மாற்றுமில்லை உரையுமில்லை.*
Gold not acquired by oneself is neither fine nor valuable. 3284.
"*Nothing is a man's truly, but what he came by duly.*"

3242. *திருடின நெல்லுக்கு மத்தளம் மரக்கால்.*
The drum is used as a measure for stolen rice.
As it has cost the thief nothing, he measures it out lavishly or at random.

3243. *நின்று போட்டதுமில்லை, குனிந்து எடுத்ததுமில்லை.*

You did not stand up to put it down, nor stoop down to take it up.

A father says this to his spendthrift son, who has had no trouble in earning what he is spending.

"*Lightly come, lightly gone.*"

3244. *வாழுகிற வீட்டுக்கு ஒரு பெண்ணும், வைக்கோல் போருக்கு ஒரு கன்றும்.*

One woman in a prosperous house, and one calf in a stack of straw.

A spendthrift woman who marries into a prosperous family will ruin the family—she will selfishly enjoy what she has never toiled for—just as a calf tied close to a stack will eat it all up.

EXAGGERATING THE VALUE OF ONE'S OWN POSSESSIONS.

சொந்தம்.

3245. *அக்கச்சி உடமை அரிசி, தங்கச்சி உடைமை தவிடு.*

If it belongs to the elder sister, it is rice, if it belongs to the younger sister, it is only bran.

Or *அக்காள் பண்டம் அரிசி, தங்கச்சி பண்டம் தவிடு.*

The elder sister thinks her own property valuable as rice, but her younger sister's property she thinks mere chaff.

"*Every potter praises his own pot, and the more if it be broken.*"

3246. *ஊரார் பண்டம் உமிபோல், தன் பண்டம் தங்கம்போல.*

The property of others is chaff, his own is pure gold.

3247. *காணாதது கண்ட கம்பங்கூழை சிந்தாது குடி அடி, சில்லி மூக்கி!*

Oh, thou silly woman, do not spill this rare gruel, drink it!

Said in ridicule of a low person, who is unduly elated by getting something a little better than that to which he is accustomed.

3248. *காக்காய்க்கும் தன் குஞ்சு பொன் குஞ்சு.*

To a crow its young are golden. 369.

"*The crow thinks her own bird the fairest.*"

"*Every cook praises his own broth.*"

3249. *தனக்கு அழகு மொட்டை, பிறருக்கு அழகு கொண்டை.*

He holds his bald head a beauty, others think so of their braided tuft.

3250. *பள்ளிப்பிள்ளை என்றால், செல்லம் குறையுமா?*

If you say 'It is only a *Palli* child,' will it have fewer caresses?

The *Pallis* or *Vanniyans* are a low caste, but a Palli mother loves her low-caste child just as much as a Brahmin mother loves her high-caste son.

DECEIVING ONE'S OWN RELATIONS.

3251. அடுத்தவனைக் கெடுக்கலாமா?
Is it right to ruin him who has come for protection? 2253.

3252. உடலுக்குள்ளே நாக்கை வழிக்கிறதா?
Do you rub the tongue with any of the members of your body?
Rubbing the tongue to cleanse it is considered a very necessary act by Hindus; but neither the hand nor any other member is allowed to touch the tongue. Should they touch it they are defiled. In the same way cheating or deceiving the members of one's own family is considered to be very shameful.

3253. உடுத்த சீலை (or புடவை) பாம்பாய்க் கடித்ததுபோல.
Just as if a cloth he had put on had bitten him like a snake. 3558, 3578.
Said when a relation, or servant, is unfaithful.

3254. குலத்துக்கு ஈனம் கோடாலிக்காம்பு.
The handle of the axe brings ruin to its own race.
It serves to fell trees like that from which it has itself been cut. Said of treacherous relatives.

3255. பிள்ளைக்குப் பிள்ளையாயிருந்து, பெட்டைப்பிள்ளையை வேலையாக்கினான்.
Though he was treated as one of my own children, he seduced a girl in my family.

3256. வேலிக்குப் போட்ட முள் காலுக்கு வினையாச்சுது.
The thorns put up for a hedge have hurt the feet. 2106.
Said if those who should protect one become one's foes.

Cf. 714 *ff.*

MOTHER.

தாய்.

3257. அழுதாலும் பிள்ளை அவளே பெறவேண்டும்.
Though she weeps, a mother must give birth to her own child. 3284.
There is no escape from the sufferings appointed to us.
"*Every bird must hatch its own eggs.*"

3258. அற்றத்துக்கு உற்ற தாய்.
A mother can be trusted with secrets.

3259. அன்னைக்கு உதவாதவன், ஆருக்கும் ஆகான்.
A son, who does not help his mother, is worthless to all men. 3272.

3260. ஆரும் ஆரும் உறவு? தாயும் பிள்ளையும் உறவு.
Who and who are relations? Mother and child are relations.
i.e. There is no closer relationship than that of mother and child.

3261. எலும்பைத் தின்று சதையைக் கொடுத்து வளர்த்தாள்.

She reared her child with meat, while she ate bones. 2159, 3285, 3294.

3262. ஒரு பிள்ளை பெற்றவளுக்கு உறியிலே சோறு, நாலு பிள்ளை பெற்றவளுக்கு நடுத்தெருவிலே ஓடு.

A mother who has had only one child has food in her store, but she who has had four children gets her food in the open street from a potsherd.

If a mother has only one child, he is sure to protect his mother, but if four, none of them thinks it his special duty to care for his mother, and she suffers want. Here: உறி=சுகம்; ஓடு=வருத்தம்.

"*Children are certain cares, but very uncertain comforts.*"

3263. ஒருவனுக்குத் தாரம், மற்றவனுக்குத் தாய்.

To one she will be a wife, to the other she will be a mother.

Of many suitors only one can marry the girl, the rest should look on her as their mother.

3264. காய்ப்பாரத்தை கொடி தாங்காதா?

Will not the creeper bear the weight of its fruits? 3266.

Will not a mother support her children?

"*A mother is like the sea that bears the greatest ships, though she, like the sea, yields to the slightest impressions.*"

3265. குருமொழி கேளாதவனும், தாய் வார்த்தைக்கு அடங்காதவனும் ஜண்டி.

He who will not hear the priest's word, and he who will not obey his mother's word are stubborn. 3274.

3266. கொடிக்குக் காய் பாரமா?

Is the fruit too heavy for the tender creeper? 3264.

A mother will find means to support her children.

3267. கோழி மிதித்து (com. மொரித்து) குஞ்சு முடம் ஆகுமா?

Will a chicken be lamed, if its mother treads on it?

"*The kick of the dam hurts not the colt.*"

3268. சாப்பிள்ளை பெற்றுத் தாலாட்டலாமா?

There will be no lullaby at the birth of a still-born child.

3269. தாயும் தகப்பனும் தவிர சகலமும் வாங்கலாம்.

One may buy everything except a mother and a father. 3320, 3575.

In Tamil, the word 'mother' precedes the word 'father' when both terms are used together.

"*Friendship is not to be bought at a fair.*"

"*Love can neither be bought nor sold, its only price is love.*"

3270. தாயில்லாத பிள்ளை தறுதலை.

A motherless child becomes a rogue. 3273.

3271. தாய் அறியாத சூல் உண்டோ?
Will a mother not know when her daughter is pregnant?

3272. தாய் பொறுக்காததை ஊர் பொறுக்குமா?
What a mother will not forgive her child, the village will not forgive either. 3259.

Or, ஊருக்கு ஆகாத பிள்ளை, தாய்க்கும் ஆகாது.

3273. தாய் முகம் காணாத பிள்ளையும், மழை முகம் காணாத பயிரும் உருப்படாது.
A child that has not seen its mother's face, and a crop that has not seen the face of the rain, will not thrive. 3270.

3274. தாய் வார்த்தை கேளாத பிள்ளை நாய் வாயில் சீலை.
A child that will not obey its mother, is like a rag in a dog's mouth. 3265.

Its end will be utter ignominy.

3275. தாயைத் தண்ணீர் துறையில் பார்த்தால், பிள்ளையை வீட்டில் பார்க்க அவசியமில்லை.
When you have seen the mother at the tank-side, there is no need to see the child at home. 2862.

The child's character can be inferred from the mother's face and conduct.

3276. தாயைப்பார்க்கிலும் சிறந்த கோவிலுமில்லை.
No temple is more beautiful than one's mother.

3277. தாயை மறக்க அடிக்கும் தயிரும் சாதமும்.
Curds and rice will make a child forget its mother.

If a child that has lost its mother is treated kindly, it will forget its mother. Also, material welfare may make a man forget spiritual things. Also, a mother-in-law's kindness may make her son-in-law forget and neglect his mother.

3278. தாய்க்குப் பின் தாரம்.
The wife after the mother.

After the mother is dead the wife should show the same kindness to her husband as his mother did.

3279. தின்னத் தின்னக் கேட்குமாம் பிள்ளை பெற்ற வயிறு.
The stomach (of her) that has borne a child asks for food continually.

A nursing mother's appetite is great.

3280. பூசணிக்காய் அத்தனை முத்து.
A pearl as big as a pumpkin.

Said in praise of a child, a jewel, or some other valuable possession.

3281. தேங்காய்க்கு மூன்று கண், எனக்கு ஒரு கண்.
The cocoanut has three eyes; I have only one.

Said by a mother who mourns because she has only one child. As this one is very dear to her, she calls it her 'eye.'

3282. நடக்கிற பிள்ளை தவறுகிறது, தாயார் செய்த புண்ணியம்.
That a child that has learnt to walk should take to crawling again is the result of its mother's virtue.

Said sarcastically about the reduced circumstances of a family.

3283. பத்தாம் பேறு பாடையில் வைக்கும்.
The tenth child will lay the mother on the bier. 3426.

3284. பிள்ளை அருமை பெற்றவளுக்குத் தெரியும்.
The preciousness of the child is known only to its mother. 3241, 3257.

3285. பிள்ளையைப் பற்றிப் பீயைத் தின்னு.
Eat excrement for the child's sake.

A mother will do or endure anything for the sake of her child. 3261, 3294.

3286. பெற்ற தாய் மூதேவி, புகுந்த தாரம் சீதேவி.
He considers his mother the goddess of ill-luck and his wife the goddess of good-luck. 3288, 3292.

3287. பெற்ற மனம் பித்து, பிள்ளை மனம் கல்லு.
The mother's heart is tender, the child's hard. 2703, 2705, 2707.

3288. பெற்றவள் வயிற்றைப் பார்ப்பாள், பெண்சாதி மடியைப் பார்ப்பாள்.
His mother will look to his stomach; his wife at his waist cloth. 3286, 3292.

The mother takes care that her son gets something to eat; the wife is only anxious to see how much money her husband brings home tied up in his waist cloth. This proverb has also an obscene meaning.

"*After the time of winning and bringing, a wife's friend you are; but when you are tired and weary, a mother's son you are.*" Kashmiri proverb.

3289. பேயானாலும், தாய் வார்த்தை தட்டலாமா?
A mother may be a devil, but may you evade her commands? 3548.

3290. பேய் பிள்ளையானாலும், தாய் தள்ளிவிடுவாளா?
Will a mother abandon her child even if it is a devil? 3575.

3291. மாதா மனம் எரிய, வாழான் ஒரு நாளும்.
She who burns her mother's heart will never prosper.

A disobedient daughter will have bad luck when she is married.

3292. முலை கொடுத்து (or ஊட்டி) வளர்த்தவள் மூதேவி, முன்றானை போட்டவள் சீதேவி.
She who has nursed you and brought you up is your evil goddess (Mudêvi), while she with whom you lie is your good goddess (Sridêvi, Lakshmi). 3286, 3288.

Said sarcastically by a mother to her married son about his wife.

3293. ராஜனானாலும் தன் தாய்க்கு மகனே.
Though a king, he is only a son to his mother. 3435, 3638.

3294. வயிற்றைக் கட்டினவளுக்கு ஆம்புடையான், வாயைக் கட்டினவளுக் குப் பிள்ளை.

She who stints her stomach has a husband, and she who muzzles her mouth has a child.

Both husband and child will thrive through her self-denial. 3261, 3283.

3295. வளர்த்த பிள்ளை சோறு போடாவிட்டாலும், வைத்த பிள்ளை சோறு போடும்.

If the child they have reared gives them no food, the child they have planted (*i.e.* the cocoanut palm) will feed them.

Providence is more reliable than the affection of a son.

3296. வாய்க்குப் பிள்ளை வயிற்றுக்கு மாற்றான்.

A child to the mouth may prove a foe to the stomach.

It is difficult to bring up children, however pleasant it may be to have them about one. The mother can eat only what is suitable for the infant; if she eats what she likes the health of the child will suffer.—Or, a pregnant woman will speak of her child with joyful anticipation, but its birth may be a danger to her own life.

3297. வாயாலே சொன்னது, தாயாரை விற்றுக் கொடுக்கவேண்டும்.

What you have promised you must give, even if you have to sell your mother.

3298. வாழுகிற பெண்ணைத் தாயார் கெடுத்ததுபோல்.

Like a mother spoiling her married daughter's happiness. 3186; 3251 *ff*.

Sometimes a mother will fetch her daughter home from her husband's house because she thinks that the girl's mother-in-law ill-treats her. This gives rise to very serious quarrels and sometimes leads to a long separation between the girl and her husband, which is bad for both. Hence the proverb refers to mistaken kindness.

CHILDREN.

பிள்ளை, குழந்தை.

THE TRAINING OF CHILDREN.

"*The tricks a colt getteth at his first backing,*
Will whilst he continueth never be lacking."

3299. அஞ்சிலே வளையாதது, ஐம்பதிலே வளையுமா?

Will that which is not bent at the age of five, bend when it is fifty years old? 437.

"*Bend the tree while it is young.*"

"*Hang a thief when he is young, and he will not steal when he is old.*"

3300. அஞ்சிலே அறியாதவன், ஐம்பதிலே அறிவானா?

Will a child who is ignorant at five, be clever at fifty?

3301. அடித்து வளர்க்காத பிள்ளையும், முறுக்கி வளர்க்காத மீசையும் செவ்வை ஆகாது.

A child brought up without beating, and a moustache that is not twirled well, will not develop properly. 3343.

3302. அடியாத மாடு படியாது.

A bullock that is not beaten will not be broken to work. 1900.

"*A rod for a fool's back.*"

3303. செடியிலே வணங்காதது, மரத்திலே வணங்குமா?

Can you bend in the tree what was not bent in the sapling?

"*The old branch breaks, if bent.*"

3304. தலை எடுக்கச்சே, கிள்ளவேண்டும்.

It should be nipped in the bud.

"*It is hard to break an old hog of an ill custom.*"

Cf. 433 *ff*; 1900 *ff*.

THE CAPACITIES OF A MAN.

3305 ஆகும் காய் பிஞ்சிலே தெரியும்.

What fruit it will be is known when it is green.

3306. கக்கின பிள்ளை தக்கும்.

A child that vomits will grow strong.

The Hindu thinks that it vomits what is harmful and so keeps good health.

3307. துளசிக்கு வாசமும், முள்ளுக்குக் கூர்மையும் முளைக்கிறபோதே தெரியும்.

The smell of tulsi, and the sharpness of the thorn are known as soon as they spring up.

"*It early pricks that will be a thorn.*"

3308. விளையும் பயிர் முளையிலே தெரியும்.

What grain it will be is known by the blade. 2609, 2973.

CHILDREN IN THE HOME.

3309. ஆனையைப் பிடிக்கிறதும், பானையில் அடைக்கிறதும், அதுவே செல்லப் பிள்ளைக்கு அடையாளம்.

To catch an elephant and put it into a pot, is a child's silly talk.

Said of a person who speaks about a great undertaking as if he were able to accomplish it easily.

3310. இல்லாத வீட்டுக்கு இலஞ்சியம்.

In a childless house (a little child) is a great boon. 3313.

3311. இளங்கன்று பயம் அறியாது.

A young calf does not know fear.

Said of a naughty child that abuses its elders.

3312. ஓடுகிற பாம்பைப் பிடிக்கிற பருவம்.
It is the young who catch a gliding snake.
The young do many dangerous things innocently.

3313. கலப்புழுவை நீக்கின கர்ணன்.
Karna, who removed a vessel fnll of worms.
From the moment Karna, as a child, went into the childless house of Dhritarâshtra, the worms disappeared from the food served in that house. (Mahabharata). The Hindu thinks that a house without children is as badly off as it would be if all the food served in it were full of worms.

3314. கன்று கூடி களம் அடித்தால், வைக்கோலும் ஆகாது, செத்தையும் ஆகாது.
If calves are yoked together to thresh corn, you will get neither straw nor rubbish. 3317, 3318.
Said of children who are set to do work that they do not know how to do, and simply spoil good material.

3315. குழந்தை பசியோ, கோவில் பசியோ?
Is the infant, or the temple hungry?
As both are dear to all, neither will ever be in want.

3316. குழந்தை தூங்குகிறதெல்லாம் அம்மையாருக்கு லாபம்.
All the time the infant sleeps is of use to its mother.

3317. சிறுபிள்ளை செய்த வேளாண்மை வீடு வந்து சேராது.
Will the crop cultivated by children ever be brought home. 644, 1238, 3314.
What is done thoughtlessly will come to naught.

3318. சிறுபிள்ளை விளையாட்டு அழிந்தது மாங்காடு (or சுண்டு எலிக்கு நாசம்).
Little children's play is destruction to a mango-grove (*or* to small rats).

3319. ஜாண் பிள்ளையானாலும், ஆண்பிள்ளை இருக்கவேண்டும்.
Though one's child is only a span long, it must be a boy. 3240.

3320. பிள்ளைச்சீர் கொள்ளக் கிடைக்குமா?
Can one buy the blessing of having children? 3269.
This cannot be had for money.

3321. பிள்ளை என்றால், எல்லாருக்கும் பிள்ளை.
If you say it is a child, it is everybody's child.
Children are dear to all.

3322. மகளுக்குக் குடல் பாக்கியம் தவிர, எல்லா பாக்கியமும் உண்டு.
My daughter has every blessing, except the blessing of having a child. 1756.
According to Hindu ideas, the possession of children is the crowning joy of life.

3323. முத்தும் பவளமும் முறையாய் (or அணியணியாய்) கோர்த்ததுபோல.
Like stringing pearls and coral in order.
Said when male and female children are born in a family alternately.

3324. வேலை முத்தோ, பிள்ளை முத்தோ?
Is work a pearl, or is a child a pearl?
A child should not be considered too precious to work, but should be put to work.

THE CONCEIT OF YOUNG PEOPLE.

வாலிபன்.

3325. அறியாப் பிள்ளையானாலும், ஆடுவோர் மூப்பு.
Though an innocent lad, he plays the old man. 1450, 1535.
"*Grey head on green shoulders.*"

3326. காலம் கண்ட கூளி.
A devil who has lived a long time!
Said of children who talk as if they were old people.

3327. பழுத்த ஓலையைப் பார்த்துக் குருத்து ஓலை சிரித்ததுபோல்.
When the young palm-leaf saw the old one, it laughed. 192.
"*Young men think old men fools, but old men know that young men be fools.*"

3328. பிஞ்சிலே பழுத்தவன்.
A precocious child.
"*Soon ripe, soon rotten.*"

3329. முட்டையிலேயே கொக்கிரகோ என்கிறவன்.
One who crows while still in the egg. 1300.
Said of a young man who plunges into pleasure too early.
"*It will be a forward cock that croweth in the shell.*"

YOUTH CONTRASTED WITH AGE.

பருவம்.

3330. இளமையில் முயற்சி, முதுமையில் காக்கும்.
Exertion in youth will preserve you when old.
"*He that saveth his dinner will have the more for his supper.*"

3331. காலம் அறிந்து பிழையாதவன், வால் அறுந்த குரங்கு ஆவான்.
He who lives without appreciating the value of his time will become like a monkey that has lost its tail.
"*If you lie upon roses when young, you'll lie upon thorns when old.*"
"*If youth knew what age would crave, it would both get and save.*"
"*A young man idle, an old man needy.*"

3332. சிற்றாள் எட்டு ஆளுக்குச் சரி.
One youth will do as much work as eight adults.

To a young man work is still a pleasant thing, and where there is a will, there is a way.

"*While the tall maid is stooping, the little one hath swept the house.*"

3333. வயசோ, வல்லக்காடோ?
Is he not young, is he not strong?

Old people say this about the young, *i.e.* young people are not afraid of encountering difficulties.

ON THE OVER-INDULGENCE OF CHILDREN.

செல்லங்கொடுத்தல்.

3334. உருக்கம் உருக்கமாய் ஊட்டி, உள்ளே போச்சுது.
The mother nurtured her child with too much tenderness, and the child shrivelled up. 203.

Said of parents who over-feed their children and destroy their digestion, so that the children become thin and weak.

"*He that has but one hog makes him fat, and he that has but one son makes him a fool.*"

3335. ஒரு பிள்ளை என்று ஊட்டி வளர்த்தாளாம், அது செரியா மாந்தகுணம் பிடித்துச் செத்ததாம்.
Since she had only one child, she over-fed it, and it got indigestion and died.

3336. ஒரு பெண் என்று ஊட்டி வளர்த்தாள், அது ஊர்மேல் போச்சுது.
Having only one girl, she nurtured her well, but the girl became a prostitute in the village.

Spoiled by her mother's indulgence, she ended as a prostitute.

"*A child may have too much of its mother's blessing.*"

3337. செல்லம் சொல்லுக்கு அஞ்சாது.
A spoiled child fears no rebuke.

"*Spare the rod and spoil the child.*"

3338. செல்லம் சீர் அழிக்கும்.
Indulgence will destroy prosperity.

"*Give a child his will, and a whelp his fill, and neither will thrive.*"

3339. செல்லம் செருக்கித் திரட்டுப்பால் குமட்டுகிறது.
Made conceited by indulgence, and loathing good milk.

3340. செல்லப்பிள்ளை சீலை உடுத்தாதாம் பிள்ளை பெறுமட்டும்.
The spoiled girl would not wear clothes till she had a child.

The idea is that over-indulgence is a sure way of making a child a prey to shame and sin.

3341. *செல்லச் சக்கிலி பிள்ளை செருப்பு செருப்பாய்த் தின்று கழிகிறது.*

The shoemaker's spoiled child ate shoe after shoe and passed them out undigested.

Said of people who give their children food that is too rich (*மூச்சுண்டை*), for them to digest.

3342. *செல்லத்தில் ஒரு பெண் பிறந்து, செட்டி தெருவு எல்லாம் நொட்டி* (*or*, *திரிந்து*) *விட்டு வந்தது.*

She was born in a rich family, but she went about mischievously in all the chetty streets.

i.e. She went to the bad.

3343. *தூக்கி வளர்த்த பிள்ளையும், தொடையில் வைத்துத் தைத்த இலையும் உருப்படாது.*

A child always in arms, and a leaf-plate kept on the thigh while being stitched together will not be well formed. 3301.

The child will be spoiled and the leaf-plate will be badly made.

"*Mother's darlings make but milk-sop heroes.*"

3344. *பூத்தானமான பிள்ளை பிறந்து, பூவால் அடிப்பட்டுச் செத்தது.*

The child when born was as delicate as a flower, but it hurt itself on a flower and died.

Said sarcastically about very sensitive people, or about a mother who is too sensitive concerning her child.

3345. *பூத்தானமான பிள்ளை ஆத்தாளைத் தாலி கட்டினதாம்.*

The child that was too tenderly treated is said to have married its mother.

The gentle treatment that it received ruined its character.

Cf. 887 *ff.*

SORROW, LAMENTATION.

துக்கம், வருத்தம்.

"Man's inhumanity to man makes countless thousand mourn." *Burns.*

N.B.—The following are chiefly used by women.

3346. *அடுப்பே வனவாசம், கடுப்பே கைலாசம்.*

The hearth is my hermitage, suffering is my heaven (Kailasa).

Said by a daughter-in-law when ill-treated by her mother-in-law, meaning that there is nothing but toil and pain for her.

3347. *அதை விட்டாலும் கதியில்லை, அப்புறம் போனாலும் விதியில்லை.*

If I leave that I do not know where to go; and if I go somewhere else no prosperity awaits me. 3364, 3384.

3348. அரிசி என்று அள்ளிப் பார்ப்பாருமில்லை, உமி என்று ஊதிப் பார்ப்பாருமில்லை.

There is no one to sift and see whether I am rice or husk. 17, 2088, 3419.

There is no one who cares for me.

3349. அன்றுமில்லை காற்று, இன்றுமில்லை குளிர்.

At that time there was no wind, now there is no coolness (pleasure).

e.g.—At the very beginning my husband did not love me, and what am I to expect now? Or, it is used by a girl whose step-mother was unkind, but who finds her mother-in-law is still more unkind.

3350. ஆர் இட்ட சாபனையோ, அடிநாளின் தீவினையோ?

Is it somebody's curse I am suffering under, or is it the result of a former birth?

3351. ஆலைக் கரும்பும், வேலைத் (கடல்) துரும்பும் ஆனேன்!

I am become a sugar-cane in the sugar-mill, and a bit of straw in the waves of the sea. 1399, 2978.

3353. இன்றைக்குச் செத்தால், நாளைக்கு இரண்டுநாள்.

If he dies to-day, to-morrow will be the day after it.

i.e. To-morrow will come whether he dies or not; said in disgust about a person of whom one is wearied.

3354. உரலுக்கு ஒரு பக்கம் இடி, மத்தளத்துக்கு இரண்டு பக்கமும் இடி.

A mortar is beaten on one side (by the pestle), but a drum is beaten on both sides. 3355.

Said by a person who suffers at the hands of several persons or by one who has many sufferings, to a person who suffers less.

3355. உரல் போய் மத்தளத்தோடே முறை இட்டதுபோல்.

Like the mortar going and telling its sorrow to the drum. 3354.

The mortar could not expect to be comforted by the drum.

3356. உழைக்கிற கழுதை எந்நாளைக்கும் உழைத்தே தீரவேண்டும்.

The hard working ass must work hard for ever.

3357. ஊர் இருக்கிறது, ஓடு இருக்கிறது.

There is a village and a potsherd. 3358, 3369, 3373, 3389.

The potsherd is the vessel in which alms begged in the village are received. The meaning is that when the worst comes to the worst one can always resort to begging.

3358. ஊர் இருக்கிறது பிச்சை போட, ஓடு இருக்கிறது வாங்கிக்கொள்ள.

The village is near to give me alms, the potsherd is ready to receive them.

i.e. I will rather go begging, than be ill-treated in this house.

3359. ஊரை வளைத்தாலும் உற்ற துணையில்லை, நாட்டை வளைத்தாலும் நல்ல துணையில்லை.

Though one wanders about the village, one finds no true help; though one wanders about the country, one finds no help.

Said in disgust by a helpless person who is left alone in his troubles.

3360. எங்கேயோ இடித்தது வானம் என்று இருந்தேன், தப்பாது என் தலையிலே இடித்தது.

I thought that the heavens would fall somewhere, but they have but fallen on my head. 3404.

The evil I thought others would have to suffer has fallen on me.

3361. எதை வாரிக் கட்டிக்கொண்டு போகிறது?

What are we going to take along with us from this world? 136, 2943.

There is no certain prosperity in this world.

3362. எருமை மூத்திரம் எக்கியத்துக்கு ஆகுமா?

Will the urine of a buffalo be used at a sacrifice? 3363.

3363. எருமை சாணி ஓமத்துக்கு ஆகுமா?

Can buffalo-dung be used as an offering? 3362.

Said in sorrow by one of the women in a family, who has been neglected at some family festival, and thus expresses her contempt for the person preferred before her.

3364. எல்லாத் தலையிலும் எட்டு எழுத்து, என் பாவி தலையிலே பத்து எழுத்து.

On every one's head eight letters are written (by Brahma), but—wretch that I am—there are ten letters on my head! 3347, 3384.

Said by a woman when asked about her welfare, implying that she is worse off than anyone else in the world. Everyone's fate is supposed to be written on his head at his birth by Brahma.

"*Every horse thinks his own pack heaviest.*"

3365. எறும்புமுதல் எண்ணுயிரம் கோடிக்குத் தெரியும்; காப்பாற்றுகிற நாராயணன் என்னைக் காப்பாற்றமாட்டானு?

All creatures, from the ant upwards (*lit.* the eighty thousand millions of creatures) know (my innocence), will not Vishnu, the Preserver, protect me? 2090.

3366. எறும்புமுதல் எண்ணுயிரம் கோடியும் அழுதது.

All creation, from the ant upwards, wept.

A lamentation from the *Drona Parva* of the *Mahabharata* referring to Arjuna's son, Abhimanyu, who had been slain in battle.

3367. என் ஈரலைக் கருக்கு அறிவாள் கொண்டு அறுக்கிறது.

The sharp edge of a sickle has cut my liver.

i.e. I am in great distress.

3368. ஒரு பணம் கொடுப்பானும், ஓயாமல் அழைப்பானும்.

He pays me only one coin, but calls me constantly.

He recompenses me miserably and demands much in return.

3369. ஓடு இருக்கிறது, நான் இருக்கிறேன்.

The potsherd is (ready), and I am (ready). 3357.

i.e. If I have to turn beggar, well, what must be, must be!

3370. கட்டை (or உடம்பு) இருக்கிறமட்டும், கஷ்டமுண்டு.

As long as we live in this body we shall have trouble. 3388.

3371. கண்ணாலே சீவன் கடகடவென்று போனாலும், வண்ணான் கழுதை சுமந்தே தீரவேண்டும்.

The washerman's ass must carry its burden to its destination, though its life is jolted out of it through its eyes. 998, 1360, 1747, 2512, 3395.

Said by daughters-in-law or others in a family, who are worried or ill-treated, implying that there is no remedy for their evil plight.

" *What can't be cured, must be endured.*"

3372. கழுவுக்கு ஏற்ற கோமுட்டி.

The Komati fit for the stake. 740, 890.

This proverb refers to an incident, that took place in "the City of Injustice." A certain man was to be impaled for a crime, but at the last moment he pointed out that a certain fat merchant (*Komati*) would be better suited for the instrument of punishment than himself and so escaped. The proverb is now used of a person who is forced to suffer for the faults of others.

3373. குளம் இருக்கிறது, நான் இருக்கிறேன்.

The pond is ready, and I am ready. 3357.

i.e. I am ready to drown myself.

3374. கொழு கொம்பில்லாத கொடிபோலானேன்.

I have become like a creeper without a support. 3378.

i.e. I am helpless and friendless.

3375. சருகு பொறுக்க நேரமன்றி, குளிர் காய நேரமில்லை.

Although there is time to gather dry leaves for fuel, there is no time to warm yourself. 3397.

3376. சந்நியாசி வீடு திண்ணையிலே.

The pilgrim's house is in a veranda (outside the house).

A pilgrim must be satisfied with any abode; also, a woman must endure any hardship.

" *Weal and woman cannot pan, but woe and woman can.*"

3377. சாகிறவரைக்கும் கஷ்டமானால், சுகம் எப்போ?

If we have to suffer till we die, when shall we get comfort?

" *We are born crying, live complaining, and die disappointed.*"

3378. சிறகு இல்லாத பறவைபோலானேன்.

I have become like a bird that has lost its wings. 536, 3374.

Said of one who has suffered great losses.

3379. தலைக்கு மிஞ்சின ஆக்கினையில்லை, கோமணத்துக்கு மிஞ்சின தரித்திரமில்லை.

There is no punishment greater than the loss of one's head, and no poverty keener than not having more than a rag.

Said to encourage a person overwhelmed by a series of calamities, implying that the worst is past.

3380. தேர் ஒண்டி தெருவிலே அலையவிட்டாயே!

You have made your family so poor, that they are obliged to take shelter (at night) under a car and to go about begging (by day).

Said by a wife to her lazy or wicked husband.

" *A dog's life, hunger and ease.*"

3381. நான் படும் பாடு நாய்தானும் படாது.

Even a dog does not suffer what I suffer. 3382.

3382. நான் படும் பாடு, பஞ்சுதான் படுமோ?

Does cotton-down suffer what I suffer? 3381, 3385.

Cotton-down is picked, put between rollers to remove the seeds, sent to the spinning wheel, and then to the loom at last.

3383. நான் பெண் பிறந்து தெருவிலே நிற்கிறேன்.

I am born a woman, but stand out in the street. 3386, 3419.

i.e. I have relations enough, but no real friend.

3384. பத்து அரிசியும் வேகவில்லை, பாவி, என் பிராணனும் போகவில்லை.

I cannot get my ten (little) rice grains boiled, and—wretch that I am—my life will not leave me! 3347, 3364.

Said in despair by a poor person who has nothing to eat.

3385. பெரும் காற்றில் இலவம் பஞ்சு பறக்கிறதுபோல்.

Flying about like the down of the silk-cotton tree in a storm. 3382.

A very common simile expressing distress and anxiety.

3386. மதி (or சந்திரன்) இல்லாத விண்ணானேன், மருந்து இல்லாத புண்ணானேன்.

I am a sky without a moon, and a sore without an ointment. 3383.

i.e. I am utterly helpless.

3387. மரம் வைத்தவன் தண்ணீர் வார்க்கமாட்டானா?

Will not he who planted the tree, water it? 2090, 2091.

God will protect those whom man neglects.

" *God never sends mouths, but he sends meat.*"

3388. மண்டையுள்ள (or, மூக்கு) வரையில் சளி போகாது.

As long as the brain (*or*, nose) remains, you will have colds in the head. 2655, 3370.

Said to one who complains about all her sorrows, and about endless quarrels.

3389. முந்தானை இருக்கிறது, நாலு வீடு இருக்கிறது.

Here is my lap or apron (to receive alms), and there are four houses to help me. 3357, 3358, 3369, 3373.

3390. முழங்கையில் பட்ட சுகம்போல் இருக்கிறேன்.

I feel as comfortable as an elbow that has been knocked.

3391. வரும் விதி வந்தால், படும் விதி படவேண்டும்.
When one's fate comes, it must be endured.
Said either about one who suffers, or to comfort one who suffers.

3392. வழி வழியாய் போகும்போது, விதி விதியாய் வருகிறது.
Though I keep to my own path, my fate comes to me.

3393. வாழ்நாளுக்கு (com. வாணுள்) ஏற்ற வயிற்றெரிச்சல்.
Life has always its anguish and troubles.
Generally said by women about family sorrows.

3394. விண் விடும் குடிக்கு விண் விடும், என் பாவி குடிக்கு விண் விடுமா!
Omens settled the choice of brides in fortunate families; alas, none turned up in my case!
This proverb is evidently of ancient origin and has reference to an omen (விண் விடுகிறது) noted by certain Sudra sub-castes when choosing wives for their sons. In this proverb the mother blames her ill fortune in not finding a girl with the wished for omen.

3395. விறகுதலையனுக்கு நோய் வந்தால், விறகு கட்டோடே போய்விடும்.
When the fuel carrier gets sick, fuel carrying is his only medicine. 3371.
There is no help for him.

3396. வீண் இழவாம் வெங்காயத்தாளாம், பிடுங்கப் பிடுங்கப் பேரிழவாம்.
It is useless toil to peal the skins from onions, the more they are pulled off the more the trouble. 1932, 1976.
Used by servants or by daughter-in-law who are constantly worried by too much work and abuse. Or, said by one who meets one difficulty after another.

3397. வேக நேரமிருந்தாலும், சாக நேரமில்லை.
Though there is time to burn, there is no time to die. 1740, 3375.

MISCELLANEOUS PROVERBS ON SORROW AND LAMENTATION.

3398. அல்லலற்ற படுக்கை அழகிலும் அழகு.
A bed free from sorrow is the greatest delight (*lit.* beauty of beauties).

3399. இன்பமும் துன்பமும் எடுத்த உடலுக்கு இயல்பு.
It is the nature of the human body to experience pleasure and pain.
This is like many others a philosophical phrase.

3400. இன்னம் இருக்கிறது தேருக்குள் சிங்காரம்.
Greater beauty is still hidden in the car.
Said in sorrow over some evil or wickedness that is gradually being revealed.

3401. எல்லாத்துக்கும் ஒரு அழுகை அழுங்கள்.
Weep for the whole at once and be done!

A bridegroom was found to be lame. During the marriage ceremony many of the relatives wept on account of this defect in him. Seeing this, the bridegroom threw off his clothes, exposed all his other defects, and used this phrase. Said by some one who knows all about a third person's faults to another person who is gradually finding them out.

3402. ஒருநாள் ஒரு யுகம்.
One single day was an age (*yuga*).

Said by a person in great distress, who finds time go very slowly.

3403. கல்லும் கரைய, மண்ணும் உருக, அழுதான்.
He wept so that stones and earth melted.

3404. கீத்திலே கனவிலே தெரியுமா?
Did any presentiment or dream forewarn me?

i.e. I never thought of it at any time. I never expected such a calamity. 3360.

3405. கோபுரம் தாங்கின பொம்மை (*or*, பூதம்) போல்.
Like a monster that bears a tower.

The reference is to those monster-images used all over the world in buildings as pillars or buttresses. Applied to persons who are burdened with the support of many people, and to those who complain of their many great sufferings and cares.

3406. சந்திரனைப் பார்த்த கண்ணுக்குச் சனியனைப் பார்த்தாற்போல.
Like the eyes that after having seen the moon, saw (the malignant) planet Saturn. 3441.

Used about a person once well-off, and subsequently reduced in circumstances.

3407. சீரங்கத்தில் உலக்கை கொடுத்ததுபோல.
Like handing over a pestle to another person at Srirangam.

At Srirangam woman pound rice for the temple for wages. Those who do so must work the whole day and there is a man to see that the work is done. If one of these women, hearing her children crying, persuades a bystander or passer-by to take her place for a while to enable her to look after her children, and does not return, the substitute is obliged to stay in her place till the sun sets. The proverb is therefore said of one who undertakes responsibilities which involve more than he expected.

3408. தலையோடே வந்தது, தலைப்பாகையோடே போச்சுது.
It came to take the head, but it took the turban only. 1008, 3417.

Used of narrow escape from danger.

3409. தேவடியாள் வீட்டில் பிள்ளை பிறந்ததுபோல.
As when a boy is born in a dancing-girl's house.

Dancing-girls are invariably prostitutes and do not care to bear children. If they do have children, they desire to have girls, that they may be brought up to their own profession—which is not regarded as a disgraceful one in India. The proverb is used to describe the sadness of a home to which misfortune has come.

3410. *நாராசம் காய்ச்சி நடுச் செவியில் விட்டாற்போல.*
As if a hot iron rod were thrust into the ear.
Said when one hears words that cause great pain to the heart.

3411. *நித்தியக் கண்டம் பூரணாயுசு.*
A long life with daily dangers.
i.e. My daily perils are endless, but my longevity is assured.
"*Long life hath long misery.*"

3412. *நேற்று வந்தாளாம் குடி, அவள் தலையில் விழுந்ததாம் இடி.*
She came yesterday to live here, and misfortune befell her at once.
Sometimes used to describe the hard lot of a new servant or daughter-in-law, whom all order about.

3413. *பிச்சைக்காரனைப் பேய் பிடித்ததாம் உச்சி உருமத்தில்* (or, *உச்சி காலம்*).
The devil seized a poor beggar in broad daylight.
The beggar had no means to buy the devil off and so could not save himself.—Applied to a great calamity or great expense that comes unexpectedly on a family. Or, said in pity of a poor man who has been ruined by a rich man.

3414. *பிரசவ வைராக்கியம், புராண வைராக்கியம், ஸ்மசான வைராக்கியம்.*
The renunciation of sexual intercourse made by a woman when suffering the pains of child birth, the renunciation of worldly things made after studying the sacred books, the renunciation of worldly things made after seeing corpses burned.
These three causes make people give up their desire for a time.
"*The chamber of sickness is the chapel of devotion.*"
"*Vows made in storms are forgotten in calms.*"
"*They who worship God merely for fear, would worship the devil should he appear.*"
"*The devil was sick, the devil a monk would be;*
The devil grew well, the devil a monk was he."

3415. *பீ மேலே நிற்கிறாப்போல்.*
Like standing on dirt.
Used of the pain felt at heart when in unpleasant company. *Cf.* the English expression: *To sit on needles.*

3416. *பொல்லாத காலம் சொல்லாமல் வந்தது.*
The bad time came without announcing itself beforehand.
Said of sudden and unexpected misfortunes.

3416*a*. *போன மச்சான் திரும்பிவந்தான்.*
The brother-in-law who took himself off has come back. 460.
Said of troubles or evils that repeat themselves at intervals. For instance of a man who gets drunk two or three times a year.

3417. *மலைபோல் வந்தது, பனிபோல் போச்சுது.*
It came like a mountain, and disappeared like dew. 3408.
Said of sudden disasters.

3418. மழை விட்டும், தூவானம் விடவில்லை.
Though the rain has stopped, the drizzle has not. 2201.
One has got through the great troubles, but their consequences remain.

ON COMFORTING.

ஆற்றல், தேற்றல்.

3420. ஆற்றுவாருமில்லை, தேற்றுவாருமில்லை.
I have no one to comfort and no one to console me.

3421. இந்தப் பெரிய கொள்ளையிலே, அப்பா! என்கப் பிள்ளையில்லை.
Though I have abundance of everything, I have not got a child to call me 'father.'
i.e. There is no one to comfort me. Riches cannot fill the heart, it will ever sigh for love.
"*Who hath none to still him, may weep out his eyes.*"

3422. என் என்பாருமில்லை, எடுத்துப் பார்ப்பாருமில்லை.
I have no one to inquire about my welfare, and no one to help me.

3423. கசிந்துவந்தவன் கண்ணைத் துடை.
Wipe the eyes of him who is weeping.

3424. தெய்வம் பண்ணின செயல் (or, திருக்கூத்து.)
It is a deed done by God.
Said to comfort one who is sorrowing for a dead friend or relation.

WOMEN.

பெண்.

GIRLS.

3425. அஞ்சாவது பெண் கெஞ்சினாலும் கிடையாது.
Though you seek humbly to marry a girl who is born fifth in her family, you will not get her.
If the fifth child in a family is a girl, she is considered to be very lucky.

3426. ஆறும்பேறு பெண்ணாய்ப் பிறந்தால் ஆறான குடித்தனம் நீறாய்விடும்.
If the sixth child be a girl, a family that is like a river (*i.e.* rich and grand) will be reduced to ashes. 3283.

3427. குமரியாயிருக்கையில் கொண்டாட்டம், கிழவியாயிருக்கையில் திண்டாட்டம்.
When young, a woman is a joy; when old, she is a vexation.

3428. சக்கிலிப் பெண்ணும், சாமைக்கதிரும் பக்குவத்தில் பார்த்தால் (*or* சமைந்தால்) அழகு.

Even a *chakkili* girl and the ears of the millet are beautiful when mature (*lit.* when they have reached puberty.)

Youth is identified with beauty. The *chakkili* are leather workers and are regarded as the lowest of the low.

3429. பெண் என்று பிறந்தபோதே, புருஷன் பிறந்திருப்பான்.

For every girl born, a husband has been born previously. 59.

"*Marriages are made in heaven.*"

WOMAN'S OBEDIENCE AND MODESTY.

3430. அடக்கத்துப் பெண்ணுக்கு அழகு ஏன்?

Why adorn an obedient woman?

Obedience itself is her beauty.

"*Beauty in woman is like a flower in spring; but virtue is the star in heaven.*"

3431. ஐந்து வயது பிள்ளைக்கு ஐம்பது வயது பெண் கால் முடக்கவேண்டும்.

A woman of fifty must sit with folded legs before a boy of five years. 3566.

i. e. A woman must always be respectful to one of the other sex. To sit on the ground with the legs stretched out straight is not thought a respectful attitude.

3432. பெண்ணுக்குக் குணம்தான் சீதனம்.

A woman's virtue is her dowry.

3433. பெண்கெள் சமர்த்து அடுப்பங்கரை வரையில்தான்.

The skill of women goes as far as the fireplace.

Cleverness is of no use to a woman outside domestic affairs.

3434. பேதைமை என்பது மாதர்களுக்கு அணிகலம்.

Simplicity (*or* Ignorance) is the ornament of women.

"*Blushing is virtue's colour.*"

"*Maidens should be mild and meek: swift to hear, and slow to speak.*"

3435. ராஜா மகளானாலும், கொண்டவனுக்குப் பெண்தான்!

Though she be a king's daughter, she is only a woman to her husband. 2549, 3293, 3638.

WOMAN'S JEWELRY, DRESS AND BEAUTY.

பெண்ணின் அழகு.

3436. *அதிசயமான ரம்பை அரிசி கொட்டுகிற தொம்பை (or தொம்பைக் கூண்டு).*

The wonderful Rhamba is only like a grain-bin. 2695, 2698.

Said to a man who is in love with a girl he has met, implying either that she is ugly and clumsy looking, or that she is engaged in mean work. Rhamba is one of the marvellously captivating courtesans in the paradise of Indra.

3437. *அந்தம் சிந்தி, அழகு ஒழுகிறது.*

That woman overflows with loveliness; beauty flows from her.

Said ironically of an ugly woman.

"*That woman is killed with beauty.*"

3438. *அவள் அழகுக்குத் தாய்வீடு.*

She is the home of beauty. 2199, 3225*a*.

அவளுக்கு அவளே ஈடு (or, ஜோடு, or, சமானம் or, சரி, or, ஒப்பு).

She alone is equal to herself.

i.e. No one can be compared with her in beauty or in goodness.

3439. *அவள் அழகுக்குப் பத்துபேர் வருவார்கள், கண் சிமிட்டினால் ஆயிரம் பேர் மயங்கிபோவார்கள்.*

Ten men will be drawn by her beauty; and, if her eyes twinkle, a thousand will be allured. 1549.

"*Beauty provoketh thieves sooner than gold.*"

"*A fair face may be a foul bargain.*"

3440. *அவள் அழகைப் பார்த்தால், கிள்ளித் தின்னலாம் என்று இருக்கிறது.*

It is as if you want to pluck and eat her beauty when you see it.

Describes great desire to enjoy a charming woman's beauty.

3441. *அவளைக் கண்ட கண்ணாலே, இன்னொருத்தியைக் காணுகிறதா?*

Will the eyes that have seen her beauty, look at another woman? 2443, 3052, 3406.

3442. *அழகு ஒழுகுகிறது, நாய் வந்து நக்குகிறது, ஓட்டைப் பானை கொண்டுவா, பிடித்துவைக்க.*

Beauty leaks from her, the dog is licking it up, bring a broken vessel to catch it in!

Sarcastically said of an ugly woman, who boasts of her beauty.

3443. *அழகிலே பிறந்த பவள கொடி.*

This coral-nymph is the first-born child of Beauty.

3444. *அழகுக்குச் செய்தது, ஆபத்துக்கு உதவும்.*

The jewels of prosperity may become the saviours of adversity.

"*Gold may be ever so red, it will go out for bread.*" Danish.

3445. இடுப்பு சுருங்குகிறது, பெண்களுக்கு அழகு.
To have a slender waist is a woman's beauty.

Also : நூல் இடையாள் or பிடி இடையாள் a waist as thin as a thread ; or so thin that a hand can clasp it.

"*A woman and a greyhound must be small in the waist.*"

3446. கந்தையைக் கட்டி வெளியே வந்தால் கண்ணூட்டி, வெள்ளையைக் கட்டி வெளியே வந்தால் வெள்ளாட்டி.
If you dress in rags and go out, you will be an object for admiration, but, if you dress up nicely and go out, people will speak ill of you.

People think an overdressed woman is a prostitute.

"*In silk and scarlet, walks many a harlot.*"

3447. காதுக்கு இட்டால், முகத்துக்கு அழகு.
If you put jewels in the ears, you adorn the face.

3448. குயில் குரலும், மயில் அழகும்போல்.
She sings like a nightingale, and is as beautiful as a peacock. 1570.

Ironically said.

3449. சேலைமேல் சேலை கட்டும் தேவ ரம்பை ஆனாலும், ஓலைமேல் எழுத்தாணி ஊன்றும் பெண் ஆகாது.
You may choose for your bride a prostitute like Rhamba, but not a girl who knows how to write.

3450. பறக்கிற கிளிப்போலிருக்கிறாள்.
She is as beautiful as a flying parrot.

3451. பார்க்கப் பதினாயிரம் கண் வேண்டும்.
Ten thousand eyes are needed to look at it. 2697.

Said of something exceedingly beautiful and rare.

3452. பிடி அழகி புகுந்தால், பெண் அழகி ஆவாள்.
If the thin woman enters, she will become beautiful.

In the negotiation previous to marriage the girl is blamed for being thin by those who want her in marriage, but they get this reply. *i.e.* Take her home and feed her well and she will soon get fat.

3453. பூவுள்ள மங்கையாம், பொன் கொடியாம், போன இடம் எல்லாம் செருப்பு அடியாம்.
It is true that she is adorned with flowers and gold, but she is beaten with slippers wherever she goes.

She appears well dressed, but is a bad character who must be treated with scorn.

"*A fair face may hide a foul heart.*"

3454. பெண்ணுக்கும் பொன்னுக்கும் தோற்பு உண்டா?
Were woman and gold ever defeated ?

"*One hair of a woman draws more than a bell rope.*"

3455. பெண்ணுக்குப் போய், பொன்னுக்குப் பின்வாங்கலாமா?

Having gone to get a girl, why withdraw on account of the price asked for her?

3456. பெண்ணுக்குப் பொன் இட்டுப்பார், சுவருக்கு மண் இட்டுப்பார்.

Put jewelry on a woman and look at her, and plaster a wall and look at it.

Both will be improved by your care. Said by a mother to one who remarks that her daughter is not exactly a beauty. Also said when something is needed to perfect a thing.

"*No woman is ugly when she is dressed.*"

3457. பெண்ணின் கோணல், பொன்னிலே நிமிரும்.

The ugliness of the girl's face will be removed by jewels.

"*He that is proud of his fine clothes gets his reputation from the tailor.*" But in India from the goldsmith!

"*Fine feathers make fine fowls.*"

3458. பொன் காய்த்த மரம்போலிருக்கிறுள்.

She is as full of jewels as a tree of fruit.

3459. பொன் குடத்துக்குப் பொட்டு இட்டுப் பார்க்கவேண்டுமோ?

Does a gold vessel need a painted spot? Of itself it is fair enough.

"*Fair faces need no paint.*"

3460. மான் கண்ணிலும் அழகு, விரைவிலும் விரைவு.

Her eyes are more beautiful, and her limbs more nimble than those of a deer.

3461. ராஜாவும், பெண்ணும், கொடியும் கிட்ட இருக்கிறதைத் தழுவிக்கொள்வார்கள்.

Kings, women and creepers will embrace what is nearest them.

MAN MUST HAVE COMPASSION ON WOMAN, AND TREAT HER KINDLY.

பெண்.

3462. ஆணுக்கு அவகேடு செய்தாலும், பெண்ணுக்குப் பிழைகேடு செய்யப்படாது.

Though you may ill-treat a man, you should never ill-treat a woman.

3463. ஆணை அடித்து வளர், பெண்ணைப் போற்றி வளர்.

Bring up a boy under strict discipline, but bring up a girl by praising her. 2264.

"*Glasses and lasses are brittle ware.*"

3464. கண்ணுலே கண்டாலும், மண்ணுலே மறைக்கவேண்டும்.

Though you see a woman's sin with your own eyes, cover it over with earth.

3465. துரோபதையை துகில் (துணி) உரிந்ததுபோல்.

Like stripping off Draupadi's clothes. 3466.

In the Mahabharata Dharmaraja played a game of chess in which Draupadi, his wife, was the prize; his opponent, Duryodhana won, and seizing Draupadi, he tried to strip her cloth off. By the grace of Krishna, however, the cloth proved endless, and he was thus unable to put her to shame. But his attempt has become proverbial for its shamelessness.

3466. பத்தினியைத் தொட்டதும், துரியோதனன் கெட்டதும்.

Touching a chaste woman was Duryodhana's ruin.

From the same story as 3465.
Also said ironically to an immoral woman who praises her own character.

3467. பெண் என்றால் பேயும் இரங்கும்.

If she says: "I am a woman," even a devil will have compassion on her.

3468. மண்மேல் நின்று பெண் ஓரம் சொல்லாதே.

Do not dare to stand on the *Earth*, while passing unjust remark on a woman. 597.

The earth is the goddess *Bhumidêvi*.

THE UNTRUSTWORTHINESS OF WOMEN.

பெண்.

3469. இராமர் மங்கையோடு இணங்கினது அவம்.

It was Rama's weakness that he yielded to a woman (to Sita).

"*Summer-sown corn and women's advice turn out well once in seven years.*"

3470. இருமனது மங்கையோடு இணங்குகிறது அவலம்.

To yield to a double-minded woman is weakness.

3471. எண்ணறக் கற்று எழுத்தற வாசித்தாலும், பெண் புத்தி பின் புத்தியே.

Though she reads and studies endlessly, a woman's thought is always an afterthought.

3472. சொல்லாததை மனையாளுக்குச் சொன்னவன் பட்ட பாடுபோல்.

Like the suffering of a husband, who tells to his wife what he ought not to tell her.

"*He that tells his wife news, is but newly married.*"

The above four proverbs are scientific in their form, and may be called literary proverbs.

WOMAN'S IMPORTANCE IN THE FAMILY.

பெண்.

3473. அரைக்காசை ஆயிரம் பொன்னுக்குகிறவளும் பெண்சாதி, ஆயிரம் பொன்னை அரைக்காசு ஆக்குகிறவளும் பெண்சாதி.

She who can convert half a copper coin into a thousand gold coins is a wife, and she who can reduce a thousand gold coins to half a copper coin is also a wife. 1794.

Economy or extravagance are alike characteristic of woman.

"*All women are good: good for something or good for nothing.*"

3474. ஈட்டுக்கும் பாட்டுக்கும் இருந்தாள் எடுகுமரி.

The burden-bearing maiden was equal to all the emergencies of life.

Said by a mother about her industrious daughter to her lazy daughters-in-law.

3475. ஏர் பிடித்தவன் என்ன செய்வான், பானை பிடித்தவள் பாக்கியம்.

The ploughman may do his work, but the comfort of the family depends on the housewife.

"*A good wife and a good name hath no mate in goods nor fame.*"

"*It shall be at the wife's will if the husband thrive.*"

3476. பெண்டுகள் சோற்றுக்குத் தெண்டமில்லை.

Women do not get their food as a charity.

Women are always doing some good at home for their food.

"*The wife that expects to have a good name is always at home, as if she were lame; and the maid that is honest, her chiefest delight is still to be doing from morning till night.*"

3477. மனைக்கொடியில்லாத மனை பாழ்.

A house without a creeper (woman) is desolate. 3500.

There must be a wife in a house, if it is to prosper.

3478. மனைவி இல்லாத புருஷன் அரை மனுஷன்.

A man without a wife is only half a man.

3479. மன்னவர்கள் ஆண்டது எல்லாம் மந்திரிகள் ஆண்மை.

The king's rule depends on the minister's skill. 3168.

Said by an elderly woman to the younger women in a family; implying:—Men go out to make money, but women manage the house.

"*As the Friday so the Sunday: as the Sunday so the week. As the good man saith, so say we; but as the good wife saith, so it must be.*"

Cf. 3156 *&c.*

WOMEN'S CLEVERNESS OR DEXTERITY.

பெண்.

"The man's a fool who thinks by force or skill
To stem the torrent of a woman's will;
For if she will, she will, you may depend on't.
And if she wont, she won't, and there's an end on't."

3480. அரைத்துட்டிலே கலியாணம், அதிலே கொஞ்சம் பாணவேடிக்கை.
She manages a wedding or a festival for a few coins, but out of them she saves a little for fireworks. 1803.

Applied to cleverness and stinginess.

"*He would get money in a desert.*"

3481. அவளுக்கு ரொம்ப தக்குத் தெரியும்.
She is up to every dodge.

"*Women in mischief are wiser than men.*"

3482. ஆனை புலி வந்தாலும் தாண்டுவாள்.
Though an elephant or a tiger come, she will leap over them.

She is equal to any difficulty.

"*Whatever a woman will she can.*"

3483. இதற்கா பயப்பட்டேன், என் ஆண்டவனே, ஆனை குதிரை வந்தாலும் தாண்டுவேன் (com. தாண்டுவேனே).
Do you think, O husband, that this frightens me; even if I meet elephants and horses I will leap over them.

Said of a bold and clever woman, or by a saucy wife when her husband threatens her.

3484. இந்திரனைச் சந்திரனை இலையாலே மறைப்பாள், எமதருமராஜனைக் கையாலே மறைப்பாள்.
She will conceal *Indiran* (a god) and the moon with a leaf, and *Death* with her hand.

"*She will scold the devil out of a haunted house.*"

3485. உலை வைத்த சந்திலே சாறு காய்ச்சுகிறது.
Where other people have put their pot on the fire, she looks for an opportunity to put her's close by, so as to have her food cooked without expense.

3486. எண்ணெய் கண்ட இடத்தில் தடவிக்கொண்டு, சீப்பு கண்ட இடத்தில் தலைவாரி (or சீவி) கொள்ளுகிறது.
Wherever she sees oil she will smear a little on her hair, and wherever she sees a comb, she will comb her hair.

3487. எத்திலே பிள்ளை பெற்று, இரவலிலே தாலாட்டுகிறது.
Cunningly she brings forth the child, and she lulls it in a borrowed cradle. 3489.

தக்காய்ச் சீவனம் பண்ணுகிறது.

3488. ஒரு கரண்டி எண்ணெய்கொண்டு பலகாரம் சுட்டுப், பந்தி விசாரித்து, வந்த பெண்டுகள் வாரி முடித்து, பெண்டுகளால் பிடிமானமில்லாமல் புறக்கடை வழியாய்ப் போய்விட்டது.

With one spoonful of oil she baked the cakes, she supplied the table, she gave oil for the hair to the women that came, but the carelessness of those women allowed what was left to be stolen through the back door.

Said ironically of one who has done much with small means.

3489. கட்டிலுள்ள இடத்தில் பிள்ளை பெற்றுச், சுக்குக் கண்ட இடத்தில் காயம் தின்பாள்.

She brings forth a child where she finds a cot, and gets the cordial where she sees dried ginger. 3487.

She makes other people bear expenses that she ought to bear herself, but at the same time makes them feel that this has happened quite by accident.

3490. சித்திரத்தைக் குத்தி (or நோண்டி) அப்புறத்தே வைப்பாள்.

She will dig out a picture painted on the wall, and place it somewhere else.

Said about great cleverness.

3492. மகாராஜன் பெண்சாதி மர்மக்காரி, யாருடன் சொன்னாலும் திறமைக்காரி.

The great king's wife has her secret sins, and, when we speak of them, she is able to defend herself.

3493. முழுப் பூசனிக்காயைச் சோற்றோடே மறைப்பாள்.

She will hide a big pumpkin under a plate of rice.

She makes the impossible possible.

3494. விலைமோரிலே வெண்ணெய் எடுத்துத் தலை மகனுக்குக் கலியாணம் பண்ணுவாள்.

She will make butter out of bought buttermilk, and perform her eldest son's wedding.

Bought buttermilk is almost as thin as water, but from this she makes butter, and by the sale of it she makes the wedding.

"*To milk a he-goat.*"

Cf. 1794 *&c. &c.*

REFERRING TO UNMARRIED WOMEN AND WIDOWS.

பெண்.

3495. அறுதலி (com. முண்டைச்சி) மகனுக்கு அங்கம் எல்லாம் சேஷ்டை.

The body of a widow's son is all mischief. 2869, 2862.

As a widow she should not get children; if she gets children, she shows thereby that she is a bad woman, and from bad comes bad.

3496. ஆருமில்லாத பெண்ணுக்கு அண்டை வீட்டுக்காரன் மாப்பிள்ளையாம்.
It is said that a neighbour is the bridegroom of a lonely woman. 3501, 3502.

Hindus are very suspicious of the virtue of women.

3497. ஆளனில்லாத துக்கம் அழுதாலும் தீராது.
The sorrow of a woman who has lost her husband will not be removed however much she weeps.

3498. ஆளனில்லாத பெண்ணுக்கு வாழ்வில்லை.
A woman without a husband has no happiness.

3499. ஆளனில்லாதவள் ஆற்று மணலுக்குச் சரி.
A woman without a husband is like the sand of a river.

She is at the mercy of circumstances, just as the sand is at the mercy of the winds.

3500. ஆளனில்லாத மங்கைக்கு அழகு பாழ்.
The beauty of a woman without a husband is in vain. 3477.

3501. இல்லாதவன் பெண்சாதி எல்லாருக்கும் தோழியா?
A poor man's wife is likely to be any man's love. 3496, 3502.

3502. இளைத்தவன் பெண்சாதி எல்லாருக்கும் மைத்துனி (com. மச்சினச்சி.)
A poor man's wife is treated by all as a sister-in-law. 3496, 3501.

All treat her familiarly or as they like.
"*A low hedge is easily leaped over.*"

3503. சுக்கிர (*or*, வெள்ளி) உதயத்தில் தாலி கட்டி, சூரிய உதயத்திற்குள் அறுத்தாள்.
She was married when Venus rose, and had to take off her thali when the sun rose, *or*, On Friday morning she was married and on Sunday morning she became a widow.

Short-lived happiness.
"*After a dream of a wedding comes a corpse.*"

3504. திருடன் பெண்சாதி என்றைக்கும் கைம்பெண்சாதி.
The thief's wife is always a widow.

Thieves' (soldiers' and sailors') wives do not know when they will be left widows, as their husbands are always in danger.

3505. வாழாத பெண்ணுக்கு மை எண்டி, பொட்டு எண்டி, மஞ்சள் குளி எண்டி, (என் அடி).
Why should she who has the misfortune to be unmarried, blacken her eyelids, paint the dot on the forehead and use saffron?

All these things should be done only by married women.

WEDDING, MARRIAGE.

கலியாணம்.

3506. அசத்துக்கு வாய்க்கப்பட்டு (வாழ்க்கைப்பட்டு) ஆயிரம் வருஷம் வாழ்வதைவிட, சத்துக்கு வாய்க்கப்பட்டுச் சட்டென்று தாலி அறுப்பதே மேலே.

It is better to be united to a virtuous man and cut off the thali after a short time, than to be united to a vile person and live with him for a thousand years.

When a woman becomes a widow the thali or marriage token is taken off.

3507. அம்மாள் தெருளுவதற்கு முன்னே, ஐயா உருளுவார்.

Before the bride comes of age, the husband will die. 3,518.

Said of the great difference in age between the bride and the bridegroom so common in India.

In plain words: ஐம்பது வயதானவனுக்கு ஐந்து வயதுப் பெண்ணு? Should a girl of five years be given in marriage to a husband of fifty, if not more?

"A certain gentleman, in a certain village, married his daughter, 10 years old, to an old man of 81 and received Rs. 2,000 for the bargain. In due course, the girl matured, and the nuptial ceremony was performed. The girl was sent to her hated husband, much against her will. She escaped from the room in the dead of night and threw herself into a well." Padfield: The Hindu at Home.

"*A young wife is an old man's post-horse to the grave.*"

3508. ஆயிரம் காலத்துப் பயிராச்சுதே.

It is a crop that will last a thousand years.

Marriage is indissoluble, therefore care should be taken to marry a girl to a fit husband.

3509. ஆருமற்றதே தாரம், ஊரில் ஒருவனே தோழன்.

Take a girl without relations for your wife, and have only one friend in your own village.

If the wife has no relations, there will be no hanger-on.

"*Go down the ladder when thou marriest a wife; go up when thou choosest a friend.*"

"*If you have one true friend, you have more than your share.*"

3510. கடல் தண்ணீர் வற்றினாலும், பள்ளிச்சி தாலி வற்றாது.

Even if the water of the sea dries up, a Palli woman's thali will not dry up.

If one husband dies she will marry again, and thus never be without a thali.

Or பள்ளிக்குப் பத்து மணை. The Palli woman has been sitting as a bride ten times.

3511. கன்னி இருக்கக் காளை (வாலிபன்) மணை ஏறலாமா?

If the girl has become a woman, her brother should not marry till she is married.

If she has not come of age, he is allowed to marry before her.

3512. கன்னிப்பூ மலரவில்லை.
The girl is not yet in blossom.
She has not come of age and cannot marry.

3513. கலியாணம் கழிந்தால், மைச்சிமிழ் கிட்டாது.
When the wedding is over, the little boxes of collyrium (eye-paint) are missing.
At Hindu weddings many little thiugs disappcar.

3514. கலியாணம் பண்ணின வீட்டில் ஆறுமாசம் கருப்பு.
In a home where a wedding has been celebrated, there will be a six months' famine, 1085, 1462, 2965.
Most Hindus borrow large sums of money for their weddings and have to suffer for it afterwards.
"*After a feast a man scratches his head.*"

3515. காட்டில் ஆனையைக் காட்டி, வீட்டில் பெண்ணைக் கொடுக்கிறது போல்.
Like pointing out an elephant in the woods, and giving a girl in marriage at home.
To promise large dowry, and afterwards not to fulfill thc promise.

3516. காயும் கனியும் உண்டானால், கார்த்திகை மாதம் கலியாணம்.
If fruit could be had in November, weddings would be solemnized even then. 3217.

3517. கிழமானாலும், கெட்டானாலும், கட்டிக்கொண்டவள் பிழைப்பாள்.
Though the man is old and worn-out, a girl should marry him to secure a livelihood.

3518. கிழவனுக்கு வாழ்க்கைப்படுகிறதைவிட, கிணற்றிலே விழுகிறது மேல்.
It is better to throw oneself into a well, than to marry an old man. 3507.

3519. குடியிலே குரங்கு ஆனாலும் கொள்ளு. *or,*
குரங்கு ஆனாலும் குலத்தில் கொள்ளவேண்டும்.
Though she be as ugly as a monkey, marry a girl of your own caste.
"*Wives must be had, be they good or bad.*"

3520. கோத்திரம் அறிந்து பெண்ணைக் கொடு, பாத்திரம் அறிந்து பிச்சை போடு.
After knowing the family of the suitor give your daughter in marriage, and after knowing the beggar give him alms.
"*Take a vine of a good soil, and a daughter of a good mother.*"

3521. சும்மா இருந்த ஒரு பெண்ணுக்கு அரைப்பணத்துத் தாலி போதாதா?
An old maid should be satisfied with a husband who spends only a few coins on the thali.
She should be glad to take anybody.

3522. *தாய் உறவோ, நாய் உறவோ ?*
Compared with relationship to one's father, relationship to one's mother is relationship to a dog.

A Hindu seeks a wife closely related to his father and not to his mother.

3523. நாக்காலே போட்ட முடி, பல்லால் கடித்து இழுத்தாலும் வருமா?
The knot tied by your tongue will not be untied, though you bite and tear it with your teeth.

"*He hath tied a knot with his tongue, that he cannot untie with his teeth.*"

3524. பத்துக்குமேலே ஒரு பறையனுக்காவது தள்ளவேண்டும்.
When a girl is over ten she should be forced into marriage, even though it be with a Pariah.

"*Marry your daughters betimes, lest they marry themselves.*"

"*Daughters and dead fish are no keeping wares.*"

3525. பழங்கால் தூர்க்கவேண்டாம், புதுக்கால் வெட்டவேண்டாம்.
Do not fill up the old channel, and do not dig new ones.

A warning against marrying with strangers and adopting new fashions.

3526. பிள்ளையாருக்குப் பெண் கொள்ளுகிறதுபோல்.
Like procuring a wife for Ganesa.

Ganesa's mother, Parvati, once asked him, if he was not going to marry; his reply was: "I shall when I meet a woman like you!" His mother got so angry over this reply, that she cursed him and ordered him to stand near the public roads to wait for a wife. Hence the images of Ganesa, or the belly-god, are placed by the public roads to this day. Said when it takes a long time for a man to find a wife.

3527. பெண் வளர்த்தாயோ, பீ வளர்த்தாயோ?
Did you bring up the girl or mere filth.

Said to one who raises objections, because the girl is too young to marry.

3528. மாப்பாயிருக்கிறமட்டும் மடியில் வைத்திருந்தேன், தோப்பானபிறகு மடியில் வைக்கலாமா?
While my daughter was a little girl, I kept her in my lap (well protected) at home, but after her coming of age, I cannot guard her safely. 3534.

3529. முந்தின சோற்றைத் தட்டினால், பிந்தின சோறு பீயும் சோறும்.
If the first food is rejected, the latter will be filth. 2974.

The first man who offers himself to marry a girl should not be rejected, as he is believed to be lucky. If he is rejected, other suitors may be doubtful characters.

3530. வேலைக்காரி என்று வேண்டியபேர் கேட்டார்கள், குடித்தனக்காரி என்று கொடுக்கமாட்டோம் என்றார்கள்.
They asked her in marriage, believing her to be hard-working; but her parents said, She manages our house well, and we will not give her away.

Said sarcastically about a girl no one will have.

HUSBAND AND WIFE.

புருஷன், பெண்சாதி.

" The gude or ill hap o' a gude or ill life
Is the gude or ill choice o' a gude or ill wife."

3531. *அசல் வீட்டுக்காரனுக்குப் பரிந்துகொண்டு, ஆம்புடையானை அடித்தாளாம்.*
She spoke affectionately with her neighbour, and beat her own husband.

3532. *அடங்காத பெண்சாதியாலே அத்தைக்கும் (மாமி) நமக்கும் பொல்லாப்பு (சண்டை).*
On account of my disobedient wife, there is strife between my mother-in-law and me.

" *Every man can rule a shrew, save he that hath her.*"

3533. *அரிசி பகையும் ஆம்புடையான் பகையும் உண்டா?*
A wife will hate rice and her husband only momentarily.

3534. *அறக்காத்தான் பெண்டு இழந்தான், ஆறுகாதவழி சுமந்து அழுதான்.*
A husband, who from jealousy shuts up his wife, while at home, and when travelling carries her on his shoulders for sixty miles, is at last cheated by her in spite of all. 3528, 3565.

" *A dishonest woman cannot be kept in, and an honest one will not.*"

3535. *ஆக்கவேண்டாம், அரைக்கவேண்டாம், பெண்ணே! என் கிட்ட இருந்தால் போதும் அடி கண்ணே!*
My dear! you shall neither cook nor grind curry stuff; if you, who are as dear to me as my eyes, are near me, it is enough.

3536. *ஆசை அறுபது நாள், மோகம் முப்பது நாள், தொண்ணூறு நாளும் போனால் துடைப்பக்கட்டை.*
After marriage there will be desire sixty days, lust will last thirty days, and after ninety days have passed, she will be considered a broomstick.

" *When a couple are newly married, the first month is honeymoon or smick-smack; the second is hither and thither; the third is thwick-thwack; the fourth :—The devil take them that brought thee and me together.*"

" *Mother, what sort of a thing is marriage? Daughter, it is spinning, bearing children and weeping.*"

3537. *ஆபத்துக்கு உதவாத பெண்சாதி அழகுக்கா வைத்திருக்கிறது?*
Is it for beauty's sake that one takes a wife, who is useless in time of adversity? 2896.

3538. *ஆபத்துக்கு உதவுவானா அவசாரி ஆம்புடையான்.*
A loose woman cannot trust her kept husband in time of trial.

3539. ஆம்புடையான் பலம் இருந்தால், குப்பை ஏறிச் சண்டை போடலாம்.
If a wife has her husband's support, she is likely to climb a dung-hill and quarrel.

If a woman is supported she will quarrel for ever.

3540. இடி விழுவானுக்கு வாழ்க்கைப்பட்டு, எந்நேரமும் இடி ஜாமம்.
A woman who has married a wretch, may find herself beaten at any time. 997, 3546.

Of her it can rightly be said: ஒருநாள் தள்ளுகிறது ஒரு யுகம், To pass a day is like passing an age.

"*Age and wedlock we all desire and repent of.*"

3541. இரண்டு பெண்சாதிக்காரனுக்குக் கொண்டை என்னத்திற்கு?
Why should a husband with two wives wear long hair?

The two wives will seize him by it in their quarrels.

"*Two women in one house, two cats and one mouse, two dogs and one bone, will never accord in one.*"

3542. இரண்டு பெண்சாதிக்காரன் பாடு திண்டாட்டம்.
A man who has two wives experiences only trouble.

3543. இளையாள் இலை தின்னி, மூத்தாள் காய் அறிவாள்.
The younger wife will sit down and eat from the leaf from which her husband has been eating; the elder wife will prepare the food.

3544. இளையாளே, வாடி! (வா அடி) மலையாளம் போவோம், மூத்தாளே வாடி! முட்டிக்கொண்டு சாவோம்!
O, younger wife, come let us go to the Malayalam country! O, elder wife, come let us knock our heads together and die!

When the younger wife is ill, the husband is willing to spend much money in taking her where she can get the best medicine, but he will spend no money on the elder wife when she is sick.

3545. உன் அப்பன்மேலே ஆணை, என் மேலே ஆசையாயிருக்கவேண்டும்.
Swear by your father that you will love me.

The wife thinks she can make her husband love her by making him take an oath.

"*Better be half hanged than ill wed.*"

3546. இழவு கொடுப்பானுக்கு வாழ்க்கைப்பட்டு, ஓட்டமே ஒழிய நடையில்லை.
After marrying a scoundrel, she must always run about. 3540.

She has to slave for his comfort.

"*Marry in haste and repent at leisure.*"

3547. ஓடிப்போன புருஷன் வந்து கூடிக்கொண்டான், உடைமைமேல் உடைமை போட்டு மினுக்கிக்கொண்டாள்.
When the run-away husband returned and joined his wife, he gave her very many ornaments and she was joyful.

"*All is well, and the man has his ware again.*"

"*Cold broth hot again, that lov'd I never,*
Old love renew'd again, that lov'd I ever."

3548. கல்லாகிலும் கணவன், புல்லாகிலும் புருஷன்.

Though hard as a stone, he is your husband; though soft as grass, he is still your husband.

Said to a woman who despises her husband, whom she should obey. 3289, 3628.

3549. கல்லைப்போல கணவனிருக்க, நெல் சோற்றுக்கு அழுவானேன்.

Why should she cry for rice, while she has a husband as firm as a rock.

3550. கழுத்து மாப்பிள்ளைக்குப் பயப்படாவிட்டாலும், வயிற்று மாப்பிள்ளைக்குப் பயப்படவேண்டும்.

Even if you do not respect him who tied the marriage token round your neck, you must respect the children he has begotten.

A good wife can easily appease her husband, but she cannot so easily overcome the impatience of the children.

3551. கற்பு என்பது, சொல் தவறாமை.

Chastity means not trangressing a husband's order.

3552. காக்கனுக்கும் போக்கனுக்கும் பூத்தாயோ புன்னை ; கண்ணாளன் வருந்தனையும் பொறுக்கலையோ புன்னை.

O, Punnai tree (Calophyllum inophyllum) hast thou blossomed for strangers? couldst thou not have waited and blossomed at the arrival of my dear husband?

A man went out into the world to make his fortune; before leaving wife and home, he planted a Calophyllum tree at the front of his house, and told his wife that he would come, when the tree had its first flowers. The day for the blossoming of the tree came, and the husband also came, but his wife did not recognize him, so she says these words in despair. (From a popular Tamil song.)

3553. குதிரை இருப்பு அறியும், கொண்ட பெண்சாதி குணம் அறிவாள்.

A horse knows its condition (its rider's will), and a wife knows her husband's mind.

3554. குறுணிக்காரனுக்கு வாழ்க்கைப்பட்டுப் பதக்கு பதக்கு என்று அடித்துக்கொண்டால் கிடைக்குமா?

After marrying a husband with a small income, will the wife get big things even if she insist on it?

" *Maids want nothing but husbands, and when they have them, they want everything.*"

3555. கைப்பொருளற்றால், கட்டிக்கழுத்தியும் பாராள்.

If the husband has no property (is reduced), even his own wife will not respect him. 1742, 3579.

" *When poverty comes in at the door, love leaps out at the window.*"

3556. கை நிறைந்த பொன்னைப் பார்க்கிலும், கண் நிறைந்த கணவன் மேல்.

It is much better for a woman to have a husband that fills her eyes (at whom she looks with delight), than to have one whose hands are full of gold.

3557. கொண்டவன் அடிக்க, கொழுந்தனார்மேல் விழுந்தாளாம்.

After the husband had punished his wife for unfaithfulness, she embraced her husband's younger brother (and thus gave evidence against herself).

3558. கொண்ட பெண்சாதியே கூர் அரிவாளாயிருந்தாள்.

His own wife became a sharp sickle in ruining her own husband. 2961, 3253, 3578.

" *Age and wedlock tame man and beast.*"

3559. கொள்ளும்வரைக்கும் கொண்டாட்டம், கொண்டபிறகு திண்டாட்டம்.

Before marriage all joy, after marriage much misery.

"*Pleasures, while they flatter, sting to death.*"

3560. கோழி தட்டிக் கூவுமா?

Is a hen able to flap her wings and crow like a cock?

A woman is not able to do the work of a man.

3561. சிவலிங்கத்தின்மேல் எலிப்போல.

Like a rat on the top of a linga.

Said of a wife who mounted her husband's head. She wilfully did what her husband told her not to do. Also: அவன் தலைமேல் ஏறியிருக்கிறாள், she has got up on her husband's head.

" *He lives under the sign of the cat's foot.*" (is henpecked).

3562. தனக்கு என்று ஒருத்தியிருந்தால், தலைமாட்டில் குந்தி அழுவாள்.

If one has a wife, she will sit down at his head and weep.

She will care for and comfort him when he is sick, or when dying.

3563. தன் பெண்சாதியைத் தான் அடிக்கத், தலையாரியைச் சீட்டுக் கேட்கிறதா?

Should one seek permission from the village watchman to beat one's own wife? 3225.

One does not need permission to exercise one's legal rights.

3564. துடியாப் பெண்டீர் மடியில் நெருப்பு.

A wife, who does not feel anxious for her husband, is like fire in the lap. 3203.

3565. நம்பமாட்டாதவன் பெண்சாதிக்கு நாற்பதுபேர் மாப்பிள்ளைமார்.

A suspicious man's wife has forty men as her husbands. 3534, 3606.

An oversuspicious person cannot see that he is fooled all through.

" *At the gate where suspicion enters, love goes out.*"

3566. *பதிவிரதா பத்தினி கதை கேட்டுவந்தேன் ; பட்டுக்கிடப்பாய்க் காலை மடக்கு.*

I have just heard a story of a very virtuous woman ; fold thy legs, thon damned fellow ! 1456, 2364, 2365, 3431.

The wife who has heard a story about a chasto wife, ought herself to try to be such a wife to her own husband. Instead of that, she begins to abuse him in a most impertinent way immediately after she has heard a sermon about the behaviour of a pious wife.

" *But be ye doers of the word and not hearers only.*"
" *Bells call others, but themselves enter not into the church.*"
" *He has one face to God, and another to the devil.*"
" *All are not saints that go to church.*"

" Pious precepts, gentle friend, never acted, wisely meant,
Are like gay and coloured flowers,—without fragrance, without scent."
R. C. DUTT : *Lays of Ancient India.*

3567. *பெண்பிள்ளை குத்துக்குப் புரிமணை.*

He is only a wisp of straw for a woman to sit on.

" *The grey mare is the better horse.*"
" *The wife wears the breeches.*"

3568. *பெண்சாதி கால்கட்டு, பிள்ளை வாய்க்கட்டு.*

A wife ties up her husband's legs, and the children his mouth. 3570.

" *Wedlock's a padlock.*"
" *Down to gehenna, or up to the throne, he rideth the fastest, who rideth alone.*" (Kipling).

3569. *பெண்சாதி முகத்தை* (com. *மூஞ்சியை*)*ப் பார்க்காவிட்டாலும், பிள்ளை முகத்தைப் பார்க்கவேண்டும்.*

If you do not look at your wife, look at your children's faces. 3206.

Though you are not kind to your wife for her own sake, you must treat her well for the sake of her children.

3570. *பெண்சாதி கால் விலங்கு, பிள்ளை சுள்ளாணி* (or *வாய்க்கட்டு*).

A wife is a fetter on her husband's legs, and a child is a bolt through this fetter to fasten it tightly. 3568.

A wife is a fetter, and a child is a gag.

" *He that has children, all his morsels are not his own.*"
" *A married man turns his staff into a stake.*"

3571. *பெண்சாதி சொந்தம், போக்கு வரத்துப் புறம்பே.*

His wife is his own, but his enjoyments are all outside. 3580.

3572. *பெண்சாதி கொண்டதும், திண்டாட்டம் பட்டதும் போதும்.*

I am more than satisfied with the woman I married, and with what I have had to suffer from her. 736, 3558, 3578.

Said of an unpleasant wife ; also, of a stay at any place of which one feels sick ; or said of people of whom one is tired.

3573. பெண் வாய்க்கும் புண்ணியவானுக்கு, பண்டம் வாய்க்கும் பாக்கியவானுக்கு.

A virtuous man will obtain a good wife, and a fortunate man will obtain wealth. 2609.

"*Be a good husband, and you will get a penny to spend, a penny to lend, and a penny for a friend.*"

3574. பேயும் அறியும் பெண்சாதி பிள்ளையை.

Even a demon knows his own wife and children. 3290.

3575. பைசாவுக்குப் பத்து பெண், கொசுறு குத்து.

One can get ten wives for a small coin, and a handful into the bargain. 3269, 3220.

"*As the market goes, wives must sell.*"

3576. மனதைப்போலிருக்கும் மங்கிலியம்.

As a wife's heart is, so will her marriage token be.

If she is good she will keep her *thali*, *i.e.*, her husband a long time.

"*A virtuous woman is a crown to her husband.*"

"*Two things prolong thy life, a quiet heart and a loving wife.*"

3577. மனப்பொருத்தம் இருந்தால், மற்றப் பொருத்தம் பார்க்கவேண்டுமோ?

If there be harmony between husband and wife, there is no need to look for astrological harmony. 2759.

It does not matter if their horoscopes do not agree.

"*Marriage with peace is the world's paradise; with strife, this life's purgatory.*"

3578. மாலை இட்ட பெண்சாதி, எமன்போல் வந்தாள்.

The woman who gave a man a garland (selected him for her husband) was *Death* to him. 1915, 3253, 3558, 3572.

"*Better be half hanged, than ill wed.*"

3579. வீட்டுக்கு இருந்தால் வெண்கலப் பெண்சாதி, வீட்டுக்கு இல்லாதே போனால் தூங்கல் பெண்சாதி.

If the house is supplied according to the wish of the wife, she is all smiles (shines like bell-metal), but if not she will be displeased and blame everyone. 3555.

3580. வீட்டுப் பெண்சாதி வேம்பு, நாட்டுப் பெண்சாதி கரும்பு.

His own wife is a margosa tree (bitter), and his wife outside the house is sugar-cane (sweet). 3571.

3581. வீணுக்குத் தாலி வேண்டும் என்று அறுத்தேனோ?

Was it wantonly and without cause that I cut off my thâli?

A widow takes off her *thâli* (marriage token) on the death of her husband. Therefore on the death of a man, the woman who takes off her *thâli* thereby shows that she was his legal wife and as such has a right to his property.

"IF JACK'S IN LOVE, HE IS NO JUDGE OF JILL'S BEAUTY."

கந்தைக்குத் தகுந்த பொந்தை. 2273.

3582. அடங்காத மனைவியும், ஆங்காரப் புருஷனும்.
An obstinate wife and a haughty husband.

"*When the husband is fire, and the wife tow, the devil easily sets them in a flame.*"

3583. அரக்குமுத்தி தண்ணீருக்குப் போனாள், புண் பிடித்தவன் பின்னாலே போனான்.
A sickly woman, who could hardly walk, went for water, and a man full of sores went after her.

3584. ஆக்கமாட்டாத அழுக நாரிக்குத், தேடமாட்டாத திருட்டுச்சாவான்.
A worthless wife unable to cook and a cursed husband unfit to earn anything.

"*Like loves like.*"

"*They were both equally bad, so the devil put them together.*"

3586. ஆம்புடையானுக்கு அழுத குறை அந்தகன் வந்து வாய்த்தான்.
Her grievance was that after she had wept to get a husband, she got a blind one.

"*A bad bush is better than an open field.*"

3587. என்னிலும் கதிகெட்டவன், என்னை வந்து மாலை இட்டான்.
One in a worse state than myself came and put a garland on me (chose me for his wife).

"*Better one house filled than two spilled.*"

3588. ஐயாவுக்கு வித்தையில்லை, அம்மாளுக்குக் கெர்வமில்லை.
As the husband is a fool and can earn nothing, his wife takes no air.

"*Like blood, like good and like age, make the happiest marriages.*"

3589. நச்சுவாயன் வீட்டிலே, நாறுவாயன் பெண் கொண்டதுபோல.
The talkative foul-mouthed man married a girl from a home as bad as his.

"*There is no goose so gray in the lake, that cannot find a gander to her make.*"

3590. சப்பாணி மாப்பிள்ளைக்குச் சந்து ஒடிந்த பெண்சாதி.
For a bridegroom who is a cripple, a bride who has broken her hip-bone will do. 2278.

"*A scald horse for a scabbed squire.*"

3591. மொட்டைச்சிக்குத் தகுந்த மூக்கறையன்.
A noseless husband suits a bald-headed woman (a widow).

"*A bad jack may have as bad a jill.*"

3592. வயிற்றெரிச்சல் பெண்சாதிக்கு மாலைக்கண் ஆம்புடையான்.
A most miserable woman has a blind husband.

"*Hedgehogs lodge among thorns, because they themselves are prickly.*"

Cf. 2259 *&c.*

REFERRING CHIEFLY TO FEMININE FAILINGS.

There are only two good women in the world: one of them is dead, and the other is not to be found.

3593. அப்பனோடே போகிறவளுக்கு, அண்ணன் ஏது, தம்பி ஏது.
What is an elder or younger brother to her, who sins with her own father. 394, 408.

"*She is as common as a barber's chair.*"

3594. அம்மி மிதித்து (com. மெரித்து) அருந்ததி பார்த்ததுபோல பேசுகிறாள்.
She speaks like one who has been standing on the grinding stone looking at Arundhati.

Arundhati was the chaste wife of Vasishta, now a star, which is shown to the bride by the bridegroom during the marriage ceremony. She stands on a grinding stone and promises him that she will be a wife like Arundhati. The grinding-stone is a symbol of Ahalya, who for committing adultery with Indra was metamorphosed into a stone. The putting the grinding-stone under the bride's feet symbolises the bride's abhorrence of Ahalya's conduct. Applied sarcastically to a woman who professes to be the wife of somebody to whom she has not been married, or to false witnesses in a case.

3595. அருக்காணி முத்து கரிக்கோலமானாள்.
The precious pearl has become a black mark.

Said of a fallen woman.

3596. அவசாரிபோகவும் ஆசையிருக்கிறது, அடிப்பான் என்று பயமுமாயிருக்கிறது.
She has a desire to go astray, but she is afraid that her husband may beat her. 3609.

Chaste of necessity. 3600.

"*Fear and shame, much sin doth tame.*"

"*Fears are divided in the midst.*"

3597. அழிந்தவள் யாரோடே போனால் என்ன?
It matters little with whom a ruined woman sins.

"*She is neither wife, widow nor maid.*"

3598. அழுகிற ஆணையும், சிரிக்கிற பெண்ணையும் நம்பப்படாது.
Do not believe a weeping man or a laughing woman.

3599. ஆயிரம்பேரிடத்தில் சிநேகம்பண்ணினாலும், ஆண்பிள்ளைக்கு என்ன?
It does not matter how many courtezans a *man* has.

The implication is that a woman has far less liberty than a man.

3599*a*. இடவசதியில்லாத பதிவிரதை.

A chaste woman who cannot find an opportunity to go astray. 3600.

3600. இடம் அகப்படாத தோஷம் மெத்த பதிவிரதை.

Having no opportunity to go astray, she is very virtuous. 3596.

"*Honest as the cat, when the meat is out of reach.*"

3601. இத்தனை பெரியவன் கையைப் பிடித்தால், எப்படி மாட்டேன் என்பது போல்.

Like saying to a rich man who lays hold of my hand: "I won't come."

Chiefly referring to a man's attempt to seduce a woman.

3602. இலை பழுப்பானாலும், குலப் பழுப்பாகாது.

Though leaves fade, a woman or a caste should not fade.

A woman should remain virtuous.

3603. ஊர் எல்லாம் சுற்றி, என் பேர் முக்தி.

I have been all round the village, and my name is Mukti (bliss). 3195, 3624.

She has led a loose life and yet praises herself.

"*A ronk-towns (a gad-about) seldom a good housewife at home.*"

3604. ஊரிலேயும் போவாள், சொன்னால் அழுவாள்.

She is a gad about, but she weeps if you say so.

"*A young whore, and old saint.*"

3605. என் எச்சிலைக் கழுவி, உன் சுத்தத்திலே வார்க்க!

Let my filth be washed off with your cleanliness.

Your cleanliness is not better than my filth.

நீ சீலமோ? Ah, do you imagine yourself pure!

3606. ஏழு அறை கட்டி (அதில்) வைத்தாலும், ஒரு தாழறையில் சோரம் போவாள்.

Though you build seven rooms, and keep her in the inner one she will find a nook in which to go astray. 3534, 3565.

"*A bag of fleas is easier to keep guard over than a woman.*"

3607. என்னடி, அவனை மசக்கிறாய்.

What are you doing, girl, are you tempting him?

3608. ஐவருக்குத் தேவி அழியாத பத்தினி.

Though Draupadi was the wife of the five Pandavas, she was quite chaste.

Ironically of one who praises herself for chastity.

3609. கண்டு பேசக் கவையுமிருக்கிறது, முகத்தில் முழிக்க வெட்கமுமிருக்கிறது.

She desires to talk to him, but she is too shy to look in his face. 3596.

"*Fain would the cat fish eat, but she's loth to wet her feet.*"

3610. கற்பில்லாத அழகு, வாசனையில்லாத பூ.

Beauty without chastity is a flower without smell.

3611. காக்காய் கர் என்றால், கணவனை அப்பா என்று கட்டிக்கொள்ளுவாளாம்.

If a crow makes a noise, she will embrace her husband and say: My dear!

She pretends to be frightened by it, that her husband may have confidence in her.

"*A wicked woman and an evil are three half-pence worse than the devil.*"

"*An eel is held by the tail surer than a woman.*"

"*You have daily to do with the devil, and pretend to be frightened at a mouse.*"

3612. வீட்டுக்கு ஒரு மொத்தை கேட்டுக்கொள்ளடி மாரியாத்தை.

O, dear goddess, you ask for a morsel of food in every house! 3195, 3603, 3619, 3624.

Said of an immodest woman who goes to any house to eat and talk.

"*Dry bread at home is better than roast meat abroad.*"

3613. குட்டமானம் தப்பி குசவனோடே போனால், சட்டையும் பண்ணான், சட்டியும் கொடான்.

If you are put out of your caste and live with a potter, he will neither respect you, nor give you pots.

3614. குளிராத வீடும், கூத்தியாரும் உண்டானால் மயிரான வேளாண்மை விளைந்தால்தான் என்ன? விளையாமல் போனால்தான் என்ன.

He who has a comfortable house and a concubine does not care whether his crops fail or succeed.

3615. கூழை குடித்தாலும், குப்பை சுமந்தாலும், குப்பைக்காட்டுப் பெண்கள் ருக்குமணி; பாலைக் குடித்தாலும், பட்டைக் கட்டினாலும், பட்டணத்துப் பெண்கள் பறக்கை (or தட்டுவாணி).

Though village-women drink water-gruel and carry manure on their heads, they are precious jewels, *or* Rukmani, (one of the wives of Krishna); though the women in cities drink milk and dress in silk, they are gad-abouts.

3616. சாக்கடை புழு என்றாலும், சக்காளத்தி என்றாலும் சரி.

Whether you say "gutter-worm" or "concubine" it is all the same.

3617. *சிரித்தாயோ, சேலை அவிழ்த்தாயோ?*

Did you laugh or did you take off your cloth? 3618.

For a woman to laugh when speaking with men is as culpable as the greatest immodesty.

"*A maid that laughs is half taken.*"

3618. *சிரித்தாயோ, சீரைக் குலைத்தாயோ?*

Did you laugh or did you destroy your good name? 3617.

If a young woman smiles while speaking, an elderly one may correct her by saying: பல்லுக்கு மேல் என்ன சிரிப்பு, why do you smile and show your teeth?

3619. *நாணமில்லாத சிறுக்கிக்கு நாலு திக்கும் வாசல்படி.*

An immodest woman will enter any door. 3612.

3620. *பட்டப் பகலிலே போகிறவளுக்குத் தட்டுக்கூடை மறைப்பா?*

Can a woman, who sins in the open daylight, hide herself with a big basket?

3621. *பெண்ணின் குணமும் அறிவேன், சம்பந்தி வாயும் அறிவேன்.*

I know the girl's character, and I also know the tongue of her parent.

The mother-in-law is called upon to interfere between her daughter-in-law, and that daughter's mother, but she says she knows their bad character too well to do so. They are both vixens.

3622. *மதனும் ரதியும்போல் வாழ்ந்திருக்கவேண்டும்.*

To live happily like Kama and his wife Radi. 2760.

3623. *முகத்துக்கு அஞ்சி மூத்தாரோடே போனால் குலத்துக்கு ஈனம்.*

If a young married woman fears to refuse an elderly man's improper advances, it will be a shame to the whole caste.

Or, when an inferior is too weak to resist his master's improper orders and does something wrong.

3624. *மூன்று வீட்டுக்கு முக்காலி, நாலு வீட்டுக்கு நாற்காலி.*

She is a footstool in three houses, and a chair in four houses. 3603, 3612.

Said of a woman who is always gossiping in other people's houses.

"*A maid oft seen, a gown oft worn, are disesteemed and held in scorn.*"

"*A woman is to be from her house three times; when she is christened, married and buried.*"

Cf. 443; 462.

MOTHER-IN-LAW.

மாமியார்.

3625. அவள் சொல் உனக்குக் குருவாக்கு (or, ரிஷிவாக்கு).

Her words are like a priest's words to you.

Said in sarcasm by a mother to her son, when she thinks that her son listens too much to his wife instead of listening to her.

" *The husband's mother is the wife's devil.*"

3626. ஆடிக்கு அழைக்காத மாமியாரைத் தேடி மயிரைப் பிடித்துச் செருப்பால் அடி.

The mother-in-law who does not send her daughter-in-law home in July, should be sought, dragged by her hair and beaten with slippers. 3629.

A married couple should never live together in July, for the first born must not be born in April, as this month is considered very unlucky.

3627. என் மகளுக்கு வாரத்துக்கு இரண்டுவொட்டி தலைக்கு ஊற்றுவேன் (this said slowly), என் மருமகளுக்குத் தீபாவளிக்குத் தலைக்கு ஊற்றுவேன் (this said quickly).

I will give my daughter a bath of oil twice a week, but my daughter-in-law will get one only at the dipâvali festival, *i. e.*, once a year.

This shews the mother-in-law's great partiality.

3628. கொடும்பாவியானாலும், கொண்ட மாமியார் வேண்டும்.

Though a mother-in-law be a wicked sinner, a house cannot do without her. 1552, 3548, 3635.

She is necessary to the welfare of the house, however bad she may be.

3629. சித்திரை மாசத்தில் செல்வன் பிறந்தால், ஆனகுடிக்கு அநர்த்தம், *or*, கெடும்.

If the first born is born in April a prosperous family will come to grief. 3626.

To avoid this calamity the mother-in-law must send her daughter-in-law to her mother's home, away from her husband, in the month of July.

3630. தான் ஆண்ட உலக்கையும், தங்கப் பூஞ்சரடும் தலை மருமகளுக்கு.

The pestle which the mother-in-law used and her gold necklace should go to the eldest daughter-in-law.

A certain daughter-in-law hated her mother-in-law, and one day being alone with her in the house struck her on the breast with the pestle or rice-pounder, so that she fell down speechless. The other women were called in, and the mother-in-law pointed to the wicked daughter-in-law, to the rice-pounder and to her own breast. The women asked the murderess for an explanation of these signs, and she said : Being the eldest of you all, I am to have the rice-pounder and the golden necklace on her breast.

3631. தென்னாலுராமன் பூனை (or குதிரை) வளர்த்ததுபோல்.

As Tennâlurâman fed the cat, *i.e.*, he fed it very scantily.

If the daughter-in-law does not receive proper food, she will say this of her mother-in-law.

3632. பானை ஒட்டினாலும் ஒட்டும், மாமி ஒட்டாள்.

Though a broken pot might be joined together again, a mother-in-law could not live in peace with her daughter-in-law. 2834, 3636*a*.

3633. பெண்ணைக் கொடுத்தாயோ, கண்ணைக் கொடுத்தாயோ?

Did you give me your daughter, or did you give me your eyes?

Said by a son-in-law to his mother-in-law:—Will we not, after taking your daughter to my home, treat her as kindly and carefully as we treat our own eyes?

3634. பெண்ணுக்கு மாமியாரும், பிள்ளைக்கு வாத்தியாரும்.

A mother-in-law for a daughter-in-law, and a teacher for a boy.

Both are alike necessary.

3635. பொன்னான மருமகளானாலும், மண்ணாலே ஒரு மாமியார் வேண்டும்.

Though the daughter-in-law be made of gold, she must have a mother-in-law of mud. 3628.

Whatever the mother-in-law's character may be, her authority is necessary for the young girl.

3636. மகன் செத்தாலும் சாகட்டும், மருமகள் கொட்டம் (*or* கெர்வம்) அடங்கினால் போதும்.

Even if my son dies, let him die, I shall be satisfied if the haughtiness of my daughter-in-law is subdued by his death.

"*Mother-in-law and daughter-in-law are a tempest and a hail storm.*"

3636*a*. மாம்பழத்திலிருக்கும் வண்டே! மாமியாருக்கும் மருமகளுக்கும் சண்டை. 3632.

O beetle within the mango-kernel, thou knowest best the strife between the mother-in-law and the daughter-in-law. 630.

No trace is visible on the surface of the kernel to show how the beetle entered it; and thus also no clear cause of strife between mother-in-law and daughter-in-law. Any trifling thing causes a quarrel between them.

3637. மாமியார் செத்த ஆறும் மாசம் மருமகள் கண்ணிலே தண்ணீர் வந்தது போல்.

Like the daughter-in-law who shed no tears for her mother-in-law, till six months after the mother-in-law was dead.

"*There is no good mother-in-law but she that wears a green gown*" (is buried under the green grass.)

"*Crocodile tears.*"—"*There will be many a dry cheek after him.*"

3638. மாமியாரும் ஒரு வீட்டு நாட்டுப்பெண்தான்.

Even the mother-in-law was once a girl from some house in the country. 3293, 3435.

"*The mother-in-law forgets that she was a daughter-in-law.*"

"*The priest forgetteth that ever he hath been holy water clerk.*"

3639. மாமியாருக்குச் சுவாமியார் இவள்.

The daughter-in-law is a god to her mother-in-law. 475.

The daughter-in-law rules the mother-in-law; a rather unusual state of things.

3640. மாமியார் மெச்சின மருமகளில்லை, மருமகள் மெச்சின மாமியாரில்லை.

No daughter-in-law praises her mother-in-law, and no mother-in-law praises her daughter-in-law. 1390.

3641. மாமியாரைக் கண்டு மருமகள் நாணுகிறதுபோல்.

As the daughter-in-law feels shy before the mother-in-law.

Said of any one who feels shy to come forward and speak freely before a superior.

3642. மாமியாரும் சாகாளோ, மனக்கவலையும் தீராதோ?

Is not my mother-in-law going to die, and put an end to my anxiety? 2928.

The daughter-in-law is longing to get rid of her mother-in-law's worry and also herself to become the mistress of the home.

3643. மாமியார் உடைத்தால் மண்பானை, மருமகள் உடைத்தால் பொன் பானை.

If the mother-in-law breaks a pot, it is only clay (of no consequence), but if the daughter-in-law breaks one, it is gold (of great consequence). 179, 180, 184.

3644. பொங்கல் போச்சுது, போய்யும் போச்சுது, பெண்ணை அனுப்படா பேயாண்டி.

The Pongal feast is over, and the day of that festival for burning up old things thrown into the street is also gone, send my wife home, thou blackguard!

A young wife leaves her mother-in-law's house and goes home to her parents for her confinement, but she must not stay there more than six months. When the time is up her husband asks for her return. Also used about money that should be returned within the fixed time.

The above refer directly to the relations between a mother-in-law and her daughter-in-law. There are a number of other proverbs more or less directly bearing on the same subject, which have been included under other headings. Some of them can be found by referring to the words மாமியார் and மருமகள் in the Index. But there are numerous proverbs which have reference to the mother-in-law by implication only. That there is such a large number of proverbs which thus refer to the mother-in-law is a proof of her immense importance in Hindu family life.

THE END.

INDEX OF THE FIRST WORD OF EACH PROVERB.

AN INDEX OF NON-INITIAL WORDS FROM THE BODY OF THE PROVERBS.